The Encyclopedia of

SACRED SEXUALITY

The Encyclopedia of
SACRED SEXUALITY

*From Aphrodisiacs and Ecstasy
to Yoni Worship and Zap-lam Yoga*

RUFUS C. CAMPHAUSEN

INNER TRADITIONS
ROCHESTER, VERMONT

Inner Traditions International
One Park Street
Rochester, Vermont 05767
www.InnerTraditions.com

LIBRARY OF CONGRESS CATALOGING-IN-PUBLICATION DATA

Camphausen, Rufus C.
The encyclopedia of sacred sexuality : from aphrodisiacs and ecstasy to yoni worship and zap-lam yoga : the complete illustrated reference, including Internet resources / Rufus C. Camphausen.
p.   cm.
Rev. and expanded ed. of The encyclopedia of erotic wisdom. 1991.
Includes bibliographical references and index.
ISBN 0-89281-719-4 (pbk. : alk. paper)
1. Sex customs—Encyclopedias.   2. Erotica—Encyclopedias.   3. Sex—Encyclopedias.
I. Camphausen, Rufus C.   The encyclopedia of erotic wisdom.   II. Title.
HQ12.C32 1999
306.7'03—dc21 98-23650
CIP

Printed and bound in the United States.

10   9   8   7   6   5   4   3   2   1

Text design by Bonnie F. Atwater. Layout by Virginia L. Scott
This book was typeset in Berkeley Oldstyle with Monsignor Elegant as the display typeface

Front matter art:
p. i: Detail from Chakra Asana image on p. 35. Ajit Mookerjee Collection.
p. ii: Rock painting at Nourlangie Rock, Alligator River, Arnhem Land, Northern Territory, Australia. Photograph by Robert Edwards.
p. v: Balinese equivalent to the Celtic sheela. Ubud, Bali. Photograph by Rufus C. Camphausen.
p. vi: A couple entwined in the lata asana. Private collection.
p. viii: A couple in Tantric practice, worshipping the divine in the other. Private collection.
p. x: Erotic temple sculpture from the Basantpur temple, Kathmandu. Photograph by Rufus C. Camphausen.
p. xii: Detail from mural on Guheshvari temple, Kathmandu. Photograph by Rufus C. Camphausen.

❧

Grateful appreciation is given for permission to use illustrations from the following works:

E. J. Brill, Leiden, Netherlands.
Robert Hans van Gulik: Sexual Life in Ancient China, 1974, p. 359, Spark of Life.

Glenn Mullin, trans. and ed.: Selected Works of the Dalai Lama II, 1985 (Snow Lion, Ithaca, N.Y.), p. 92, Niguma.

Thames and Hudson, London.
Dolf Hartsuiker: Sadhus: Holy Men of India, 1993, Cannabis Sativa.
Ajit Mookerjee and Madhu Khanna: The Tantric Way, 1977, p. 17, Shakti; p. 44, Coco-de-mer.
Philip Rawson: The Art of Tantra, 1973, illustration 37, Yoni; illustration 67, Kundalini; illustration 68, Serpent Energy; illustration 82, Defloration; illustration 103, Chakra Asana.
Philip Rawson and Laszlo Legaza: Tao, 1973, p. 99, Dragon Veins.

Weidenfeld and Nicolson Ltd., London.
David L. Snellgrove and Hugh Edward Richardson: A Cultural History of Tibet, 1986, p. 123, Bön-po.

The author has done the utmost to settle copyright issues and obtain permission for all illustrations. Those who nevertheless believe they can claim certain rights are referred to Inner Traditions International, Rochester, Vermont.

To the pure in heart everything is pure.
KAULAVALI NIRNAYA TANTRA

*There is nothing simple about what goes on in the intimacies
of sex. Men and women need as much insight as possible in living
together through the ups and downs of sexual passion.*
JOSEPHINE LOWNDES-SEVELY, *EVE'S SECRETS*

The good can even be better.
ROBERT ANTON WILSON, *SEX AND DRUGS*

*"Why must I lie beneath you?" she asked.
"I also was made from dust, and am therefore your equal."*
LILITH, IN CONVERSATION WITH ADAM,
FROM A RABBINICAL LEGEND

*"We fight for God, messire. Have you as great a motive?"
"Yes, I do," said Roland. "I fight for Love."*
ROBERT SHEA, *ALL THINGS ARE LIGHTS*

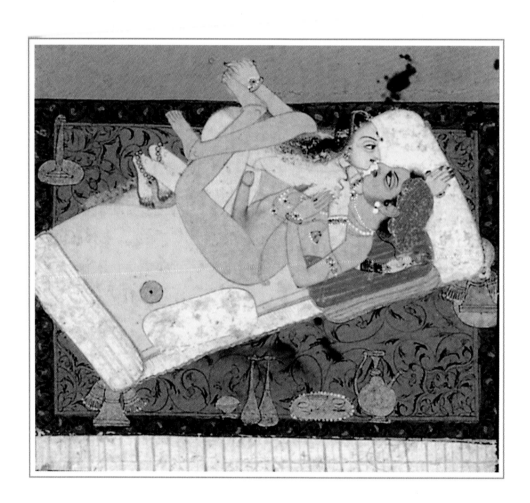

Contents

ΛCKNOWLEDGMENTS

My debt to all the authors quoted in the book or mentioned in the bibliography is evident. Nevertheless, among the many, I would like to pay tribute especially to a few. The work of Robert Briffault (*The Mothers*), unfortunately not reprinted since 1927 and less well known than the comparable work by James Frazer (*The Golden Bough*), was important to me not only for its invaluable mass of anthropological data but for his unique, woman-centered approach to the topic at hand. Among my female teachers and authors, apart from my intimate friends, I especially admire Sister Niguma, Lady Yeshe Tsogyal, June Campbell, Ginette Paris, Miranda Shaw, and the late Marija Gimbutas for both their scientific work and their sensitive, understanding views. Among other "giants of knowledge" on human affairs, I am indebted to Mircea Eliade, John Lilly, Norman O. Brown, Lyall Watson, and Robert Anton Wilson for each of their individual attempts at objectivity, relativity, and honesty.

I also take this opportunity for expressing my sincere thanks to a number of friends whose efforts have aided the difficult and time-consuming task of writing and researching the present work. Although they are too numerous for me to name them all, I nevertheless want to make some exceptions. Apart from my friend, lover, and companion Christina Camphausen, who has nurtured and sustained me on all levels during the gestation of this and all my earlier books, I would like to name especially Jane Sperr for having both challenged and stimulated me with her independent thoughts and valuable information; and John C., David Kinsella, and Paul Throne for supplying very specialized information I would not have found otherwise. Last but not least, as with all my previous books, this one would not have become what it is without the decidedly friendly and fully professional help of senior editor Jeanie Levitan and her many helpers at Inner Traditions International.

To all those involved, named or unnamed, I express my thanks with the beautiful Hawaiian term *mahalo lui noa* ("Thank you great and far").

Note to the Reader on Using the Encyclopedia

This encyclopedia has been designed and prepared to provide easy, meaningful, and intelligent access to a variety of lesser-known facts concerning eros and sexuality. Its entries deal with information ranging from aphrodisiacs to ancient deities and demons, from erotic symbolism to lesser-known sexual techniques and exercises, from mystery schools and religious sects concerned with sexual activity to worship directed toward male and female energies and/or the genitals themselves. Whether this information is medical, psychological, historical, or anthropological, the entries in this work have been selected in accordance with these criteria. Therefore no entries are included, for example, about such well-known and often-written-about matters as AIDS, fetishism, Freudian theory, homosexuality, or sexual hygiene.

The encyclopedia's scope embraces inner and outer Tantric and Taoist teachings along with the whispered secrets of Western alchemists and cabalists, the erotic rituals and beliefs of our ancestors along with up-to-date scientific knowledge of brain, mind, and body—wherever these fields of wisdom concern the erotic and sexual.

A reader opening *The Encyclopedia of Sacred Sexuality* for the first time should note the following about its use and design:

1. Extensive cross-references have been made that can guide you on a mental odyssey—from almost any point of departure—further and deeper into related areas of your interest. All terms with an asterisk (*) indicate that the term has a meaningful entry in this encyclopedia; be assured that cross-references have been selected carefully and will not lead you on a frustrating chase to all passing comments that have little or no information to add.

2. Because many of the terms discussed in these pages have double or multiple meanings, the following rule has been applied throughout the text: If, for example, the Sanskrit term *mudra* has five different meanings, the term will be referred to as *mudra*/1, *mudra*/2, and so on, accordingly.

3. In the appendix, a substantial number of lists have been provided for those readers who are interested in a specific, subject-related pursuit. With the help of these listings you can focus your search, for example, on specialized areas such as these:

   • Sacred and/or erotic primary literature (index 13)
   • Aphrodisiacs derived from animal substances (index 5.3)
   • Religious groups, sects, and schools (index 2)
   • Festivals, rituals, and customs (index 6)
   • Sexual biochemistry (index 11) and electromagnetism (index 12)

   Other listings of key words allow access to all entries related to a certain cultural background. They give access to, for example, all Chinese or all American data.

4. Having a large number of foreign-language entries (including Sanskrit, Chinese, Greek, and Latin, for instance) is unavoidable in a book such as this. In most of the entries that follow, the originating language and/or cultural background is specified, and translations have been provided as often as possible.

5. A variety of pictorial images have been collected for this work. They have been chosen in an attempt to balance the aesthetic with the unique, the erotic with the scientifically interesting—preference being

given to material not usually available except in rather specialized literature. Many illustrations have been commissioned to artist Christina Camphausen, who has prepared a unique collection of artwork not available elsewhere.

6. Interesting quotations from sacred and/or erotic scriptures have been included in many of the entries as well as at the beginning of each letter of the alphabet.

7. A selected bibliography provides recommended reading for further study, the selection based on the quality and/or uniqueness of the material.

8. In publishing this material, neither the author nor the publisher intends to promote all practices described in this book. However, we believe that personal tastes and mutual consent between mature men and women, not arbitrary regulation by any administrative body, is the one and only guideline to be followed in matters of sexuality. See also the disclaimer on page v.

ABBREVIATIONS ARE USED IN THIS BOOK AS FOLLOWS:

b.	born (year of birth)
B.C.E.	before the common era (instead of B.C., before Christ)
c.	circa (approximate date of birth or death)
C.E.	common era (instead of A.D., *anno Domini*, or "in the year of the Lord")
Chin.	Chinese
d.	died (year of death)
Jap.	Japanese
Skt.	Sanskrit
Tib.	Tibetan

"Just what is sacred sexuality?"

*"What if we all helped each other to manifest
our most beautiful, sexy, intelligent, creative,
and adventurous inner selves, instead of
cooperating to suppress them?"*

PAT CALIFIA ON THE COVER OF *SEX CHANGES*

On first glance, the quote above sounds more like a hedonist's dream than anything we usually associate with sacred or spiritual teachings. But it does in fact present in a nutshell what hundreds of learned and enlightened women and men have tried to teach humanity for the past millennia. Imagine, for a moment, that Califia's words had come from the lips of the *Dalai Lama rather than from the pen of a woman known for her radical approach to sexuality. We would marvel at the *bodhisattva-like compassion in these words, which ask us not only to be our true selves but also to love our neighbor and aid her or him in the quest toward that liberation and fulfillment.

The comparison shows that we can learn as much from the words of a lesbian sadomasochist as we can from a celibate Nobel laureate, at least in this case where wise crone Califia has tapped straight into the cosmic noosphere† and then right into the heart of the matter.

Whereas the hedonic personality will follow the often misunderstood "Do What Thou Wilt!" of Aleister *Crowley, one who seriously practices sacred sexuality will rejoice in the freedom and bliss of the other and in the beauty of empathic synergy that can be achieved when sexuality is taken beyond self-gratification, beyond physical need, beyond its being a genetic strategy of species survival and into a realm of cooperative development and mutual gifts of pleasure.

Several years ago I wrote a column for a Dutch magazine with the subtitle "Intimate Initiations, Heathen Hedonism, Sacred Sexuality." At a family reunion during those years, one of my brothers-in-law approached me with the following question: "Now can you tell me just *what* sacred sexuality means!?!" His intonation left no doubt that, to his mind, the terms *sacred* and *sexuality* were incompatible, like a naturally impossible and thus doomed mating between two different species.

Unfortunately, there are many who, like this otherwise well-educated man, have never come into contact with concepts and values of cultures other than their own, where indeed the sacred is seen as incompatible with the body and also in full conflict with sexuality—in other words, the truly sacred is regarded as more or less nonhuman by definition.

The fact that such a view is a very limited and biased one is borne out by many recent publications concerning *"Tantra" or "spiritual sex" by innumerable "Tantra" groups from Hawaii to New Zealand to Amsterdam, and it is again evidenced in great detail in many of the more than 1200 items collected and presented in this encyclopedia. In many other cultures that have arisen on this planet, and with many peoples past and present, the sacred and the sexual are not at all dichotomous. Instead, wise women and men taught the next generation that sexuality without a spiritual dimension is not the way of humanity; hence the Sanskrit words *pashu* ("animal") for those who are slaves to their instincts and *vira* ("heroine, hero") for those who are both educated and initiated. Although these are Sanskrit terms

---

†Term coined by Pierre Teillhard de Chardin for the concept of a "cosmic consciousness" or "universal brain" surrounding our planet.

from an ancient Hindu culture almost lost, the concept was shared by many other peoples and societies who merged sacred concepts with erotic arts into a vision of why being born human is preferred to being born a pig or a rabbit.

From the temples of Knossos to those of Khajuraho, from *Sodom and Gomorrah in the Near East to Mohenjo Daro at the Indus River, and from Lesbos to Lhasa to Luxor: wherever we look at the interface between sexuality and religion in prepatriarchal times or nonpatriarchal cultures we see universe and life celebrated in ways that combine the body with the spirit—and thus combine eros with religio. The marriage between these two is the real holy matrimony, or *hieros gamos—a marriage that is fruitful in ways other than in the more or less prescribed one of creating offspring. Sacred sexuality, whether soft or radical, of the right- or left-handed path, is an acceptance of what it means to be human. It is an essential component in the nurturing process of any self-determined, sensitive, unique individual.

> My impression is that sexual abstinence does not promote the development of energetic, independent men of action, original thinkers or bold innovators and reformers; far more frequently it develops well-behaved weaklings who are subsequently lost in the great multitude (Sigmund Freud, *Collected Works*).

The age-old teachings of Taoist masters, of Tantric adepts, and of Near Eastern and European priestesses and priests can often supply us with ample and good advice on how to integrate body and mind, love and sexuality, spiritual exercise and inner, alchemical techniques. Hindu Tantra and Tantric Buddhism are not free from all failings or fallacy, but both schools have understood and integrated the basic fact that we are all equal but also individually different. Thus, in these enlightened teachings, there is room for the celibate as well as for the shy, for the exhibitionist as well as for the hedonist. The Tantric saying "One must rise by that by which one falls" is a message for each of these types and for all of us. It implies that there is a way available for us to use our individual makeup and preferences in order to find both peace and joy, fulfillment and liberation—as long as whatever path we choose is the proverbial path "with a heart."

Although the realities of so many present-day relationships are not very encouraging, and divorce has become a common phenomenon, I wish to encourage any reader to resist thinking that sacred sexuality is simply another romantic notion, in the same way that many people have been led to believe that love is just a romantic notion and more or less impossible to find in real life.

Sexuality, approached openly, honestly, and with respect for self and other, is not just one of humanity's major evolutionary drives and a possibility for great mental and physical pleasure. Its function also is to be a most powerful and pleasant means to discover one's inner self, exorcise one's demons, and develop one's potential—in loving communication and cooperation with others.

Whether or not we find sacred sexuality in our life depends mostly on ourselves, on the way we look at self and other and at our sexuality. Once we do know who we actually are, the next step is finding and having at least one companion whose outlook on these matters is sufficiently close to ours. Such a partner does not necessarily have to be the one great love of our life; she or he simply should be on the same path. This necessarily includes that he or she is respectful, loving, and compassionate; ready and able to learn as well as to teach, and to receive as well as to give. It is really as simple as that.

Then, the delightfully dangerous journey can begin to "manifest our most beautiful, sexy, intelligent, creative, and adventurous inner selves." Beyond all theories and techniques, beyond all rituals and requirements discussed in this book and others, this is the heart-essence of the teachings.

Amen.

THE VARIETY OF THE SEXUAL EXPERIENCE

The forces and energies we usually categorize under terms such as *eros* and *sexuality* can certainly be classified among the most basic and necessary "ingredients" for the evolution of life and the continuing evolution of humanity. In a certain sense, these forces (instinctive fertility, mutual attraction, love, pleasure, and so forth) will probably defy forever any attempt at complete recognition, examination, and analysis (on a verbal, intellectual level) because they are too close to home, too physical, and too emotional (in humans) to allow any "objective" approach.

However, although the deepest and fullest portent of the energies represented by Eros and *Aphrodite may elude our attempts at capturing their true essence, thus rendering any "judgment" superfluous, we are—at this moment in time— able to compare the different approaches that have been taken to this universal theme by different cultures, religions, and societies of past and present.

To introduce the reader to these varieties of sexual experience is one of the objectives of this book. An acquaintance with such knowledge seems necessary especially now, at the start of a new millennium—a time in which we can watch our contemporary world becoming a global village, or rather an international supermarket, in which all varieties of local custom and "moral" outlook are making room, more or less under pressure, for one general diet that is supposed to suit anyone and everyone. Even the overdue breakdown of many general Judeo-Christian taboos, as happened during the famed "sexual revolution" of the 1960s, has often served only to bring about, simply, a more materialist, "no-nonsense" approach to matters erotic, aiding an ongoing devolution and eventual commercialization of the sexual impulse. In a time of TV spots promoting *monogamy and "safe sex" (and the sales of condoms), "phone sex," "computer sex," and prenuptial contracts, sexuality is more and more being emptied of all emotional, psychosomatic, and spiritual content and considerations. Even the legalization of prostitution (in some enlightened nations), although wise, is only one more aspect of this continuously growing materialistic attitude.

When thinking of sexuality, people today are often concerned mainly with material questions: with whether or not they may catch the AIDS virus, with birth or abortion, with pleasure or pain, with (premature) *ejaculation and clitoral or vaginal *orgasms. At least one complete dimension —the mystery of being male or female and of how these two can interact creatively in individually and socially fulfilling ways—is most often overlooked and neglected by the disciples of the no-nonsense approach.

A continuation of this development may mean that humanity comes to losing as much of its heritage and potential as is now being lost by the ongoing destruction of nature's variety of plants and animals and of humanity's diverse offspring, in the form of tribal communities and their languages.

Another objective of *The Encyclopedia of Sacred Sexuality* is therefore to introduce and clarify concepts from other cultures in which the erotic impulse has not been divorced from religious worship and spirituality, and in which the human body has not been divided into a good, upper part and a bad part "below the belt."

Often these teachings from other cultures and earlier times sound strange or almost alien at first encounter, or if received only as pieces of unrelated information. However, if one follows the appropriate lines of thought (assisted by the encyclopedia's cross-references or the topical indexes), the teachings of those cultures can often provide us with new and important insights into the topic at hand.

Still another objective of this book has been to introduce a new and meaningful terminology, often borrowed from Eastern languages, that can serve to change our way of thinking by replacing the well-worn and often prejudiced language of our own Western culture. Such terminology can also serve to show how much more open and honest other societies have often been in matters that are—even today—difficult to express in our contemporary languages. English, Dutch, and German, for example, have all developed within the Judeo-Christian background of contempt for the body and guilt about sexuality. Their "erotic" vocabularies often provide only scatological and negatively tinted words or those used by the medical profession, which again are too clinical and cold, lacking sensitivity or respect. A very different approach is evident in languages that developed in societies that did not declare human sexuality as vile and filthy but rather viewed the body as a sacred temple and sexuality as one more possibility to be enlisted in one's individual, psychological, and spiritual fulfillment. *The Encyclopedia of Sacred Sexuality* provides its readers with more than anthropological data regarding the erotic rituals, sexual techniques, and different moral outlook of lost or distant peoples. Unfortunately, even in our generally well-informed and rather scientifically oriented times, the sexual aspects of life are seldom discussed and taught truly openly and honestly. The many still-existing taboos and false preconceptions concerning the reproductive systems of men and women prevent people from really appreciating those complicated, sophisticated, and beautiful parts and processes of their bodies that are part and parcel of all sexual activity. *The Encyclopedia of Sacred Sexuality* therefore includes detailed discussions of topics such as the female and male *clitoris, male and female ejaculation, and the biochemical and electromagnetic powers of menstrual and other fluids. Many of the as yet not widely published advances in the biological and medical sciences, in the framework of our topic, have been included here. With the help of these unique, cross-cultural, and interdisciplinary facts, the reader will be able to extend her or his knowledge, and perhaps appreciation, of sexuality—and to recognize the ambivalence and arbitrariness of all local custom, of rules written and unwritten, especially those of the twentieth-century global supermarket.

THE GENERALIZED PRINCIPLE OF HUMAN SEXUALITY

Among all known cultures of all known times and all known places, there is but one generalized principle concerning human sexuality and the varied forms of expression it finds. This principle exists in spite of the incredible variety among humans concerning erotic activities, sexual or sex-related concepts and rituals, gender roles, forms of relationship, customs, and taboos.

The principle can be stated in one simple sentence: **It is the nature of every *group* to *guide* and/or *control* the sexual development of its members, as well as the individual and/or communal expression of their sexual energy.**

In this context, the term *group* represents and embraces all related entities such as family, clan, tribe, people, society, or culture: any form of communal living in relatively close proximity. The term *guide* indicates life-affirming, positive, and respectful approaches to educating and informing young members of the group. It is an important part of this approach to inform members that differences in tastes and preferences do exist, that individual choice is possible and desirable, and that there are few actual limits within the bounds of respect and consent. Although few groups have achieved this level of civilization, the generalized principle does provide for the best of all possible worlds. The term *control* indicates enslaving, guilt-creating, negative, forceful approaches to imprinting and programming young members of the group. An important strategy of such an approach is to negate the possibility of personal choices and preferences and to punish or denigrate anyone not adhering to the particular set of locally accepted behavior. Although this approach is the one most commonly practiced in human history, we should recognize it as disrespectful, nonenlightened, counterproductive, and, in the final analysis, uncivilized. It is an approach not at all required for adherence to the generalized principle.

This generalized principle does not concern itself with any possible or probable local detail—technical and/or conceptual—but with humanity as a whole. The application of this principle—in one way or another and more or less successfully from case to case—gives rise to a specific and local psychological "climate" within which any given individual grows up, lives, flourishes and/or withers in varying degrees, and then dies.

Fortunately there are many possible varieties (nuances, tones, shades, hues) that exist between loving and respectful guidance and calculating and forced control, which will be evidenced in the pages of this encyclopedia that follow.

THE
ENCYCLOPEDIA

A

If you don't know the way of intercourse, partaking of herbs is of no benefit.

*P'ENG TSU

ABRAHAM

(C. 2000–1900 B.C.E.)

The dates for birth and death of this archetypal patriarch are tentative and approximate, based on reports that he lived to the proud age of 100 and died in about 1900 B.C.E.

Abraham is one in a succession of many male leaders who have scorched the earth—and millions of human beings along with it—in their attempts to control and dominate everyone around them, especially the women. He was instrumental in the destruction of some cities in the Near East—like *Sodom and Gomorrah—and of people who celebrated life and sexuality and whose religions were often oriented toward the Great Goddess. Abraham, a hero not only of the *Bible but also of Islam, where he is called a "friend of Allah," was also involved in the institution of *circumcision and with the Islamic Holy of Holies, the *Ka'bah.

SEE ALSO *ZEUS

ABSINTHE

A strong *aphrodisiac by reputation, absinthe is a green liquor originally made in France from the oil of *Artemisia absinthium* (wormwood) with the addition of marjoram, anise, and other herbal oils. This plant was considered sacred to, and its name is derived from, the Greek goddess Artemis. The Greeks believed that merely by being placed under one's bed, absinthe would work its "magic" and aid the sexual passions. Absinthe was known in England as "green ginger."

In most countries absinthe has been banned because of its danger to health in general and is now illegal. Any regular use can easily result in muscle and gastric spasms caused by the wormwood, the main active ingredient of this drink.

ABTAGIGI

A Sumerian title that translates as "She who sends messages of desire." It is used for *Ishtar in her role as patroness of *ritual promiscuity and *ritual prostitution.

ACCA LARENTIA

Etruscan "lady mother," a goddess of sexuality in whose worship *ritual prostitution played an important role. A semidivine prostitute, she passed into Roman mythology as a benefactress of the lower classes and as the she-wolf foster mother of Remus and Romulus, the mythical founders of Rome. Her festival, the Larentalia, took place annually on December 23.

ACCLIVITY

(FROM LATIN *ACCLIVITAS*, "ASCENT")

Similar to the Eastern *oli techniques, this practice is used to direct ethereal, erotic essences upward toward the *brain in order to aid illumination. Acclivity was advocated mainly by the brethren of the *Free Spirit Movement, who thought of it as an "upward movement of the soul" during sexual union.

ADAMITES

A second-century Christian sect that aimed to attain a natural and innocent state similar to that of Adam, and of the biblical paradise, by wearing no clothes. Similar "naked holy men" are known from India and Arabia, as for example, the wandering saints known as *Maslub or the sect of the *Nagna. In later times, any group engaging in public nudity—often for purposes of political demonstration—was termed *adamite*. This happened, to name but a few examples, in fourteenth-century Cologne (Germany), fifteenth-century Lyon (France), and eighteenth-century Amsterdam (Netherlands).

SEE ALSO *BOBOMILES

ADAMU

A Chaldean goddess whose name translates as "red." She is regarded as the female principle of matter, specifically of *blood and *menstrual fluid.

ADRENAL GLANDS

Two glands of the *endocrine system, one atop each kidney, which secrete several highly influential substances affecting the whole being. Among them are the hormones known as *androgens, *estrogens, and *progestogens, as well as adrenaline and noradrenaline, which energize the body at times of stress.

ADVAITA VEDANTA

Based on the *Sanskrit advaita ("non-two-ness"), the term actually translates as "the nondual end of the Vedas." Advaita Vedanta refers to the various schools of *Hinduism with a strong or exclusively nondualist philosophy, based on the metaphysics expounded in the *Vedas, the *Upanishads, and related scriptures.

Often the term is also used as a name for the absolute nondualist teachings of Shankara (C. 788–822 C.E.), a system also known as Kevala Advaita. According to this philosopher, all of reality is fundamentally united—one, and not two—and essentially divine.

SEE ALSO *VEDANTA

ADYA SHAKTI

As is so often the case in Hindu, Buddhist, or Tantric terminology, one can approach an explanation of this term from two different angles. One way to interpret the Sanskrit words Adya Shakti, in a philosophical and scientific manner, is to say that they represent the most basic and principal energy of the universe, an energy that is conceived as being female in essence. From another point of view we can also state that Adya Shakti is a name for the goddess as genetrix of all and everything, as primeval energy and ultimate ground, the creative center of the universe.

A unique stone altar of *Shakti in this aspect is now in the museum of Alampur in Andhra Pradesh, India. The eleventh-century sculpture shows the goddess's *yoni between her widely opened thighs, ready to receive *flowers, touches, and kisses from her worshippers.

SEE ALSO *KAMESHWARI, *YOGANIDRA ASANA

AGAMAS

1. In Hinduism, the Agamas (Skt. "Source of the Teaching") constitute a class of scriptures that mainly contain *Shaiva teachings concerning ritual and cosmology. They are written in the form of supposed dialogues between the goddess *Parvati (or *Shakti) and the god *Shiva, and mark the appearance of *Shakta influence among the Shaiva groups in Tamil Nadu, a South Indian province. Among the approximately 200 texts, 28 are regarded as the Shaiva equivalent to the northern *Vedas. Like the Mahabharata, they are sometimes called the Fifth Veda. Little is known about these texts, as they have not yet been studied or researched in detail. 2. In Buddhism, the term is used for several texts belonging to the Tripitaka, texts without bearing on our topic.

AGHORA
(SKT. "NONTERRIFIED")

1. A form or manifestation of the Indian god *Shiva, here in a black and fierce aspect. 2. A name for one of the more extreme Indian *Vamacara sects founded by an adept known as Kanipa. Aghora teachings often concentrate on a forcible conversion of a limited human personality into a divine personality through the use of drugs, sexuality, and rituals that often take place in cemeteries. The members seem to delight in breaking every rule in the book of social conventions and generally accepted behavior. The practitioners of Aghora are known as Aghoris. According to Mircea Eliade, Aghoris were involved with the temple of *Kamakhya in *Assam and "were famous for their cruelties and orgies" (p. 305), a fact that often gave the general designation "Tantric yogi" a bad name.

SEE ALSO *BHOGIS

AGRAT BAT MAHALAT

A Near Eastern, Semitic goddess or *female sexual demon known for her role as sexual temptress and seductress. According to the *Talmud she is the "spirit of uncleanness," a designation stemming from her association with unbridled, instinctive sexuality.

SEE ALSO *SHEKINAH

AJNA CHAKRA

The "brow" chakra, one of the later additions to the older Tantric system of only four *chakras. It is now regarded as the sixth chakra.

LOCATION: Symbolically on the forehead, between the eyebrows; actually inside the brain, first cervical vertebra, plexus cavernosus

ENDOCRINE GLAND: *Pituitary

RULING *SHAKTI: Hakini
COLOR: Indigo
LOTUS: Two-petaled, milky white
ASSOCIATIONS: Cognition, psychic energies, synthesis

ALAMBUSHA   SEE *NADIS

ALCALOIDS   SEE *ALKALOIDS

ALCHEMY

After all that has been written on alchemy in both East and West, we must clarify that the popular notion of alchemists, as "mere" early and relatively ignorant chemists, is for the greater part a complete misunderstanding. The aim of true, inner alchemists was never to turn lead into *gold—an activity that was left to their materialistic colleagues who did not grasp the true nature of the "great work." Though less well known than the exoteric alchemists of Europe, the typical scientific (al)chemists of China and India also tried to make silver, gold, and gemstones; to transform wine into milk; and to make wine odorless. One of the oldest *Tantras, the Matrikabheda Tantra of the fourth century, is almost entirely devoted to secrets of alchemy.

Nevertheless, apart from such obviously exoteric attempts at the transmutation of certain substances (which is really chemistry), the Chinese, Indian, and European true art has always been an *inner alchemy: aiming at the completion and perfection of the human being. Certain alchemists throughout the ages have discovered, like the Tantric and Taoist adepts, that the energies released before, during, and after erotic play can be harnessed toward that goal. When Kenneth Grant writes that the "alchemist's metals were living substances" (reported by Redgrove, p. 147) he refers to erotic secretions, especially those of women. One of the best works on this subject may be that by Johannes Fabricius (1976; rev. ed. 1989).

SEE ALSO *ALEMBIC, *LO HUNG, *SRI VIDYA, *VAUGHAN, THOMAS, *YONITATTVA

ALCOHOL

Alcohol becomes an *anaphrodisiac when consumed in large quantities and has been identified as a major cause of what is called "secondary impotence" in men. However, tradition and experience also indicate clearly that wine, and drinks distilled from wine—such as Armagnac, cognac, and Metaxa—do have *aphrodisiac qualities, as do herbal liqueurs such as Benedictine and Chartreuse, when used in "appropriate" amounts. Note that the last two drinks were "invented" by monks and produced in their monasteries.

SEE ALSO *ABSINTHE, *MADYA

ALEMBIC
(FROM ARABIC *AL-ANBIQ*)

Generally speaking, the term *alembic* indicates a chemical or alchemical instrument used in distilling fluids, but it was also used as code (*see* *Secret Language) for the uterus (*see* *Yoni Topography/18).

ALGOLAGNIA

A term used to indicate the use and transformation of pain into a sexually arousing pleasure. This is not to be confused with the de facto addiction to pain as it occurs in classical *sadomasochism, though one must be aware that the line between these two is very thin and can easily be crossed.

ALCHEMY. *The Ninth Key of Alchemy:*
woman and man unite atop a fertilized egg.
Fifteenth-century engraving
by Basilius Valentinus.

Whereas sadomasochistic tendencies are often found in *puritanical fanaticism and in some of the more aggressive sexual preferences, algolagnia is much more at home in the realm of scratching with one's fingernails, love bites, and pinching the right places with the right amount of strength. Many couples avoid such techniques for expressing and arousing passion because of a fear, imprinted by society, that they might be dealing in sadomasochism.

The *Kama Sutra recommends and extensively describes techniques such as biting, scratching, and well-directed blows to certain body parts as an integral part of erotic play. In general, the dividing line between SM and algolagnia mainly depends, as with most things sexual, on a given society's general *sexual imprinting and local moral standards.

A prime example of painful sexual practices that will sound very strange to most readers—but regarded not only as normal but as absolutely "necessary" by the lovers themselves—can be found in Bronislaw Malinowski's famous study *Sexual Life of Savages*, first published in 1884. These "savages" not only are fond of biting off their lovers' eyelashes (*see* *Mitakuku), but also are given to heavy, blood-drawing scratching (*see* *Kimali).

SEE ALSO *KHLYSTI, *PURITANICAL FANATICISM

ALIPHATIC ACIDS
A number of odor-dispensing substances found in the vagina of most women.

SEE ALSO *SCENT AURA, *YONI TOPOGRAPHY/9

ALKALOIDS
Many of the better-known psychoactive plants contain alkaloid substances that are responsible for their specific psychosomatic effects. The alkaloid's function in the biological life of these plants themselves, however, is in most cases yet unknown to science. The following list of such plants and the chemicals derived from them shows a strange collection of legal and illegal drugs, poisons, and medicines used by humans as well as by animals:

coca leaves	* cocaine
cocoa plant	* cocoa
tea, coffee	caffeine
spotted hemlock	conine
* *fo-ti-tieng*	(consumed as an herb)
ergot fungus	lysergic acid diethylamide (*LSD)
* peyote cactus	* mescaline
opium poppy	* opium (morphine, heroin)
tobacco leaves	nicotine
* *Psilocybe mexicana*	* psilocybin, psilocin
quebracho tree	* quebrachin
cinchona bark	* quinine
castor beans	ricinine
Strychnos nux vomica	strychnine
yohimbe tree	* yohimbine

Along with the fact that many of these plants and their derivatives are now illegal in most nations, some authors have always tried to warn potential users not only of addiction but of possible death resulting from their use. For example, in his book on *aphrodisiacs, H. E. Wedeck writes the following under the heading "Poison Plants": "The most virulent plants are those that contain alkaloids as active principles. Some of these alkaloids form active principles in certain aphrodisiac compounds. Such compounds are generally fatal" (p. 194). Similar yet nonalkaloid drugs are, for example, *Amanita muscaria* and *MDMA.

AL'LAT
When we look closely at what is known about pre-Islamic worship of the Goddess we find foremost the goddess Al'Lat. Her name/title merely means "goddess," quite similar to calling Jehovah and Allah "the Lord" or simply "God." Al'Lat, however, is one of the deities of the moon who come in three aspects, similar to the Greek goddess manifested as Kore, Demeter, and Hecate. Each of these aspects corresponds to a phase of the moon and a phase in the life of women. The crescent moon is the *virgin, the full moon corresponds to the mother, and the waning moon hints at the crone, the wise old woman who has often been made into a witch. The Arabian Al'Lat is thus known under three other names, each one considered, by the initiate, to be but one manifestation of her totality. First, there is the maiden Q're, or Qure, the crescent moon. Second, we find the full-moon/mother aspect, *Al'Uzza, "the strong one," and last but not least is Al'Menat, a waning yet wise goddess of fate, prophecy, and divination. Islamic tradition views these three as "the daughters of Allah," but M. J. Vermaseren points out that Al'Lat is, grammatically, the feminine form of Allah, and vice versa (p. 22).

Al'Lat is that Arabian Great Goddess who was worshipped at the *Ka'bah, until the time when her shrine was taken over by the prophet Muhammad and when *matriarchy had to give way to male domination.

ALLEGRO, JOHN M.
(B. 1923)
A distinguished English scientist in the discipline of comparative Semitic philology. His research includes translations of the Dead Sea Scroll fragments and of ancient Sumerian texts. Allegro has published several books dealing with languages, myths, and history of this area and with the roots of Judaism and Christianity. His most famous and controversial work is *The Sacred Mushroom and the Cross*, written in 1970 and revised and enlarged in 1973. This work deals specifically with *Amanita muscaria* and its role in Christian mythology and ritual.

SEE ALSO *BACCHUS, *SEMEN, *SUMERIAN WRITING

ALMOND
In Phrygian mythology the almond is said to have sprung from the genitals of the goddess *Cybele. It is against this background that we must view the *yoni symbology of the vesica piscis or *mandorla.

SEE ALSO *EROTIC SYMBOLISM

ALOKA   SEE *BODHISATTVA DAKINIS

ALPHA ANDROSTEROL
A synthesized compound based on a *pheromone isolated from human sweat. The compound is closely related to the human *sex hormones and it smells, in purified form, very much like *sandalwood. Alpha androsterol is very similar to a pheromone found in boars, which is used by pig breeders to make a sow receptive to artificial insemination.

ALPHAISM
A term used in the *Great Brotherhood of God for the first degree of sexual initiation and practice. Alphaism consists mainly of observing what has been termed magical chastity, a type of *chastity that demands that all erotic activity and all sexual union be of a dedicated, ritual type. Further, it demands even mental chastity—that is, not thinking or fantasizing about sex except when actually engaged in sexual activity.

SEE ALSO *DIANISM, *QODOSH

AL'UZZA
One aspect of the *triple goddess known as *Al'Lat, it seems that especially Al'Uzza was worshipped at the *Ka'bah, where she was served by seven priestesses and where her worshippers circled the holy stone, in total nudity, seven times—once for each of the ancient seven planets. The sacred place with its life-giving well, Zamzam, right next to it attracted pilgrims from all over the Arabian Peninsula and its neighboring regions. Here, with the black *sacred stone—a symbol of her *yoni—in an oasis of life-giving waters, the goddess resided in her aspect as Earth Mother, creatrix of life and helper of women in childbirth. To this image and focus of energies people come to pray, to ask for offspring and protection, and to celebrate life. We now can appreciate why *Abraham, who with his wife Sarah was barren for many years, came here to make love with *Hagar—and why Muhammad, being fed up with women ruling his life, needed to conquer this very spot in order to put Allah, himself, and his male followers in control.

The Arabian philosopher and alchemist Al-Kindy (810–872 C.E.), as *Burton and Briffault inform us, let the world of the ninth century know in his "The Apology" that the moon goddess Al'Uzza was enshrined in the Ka'bah, where she was attended by her priestesses (Burton, vol. 2, p. 161; Briffault, vol. 3, p. 79). Another source tells of the probability that "Al'Uzza may be connected to the name of the predynastic Egyptian cobra goddess Ua Zit, who is closely linked with the image of *Isis" (Stone, 1984, p. 124).

AMANITA MUSCARIA
Botanical name for the psychotropic mushroom commonly known as fly agaric, a name stemming from the fact that its toxic substance, *muscarine, is used to kill flies; but it is also fatal to humans. It is now believed that this was the major ingredient in what Indian texts and adepts know as the sacred drug called *soma, an ancient type of *LSD. The fungus is toxic, and an overdose can easily be fatal, though the toxic dose varies according to individual. Because of this potential danger, it was/is usually first given to a cow, which "preprocesses" it, and only then the user will drink the less poisonous substance contained in the cow's urine.

Not only in India was/is this mushroom known and highly valued as a sacred plant/drug, but Siberian shamans and early Sumerian priests also made use of it to aid them in their explorations of other realities. The prime exponents of the ancient world's many cults based on the ritual use of *Amanita muscaria* were the *Bacchantes, the all-female group of worshippers associated with the god *Bacchus.

In his famous work *The Sacred Mushroom and the Cross*, John M. *Allegro comes to the conclusion that the early use of *Amanita muscaria* by the Sumerians and their neighbors involved a mixture of *phallic worship (the mushroom being a phallic symbol), *ritual promiscuity, and the achievement of visionary experiences induced by the drug. Allegro offers a variety of evidence to support his findings that it is this very mystery religion that lies at the root of Christianity. In short, Allegro says that "Jesus, like the Dionysus of the related Bacchic religion, is but a personification of the sacred fungus, the 'smeared' or anointed, the 'Christ,' the phallic representation of the ancient fertility god" (1972, p. 39); in other words, he is Yahweh/Jehovah, Jove/Jupiter, and also *Zeus.

SEE ALSO *DIONYSUS, *MAGIC MUSHROOMS

AMA-NO-UZUME

A *Shinto deity known as the "dread female of heaven." Similar to the Greek *Baubo, she is mainly known for her *yoni magic, displaying her "heavenly gate" in public before all the other divinities. This myth, celebrated in the *kagura festival, probably gave rise to the early Japanese stone sculptures in which a woman is shown displaying her *yoni, quite similar to the Celtic figures of the *Sheela-na-gig.

SEE ALSO *SARUTAHIKO

AMARNATHA CAVE

Discovered in remote times by a wandering shepherd, this cave is now one of India's foremost places of pilgrimage, where about 100,000 devotees meet annually. The cave holds—so Indian tradition tells—the *lingam of the god *Shiva, modeled by Nature herself as a stalagmite of ice more than three meters tall. Every August, this lingam of ice grows anew; then it withers away again afterward.

SEE ALSO *KASHMIR, *PHALLIC WORSHIP, *SHIVALINGA

AMAROLI   SEE *OLI TECHNIQUES

AMATERASU-O-MI-KAMI

Japanese goddess of the sun, literally "heaven radiant great divinity," and highest of all *Shinto deities. The famous myth of her withdrawal into a cave, caused by her indigna-

tion at the deeds of her divine brother, thus casting the world into general darkness, is celebrated in the *kagura festival. According to Japanese tradition, this cave, with the name Ama-no-Iwato, or "heavenly rock dwelling," is located at Takachiho on the island of Kyushu.

AMAURIANS

A thirteenth-century "heretical" and anarchist sect in France, which—according to Norman Cohn's *The Pursuit of the Millennium*—committed, in the words of an abbot, "adulteries and other acts which give pleasure to the body. And to the women with whom they sinned . . . they promised that these sins would not be punished." Incidentally, the Amaurians thought themselves to be "gods," and like some other heretical groups, they could be regarded as Western Tantrics.

AMARNATHA CAVE. *The sacred *lingam of natural ice in the *Amarnatha cave, 30 kilometers east of Pahalgam, Eastern Kashmir.*

AMBER

Amber, a sweet-smelling resin from a particular tree native to *Assam, not only is regarded as an *aphrodisiac scent but is believed to have purifying and healing powers. This type of amber comes in two varieties. The dark, almost black amber is regarded as female, and the lighter, less sweet, less heavy-smelling variety is seen as male in essence. Amber is won from the tree's roots and then crystallized; the crystalline substance continues to grow slightly, over years. Its strong aroma, if it is kept in a closed container, will last indefinitely. The use of amber—as a perfume and a medicine—was known to shamans and medicine men among American Indians, practitioners of *Sufism, and tribal peoples in the Far East.

This type of amber has little to do with the semiprecious "stones" by the same name that are found in the sea or earth. That amber is a fossilized transformation, by pressure and age, of a similar resin from ancient pine trees.

Sometimes the term amber is also—unknowingly?—used for the substance known as *ambergris.

AMBERGRIS
(FROM FRENCH AMBRE GRIS, "GRAY AMBER")

A waxy substance often found on the shores or in the waters of tropical seas. The sources of this substance are the few sperm whales left alive today, which secrete ambergris from their intestines. The largest piece of this substance ever found weighed 418 kilograms. Like *civet, it is mainly used in the preparation of strong and erotic perfumes. It was also used as an *aphrodisiac, laced in chocolate candies at the courts of seventeenth-century France. In Persia, little pills were made from powdered gold, rubies, pearls, and ambergris, and drinking ambergris in one's coffee is a widespread custom in many Oriental countries. Besides enhancing desire, the substance is also believed to have healing and life-preserving properties, and in Eastern countries it is often used as a spice. Known and sold most often under the name amber, it is a rare and costly substance. Many stores in the United States and the Caribbean islands offer ambergris oil, which is often, unfortunately, a synthetic.

AMPALLANG

Name for a small shaft made of bone or metal that is inserted in a hole bored through the penile glans (see *Lingam Topography/7). Although in literature this form of piercing is often wrongly discussed with male circumcision, the two are unrelated. The ampallang is clearly a genital adornment and, according to those who really know, a genital enhancement.

A visit to the Sarawak Museum in Kuching, Borneo, proved very enlightening as to the origins of this practice. Here it was shown that the ampallang practice originated as a means, both magical and practical, and was motivated by the desire to acquire the stamina and strength—and perhaps even the size—of a rhino. The rhinoceros of Borneo has, clearly visible, a small diagonal bone in his member. During maturity, by way of calcification through urine, this natural ampallang even grows in size—something that also happens to men who never take the insert out of their flesh. Tribal ampallang wearers often announce their status by having a special mark tattooed on their shoulder

The practice is known not only among the Dayak of Borneo but also in other areas of Oceania, and it results in a phallus not only adorned but apparently more stimulating to the men's sexual partners. The local women compare making love without an ampallang to the taste of plain rice, whereas sexual union enhanced by an ampallang is seen as much more exciting—in their words, as rice with salt. In the recent decade, with its renaissance of body adornment and modification, the ampallang has begun to appear in the bedrooms of the Western hemisphere as well.

SEE ALSO *CIRCUMCISION/MALE/4, *LABIAESTHETICS

AMPLEXUS RESERVATUS

Technical term used by the Catholic Church for a practice much abhorred by the Church, in which both man and woman have sexual union not aimed at procreation, without *ejaculation. In 1952 the Irish Ecclesiastical Record, an official publication of the Vatican, carried a "warning" to all those writers who have "praised and recommended" this practice "in an unreserved and shamelessly detailed manner," as J. *Lowndes-Sevely reports (p. 62).

SEE ALSO *COITUS RESERVATUS, *KAREZZA

AMRITA
(SKT., "IMMORTAL")

Term for the famous "nectar of immortality" or "water of life" known to adepts of *Tantra, *Taoism, *sexual magick, and *inner alchemy. Sometimes the term was also used to indicate the sacred drug usually known as *soma.

AMSAK SEE IMSAK

ANAHATA CHAKRA
(SKT., "UNSTRUCK")

The "heart" *chakra;* one of the *chakras* of the earlier Tantric tradition and now the fourth *chakra.* This can be compared to one of the three Taoist *tan-t'ien, and it is known among the *Sufi as the "secret center."

> LOCATION: Center of chest in the heart region, first thoracic vertebra, plexus cardiacus
> ENDOCRINE GLAND: Thymus
> RULING *SHAKTI: Kakini
> COLOR: Gray-blue
> LOTUS: 15-petaled, red
> ASSOCIATIONS: Touch, compassion, consciousness

ANANDA

Sanskrit term for the principle of joy, bliss, transcendence, and spiritual *ecstasy.

ANANGA RANGA

Written or compiled by the sixteenth-century Indian author Kalyanamalla, this manual of erotic arts was translated into English in 1873. Similar to the *Kama Sutra, the *Koka Shastra, or the *Ars Amatoria, it deals with a great variety of erotic, sexual, and moral subjects from hygiene to incantations, from *aphrodisiac love philters to sexual positions and the "how to" of seducing members of the opposite gender. Although the Kama Sutra is the most famous of these books, the Ananga Ranga is probably the best and most complete guide to the erotic ideas and concepts of India. An 1885 translation by Richard *Burton has often been criticized as being insufficiently scientific, but his many annotations and his general knowledge of Oriental customs make his a valuable work.

> SEE ALSO *POMPOIR, *SHANKHINI NADI

ANAPHRODISIACS

As counterpart to *aphrodisiacs, this term indicates plants, formulas, and practices that have the effect of reducing sexual desire. Among the better known are valerian, vinegar, lemonade, cold showers, tobacco, and the extensive use of alcohol. So in case you want, don't!

ANAT

In the *Bible this goddess is mentioned as Anath, and there are several alternative spellings of her name: Anata, Anit, Antu. She is the Ugaritic Great Goddess of life and death and the Canaanite "lady of the mountain." Known as *virgin, mother, and whore, she is also famous as an aggressive and ruthless warrior-goddess who wades in the *blood of her human victims. Anat was introduced into Egypt by the Hyksos and was there partly identified with *Hathor, from whom she acquired her symbolic cow horns. The Egyptians regarded her, together with *Astarte, as daughter of the god Ra, or Re (the sun), and Pharaoh Ramses III (who ruled from 1198 to 1166 B.C.E.) used both goddesses as divine protectors on his battle shield. Anat—as a goddess of fertility and sexuality—is sometimes depicted together with the *ithyphallic *Min. She is said to have given birth to a wild bull that sprang from her union with her brother and lover, the Ugaritic/Syrian god Baal.

ANDROGENS

The androgens are steroid hormones manufactured in glands of the *endocrine system. The term is used for male *sex hormones such as *androstenone and *testosterone. Their female counterparts are the *estrogens.

> SEE ALSO *ALPHA ANDROSTEROL

ANDROSTENONE

An active male hormone or *androgen, the first ever to have been discovered/isolated (1931) by medical science. It is found in perspiration and *saliva and is also produced by bacteria in the armpits. Its *scent is described as musky and sometimes as flowery. Men produce larger amounts than women, but women are more sensitive in detecting this odor.

In an experiment at Birmingham University, a waiting-room chair was sprayed with varying amounts of this substance. While men seemed repelled by the chair, especially at the higher doses, most women "seemed actively attracted" to it, according to Lyall Watson (1989, pp. 87 ff.).

Some of the preliminary and tentative results of a worldwide "smell survey" indicate that many people, especially males (and in particular Americans), cannot smell this substance at all. However, since it is known that repeated exposure improves the ability to detect its molecules in the air, this may not be a genetic trait but rather a result of excessive "hygiene": eliminating or hiding real body scents for most of one's life. The percentage of women and men who are able to smell it is shown in the following table:

WOMEN	MEN	REGION
85.3	78.4	Africa
84.2	75.9	Europe (except United Kingdom)
82.8	74.5	Asia
82.5	70.8	Caribbean islands
82.3	75.4	Latin America
82.1	75.8	Australia
79.1	70.0	United Kingdon
70.5	62.8	United States of America

(From Gilbert and Wysocki)

One ounce of androstenone can cost as much as $200,000.

ANGEL WATER

A Portuguese *aphrodisiac cocktail that was, writes H. E. Wedeck, popular in the eighteenth century. The following recipe can be found in his 1962 *Dictionary of Aphrodisiacs*:

1 pint orange flower water

1 pint *rose water

1/2 pint myrtle water

2/3 distilled spirit of *musk [sic]

2/3 spirit of *ambergris [sic]

ANKH

Also known as the crux ansata, the Egyptian ankh is a probable precursor to the Christian cross. Most often simply explained as a symbol of life, it is popularly known in present-day Egypt as the key to the Nile: the key to Egypt's fertile water and earth.

The ankh quite obviously represents the union of *yoni and *lingam: of both male and female energies that combine to create all things. We can detect here the remnants of fertility symbolism, which is still reflected in the modern connection with the Nile. A male-female symbolism is also inherent in the Christian cross, where the horizontal line, or beam, represents the female and earthy pole and the vertical stands for the celestial, male, active forces, almost as if one were to insert a closed *yang line of the *I Ching vertically into an open *yin line.

SEE ALSO *DUALISM, *EROTIC SYMBOLISM

ANNA FURRINA AND/OR ANNA PERENNA

An Etruscan, and subsequently Roman, goddess whose *fertility festivals were aimed at stimulating the fertility of both plants and humans. Her worship also involved *ritual prostitution.

ANTHROPOPHAGY. *The widespread practice of *cannibalism is symbolized by the outstretched, lolling tongue. Wolfgang Winter (1948, Berlin) has accumulated much evidence for this, especially as related to ritual masks. Indonesian mask from Ubud, Bali. Photograph by Rufus C. Camphausen.*

ANTHROPOPHAGY
(FROM GREEK *ANTHROPOS*, "HUMAN," AND *PHAGIA*, "EATING")

A term that indicates the practice of cannibalism, a phenomenon once common in most human societies. Contrary to popular opinion, anthropophagy was (or is) not practiced only by so-called primitives or savages, or only during the Stone Age or merely somewhere in the jungles of New Guinea, Africa, or South America. Among the adherents of such ritual feasting were the Chinese, Tibetans, Indians, Aztecs, English, Germans, Indonesians, Filipinos, and many more.

A most special treat for the cannibal was the consumption of human brain, the eating of which was thought to confer the dead person's life force, intelligence, daring, and strength. According to Oscar *Kiss-Maerth, the eating of brain from a monkey or human being clearly has *aphrodisiac effects. In fact, author Kiss-Maerth tried monkey brain himself in order to establish the truth of the matter, and he found out it was true!

In India, within the circles of *Tantra, the meat of a sacrified human is known as *mahamamsa (Skt., maha, "great," and mamsa, "flesh, meat"). The term occurs in the *Nila Tantra where the text discusses various types of *sacrifice. It does not actually refer to the consumption of the flesh, but usually the term mamsa is used for meat eaten during certain rituals.

APHRODISIACS

Term for a variety of substances that stimulate desire and/or enchance sexual activity, hence the name reminiscent of *Aprodite, the Near Eastern and Greek goddess of love and desire.

Most of these substances are based on plants; others derive from secretions or body parts of certain animals (*musk, *civet, *caviar). Aphrodisiacs mentioned in this encyclopedia range from *cinnamon to *zinc, from *garlic to *oysters, and from *goat's milk to *LSD and *jasmine scent to *wheat germ. As the reader can see even from this short list, many aphrodisiacs can be obtained by anyone in a local store, but the more esoteric ones, like *bird nests, can be obtained only through specialized distributors. Much of the information concerning the traditional aphrodisiacs derives from Chinese, Arabian, Indian, and Greek sources, and often several substances are combined into recipes for certain success in matters erotic. A typical example of such a prescription—this one from Morocco—combines *honey, *sesame, *cannabis, and *spanish fly. During recent years, however, and even before the human *pheromones were discovered, several companies started to bring out attractants containing animal pheromones, which by definition cannot affect humans. Thus, most of these modern aphrodisiacs are no better than the ancient ones, and rely more on a psychological effect of the wearer than on actual influence on the other. Perhaps the whole question of influence will change radically with the arrival of more and more compounds based on and containing human-based pheromones, the first of which have already arrived in the marketplace.

One of the most powerful aphrodisiacs, however, is available to everyone but should prove quite difficult to buy or eat.

That substance is the brain of humans, monkeys, and certain other animals. Research as well as personal testing—in this case with monkey brain—have convinced author Oscar *Kiss-Maerth that the cannibalist practices of our ancestors, involving the eating of the brain, indeed have a powerful boosting effect on one's sexual desire and virility. Come to think of it, I myself much prefer the type of stimulation proposed by Timothy Leary (1920 96), who once stated that "intelligence is the ultimate aphrodisiac." Those who would like to pursue this specific topic throughout the encyclopedia will find a helpful listing in index 5.3 on page 274.

SEE ALSO *BRAIN (AS APHRODISIAC), *GAYATRI MANTRA, *TANTRIC PERFUMES

APHRODITE
(GREEK, "DESIRE," "INTERCOURSE")

Aphrodite is one of the few goddesses of ancient times who is still well known—albeit incompletely—in the present day. Although her cult has its roots in the region that today constitutes Turkey and Cyprus, she has become known as a Greek/European deity.

Aphrodite was, according to her various myths, born from the sperm of the last *ejaculation of the dying god Uranos as he was being castrated by his son Cronos, and most of her psychological and social attributes are reflections of this primal association with sexuality: love, desire, seduction, and *ecstasy, the latter sometimes in connection with *opium and other drugs.

A great goddess such as Aphrodite often acquires—throughout the ages and among the peoples who worship her—a great number of symbolic associations. Although the *dove is her primary sacred animal, she also has ties with the sparrow, the wryneck (a type of woodpecker), and the dolphin. Among plants, the *lily, *rose, *apple, *pomegranate, *myrtle, and *quince are sacred to her, as well as *opium poppy, *mandrake, and the *aphrodisiac scents of fennel, *myrrh, and *cinnamon. Other symobls are her famous girdle of *gold and the *scallop (Greek kteis, or *yoni).

Aphrodite's names are many; here is a collection of those pertaining to our inquiry:

Aphrodite Ambologear	"She who postpones old age"
Aphrodite Hetaera	"Aphrodite the harlot" (refers to her involvement with *ritual and *secular prostitution)
Aphrodite Kallipygos	"She of the lovely behind"

Aphrodite Ourania	"Aphrodite of the heavens"
Aphrodite Pandemos	"Aphrodite of all the people"
Aphrodite Peribaso	"Aphrodite the streetwalker"
Aphrodite Philommeides	"Smile-loving Aphrodite" (most likely a wordplay referring to *philommedes*, which translates as "penis-loving" or "genital-loving")
Aphrodite Porne	"Aphrodite the arousing one"
Aphrodite Trymalitis	"Aphrodite as goddess of ultimate sexual consummation"

Further epitaphs are "Aphrodite of copulation," "Aphrodite who rides astride," "Aphrodite who opens herself up," "Aphrodite the persuasive," "Aphrodite the sideglancer," "Aphrodite who contrives ways and means for lovers," "Aphrodite of the *mandrake," "she who lulls the senses (*opium) and gives sweet sleep."

APOCRINE GLANDS SEE *SCENT GLANDS

APPLE
It is not by accident that an apple is featured so importantly in the biblical book of Genesis as well as in the Greek myth of Paris and Helen of Troy (C. 1200 B.C.E.). In both Greece and Rome the apple was considered an amorous gift, was a sacred plant associated with *Aphrodite/*Venus, and was beloved by lovers, who exchanged apples, or threw them at one another. An interesting bit of information connecting this erotic apple to the *perspiration from someone's armpits is recounted in the entry on *scent glands.

APRICOT
Like the *peach or fig, the apricot derives its use as a symbol of the *yoni from its general shape.

SEE ALSO *EROTIC SYMBOLISM, *YONI SYMBOLOGY

APRIUS SEE *PRIAPUS

APSARASAS
(SKT., "MOVING IN WATER")
A group of female Indian deities generally associated with water, though they are also known as shape-shifters who can assume any form at will. They appear most often as magnificent women, the "daughters of joy," with rich, long hair and *breasts smelling of *sandalwood. One of their

APSARASA. *"Daughter of Joy," an *apsarasa from the Vishnu temple in Srirangam, Tamil Nadu, India. Photograph by Bodo Willrich, Bad Vilbel, Germany.*

functions is to tempt, seduce, or test potential male initiates, ascetics, hermits, and so forth, and they are said to do so to the point of madness. On the other hand, they accompany fallen warriors to their well-deserved afterlife. Many of the female figures depicted in and on temples such as *Khajuraho are *apsarasas* and *yakshinis,* and they can be compared to the European concept of the *nymphs.

AQUA VITAE
Latin term meaning the "water of life," used for erotic fluid secretions in general, especially for female ones.

SEE ALSO *FEMALE LOVE JUICES

ARGININE

One of the eight essential amino acids, arginine is especially important to male sexual functioning. Sperm cells, which have to be produced and replaced after each *ejaculation, are made up of 80 percent arginine. However, a deficiency leads to loss of sexual interest in both men and women.

SEE ALSO *SEMEN

ARGHA

A *yoni-shaped ritual chalice, an *argha* (named for a *Sanskrit word for "bowl") is used to pour libations on a woman's yoni in order to bestow on her the energies of the Goddess.

SEE ALSO *STRI PUJA/1, *YONI PUJA

ARIADNE AND/OR ARIAGNE

A Greek goddess whose myth matches her with the male archetype known as the vegetation god (*see* *Attis) and whose worship included the rite called *hieros gamos. In her case it is a celebration of her sacred marriage with her lover *Dionysus. As a pair, they were worshipped together on the Greek islands of Crete, Naxos, and Los.

ARS AMANDI

The "art of love" as practiced by the brethren of the *Free Spirit Movement, the art being what is usually known as *coitus reservatus.

ARS AMATORIA

"The Art of Loving" is probably the most important erotic poem by Ovid (43 B.C.E.–17 C.E.). The poem instructs men and women on how to attract the attention of members of the other sex. Written in the year 1, its major message is that in order to be loved, one must love. Nevertheless, Ovid was exiled from Rome, partly because of the *Ars Amatoria* and partly because of his sexual involvement with Julia, daughter of the Roman emperor Augustus (63 B.C.E.–14 C.E.).

ARSENIC   SEE *MENSTRUAL FLUID, *YONIMANDALA

ARTEMIS   SEE *EPHESIAN ARTEMIS

ARYAN INVASION THEORY

In this book, the reader will find various items that refer to the established theory and widely held belief that Indian

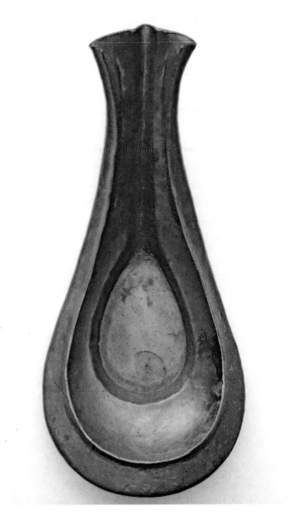

ARGHA. *A beautiful example of a ritual chalice from India. Height, 30 cm. Vincent Dame Collection, Amsterdam. Photograph by Remus Dame.*

civilization as we know it has been formed by the confluence of two often clashing cultures. First was one of the subcontinent's indigenous peoples and their customs, ranging from tribal Assamese and Dravidian worshippers of the Goddess to the highly advanced civilization along the rivers Indus and *Sarasvati. Along came, so goes the theory, an iron-based people from the northwest, people with patriarchal concepts who invaded and began to dominate Indian life, for example, creating the caste system that made indigenous peoples second- and third-class citizens.

However, in recent years this Aryan invasion theory has been challenged on many grounds by both new liguistical and new archaeological insights, mainly from Indian scientists. As this discussion is far from resolved, and especially because even Indian scholars are still divided into two camps on these issues, it is not yet possible to replace the current theory with a seamless new one. We'll have to await further developments before history can be rewritten, if indeed it needs to be.

ASAG

Term for traditional period of *nuptial continence that was observed in parts of medieval France. The newlyweds would sleep the first three nights without touching each other. The lovers lay in bed naked but with a sword, as a symbol of chastity, between their bodies (Nelli, p. 95).

SEE ALSO *STRI PUJA/2

ASANA

General generic name for any of several exercises or positions in Tantric or other yogas. Individually, each *asana* has a specific name, such as **bhaga, *chakra,* or *lata asana.* Such *asanas* are designed with specific goals: some speed up or slow down blood circulation, others change the electromagnetic polarities of the human body, and still others aid in the exchange of sexual energies with a partner. There is as yet no work that shows and explains all of the Tantric sexual *asanas,* but several of them are described in detail, and often depicted, in *Sexual Secrets* by Nik Douglas and Penny Slinger, and in Kamala Devi's *The Eastern Way of Love.* The latter, though otherwise quite a strange book, written as an exotic love manual for the not very imaginative American "husband and wife," does have its merits in this area. Taoist exercises and positions, sometimes similar to the Indian *asanas,* have been published by Mantak Chia and by H. S. Levi and A. Ishihara (see bibliography).

SEE ALSO *BANDHA, *MAITHUNA VIPARITA, *SHAKTI ASANA

ASHERAH

Most often said to be the Hebrew name for *Astarte and also used to indicate the wooden pillars associated with her shrines and sacred places. Originally, however, Asherah was an independent Near Eastern deity and was called "she who gives birth (to gods)" and "wet nurse of the gods." Her worship included *ritual prostitution.

ASHTORETH

A biblical name for the goddess *Astarte/*Ishtar, who appears in several books of the Old Testament: Genesis 14:5, Judges 2:13 and 10:6, I Kings 11:5, and II Kings 23:13.

ASS

An animal famous for its sexual playfulness and virility and consequently often identified with phallic/erotic male deities such as *Dionysus. On Greek vases the ass is often shown with an erect phallus, and some Greek men went so far as to carry a *testicle of an ass as an amulet to increase their potency. It is also not by chance that the most famous classical story of erotic adventure, magic, and religion is "The Golden Ass." Its Roman/Algerian author, Lucius Apuleius (b. 123 C.E.), later became an initiate of the goddesses *Cybele and Isis, and he also wrote of the Thracian/Greek witches' preference for the *female superior position.

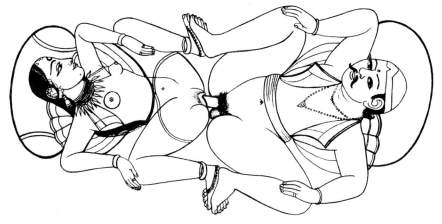

Asana. *The aim of ritual union is not always the romantic, face-to-face encounter for which many westerners aim. This couple has arranged arms, legs, and feet to create a closed circuit that directs the sexual energy to flow in a continuous loop. Drawing by Penny Slinger, after a nineteenth-century miniature in the collection of the King of Nepal.*

ASSAM

Next to *Bengal, Assam is the region that has been most prominent in the development of *Tantra and *Shakta. Politically, Assam has been one of the Indian provinces since 1947, and it is much troubled by ethnic and religious unrest.

In the past, however, Assam was part of the famous nation of Kamrup, or Kamarupa, and we can find it mentioned under this name in many ancient scriptures. Assam is a province full of tribal peoples with roots in India, China, and Burma and has been—and still is—a melting pot of influences from all of these cultures. One finds in Assam the *Kamakhya Pitha with its unique *Yonimandala. In eighth-century Pagan, a nearby city in Burma, Tantric worship was known and sexual rituals were held, showing that the area of and around Assam has been a Tantric stronghold where influences from India and *Mahacina came together.

Unfortunately, the Indian government has restricted travel into Assam for many years, partly because of frictions with local tribal people and partly because of the recurring tensions during the 1990s between the central government and those who fight for independence.

ASTARTE

This "queen of heaven" and Great Goddess, with a *dove as her symbolic animal, was worshipped mainly by the Canaanites, Assyrians, and Phoenicians. She was also venerated by some early Hebrew tribes, by whom she was called "the goddess of Sidon," often side by side with Yahweh/Yehovah—as at the archaeological site of Mizpah, where temples stood to both deities. In the Upper Egypt of 500 B.C.E., the local Hebrew immigrants/slaves worshipped her as the goddess of the moon and as divine consort.

Astarte is a true western Semitic equivalent to the Mesopotamian *Ishtar, and if the two deities are not actually one and the same, they are at least two very similar expressions of one goddess-oriented religion that prevailed for several millennia in western Asia. Other related names are Ashdar or Astar, names that were also used for Ishtar. Both she and Astarte had a brother and lover, named Tammuz or Dumuzi, who was a vegetation god like *Attis. Astarte's fame and the religious tolerance of Egypt led to her being officially admitted into the Egyptian pantheon about 1500 B.C.E., though here she was mainly regarded as a goddess of battlefields, soldiers, and horses. Elsewhere her religion embraced *ritual prostitution and the rite of *hieros gamos.

SEE ALSO *SACRED STONES

ATARGATIS

Near Eastern goddess of the moon who was worshipped mainly in the Levant: today's Turkey, Syria, Israel, and Lebanon. Atargatis is one of the independent *virgins, and her myth speaks of a union with the archetypal vegetation god and of *incest. She was often worshipped in a more or less public *orgy that usually involved both *ritual prostitution and *ritual promiscuity.

ATHARVA VEDA SEE *VEDAS

ATTIS

Husband/lover of the Near Eastern goddess *Cybele, whose myth is responsible for the annual *castration rites of her priests. Many myths of the Mediterranean and Near Eastern Great Goddesses feature this type of male vegetation god, and their stories sound very much alike. Attis is closely related to Tammuz and Dumuzi in the cult of *Astarte

AUPARISHTAKA

Literally, this *Sanskrit term means "mouth-congress" and is similar to the English term "oral sex," that is, *fellatio and *cunnilingus. The practice is held in high regard by certain Tantric groups and in *sexual magick but is, of course, condemned by almost everyone else, whether Hindu or Christian.

AURA SEMINALIS

Similar to the Indian concepts of *bindu and *ojas, this word was used by European alchemists to denote the metaphysical, subtle dimension of male *semen. Together with the *liquor vitae, its physical counterpart, the aura seminalis is, according to esoteric theory, one of the two major constituents of semen.

SEE ALSO *SEMINAL VISCOSITY, *SEXUAL BIOCHEMISTRY AND ELECTROMAGNETISM

AUTOSEXUAL MAGICAL PRACTICE SEE *MASTURBATION

B

Divided into two parts, I create.

DEVI BHAGAVATA

BABYLON

Famous ancient metropolis on the banks of the river Euphrates, which flourished—with ups and downs—from about 2300 B.C.E. until 482 B.C.E., when it was finally destroyed by the Persians. Along with *Sodom and Gomorrah, Babylon—and its religion, deities, people, and morals—has had much "bad press" and was, to the Jews of the Old Testament, a place "full of abominations." This was—along with political reasons—due to the fact that Babylonians worshipped the goddess *Ishtar, were polytheistic, and were famous for their promiscuity and the practice of *ritual prostitution. In fact, the city became known as "the great whore," and the "Whore of Babylon" also features prominently in the biblical apocalypse. The women in the temple of *Bit-Shagatha may not have been ritual prostitutes in the true sense of priestesses and trained adepts in the arts of ecstasy and delight but rather women for whom such "initiation" was deemed educational. However, Babylon also knew the institution of the *kaluttu*, or "house of the bride." These were cloisterlike buildings attached to the temples where the *qadeshtu*—consecrated and sacred *hierodules—lived and worked. The city, of course, also had its share of common taverns and brothels associated with *secular prostitution.

SEE ALSO *RITUAL PROMISCUITY, *SCARLET WOMAN

BACCHANTES

The female worshippers of *Bacchus. The Bacchantes, whose proverbial bouts of violence and unchecked sexuality were always succeeded by introspective withdrawal and calm silence, not only were intoxicated by love, wine, and adoration of their deity but also used the mushroom *Amanita muscaria* in their rites. The almost manic-depressive pattern of behavior for which they are known is consistent with the behavior this drug induces in most of its users. The Bacchantes' Greek equivalent are the *maenads.

BACCHUS

Ancient Roman god of wine and erotic ecstasy, whose association with the goat, licentious festivals, and the ecstatic rapture of the *Bacchantes is well known. According to philologist John M. *Allegro, the name is linguistically derived from the Sumerian word *balag Ush* (pronounced with the *l* silent), which means "erect penis." Myths, imagery, and associated rituals make it clear that he represents a Roman development of the Greek god *Dionysus, whose other Greek name was Bakkhos.

BANALINGA

A specific form of the *shivalinga, a symbol and an energy that, S. C. Banerjee writes, is supposed to "reside in the triangle of the *anahata chakra*" (Banerjee, p. 549)

BANDHA

(SKT., "KNOT," BONDAGE)

Term for various yogic techniques aiding in the control of physical processes and energies such as one's breath or, for example, the control of *ejaculation by certain muscular contractions. The term is used in combined words such as the *muladhara bandha*.

SEE ALSO *ASANA, *MUDRA/3

BARDO

(TIB., "IN-BETWEEN STATE")

It is true that the Tibetan term *bar-do* (and/or *zhi-khro*) is used to indicate the intermediate phases one has to pass through between death and one's next rebirth or reincarnation, according to these teachings. However, *bardo* also stands for other special states of mind, not all of which are connected with death. These states are differentiated as follows:

1. *skyes-gnas bar-do:* intermediate state of ordinary consciousness; the ordinary waking state
2. *rmi-lam bar-do:* intermediate state of dreaming
3. *bsam-gtan bar-do:* intermediate state of meditation
4. *'hi-kha'i bar-do:* intermediate state of dying, of the moment of death
5. *chos-nyid bar-do:* intermediate state of reality
6. *srid-pa bar-do:* intermediate state of rebirth, of becoming

As can be seen from these translations, only states 4 through 6 are part of the period during which an individual is believed to remain in a kind of limbo between death and (re)birth: a period that lasts—according to the Tibetan teachings—forty-nine days.

BARDO THÖDOL

According to tradition, a text based on oral teachings by *Padmasambhava and recorded in written form in about 760. After having been hidden as a so-called *terma,* the text was then rediscovered (and extended) by the *terton Karma Lingpa in the fourteenth century. The text is part of the *Kargling Zhikhro collection of the *Dzogchen tradition and shows traces of earlier and originally pre-Buddhist Tibetan thought, as is indicated by symbolism and divinities that are part of the shamanic *Bön religion. By way of the early misrepresentation of the text by Evans-Wentz (1878–1957), the Western reader has come to know this text as *The Tibetan Book of the Dead,* a translation that has misguided many readers. A much better translation is *Liberation by Hearing During One's Existence in the Bardo.*

The text is read aloud (i.e., liberation by hearing) to someone in *bardo,* sometimes as pure instruction for meditation and also, at the time of death, to prepare the mind for the adventures ahead in the form of *rebirth or *reincarnation.

BARTHOLIN GLANDS   SEE *YONI
TOPOGRAPHY/12

BASA ANDERE
(BASQUE, "FOREST-WOMAN")

In Basque legend, Basa Andere is said to be a beautiful woman, "perfectly shaped" for love and covered all over with soft, golden hair like a cat's. This Basque "wild lady" can usually be met near a sunlit stream in a forest, where she awaits the wanderer while combing the hair of her soft belly with a golden comb. She will smile lovingly at the man, lie back with open legs, and offer him first a view of the beautiful moist flower between her thighs and then entrance into her warm and fragrant body. It is said that the pleasure of making love to Basa Andere is so intense that a man will die from it at the height of his orgasm. The dead are found with their backs arched in the agony of unimaginable pleasure.

SEE ALSO *LAMIA

BASIL

This aromatic green herb, commonly at home in the Italian kitchen, is also reputed to cure the "deficiency of *Venus," that is, the lack of erotic impulse. Italian girls also used this alleged *aphrodisiac as a love charm.

BAUBO

The story of the Greek goddesses Demeter and Baubo is an example of *yoni magic in which Baubo spontaneously and unexpectedly raises her skirt and makes Demeter take a good look at her genitals. The strange and mysterious part of this myth is the fact that this did not happen in a setting of gaiety, erotic stimulation, or drunkenness, but in a moment of utter despair and sadness, with Demeter in tears over the loss of her daughter Kore.

The French psychologist and author Georges Devereux has written an extensive analytical study on the figure of Baubo. His explanation of this particular myth may be close to the original meaning: that Baubo's exhibitionist action may have been intended as a reminder to the grief-stricken Demeter that she—as a woman, but especially as the goddess of fertility—carries in herself the means of giving birth to new life. Demeter's attachment and pain concerning her daughter, now abducted to the realm of Pluto (the Greek god of death), had made her forget about the creative power of the yoni/woman who endlessly creates life. She is reminded that life is by definition temporary and that all life will someday turn back to the womb of Earth in an endless and unceasing cycle of transformation and rebirth. On seeing Baubo pointing out her yoni, Demeter is said to have burst into a liberating laughter.

SEE ALSO *KAGURA

BEANS and BEAN FLOWERS

Because of their alleged powers to arouse and stimulate the emotions, bean flowers were used as love charms by the

Romans, who considered the plants to be sacred. For the Teutonic peoples, the bean was a symbol of sexual pleasure and eroticism and it is possible that the Romans picked it up from them, or vice versa.

SEE ALSO *EROTIC SYMBOLISM

BEBHIONN AND/OR BEBIND

A dark Celtic/Irish goddess whose worship included *ritual prostitution.

BEDROOM ARTS

Whether people make love in their gardens, on the beach, or under the Christmas tree, the erotic arts have—in urban societies—a foremost connection with the bedroom. "Bedroom arts" is a Chinese expression, and the following quotation shows that here the idea of the bedroom does not stand for a marital tussle between the sheets with all the lights out but rather for a mature art, science, and magic that makes use of the erotic and sexual energies:

> The Bedroom Arts comprise the entire Supreme Way and can themselves suffice to help one achieve the goal of Immortality. These arts are said to enable a person to avert calamities and become freed from misdeeds, even to change bad luck into good fortune.

This quote by the Taoist scholar *Ko Hung may be a bit of an exaggeration, but it would do well on the walls or doors of many contemporary bedrooms, where all too often people merely frustrate and abuse one another.

BEE POLLEN SEE *HONEY

BENGAL

Besides *Assam, *Kashmir, and—to a lesser extent—*Kerala, Bengal is one of the major areas where Tantric teachings originated and have flourished. Many of the *Tantras were originally written in Bengali script, though many of them are extant today only in their respective Chinese or Tibetan translations. We must realize, however, that what was known as Bengal in the past was divided between India and Bangladesh, the Indian portion being the state of West Bengal, and the area that is now Bangladesh having once been known as Eastern Bengal.

SEE ALSO *KALIGHAT, *NALANDA UNIVERSITY, *SAHAJA, *YONIPUSHPA, *YONI TANTRA

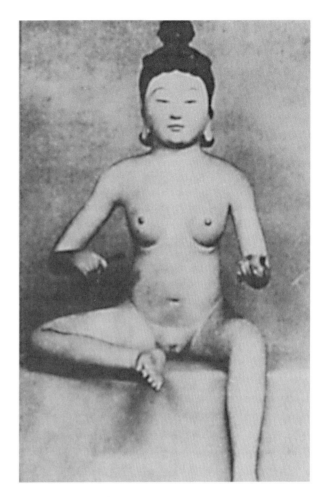

BENZAI TENNYO OR BENTEN. *A wooden statue of the Japanese goddess *Benzai Tennyo. Kamakura period (1185–1333).*

BENI UDHRI
(ARABIC, "SONS OF VIRGINITY")

Name of an Arab/Bedouin tribe, the members of which practice and advocate *coitus reservatus.

BENZAI TENNYO AND/OR BENTEN

A Japanese goddess associated with sexuality and fertility. Her worship features the rite called *hieros gamos. She also represents the art of music and is seen as a goddess granting good fortune and wealth.

BHAGA

A *Sanskrit term, the meaning of which ranges from "luck" and "wealth" to "womb" and "*yoni." It is based on the same root (bhag) as terms like bhagananda ("ecstasy"), bhagat ("devotee"), bhagavat-cetana ("mother, divine consciousness"), bhagavatisakti ("divine power"), *bhagini ("independent woman"), bhagwan ("divine one"), bhagpith ("mons pubis"), and bhagshishnaka ("clitoris"), and is most often used in connection with the Goddess and her major symbol. It also signifies that aspect of our being called bhagavat, "the divine enjoyer" of things both erotic and nonerotic.

There is also a Bhaga River in Himachal Pradesh, India.

BHAGA ASANA
(SKT., "VULVA EXERCISE")

A powerful physical technique used by female Tantric adepts, *devadasis, and other women trained in the erotic and sexual arts. The *yoni/vagina embraces the *lingam/penis fully and "locks" it—by means of the powerful female genital muscles (such as the pubococcygeus)—in a prolonged erection, a span of time during which the partners can then manipulate certain internal processes and the flow of their subtle energies. The contraction of these muscles can, of course, also be done by a woman alone. This is done not only as an exercise but also for self-stimulation. It is in this pose that the goddess *Kameshvari is thought to sit in her famous statue at Bheraghat.

Similar techniques were known to Arab and African women and are described in more detail under the headings *kabbazah and *pelvic floor potential. Among the Tamils of India, and in the *Ananga Ranga, the exercise is known as *pompoir.

BHAGAYAGJA

A more clearly "sexual" form of a *yoni puja that is celebrated only among the most radical *Vamacara groups.

Whereas the *yogini taking part in the *ahasya puja is often an initiated woman specifically trained not to become sexually aroused by all the attention to her body, in this case the sexual energies are awakened on purpose, namely, to create the subtle energy and/or liquid that is called *yonitattva. Thus, the *yoni is not only adored and worshipped but also stimulated and excited, sometimes even penetrated, depending on which holy scripture a specific sect follows. No mixture of yogurt, honey, or oil is consumed by these worshippers. The most esoteric of Tantrics, in their most secret modes of worship, consume the juices of love produced by the woman/Goddess or produced by mingling the female juices

with those of the male. Two-thirds of the "divine nectar" thus generated is then mixed with wine and drunk by the congregation; the remaining one-third is offered to the Goddess.

Sometimes a bhagayagja is also celebrated with a menstruating woman, producing an even more powerful liquid known as *yonipushpa (Skt., "yoni flower"). Although this is a practice forbidden by most texts and within many sects, it is specifically advocated in the *Yoni Tantra.

BHAGINI

First and foremost, this *Sanskrit term signifies an autonomous, independent woman not bound to any man, similar to the original concept of the term *virgin. The existence of this term indicates that not all times or cultures have regarded women as intrinsically bound to men or destined to bear offspring. Even though *Hinduism, like other patriarchal and monotheistic religions, has tried its best to deny women this freedom more or less successfully, the term hints at the previous existence of cultures where *matriarchy, or at least *matriliny, was the way of life.

When prefixed with the root syllable bhag, which is the base of *bhaga, the term becomes doubly female and doubly independent, as it then signifies a woman who "eats of and enjoys the bhag" (Thadani, p. 63), that is, makes love to women by way of bhag-lila (Skt., "yoni play"), *cunnilingus, *Shakti asana, or other techniques.

BHAIRAVI

One of the many names used for the goddess *Kali, whereas Bhairava is a name for the god *Shiva.

SEE ALSO *KUMARI PUJA, *NIRUTTARA TANTRA

BHAIRAVI CHAKRA

A Tantric ritual observance named after *Bhairavi, who was worshipped widely in India. From texts such as the *Mahanirvana Tantra, the *Kularnava Tantra, and the *Kaulavali Nirnaya Tantra it becomes apparent that during this ritual women and men worship and celebrate making use of the five classical, unadulterated *makara—including the drinking of wine and sexual union.

BHAKTI
(SKT., "DEVOTION")

The yoga of loving devotion and unconditional surrender to either a deity or one's teacher(s). The aim of this type of "love" is conscious unity with the deity, similar to the aim of certain Christian mystics, especially women, who experience ecstatic and almost erotic union with Christ.

SEE ALSO *PREMA, *SUFISM

BHANG

Popular Indian way of using *Cannabis sativa. The plant's leaves are crushed into a powder, which is then mixed into a milkshake or another type of drink. R. A. Wilson reports that it is often "served at wedding banquets in India and is said to produce greater conviviality than any alcoholic beverage" (1988, p. 176).

BHAIRAVI. *The goddess* *Bhairavi.
*Eighteenth-century painting
from the Punjab, India.
Ajit Mookerjee Collection, New Delhi.*

BHOGA
(SKT, "ENJOYMENT, SENSORY PLEASURE")

A term indicating a "path to spiritual attainment and liberation," which is based on the enjoyment of so-called worldly experiences. *Bhoga* is the "sensuous appreciation of life" (Narain and Arya, p. 23) and has a meaning quite similar to the English term *hedonism*. The term has also been interpreted as "enjoyment as a principle of creation" (Rawson, *Art of Tantra,* p. 205).

BHOGI

The Sanskrit term *bhogi* refers to someone who has volunteered to die in a human *sacrifice, a practice that was known in India until its suppression by the British government during the nineteenth century. *Kalighat and the temple of *Kamakhya in *Assam are examples of two places where such sacrifices frequently took place. From the moment someone announced the will to serve as a *bhogi,* he or she received sacred status and was granted any wish (*see* *Bhoga) and luxury. In the case of men, notes Mircea Eliade, an especially attractive offer was that "they were allowed as many women as they wished" (Eliade, p. 306). Considering that human sacrifice is an ancient practice connected to the early fertility cults—and that the temples mentioned above are associated with Tantric yogis, *Kapalikas, and followers of *Aghora—Eliade's theory, in which he states that *Shakta and *Tantra are largely a revival of the ancient tradition of fecundity (in which sexualtiy and death are closely connected), becomes plausible.

SEE ALSO *ATTIS, *KALI, *KALIKA PURANA

BHUKTI
(SKT, "SENSUALITY")

The Tantric concept of the type of sensuality that can lead to liberation and salvation.

BIBLE

The Bible, especially the Old Testament, provides us with much source material about the many peoples, cultures, and religions that once existed in the ancient Near East and Mesopotamia.

What is known as the Bible consists of texts written by many authors during a span of time covering the centuries from about 1000 B.C.E. to approximately 100 C.E. Besides the Old Testament, sometimes called the Hebrew Bible, and

the New Testament, recognized by Christians only, the oldest versions also include the Apocrypha: texts later omitted by Jews and by most Christian sects.

A subdivision of the Old Testament, the first five books, is known to Christians as the Pentateuch and to Jews as the Torah. These books, which include Genesis and Exodus, also form the basis for the *Zohar. References to this mythical or historical material, often with quotes, can be found in each of the following entries: *Abraham, *Ashtoreth, *Babylon, *Bit-Shagatha, *Circumcision, *Coitus Interruptus, *Ecstasy, *Elephant, *Ephesian Artemis, *Ishtar, *Lilith, *Mandrake, *Matrilocality, *Niddah, *Olfactory Delights, *Origen, *Phallic Worship, *Pomegranate, *Scarlet Woman, *Secret Language, *Serpent, *Shekinah, *Shunamism, *Sodom and Gomorrah, *Song of Songs, *Wine of the Navel.

BIJA
(SKT., "SEED," "POTENTIAL")

1. A "seed" in the sense of being a primal constituent of the universe. 2. A tiny "seed" sound with the stored potential of growing into a full-fledged "big bang." 3. A sound syllable used in meditation and *mantra repetition, for example, *hrim* or *hum*.

BINDU
(SKT., "PARTICLE, SPOT, DOT")

A difficult concept to translate into contemporary Western languages, the term *bindu* indicates a "seed," "source," and/or "point" very much in the sense of the Occidental *monad*. Therefore, the *bindu* is often symbolized and represented, in the cosmic diagrams called *yantra, by a simple dot. Though the *bindu* is sometimes interpreted as being essentially male, and is then identified with male *semen or its subtle essence, it can be seen as more or less neutral in terms such as *sona bindu* (red ovum) and *sita bindu* (white semen). We would do well to imagine it as an enfolded, not

*B*HOGA. *Many Tantrics believe that the path to spiritual attainment and liberation can be achieved through a thoroughly sensuous appreciation of life, including so-called worldly pleasures such as sexuality. Unusually large Nepalese painting on card, c. 1830. Photograph courtesy of Nik Douglas.*

yet unfolded, state of "seed energy" in the same sense in which an embryonic *gonad is not yet differentiated into either ovaries or testes. S. C. Banerjee, however, notes that this concept is somewhat more complex, and that the Tantric text Kamakala Vilasa informs us of "two Bindus, white and red," where the former represents the energy of the male *Shiva and the latter that of the female *Shakti. They are "Siva and Sakti in their mutual enjoyment" and they "expand and contract alternately. They are the root of creation of word and meaning which sometimes unite and sometimes separate from each other" (p. 209).

See also *Sri Yantra

BIRD NEST SOUP

A spicy soup made from the nests of certain sea swallows is recommended to us by the Chinese. The edible nests of the vulture swallow not only are famous for their *aphrodisiac properties but are very rare. Difficult and dangerous to collect, they are found mainly in the deep and dark caves of Sarawak (Malaysian Borneo), where heat, humidity, darkness, and poisonous insects often lead to accidents. Nests of the first quality are of a light color, have not been used for raising young birds, and consist of nothing but the unique spittle that is secreted for this purpose by the swallows. Less valued are used nests, which also contain feathers and are of a darker color.

The collectors "harvest" the nests four or five times per year by climbing on bamboo poles to the cave's ceiling, often 40 to 50 meters high, where they steal the nests and thus stimulate the birds to begin building new ones. The nests are taken back to the village and then cleaned, pressed, dried, and packaged before they are exported, mainly to places in China, for consumption by people who can afford this delicacy. A connoisseur in Hong Kong, Taiwan, or China has to pay about $50 for a mere three to four grams of this "white gold," as the material is called by its collectors. For some, the nests are truly the source of great riches. One privately owned cave—the owner is a tribal chief—with a population of about five thousand swallows generates a yearly income of about $100,000. One nationally owned, or public, cave is known to have a population of some two million birds and will probably soon be "harvested." The Malaysian government is presently preparing an exploitation plan that will ensure the well-being of the species and—naturally—of the country's economy.

NOTE: The information on bird nest soup is based on Werner Fend's 1989 television documentary *Die Nestrauber von Borneo* (see the bibliography).

BIT-SHAGATHA

In Babylon, every woman had to enter this temple of the Great Goddess once in her life and become, temporarily, a ritual prostitute. Dressed in her finest clothes, such a woman had to wait in the temple for a passing stranger who requested her "services" by saying "I beseech Our Lady to favour Thee" (Briffault, vol. 3, p. 219). The name *Bit-Shagatha* translates as "place of union."

Similar rules and customs were observed in various ways in many Near Eastern cultures, often before or at a time of marriage. In Cyprus as well as in Lydia and Armenia, every girl or woman was under the obligation to become a temporary prostitute before she married, and the rule applied to members of all levels of society, including the nobility. It appears that Lydian women were, in later life, still proud of their devotional activities: Some of them—those who were wealthier—had monuments erected to commemorate their deeds. In these examples, the line separating *ritual prostitution from *ritual promiscuity is quite thin, and a clear classification is difficult to achieve. However, reading related entries with the help of index 7 (page 276) will give a good idea of the variety—and the similarity—of such ancient sexual customs.

SEE ALSO *BRIDAL PROSTITUTION

BLACK MASS

This infamous and notorious mass, performed by certain groups, especially those within satanism, is a sexual rite during which a celebrant or priest unites with a dedicated woman. Different sects go about the rite in different manners and use a variety of erotic/sexual stimulation techniques in order to arouse the congregation. The main feature of the mass is ritual sexual union between the "priest" and a woman, often a prostitute and sometimes a member, whose naked body serves as a living altar. It is quite clear from the imagery involved that this rite is based—to whatever degree—on the mass of Christianity as well as on rituals gleaned from *Tantra. And in fact, historically the black mass has included among its practitioners a number of defrocked priests. One such priest was Joseph-Antoine Boullan (see *Spectrophilia), whose life story is the basis of the novel *La-Bas* by J. K. Huysmans (1848–1907). The book describes a black mass in detail.

SEE ALSO *STRI PUJA/1

BLACK PAGODA   SEE *KONARAK

BLOOD

Blood, of course, has been feared, honored, spilled, magically used, and declared sacred in all cultures and religions. Almost everywhere it is the most basic symbol of the life force.

Especially interesting to our topic is the fact that many of the *flowers and plants that are symbolically associated with eros, and even some *aphrodisiacs, are said to have sprung from the blood of one or another deity. Like the red *rose, which is supposed to have grown from the blood of Christ, so the *violet comes from *Attis, the *pomegranate from *Dionysus, and many herbs—as well as wheat—come from the blood of *Osiris. A similar mythical idea concerns the birth of *Aphrodite/Venus. This goddess of sexuality and love, however, springs not from real blood but from *semen, a life juice also known as "blood of the red lion." Blood, whether it is given to Earth to drink or burned for the benefit of Heaven, is the central mystery of all human and animal *sacrifice. It is of special importance in the Australian Aboriginal custom of *subincision but also in many rites surrounding *defloration and *virginity. Though the spilled blood itself is not given great importance in the rites of male *circumcision, it is quite reasonable to assume that the "covenant" made at this time with God, Allah, or another deity is sealed by this spilling of *red blood, and we can thus identify circumcision as a blood sacrifice.

The specific myths and customs surrounding menstrual blood are discussed under *Menstrual Fluid, and the magical energy thought to be inherent in this blood is dealt with in *Moon Magic.

BLOOD OF THE RED LION

Alchemical term/code for male *semen.

BLUE FLAME TANTRA

One of the most recent among the many Neo-Tantric groups arising across the Western world is this one founded by Mark Roberts, a widely traveled author and researcher who was also an active pagan priest in the 1970s and was featured in Margot Alder's book *Drawing Down the Moon*.

In his paper "The Tantra of the Blue Flame," he describes this form of Tantra as being steeped in the tradition of ancient *matriarchy, fully centered on women and their empowerment and independence, and open to persons of both genders who can and will engage in *yoni *puja* and *yoni worship.

The name Blue Flame Tantra was inspired—apart from literary research—by his contact with a priestess of the famous *Javalamukhi shrine, where the tongue of *Kali and/or Sati is believed to be present in the form of eternally burning blue flames. Different from other *Vamacara schools, Blue Flame Tantra focuses solely on those forms of ritual sexuality that do not involve penetration, are mainly oral in nature, and are focused on the *yoni. As such, apart from the *asanas* recommended by Roberts in his paper, the main practice is *cunnilingus, though the *Shakti *asana* also fits this teaching and/or preference.

BLUE-GREEN HALO

Not unlike the *fivefold light, this halo/aura is said to occur when someone undergoes prolonged sexual stimulation without or until *orgasm and/or *ejaculation.

SEE ALSO *SHAKTI ASANA

BODHISATTVA

(TIB., *BYANG-CHUB-SEMS-DPA'*, OR *DBANG-PHYUG*)

Translating the Tibetan term, one arrives at "heroically committed to pure and total presence," but in a more practical sense, a bodhisattva is better defined as an enlightened being dedicated to the liberation of others. A man or woman who takes the bodhisattva vow makes the commitment to return to the cycle of life until all beings are equally liberated. Although most Buddhist texts usually speak of male bodhisattvas, with the exception of *Kuan-yin, the Tibetan pantheon contains at least eight female bodhisattvas, the *bodhisattva *dakinis*.

BODHISATTVA DAKINIS

The *Bardo Thödol speaks of eight female *bodhisattvas appearing in groups of two during the second to the fifth days of the *bardo*. The deities in question are these:

1. Lasya, who rules the human sense of vision and draws all eyes toward her by performing dance and mudras. Thus she is seen as the divine archetype of

the female temptress, displaying the physical beauty, dignity, majesty, and seductiveness of the feminine principle.
2. Pushpa (Skt., *puspa*, "flower"), the goddess of flowers and the natural environment as well as the bodhisattva of vision and sight.
3. Dhupa, the goddess of air, smell, and scent, who carries and burns wonderful incense.
4. Ghanta, goddess of feelings, carrying an essence of herbs, representing sensory perception.
5. Gita, the bodhisattva of singing and changing.
6. Mala, the bodhisattva of adornments, necklaces, and garlands.
7. Naivedya, who offers the nourishment of meditation that is necessary for skillful action.
8. Aloka, who carries the torch of boundless white light.

BODY

For a listing of all entries concerned with parts of the human body, especially *brain and *genitals, consult index 10 on page 278.

BOGOMILES

A group of Christian heretics that was active in the Balkan states from about the tenth to the fifteenth century. The original Bogomiles were in large number monks who had been expelled from the monasteries of Mount Athos in Greece. They not only went unclothed, like the *Adamites, but actively preached against the institutions and rules of the church. They told people to dissolve their marriages and advocated free sexual relations.

SEE ALSO *FREE SPIRIT MOVEMENT, *SAHAJA

BÖN

(TIB., "INVOCATION")

Name for the pre-Buddhist religious tradition of the Tibetan Himalayas, many teachings and rituals of which were finally absorbed into *Vajrayana. Practitioners of Bön are called Bön-po.

Although Bön was previously believed to be a purely shamanic system of belief like those found elsewhere, more and more scholars have begun to agree with a hitherto controversial theory that early Bön was a combination of Himalayan shamanism and early Buddhist Tantra (before the arrival of *Padmasambhava) and elements of Mithraism

Bön. A Bön-po lama (priest and/or shaman) in his chapel at Tarap (Dolpo), Tibet. Photograph by C. Jest.—

arriving from fifth-century Persia via the silk route. (For more details, I refer the reader to chapter 2 of June Campbell's excellent *Traveller in Space.*)

But Bön's independent existence was not to last long. Only a few centuries later, the hitherto not highly organized Bön-po quickly lost ground as well as believers when Indian Tantric masters such as *Indrabhuti and Padmasambhava began teaching in Tibet in the seventh and eighth centuries. Philosophically and politically, they were not able to withstand the intellectual sophistication and increasing dominance of *Buddhism, which by 779 had risen to the position of state religion.

By the late eighth century, a movement known as Reformed Bön had evolved, which claimed as its founder the master Tönpa Shenrab, an early third-century shaman and priest. This new Bön had borrowed heavily from the *Nyingmapa and was now able to compete with the organized Buddhist schools and sects, having evolved a mythic-historical lineage and written teachings. After the philosophical debate and magical competition in 792, won by the Vajrayana adepts, the original and unreformed swastika Bön-po were banned from Tibet, and the Reformed Bön was

grudgingly accepted, by force of Padmasambhava's decree, as a fringe religion and allowed to operate in Tibet. In the centuries to follow, Bön developed alongside the Nyingma, and sometimes their teachings were almost similar, each influencing the other. One of the major texts of Tibetan Buddhism, the *Bardo Thödol, is strongly influenced by Bön and may even be of Bön origin with Buddhist overlays. By the eleventh century this new Bön had gained some ground, and its teachings have been transmitted ever since, on a small scale, even into the present time.

Since the late 1980s, Bön teachers have traveled throughout Europe and the United States—especially Lama Tendzin Namdek Lopon and his student Lama Tendzin Wangyal—in order to make their cultural and spiritual heritage, now once more threatened with extinction by the Chinese occupation of Tibet, accessible to others. The Tibetan teacher Namkhai Norbu, also operating in the West, is another one of the few to carry on some of these teachings, especially the Bön mode of *Dzogchen. The approximate date for a first Bön monastery (gYas-ru dben-sa, founded by gYung-drung bla-ma [eleventh century]) is the year 1080.

SEE ALSO *KERIMA, *MACHIG LAPDRON, *PHRAMENMA

BRAHMA APERTURE

In terms of subtle physiology, this is an opening at the top of the skull through which light or other waves/rays of energy can enter the human system. This opening, sometimes called the golden passage, is also used for leaving one's body at the time of death. At that moment all other openings of the body, where one's consciousness could otherwise exit, need to be closed. The actual *Sanskrit term for this opening is brahmarandhra.

Brahma is the name of one of the major gods of the all-male *Hindu trinity, the other two being Vishnu and *Shiva.

SEE ALSO *PINEAL GLAND, *SAHASRAHA CHAKRA, *TANTRIC VISUALIZATION

BRAHMA NADI

The "royal road," a delicate *nadi situated in the center of the *sushumna, in the interior of the cerebrospinal axis. Some authors see the term brahma nadi merely as a synonym for the sushumna nadi itself.

BRAHMANAS

A designation for several clerical compositions associated with the *Vedas, or Vedic Samhitas, mainly explaining and expounding Vedic sacrificial rituals and their underlying symbolism. The oldest of the Brahmanas, the Shatapatha Brahmana of the Yajur Veda, has been dated to approximately 900 B.C.E., but most of the works were apparently written during the eighth to fifth centuries B.C.E. The texts are closely interwoven with other Vedic literature such as the *Upanishads, the latter of which often show strong influences from the mysticism prevalent in many of the Brahmanas.

It is mainly through these scriptures that the Sanskrit term brahman acquired its meaning of "the Absolute" in the sense of a universal divine principle. Earlier, the term meant simply "to grow," "vast," and "expanse." This term for the highly abstract, philosophical concept of a "highest principle" should not be confused with Brahma, the god of creation in the classical all-male trinity of *Brahmanism and/or *Hinduism.

BRAHMARANDHRA   SEE *BRAHMA APERTURE

BRAHMANISM

A term used to indicate the specific religious beliefs and practices prevalent in India before and during the formative years of *Buddhism (c. 500 B.C.E. to 100 C.E.). An orthodox form of *Hinduism, it derives its name from the highest members of India's caste system, the priests known as Brahmans, and from the Indian concept of Brahman (see *Brahmanas). Brahmanism was mainly concerned with the various rituals and sacrifices proscribed by the *Vedas and took strong opposition to later developments such as *Shakta and *Tantra.

BRAIN

The human brain is such a delicate and sophisticated system—from the communication, storage, and processing of data from the senses, to memory, motoric control, and so forth—that biology and neurology have yet to apprehend the fine structure and function of the brain in its entirety. In order to provide the most basic background information necessary to understand certain other entries, we have included short descriptions of those subdivisions and functions relevant to our topic, in alphabetical order:

AMYGDALA   The "almond," previously thought to mainly control emotions such as fear and aggression; it is now known that this part of the brain also receives signals from the *VNO in our noses, which in turn are stimulated by human *pheromones. From here, such signals are mediated to the hypothalamus.

BRAIN STEM   Includes the pons, the medulla, the reticular activating system, and the midbrain. A central stalklike structure connecting the spinal cord and the cerebral hemispheres. The brain stem receives signals from the skin and muscles of the head and neck—muscles it also controls. Containing neurons of almost all the cranial nerves, it is essential for the processing of sensory information.

CEREBELLUM ("LITTLE BRAIN")   Located at the back of the skull, it processes signals from the muscles, joints, and tendons. Together with the subcortical basal ganglia, it controls posture and equilibrium and modulates motor movement.

CEREBRAL CORTEX (OR NEOCORTEX)   The cortex ("bark") is the wrinkled outer layer of nervous tissue known as gray matter. It receives and interprets sensory impulses, contains centers of consciousness and rational thought, and is the body's ultimate control center. The cortex is subdivided into four lobes, each of which is duplicated on either side of the brain. These are known as the temporal, frontal, parietal, and occipital lobes.

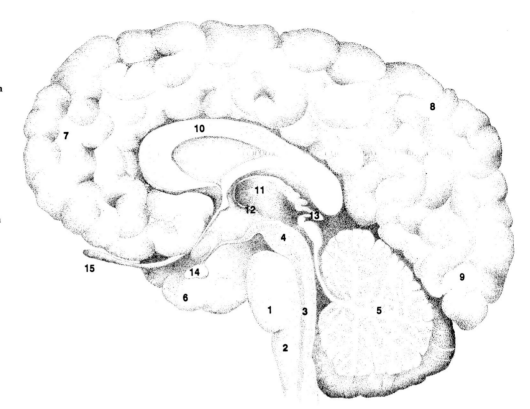

1. Pons
2. Medulla
3. Reticular
   activating system
4. Midbrain
5. Cerebellum
6. Temporal lobe
7. Frontal lobe
8. Parietal lobe
9. Occipital lobe
10. Corpus callosum
11. Thalamus
12. Hypothalamus
13. Epithalamus
    (pineal)
14. Pituitary
    (hypophysis)
15. Olfactory bulb

Brain. *A cross-section of the human *brain. Illustration by Christina Camphausen.*

Studies of people with an impaired temporal lobe have shown that it is involved with sexual interest, feelings, anger, fear, and auditory and visual hallucinations.

CEREBRAL HEMISPHERES   These much-discussed "left and right lobes of the brain" are concerned with the so-called higher perceptual, cognitive, and motor functions.

CEREBRUM (INCLUDES CEREBRAL HEMISPHERES, CORPUS CALLOSUM, CORTEX)   The largest and uppermost part of the brain, which is divided into the two cerebral hemispheres, connected by the corpus callosum. The hemispheres are covered by the cerebral cortex.

DIENCEPHALON   Includes the thalamus, hypothalamus, subthalamus, and epithalamus. The oldest and innermost layer of the forebrain, the diencephalon has key functions in the transmission of sensory and motor information and has control (through the hypothalamus) of endocrine functions. The pituitary (attached to the hypothalamus) and pineal glands can also be regarded as part of this system.

HYPOTHALAMUS ("BELOW THE INNER CHAMBER")   A small structure responsible for "general maintenance": hypothalamic hormones govern such basic body functions as heart rate, blood pressure, temperature, hunger, and thirst. These hormones are released by the pituitary, a gland attached by a stalk to the base of the hypothalamus. Together with the limbic system, the hypothalamus is also involved with our emotions and the sexual drive, especially via signals from the *VNO to the amygdala.

LIMBIC SYSTEM   Includes the amygdala, hippocampus, and olfactory bulbs; earlier called the rhinencephalon, or "nose brain." This is the "bordering" system of neural structures deep within the forebrain, believed to be the primary seat of emotions. Here are the centers of joy, pleasure, rage, and fear. Because the limbic system is able to activate the hypothalamus, it can also influence the endocrine system to some degree. The limbic system is involved with memory—to which the olfactory sense is tied most directly—and perhaps with dreams. It also governs basic, instinctive activities such as self-preservation, reproduction and sexuality, fear, and aggression.

OLFACTORY BULBS   Two "relay stations" for sensory input from receptor cells in the nose, leading into the olfactory nerves.

PARIETAL LOBE   The middle division of the cortex, which contains the motor cortex (concerned with the coordination of movement) and the somatosensory cortex (concerned with skin-surface sensations such as temperature, touch/pressure, pain, and so on).

THALAMUS ("INNER CHAMBER")   A structure located atop the brain stem that relays all sensory nerve impulses, except those of the olfactory system, to the cortex. It has been suggested that the various phenomena of extrasensory perception *(*siddhis)* may be due to a special sensitivity of the thalamus.

BRAIN (AS *APHRODISIAC)

Along with the digestion of primate brains—human or monkey—as described under *anthropophagy, there are several other "recipes" involving brain from a variety of other animals. The medieval philosopher, alchemist, and hermeticist Albertus Magnus (c. 1200–1280) recommended powdered brain of partridge mixed into a glass of red wine.

According to H. E. Wedeck, the brains of calf, lamb, and piglet, if eaten young and fresh, are reputedly erotic in their effects and assist the libido. He also reports that doves' brains are eaten with similar intent (pp. 49, 77).

BREASTS

It is certainly no "neglected wisdom" that the nipples and breasts, especially those of women, are major erotically charged areas (*marmas*) of the body. Lesser known is the fact that these *twin peaks contain *scent glands and can, under the right circumstances, discharge more and other substances than milk for a newborn child. In both East and West such secretions have been recognized and have names such as *witches' milk, *white snow, and *peach juice of immortality. One of the female adepts of Taoist *inner alchemy describes the feeling that can occur during or after a woman's meditation if it is done "after midnight and before dawn." According to this ancient Taoist text, a woman may feel a

BREASTS. *A natural symbol of the Goddess's *breasts: the hills known as the Paps of Anu.*

stream of energy "between the breasts that thrusts out, divides and goes into the breasts, right through the nipples, which then erect" (Cleary, ed., 1989, p. 97). Texts and thoughts concerning such topics as "mammary metaphysics" and "the breast repressed" can be found in Robert Anton Wilson's *Ishtar Rising*, a revised edition of his earlier *Book of the Breast*.

Ancient peoples who worshipped the Goddess in one or another form often saw mountains and hills, and certainly twin peaks, as breasts of their deity. An example of this can be found in the Paps of Anu, or "Two Breasts of the Great Queen," two softly rounded twin hills in a landscape of the Irish county of Kerry, considered sacred ground of the goddess called Anu and/or Danu and also of the Irish goddess of slaughter known as Morigna. In the latter's name, human sacrifice was practiced here; women were suspended from trees, and their breasts, symbols of nourishment, were ritually severed.

SEE ALSO *APSARASAS, *EPHESIAN ARTEMIS, *PITHAS, *SURYACANDRASIDDHI

BREATH

In both East and West, breath plays an important role in the magic of sexuality. Taoist adepts—although too often concerned with benefits for the male partner only—show us in their teachings that the exchange of breath helps us absorb the opposite energies of *yin or *yang. The type of energy that is abundant in one's male or female partner(s) is exactly that energy needed by oneself in order to become whole. It needs to be said that many breathing techniques, especially those designed to arouse the *kundalini, are not without danger if one has not been instructed and guided by an experienced teacher. This also holds true for Taoist techniques such as *t'ai-hsi and related exercises.

For further information concerning sexual associations with breath *see* *Conspiration, *Ho-ch'i, *Insufflation, *Shunamism, and *Sympneumata. The Sanskrit term for all exercises concerned with breath, both sexual and nonsexual, is *pranayama.

BREATH RETENTION

A technique regarded highly by both Tantric and Taoist male practitioners as helpful in avoiding *ejaculation, the outward flow of their precious *semen.

SEE ALSO *RETENTION OF SEMEN

BRETHREN OF THE FREE SPIRIT   SEE
*FREE SPIRIT MOVEMENT

BRIDAL PROSTITUTION

Somewhere in between *ritual promiscuity, *sacred and *secular prostitution, and marriage, there are some customs that can best be called bridal prostitution, also known as *Nasamonian marriage.

Bridal prostitution was a custom known by several peoples around the globe. In Nicaragua, a young marriageable girl or woman would be sent by her parents on a journey to earn money for her marriage. Such girls would then roam the country and prostitute themselves until they had earned enough to buy a house or set up a trade, in which case they would return home to their parents and subsequently marry.

Among the Amorites, it was a law "that she who was about to marry should sit in fornication seven days by the gate" (from Testament of Judah, citied by Briffault, vol. 3, p. 220). Also, the *Bible contains repeated references to such promiscuity, *ritual prostitution, and other "abominations." Ezekiel 8:14 (592–550 B.C.E.) clearly shows that worshippers of *Ishtar could be found right outside the temple of the god Yahweh, a fact that both the god and his prophet did not like at all. Again, the priest Eli refers to such customs when he scolds his sons because they "lay with the women that assembled at the door of the tabernacle of the congregation" (I Samuel 2:22–24).

Among the Bohindu (an African tribe of the Congo River basin in what is now Zaire), the husband has to remain in *nuptial continence until his wife has conceived and is pregnant by another lover. Similar observations have been made in Australia and Oceania; in Cuba, Puerto Rico, and Peru; and in peoples of Ethiopia and other East African nations. In Europe, it was practiced at one time on the Balearic Islands.

SEE ALSO *OTIV BOMBARI

BUDDHA-FACE
(CHIN., FO-CHUANG)

A Chinese custom of the Sung period (*see* *Chinese dynasties), which R. H. van Gulik suggests has sexual/Tantric implications (pp. 74, 238). The female partner (*Shakti) prepares her face with makeup according to a special prescription. The face is covered entirely in gold or yellow, and special emphasis is then given to the lips (painted large and red) and the eyebrows (black), thus creating a Buddha-like or goddesslike mask. Such preparation may aid the man's mind in viewing the woman as a representative of the Shakti who will impart her energies to him.

BUDDHISM

As is true for most other religions, the Buddha dharma ("Buddha teaching") is not such a homogenous set of beliefs as it may seem to an outsider on first examination. The teachings of Siddhartha Gautama (c. 563–483 B.C.E.), the historical Buddha, have been adapted to many societies and have been influenced by many local customs and beliefs.

Though Buddhism originally developed in India, the major Buddhist countries today are Bhutan, Burma, Japan, Kampuchea (Cambodia), Korea, Laos, Malaysia, Mongolia, Nepal, Sri Lanka (Ceylon), Taiwan, Thailand, Tibet, and Vietnam. In India itself it has played only a marginal role since the thirteenth century; there it exists today mainly in India's Himalayan territories, such as northern *Assam, Darjeeling, Ladakh, and Sikkim—regions that have not always belonged to India and that were culturally influenced by Tibet.

Basically, Buddhism knows two major subdivisions: *Hinayana and *Mahayana, a division that arose in the first century. However, two other terms are often used that seem equally distinct divisions: *Vajrayana and Zen. Formally, these two schools are part of Mahayana, but by virtue of their large sphere of influence, they are often regarded as equally major divisions of Buddhism as a whole. Today, Buddhism also attracts growing numbers of adherents in Europe and the United States.

BURTON, SIR RICHARD FRANCIS
(1821–1890)

Orientalist, philosopher, and adventurous traveler who was one of the first Europeans to go to East Africa and who discovered Lake Taganyika. He also dared to visit Mecca and the *Ka'bah, places forbidden to all non-Muslims on the penalty of death. His knowledge of Arabic languages and his disguise as an Afghan pilgrim made his mission possible and saved his life. Between 1864 and 1875 he served as British consul in São Paulo (Brazil), Damascus (Lebanon), and Trieste (Italy). Throughout his life he studied anthropology and was interested especially in the sexual mores and erotic literature of all cultures.

Burton, a rebel and eccentric outsider to Victorian society,

translated several interesting works such as the *Kama Sutra (1883), the *Perfumed Garden (1886), and the 16 volumes of the tales of the Arabian Nights, for which he was knighted in 1887. All these texts now belong to the classics of erotic literature. Unfortunately, on the night of Burton's death, his wife, Isabel, burned 41 unpublished manuscripts and all of his notes, thus hoping to preserve her husband's reputation!

Burton is one of the main characters in William Harrison's 1982 novel *Burton and Speke,* republished in 1989 under the title *Mountains of the Moon.*

SEE ALSO *KABBAZAH

BUDDHISM. *Bodhidharma (470–543 C.E.), the first patriarch of Chinese and Japanese *Buddhism, in an unusually excited condition. Japanese silk scroll.*

C

From a solar orb,

red like hibiscus, the secret form

of *Chinnamasta appears.

She is as effulgent as ten million suns;

she drinks the blood which gushes from her neck.

She is full of sexual promise,

sixteen years of age.

CHINNAMASTA STOTRA

NOTE: An entry expected to have the initial letter *C* may sometimes be found under *K*. Sanskrit terms such as *Cakra* and *Candali* are written as *Chakra* and *Chandali*.

CAMEL

Oriental erotic manuals such as the *Perfumed Garden often note that the camel provides various stimulating substances. According to Arab tradition, camel milk—mixed with *honey and taken as a drink every day for a week—produces marked potency in men. The camel's fat, melted down from its hump, is said to be a general *aphrodisiac.

CANNABIS SATIVA

Botanical name for the Indian hemp plant, the origin of preparations such as marijuana, hashish, *bhang, *charas, and *majoon. It is well known among users of hashish and marijuana that *THC, the main active chemical ingredient of cannabis, is—among other things—a strong *aphrodisiac, a fact even recognized by the *Encyclopaedia Britannica*. A famous description of the erotic fantasies that can be induced by cannabis is "Les Paradis Artificiels" by the French user and poet Charles Baudelaire (1821–1867), in which he also describes cannabis and *opium in their botanical and historical contexts.

Erotically minded Indians developed a special aphrodisiac recipe in which bhang is mixed with sugar, *musk, and *ambergris (Waddell, p. 15). It is also certain that ganja, the Indian name for marijuana, was used by many Tantric adepts, for example in the *Panchatattva ritual. The following lines from a song by Saraha make it clear that early Tantrics such as the 84 *Mahasiddhas were acquainted with the use of cannabis: "The Sabara girl is sitting on a high hill. She has peacock feathers on her head and a garland of ganja around her neck. Her dear Sabara is mad, intoxicated by love for her" (Dowman, 1985, p. 65).

Keith Dowman comments that the image associated with the Sabaras, a "wild" and aboriginal hill tribe, is that of a yogi crazed with passion for his female companion, intoxicated by smoking cannabis, covered in ashes, and drinking *alcohol from a skull cup. For Saraha this seems to be an appropriate image of the early Tantrics, and it sounds much like a description of the *Kapalikas. But the use of cannabis is certainly not an all-Indian affair. The plant was known and used in China, Persia, Afghanistan, and the Arabic countries; among the American Indians; and also in Europe among the Greeks, Romans, Scythians, and Vikings. Today, although cannabis preparations are illegal in most countries, millions of our contemporary neighbors in East and West use (or have used) it on a more or less regular basis. One of the few enlightened and civilized countries in its approach to hashish is the Netherlands, where only large-scale sale is punished but use and possession are not.

The best and most exquisite erotic sensation, in this context, can be achieved by using the concentrated oil of cannabis, eating majoon, or drinking bhang, rather than smoking leaves or other preparations.

SEE ALSO *NIZARI ISMA'ILIS

CANNIBALISM   SEE *ANTHROPOPHAGY

CANOPUS

1. An Egyptian city in the Nile delta that was, according to the historian Strabo (63 B.C.E.–21 C.E.), notorious for its festive indulgences and wild sexual activities. Such a descrip-

CANNABIS SATIVA. *As do many of his fellow practitioners, the wandering ascetic Naga Baba Hari Giri smokes cannabis several times each day, thus opening his mind more fully to divine guidance and inspiration from the god *Shiva.*
Photograph by Dolf Hartsuiker.

tion is often used by Greek writers when they refer to places and rituals of peoples whose religions incorporated *ritual promiscuity, *ritual prostitution, and genital worship (incidentally some of the "sins" for which the biblical *Sodom and Gomorrah had to be destroyed by the command of the god Elohim). That such a city bears the name of the star to which the sacred *Ka'bah is oriented is surely no coincidence. **2.** Canopus, or alpha Carinae, is the main star of the Carina nebula (keel constellation). This star, though less

known than its famous competitor Sirius, is one of the more important stars in the heavens. According to Rodney Collin, probably the most brilliant of *Gurdjieff's students, it is either Canopus or Sirius that constitutes the gravitational center of Charlier's Local System, a stellar subsystem that also includes our local sun and planets (pp. 14, 27).

CANTHARIDES/CANTHARIDIN

Cantharidin is the active chemical substance of cantharides, the scientific name for what is popularly known as *Spanish fly.

CARDAMOM SEEDS

These seeds are used as a minor meditation symbol in an intimate Tantric ritual. After a number of other preparations, such as *nyasa, the two practitioners each open such a seed and meditate on its shape, which resembles that of the *yoni.

In Arab countries cardamom is known as one of many kitchen herbs with *aphrodisiac properties. A typical dish to enhance erotic feelings would be a mixture of cardamom seeds, ginger, and *cinnamon, pounded into a powder and sprinkled over boiled *onions.

CARMINA PRIAPEA

A collection of erotic/obscene poems and hymns dedicated to the phallic god *Priapus and his potency.

CARNIVAL

Derived from pre-Christian orgiastic *fertility festivals, the bawdy and licentious festival of Carnival was grudgingly tolerated by the Christian clergy as an outlet for the otherwise repressed sexuality of the "common folk." Like the Japanese *matsuri ceremonies, Carnival also often incorporates features of *phallic worship. During the Carnival procession in Trani (Italy) for example, a gigantic wooden statue of *Priapus was carried through the city, and its huge and prominent phallus was called Il Santo Membro, "the holy member."

Such festivals, where the normal laws, rules, and moral codes were temporarily suspended, have been allowed and organized in many cultures. Those in power have apparently always recognized that at least once a year people need an opportunity to let go of artificial, social restraints and live some of their repressed dreams.

SEE ALSO *KHLYSTI

CARTE BLANCHE

Priests, bishops, rishis, fakirs, yogis, and saints: in whatever guise these and other traveling "holy men" roamed their respective countries, they often had a kind of sexual "carte blanche" and were allowed, or even asked and sometimes paid, to make love to any woman they picked out of the crowd or visited at her home. The background of such a custom can also be found in common *phallic worship, in *Nasamonian marriage customs, and in the fact that priests and sacred kings sometimes were the chosen agents for the *defloration of a young bride. Robert Briffault writes that the "notion that for a woman to have intercourse with a person of holy or divine character is desirable and meritorious is very general" (vol. 3, p. 227).

FAR EAST   It was once believed throughout India in general that the blood, or rather the *semen, of sacred persons had generative powers. It is against this background that we must view the information that since ancient times the holy rishis have been asked by nobles and kings to have intercourse with the latter's daughters and wives, and that fakirs, yogis, and holy persons of all kinds were regarded as being free to make love to any woman. Married women, although otherwise bound by strict moral codes, would go unpunished if their partner was a sacred personage, a rule we meet also in the affairs of the *gopis with the god Krishna. Women of the Gond tribe sing joyous songs about the sexual gratification they expect to receive from the arrival of such a saint in their village.

Not only was the Taoist or Buddhist priest in Kampuchea (Cambodia) required to serve in the defloration of young brides, but also he was expected to repeat sexual union with these women once annually.

SEE ALSO *PHALLIC WORSHIP

NEAR EAST   The prelates among the semi-Christian Yezidi sect of Armenia led a somewhat nomadic life, traveling up and down the country to preach their gospel. Whenever they arrived at a village, they were immediately married to a woman of their choice for the time of their stay. The woman so chosen gained strongly in social status and herself became a holy personage of the village.

In Lycia (southwest Turkey) the priestlike dede of the Tachtadshy people had the right, and was expected, to have sexual union with any woman he so desired. The women's husbands felt "considerably honoured by this distinction" (Petersen and von Luschan, p. 199).

SEE ALSO *MASLUB

THE AMERICAS   Among the tribes of the Huron and Algonquian, young women will follow their shamanic medicine man when he goes into "solitude," where they share in his communication with the higher powers. In Central and South America, notably in Guiana, Brazil, and Patagonia, a young bride was required to have intercourse with the local shaman/priest before getting married. The shaman, therefore, was always the one-time lover of almost all of the women of his specific tribe.

Among the Eskimos of Greenland, the women think themselves honored and fortunate if they can unite with an *angikok,* or "prophet," and sometimes their husbands will even pay such a man; this is a practice we may interpret as a male version of *ritual prostitution.

SEE ALSO *BRIDAL PROSTITUTION, *CHILDREN OF GOD, *RITUAL PROMISCUITY

CASTRATION

There are several forms of castration and an even greater variety of motivations for this mutilation or *dismemberment, which we should reckon among the true *perversions.

Where castration was not used as punishment or as mere senseless mutilation of enemies during and after battle, it consisted mainly of two forms. One form entails the cutting off of the *testicles only, which has been called the "minor seal" and was the most common procedure used for eunuchs in Rome, Arabia, and Persia. The other form, the "great sacred seal," was often used by religiously motivated sects, and in that procedure both testicles and the *lingam were cut away. Other variations include severing the phallus but leaving the testicles unharmed (China) or cutting out one testicle only.

When the philosopher *Origen and the *Valerians undertook self-castration they were—according to the prevalent zeitgeist—doing so in order to restrain themselves finally and absolutely from erotic temptation and from what they conceived of as sin. Earlier cultures have used castration not in order to escape women but rather in order to be like them. When Attis and (celebrating his deed) the priests of *Cybele castrated themselves they were doing so in order to become priest/eunuchs, almost priestesses, thus to be allowed to live in the temple and to serve the Goddess.

Christianity has also made thousands of young boys into victims of the "sacred knife." Until at least 1890, it was customary—for the pleasure of popes and bishops—to castrate young boys who were to sing with their beautiful and clear soprano voices in the Vatican's choir.

At other times, castrati were cast in female opera roles simply because women were not allowed to perform on stage—very similar to the Japanese custom of having men play female roles in Kabuki theater.

Depending on the age of the victim, castration effects certain changes in hormonal production and functioning. This is the biochemical reason for the choirboys' soprano voices and for the lack of beard in those who are castrated before reaching puberty.

SEE ALSO *CIRCUMCISION, *DISMEMBERMENT, *SKOPTSI, *SUBINCISION

CAVIAR

Highly regarded as an *aphrodisiac among those who are financially willing and able to wine and dine at exclusive prices. Whether it is the caviar or the accompanying social circumstances, the champagne, and the general atmosphere that are conducive to erotic intensity has not been seriously studied.

CEREBELLUM   SEE *BRAIN

CERVIX   SEE *YONI TOPOGRAPHY/17

CHAKRA
(SKT., "CIRCLE, WHEEL")
1. A term used in Tantric physiology for several centers of subtle energy within the human body (*see* *Chakra/ Physiological). **2.** A term used for several types or modes of "circle worship," Tantric rituals such as the *chakra puja or the *deva, *gana, or *raja chakras.

CHAKRA (PHYSIOLOGICAL)

In Tantric texts, this is the technical term for those major and minor centers of subtle, or "psychic," energy that are situated in the subtle body "along the spinal column" of the human organism. Although we here will use mainly *Sanskrit terms and images such as *chakra,* lotus, *nadi,* and so on as they are used in India, Nepal, and Tibet, it must be made clear that similar centers with similar functions are also known in Chinese teachings (*tan-t'ien*) and among the *Sufi.

According to Tantra, these *chakras* are connected to one another by channels called *nadis and are often imagined and depicted as circles surrounded by a specific number of lotus petals, each having its own traditionally associated color, sound, deity, and so on. However, Robert S. de Ropp is refreshingly clear when he points out that it is merely a

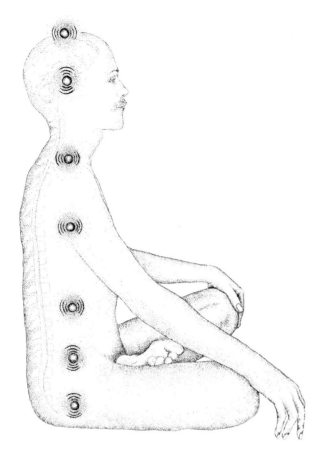

Cʜᴀᴋʀᴀ. *The seven major* chakras.
Illustration by Christina Camphausen.

developed only after the tenth century (*Tantra Yoga*, p. 56) and seems to be a departure from the earlier tradition. (For details on these four centers *see* *Manipura, *Sahasrara, *Vishuddha, and *Anahata Chakra.)

The most publicized system, the later Tantric and yogic development of seven *chakras*, has become—at least in the West—an accepted standard (see illustration). This "modern" system may have developed as both Eastern and Western medical science matured and discovered the function of the seven important glands that make up the human *endocrine system, a system that fits rather perfectly with the location of the centers in the later tradition of seven. Details on the three additional centers can be found under *Muladhara, *Svadhishtana, and *Ajna Chakra.

Apart from such major *chakras* there are—in the Tantric system—other lesser-known and so-called secondary *chakras* such as these:

ananda kanda chakra	in the heart region
lalana chakra	at the base of the palate
manas chakra	in the head
soma chakra	in the head

CHAKRA ASANA

Defined as a "sexo-yogic circle-pose" by Ajit Mookerjee (Mookerjee and Khanna, p. 197), this is actually one of the most physically difficult sexual *asanas, for which the male partner especially has to be well trained and extremely subtle. The bent and twisted spinal column effects a certain pattern of energies.

CHAKRA PUJA

Most writers are quite secretive about this and say nothing more than that it is a "communal ritual of union" (Mookerjee and Khanna, p. 197). The term can best be translated as "circle worship" and is applied to a Tantric *puja* involving between eight and 48 men and women, present in equal numbers. Generally under the guidance of a *chakresvara*, they worship the Goddess and life in a nighttime celebration that includes sexual union. Several contemporary authors, including N. N. Bhattacharyya (p. 278) and Nik Douglas (*Tantra Yoga*, p. 14), report that the *chakra puja* was still celebrated in the 1970s and that the tradition is probably still alive today.

In a sense these rituals can be compared to the *hieros gamos or the sacramental *orgies that were common during

"decorative convention" that "portrays these centres as lotuses each having a different colour, a different number of petals" (p. 143). In fact, there are no flowers, petals, or colors. Each *chakra* is a vortex of energy that whirls and swirls, invisible to normal perception, and we can visualize them in our minds in various ways. We might as well describe them as spiral galaxies or as supersensitive antennae—transmitting as well as receiving—tuned to subtle, yet powerful, energies.

The number of *chakras* said to exist in a human being, even the number of the major ones, varies in different schools; there are systems that count four (early *Tantra and *Sufism) or seven (yoga and later Tantra) such centers. Although it is sometimes stated that this divergence of opinion is due to cultural differences, it has been pointed out that the most ancient system is that of four (in India). According to Nik Douglas, the system of seven centers was *fertility rites among Near Eastern and European peoples, the major difference being that these were expurgated from their associated cultures by a Judeo-Christian priesthood that has elevated guilt and shame above love and life.

SEE ALSO *CHAKRA, *CHOLI MARG, *PANCHAMAKARA, *STRI PUJA

CHAKRESVARA
A kind of "high priest" who guides and leads a *chakra puja* and who—in the center of the circle—practices *maithuna* with the chosen *Shakti.

CHAMBER OF SIX COMBINATIONS
It is into this secret "chamber" of the human *brain that a male adept of Taoist sexual alchemy draws the *yin fluid provided him by his female partner(s).

SEE ALSO *GOLDEN ELIXIR, *TAN-T'IEN

CHANDALI
In the *Yoni Tantra this term is used for a woman on the first day of her menstruation. That a term for this very specific condition, occurring merely one day a month, exists at all shows how Tantric attention was focused on the *menstrual fluid.

In Tibet, Chandali is also the name of a deity who appears, as a member of the Gauri, on the 12th day of the *bardo.

CHANDAMAHAROSANA
(SKT., *CANDAMAHAROSANA*, "FIERCE AND GREATLY WRATHFUL ONE")
A buddha/yidam who is one of the two conversants in the *Chandamaharosana Tantra. At one point in that text, he makes the interesting statement that he carries his weapons not only to battle with evil of all sorts but especially to protect women from men who fail to honor them.

CHAKRA ASANA. *For experienced adepts only: the* *chakra asana.
Eighteenth-century gouache, Nepal.
Ajit Mookerjee Collection, New Delhi.*

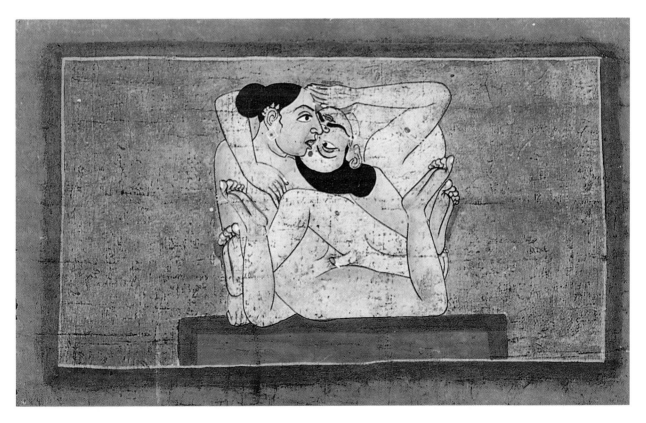

CHANDAMAHAROSANA TANTRA

(SKT., *CANDAMAHAROSANATANTRA*, "TANTRA OF THE GREAT LUNAR ELIXIR")

An early and most secret Buddhist Tantra that espouses *Shakta ideas and concepts. The text is set as a conversation between the *Vajrayogini and her consort *Chandamaharosana.

Here are a few quotes from the translation by C. S. George that show very well how clearly left-handed (*Vamacara) and nondual this work is:

- "I must practice devotion to women until I realize the essence of enlightenment."
- "Take refuge in the *yoni of an esteemed woman."
- "Never should the practitioner think in terms of pure or impure; never should he think in terms of edible or inedible, to be done or not to be done; in terms of 'suitable for love-making' or 'unsuitable for love-making.' By so doing, the yogi is cursed and all *siddhis will leave him."

Together with the *Hevajra Tantra and the Chakrasamvara Tantra, this text is one of the major *yogini tantras*, also classified collectively (together with the *mahayoga tantras*) as *anuttara yoga tantras*.

SEE ALSO *CUNNILINGUS, *MAITHUNA

CHANG TAO-LING

(34–156 C.E.)

A Chinese adept and founder of one of the more important Taoist schools, the *Five Pecks of Rice Taoism. He combined the teachings of Lao-tzu's *Taoism with those he himself studied "across the Western mountains." From a Chinese point of view such a journey would have brought him to either *Assam, *Bengal, Tibet, or Nepal. According to Benjamin Walker, it was Chang Tao-ling who introduced many of the sexual exercises into Taoism.

CHARAS

Indian name for a very potent, hashishlike, and resinous *aphrodisiac made from *cannabis sativa*. It is much stronger than common marijuana or hashish and often has effects similar to those of *LSD.

CHARIS

A goddess of love whose emanations are known as *Charites and in whose temple *ritual prostitution was practiced.

CHARITES

Original Greek name for the famous Graces, who were seen as emanations of the goddess *Charis. Though they have become known as the Three Graces, mythological studies reveal the names of six individual goddesses who belong to this group. They represent the energy of loving-kindness that is alternately translated as love, grace, or charity. Far from the meaning that *charity* has acquired in later interpretations, the original Charites were involved with fertility, erotic delight, and *ritual prostitution. Their members are Aglaia, Auxo, Euphrosyne, Hegemone, Pasithea, and Thalia.

CHASTITY

Not always, as in Christianity and many other schools of religious belief, is chastity a spiritual requirement for avoiding "sins of the flesh." On the contrary, it is often used as an instrument to prepare for heated and passionate sexual union during *fertility festivals and ritual *orgies or similar celebrations. Greek women, for example, who were to participate in the unrestrained, all-female *thesmophoria* were required to abstain from erotic activity for nine days.

A number of schools involved with *Tantra or *sexual magick have, not surprisingly, condemned chastity in the "moral" sense. In the Secret Instruction of the Eighth Degree, a manual of the *Ordo Templi Orientis, for example, chastity is described as a "corruption" and "castration" of humanity, and the blame for this is laid at the door of "that tyranny and superstition which is called Christianity" (King, 1986, p. 188).

SEE ALSO *ALPHAISM, *ENCRATISM, *KHLYSTI, *NUPTIAL CONTINENCE

CHEN-JEN

1. The "pure" or "true" human being, an ideal of *Taoism.
2. A Chinese Buddhist/Taoist sect that emphasizes the use of *mandala, *yantra, and *mantra.

CH'I

(CHIN., "BREATH, ENERGY, ETHER")

Term referring to the vital energy, life force, and/or cosmic spirit animating all of life. Says *Ko Hung: "There is noth-

CH'I. *The Chinese character* *ch'i:*
breath, bioenergy, ether.

ing which does not require ch'i to remain alive." This "vital breath" can be generated, concentrated, and recharged by various techniques, and it plays an important part in the various Eastern martial arts. *Ch'i* is associated with the middle *tan-t'ien* and must not be confused with the sexual energy called *ching*. The forces of *yin and *yang are sometimes spoken of as two complementary "types" of *ch'i*, and the aim of Taoist *inner alchemy is the union of these two forces, a union that can be achieved by meditation, breathing exercises, and erotic techniques.

The equivalent Japanese term is *ki*.

CHI-CHI

In the Chinese *I Ching, or "Book of Changes," *chi-chi* is the 63rd hexagram and is translated into English as "completion." The hexagram (six lines) consists of two trigrams: above *k'an*, or "water," and below *li*, or "fire." Interestingly enough, these two trigrams are mirror images of each other, and they symbolize—in the context of Taoist *inner

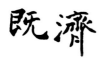

63. *Chi Chi / After Completion*

CHI-CHI. *The hexagram* *chi-chi:*
water above fire, or "matters completed."

alchemy—woman (above) and man (below).

In alchemical imagery this is symbolized as a cauldron of water above a fiery furnace and thus represents alchemical fusion, the ultimate quest for the Taoist adepts of *dual cultivation.

SEE ALSO *VIPARITA RATI

CH'IEN

1. One of the eight trigrams of the *I Ching, consisting of three yang lines and signifying heaven, or pure *yang. **2.** One of the I Ching's 64 hexagrams, consisting of twice the trigram ch'ien. **3.** In the context of *inner alchemy it refers to the furnace as opposed to *k'un*, the cauldron.

CHILDREN OF GOD

The different sexual/religious customs of our ancestors— *ritual promiscuity, *ritual prostitution, and *defloration by priests or relatives—in all "corners" of the world made, naturally, many participating women pregnant with children from such unions. Such children were not—as happens to extramarital children in many of our present societies— stigmatized, but were considered offspring of the god(s), and often these children were the pride of the mother.

CHINESE DYNASTIES

For data concerning the phases in Chinese history and the huge empire's different dynasties, see index 27 on page 290.

CHING AND/OR CHING-CH'I

Though this is the technical term for sperm or *semen, this Chinese word refers, in the context of *Taoism, to sexual energy in general and/or to both ovarian and spermatic essences and energies. This sexual *ching* energy, akin to Freud's libido but quite distinct from the vital force called *ch'i*, is associated with the lowest of the three *tan-t'ien. It is this energy that is "'the substance' on which the alchemical firing and transforming process works" (Rawson and Legeza, p. 27). The Taoist's concern about the loss of vital energy during male *ejaculation stems from the belief that death will ensue once the *ching* energy is used up. According to the same belief, the male is able to replenish his *ching* and even to store it by absorbing as much female *yin energy as possible.

SEE ALSO *EMERALD PILLOW, *HUAN-CH'ING PU-NAO, *RETENTION OF SEMEN

CHING-TAO

A Chinese technical term for the male *perineum, important in the control of both erection and *ejaculation.

SEE ALSO *HUI-JIN

CHINNAMASTA

Like *Kali and *Tara, Chinnamasta is one of the 10 most important goddesses for the followers of *Tantra and *Shakta. Her name is variously translated as "she of the cut neck" or "the headless one."

Chinnamasta is a goddess concerned with sex/life/death and the idea of *blood as a life force. She represents *Shakti in both her destructive and creative aspects, signifying apparent dissolution and a return to what is called "the first cause." In paintings she is presented as a woman with a severed head; two streams of blood flow from her neck, bestowing her own life force onto Varnani and *Dakini, the two female figures beside her. It is she who distributes—by way of her blood—her "vital essence" or "life energy" to all beings. The whole scene just described above is often set inside a huge lotus that arises from the sexual union of a male/female pair, *Kama and *Rati, both deities of love, lust, and desire. As David Kinsley reports (1997, p. 157), Chinnamasta's mantra, containing the sexually charged syllable klim, is believed by men to attract women to them. The same author, in his in-depth study of this goddess, also shows once and for all that the *dismemberment imagery connected to Chinnamasta is not at all merely symbolic. He reports (1997, pp. 151–52) that real decapitation of humans happened at her temples and that even "to this day," that is, 1997, devotees sometimes cut off their own tongues as a sacrifice to the goddess at *Jvalamukhi, the temple of Kali's tongues.

SEE ALSO *VAJRA YOGINI, *YONI TANTRA, AND THE QUOTATION ON PAGE 32.

CHIN-TAN
(CHIN., "GOLDEN CINNABAR")

Originally a term used in Chinese outer, or exoteric, *alchemy for what is also known as "golden pill" or "golden fetus," similar to the quested essence of the alchemical *gold that was sought in Western alchemy. Later—from the Sung dynasty onward—the term was mainly used in *inner alchemy and became indicative of the erotic/sexual interpretation of the *golden elixir and the *golden flower.

CHITRINI

1. One of the *female archetypes of Indian erotic literature. The Sanskrit word chitrini can best be rendered as "fancy woman" yet is sometimes translated as "picture woman" or "art woman." Of the chitrini, it is said that she is interested more than others in much foreplay, especially enjoying manual stimulation of her *breasts and nipples. Her *yoni is easily and quickly lubricated, with little pubic hair, and she is especially partial to sexual union in a forest. This woman most enjoys lovemaking in the first quarter of the night. She is very proficient in the *sixty-four arts. The chitrini's love juice is said to be exceptionally hot, to smell sweet, and to taste like *honey.

SEE ALSO *FEMALE LOVE JUICES

2. Name for one of the *nadis within the human subtle body. Sometimes used as a synonym for the *sushumna and sometimes seen as a subdivision of that subtle channel.

CHÖD
(TIB., GCOD, "SEVERANCE, CUTTING")

One tradition of Tibetan *Vajrayana comprising features from shamanic *Bön and early *Tantra. Because of Chöd's esotericism, on one hand, and its specific, dangerously "magical" rituals, on the other, it is often conveniently "forgotten" and generally receives little attention in works about Tibetan Buddhism.

The Tibetan gCod translates as cutting, severing, and/or dismemberment—terms to be understood mainly in a symbolic and/or psychological sense as a radical liberation from one's ego and all that it usually fears. However, to a Tibetan, in whose culture the deceased were actually left on a charnel ground and their bodies at the mercy of vultures and other carrion animals, such visions of dismemberment also represented a "soon to come" reality.

In a typical Chöd ritual, the practitioner visualizes the "cutting up" and offering of his or her body, a rather universal shamanic trance practice during which the adept's body is disassembled into pieces, which—if all goes well—are later reassembled once again by deities, *demons, and similar entities from the beyond.

As a whole, Chöd was inspired by the teachings of the Indian adepts Phadampa Sangye and Kamalasila, and its adherents regard the Prajnaparamita Sutra as the school's most important sacred text.

A certain distinction exists between pho-gCod (male

Chöd) and mo-gCod (female Chöd). The school of male Chöd was founded by sKyo Sa-skya ye-shes (eleventh century). The other, female development of Chöd is based in the teachings of the unique and fascinating *Machig Lapdron, the Dakini Guru of this lineage and an incarnation of *Yeshe Tsogyal.

CHOLESTEROL

Today considered mainly a harmful substance, present in dairy products and involved with problems of the heart, cholesterol is important for the manufacture of hormones such as *progestogens, *estrogens, and *androgens.

CHOLI MARG

A Tantric ritual not very different from a *chakra puja but with an added element of randomness. The participating women, when entering the place of worship, take off their cholis (a blouselike upper-body garment worn with a sari) and leave them at the entrance. These are picked up by the men, who arrive later, and it is thus determined—by synchronicity or "chance"—who will be partner to whom during the celebration. The possible choices do not exclude *incest.

An almost identical ritual was observed by certain tribes or sects of the Near East: the Nessereah and the Ali Ullaheeahs, both regarded as pagans by their Islamic neighbors. The women's undergarments would be hung on the wall, and partners would be determined as each man picked one up (Briffault, vol. 3, p. 221).

CHU-LIN CH'I-HSIEN

This Chinese term, which translates as "the seven sages of the bamboo grove," refers to seven legendary Taoist scholars/ adepts of the third century who can best be compared with the Tibetan adepts of *crazy wisdom and some of the *Mahasiddhas. The masters in question are famous for seeking harmony with the universe by indulging in wine (*madya) and for following all their impulses in a natural, spontaneous way, thus defying all moral and ethical standards of their time.

CINNABAR

1. As a natural substance, cinnabar is a crystalline stone of a rose-purple hue. Chemically speaking it is a sulfur of mercury, often used as a red pigment in Chinese and Indian paintings. **2.** In Taoist *inner alchemy, cinnabar is one of the key symbols in the process of the transformation of energies; it is to the Chinese what *gold is to the Western alchemist. On its highest and most abstract level, cinnabar is the symbol for the "nuclear energy of joined *yang and *yin, which is to be fired in the internal crucible by alchemical yoga" (Rawson and Legeza, p. 26) in order to generate longevity or immortality.

Three of the Taoist subtle centers (*chakras) are called "fields of cinnabar," or *tan-t'ien; the female womb, or uterus, is called "cinnabar cave"; and the Taoist code for the valuable female *yin fluid used in sexual alchemy is "red cinnabar."

CINNABAR CAVE   SEE CINNABAR/2

CINNABAR FIELDS   SEE *TAN-T'IEN

CINNAMON

An easily obtained *aphrodisiac that is known and used in almost every household, though not in the sense here discussed. Cinnamon is the dried inner bark of an Indian tree and was already known to King *Solomon. In his *Song of Songs he mentions it among other well-known aphrodisiacs and fertility symbols. An "erotic recipe" involving cinnamon is to be found under *Cardamom Seeds.

CIRCE

A sister deity or *demon of the Cretan *Pasiphae, Circe features as enchantress and seductress in the myths surrounding the Greek hero Odysseus. The German language has a synonym for seduction that is derived from her name: becircen.

CIRCUMCISION (GENERAL)

Among the sexually oriented *perversions of humanity—*infibulation, *castration, *subincision, and a few others—circumcision may be counted as the one most commonly practiced. Many cultures and religions have demanded it, and its victims have been both women and men; yet, the operation and its consequences are in general much easier to bear and to live with in the case of males. (Although it definitely does hurt!) An especially painful exception to this general rule is the practice of subincision among the Australian Aborigines.

Whereas a boy victimized in this way by the religious

CINNABAR. *Although India has no native sources of *cinnabar, the valuable substance
has often been fetched from Afghanistan, Chitral, and Nepal, to be used in alchemy and as a pigment for painting.
Early nineteenth-century painting on paper, Rajasthan, India.
Photograph courtesy of Nik Douglas.*

and moral customs of his parents in most cases "merely" has to endure one single cut (preputial excision), which severs or shortens his foreskin, the female victim usually has to undergo the "trimming" of her clitoris and sometimes of both the labia minora and majora. In many older cultures, both the young men and women were advised, expected, or ordered to perform intercourse immediately or shortly after the operation, surely a painful experience by all standards. However, considering that the pain inflicted by the procedure may have lessened under the influence of pleasure and lust, the rule should be regarded as a well-meant and—

under the circumstances—perhaps a wholesome and healing custom.

According to the *Encyclopaedia Britannica,* only very few peoples "were unacquainted with the practice," and it names the "Indo-Germanic, the Mongol, and the Finno-Ugric speaking peoples." Because of the great differences in custom, we have divided the data into specific male and female entries.

One problem in abolishing these practices is that they are deeply ingrained in the social structure and value system of a given society. Even the women themselves, out of a sense of belonging, often actually want to be circumcised. Europeans and Americans who are working to have this practice abolished everywhere by the year 2000 must tread carefully and realize how much time it takes to make changes in custom and consciousness in any culture.

CIRCUMCISION (FEMALE)

Most of the practices described as female circumcision would be better categorized under the more precise terms of incision, excision, clitoridectomy, and infibulation. The least traumatic of all these practices is incision, in which one "merely" makes a slight cut into the clitoral crown (glans clitoridis) or the clitoral hood. Excision goes a step further. In this form, closely related to male circumcision, the clitoral hood, or "female foreskin," is completely cut away. For information on the two most extreme procedures, *clitoridectomy and *infibulation, see those respective entries. The variety of practices, and the respective circumstances surrounding the events, is so great that the present entry can function as a general overview only.

FAR EAST   In India, where circumcision originally was limited to *defloration by means of a local razor cut, the later Baluchis often circumcised part of a girl's clitoris at a very early age—a type of clitoridectomy. Several other countries in Asia practice(d) infibulation.

NEAR EAST   *Arabia:* According to Arabian tradition, female circumcision historically preceded that of males and is said to have originated with some of the *Bible's famous figures.

Israel: Although the historian Strabo (63 B.C.E.–21 C.E.) states otherwise, and though it has been said that the Virgin Mary was circumcised (Maury), it seems that the Jewish people did not generally practice this custom on girls. (More information is given at "Africa," below.)

Egypt: Clitoridectomy is still practiced, both in rural areas and in the cities, where people are more educated and more "modern." Considering that the type of major circumcision that is usual in Sudan is known as Pharaonic circumcision, we can assume that the Egyptians probably practiced infibulation in past times.

THE AMERICAS   Several tribes of the Amazon forests, and also the Conivos of northern Peru, celebrate circumcision by holding a merry feast with much drinking. At some point the young woman—semiconscious from the alcohol—is stretched out on a stage with all of the tribe looking on. One of the old women then deflowers the bride with a bamboo knife and also "frees" the clitoris from its hood. An artificial clay phallus with the true dimensions of her future husband's *lingam is then moistened and inserted into her *yoni before she is handed over to her husband.

EUROPE   Among the Russian/Rumanian *Skoptsi sect, both male and female circumcision, and sometimes even *castration, was a general and required practice.

OCEANIA AND AUSTRALIA   The Australian Arunta, also known for their painful *subincision of boys, use a flint knife for the operation they call *atna-aritha-kuma*, the "cutting of the vulva." What was originally meant to be an artificial *defloration is here turned into a thorough circumcision, cutting clitoris, labia, and hymen and continuing down through most of the *perineum. The more "normal" clitoridectomy was done among tribes of Celebes, Malaysia, and Indonesia.

AFRICA   Circumcision is very widespread in all its forms and was (and is) observed in almost every part of Africa, sometimes under the influence of old tribal customs, sometimes under that of Islam. Though some nations have meanwhile prohibited both infibulation and clitoridectomy, as did Kenya under President D. A. Moi in 1982, it takes a long time to change a "religious" custom that is deeply ingrained in a given culture's collective (un)consciousness.

An article in the Dutch magazine *Onze Wereld* (February 1990) lists more than 20 nations where excision and clitoridectomy are still practiced. Among them are Egypt, Niger, Ethiopia, Kenya, Ghana, Ivory Coast, Yemen, and also parts of Zaire and Tanzania. In some of these African nations (Sudan, Somalia) infibulation is also still commonly "executed."

The pre-Talmudic Jews of Abyssinia (now Ethiopia) used to regard female circumcision as obligatory, and the early Copts also observed the custom without exception. These painful operations, which lack any respect for the female body and soul, have—such is human nature—been rationalized here and there with strange theories. In India, for example, the Bahui tribe of Baluchistan and the Kelal—a fisherman caste—claim that snipping the tip of the clitoris will overcome barrenness or may help to achieve conception of a male child in a woman who until then has borne "only" girls.

CIRCUMCISION (MALE)

NEAR EAST   *Arabia:* Arab tribes used to cut the foreskin of their male youths in the presence of a boy's father and his future bride. If a boy cried, the father sometimes would kill his son for having shamed the family. One-fifth of the boys used to die anyway from the resulting infections and fevers.

Ever since the time of *Abraham, Hebrews have circumcised their sons on the eighth day after birth as part of Abraham's convenant with God. This "Law of Moses" (Acts 15) is still observed today. The Arab prophet Muhammad (c. 570–632 C.E.) also pronounced circumcision to be obligatory for all men, and it still is. Non-Arabic converts to the Islamic religion are known to undergo the operation supported by all the professionalism of modern medical technology.

THE AMERICAS   Among North and South American Indians male circumcision was, and is, not the rule; whenever it is done it is merely a small cut, a minor scarification of the foreskin.

Circumcision is, on the other hand, widespread in the contemporary United States, and 80 percent of newborn boys are circumcised on the fourth day of life. The child's parents are charged for this "elective" operation. The American Medical Association claims it is done on grounds of sexual hygiene, but world health statistics do not verify any such benefit. The resulting easy availability of foreskin has even led to its use in skin transplants needed by victims of fire or other accidents.

EUROPE   In the wake of contemporary standard circumcision as practiced in the United Sates, England also shows more and more inclination for having its young boys go through this unnecessary and traumatic experience.

OCEANIA AND AUSTRALIA   Throughout the Polynesian and Melanesian Islands, circumcision is of a different type than is normally encountered elsewhere in the world. Instead of cutting away the foreskin, these peoples simply cut a straight slit into the skin that results in a very visible scar. In Indonesia and the Malayan Islands, this practice has today been replaced by the Islamic "normal" excision of the foreskin.

The same Australian tribes who also practice female circumcision, in this case including a ghastly subincision of the *perineum, use male *subincision as part of their *puberty rites, thus making the boys "menstruate."

Yet another form of phallic modification is known in Indonesian Nias, Borneo, Celebes, New Guinea, and some Philippine islands. In this case, a hole is bored through the penis, and objects are inserted into and through the wounds. These objects stay there permanently and cause a number of problems in sexual intercourse, though they may, perhaps, also add to pleasurable stimulation (*see* *Ampallang).

AFRICA   The practice of circumcision in tribal Africa involved the making of small, straight slits and sometimes the boring of a kind of buttonhole into the foreskin, through which the phallic glans was then thrust. Similar to the Australian Aborigines' custom of subincision, this rite very much hints at the men's conscious mimicry of female *defloration.

Since the arrival and success of Islam, most of these techniques have been replaced by the "normal" amputation of the whole prepuce as it is practiced today on many male American children and on Muslim and Jewish boys all over the world.

CIVET, CIVETONE

An oily, yellow secretion from the sexual glands of the ferocious and untamable civet cat (*Viverra civetta*), which is used as a fixative in many of the more heavy, sweet, and erotic perfumes. Undiluted, this substance is so strong as to be hazardous to one's health—leading to nosebleeds and possibly to death—yet, once diluted it is most pleasing and similar to *musk, though it is of a finer scent and has more floral than animal overtones. Civet has been used to attract the opposite sex by rubbing it onto one's body, preferably on the throat and/or beneath the breasts. The civet cat lives in Burma, Thailand, and Ethiopia, and the African animals in particular are used for the extraction of civet.

CLITORAL BULBS   SEE *YONI TOGOGRAPHY/3

CLITORAL HOOD   SEE *YONI TOPOGRAPHY/5

CLITORIDECTOMY

Contrary to most of the practices described in this book, this practice does not simply constitute another piece in the puzzle of humanity's quest for sexual knowledge, but together with *infibulation, *subincision, and *castration it is rather one of the true *perversions. We have included it here only to show the outrageous lengths to which some societies have gone in their disrespect for the individual, especially apparent in the case of women and their bodies, minds, and sexuality.

Clitoridectomy—however scientific and learned this Latin term may sound—is in reality simply oppression and butchery of a very primitive kind. A girl, usually at about the age of six, will unexpectedly be seized at night and find herself held by many strong hands. With her legs forced wide apart, she lies half-naked, surrounded by her parents and other members of the family, while a woman deftly cuts off the girl's clitoral crown, clitoral hood, and labia minora. Mostly this is done with a crude knife and without any anesthetic. The "operation" not only is an extremely painful and truly traumatic experience but most often destroys once and for all any possibility of sexual pleasure and/or orgasm for the girl/woman in question. That this is done with the consent—and in the presence—of all those she would usually turn to for help must certainly be an added dimension of terror for the child.

The description above is based on an account by Nawal el Saadawi (b. 1931) of her personal experience in 1937. As an adult she became an Egyptian government official and published several books in an attempt to spare girls in the future from this and other torments; however, even though she was Egypt's director of public health, her works were censored, and she herself was finally dismissed from her post. One must realize that clitoridectomy is not something of the past or something that happens to a few unfortunate girls. Even in 1993, there were approximately 26 countries worldwide, often Islamic, in which the astonishing number of about 30 million women were abused in this way (French, p. 255). For a list of countries involved, see *Circumcision. In some societies, this practice is extended by an even worse procedure: *infibulation.

CLITORIS SEE *MADANAHATRA, *YONI TOPOGRAPHY/11

CLOUDS AND RAIN
(CHIN., YUN-YU)

According to R. H. van Gulik, the Chinese expression yun-yu is the "standard literary expression for the sexual act." However, considering that Chinese sexological literature associates these "clouds" with *female love juices and the "rain" with a man's *semen, it would rather seem to be an image of *orgasm, and one can find it used in this way in erotic novels. Poetic and flowery expressions like this one for sexual union abound in most of the *pillow books. Another one, for example, is "to share pillow and couch." Homosexual activity, on the other hand, is designated as "the reverse clouds and the inverted rain" (van Gulik, pp. 39–40).

SEE ALSO *LINGAM TERMINOLOGY, *YONI TERMINOLOGY

COCAINE

An *alkaloid made from the leaves of the coca bush. It is widely known and used for its *aphrodisiac and energy-enhancing properties. Not only is it illegal, but its habitual use can lead to diseases of the nasal tract, eventual physical depletion, and, in some people, acute paranoia.

COCK

An animal that features as a symbol of human desire in the Tibetan *mandala known as the wheel of life: a graphic representation of the complete cycle of existence. In France, the cock has been interpreted as a symbol of independence and freedom. Interestingly enough, the cock was a phallic totem among the Romans, and even today it is a vernacular term for the *lingam. According to Barbara Walker, the Vatican's ancient treasures include a bronze image of a cock represented by the head of a penis on the torso of a man. The sculpture's pedestal is inscribed with the words "The Saviour of the World" (Walker, 1988, p. 397).

COCOA

This plant, immediately associated by most people with chocolate, cholocate drinks, and children, contains the *alkaloid theobromine. The substance, when taken in large quantities, has *aphrodisiac qualities—a fact demonstrated by a study on workers in a chocolate factory who ate excessive amounts of their products.

COCO-DE-MER

The fruit of a special type of coconut palm that grows only on the Seychelle Islands off the southern coast of India. They are huge double coconuts, the shape of which resembles a woman's parted thighs with the vulva clearly visible. From the Indian point of view, such coconuts—when found on their shorelines—were simply coco-de-mer ("coconut from the sea"). This fruit—apparently born from the female

C OCO-DE-MER. A *coco-de-mer, regarded in India
as a sacred symbol of the *yoni.
Ajit Mookerjee Collection, New Delhi.

element water, and with its obvious yonilike shape—
became a major symbol of the Great Goddess and her *yoni.

COCONUT

According to the ancient Indian texts of the Yajur *Veda, the
coconut is a fruit of specific interest to men. Aside from its
general property of purifying the bladder, it is also said to
increase a man's semen. A drink made from coconut milk
and *honey is reputed to promote sexual appetitie. In New
Guinea, the meat and milk of coconuts would be used,
mixed with sperm, for a variety of purposes.

SEE ALSO *SPERM MAGIC

COITUS A TERGO

Sexual union with *lingam entering *yoni from behind. Not
to be confused with *venus aversa.

COITUS INTERRUPTUS

Withdrawal of the *lingam just before *ejaculation occurs.
This technique is used as a contraceptive method, although it
is not very safe with inexperienced men. The practice was
known of old and is described even in the Bible, although it

is usually interpreted as speaking of onanism, or *masturbation: "And it came to pass, when he went in unto his brother's
wife, that he [Onan] spilled it on the ground" (Genesis 38:9).
According to some Jewish legends, coitus interruptus was one
of the major reasons for humanity's divine punishment in the
form of the great flood. The technique is necessary in sexual
union according to systems such as *karezza and *imsak.

COITUS PROLONGATUS

Prolonged sexual union through controlled postponement
or complete inhibition of *orgasm and/or *ejaculation.

SEE ALSO *IMSAK, *KABBAZAH

COITUS RESERVATUS

A mode of union in which the man refrains from *ejaculation. If both partners withhold their juices, it is called *coitus
sublimatus or *amplexus reservatus, a sort of "dry" orgasm.

COITUS SUBLIMATUS

A term used in *karezza for a form of sexual union during
which both partners refrain from *orgasm and/or *ejaculation yet do exchange subtle or "spiritual" fluids.

COLOR SYMBOLISM   SEE *GOLD, *LIGHT, *RED, *VIOLET

CONCH SHELL

A typical symbol of the feminine in general and specifically
of the *yoni. In Tibet and India, conch shells are used as
musical instruments, and the sound that emerges from the
shell's spirals is considered to be a symbol of eternity and of
pure, primordial space.

SEE ALSO *COWRIE SHELL, *SHANKHINI

CONFUCIUS, CONFUCIANISM   SEE *K'UNG-TZU

CONGRESSUS SUBTILIS

Alleged sexual union with a nonphysical or astral entity, for
example an *incubus, a *succubus, or the spirit of someone
dead. Also known as congressus cum daemone.

SEE ALSO *KA'A, *SPECTROPHILIA

CONISALUS

A very specialized male deity connected with the perspiration of couples during sexual union.

CONSPIRATION

A technique used to harmonize breathing between two or more persons. This method of coordinated breathing has been used successfully to control a given individual's psyche, especially to arouse his or her sexual desire.

As with all powerful techniques of energy manipulation this can also be, and has been, used in both black/egoistic and white/altruistic ways. Both Aleister *Crowley and G. I. *Gurdjieff are known to have mastered and used this method. In his book *God Is My Adventure,* R. Landau recalls the experience of an attractive woman who dined in a restaurant at a table next to Gurdjieff's. Shortly after Gurdjieff had begun breathing in a peculiar pattern, the woman went pale and was quite shocked. She later explained that she "suddenly felt as if I had been struck right through my sexual center" (quoted by C. Wilson, 1984, p. 397).

CONSTRICTOR CUNNUS   SEE *YONI
TOPOGRAPHY/25

CORDAX

Name of an ancient Greek *dance that expresses and pro-

C<small>OITUS A</small> T<small>ERGO</small>. *Fifth-century Greek bowl (detail)
depicting *coitus a tergo.
Private collection of Coen vanEmde Boas.*

vokes sexual desire. Dedicated to the goddess Artemis Cordaka, the dance involves stripping off all garments, exhibitionism, and swaying, erotic movements.

CORPUS CAVERNOSUM
(LATIN, "BODY OF CAVES")

Before 1987, *corpus cavernosum* was the term mainly used to indicate the erectile part of the *lingam, when it was not yet recognized as a male clitoris. Now the term indicates the erectile tissue that constitutes the shaft and the two crura (legs) of the clitoris, in both the female and male varieties. It consists of involuntary muscles and a great number of cavities, which can become filled with blood. This tissue can become bone-hard during sexual excitement.

S<small>EE ALSO</small> *C<small>ORPUS</small> S<small>PONGIOSUM</small>, *L<small>INGAM</small> T<small>OPOGRA-</small>
<small>PHY</small>/11, *Y<small>ONI</small> T<small>OPOGRAPHY</small>/11

CORPUS LUTEUM

The so-called yellow body in the human female, where the manufacture of the hormones *progesterone (formerly called luteum) and *estrogen takes place.

S<small>EE ALSO</small> *M<small>ENSTRUAL</small>/O<small>VARIAN</small> C<small>YCLE</small>

CORPUS SPONGIOSUM
(LATIN, "SPONGY BODY")

Erectile tissue that makes up the clitoral crown (or glans), the bulbs below the labia majora, and the urethral sponge. Different from the *corpus cavernosum, this tissue remains soft and elastic when erect.

S<small>EE ALSO</small> *Y<small>ONI</small> T<small>OPOGRAPHY</small>/3, 6, 14

CORAL ESSENCE   SEE *MENSTRUAL FLUID

COTYTTO

A Thracian goddess of sexuality in whose honor secret *orgies were organized by her worshippers. In southern Greece she later became the Athenian goddess of licentious *ritual promiscuity.

COURTESANS

Prostitution, sometimes *sacred and often *secular, was a generally accepted feature of social life in much of Greek and Roman history, and there were some 50 terms to differentiate and indicate the class, social status, location, specialties, and appearance of various courtesans. Although the word *courtesan* originally indicated merely a "lady at court," the word acquired its meaning of "high-class prostitute" during the European Renaissance. In that age, the courtesans—generally educated, elegant, intelligent, and successful women—styled themselves after the Greek *hetaerai.

See also *Fruit de Mer

COWPER'S GLANDS   SEE *LINGAM TOPOGRAPHY/12

COWRIE SHELL

In a great many cultures, the beautiful cowrie has been a symbol of the divine *yoni and therefore has been used as a fertility charm. It was believed to have healing and regenerative powers. Whether it was worn in necklaces or put in graves to accompany the dead on their way to a new cycle, the cowrie provided the devotee with an especially intimate connection with the Great Mother.

Cowrie shells were held sacred in such diverse societies as those of the Polynesian Islands, Africa, India, and the Mediterranean area, as well as in the Europe of 20,000 B.C.E. There is an Indian goddess called Kauri who is connected to both the sacred yoni and the cowrie shell. Cowrie shells were one of the earliest forms of money, in Africa and Asia, and have been used as such even into the twentieth century, for example, among tribes of Papua New Guinea.

See also *Conch Shell

CRAZY WISDOM

A phrase describing an unorthodox and rather informal Tantric tradition that has its origins with the *Mahasiddhas, including such illustrious masters as *Tilopa and *Naropa. The tradition, though not a formal one, knows such famous exponents as *Drukpa Kunleg and was recently represented by the Tibetan teacher and author Chogyam *Trungpa, whose lifestyle scandalized many of his European and American disciples.

CROMLECH

1. A term often used for a circle of large standing stones (*see* *Megaliths) such as are found mainly in Celtic regions. The term derives from the Welsh *crom* ("curved") and *lech* ("stone"). Occasionally such a circle surrounds one or more *dolmens. **2.** Sometimes used as a synonym for *dolmen.*

CROSS   SEE *ANKH

CROWLEY, ALEISTER
(1875–1947)

Edward Alexander Crowley is regarded by some as the greatest magician of the twentieth century and by others as an egomaniac "great beast" addicted to power, sex, and drugs of all kinds. This is an indication of how controversial and uncompromising a man he was. Whatever category the reader may prefer to place him in, Crowley certainly has provided us with several unique texts and insights concerning philosophical and hermetic matters, human nature, the human mind, and last but not least, various magical uses of sexual energy, for example, *erotocomatose lucidity. Crowley also became a member, and later the spiritual head, of the *Ordo Templi Orientis.

In an attempt to re-create some of the ancient practices such as *phallic worship, *yoni worship, and *ritual prostitution, Crowley founded, in 1920, the Abbey of Thelema at Cefalu in Sicily. He also created his own versions of erotic rituals and tried to fashion some of his female acquaintances into Tantric *yoginis* (see *Yogini/2), "bestowing" on them the title and office of *Scarlet Woman. He did not heed the warning of the *Parasurama-kalpa Sutra, and his several attempts to have secular prostitutes turn quickly and easily into trained and sacred initiates failed without exception. This failure, of course, must not be attributed to the women alone. To a large extent it was certainly Crowley's own inability to understand and deal with women, though European society, education, and moral standards certainly did not help. Crowley has strongly influenced such important artists as the contemporary filmmaker Kenneth Anger and the fine artist Austin Osman Spare (1888–1956).

See also *Conspiration, *Nuit, *Reincarnation

CRUX ANSATA   SEE *ANKH

CUNNILINGUS

Latin technical term for kissing, licking, or sucking the cunnus, or *yoni. Though its male counterpart, *fellatio, is often depicted in the temples of *Konarak and *Khajuraho, depictions of cunnilingus are rare.

That the practice, however, was and is a major form of sacred sexuality—and thus Tantric worship—is borne out by its clear description in several sacred texts. The

CUNNILINGUS. *In Chinese sexual alchemy, the mutually pleasureable practice of *cunnilingus is sometimes diverted into a form of sexual vampirism. Not spending any of his own essence, the man—intent on longevity— will absorb as much female essence as possible; a second woman is often close at hand. Late nineteenth-century painting on silk, China. Photograph courtesy of Nik Douglas.*

Chakrasamvara Tantra, for example, clearly states that a skillful practitioner "worships the yogini's stainless lotus of light." And for those who may not believe that the *lotus referred to here is the *yoni of flesh and blood, the following quote attributed to the goddess *Vajrayogini will end all doubts: "I will bestow supreme success on one who ritually worships my lotus, bearer of all bliss" (quoted in Miranda Shaw, p. 155).

In her *Passionate Enlightenment,* Shaw continues by paraphrasing a verse from the *Chandamaharosana Tantra,* which says that the man should "declare his devotion and humble servitude to her, asking her to grace him with a loving glance. She will then draw him to her and kiss him, direct his mouth to between her thighs, and embrace and pinch him playfully."

The fact that ritual cunnilingus can as well involve two women rather than the usual male/female pair has been shown by Giti Thadani in her attempt to write a history of lesbian love in India. The existence of a beautiful statue of two women engaged in cunnilingus in the eleventh-century

Rajarani Temple in Bhuveshvar, Orissa, is reflected in a Tibetan text by *Yeshe Tsogyal. Her experience is retold under *Menstrual Fluid.

All of the above combined, together with what we know about *yonitattva, *yonipushpa, and the Taoist's third *Medicine of the Three Peaks, can only lead to one conclusion: that cunnilingus is a beneficial and preferred type of worship, even if ridiculous "laws" exist in some countries—and in 24 states of the United States (according to K. R. Stuldas, *The Clitoral Kiss*)—trying to enforce the Roman Catholic assertion that all sexuality should be aimed toward procreation.

CUPID

The Roman version of the Greek *Eros.

CUSTOMS

A special listing that provides access to all entries related to festivals, rituals, and customs has been prepared in index 6 on page 275.

CYBELE

A Near Eastern goddess whose worship spread into Greece, Rome, and other neighboring cultures. Even in Athens's Agora there is a temple dedicated to her, known as the Metroon, or "temple of the mother." Cybele was involved with *ritual prostitution, *castration, and *fertility rites focusing on *Attis, one of the many vegetation gods. The cult of this Phrygian goddess has resulted in archaeological monuments ranging in time from 6000 B.C.E. to the end of the Roman Empire. Recent finds have established that she was also worshipped among the Thracian peoples.

In his work on the Christian Black Virgins and their origins, Ean Begg relates Cybele to the *Ka'bah: "Her name is etymologically linked with the words for crypt, cave, head and dome and is distantly related to the Ka'aba, the cube shaped Holy of Holies in Mecca that contains the feminine black stone venerated by Islam" (p. 57). Cybele, like the *Ephesian Artemis and many other female deities, was venerated in the form of a black stone. Once it had been brought to Rome, both stone and goddess were worshipped in the Roman Empire until the fourth century C.E. The Roman name for this goddess was Mater Kubile.

SEE ALSO *ALMOND, *SACRED STONES

D

*Because all women are *Dakinis, an intense, integral sexual encounter or relationship is a means to attain *siddhi.*

KEITH DOWMAN, *SKY DANCER*

DAGPO KAGYUD

One of the original two schools that form the *Kagyudpa tradition. The school is based on the teachings of Dagpo Lharje Gampopa (1079–1153), who founded this tradition in 1125, having combined the *Mahamudra teachings with those of the Naro-chos-drug.

Among the members of this school were many inventive and nonconformist monks and masters, and their activities and teachings led to a variety of subdivisions. Four schools were founded by direct students of Gampopa. They are collectively known as "golden lineages" or simply as "the four major schools":

- **Barom** (or Baram) **Kagyud** (Tib., 'Ba-rom) founded by Barom Darma Wangchuk.
- **Karma** (or Kamstang) **Kagyud**, founded by Dusum Khyenpa (1110–1193), the first *Karmapa.
- **Tsalpa** (or Tselpa) **Kagyud** (Tib., Tshal-pa), founded by Zhang Yudakpa Tsondu Dakpa (1123–1193).
- **Phagmo Drupa** (or Pagtru) **Kagyud**, founded by Phagmo Drupa Dorje Gyelpo (1100–1170).

From this latter teacher, and the school named after him, derive the "minor" or "lesser" Kagyud schools, each founded by one of his direct students:

- **Drikung** (or Brigung) **Kagyud**, founded by Drikung Kyopa Jigten Gonpo (1143–1217).

- **Drugpa** (or Brug pa) **Kagyud**, founded by Choje Gyare Yeshe Dorje, better known as Linchenrepa (1128–1189). Thus, the school is also known as Linre Kagyud.
- Martzang (or Martsang) Kagyud (Tib., *sMar-tsang-pa*), founded by Marpa Rinchen Lodoe.
- Shungseb (or Shugsep) Kagyud (Tib., *Shugs-gseb-pa*), founded by Chokyi Sengey.
- **Taglung** (or Taklung) **Kagyud**, founded by Taglung Thangpa Tashe Pel (1142–1210).
- Trophu (or Khrophu) Kagyud (Tib., *Tr'op'u*) founded by Rinpoche Gyaltsa.
- Yamsang (or Yazang) Kagyud (Tib., *gYa'abzang*) founded by Yeshi Senge.
- Yelpa (or Yerpa) Kagyud (Tib., *Yel-pa*) founded by Yelpa Yeshe Tseg.

NOTE: All schools given in **bold** letters are still alive today, with monasteries in India, Nepal, Sikkim, Bhutan, Ladakh, Europe, Australia, and the United States.

DAIMON

In most contemporary literature and speech, the terms *daimon* (Greek), *daemon* (Latin), and *demon appear to be synonyms; sometimes there is not even a distinction made between demons and angels. One should be aware, however, that in ancient Greece, a daimon was most often regarded as a beneficent personal guardian spirit or—in modern psychological terminology—as one's "higher self." Such a definition is a far cry from the usual concept of a demon as an evil and/or unclean entity, as both daimons and demons are defined and described in the Bible and similar texts.

In Latin, the language of the Roman empire with its many imported, adopted, and adapted customs and deities, the Greek daimon became a daemon; here she or he acquired the qualities good/beneficent (Latin, *agathodaemon*) and bad/malefic (Latin, *cacodaemon*).

DAISEI SHOKUSHU

A modern-day Japanese sect, "the religion of primal creation," founded by *Shinto priest and artist Kobu Morimaru. His painting of the goddess *Kuan-yin is very interesting in that it shows her with uniquely erotic attributes, quite unlike her offical and common version.

DAKINI

1. A group of "sky walkers" or "queens of space" whose number is said to be "one hundred thousand myriads" and who appear in both Hindu and Buddhist Tantra. In popular Hindu Tantrism and folklore they are semidivine beings and are most often seen as malignant spirits, *demons, or witchlike hags. In Buddhist Ladakh, an originally Tibetan region now in northwest India, they enjoy a much better reputation. For example, 500,000 of them are still today invited to a local celebration of marriage in order to bestow their blessings and good fortune on the young couple. The *dakinis* play an important role in the esoteric tradition of Tantric Buddhism, or *Vajrayana, where each of them is regarded as the personification of a certain level of wisdom/initiation. The large number and variety of *dakinis* prevents us from discussing them here in detail.

SEE ALSO *BODHISATTVA DAKINIS, *SURYACANDRASIDDHI

2. The equivalent Tibetan term, *khadroma,* when we translate the individual syllables, shows these deities to be "females who move on the highest level of reality," whose nakedness symbolizes the diamond clarity of truth unveiled.

3. Quite often the term *dakini* seems to have been used not for a deity but as a name of honor for a living woman who had achieved a high degree of initiation and accomplishment or who was seen as a true incarnation of a goddess. In the biography of the great Tantric adept *Padmasambhava, for example, five *dakinis* are mentioned as being among his direct disciples. These are clearly five women, all of whom were very much alive and physical and who were the yogi's companions and lovers, having "access to the Master's heart." Because of such role models, the term *dakini* is also used as a title for the participating woman in *maithuna,* just as is done with the terms *prajna, *vidya, and *Shakti.

SEE ALSO *NIGUMA, *YESHE TSOGYAL

4. A figure called Dakini also occurs in the image of *Chinnamasta, and it is also the name of the deity who represents the energy of—or the Shakti presiding over—the *muladhara chakra.

DAKSHINACARA

The "right-hand way" of *Tantra, the followers of which are called Dakshinacharins and who renounce many of the truly Tantric techniques and are mainly *bhakti yoga–oriented. Here sexual activity is merely symbolic/mental, and several of the five *makara acquire a different interpretation.

The reformation from "left" to "right" is often attributed to the influence of the scholar, philosopher, and teacher Shankara (788–820 C.E.). He and others like him actually tried to compromise between the new and radical teachings of Tantra and the more orthodox Vedic tradition. The Sanskrit word daksina indicates both "right" and "southern." A temple, for example, with the name Dakshin-Kali, found in both India and Nepal, does not signify a "right" *Kali, but more likely "she whose worship derives from southern India." Such a temple does not necessarily have to be a sacred place of Dakshinacara.

DAKSHINAMARGA   SEE *DAKSHINACARA

DALAI LAMA, HIS HOLINESS THE

Honorary religious title meaning "the teacher whose wisdom is great as an ocean." The term dalai is a Western adaptation of ta-le, the Mongolian version of the Tibetan gyatso (Tib., rGya-mtsho), "Ocean of Wisdom." The true Tibetan title for the Dalai Lama, as it is used in Tibet, is rGyalba, indicating the "supreme head" of the school, believed to be an incarnation of Avalokiteshvara. The title of Dalai Lama was first bestowed (1578) on Sonam Gyatso, then Grand Lama of the *Gelugpa school, by the Mongol leader Altan Khan, when he and his Mongols officially adopted *Buddhism. Sonam Gyatso, who was seen as an incarnation of Gendun Drub, by way of Gendun Gyatso, has come to be known since then as the third Dalai Lama. Sonam Gyatso (third) promised the Mongolians that his future incarnation would be among them. As promised, Yonten Tyatso (fourth) was a direct descendant of Altan Khan and the only Dalai Lama ever to be born outside Tibet. Similar to the *Karmapa, both the title and office have since been carried through time by an unbroken series of *reincarnations. However, the present (14th) Dalai Lama, Nobel prize-winner Tenzin Gyatso, has announced that he represents "the end of the line" and has decided not to reincarnate in the future.

1. Gendun Drub	1391–1474	
2. Gendun Gyatso	1475–1542 (see *Tantric Visualization)	
3. Sonam Gyatso	1543–1588	
4. Yonten Gyatso	1589–1617 (Mongolian)	
5. Ngawang Lobzang Gyatso	1618–1682 (The Great Fifth)	
6. Tsangyang Gyatso	1684–1706	
7. Kalzang Gyatso	1708–1757	
8. Jampal Gyatso	1758–1804	
9. Lungtok Gyatso	1805–1815	
10. Tsultrim Gyatso	1816–1837	
11. Khedrub Gyatso	1838–1856	
12. Trinle Gyatso	1857–1875	
13. Tubten Gyatso	1876–1933	
14. Tendzin Gyatso	born 1935, enthroned 1940	

DANCE

As one of the arts that lend themselves excellently to erotic stimulation, dance figures in a variety of cultures, rituals, and customs. Here is a list of entries where dance plays a role: *Cordax, *Devadasis, *Gopis, *Graces, *Hetaerai, *Horae, *Kagura, *Khlysti, *Lasya, *Maithuna Viparita, *Maypole Dances, *Ritual Promiscuity, *Ritual Prostitution, *Sarasvati/2, *Sexual Hospitality, *Sixty-four Arts, *Tantric Visualization.

DEFLORATION

It is a great pity that most contemporary women have to undergo this unique, important, and potentially initiatory moment "at the hands" of a male who is usually inexperienced, often frightened and impulsive, or even downright primitive in his sexual expression and sensitivities.

Other cultures, sometimes less patriarchal ones without the trappings of original sin and extensive sexual repression, have recognized the moment of defloration as an important psychosomatic event and have often surrounded it with special care and attention, however strange, gross, or "barbaric" such efforts may seem to us. Such sacred proceedings can take many forms, and though not all of them are gentle or can be recommended, they may easily be preferred to the college student's "sport" of "breaking in" a *virgin, or the fearful and tearful fumbling in the back of a car or an unlit tent.

Whenever defloration is done by a priest, a mother, or a midwife/shamanness, we must realize that often the reason behind this is a deep-rooted fear that the "magical" *blood, with a force seen as similar to the dark blood of menstruation, could cause harm to the future husband (see *Nasamonian Marriage Custom). Another reason for some

D ANCE. *A *dance of the Bavenda in southern Africa,
designed to invoke the powers of fertility. Photograph by Peter Carmichael.*

defloration customs is to provide proof of a potential bride's previous chastity and frequently had/has to do with the bridal price a husband has to pay to her family. What in Sicily, Spain, and Greece, and among Jews, Christians, and Copts, later became the custom of showing off a bloodied gown or cloth to one's neighbors has its roots in such actual and often public defloration customs of earlier times.

The attention given to a virgin's defloration is nonetheless not always directed at proving her chastity, at diverting the feared energy of her blood, or at the personal "initiation" of the girl who is becoming a sexual woman. The sexual and fertile potential of a physical virgin and the release of the strong psychic energies inherent in her "first blood" have often been harnessed in the service of the tribe or the community.

As to a required or preferred age for deflowering a girl, we can find no consistent pattern, but most often it is done before the girl reaches puberty.

FAR EAST   In Kampuchea (Cambodia), it was the duty and privilege of the Buddhist or Taoist priest to deflower a bride before her marriage.

In Burma, ritual defloration was used to ensure crop fertility.

In Nepal, the worship of the *living goddess also involves the *kumari puja, a ritual during which defloration sometimes takes place. Young Nepalese girls intending to become *devadasis are "deflowered by the temple priest who makes her sit on a stone linga" (Devi, p. 133), a symbol of the divine *Shivalinga.

India values defloration of a *kumari very highly, and the kumari puja is seen as indispensable for Tantric devotees. Certain rishis and yogis were known to take "vows of penance," for example, to deflower two thousand virgins, and those who had taken such a vow would then travel up and down the country in order to fulfill this

DEFLORATION. *Defloration as *initiation, using *lingams of stone. Eighteenth-century gouache, Rajasthan, India. Ajit Mookerjee Collection, New Delhi.

charitable obligation (Briffault, vol. 3, p. 229). The fact that the *Sanskrit language even has a specialized term, *svapuspa,* denoting the first *menstrual fluid after defloration, is also significant. Certain Indian tribes practice defloration together with a girl's *circumcision.

NEAR EAST   In ancient, pre-Islamic Egypt, defloration was often done digitally (that is, using a finger) and in the presence of both mothers of the marrying couple. Another accepted way for a young Egyptian girl to lose her physical virginity was by participating—before puberty—in one of several celebrations that included *ritual promiscuity.

EUROPE   In Italy, the priests of *Priapus deflowered young female devotees by means of artificial phalli representing the diety. In ancient Ireland, it was the privilege and duty of the king to deflower all brides before they were taken to their respective husbands. In an ancient Irish record, the legendary King Conchobar is praised for his diligent devotion to these duties, and he was said to have taken the virginity of "every maid in Ulster" (Briffault, vol. 3, p. 230). From customs such as these stems the concept of the *Jus Primae Noctis.

SEE ALSO *TUTINUS

THE AMERICAS   *North America:* Among the Kushkuwak tribe of Alaska, a young girl would be deflowered by the local shaman, and only afterward was she deemed "worthy" to take part in any religious celebration.

Latin America: In Peru, a mother would break her daughter's hymen with her own hands in a public assembly. In Mexico, a Tahu husband took his bride to a priest immediately after marriage, and the latter would, after spending the night with the girl, report on the condition of her virginity. Other Mexican tribes let the priest deflower a girl by hand when she was only a few months old, the mother repeating this once more at the age of six. Jivaro girls of Ecuador were deflowered with a bone, and similar customs are known from Brazil and Paraguay.

OCEANIA AND AUSTRALIA   The birde of a Samoan chief would be deflowered digitally or with a shark's tooth, with much ceremony and before many spectators, by the bridegroom himself or by a relative. Such "instrumental" defloration was also performed in the Philippines, the Pulau Islands of Indonesia, and mainland Australia, using sticks or similar tools.

Members of the Australian Arunta tribe practice a type of defloration that includes thorough *circumcision.

AFRICA   *Sudan:* A future husband in Nubia was expected to test the intended bride's virginity when she was nine years old and would—one year later—dilate her hymen slowly and gradually on several successive days.

Morocco: Among the Zhara people, the spiritual leader, or *rusma,* was required to deflower every young bride before she could be married to her future husband. A figure called "the man who is asked to oblige" was known to many tribes of Central Africa. It was he who made love to a girl only moments after she had been deflowered and undergone circumcision.

DEMON

Generally—in most religious systems, spiritual philosophies, and esoteric schools—the term *demon* denotes an evil spirit, a force, influence, or power opposed to personal and/or human evolution and fulfillment. However, one should also be aware that the demons described and maligned by one religious system or culture frequently are or were the deities of another one—a process that can easily be discerned from cases such as that of *Lilith.

SEE ALSO *DAIMON

DEVA

General Sanskrit term for "god," yet sometimes, depending on the context, also used for individual deities such as *Shiva or others.

DEVA CHAKRA

Like the *raja* and *vira chakras,* this is a ritual in which one man engages in *maithuna* with five women, in this case a selection of *veshyas: women who practice *ritual prostitution. The participants in a *deva chakra* are, according to D. N. Bose (who quotes an unidentified *Tantra), as follows (all quotes from Bose and Haldar, p. 144):

- one *raja veshya,* a "royal harlot" normally "devoted to the service of the king"
- one *gupta veshya,* a "secret prostitute" who "belongs to the family"
- one *deva veshya,* a "dancing girl" and "celestial prostitute" (*see also* *Devadasis)
- one *brahma veshya,* one of the prostitutes who "visit sacred shrines"

- one *nagari,* a title that is given to any young girl during her menstruation
- one male would-be initiate

SEE ALSO *VESHYA

DEVADASIS

Translated, this Sanskrit term means "servants of the gods." It is a collective name for those girls and women who were both refined temple dancers and well-trained *courtesans serving in the temples of *Kama, the Indian god of love. Sometimes the girls were bought by the temple trustees from poor and needy families; most often they were given to the temple by pious parents. Such dedication was considered a sure ticket to heaven. The *devadasis* were mainly a phenomenon of southern India and were found there until quite recently. The famous temple at Somnath had—at its peak—more than 500 *devadasis.* The ruling king, as representative of the Divine, could make free use of their services.

Nepal has also known its *devadasis* until the custom was quite recently banned by the late King Mahendra (1920–1972), who ruled Nepal from 1955 until his death. However, a 1982 Nepali publication stated that "this custom of devadasi has almost disappeared in Nepal" (Majipuria, 1982, p. 133), indicating that it actually still lives on.

SEE ALSO *DEFLORATION, *DEVA CHAKRA

DEVI

General Sanskrit term of "goddess," and sometimes, depending on the context, also used for individual deities such as *Kali, Sati, or others.

DEVI MAHATMYA
(SKT., "GLORIFICATION OF THE GREAT GODDESS")

A very interesting work in that it is the very first large and comprehensive text within *Sanskrit literature that specifically deals with the Indian tradition of the Great Goddess (Skt., *devi*). Although the text was certainly influenced by Vedic Brahmanism, in itself it is a major scripture of *Shakta, apparently evolving and attempting to reestablish the position the Goddess had held in pre-Aryan, pre-Vedic times.

The Devi Mahatmya, actually a part of the Markandeya Purana but clearly having an independent status, reminds us that the ultimate reality of the most ancient human traditions has always been recognized as female, and venerated in the form of a goddess. The Goddess is described here in her manifold aspects, among them the archetypal virgin (*Kumari) and mother (Ambika), wanton (*Kamakhya) and virtuous woman (Sati): apparent dualities that in fact are merely possibilities of manifestation.

SEE ALSO *ARYAN INVASION THEORY

DEVI PURANA

One of the Puranas of the *Shakta school, written at some time during the sixth century C.E. in Bengal. Like the slightly earlier *Devi Mahatmya, the Devi Purana makes obvious references to a pre-Vedic worship of the Goddess in India, and it declares the worship of her open to members of all castes. The text is available only in Bengali with Hindi commentaries.

DEW OF ECSTASY

1. A concept like *ros, *amrita, and *soma: an essence that is thought to be created or stimulated by techniques of *retention of semen.

SEE ALSO *ECSTASY, *PINEAL GLAND

2. A secret code indicating vaginal secretions, or *female love juices.

DHUPA   SEE *BODHISATTVA DAKINIS

DIANA OF EPHESUS   SEE *EPHESIAN ARTEMIS

DIANISM

The next stage after *alphaism, dianism is the second degree of initiation in *sexual magick as practiced by the *Great Brotherhood of God and perhaps similar organizations. Dianism entails sexual union, but similarly to *imsak, it requires the *retention of semen. Dianisic unions are usually held in the dark in order to minimize emotional, individually oriented attachments and behavior, and with the understanding that one unites with a "divine lover," the latter having certainly been gleaned from Tantric teachings.

SEE ALSO *QODOSH

DIGAMBARA
(SKT., "CLOTHED WITH AIR," "SKY-CLAD")

A name indicating that the person in question is a member of the Digambara sect, a group of *Jaina devotees who do not wish to possess even clothes and who therefore walk about the country entirely naked. Generally speaking, the

Digambara, like the *Kapalikas, are part of the *Vamacara, or "way of the left hand." More specifically, they constitute a subsect of the Tantric *Kula, but with a Jainist orientation.

SEE ALSO *ADAMITES, *NAGNA

DIKSHA

Sanskrit term for *initiation by one's spiritual teacher, during which the pupil receives a personal *mantra and is introduced to the spiritual and philosophical tenets of the school or sect in question.

DIONYSUS

Originally a Thracian deity, Dionysus became the Greek representative of *ecstasy, trance, hysteria, and frenzy and was associated with wine as well as sexuality. Dionysus, the latest and last of the deities "admitted" into the circle of Olympic gods and goddesses, represents the type of male who has, lives, and shows his emotions in a way that is usually seen as a typically female trait: He actually feels rather than just talks about his feelings.

When we read in his myths that Dionysus emerged—that is, was born—from the thigh of *Zeus, we must realize that the term *thigh* was often used as a code for the phallus, or *lingam. This usage occurs, for example, in Genesis, where an oath is sworn on someone's thigh (*see* *Phallic Worship/2). His cult was carried to Rome, where he was worshipped as *Bacchus and where his female initiates, the *maenads, came to be known as the *Bacchantes.

SEE ALSO *AMANITA MUSCARIA, *GOAT

DISMEMBERMENT

Several myths are known—from Greece, Egypt, Africa, and the Far East—in which the dismemberment of a certain deity plays an important role, signifying and symbolizing death and *rebirth, disintegration and reintegration. Such gods as *Osiris, *Dionysus, and *Shiva were dismembered and individual pieces were scattered; sometimes, as with Osiris, they were searched for, found, and reunited, in this case by his sister, wife, and lover, Isis. Similar myths, and ceremonies recapturing those divine events, are also known in the *Bön of pre-Buddhist Tibet and among the African Yoruba. In India, apart from Shiva's 12 *jyotirlingas,* we also find such a myth in connection with the goddess Sati, whose body was dismembered and scattered all over India and the neighboring lands. This myth has given rise to the holy places called *pithas.

Quite often in these myths, the *lingam or *yoni of the deity in question receives special literary treatment, being regarded as symbol and seat of the deity's most essential powers. Such myths probably stem from an older layer of religious and spiritual psychology and cosmology. The shamans, both male and female, of many peoples often report making journeys into the "otherworld," where they are dismembered by *demons and deities but are reintegrated before they return to their fleshy body.

SEE ALSO *BREASTS, *CHINNAMASTA, *CHÖD

DIVYA

A Sanskrit term meaning "divine" and "heavenly." It indicates a Tantric initiate of the first and highest degree. The *divya* man is considered to be the best possible male partner for Tantric ritual.

SEE ALSO *DIVYA CHAKRA, *DIVYA SHAKTI, *DIVYA SIDDHIS, *PASHU, *VIRA

DIVYA CHAKRA

A Tantric ritual, performed for and by initiates of the *divya* level only, which is described in the *Mahanirvana Tantra. No *pashu* man is allowed to participate in this ritual; neither is any woman who has sexual union with a *pashu* or with many *vira* men. If this sounds like a new and Tantric version of the *Hindu caste system, one must realize that *vira,* and especially *pashu,* are psychological types and are classifications that are not based on birth and family.

SEE ALSO *KULA PUJA

DIVYA SHAKTI

A designation for the *veshya* women participating in Tantric ritual and *maithuna. The woman is seen as representing and transmitting divine energy to her male partner.

SEE ALSO *VIRA SHAKTI

DIVYA SIDDHIS

A term to indicate the divine (*divya*) powers (*siddhis*) that can result from meditation and other yogic, Tantric techniques and exercises. Whereas in most schools of *Hinduism and *Buddhism the conscious development and use of the *siddhis* is not encouraged (they are seen as distracting side effects), several *Tantras describe them clearly and outline the paths to their achievement.

DOLMEN

Celtic name ("stone table") for a certain type of *megalithic temple or tomb in which a capstone rests on three or more vertically erected stones. Among the megaliths, the dolmen symbolizes the *yoni as the female "womb fate" and is associated with the powers of birth and *rebirth and with the "beyond." One of the most intersting dolmens is that of Crucuno in France, where the incoming sunlight, during the autumn equinox on September 21, creates a downward-pointing *triangle, a symbol of the Great Mother's yoni. In centuries past, young girls would lie naked on these so-called "hot stones" in order to find the man of their dreams. The German magazine *Esotera* reported in June 1989 that even today some French women sit on dolmens in order to enhance their fertility.

DOLMEN. *Autumn equinox at the *dolmen of Crucuno, near Carnac, France. Photograph by Andritzky.*

Dolmens can be found throughout Europe as well as in India. In literature, these too are usually referred to by their Celtic name.

SEE ALSO *CROMLECH, *MENHIR

DORJE

This is a transcription of the Tibetan name for the Sanskrit *vajra.*

DOVE

Surprising as it may be to those who know the dove mainly as a Christian symbol signifying peace, mythological research makes it quite clear that the dove is a sacred animal to such pre-Christian Syrian, Greek, and Roman goddesses as *Astarte, *Apohrodite, and Juno, all noted for their connections with sexuality and fertility.

Not only in the European/Mediterranean region but also in India the dove is known as a bird of sexual passion, and its *Sanskrit name, *paravata,* also means "lust." The Indian dove goddess is often shown in sexual union with a phallic *serpent, a symbol that signifies life. Against this background, the dove is also a symbol associated with the *yoni.

I was able to understand these attributions fully only after making love once on a beautiful spring morning. As we were quietly playing with each other after a night of orgasmic joy, a dove on the balcony began making almost exactly the sounds we had previously heard from each other: little sounds of gentle and contented pleasure and love.

On quite a different note, it has been reported that doves' *brains have been used in meals designed to have *aphrodisiac effects.

DRAGON VEINS

A concept from Chinese geomancy (divination by means of the lines of geographic features), comparable to the European ley lines but also applied to the human subtle body. In the latter case, the dragon veins are channels or arteries of subtle energy comparable to the Tantric *nadis* and the Egyptian *metu* (Rawson and Legeza, p. 99)

DRUGS AND SEXUAL INITIATION

Several deities from different cultures indicate that almost everywhere humans have often connected sexuality and the use of psychotropic drugs in their *initiation ceremonies. In China, we find the goddess Fu-pao; among the Celtic Irish,

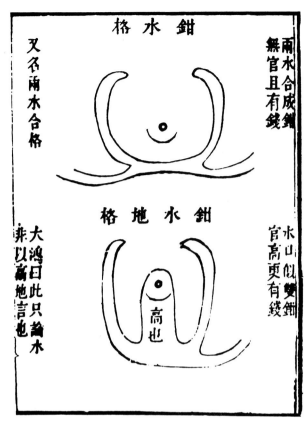

格水鉗

又名兩水合格

兩水合成鉗 無官且有錢

格 地 水 鉗

大鴻曰此只論水 并以高地言也

水山似雙鉗 官高更有錢

高也

Dragon Veins. *Illustration of *dragon veins from the 1744–45 edition of the Shui-lung Ching, a Chinese work on geomancy.*

the goddess Graine (or Grainne); and in India the example of Mahi, all deities who initiate their worshippers into their wisdom with the help of drugs and sexual celebrations. The South American Warrau tribe knows a goddess named Korobonako (or Korobona), who not only is a similar deity but is regarded as the creatrix of humans.

See also *Dionysus, *Madya, *Sexual Imprinting

DRUKPA KUNLEG
(1455–1570)

Tibetan Tantric master famous for his spiritual and sexual exploits. His name translates as "perfectly good dragon."

Naljorpa Drukpa Kunga Legpa Zangpo—his full name and title—became the cultural hero of Bhutan, where he "subdued the local demons" and taught the precepts of *Vajrayana, thus converting Bhutan to *Buddhism. The man himself stems from the lineage of the Drugpa school of

the *Kagyudpa, but he soon chose to live the life of an unorthodox wandering "holy madman," not unlike the early *Mahasiddhas. Drukpa Kunleg was regarded as the incarnation of two of these Mahasiddhas, and like them he wrote songs in the ancient style.

A number of the master's songs, episodes from his life, and tales beloved and valued by the people of Bhutan, Ladakh, Nepal, and Tibet have been collected, translated, and published by Keith Dowman as *The Divine Madman* (1983). The stories provide insights into sixteenth-century life in the Himalayas and into the (in)famous Tantric tradition that has been called *crazy wisdom.

A typical discourse of the master, this one given in the southern valleys of Bhutan, runs like this:

> *Although the clitoris is suitably triangular,*
> *It is ineligible as devil-food for the local god's worship.*
> *Although love-juice can never dry up in the sun,*
> *It is unsuited for tea to quench thirst.*
> *Although a scrotum can hang very low,*
> *It is an unsuitable bag for the hermitage's victuals.*
> *Although a penis has a sound shaft and a large head,*
> *It is not a hammer to strike a nail.*
> *Although your mind may be virtuous and pure,*
> *The Buddha's teaching is not accomplished by staying home.*
> *The teaching of the Tantric Mysteries is most profound,*
> *But liberation cannot be gained without profound experience.*
> *Drukpa Kunleg may show you the way,*
> *But you must traverse the path by yourself.*
>
> Dowman, p. 140

DUAL CULTIVATION

Taoist set of techniques of "sexual yoga" that calls for "absence of lust and strict seminal continence." The goal of dual cultivation is the internal manufacture of a liquid called *golden elixir, which is thought to help achieve longevity and a "mystical union with the Tao." The famous Taoist master Yü Yen comments on the practice as follows: "At each copulation of heaven and earth draw to yourself the secret sources of yin and yang"—a sentence that John Blofeld interprets for us as

"When you and your partner came together, combine the two vital fluids and draw them into your body."

The teachings of dual cultivation and similar secrets of Taoist *alchemy and *sexual magick are thought to originate with the legendary *Yellow Emperor. He, in turn, had received his instructions from the *Three Lady Immortals, "fragments of whose treatises still survive" (all quotes from Blofeld, pp. 132–33).

DUALISM AND THE PROMISE OF UNION

Both man and woman are considered the living, in-the-flesh and on-the-spot manifestations and representatives of the omnipresent dualism that permeates all and everything—above and below—from galactic clusters to quantum-probability states. It is this inherent dualism that forms the basis of the Chinese *yin and *yang, the Tibetan *yab-yum, and what Occidental science prefers to call positive and negative charges or active and passive principles.

In order to provide the reader with food for thought and contemplation, we will list here a limited number of such dual forces and the states in which they manifest: dual forces that simply cannot exist—as we need to remind ourselves again and again—without their opposite, forces that ultimately want and need to be unified. The secret of all dualisms, even that of good and bad, lies in the fact that they exist beyond and in spite of the all-too-human preference for simple "either/or" solutions, and that both universe and life show an inherent tendency for complex and synergetic patterns of "and . . . and . . . and."

FEMALE	MALE
*yin	*yang
earth	air
water	fire
*Shakti	*Shiva
*yoni	*lingam
Earth	Heaven
*ghanta	*vajra
wave	particle
cave	mountain
energy	matter
crucible	forge
alkali	acid
negative	positive
enfolded	unfolded
*estrogen	*testosterone

FEMALE	MALE
profound cognition	skillful means
right *brain	left brain
introvert	extrovert
centrifugal	centripetal
passive	active
inside	outside
white tiger	green dragon
white eagle	red lion
dark	light
ovum	sperm
life	death
space	time
black	*red
cold	hot
wet	dry
*xx	*xy
0	1

DURGA

One of the major goddesses of *Hinduism and *Tantra, much venerated especially in *Bengal. Her worship was and is so widespread and manifold that she is sometimes seen as an individual goddess and at other times as "merely" a name for, or an aspect of, *Shakti and/or *Kali.

Durga is a very complex goddess and is venerated in many sects and schools. The earliest mention of this deity can be found in the Mahabharata, where she is a *virgin delighting in *wine, flesh, and animal *sacrifice; she is the fierce goddess who slew the terrible demon Mahisha. In another passage she is regarded as "the wife of *Shiva" and as such is addressed as Uma. Durga worship became more widespread between the fourth and seventh centuries, when many more texts began to mention her. This development mirrors the resurgence of Goddess worship in general and the early beginnings of what is now called *Shakta.

SEE ALSO *CHINNAMASTA

DUTI

1. A female intermediary, a woman who acts as a go-between for two (secret) lovers. Such a service was often instrumental in Indian love affairs; the *Kama Sutra, for example, mentions such women very often. 2. Often the term is used as a synonym for a *dakini or *yogini—that is, a woman who has been empowered to act as a sexual initiatrix.

Dᴜʀɢᴀ. *A Nepalese statue showing the goddess *Durga*
as a many-armed, multifaceted deity. Each of the attributes held by
her many hands signifies one of her powers and responsibilities.
Photograph by Kevin Bubriski.

DUTIYAGA

Other than in most of the known Tantric rituals, where worship is a group activity, *dutiyaga* designates the union of only two Tantric devotees, a woman and a man. During *maithuna* the woman's *yoni represents, and is visualized as, a "sacrificial fire into which the semen of the male partner, conceived as clarified butter, is offered" (Banerjee, p. 553).

DZOGCHEN

The term *Dzogchen* is the short form of the Tibetan *rDzogs-pa ch'en-po* (Skt., *mahasandhi*), which means "Great Perfection" or "Great Completion." Less literally taken, *Dzogchen* has been defined as "the self-perfected state of the individual" (Norbu, *Dzog Chen and Zen*, p. 31), "the state of total completeness" (Norbu, *Primordial Experience*, p. ix), or "the teaching of spontaneous self-perfection" (Norbu, *The Crystal*, p. 146).

Dzogchen is often regarded as the name of a specific school of *Vajrayana Buddhism, but it is simply the Tibetan designation for the highest stage of the *Inner Tantras and has much in common with the *mahamudra and certain *Lamdre teachings of other Tibetan schools.

Dzogchen is, or was, sometimes regarded as a heretical school, especially by the *Gelugpa, mainly because it shares certain points of view with Chinese Ch'an (Zen) Buddhism (influenced by *Taoism) and with the *Shaiva tradition of *Kashmir. Thus, the Dzogchen texts have been consciously left out of the Buddhist *Kanjur, the famous thirteenth-century collection of sacred texts by Bu-ston. However, adherents of the Gelugpa and other schools (for example, the fifth *Dalai Lama) have recognized the power of Dzogchen teachings and have often practiced them, in secret if necessary.

Dzogchen teachings have been transmitted mainly by the *Nyingmapa, the first and oldest of all Tibetan schools. The tradition is still very much alive and is represented in the West, especially by the incarnated Tibetan lama Namkhai Norbu. Because of his unique training and background; his knowlege of Tibetan, Chinese, Mongolian, and modern Western languages; and his diligent research into the earliest beginnings of the Tibetan culture (see *Zhang Zhung), it has become known that Dzogchen has roots independent from Buddhism (see *Bön) and that important aspects of it predate the Buddhist teachings that came to Tibet from India.

One of the interesting and rather unique features of the Dzogchen teachings is the nonhierarchic method that is used—a method that leaves the student/practitioner much room for her or his individuality and for the social role he or she happens to play in life. A Dzogchen teacher will not, as is the case with many other masters or gurus, demand blind obedience in the sense of "Follow my rules unquestioningly and obey all my precepts!" Instead, he or she simply tries to transmit a particular knowledge, to awaken the student's mind, and to make the individual aware of the primordial, inborn nature of consciousness. Such a Dzogchen master will say, "Open your inner eye and observe yourself. Stop seeking an external lamp to enlighten you from outside, but light your own inner lamp. Thus the teachings will come to live in you, and you in the teachings. The teaching must become a living knowledge in all one's daily activities. This is the essence of the practice, and besides that there is nothing in particular to be done" (both quotes from Norbu, *Dzog Chen and Zen*, p. 7).

In the history of this ancient tradition, the almost forgotten kingdoms of Zhang Zhung and *Uddiyana play a major role. Both regions have often been regarded as purely legendary, but they are now recognized as kingdoms with distinct traditions that have strongly influenced the cultural development of Tibet and some of its neighbors. Dzogchen is often compared to Chinese Ch'an Buddhism and has even been called Tibetan Zen. To a degree the comparison certainly holds, and is an observant one. A typical Dzogchen

anecdote that sounds uncannily similar to many famous teaching stories known from Ch'an/Zen will illustrate the point. A visitor came to see the well-known Dzogchen master Yundon Dorje Bal (1284–1365). The visitor asked, "You Dzogchen practitioners, you are always doing meditation, right?" Yundon Dorje Bal answered, "What am I supposed to be meditating upon?" "Ah," the visitor then said, "then you practitioners of Dzogchen do not meditate?" This time the master's reply was "When am I ever distracted?"

Also in regard to the important question of mindfulness—important at least for Buddhist practitioners—Zen and Dzogchen both show a similarly deep appreciation for a particular advice of Siddhartha Guatama Shakyamuni Buddha (563–483 B.C.E.) on these matters. The Buddha said, as is recorded in the Prajnaparamita Sutra, that when standing, one is to be mindful of standing; when sleeping, to be mindful of sleeping; when being well or ill, to be fully mindful of either condition. Another way in which masters of Dzogchen and Zen sound very much alike is that both do not cease to declare that they are not "religious" but simply a way of knowledge. Both define themselves as philosophical and/or psychological systems transcending any religious and cultural limit. Such striking similarities between the two systems, however, can easily lead us to overlook the major difference, which is the difference between the sutric *Mahayana Buddhism of the Zen monk and the *Bön/*Tantra–inspired nongradual path of the independent Dzogchen practitioner. Dzogchen also knows and teaches a principle of nonaction (Tib., *bya-bral*, "pure potential") similar to the *wu-wei* (Chin., "action within nonaction") of Taoism and Ch'an Buddhism.

A detailed and sensitive discussion of Dzogchen's philosophical and psychological precepts and techniques can be found in *Sky Dancer* by Keith Dowman (pp. 217–52). Sometimes these teachings are referred to as "Sacred Great Perfection." However, even if the term *Dzogchen* does not appear in a given text at all—as in the tradition's most early texts—the teachings can be recognized by terms and expressions that are virtual synonyms: "spontaneously perfect" (Tib., *lhun-grub*), "the state of pure and total presence" (Tib., *byang-chub kyi-sems;* Skt., *bodhichitta*), "the very core of the state of pure and total presence" (Tib., *snying-po byang-chub kyi-sems*), "the primordial ground of the very core of the state of pure and total presence" (Tib., *ye-gzhi snying-po byang-chub kyi-sems*), and "the all-inclusive state of the individual" (Tib., *bdag-nyid chen-po*).

C

ECSTASY (DRUG)

Code for an amphetamine drug (*MDMA) that is also known by its street names XTC or Adam. The abbreviation XTC, and the erotic experiences sometimes associated with the drug, have led to the nickname and pronunciation "ecstasy."

ECSTASY (PSYCHOSOMATIC)

Speaking of possible biochemical events that accompany the ecstatic state of mind, the biologist John N. Bleibtreu stated in 1968 that it becomes increasingly difficult to avoid the conclusion that "the substances controlling both its [ecstasy's] sexual and transcendental manifestations are probably manufactured in the *pineal gland" (Bleibtreu, p. 78).

A statement like this elicits one's recollection of the *soma, or "nectar of ecstasy," known to Indian adepts; of the *ros, or "fiery dew," of certain Rosicrucian societies; and of the Taoist *kan-lu, or "golden nectar." All these are names and images for a certain fluid/energy that is thought to fill some secret cavern in the *brain, whence it drips down into the body and aids in mystical illumination and the achievement of longevity—this often in connection with sexual exercises and erotic ecstasy.

SEE ALSO *NI-WAN, *SAHASRAHA CHAKRA

As is so often the case, we can find a quote in the Bible to shed some symbolic light on our quest for knowledge, and we find it, of course, in King *Solomon's grand poem of love where it says, "Open to me, my sister, my love, . . . for my head is filled with dew" (Song of Songs 5:2). Solomon, as one of the early cabalists, knew of course about the pineal and its secretions. Cabalistic initiates speak of a crystalline dew and teach secret ways to draw this "celestial" fluid down into the body, where it will then benefit the man or woman who accomplishes this. Such teachings are—though shrouded in somewhat mysterious language—given in the Book of Concealment that forms part of the *Zohar.

Only a little later in time (c. 800 B.C.E.) we find that Homer refers to an "immortal fluid" that drips down from the back of the head and helps to attain longevity—a claim that has also been made by Taoist masters about the "golden nectar," or *kan-lu, that they synthesize internally from the *yin and *yang essences and energies.

Modern science at last seems to be slowly approaching an understanding of the pineal gland that will ultimately back up some of these esoteric claims. The gland, as is discussed under *Pineal Gland, not only has a connection with the onset of puberty but is apparently different in the two sexes—at least, it is larger in women. This, to me, seems to correspond to a concept known to Taoist and Tantric initiates: that a woman's yin essence, aroused in erotic play, is much more abundant than a man's yang energies and in fact is regarded as inexhaustible. This Taoist concept of yin essence is expressed in Tantric terms in the idea of *Shakti and can best be described in modern Western languages with the word *gynergy.

The Taoist idea that erotic activity without male emission will lead to general well-being and to longevity may now also be approached from a biological point of view. Research has shown that the pineal gland gradually becomes less active as aging progresses. In about 70 percent of human beings, the gland calcifies by the age of 60. Could it be, we must now ask ourselves collectively, that the exercises and visualizations, the physical and mental processes, that are activated in Taoist *dual cultivation and in the Tantric *maithuna can help to keep the pineal gland active and young, to keep the "third eye" open, and to keep hormones, fluids, and energy flowing and "dripping" into our bodies and souls?

ECTOHORMONES   SEE *PHEROMONES

EGGS

The commonly known association of eggs with male sexual performance stems mainly from Arab sources, though it has become folk wisdom almost everywhere. Advice ranges from eating three egg yolks every day to following a French recipe that calls for drinking egg yolk in a glass of cognac. Arab recipes also speak of a dish prepared from fried eggs, which are then soaked in *honey, or of eggs boiled with pepper, *cinnamon, and *myrrh. The eating or drinking of eggs, combined with thoughts concerning their *aphrodisiac properties, will, besides their normal nutritional effects, probably help some men assert their ego and boost morale in general.

EIGHT VALLEYS

Sexuality and erotic play obviously has been studied in Eastern cultures as both an art and a science. The "eight valleys" are a prime example of Chinese inquisitiveness and pedantry in these matters. Here the *yoni is subdivided into eight categories, each indicating a certain depth of the vaginal tunnel:

Lute String	2 cm
Water-Chestnut Teeth	5 cm
Little Stream	8 cm (perhaps the *G-spot?)
Black Pearl	10 cm
Valley Proper	12 cm
Deep Chamber	15 cm
Inner Door	18 cm
North Pole	20 cm

EJACULATION (FEMALE)

Many, though not all, women can or do have an ejaculation, especially when the *G-spot of the *urethral sponge and/or the female *prostatic gland is stimulated manually. The *female love juices that then exit via the urethra have been tested, and it has been established that they contain only a minimal amount of urine and consist mostly of a liquid very much like the male prostatic fluid. Such ejaculation may well occur during intercourse with penetration, but Josephine *Lowndes-Sevely explains very convincingly that it can hardly be detected—visually or tactilely—in that situation. Other types of stimulation can often lead to small, but clearly visible and tangible, showers of droplets.

The fact that female ejaculation seems less powerful than that of the male can be explained by the differing number of ducts leading to the urethra. Whereas the male fluid emerges via only two such channels, the ducts of the female system number 31, making the pressure much more diffused.

Even though patriarchal "scientific consensus" had not as of 1998 accepted the female potential for ejaculation, the Vatican has done so since ages past, as can be concluded from the official papal condemnation of *amplexus reservatus.

In recent publications concerning the so-called G-spot, many authors have pointed out that women who experience ejaculation often fear that they are urinating rather than simply "coming." Similar references have been made by anthropologists of the nineteenth and twentieth centuries in studying the sexual behavior of peoples in the South Pacific. This faulty concept can be understood when we remind ourselves that the ejaculate is actually expelled by the urethra, not the vagina, and that its amount can be quite large. Lowndes-Sevely reports that the fluid from the prostatic glands can amount to 126 milliliters: a quarter of a cup (p. 92).

That female ejaculate is often thought to be urine, rather than being recognized for what it truly is, is merely a question of general consensus. The famous researchers of human sexuality, William Masters, Virginia Johnson, and Alfred Kinsey, have contributed to the urine myth, and earlier researchers such as Regnier de Graff, Ernest *Grafenberg, Theodoor van der Velde, and others have been falsely discredited by them. A new paradigm, which takes into account the ejaculatory potential of the urethral sponge and/or the female prostatic glands, is now arising and will help many women—and men—to experience this variety of sexual response consciously and clearly.

SEE ALSO *MASS OF THE HOLY GHOST, *NURE, *NYMPHAE, *ORGASM, *YONITATTVA, *YONI TOPOGRAPHY/ 13, 14, 15

EJACULATION (MALE)

At ejaculation, 200 million to 500 million sperm cells from the epididymis move through the spermatic ducts, where fluid secretions from the seminal vesicles and the *prostatic glands are added, altogether making up about 3 to 5 milliliters of *semen that is expelled with great force by the action of muscles in the urethral walls. (For explanations of medical terms and further information on the constituents of semen, see *Lingam Topography/13, 15, 19, 21, 22.)

Whereas suppression of female ejaculation is relatively seldom if at all recognized (see *Karezza and *Coitus Sublimatus), male *retention of semen is much more often called for, for example, in certain schools of *Taoism and *Tantra. Other schools or sects, however, value both male and female ejaculates and secretions, which are seen as sacred and powerful substances, the mingling of which connects and balances the male and female energies on both a subtle and a physical level. Sometimes such a mixture is then redistributed among—and drunk by—the partners/participants. The *Niruttara Tantra even states that the emission of seminal fluid is the highest goal of *sadhana and is to be compared to Nirvana, the state of total liberation.

SEE ALSO *DUTIYAGA, *GUPTASADHANA TANTRA, *MASS OF THE HOLY GHOST, *ORGASM, *YONI TANTRA, *YONITATTVA

EKALINGA

A specialized term indicating a *shivalinga, a sacred *lingam of the god Shiva, that is the only and exclusive one in a vicinity of several kilometers. The *Kaulavali Tantra describes such places in detail and mentions, among others, the top of a mountain, a cemetery, an empty house, and the crossing point of four roads.

ELEPHANT

In India and China as well as in Jewish lands, this animal was considered a symbol of a powerful sexual drive. Not only does India know and worship elephant deities such as *Ganesh and *Matangi, but this animal is so sacred that mythology ascribes the birth of the historical Buddha, the founder and main teacher of *Buddhism, to a miraculous "impregnation" of his mother by a white elephant—comparable to the Christian myth of Mary's conception of Jesus with the help of an angel. The well-known Behemoth of Hebrew legend, who was once worshipped in the city of Elephantine at the shores of the Nile, was an elephant whose "strength is in his loins, and his force is in the navel of his belly" (Job 40:16). Also *Radha, the main character of the *gopis, is associated with this animal: her name translates as "she-elephant."

SEE ALSO *HASTINI, *MUSK

ELEUTHERIANS

General term for various medieval, Christian heretic sects; for example, the *Free Spirit Movement.

ELIXIR

An alchemical term similar to the Sanskrit *amrita and referring to a transmuted "first matter," or *prima materia.

ELIXIR RUBEUS
(LATIN, "RED ELIXIR")

According to alchemists and sex magicians, this is a potent ingredient in *menstrual fluid, the power of which is especially strong during the full moon.

SEE ALSO *MOON MAGIC

ELLAMMA   SEE *YELLAMMA

EMA

Used by Japanese *Shinto worshippers, these are wooden prayer tablets that are posted at shrines to ensure the attention and cooperation of *kami*, the Shinto term approximating our concepts of deity or spirit. Unthinkable in most of our present major religions, such *ema* sometimes feature male or female genitals, making them an expression of *phallic or *yoni worship.

E MA. *Typical examples of Japanese *ema*
offered at *Shinto sanctuaries.*

EMERALD PILLOW

Chinese technical term for the cranial pump in the human *brain, which is regarded as a "storage place" for the sexual energies know as *ching-ch'i.

EMPUSAE

The "forcers-in," a group of *female sexual demons and/or "vampires" known in Greece and the Middle East. They are similar to the offspring of *Lilith and are thought to seduce men and to suck out their *blood. The concept probably stems from a general male fear of the sexually independent woman who is able to drain his vital strength, a fear that probably constitutes the psychological basis for Eastern and Western techniques for the *retention of semen.

SEE ALSO *SUCCUBUS

ENCRATISM

A method of abstinence from all sexual activity, or at least from any sexual emission, for a certain period of time. This is said to result in a vacuumlike field of energies that, once strong enough, will attract the sexual attention of members of the opposite sex.

SEE ALSO *CHASTITY

ENDOCRINE SYSTEM

A term used to indicate a variety of ductless glands and their chemical (inter)actions. The common denominator of these seven glands is that they secrete their respective chemical messengers, the hormones, directly into the bloodstream, as opposed to a distribution by way of ducts. By way of these hormones, the system regulates and coordinates a large variety of chemical processes in the tissues and organs of the body, resulting in specific psychosomatic (re)actions and, ultimately, certain emotions and behavior.

In the classical concept of the endocrine system, its overall activities were believed to be governed or regulated by the *pituitary as a master gland. However, as had been speculated for many years, it has become clear that the pituitary is not the master but rather a high-level executive in the service of the hypothalamus (see *Brain).

A closer look at the seven endocrine glands reveals that some of them are, in fact, only glandlike secretory bodies, whereas others are collections of several associated glands acting in concert. It is therefore preferable not to speak always of glands, but rather of centers of endocrine activity.

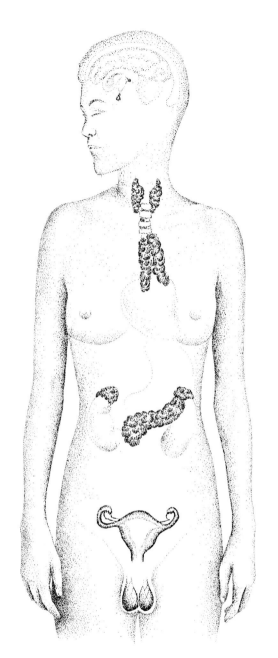

ENDOCRINE SYSTEM. *The seven glandular centers of the human *endocrine system. Illustration by Christina Camphausen.*

In the new and revised concept, the brain's hypothalamus stimulates the pituitary by way of certain hypothalamic hormones or releasing factors. This triggers the manufacture and/or release of other hormones from the pituitary, which in turn triggers subsequent action in other centers of endocrine activity.

These centers seem to be the physical/medical equivalents of the subtle centers of energy known as *chakras:

* pineal	7	*sahasrara chakra
* pituitary	6	*ajna chakra
thyroid/parathyroid	5	*vishuddha chakra
thymus	4	*anahata chakra
* adrenals	3	*manipura chakra
pancreas	2	*svadhishtana chakra
* ovaries/testes	1	*muladhara chakra

EOS

Usually known as the Greek goddess of dawn, Eos is one of the few female deities who sometimes "forced" their attentions on beautiful young men.

SEE ALSO *USHAS, *ZEUS

EPHESIAN ARTEMIS

An ancient Near Eastern and Greek goddess of fertility and sexuality who was worshipped especially in Anatolia. She is quite different from the later Roman version of the *virgin huntress Diana, who was styled after the Artemis remodeled by the Greeks. One of the earliest figures of this goddess was cut from a black meteorite—a sacred stone similar to that of the *Ka'bah—and shows her as a beautiful, many-breasted goddess. In the New Testament (Acts 19:24–37) we can read of St. Paul's lonely crusade against the worship of Artemis/Diana and also that her image "fell down from Jupiter" (Acts 19:35).

SEE ALSO *BREASTS, *CORDAX

EPIDIDYMIS   SEE *LINGAM TOPOGRAPHY/22

EROGENOUS ZONES   SEE *MARMAS

EROS

Everyone is acquainted with the cute, naked, and babylike image of this mischievous boy-child who aims his arrows at two people's hearts and thus ignites love between the couple. This image has overtones of love being fated and represents quite playfully the common wisdom that people—when it comes to love, courtship, and choice of partner—are not in complete control of themselves. However, such a "god of love" can hardly serve to symbolize the actual powerful elemental and psychic forces that are active in a loving and carnal union, and we thus feel the need for an image like

*Aphrodite or *Pan in order to gain access to these forces. But there is another and much more elemental Eros, too. To discover him or her (this true Eros is not limited to being either male or female) we must look at the Greco-Egyptian *Orphic mysteries, in which we meet no child but a powerful deity who is both goddess and god, man and woman.

EROTIC SYMBOLISM

Throughout this encyclopedia there are references and entries concerned with symbology and symbolical language. Plants, fruits, and natural features such as caves and mountains were seen as being associated with one or other male or female deity—often determined by their shape—and have thus been declared sacred by our ancestors. In the case of animals, it was their observed extraordinary fertility and sexual activity that usually led to such status. Some such cases are also discussed in this book. In order to provide access to this information, index 8 (p. 276) lists all entries concerned with erotic symbols in nature, art, and language.

Besides such natural symbols, most cultures have developed a sacred art and architecture using appropriate symbology to express one or more of their beliefs and to symbolize, in a more or less abstracted form, the male and female energies, powers, and physical attributes. These works do not always have to be such artful and sophisticated sculptures as the temples of *Khajuraho; artists have expressed the union of male and female powers in much more simple forms as well—for example, as a *yonilinga mudra or *yoniyugma, or as *megaliths.

Another aspect of symbolism can be found in language, where expressions and code words are often in "double-talk," concealing an erotic, sexual meaning below the surface of the apparently obvious. This topic can best be approached through the entries on *secret language, *lingam terminology, *om mani padme hum, and *yoni terminology.

SEE ALSO *MAYPOLE DANCES, *YONILINGA

EROTOCOMATOSE LUCIDITY

A state of consciousness achieved through complete physical and emotional exhaustion, brought about by inducing successive orgasms "by every known means" alternating with short periods of exhausted sleep.

A technique of ritual sexuality publicized by Aleister *Crowley, although the term itself was coined by Mrs. Ida

EPHESIAN ARTEMIS. *The many-breasted *Ephesian Artemis. Eighteenth-century engraving (frontispiece of the Actorum chymicorum holmiensium, Stockholm, 1712).*

Nelidoff, an initiate (ninth degree) of the *Ordo Templi Orientis's "Sovereign Sanctuary." Crowley used her formula, akin to what Austin Osman Spare called the death posture, in his secret enchiridion of the *O.T.O. Erotocomatose lucidity, likely adapted from Indian *Tantra and/or Chinese *Taoism, seems to have been practiced in the circles of the *O.T.O. and affiliated secret societies (such as the Argentum Astrum) as one of the techniques of what is often called *sexual magick.

The person about to be led into trance is brought to complete sexual exhaustion by the attentions and ministrations of "one or more chosen and experienced attendants." The alternation of this state with brief periods of sleep is continued "until the candidate is in a state which is neither sleep nor waking" and in which her or his spirit is "set free" (all quotes from Crowley's *De Arte Magica,* An. 10).

The lucidity (or transcendent awareness) reached this way is a state in which the person is then able to experience separate realities. Perhaps this state of mind, independent from the techniques used to achieve it, can be compared to the highest form of concentrated passionate energy known in *Sanskrit as *maharaga.* It is very likely that Tantric rituals such as the *pancha chakra* (five women and one man) and the *yogini chakra* (two women and one man) were designed for achieving this very type of lucidity.

EROTOMANIA

A general term indicating a sexual desire so strong that it manifests itself as a constant urge for recurrent gential satisfaction. The gender-specific expressions of this condition are known as *satyriasis (male) and *nymphomania (female).

ERZULI

A *Voodoo goddess connected with love, sexuality, wet dreams, and jealousy. Erzuli, my personal choice among her many names, is also known as Ezili and Madame Saint Urzuli. Coming to her worshippers mainly in dreams, she plays the part of *incubus/*succubus, of astral lover and seducer. However, her "ministrations" are seen here as beneficial, and she is said to heal by inducing erotic dreams and nocturnal, "unconscious" *ejaculation. As with other Voodoo loa (deities/spirits), the contemporary worship of Erzuli is sometimes accompanied by offerings consisting of such modern consumer goods as champagne and expensive perfumes: a sign that the tradition really is alive and still changing with the times.

ESCARGOTS

In France these snails are considered an excellent *aphrodisiac food, a property that had already been known to the ancient Greeks.

ESOTERIC
("INNER, SECRET")

In opposition to exoteric ("outer"), the term esoteric is often used to suggest the *occult. The word has given rise to terms and concepts such as esotericism, esoteric teachings, esoteric schools, and others.

ESP (EXTRASENSORY PERCEPTION)   SEE
*DIVYA SIDDHIS, *SIDDHIS

ESTRADIOL

Female sexual hormone. As the major *estrogen produced in an embryo's *gonads, estradiol is instrumental in the formation of the female genitals. In later life, it will be involved in the menstrual cycle and in eventual pregnancies. Estradiol levels are about 100 times higher than normal at the time of delivery but return to normal within seven days

afterward. It has also been shown that intercourse and orgasm are more likely to occur when estradiol levels are high (Udry and Morris, p. 593).

ESTRIOL

A female hormone, mainly instrumental in pregnancy. At the time of delivery, estriol levels are about one thousand times higher than normal; they return to normal two to three weeks afterward.

ESTROGEN
(FROM LATIN *ESTRUS)

One of the *estrogens and involved in the human *menstrual/ovarian cycle. Estrogen has also been found in the roots of *licorice.

ESTROGENS

General term for a group of female steroid sex hormones such as *estrogen and *estrone. Most estrogens are involved in women's *menstrual/ovarian cycle, but some—responsible for the healthy growth and functioning of skin and mucous membranes—are present and active in men, too. Estrogens are manufactured in several *endocrine glands, including the *adrenals and the ovaries and/or testes.

SEE ALSO *ANDROGENS

ESTRONE

One of the *estrogens and the first *sex hormone to be discovered (1927) and isolated (1929).

ESTRUS

Term used to indicate sexual "heat" in nonhuman females. In 1927, German researchers found that the urine of pregnant women induced estrus in mice and rats, and this observation led to the first discovery of one of the *estrogens, or female sex hormones, called *estrone. The term estrus itself is derived from the goddess of fertility, Oestre. It is also this deity who lent her name to the spring festival of Easter, the German Ostern.

EVOCATION

A ritual for summoning a spirit—or other entity/being from beyond the world of the human senses—in order to establish communication.

EXERCISES AND TECHNIQUES

Along with information about literature, rituals, festivals, and general customs concerning eros and sexuality, there are, throughout this encyclopedia, many entries that constitute actual and more or less practical exercises and techniques for individuals and/or heterosexual couples. Such entries are listed, for your convenience, in index 9, on page 277. For more detailed and practical information, however, it is necessary to turn to some of the works listed in the bibliography beginning on page 294.

*As one falls to the ground,
one must lift oneself by aid of the ground.*

*KULARNAVA TANTRA

FACULTY X   SEE *SIDDHIS

FALLOPIAN TUBES   SEE *YONI TOPOGRAPHY/19

FALLOW FIELDS   SEE *TAN-T'IEN

FANG-CHUNG SHU
(CHIN., "ARTS OF THE INNER CHAMBER")

In *Taoism this is a general term indicating all sexual exercises and techniques that lead to mystical union with the *Tao and/or to the achievement of immortality. Among them are the rituals of *ho-ch'i, the teachings of the *Three Lady Immortals, and all the sexual exercises of *inner alchemy that aim at developing the inner elixir, or *nei-tan. The philosophy behind Taoist sexual exercises is based on the concept that the union of Heaven (male) and Earth (female) gave rise to all things and all beings. The Taoist adepts, both female and male, partake of that primordial creative process by once more, on a human scale, repeating and reenacting this union, thereby experiencing the Tao and uniting with its flow of energy. Outside China, such concepts have led to the practice of the *hieros gamos.

The various techniques and rituals of *fang-chung shu* were practiced both privately and publicly until about the seventh century, when a dominating Confucian morality outlawed such practices.

The ideal *fang-chung shu* exercises should be aimed at a free, knowing, and consenting exchange of energies and liquids between the two partners. However, certain adepts, especially men, have used (and still use) their training and knowledge to merely extract women's energies—especially those of *virgins—in order to accumulate them for their own benefit only: a practice that could be called sexual vampirism. A novel by Colin Wilson, *Lifeforce,* provides interesting reading on this subject. Although the plot may be somewhat lacking, Wilson's novel incorporates much occult, erotic knowledge that is not found elsewhere in so concentrated a manner.

SEE ALSO *DUAL CULTIVATION, *HO-CH'I, *HUAN-CH'ING PU-NAO, *WEB OF HEAVEN AND EARTH

FANG-SHIH
(CHIN., "MASTERS OF PRESCRIPTION")

Collective term for the pre-Taoist shamanic "magicians" who have much in common with the Indian/Tantric *Mahasiddhas. They were adepts at techniques such as divination, esoteric sexual practices, breathing exercises, and the making of talismans. They also used and prescribed psychoactive drugs. The *fang-shih* played an important role in the establishment of religious *Taoism and are known to have used the *I Ching. One of their most influential representatives was the adept *Li Shao-chün.

FELLATIO

Technical term for the practice of kissing, licking, or sucking the *lingam, a practice known in China as "playing the flute." The erotic sculptures of the temples at *Khajuraho and

*Konarak include several images involving fellatio. There are places in the world today—for example, in many states of the United States—where this not only is regarded as a *perversion but actually is illegal and liable to punishment.

Other cultures have been more open-minded, realistic, and honest, and a person's sexual preferences were often common knowledge. It is said of the Egyptian queen Cleopatra that she engaged in fellatio with thousands of men, once even with 100 men at a single dinner party. Some of her nicknames were "she of the wide mouth" or—among the Greeks—"the great swallower." Fellatio was also used, according to Epiphanus (see *Gnosticism), as a ritual technique among some Gnostic sects.

An alternative, older term for fellatio is *penilinctus,* reminding us of the opposite and complementary practice, *cunnilingus.

FEMALE ARCHETYPES

Indian texts on love and sexuality such as the *Kama Sutra, the *Ananga Ranga, and the *Koka Shastra speak of four basic and quite different (arche)types of woman. Although the descriptions of these female models abound with superficial information as to type of voice, and size and form of *lips and *breasts (not included in this encyclopedia), they do contain some psychological and sexological insights that are of interest. These are no more doubtful and debatable than any other attempts at classifying human beings, their behavior, and their psychological "makeup."

The descriptions of such "types" given in this encyclopedia are intended not as truly serious material for study (although it serves partners well to talk about and play with these images) but rather to show that Indian erotology has given extensive thought to the variety of desires and preferences in women, which is more than can be said about most contemporary masculine approaches. The respectful and sensitive lover or husband will do well to explore such advice and to adjust his erotic practices to suit that of the woman or women involved.

For detailed information see the entries *Chitrini ("fancy woman"), *Hastini ("elephant woman"), *Padmini ("lotus woman"), and *Shankhini ("conch woman").

According to a Western version of such classification, that of Jungian psychology as introduced by Toni Wolff in 1934, the four female archetypes are as follows: mother, amazon, *hetaera, and medium (or better, the medial feminine).

SEE ALSO *MALE ARCHETYPES, *VESHYA

FEMALE LOVE JUICES

With the information we have today concerning the female *prostatic glands and female *ejaculation it becomes possible to take a close look at the biochemical makeup of women's "sexual secretions," or, as we prefer to call them, the juices of love. On the basis of information provided by Josephine *Lowndes-Sevely we can make the following list of the various liquids from which the female ejaculate is made up:

• fluids from the prostatic (paraurethral) glands
• fluids from the vulvovaginal (Bartholin) glands
• fluids from the lining of the uterus
• fluids from the fallopian tubes
• secretions from the sweat glands of the vulva
• secretions from the sebaceous glands of the vulva
• mucus from the cervix
• cells from the lining of the upper vagina
• a minute amount of urine

Apart from these "scientific" constituents, which also determine a woman's *scent aura, Tantrics and Taoists know several different secretions from the *yoni, *lips, and *breasts, and they use terms for them such as *dew of ecstasy or *kama salila.

For a discussion of male love juices, see the entries *Lingam Topography/19–22 and *Semen. Index 11 (p. 279) lists all entries connected with female and male *sexual biochemistry.

FEMALE SEXUAL DEMONS

Throughout the world we find a particular type of female deity of whom it is said that she either seduces or sexually assaults men, and in general the male does not survive the special treatment given to him. The image recalls the behavior of certain animals—especially the black widow spider—who are known to kill the male after sexual intercourse. One obvious example of this type of seductive vampire and sexual killer—a fantasy that probably cannot be attributed solely to either the male or the female mind—can be found in the stories surrounding the southern European deity, *demon, or spirit *Basa Andere, a mythical female of Basque folklore.

SEE ALSO *KALI, *LAMIA, *LILITH, *RATI, *SUCCUBUS

FEMALE SUPERIOR POSITION

One of the "achievements" of the Western world's so-called sexual revolution of the 1960s and 1970s is the reestablishment of this ancient mode of sexual union. However, what now seems an achievement was once a more normal state of affairs among several peoples and, of course, in *Tantra and similar sexual teachings. "That Greek witches who worshipped Hecate favored the superior posture, we know from Apuleius; and it occurs in early Sumerian representations of the sexual act," state Graves and Patai (p. 60). For references in other cultures and languages *see* the Egyptian deities *Geb and *Nuit, the Sanskrit term *viparita rati, the Tibetan *yab-yum, and the Taoist *chi-chi. In his well-researched romantic novel on the Cathar "heretics" and the medieval tradition of courtly love, Robert Shea suggests that this position was known as "the secret position of love": "The sight filled her with delight. He knows the secret position of Love, she thought. He must know the entire rite. We can enter the gates of paradise tonight" (p. 193).

SEE ALSO *ASS

FENNEL

Known mainly for its strengthening effects on health in general, fennel is also reputed to be an *aphrodisiac. An Indian recipe gives directions on how to mix fennel sap and milk with *honey, *licorice, and sugar into a "sacred" drink. Mediterranean peoples also knew about fennel's properties, and prepared fennel soup in order to stimulate desire.

FERTILITY FESTIVALS AND RITES

Once a certain culture changes its basic pattern of life from nomadic hunting and gathering to the more settled way of agrarian communities and village life, there arises a stronger need to aid Mother Nature and magically influence the deities in charge of vegetation.

Such magical attempts were designed by the ancients to manipulate natural forces and/or to excite the male and female divinities to carry out their fertility-oriented sexual duties. Sometimes these took the form of lusty, public revelries as they are described under *Ritual Promiscuity, but they have also been institutionalized in more formal rituals such as the *hieros gamos ("sacred marriage"). However, quite often the lines of distinction are not clear-cut. One interesting example of such a mixture of the formal and informal can be found in the Chinese practice called the *Web of Heaven and Earth.

It is quite likely that even the very abstracted, knowledgeable, and sophisticated forms of later Tantric and Taoist worship have their roots in such fertility-oriented village activities, although the original extroverted goal has been transformed into an introverted one. Whereas once all efforts were directed outward, toward nature and its growth processes, they later became inwardly oriented, toward one's own personal becoming, enlightenment, and liberation.

SEE ALSO *CARNIVAL, *DOLMEN, *FLORALIA, *HO-CH'I, *LIBERALIA, *MENHIR, *PANCHAMAKARA, *SATURNALIA, *SIXTY-FOUR YOGINI PITHA

FESTIVALS

Index 6 (p. 275) gives access to all entries related to festivals, rituals, and customs.

FIELD(S) OF CINNABAR   SEE *TAN-T'IEN

FIERY DEW   SEE *ROS

FIVEFOLD LIGHT

The stream of luminescent energy/light originating in the crown *chakra (Skt., *sahasrara chakra) during *maithuna or other sexual exercises and reaching downward via the system of *nadis to the genitals.

SEE ALSO *BLUE-GREEN HALO, *SHAKTI ASANA

FIVE PECKS OF RICE TAOISM

One of the major schools of "religious Taoism," or *Tao-chiao, the Chinese name of which is Wu-tou-mi Tao. The school was founded during the second century by the alchemist and healer *Chang Tao-ling, who is said to have succeeded in attaining immortality, and who is venerated as a "celestial master." Among the ritual practices of Wu-tou-mi Tao we find the orgiastic *ho-ch'i.

FLORA

Roman equivalent to and development of the Greek goddess Chloris. Most often described as a beautiful goddess of *flowers, writers usually seem not to mention that her worship included an annual *orgy of *ritual promiscuity. Several sources claim that Flora was a deified prostitute.

FLORALIA

Annual *fertility festival dedicated to the goddess *Flora, during which the participants liberally enjoyed wine and sexual union.

SEE ALSO *PANCHAMAKARA, *RITUAL PROMISCUITY

FLOWERS

All three of the flowers that symbolize the Goddess, the *yoni, and the concept of femininity as such—that is, the *lily, the *lotus, and the *rose—have rather ambivalent meaning. On one hand, they can be of an earthy, passionate character (when they are *red in color) and represent desire, love, pleasure, consummation, and fertility; on the other hand, they can be used to symbolize spiritual purity, physical virginity, and sexual innocence (mostly when white, *gold, or blue). It is therefore especially important to consciously note in which color the flower is represented. Worship of the Roman *Flora, a goddess of flowers, was a very sexual affair.

SEE ALSO *YONIPUSHPA

FLY AGARIC   SEE *AMANITA MUSCARIA

FORESKIN SEE *CIRCUMCISION, *LINGAM TOPOGRAPHY/5

FORTUNA VIRILIS

Ancient Roman goddess thought to "steer" and "stir" men's lives. She was also associated with *ritual promiscuity and *phallic worship.

FO-TI-TIENG
(CHIN., "ELIXIR OF LONGEVITY")

A plant (Hydrocotyle asiatica minor) found in the marshes of tropical Asia. Although largely ignored by science in general, it has been studied independently by the French biochemist Jules Lepine and by Professor Menier. They agree that the plant contains an *alkaloid that has a rejuvenating effect on the nerves, brain cells, and *endocrine system. This seems to give credit to the claim of the Indian sage Nanddo Narian, who said, at the age of 107, that the herb can give one control over the processes of disease and decay.

Another sage, the Chinese herbalist and physician Li Chung Yun (1677–1933), advocated the daily use of the herb and seems to have followed his own advice very well. He was in fact—and this is a matter of record with the Chinese government—256 years old and had been married 24 times when he died in 1933 (reported by J. C. Cooper in Chinese Alchemy).

FRATERNAL POLYANDRY

Term for a marriage custom in which one woman marries all the brothers of a given family. As such it is the exact opposite to *sororal polygyny and is known, for example, in Tibet and Nepal.

SEE ALSO *POLYANDRY/1

FRATRES RORIS COCTIS

The "brethren of the fiery dew," a branch of seemingly Tantric Rosicrucians who experimented with the fluid/energy known as *ros.

FREE SPIRIT MOVEMENT

A rather loose association of medieval, heretical Christians that was originally known as the Sect of the New Spirit and is one of the Eleutherian sects. Part of this loose association was sects or groups whose involvement with erotic activity and so-called license meant that they were considered heretical sinners to be persecuted and condemned. Such sects—for example the Familists and Perfectionists—practiced techniques such as *acclivity and *coitus reservatus.

SEE ALSO *BENI UDHRI, *KAREZZA, *NOYES, JOHN HUMPHREY

FREY

Phallic Teutonic god, not to be confused with the goddess *Freya.

FREYA AND/OR FREA

Northern European (Teutonic/Scandinavian) goddess of love and sexuality and leading member of the Valkyries, the warriors' weavers of fate and their female, astral companions. In the myths about her, Freya is married but also totally promiscuous. She also practices *incest with her brother, and her worship included *ritual prostitution.

FRUIT DE MER

Most seafood, be it fish (especially trout and salmon), clams, prawns, *oysters, or *caviar, is reputed to have *aphrodisiac qualities and powers. Most likely this is due to the unusually high content of minerals and trace elements (for example phosphorus and *zinc) in such food. According to the Greek poet Asclepiades, it was customary to take along 24 prawns, plus 3 large and 10 small fish, when going to visit a *courtesan.

FSH

Abbreviation for the follicle-stimulating hormone, which is instrumental in the female *menstrual/ovarian cycle. It is produced in the *pituitary gland.

FUGU

Probably the most popular yet fatally risky *aphrodisiac in Japan is fugu, a dish made from an often highly poisonous fish and hot sake (rice wine). Approximately 400 to 500 people die annually from ingesting this toxin, taking the chance on either receiving a sexual high or being stricken by a deadly nerve poison, which, if the fish carries it, will immediately attack one's heart or lungs. Well-to-do lovers therefore hire a taste tester, who takes the risk in return for very substantial payment.

FUSION OF K'AN AND LI

Two of the *I Ching's hexagrams, *k'an (number 29) and *li (number 30), are of great importance in the symbology and imagery of Chinese *inner alchemy, its view of *subtle physiology, and the sexual techniques known as *fang-chung shu. The fusion of the two energies represented by k'an (female, moon, water) and li (male, sun, fire) is seen as a means to create, concentrate, or awaken the elixir of life within the bodies of the practitioners.

SEE ALSO *CHI-CHI, *LUNG-HU, *ORGASM

Do not suppress your feelings, choose whatever you will, and do whatever you desire, for in this way you please the Goddess. Perfection can be attained by satisfying all one's desires.

*GUHYASAMAJA TANTRA

GANA CHAKRA

(SKT., *GANACAKRA*; TIB., *KYI 'KHOR-LO*)

Based on gana ("gathering") and chakra ("circle"), this is a generic term for a variety of Tantric assemblies, or feasts, in which practitioners met to perform *mantra, to create and empower sacred tools and ornaments, to worship, and to practice various Tantric rituals. Sometimes, as reported by Miranda Shaw throughout her excellent book *Passionate Enlightenment*, such assemblies consisted solely or mainly of female adepts who would only occasionally allow a male Tantric to join their celebrations and thus be initiated to the teachings of these living *yoginis. Tantric literature abounds with such examples of female-to-male initiation, ranging from texts such as the *Hevajra Tantra to personal songs of yogis and reports of pilgrims until at least the twelfth century.

Often, such gatherings were held at charnel- or cremation-grounds; sometimes they occurred at or near well-known temples of the Goddess, such as *Javalamukhi or *Kamakhya Pitha.

Special forms of the gana chakra are known as *bhairavi chakra*, *chakra puja, *tattva chakra*, *yogini chakra*, and *yogini gana.

GANESH

A god of the *Hindu pantheon (the "lord of hosts") and known throughout India and Nepal, where he is usually depicted as a four-armed, *elephant-headed divine being. Although most often worshipped as a deity granting spiritual and material success, Ganesh sometimes is an *ithyphallic god. In the Negesvara temple at Kumbhakonam in India, he is depicted and worshipped in this aspect, with *lingam erect and his hand touching (*see* *Nyasa) the *yoni of his divine partner, or *Shakti. Among his major symbols are the *conch shell and the *lily.

SEE ALSO *MATANGI

GARAB DORJE

(TIB., *DGA-RAB RDO-RJE*; SKT., PRAHEVAJRA; B. 184 B.C.E.)

Born in *Uddiyana only a few generations after the historical Buddha, this early yogic and Tantric adept is generally regarded as the actual originator of *Dzogchen.

Garab Dorje is regarded as an emanation of the Buddha Vajrasattva. He is especially famous for his "three final sayings" or "three incisive precepts" (Tib., *tshig-gsum gnad-brdegs*), his last testament (Tib., *zhal 'chems*) in the form of three essential statements that sum up the teachings of Dzogchen:

1. direct introduction to one's own nature (Tib., *ngo rang thog-tu sprod-pa*),
2. direct discovery of this unique state (Tib., *thag gcig thog-tu bcad-pa*),
3. directly continuing with confidence in liberation (Tib., *gdeng grol thog-tu bca'pa*) (based on Reynolds, 1989, p. 42).

GARLIC

In both Orient and Occident, garlic is famous as a health- and strength-promoting spice/vegetable, and it is often included in erotically stimulating dishes. To the Ainu of Japan, the plant was very sacred and had a status comparable to that of the Greek ambrosia of the gods. The Ammites of China, reportedly a very lascivious people, also credit much of their lustful activities to their extensive consumption of garlic.

Scientists have recently discovered that the main chemical ingredient in garlic's strong-smelling oil is the same as one of the constituents of the *female love juices. It also contains iodine, which is necessary for the proper function of the thyroid gland of the human *endocrine system.

GATE OF JEWELS

A Japanese expression for the vagina (see *Yoni Topography/9).

GAUDA SAMPRADAYA

A sect of *Vamacara background whose members advocate the idea that all things are emanations of the Great Goddess's energy and who practice their rituals with the *panchamakara.

GAURIPATTA

The *yoni-shaped pedestal in a *yonilinga statue, upon which the lingam is placed.

GAYATRI MANTRA

The Gayatri is one of the most sacred verses from the ancient Rig *Veda and is addressed to the goddess Savitri, whose lover/partner is the god *Brahma. It is a multipurpose *mantra designed for psychic protection, the enhancement of sensuality, the focusing of healing energies, or the welfare of one's family.

The Gayatri is composed of 24 different "submantras," each dedicated to a certain deity and representing an associated energy. The daily repetition of the mantra, or any of its specific parts, is thought to bring about the desired effect. Here are a few examples pertinent to our topic: **1.** The Chandra Gayatri (part 10 of the whole) subdues depression, anxiety, pessimism, and neurosis. **2.** The Varuna Gayatri (part 12) increases love between a man and woman. **3.** The Kama Gayatri (part 22) increases sensuality, sexual satisfaction, vigor, and vitality.

GAYATRI MANTRA.

ॐ
जलविम्बाय विद्महे,
नीलपुरूषाय धीमहि।
तन्नो वरुण:प्रचोदयात्॥

Varuna Gayatri: To increase love between man and woman.

ॐ
कामदेवाय विद्महे,
पुष्पवाणाय धीमहि।
तन्नो काम: प्रचोदयात् ॥

Kama Gayatri: To increase sensuality, sexual satisfaction, sexual power, vitality, vigor, and stamina.

GEB

The early Egyptian god of Earth—one of the few male figures with this particular function—is most often shown with a large, erect *lingam that he has just withdrawn from *Nuit, the sky goddess, after their all-creating embrace. The male Geb, as Earth, is on his back, with Nuit, the Sky, arched above him.

SEE ALSO *MIN, *VIPARITA RATI

GELUGPA
(TIB., DGE-LUGS-PA; "VIRTUOUS DOCTRINE")

This school, the "Model of Virtue," is the best-known and most widespread school of *Vajrayana today. The Gelugpa, sometimes referred to as the Yellow Hat School, is rooted in the *Kadampa tradition and in that school's reformation under Tsongkapa (1357–1419), a teacher of *Sakya background who preferred a strict, monastic discipline and who found the Kadampa monks not virtuous enough, not to mention the wandering Tantrics of the time who only much later became organized as the *Nyingmapa.

Following the foundation of the first Gelugpa monastery in 1409, Ganden (Tib., *Ri-bo dGa-'ldan*), the Gelugpa strongly expanded during the fifteenth century, with the building of many strongholds between 1416 and 1447.

About 1475, a violent struggle for power broke out between the Gelugpa Kagyud and the Phagmo and the *Karma Kagyud. After the third Dalai Lama went to seek outside help from the Mongols (1560) in order to establish Gelugpa rule, the opposition began to weaken. However, the actual consolidation of Gelugpa power came only during 1642–1659, under the Great Fifth Dalai Lama. This included confiscation of non-Gelugpa monasteries and the burning of texts that originated with the *Jonangpa.

The Gelugpa emphasized the study of logic and philosophy and became the dominating force in Tibet, assuming both religious and secular leadership. The Gelugpa teachings are continued through the lineage of His Holiness the *Dalai Lama and are very much alive in Tibet, Nepal, northern India, and Western countries. In Gelugpa publications, it is often pointed out that the school also absorbed and thus represents all major teachings of the other Vajrayana branches.

GENITALS

For a description of male and female genitals, *see* *Lingam Topography and *Yoni Topography.

GENITAL TERMINOLOGY

Everywhere in the world people have invented words and phrases for their own and others' genitals. Sometimes such words were meant to remain more or less secret, inside a certain group, and constituted a kind of code. At other times, the words were those of honest, sheer delight with the organs of pleasure and can be recognized as terms of endearment as one makes them up for friends and beloved ones. However, those religions and societies—one can hardly call them "civilizations"—where sexual pleasures were inhibited, deplored, and outlawed most often develop a genital terminology that is merely vulgar and whose words are those of fear rather than awe, scatological rather than delightful.

Such repressed societies also had their "deviant" members, those who did not share the negative sentiments and knew the psychological, spiritual, and health-promoting forces of eros and sexuality. Such people, often labeled as heretics and/or hedonists, also invented their respective language for acts and parts of physical love. Especially in *Tantra, *Taosim, and *alchemy, such terms were often coined and chosen to make them unrecognizable by outsiders—a language evolving from a need for secrecy in times when sexual experimentation, sacred or profane, was not socially accepted or encouraged. Often these were everyday words that also had a simple, exoteric meaning. We find here words that are drawn from nature—the names of fruits, plants, and animals, for example—or from humanity's own inventions in the world of agricultural and industrial tools: words such as *plow, hammer,* and *anvil.*

Two interesting lists of terms and names that have been, and can be, used instead of *vagina* or *phallus, cunt* or *prick,* are supplied under the headings *Lingam Terminology and *Yoni Terminology.

GENITAL WORSHIP   SEE *PHALLIC WORSHIP, *YONI WORSHIP

GHANTA
(SKT., "BELL")

1. The bell in Tantric ritual that is symbolic of the feminine energies, contrasting with the male *vajra. Images of

GHANTA. *A Tibetan* *ghanta, *symbolizing female energy.*
Illustration by Christina Camphausen.

Buddhas and other *Vajrayana dignitaries often show them with the *ghanta* in one hand and the *vajra* in the other. **2.** A code for the *yoni. **3.** Name for one of the eight *bodhisattva *dakinis*.

GHAZYE

The Arabian clan known as the Barmaky traditionally brought forth specially revered and honored prostitutes who are known as *ghowazy* (singular: *ghazye*). When ceasing their enterprise these prostitutes were coveted wives for sheiks or other dignitaries; they were women who often had been on the holy pilgrimage to the *Ka'bah at Mecca and had thus become *hajji*. Such women belong to neither of the categories of *sacred or *secular prostitution; rather, they occupy a position somewhere between those two.

GIANT OF CERNE ABBAS

The Cerne Abbas Giant in Dorset, England, is a first-century B.C.E. earth sculpture representing a fertility god known as Hercules. The huge ithyphallic figure, cut into the hillside, is 60 meters tall and features a phallus about 12 meters long. Local women who desperately wanted to become pregnant were known to sleep on the phallus overnight. According to John Sharkey, local folk tradition has continued this *phallic worship into modern times: Ritual cleaning—once every seven years—of the giant is done on May Eve, and *Maypole dances and games also continue to be held on the site.

GINGER

Sweet ginger, ginger jam, ginger with *honey, or ginger with pepper—the possibilities are almost as manifold as the praise this plant has received as an *aphrodisiac among Chinese, Turkish, Indian, and Arabian physicians, lovers, and erotologists.

GINSENG

Famous both as an *aphrodisiac and as a general preventive medicine, ginseng (*Panax quinquefolium*) has been chewed daily, for about the past five thousand years, by Korean and Chinese men, who often father children while in their 60s and 70s. Ginseng was known in India, too, and is mentioned in the Atharva *Veda as bestowing the "power of a bull" on men both young and old.

Recent scientific research in the Soviet Union has shown that ginseng root contains a combination of substances (panaquilom, panaxim, schingenin) that strengthen the heart and nervous system and promote the flow of hormones. The Russian scientists have also discovered a subtle mitogenic radiation that is generated by the root. This radiation is, in terms of the electromagnetic spectrum, close to ultraviolet (*see* *Violet), and stimulates the growth of the tissues that form the *endocrine system.

Ginseng can be acquired in many qualities and accompanying price tags, from "imperial Chinese" at the top, through Korean, to Japanese ginseng at the bottom of the scale; one does well to be informed and attentive when purchasing the roots. Ginseng is equally beneficial for both men and women, and its aphrodisiac effect can often be felt after a short time of use.

GITA   SEE *BODHISATTVA DAKINIS

GLANS CLITORIDIS   SEE *YONI TOPOGRAPHY/6, 7

GLANS PENIS   SEE *LINGAM TOPOGRAPHY/6, 7

GNOSTICISM

A generic term for all Gnostic sects and schools that arose, mainly in Syria and Egypt, during the early days of Christianity. Most of the Gnostics, the believers in gnosis (higher spiritual knowledge), were seen as heretical by the Christian church fathers. Gnosticism has its spiritual, philosophical roots not only in Christianity but also in the teachings of the Persian Zoroaster/Zarathustra (c. 600 B.C.E.) and some of the religious beliefs of Greece, Egypt, and India. It was not only the Gnostics' insistence that knowledge rather than blind faith is the main spiritual goal and achievement that caused them to be declared heretic but also the "abominable" ritual practices featured by some of their sects. Although little is known about most of the sects' actual life and rituals, there is one exceptional eyewitness account by the then 20-year-old Epiphanus of Salamis (315–403 C.E.), a church father who later became famous for his relentless fight against all "heretics." This report, published in the Netherlands by the late G. Meuleman in 1991, records the shocked words of poor young Epiphanus, who took part in the Easter celebrations of a Gnostic group, apparently an *orgy of *ritual promiscuity.

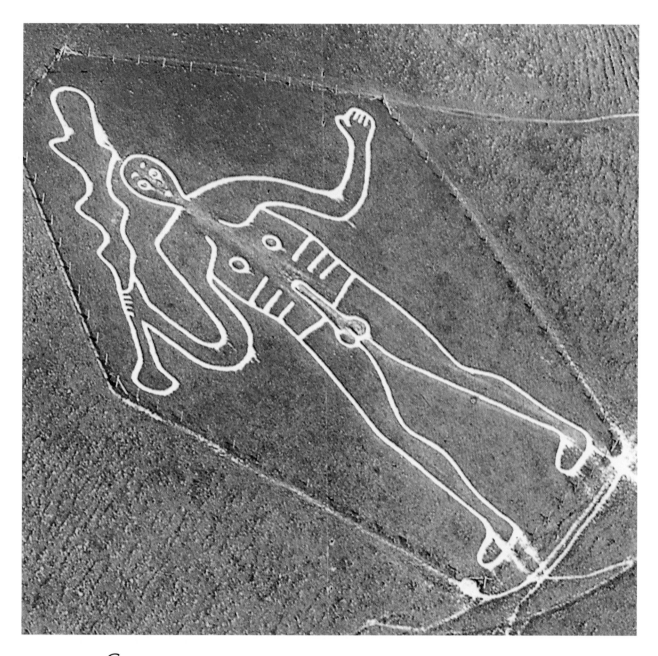

GIANT OF CERNE ABBAS. *The *Giant of Cerne Abbas (c. first century B.C.E.), Dorset, England.*
Photograph from The Tourist Guide to Dorset.

Similar to certain Tantric rituals, the celebrations began with the consumption of wine and food, after which "the unhappy ones" (Epiphanus's words) united in sexual union with their spiritual brothers and sisters. Epiphanus never clearly says that he himself did not take part but merely shows himself to be outraged, especially by what followed.

The men and women would collect in their hands the mixed love juices of their union, symbolically offer them to their deity, and then proceed to "eat it and celebrate the eucharist with their own sperm," declaring it to be "the body of Christ." Epiphanus reports that the same is done with the women's *menstrual fluid and also that the celebrants are careful to avoid conception during such ritual intercourse. In other instances this particular Gnostic sect, one of more than 60 sects active during Epiphanus's time, used the collected juices in other ways. Similar to the *sperm magic known in New Guinea, the participants would cover their naked bodies in their love secretions, a gesture intended as a means of aiding them in the desired "direct access to God."

SEE ALSO *YONI TANTRA

GOAT

An animal symbolically used to indicate the male sexual energy inherent in the processes of fertility and creation. The goat appears in myths and in images of gods such as *Pan. The goat is sacred to *Aphrodite and *Dionysus and figures exclusively in the Christian versions of the devil. William Blake wrote, "The lust of the goat is the bounty of god." In India, a prescription to attain the goat's strength and virility was to drink sweetened milk in which a goat's testicle had been boiled, and the first-century Greek physician Dioscorides prescribed young cabbage steeped in goat's milk.

The major *nymph of Basque myth (also viewed as a goddess or witch), whose name is Mari, is depicted as having a goat's foot and also demands that goats be sacrificed to her.

GODS AND GODDESSES

Several entries in this encyclopedia are concerned with male and female deitites—erotic, sexual, or fertility-related—who held more or less important places in the worship of their respective cultures. Two lists provide access to the names of all deities occurring in this book.

The first is index 3, "Woman As Goddess, Demoness, and Cultural Heroine" (p. 272). Most entries in this index are concerned with female deities, including lesser-known ones, in whose worship and ritual the erotic, sexual element or their power of fertility plays an important role. No discrimination is made between Great Goddesses, minor female deities such as *nymphs, and ancient deities made into *demons by succeeding religious and political systems. All too often, such discrimination is arbitrary and does not reflect the status of such a goddess in the originating culture. For some background information see *Female Sexual Demons and *Yoni Worship.

The second list is index 4, "Man as God, Demon, and Cultural Hero" (p. 273). As with index 3, most entries in this index are concerned with deities in whose worship and connected ritual the erotic, sexual element or their power of fertility is a paramount feature. Other deities are also listed, however, if the related information can contribute, in the context of our pursuit, to our general knowledge and understanding.

SEE ALSO *PHALLIC WORSHIP

GOLD

The gold of the Western student of *alchemy can be compared to the *cinnabar of the Chinese adept. The Taoist alchemist, however, also uses the image of gold and jade in order to indicate great worth or "preciousness," as in *golden elixir, *golden flower, and *golden tongue.

GOLDEN ELIXIR OR GOLDEN LIQUID

An elixir created during sexual union, which—according to Taoist adepts of *inner alchemy and *dual cultivation—is instrumental in achieving longevity and even immortality. This liquid and/or subtle energy is created by the mingling and drawing into the body of the sexual secretions of both male and female practitioners. This "manufacture" of the quested essence simultaneously leads to a mystical state of awareness and a merging of the individual with the Tao, the all-permeating cosmic principle.

Some Chinese texts speak of a golden pill, golden fetus, or *golden flower, but most often these terms are simply alchemical code words hinting at the same mixture of male and female secretions/energies.

SEE ALSO *CHIN-TAN, *FEMALE LOVE JUICES, *SECRET LANGUAGE, *SEMEN

GOLDEN FLOWER   SEE *TEACHINGS OF THE GOLDEN FLOWER OF THE SUPREME ONE

GOLDEN LIQUID   SEE *GOLDEN ELIXIR

GOLDEN NECTAR   SEE *KAN-LU

GOLDEN PASSAGE   SEE *BRAHMA APERTURE

GOLDEN TONGUE

A Chinese/Taoist expression for the female clitoris.

GOLODBHAVA

Special Indian term for the *menstrual fluid issued by a widow.

SEE ALSO *CHANDALI, *KUNDODBHAVA

GONADS

The indifferent gonads are the so-called sex glands of an embryo from which, approximately seven weeks after conception, the still sexually neutral or androgynous embryo develops its gender-specific genital organs, in particular the fully developed gonads: the ovaries and testes. This process is catalyzed by the female and male *sex hormones.

SEE ALSO *LINGAM TOPOGRAPHY/20, *YONI TOPOGRAPHY/20

GOPIS

(SKT., "COW-GIRLS")

Collective name for the legendary cow-herding maidens of Krishna's erotic adventures. The most famous among them—and Krishna's favorite—is known as *Radha. Most interesting is the fact that the *gopis* were mostly married women whose absence from home and their love affairs with Krishna went "unnoticed" by their husbands, indicating perhaps that such extramarital affairs were no reason for concern and unrest.

Such *parakiya* relationships, however, were actually denounced and tabooed by maintream Indian society, so much so that a special group of teachings—*Sahijiya—was developed in order to give sacred and ritual status to such "unlawful" relationships. The *fertility festival of Holi, or Holaka, is a reenactment of this mythical theme with circle dances, lovemaking, and general merriment.

Some interpreters make it sound as if the *gopis'* love for Krishna was not physical and was solely an expression of *bhakti.

SEE ALSO *FERTILITY FESTIVALS

GRACES

The Roman concept of these three deities is borrowed from the greek *Charites, emanations of the goddess *Charis. This connection also lies at the root of the Latin term *caritas* and thus of the English word *charity,* a trait typical of the Graces. The Three Graces are often seen as the "maidens" of *Aphrodite and are, in a way, extensions or manifestations of that deity. These maidens—Aglaia ("the bright one"), Euphrosyne ("the glad one"), and Thalia ("the one of

GOPIS. *A scene from the Basantpur temple in the center of Kathmandu showing six women during sexual play with one man, guiding him to unknown heights of ecstasy and unknown depths of exhaustion, an exercise inspired by the erotic adventures between the *gopis and the god Krishna. Photograph by Rufus C. Camphausen.*

abundance")—surround Aphrodite in their *dance and create an atmosphere of youthful vigor and maidenly grace, of charm and delight. Although they are generally regarded as personifications of beauty, love, and pleasure, they represent later, in medieval art, the virtues of charity, beauty, and love. Each of the Graces has a symbol identifying her; they are, respectively, the *rose, the myrtle, and the *apple.

GRAFENBERG, ERNEST
(1881–1957)

German obstetrician and gynecologist who first proposed in the 1940s the existence of an erotically sensitive area now popularly known as the *G-spot. He described it as a "zone of erogenous feeling . . . located in the anterior wall of the vagina." Grafenberg's "zone" became popularly known and discussed 40 years later, when Alice Kahn Ladas, Beverly Whipple, and John Perry published their own theory concerning his original findings. The area was called the G-spot after this early "discoverer."

GRAIL

First featured in so-called pagan religions as a symbol or container for the water, blood, and life energy of the Great Goddess, the grail later became a Christian symbol for a vessel holding the *blood of Christ, connected with the Eucharist (literally, "thanksgiving").

Lady Harris, Aleister *Crowley, and others saw or see this cup as holding rather the "wine of the sacrament," which is—as Francis King (b. 1934) points out in his Tantra for Westerners—"on the most physical level the mingled male and female secretions of the particpants in the rites of left-handed Tantra."

SEE ALSO *SCARLET WOMAN

GREAT BROTHERHOOD OF GOD

An occult group, publicized by Louis T. Culling (b. 1893), in which *sexual magick, specifically *alphaism, *dianism, and *qodosh, are practiced. Culling's GBG can be regarded as an offspring of Aleister *Crowley and his *Ordo Templi Orientis, and GBG publications are full of praise for, and of quotes from, Crowley's work. In Sex Magick, a revised edition of his earlier Manual of Sex Magick, Culling also cites *Sufism as being at the root of the order's teachings.

GROUP MARRIAGE

A custom that has been known in many cultures and tribal societies, but especially among North American Indians and Eskimos. It is, in a certain sense, a combination of *polyandry and *polygamy. With the rise of Christianity, its missionaries, and its successive political and economic world dominance, all these earlier forms of marriage became suppressed, outlawed, and then almost forgotten.

A prime example of group marriage is discussed in Robert Briffault's The Mothers, where he explains that Tibetan marriage customs are best described by this term and not, as is more commonly stated, by the terms polyandry or polygamy. By virtue of a single marriage contract, whole groups of brothers married whole groups of sisters.

Many of the communes that were formed among the youth of Europe and the United States during the 1960s and 1970s, if they included free sexual relations among their members, were in fact merely a reinvention of this ancient custom.

G-SPOT

Popular term for a particularly sensitive area in the vagina, about halfway between the pubic bone and the cervix (see illustration p. 261) at the rear of the urethra; named after Ernest *Grafenberg. When authors Alice Kahn Ladas, Beverly Whipple, and John Perry first published their book The G-Spot in 1982, their findings were not entirely convincing, and the existence of the "new" erogenous zone—especially of its alleged ability to ejaculate an orgasmic fluid—was not officially recognized by most doctors and medical scientists. Leading scientific journals still do not publish the results of any research on the G-spot, thereby declaring it "unscientific." Yet, a growing number of women, as well as men, now know of it through experience and do not need to be convinced by theory.

In reviewing the available evidence, meanwhile, the conclusion must be drawn that there is no actual G-spot in the sense in which it has been promoted, although the "discovery" certainly has led to a better understanding of what actually goes on. The G-spot is in fact merely a simple label for a rather complicated and sophisticated part of the *yoni, a part that is erotically sensitive and that is also responsible for female *ejaculation. For simplicity's sake, the label can of course be used, but without a consideration of the biological facts, it may only lead to new misconceptions. There can be no question, for example, whether or not each women "possesses" a G-spot: She does! The distinction, whether or not she feels it, depends on a wide variety of physical and psychological factors, and it is certainly conceivable that not every woman is particularly sensitive in this area, just as there are worlds of differences in the sensitivity of nipples and other erogenous zones.

The area we are concerned with is actually the urethral sponge—an area of spongy tissue (*corpus spongiosum) that also contains clusters of nerve endings, blood vessels, *paraurethral glands, and ducts—which covers the female urethra on all sides. During sexual stimulation—by finger pressure or certain positions and movements of the *lingam—the sponge can become engorged with blood, swell, and thus become distinguishable to touch. A number of reasearchers in both Israel and the United States have meanwhile established that the tissue in the G-spot area contains an enzyme that is usually found only in the male *prostatic glands. This may indicate that we are dealing here with a female version of the prostatic glands, a collection of glands that in men is also rather sensitive to touch and pressure. The existence of these hitherto unknown glands in this place may also explain the fluid secretions many women experience during or after G-spot stimulation. To those not yet practically acquainted with the G-spot, it presents an interesting paradox and invites adventurous exploration: In order to find it, one has to stimulate it—and to do just that, one has to find it!

SEE ALSO *YONI TOPOGRAPHY/13–15

GUHE

The main term used in Nepal for the vulva (*yoni), another being *jaldri*. The equivalent male term is *guhya*.

GUHESHVARI

1. The "lady of mysteries," a secret Tantric form of the Goddess as sexual initiatrix and one of the *yoginis. Sometimes the term is also used to indicate such an initiatrix who is of flesh and blood. **2.** Like *Taleju, she is a Nepalese "hybrid" goddess worshipped by both Hindus and Buddhists. Guheshvari is believed, in Nepal, to be the divine presence of the *guhe of the goddess Sati, giving her beautiful temple outside Kathmandu the status of a sacred *pitha, although Indian mythography points to *Assam and its *Kamakhya Pitha as the place where the goddess's yoni fell from the sky. Only 1 kilometer away from Pashupatinath, Nepal's famous temple of *Shiva, the temple of Guheshvari features an oval, golden platform shaped in the form of a *yoni, with an "unfathomable opening" (Majupuria, 1982, p. 25) at its center that is always kept covered by a silver ceremonial water vessel.

GUHYA

Nepali term equivalent to the Sanskrit *lingam.

SEE ALSO *GUHE, *GUHYASAMAJA TANTRA

GUHYASAMAJA TANTRA

This "assembly of secrets" is probably the earliest and most important of Buddhist Tantric scriptures, and it is attributed to Asanga, the fourth-century Yogacara master. This treatise, sometimes simply referred to as the Samaja Tantra, represents one of the root texts that were instrumental in the development of *Vajrayana and belongs to the highest class of its teachings, the Anuttara Yoga Tantra. The general tone of this early text can be judged from the following quote: "No one succeeds in attaining perfection by employing difficult and vexing operations; but perfection can be gained by satisfying all one's desires."

The text speaks of the virtues inherent in desire and sensory enjoyment, of the well-being of body and mind, and of realizing the "Buddha nature" through the union of female and male. It differs from many later texts in not condemning male *ejaculation but says that when "the diamond [*vajra/*lingam] is connected to the *lotus blossom [*yoni] in the union of both polarities, one worships the Buddhas and the diamond beings with the drops of one's semen." We also read that the male adept, or yogi, lets his *semen flow out "continuously in the form of *mandalas" (translated from the German edition of the Guhyasamaja Tantra, Gang, pp. 145ff.).

The ancient Tantra also states that if psychic powers, or *siddhis, are to be acquired, women must be associated with those who attempt to reach this goal. The text of this *Tantra—also sometimes called Tathagata Guhyaka—allows for sexual union between siblings and between mother and son, indicating that even within the fold of *Buddhism (with its unequivocal prohibition of "adultery" and its demand for continence) Tantra preserved its radical element of civil disobedience. This is also evident in works such as the *Prajnopaya-viniscaya Siddhi.

SEE ALSO *INCEST; FOR ANOTHER QUOTATION SEE THE EPIGRAPH ON P. 75.

GUHESHVARI. *Main portal to the temple of *Guheshvari, a temple to which no Westerner gets access unless being able to prove she or he has first become a Hindu. Located near the more famous temple of Pashupathinath, at the outskirts of Kathmandu, Nepal. Photograph by Rufus C. Camphausen.*

GUNAS

In Hindu philosophy these are the three "basic ingredients" or "fundamental qualities" of cosmos and being. All objects of the manifested world are thought to be composed of a particular mixture of three *gunas*, which influence the unfoldment of all matter and nature (*see* *Prakriti), as follows: **1.** *Tamas*, the generalized principle of inertia (and of related phenomena such as density, stability, and matter). **2.** *Rajas*, the generalized principle of motion (activity, creativity). **3.** *Sattva*, the generalized principle of order (time, structure).

GUPTASADHANA TANTRA

A small treatise of unknown age and authorship. Like the *Yoni Tantra, it lists, with slight changes, the nine types of women who are encouraged to take part in Tantric worship and who are known as *navakanyas. The text gives preference to the beautiful daughters of good conduct who come from the castes and professions mentioned by the Yoni Tantra, rather than to mature and married women.

The text, judging by the practices it recommends and advocates, is certainly of *Vamacara origin, and it clearly states that *initiation by a female preceptor is not only allowed but salutary and conducive to the attainment of all one's desires.

Chapter 4 describes a shortcut, or "royal road," for men, toward the attainment of freedom from disease, defeat of enemies, love, and wealth. The ritual, described by S. C. Banerjee, is as follows: "One's own or another man's wife, who is initiated" and "free from hate and shame" is worshipped in a way that includes the washing of her feet and the recitation of *mantras over the various parts of her body. "She is to be looked upon as the desired deity, and the devotee should imagine himself as Shiva. Then he should put betel leaves into her mouth as well as into his own, and with her permission perform intercourse according to the rules. At the time of copulation, *semen should be offered to Mahadevi [Skt., "Great Goddess"]" (p. 185).

SEE ALSO MANTRA, *PAAN, *SADHANA, *SHIVALINGA

GURDJIEFF, GEORGE IVANOVICH
(1873–1949)

Russian mystic, magician, psychotherapist, musician, and adventurous seeker-of-truth. He was the founder and head of a spiritual and philosophical school or discipline that has become known as the Fourth Way. His system incorporates strong elements of *Sufi teachings, and its focus is on self-discipline, personal integration, and demanding exercises, including much work in the sense of actual manual labor. Gurdjieff traveled widely, including through Mongolia and Tibet, where he studied with teachers and adepts of varied traditions. One of his teachers was the Mongolian Shamzaran Badmaev (d. 1919), a former medical adviser to the Russian court. A physician well versed in Mongolian, Chinese, and Tibetan medicine, this man was also a specialist in both the physical and mental disorders of women. It was from such men that Gurdjieff most certainly learned of Tantric sexuality, and the fact that he later fathered several children with some of his female pupils seems to indicate that he became a lifelong practitioner. A little-publicized sexual episode involving Gurdjieff is recounted in our description of the breathing method called *conspiration.

Gurdjieff influenced several unique and interesting minds, such as those of P. D. Ouspensky, Rodney Collin, J. G. Bennett, Maurice Nicoll, Robert S. de Ropp, and A. R. Orage, all authors who in their own way continued the propagation of the Fourth Way teachings. Among culturally influential people who have been strongly affected by

Gurdjieff we can find, for example, the painter Georgia O'Keeffe, architect Frank Lloyd Wright, filmmaker A. Jodorowsky, author Rudyard Kipling, and physiologist Moshe Feldenkrais.

GYNERGY

Contemporary term in Western languages indicating the female erotic/sexual energies that are stimulated, concentrated, and shared in sacred sexuality and, ultimately, in life and society. Compare here the Sanskrit terms *kalas, *najika siddhi, and *Shakti, and also the Taoist *yin essence.

H

At all times, whether washing one's feet or eating, rinsing the mouth, rubbing the hands, girding the hips with a loincloth, going out, making conversation, walking, standing, in wrath, in laughter, the wise man should always worship and honour the lady.

*HEVAJRA TANTRA

HAGAR

The story connecting Hagar, *Abraham, and the holy *Ka'bah can best be retold by combining Islamic tradition with the legends of Genesis. There we are told that stern, old Abraham, though married to Sarah at the time, made love to his young slave Hagar at the sacred shrine of the goddess *Al'Lat, and she conceived from this union her, and his, first son, Ishmael. However, the birth of Abraham's firstborn was not without problems. Water was scarce there in the desert, and shortly after the actual birth, mother and baby suffered badly from thirst. Desperately running back and forth, Hagar could not find any water, and the child's life became endangered. In his great compassion, and because Ishmael was destined to be the ancestor of all Arabian peoples, Allah—or Elohim, depending on the text—miraculously made a spring appear in order to save them from certain death.

Today the holy well Zamzam is part of the Great Mosque and has cooled the throats of millions of pilgrims who drink here from modern faucets. The miracle of the well's origin is still remembered and praised by the pilgrims to Mecca. Part of the prescribed ritual of the *hajj* is the *sa'i*: running seven times along the road between Al-Safa and Al-Marwah as a reenactment of Hagar's search for water, a run of little less than 3,000 meters.

The figure of Hagar, as known to local peoples, predates even these legends, however, and originally Hagar may have been "a desert mountain-goddess; her son's name means 'the

goddess's favourite,' and the Ishmaelite people were goddess worshippers" (Monaghan, p. 126).

SEE ALSO *LILITH

HALVAH   SEE *SESAME

HARDHAKALA
Sanskrit term used to express either of the following: **1.** The drawing of a *yoni when it is part of a mystic diagram or *yantra. **2.** The so-called wave of bliss that results from the union of *Shiva and *Shakti.

HAREM
When we consider the institution known as the harem, and the fact that the word originally indicated a "temple of women" or "sanctuary" (Arabic *harim*), it seems that the popularly known harem has become a personalized version of the earlier temples where *ritual prostitution is practiced. Although the harem was and is a questionable institution, the women who lived there often enjoyed a much better life

H AREM. *Three harem ladies entertaining their master;
a typical image of the *harem as a private playground.
Twentieth-century painting. Private collection.*

than their supposedly free sisters in the oustide world. Harem ladies, at least those at the top in the "pecking order," were often influential and powerful women. Harems were known not only in Arabia but also, in one or another form, in Persia, India, and China. The expression *temple of women* seems quite well chosen when we consider that early church fathers in England often complained that the king and male nobles used female monasteries as their harems.

HASTINI

The "elephant woman," one of the "female archetypes" of Indian erotic literature. In some texts this type of woman is called *karini*. The *hastini* seems to prefer mountain scenery for sexual union and is said to be difficult to satisfy, partly because of her large *yoni and partly because she is given to some of the more extreme desires, in love as well as food. The *hastini* enjoys much clitoral stimulation and is not averse to a little rough handling. Her love juice is said to taste and smell like an elephant's tears in spring. The smell of these "tears" refers to the smell of "sweat," or *musk, that collects on a rutting male *elephant's forehead.

SEE ALSO *ALGOLAGNIA

HATHOR

Near Eastern and Egyptian goddess usually depicted and visualized as a fertile, cosmic cow. Although in some aspects she is associated with the dark sides of life such as war and death, Hathor is very often seen as a goddess of desire, sexuality, and pleasure. Her worship included *ritual prostitution.

HEAVENLY FIRE OF THE HEART

A *Taoist center of the subtle body. During meditation and/or sexual union, one's vital breath is transformed and circulated throughout body and brain. On its way downward (see illustration on p. 225) the subtle energy passes the heart, picks up its fiery energy (the "heavenly fire"), and transports it to the furnace of the lower *tan-t'ien.

SEE ALSO *SUBTLE PHYSIOLOGY, *THREE GATES

HEDONIC ENGINEERING

A term used in the sociopsychological works of Timothy Leary (1920–1996) and Robert Anton Wilson (b. 1932) for the techniques and practices used to recondition and reimprint the original, mostly repressive *sexual imprinting most of us receive from family and society. Several tech-

niques of *Tantra, the use of psychotropic substances and *aphrodisiacs, and knowledge and information about sexuality and the human nervous system can play a pivotal part in such reimprinting. Hedonic engineering can, of course, also be used to simply create a new sexual imprint. The well-designed ceremonies of the *Nizari Isma'ilis, creating a kind of *erotocomatose lucidity in their would-be assassins, are an obvious example of this.

HERMAPHRODITE

The mythical figure and/or symbol that combined the god Hermes and the goddess *Aphrodite into a double-sexed personality, though it is sometimes interpreted as being neutral and nonsexual. This must not be confused with the concept of androgyny, in which the male and female poles do not physically coexist but are seen as existing in an integrated way on a psychological level, with repression of neither and each complementing the other. To the ancient alchemist, the hermaphrodite represented perfection. Symbolically this image can be compared to those of the hexagram *chi-chi and the Chinese symbol of *yin and *yang.

Though families and individuals themselves often keep it as secret as possible, hermaphroditic children are still being born. Most often the male part of a hermaphrodite's genitals is surgically removed, and the child is dressed and "trained" (*see* *Sexual Imprinting) as a girl. If you are not really a "man," within the black-and-white definition of society, you must be a woman: Our patriarchal culture cannot bear ambiguity or anything undefined and "in between."

HERMAPHRODITE. *A *hermaphrodite and the god *Pan. Nineteenth-century reproduction of a fresco from Pompeii. Private collection of Coen vanEmde Boas.*

HETAERAE
(GREEK, "FEMALE COMPANIONS")

Marriage in ancient Greece was seldom based on love and sexual attraction. Men often had a wife merely for providing offspring—and it had better be a boy! Sexuality and erotic pleasures were—if directed at women at all—found in contacts with the unmarried, free, and sophisticated "female companions."

The hetaerae were Greek society's version of the refined courtesan, and some of these women seem to have enjoyed a rather high social status. Similar to a Japanese geisha, a hetaera (singular) was a well-trained musician and dancer and an especially skilled adept of erotic delights, and it was through these qualities that the most successful of them attained considerable wealth together with the accompanying social power. The hetaera, representing the image of woman as comrade and friend, is one of the four Jungian *female archetypes.

HEVAJRA TANTRA

A Buddhist *Tantra of 20 chapters that is supposed to have originated in the eighth century. The deity Hevajra is a personified symbol for the Buddhist concept of a "supreme being" in a state of nonduality and is most often imagined or shown in a position of *yab-yum with the Shakti. The Hevajra Tantra teaches the *Union of Skillful Means (Skt., upaya) and Profound Cognition (*prajna) and states that sexual union can be helpful in achieving the powers called *siddhis. The text "quotes" the god Hevajra as saying: "I dwell in the *yoni of the female in the form of *semen."

For other quotations from this text see *Triangle and pages 85 and 186.

HEXAGRAM   SEE *I CHING, *YONIYUGMA

HIERODULES

The Greek term, actually hierodouloi, for the priestesses and women who practiced *ritual prostitution, comparable to the *ishtarishtu and *qadeshtu of the Near East. Hierodules served at the temples of *Aphrodite at Phoenician Byblos, Cyprian Paphos, and Greek Corinth. Roman Sicily also had its hierodules, who served Venus Ericyna on Mount Eryx.

SEE ALSO *VENUS

HIEROS GAMOS

This ritual, also known as sacred marriage, is sometimes explained in purely abstract, psychological terms as being representative of a "union of differentiated opposites" (Monick, p. 69). Of course, such a definition is not false, men and women being such opposites, but it completely disregards the reality of the actual celebrations as they were held by many peoples in the past.

Kings and queens, pharaonic couples (sometimes brother and sister), or priest and priestess—such personages would join in sexual union once a year in order to ensure general fertility and the well-being of "their" people. Such a celebration was often held in public and would in some cultures be followed by a general *orgy among the onlookers, be they a select group of initiates or the common townsfolk.

SEE ALSO *RITUAL PROMISCUITY, *WEB OF HEAVEN AND EARTH

HINAYANA

The small or lesser vehicle, indicating the southern branch of *Buddhism, which developed in India and Sri Lanka, whence it spread to several southeast Asian countries. Originally, the term was used, deprecatingly, by adherents of *Mahayana.

The development of Hinayana took place during the centuries following the death of Siddhartha Gautama Shakyamuni Buddha (in 483 B.C.E.). Out of the original Buddhist community arose several separate schools brought about by disagreements and different priorities in interpreting the Buddha's teachings. One of these developments was the eventual rise of *Mahayana. Of all the early Hinayana schools, only *Theravada has survived; it still exits today in countries such as Burma, Kampuchea (Cambodia), Laos, Sri Lanka, and Thailand as well as in the West.

One of the major flaws in traditional Hinayana teaching is the precept that only if one is (re)born as a man (male) and becomes a monk can one hope to attain enlightenment and liberation from the endless cycle of birth and death. In opposition to such teaching, the various schools of Mahayana assert that all beings equally possess the seed of Buddhahood. The goddess *Tara, for example, vowed to be reborn over and over again as a woman until all sentient beings would be liberated.

SEE ALSO *REBIRTH, *REINCARNATION

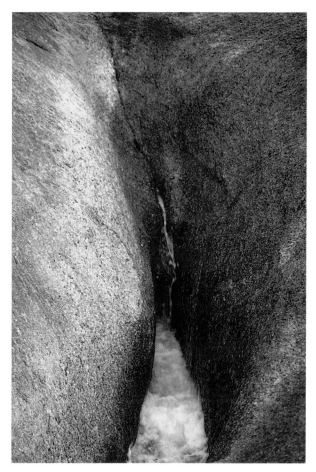

Hinta Hinyaai. *Located on the island of *Koh Samui (Thailand), *Hinta Hinyaai is a famous natural rock formation in the shape of the male and female genitals. In Thai,* Hinta *means "Grandfather Stone" and* Hinyaai *translates as "Grandmother Stone," suggesting that these rock formations are regarded as divine ancestors. Photographs by Christina Camphausen (Hinta) and Rufus C. Camphausen (Hinyaai).*

HINDUISM

An almost outdated and all too general term that often indicates little more than that a certain school of thought has come forth out of India (Persian, *Hind*), a country that virtually teems with different religious systems, sects, and schools. Using the term *Hindu* to describe a person indicates mainly that she or he does not belong to one of the other religions existing in India: *Jainism, *Buddhism, Islam, Sikhism, or Christianity. Today, the major traditions of Hindu worship are known as Shaivism (centered on the god *Shiva), Vaishnavism (devotees of the god Vishnu), *Shakta, and *Tantra. Historically speaking, so-called Hinduism also embraces what is known as Vedanta, a school of thought based on the ancient *Vedas, which arose at the time of India's invasion by Indo-Europeans. Sometimes, this classical Vedic Hinduism is referred to as Brahmanism, a name based on the highest caste: the priests known as Brahmans.

HINTA HINYAAI

On the Thai island of Koh Samui, at the coast near Lamai, natural rock formations in the shape of the human genitals have become places of prayer and pilgrimage.

Here, where tourists now bring their cameras and their giggles of shame and surprise, local people bring flowers in the early morning as their ancestors did for many generations.

Interestingly enough, there is only one very obviously

phallic statue here: Hinta—the Grandfather Stone, although there are two less-obvious vulva-shaped places. The best known of these, Hinyaai—the Grandmother Stone—is far down the cliff and is often hidden from view by the restless sea, wave after wave lapping the mossy cleft. The second one, dry but more detailed—not mentioned by the professional guides and thus missed by many visitors—is found when you look from the sea at the high wall of dark rocks to the right of the narrow road now lined with stalls selling drinks, food, and souvenirs to pilgrims and tourists alike.

HO-CH'I

1. Chinese/Taoist term for the "unification of breaths," a technique that aims to merge the male and female energies of *yang and *yin during sexual union. **2.** *Ho-ch'i* is also the name of a recurring communal sexual ritual held in ancient China, beginning with the time of the Han dynasty, at each new and full moon. Later Buddhist sources, much opposed to such practices, described the celebration as a "riotous *orgy of outrageous and disgusting licence" (*Encyclopaedia Britannica*). Such collective orgies were practiced by the schools of religious Taoism known as the *Way of Supreme Peace and *Five Pecks of Rice Taoism until the time of the Sung dynasty. One aim of the *ho-ch'i* celebration was to have sexual union with as many partners as possible, thereby increasing one's own sexual energy. This was thought necessary to help one achieve the Taoist goal of immortality.

HOLED STONES

A specific type of *megalith used in ancient Europe to facilitate fertility and the healing of diseased children. One of the best known is part of the famous Men-an-Tol megalith site in Cornwall, southern England. Here, the placement of the holed stone (1 meter tall) together with a *menhir (1.3 meters tall) on each side shows clearly that the holed stone represents the *yoni of the Earth Mother. Marriages were closed at such a sacred site, infertile women would crawl through the stone to remedy this condition, and sick infants were passed one or more times through the hole to be healed, symbolically being given a new birth.

Archeological findings at Men-an-Tol indicate that the center stone, the yoni, was once surrounded by a complete megalithic circle, a *cromlech.

HONEY

Many Oriental recipes, prescriptions, and concoctions are prepared with honey. Halvah, for example, is made from honey, *sesame, and nuts; there is a Moroccan recipe (*majoon) that mixes honey and *cannabis, and there are others that mix honey with *camel milk or the sap of *fennel, with *coconut, *egg, or *ginger. Honey's properties are due to the bee pollen it contains. This pollen, with it's high content of *vitamins B and C and minerals, positively affects the production of *sex hormones. Honey can also provide a general, and instant, boost of energy; it is a food that needs minimal time for digestion and absorption into the body.

In ancient India, a *chitrini's love juice was said to taste like honey. And more recently in a book on the *G-spot, authors Ladas, Whipple, and Perry quote a woman saying that the flavor of *female love juices varies and "changes four times during the month," at times being "very very sweet, better than any honey" (pp. 74 ff.).

HORAE

According to Barbara Walker, these Greek "ladies of the hour" had much in common with the *houris and other "harlots" and were probably temple dancers and/or *ritual prostitutes. We know of a traditional circle dance called the hora that is performed by "sacred harlots" every hour of the night, a custom also known in Egypt and performed by all-female temple dancers. In Hebrew, the word hor is used to indicate "cave, pit, hole" and is also used for *yoni.

The horae also have connections with the flow of time in nature—that is, with the seasons of the year. In personifying such aspects of natural order, one can easily imagine that they came to represent certain aspects of the social order as well: justice, peace, law, and so forth. Some of the deities belonging to this group are Thallo, Carpo, Dike, Eirene, and Eunomia.

It is quite probable that the English term whore and the German Hure developed their sound and meaning from these horae.

HOURIS

Especially beautiful Arab/Islamic spirits and trained adepts of the erotic arts similar to the *apsarasas and *horae. They are thought by believers to inhabit the paradise promised to the faithful.

HSING-CH'I

General Chinese term for all techniques involving the use and control of one's breath; comparable to the Sanskrit *pranayama.

SEE ALSO *HO-CH'I

HSUAN NÜ

The "dark girl" or "mysterious maid" and one of the *Three Lady Immortals.

HSUEH

Chinese term for the ova and ovaries, which, according to Taoist teachings, contain the female *yin energy.

HUAN-CH'ING PU-NAO

A Chinese technical term that translates as "letting the *semen return and strengthen the *brain." The term refers to a sexual technique for strengthening the male *ching energy and aiding in the prolongation of life or the attainment of immortality. Just prior to *ejaculation the man's *lingam is sealed off by finger pressure from either partner. With a deep exhalation of breath and grinding of teeth the ching (semen/energy) is directed upward toward the highest *tan-t'ien. According to the Taoist adepts, this allows the ching (seminal essence) to mingle and unite with the *ch'i (vital energy), a process that has rejuvenating effects on the practitioner's general health and total being.

SEE ALSO *OLI TECHNIQUES, *RETENTION OF SEMEN

HUANG-TI   SEE *YELLOW EMPEROR

HUANG-T'ING CHING

A third-century Taoist treatise, the title of which translates as The Classic Treatise of the Yellow Castle, with "yellow castle" being a reference to the human heart.

The Huang-t'ing Ching is purposely designed to be recited, not simply read; the recitation aids in the visualization and invocation of the "body deities" named in the work. The text contains descriptions and instructions concerning fang-chung shu (sexual techniques), *hsing-ch'i (breathing exercises), and other practices aiming at achieving immortality, a pursuit that plays a large role in the inner alchemy of Taoism.

Considering the text's early date, it could have been a medium for the often discussed Chinese influence on the first Indian *Tantras, texts that appeared three hundred to four hundred years later. The text should not be confused with Huang-ti nei-ching, the Yellow Emporer's famous classical work on Chinese medicine.

SEE ALSO *MAHACINACARA-SARA TANTRA

HUI AND/OR HUI-JIN

Chinese for a woman's *perineum, a point midway between anus and vagina, which is thought to be the seat of *yin energy (Chia and Chia, p. 77).

SEE ALSO *CHING-TAO

HUN
(CHIN., "SPIRIT SOUL," "BREATH SOUL.")

One of the two subdivisions of the soul present in all humans, according to Taoist teachings. *Hun* is the subtle and luminous element of the male *yang energy that is concentrated precisely between the eyebrows. The male/active *hun* needs to be balanced with the female/*yin "body soul," or *p'o.

SEE ALSO *PITUITARY GLAND

HYMEN   SEE VIRGINITY/2, YONI TOPOGRAPHY/10

It is the duty of the man to consider the tastes of woman and to be tough or tender, according to his beloved's wishes.

*KOKA SHASTRA

I CHING

The ancient Chinese/Taoist "Book of Changes," a book of wisdom and divination developed during the early phases of Chinese culture (about five thousand years ago) and still very much in use today—including by many of the spiritually and philosophically eclectic people in modern Western societies. The present form of the I Ching, however, has been heavily influenced by the Confucianism of *K'ung-tzu and is thus not entirely Taoist, as it must have been when it was used by the *fang-shih. The philosophical and divinitory

basis of the I Ching is found in the permutations, the many stages of intermingling, of the forces of *yin (female, Earth) and *yang (male, Heaven). From these two forces develop the 8 trigrams that in turn combine in manifold ways into the 64 hexagrams that constitute the I Ching. This continuous interaction of the two basic forces of the universe produces *i* (change), which is seen as the movement of the *Tao.

Some of the I Ching's symbology also plays an important role in Taoist *inner alchemy and *subtle physiology, and the I Ching commentaries themselves include the following interesting statement: "The constant intermingling of Heaven and Earth gives shape to all things. The sexual union of man and woman gives life to all things" (quoted in van Gulik, p. 37).

SEE ALSO *CHI-CHI, *CH'IEN, *K'AN, *K'UN, *LI, *ORGASM, *SIXTY-FOUR YOGINI PITHA

IDA   SEE *NADI

I-KUAN-TAO

A Taoist group, existing in twentieth-century communist China but suppressed about 1950, which seems to have continued sexual practices as they were known among the earlier *K'un-tan and *Yellow Turban schools. A newspaper of November 20, 1950, reported that its "shamelessly lustful leaders" had their members engage in *ritual promiscuity (van Gulik, p. 90).

IMSAK
(ARABIC, "RETENTION")

Arabic term for a set of techniques to achieve prolonged erection and coition by means of repeated *coitus interruptus and *retention of semen. *Imsak* basically calls for conscious control during sexual union by both partners: not allowing *ejaculation to happen and simultaneously keeping up the erotic tension in mind and body. Whenever a critical stage is felt to approach, the lingam is withdrawn. Both man and woman willfully do their best to allow for as many cycles of reentry and withdrawal as are desired and possible. Different from *karezza, imsak "allows" the practitioners to stage a grand finale and to let *orgasm and/or ejaculation—the quality of which will often and understandably be extraordinary—take place.

Imsak provides certain guidelines according to which the

man makes, for example, ten calculated thrusts before once again withdrawing: three times slow and shallow, two times fast and deep, three fast and shallow, ending the cycle with two very slow and deep penetrations. Once one has gained some experience with a given partner, however, spontaneity is possible, but still only if the intention is singularly pointed and attention remains focused.

On the woman's part, it is excellent if she has developed her *pelvic floor potential (*pompoir) to a certain degree, enabling her to have more control over the inserted lingam.

The *Sanskrit term for this exercise is amsak.

SEE ALSO *KABBAZAH

INANNA AND/OR INNIN

The Sumerian great queen, or "lady of Heaven" (Ninanna), who is known to us mainly from the Gilgamesh epic and from the myths concerning her relation in life and death to her brother and lover, the fertility and vegetation god Dumuzi. Inanna was a goddess associated—in terms of symbology—with the moon, the planet *Venus, and the *serpent. As she was explicitly a goddess of sexuality and fertility, her worship included *ritual prostitution. During and after the decline of the Sumerian kingdom, Inanna was replaced by the Semitic goddess *Ishtar, who became the one to be invoked at Inanna's original temples at the cities of Erech, Kish, and Ur.

INARI

A Japanese goddess responsible for the fertility of plants. In this connection she is also involved with *ritual prostitution, which is seen, in this case, as helpful in promoting a good harvest.

INCEST

Sexual union between close members of the same family is probably the most widespread taboo known to humanity, although it is not the most ancient one. This fact has not prevented thousands of individuals in many societies, including most or all modern ones, from having broken this taboo as frequently as all others, or more. The original reasoning against incestuous sexual relations was based on humanity's recognition—truly experienced and learned the hard way—of genetic laws. After men and women became aware that conception and birth were the outcome of sexual union between male and female, they found that miscar-

riages and misformed offspring could result from unions of the same *blood.

In recent years, incest has become—at least in Europe and North America—a much-discussed item on the sociopolitical agenda. Although the cases in question generally represent one specific form—criminal abuse of girls and boys by one of their parents or other family members—general "morality," past and present, condemns all forms of incest. However, mythology and history know many cultures where such a general judgment has not been shared and where the rules have been suspended for certain persons and for members of certain social, political, or religious groups.

Several of the important deities in the Greek and Egyptian pantheon—for example, *Zeus and *Osiris—are known for their incestuous exploits. Osiris not only marries his sister Isis—a practice often copied among the royal families of Egypt—but also makes love with Nephtys, his second sister and the wife of their common brother, Seth. Later in the myth, Isis also enters into a sexual relationship with her son Horus.

We see in such examples that for gods and goddesses, and therefore sometimes for their representatives on Earth, normal rules often do not apply. Likewise, certain Tantric sects and schools often broke with normal codes of behavior in this area. Incest is allowed or recommended in one or more of the possible varieties (father/daughter, mother/son, sister/brother) in the *Guhyasamaja Tantra and the *Prajnopaya-viniscaya Siddhi. A famous Tibetan/Bhutanese tale of incest, from the songs of *Drukpa Kunleg, is well loved in those countries and is often told when people sit around their hearth, accompanied by general merriment and a few beers. In this tale the hero begs his unconsenting mother to make love to him. When she finally gives in and they have "done the deed," he runs out into the marketplace and informs everyone in the village that his mother has just committed incest. We can recognize that in the places where this story is told, incest is also outside the norm but that nonetheless one can speak of it: The participants are not, as would have happened in many other cultures, condemned and burned at the stake.

Such a story raises the interesting question whether or not incest should be allowed between consenting adults, provided that no children are produced from the union. The mental and spiritual torments of the eponymous character of Robert Musil's *The Man without Qualities* and his sister would not have been necessary if they had realized the true nature of the incest taboo and its practical, genetic dimensions. Yet they, like many people, have fallen into the trap set by religious leaders and lawmakers who have overzealously declared physical, sexual expressions of love between blood relations as unnatural and inhuman, embedding deep feelings of guilt in our individual and collective psyche. An enlightened society, in which mental or chemical control makes contraception possible, could and should allow incest between consenting adults. Such tolerance, together with a generally wise and free attitude concerning sexual matters, would probably reduce neurosis and true sexual abuse and misconduct, occurrences all too common in present-day "moral" societies.

According to Epiphanus (*see* *Gnosticism), incest between brothers and sisters was practiced as a ritual technique among some Gnostic sects.

SEE ALSO *MATRIYONI, *MBOZE

INCUBUS

The nonphysical, immaterial male sexual partner in *congressus subtilis*. According to Hebrew legends the incubi are the children of *Lilith and can assume either sex in order to have intercourse with humans.

SEE ALSO *SUCCUBUS

INDOLE

The active chemical ingredient (related to methyl alcohol) in several powerful scents with *aphrodisiac properties. Indole is present in plants such as *lilac, Madonna lily, narcissus, privet, orange blossom, and *tuberose, and also in the *civet secreted by the cat of the same name. When inhaled in small quantities, all these scents are sweet and very pleasing to the olfactory system, but if inhaled in excess (strength or duration) they can lead to nausea, headaches, and depression. Considering that indole is also one of the substances produced by the human scent glands, the question why or whether such essential oils are aphrodisiacs is an academic one.

SEE ALSO *OLFACTORY DELIGHTS

INDRABHUTI

Several "enlightened kings" (*indra* meaning "king," *bhuti* or *bhodi* meaning "wisdom, enlightenment") bear the name Indrabhuti, and their exact dates and indentifications are still subject to further research. Following Keith Dowman's detailed research in *Masters of Mahamudra,* we arrive at the following simplified data:

1. Indrabhuti the Great (seventh century), also known as King Dza, the so-called first Tantric and the adoptive father of *Padmasambhava
2. Indrabhuti II (also known as King Dza and/or Son of King Dza)
3. Indrabhuti III (late ninth century), one of the *Mahasiddhas and brother of Lakshminkara, probably the author of the Buddhist Tantra known as *Jnanasiddhi

INFIBULATION

Contrary to most of the entries in this book, infibulation does not simply consitute another piece in the puzzle of humanity's quest for sexual knowledge—of self and other—and for erotic pleasures from which we can learn or that we may even revive. Infibulation is a specific, and the worst, type of *circumcision. It is included here only to make evident to what extent some male-dominated societies are prepared to go in order to ensure their men's exclusive "possession" of a woman and to make sure that the children she bears are those of her "rightful husband." It is, together with *clitoridectomy, *castration, and *subincision, one of the true *perversions. The deformed feet of Chinese women, the European use of chastity belts, and other appalling practices that women have had to undergo in various cultures all seem lesser crimes compared with infibulation and the psychological and physical pain and imprisonment it involves.

Infibulation is usually done together with clitoridectomy, another practice prescribed in many societies. In the Sudan, where infibulation, although illegal, is still widely practiced, the operation is known as pharaonic circumcision, pointing perhaps to an Egyptian origin. This male invention is often seen as a religious practice but is actually only another tool of repression in the hands of certain alpha males. The actual procedure consists first of cutting away the clitoral crown and hood as well as the labia minora. Then part of the large lips are also cut off, and the wounds are expected to close up the vagina's entrance except for a small and necessary opening. Often this is achieved by actually sewing the wound together, or sometimes by immobilizing the victim until it has closed by itself and adhesion has been com-

INITIATION. *For their *initiation, male Australian Aborigines often pretend to be women. Photograph by Axel Poignaut.*

pleted. Months or years later, for the consummation of marriage, the scar tissue must be opened again, sometimes by the husband, and often it has to be opened once more, by a "midwife," shortly before birth. The most unfortunate women have to undergo this outrage again and again between successive births.

For ages, the women—girls, mothers, aunts, tribal queens, and midwives—in cultures that require infibulation have acquiesced in this practice, usually with a degree of consent that is difficult for people in Western cultures to imagine. Infibulation is still practiced, as reported in 1985, in Sudan, Ethiopia, Somalia, Djibouti, Kenya, Nigeria, Mali, and the whole of the Arabian peninsula (French, pp. 255ff.).

In 1925, Burma, Java, and Thailand still also belonged on that list.

INITIATION

Describing the many types of initiation existing in the world of religion would require a study several volumes long, and most religious rites of initiation have little or no connection to eros and sexuality. Most initiation rituals, sexual or not, were to be kept a secret, and we are fortunate to know anything about them at all.

One of the few examples we do have, in literary form, of a secret and sexual initiation is described very briefly by Giuseppe Tucci, one of the leading Western authorities on

Tibetan studies. Though Tucci generally prefers to see the Tantric sexual rituals as merely symbolic, and he actually labels literal practice as a deviation from the intended and abstract meaning, his scientific honesty led him to write about a sexual initiation in a short exposition of Anuyoga. In discussing the "union of father and mother" or *yab-yum in this case of the initiating lama and his female partner (Tucci calls her *paredra,* a term similar to *mudra/4), he says the following:

> The symbolic power of this process, in which
> Enlightenment is equated with the semen resulting
> from the union, permeates the whole scheme. The
> same is true for the second set of consecretions . . . in
> the course of which the initiand himself becomes the
> actor, for he united himself with the paredra. In the
> secret initiation, when the Thought of Enlightenment,
> here equated with the semen of the lama embracing
> the paredra, is placed on the tongue, then this is the
> consecration of the "vessel." When one tastes it, the
> consecration is granted (pp. 79–80, 103).

He goes on to say that in this second consecration, the woman takes over the initiation from the lama, the master or "priest," who has been leading the earlier initiation. Tucci also admits that even one of the reformed *Gelugpa teachers of the fifteenth century stated that the performance of such rituals requires the presence of an experienced female scholar of the 64 methods of love.

The *Sanskrit term for initiation by one's spiritual teacher, man or woman, is *diksha.* Very different types of initiation, often classified as *puberty rites, are described in the entries *Circumcision and *Defloration.

SEE ALSO *DRUGS AND SEXUAL INITIATION, *SPARSHA DIKSHA

INNER ALCHEMY

The alchemists of China and Europe were concerned with the careful balancing of the subtle energies and cosmic forces at the root of, and active in, all subtle, physical, and mental activities and manifestations. Inner alchemy is not necessarily erotic in nature, but many of its techniques play an important role in the sexual *asanas of *Tantra, *Taoism, and *sexual magick.

SEE ALSO *NEI-TAN, *RETENTION OF SEMEN, THOMAS *VAUGHAN, *YONITATTVA

INNER TANTRAS
(TIB., NANG RGYUD)

NOTE: Outside the *Nyingmapa school, these Inner Tantras are often named Anuttara Tantra (Tib., *bla-med-rnal-'byor rgyud;* Skt., *anuttarayoga-tantra,* "Unexcelled Yogatantra"), a collective classification of texts that originally were categorized as *yogini* Tantras and *mahayoga* Tantras.

The Inner or Higher Tantras are subdivided into three groups, a division that corresponds to the seventh to the ninth level of the *Nine Vehicles. Among the Nyingmapa and in most *Dzogchen texts, these three levels are known as Mahayoga, Anuyoga, and Atiyoga, whereas other schools call them father Tantras, mother Tantras, and nondual Tantras. These texts, including the *Guhyasamaja Tantra and the *Hevajra Tantra, mainly teach nonaction and the identity of path and goal, or, in other words, the fusion of method and goal.

LEVEL 7: MAHAYOGA (SKT., MAHAYOGA, "YOGA OF GREAT ACTION"; TIB., RNAL-'BYOR CH'EN-PO) OR "FATHER TANTRAS" (TIB., PHA-RGYUD; SKT. PITRYOGA) These are teachings that mainly concentrate on the generation process (Tib., *bskyed-rim*), i.e., the creative stage that corresponds to method. There is an emphasis on "skillfull means" (Skt., *upaya*) and on making use of elaborate mandalas. Mahayoga is once again subdivided into a Tantra section (Tib., *rgyud-sde*) and a *sadhana* (Skt., "accomplishment") section (Tib., *sgrub-sde*). The major text of this level is the Guhyagarbha (Tib., *gSang-ba snying-po,* "The Secret Heart" or "Essence of Secrets").

LEVEL 8: ANUYOGA (TIB., RJES-SU RNAL-'BYOR) OR "MOTHER TANTRAS" (TIB., MA-RGYUD; SKT., MATRYOGA) With the vehicles 8 and 9, one actually leaves the gradual path that is typical for *Mahayana-oriented Buddhism and enters the nongradual method that finally culminates in *Dzogchen. Anuyoga represents the teachings of the Perfection Process (Tib., *rDzogs-rim*) or the fulfillment stage, with an emphasis on perfect insight. The specialty here lies in eradicating previous mental conditioning, belief systems, and purely relative convictions, thus opening the way to a cessation of thought. In contemporary psychological terminology it could be called "reprogramming the human biocomputer" (Lilly, *Human Biocomputer*).

The practice at this level focuses strongly on the subtle body, its channels, and its energies (Tib., *rtsa rlung*).

A specific practice of the Anuyoga stage that makes use of sexual techniques and energies is known as *Zap-lam. In order to learn and practice the teachings of this stage, the practitioner should have undergone the third, Secret (or Mystic) Initiation (Skt., guhyabhiseka). For a description of that, see *Initiation. Major texts of this level are the Chakrasamvara Tantra, the Hayagriva Tantra, and the *Hevajra Tantra.

LEVEL 9: ATIYOGA (TIB., rDzOGS-PA CH'EN-PO, "GREAT PERFECTION"; SKT., MAHASANDHI, "GREAT COMPLETION"; AND/OR TIB., SHIN-TU rNAL-'BYOR) OR NONDUAL TANTRAS (SKT., ADVITIATANTRA, ADVAITAYOGA) OR PRIMORDIAL YOGA (TIB., GDOD-MA'I RNAL'BYOR) This, in fact, is the level of the *Dzogchen and *Mahamudra teachings and represents the highest possible achievement: the unification of path and goal that leads one to true Buddhahood. In addition to the initiations of the previous stages, the practitioner now receives the fourth, or Word, Initiation (Tib., tshig-dbang; Skt., caturthabhiseka), which empowers her or him to receive and understand these highest teachings. On this level one learns about the equality and union of the two earlier stages (7 and 8), and in practice, emphasis is put on entering the state of nondiscriminating contemplation (Tib., ting-nge-'dzin; Skt., samadhi).

The Dzogchen Atiyoga teachings, introduced into Tibet by *Vairochana, *Vimalamitra, and *Padmasamb-hava, exist in three series, classes, or categories of written texts. The Semde (Tib., sems-sde, "The Nature of the Mind-Class," "Mind Series") teachings are somewhat like the gradual method of many other Buddhist schools. These rather intellectual teachings lead the student to knowledge by way of consecutive, step-by-step instructions on how to enter the state of mind known as contemplation. An important Tantra of this class, written by *Longchenpa, is known as "The King Who Creates Everything" (Tib., kun-byed rGyal-po)—a title that refers to the human mind. The text has been translated into English and published as "You Are the Eyes of the World" (Longchenpa, 1987). The Six Vajra Verses, originally written in the language of *Uddiyana, also belong to this class of teachings (see Norbu, Crystal and Dzogchen).

The Longde (Londe, Tib., klong-sde, "Primordial Space Class," "Space Series," or "Expansive Category") teachings are designed to lead the student more directly toward a thorough and doubt-free experience of his or her primordial state. Both the Semde and Longde teachings were brought to Tibet by *Vairochana and represent the early oral tradition (Tib., bKa'-ma, "audio transmission") he received from *Garab Dorje in Uddiyana.

The Mannagde (Mengagde, Tib., man-ngag gi sde, "Secret Precept Class," "Secret Instructions Series," "Concealed Instruction Category," "Secret Oral Transmission Class"; Skt., Upadesa) teachings derive from *Vimalamitra and *Padmasambhava and consist mainly of *termas, among them the *Vima Nyingthig and 17 Tantras hidden by Vimalamitra's student Tingzin Zangpo (Tib., ting 'dzin bzang po) and revealed by *terton Donma Lungyal (Tib., dong ma lhung rGyal) (Norbu, Dzog Chen and Zen, pp. 19, 37).

The Mannagde level of Dzogchen Atiyoga knows two types of training, each of which may be practiced as a path in itself. Trekchod (Trekchöd, Thregchod, Trekchod, Tib., mKhregs-Ch'od, "cutting through") is the method of "cutting through to the essence" or the "destruction of solidity." It involves the actualization of one's innermost awareness, one's primordial wisdom nature. Thogal (Thodgal, Togal, Tib., Thod-rGal, "direct approach") is the method of "direct crossing," with an emphasis on spontaneity (Tib., lhun-grub).

Once more, the reader should remember that different schools apply different classifications and sometimes see other texts as more important. Which of the major (Buddhist) Tantric texts belongs to which stage and group, however, is a question often debated among the different schools and one that varies from account to account. An extensive discussion of this problem, from a *Gelugpa point of view, is provided in mKhas grub-rje's (1385–1438) "Fundamentals of Buddhist Tantras" (F. D. Lessing and L. A. Wayman, 1990).

INNER YANG

Although *yang is generally a male energy, this is a Taoist term for the subtle glandular secretions generated in the *yoni of a woman in *ecstasy. The rejuvenating effects of sexual union are ascribed to these subtle fluids or energies.

SEE ALSO *FEMALE LOVE JUICES, *SEXUAL BIOCHEMISTRY

INQUISITION

General name for an enforcement agency comparable to the Nazi SS that was established by the Roman Catholic Church in 1233 in order to suppress whatever was deemed and declared a heresy. The Spanish Inquisition, which was not officially abolished until 1834, used methods that included the torture, rape, burning, and drowning of its victims to keep the population within the fold of the "holy church." Among those considered heretics were a huge number of women—so called witches—and, of course, all those suspected of "deviant" sexual tastes.

INSUFFLATION

One of the techniques in which one's *breath is used to influence another being and to manipulate subtle energies. This can be used either for the purpose of healing, as a means of transpowering (transmitting power or energy from one entity to another), or—similar to *conspiration—for sexual control.

INTRAJACULATION

By means of pressure on the *perineum, the flow of male semen is directed inward rather than outward (ejaculation). Medical research has establised that the sperm thus arrives in the bladder, though this does not necessarily prove the exercise to be fruitless.

SEE ALSO *KHECHARI MUDRA, *OLI TECHNIQUES

ISCHIOCAVERNOSUS MUSCLE

A muscle running along both crura (legs) of the female clitoris. They are part of the muscles discussed in *pelvic floor potential.

ISHTAR

Also written and spelled as Ishara, Istar, or Istaru, this Akkadian/Babylonian Great Goddess represents a later and more complex development of the Sumerian *Inanna, and her son/lover Tammuz plays the role of the vegetation god *Attis. Not only is she an embodiment of sexuality and fertility, a "lady of battle," and a goddess of healing, but also it is she who bestowed the ancient kings with the right to rule over her/their people. Her fame reached into the Hittite and Hurrian lands of Anatolia, to Sumer and Egypt, and to the Assyrians. Especially in Assyria and Egypt she was revered as a goddess of battle and is depicted with bow, quiver, and sword; her prowess is symbolized by the lioness she rides as a steed.

In other sacred texts Ishtar is described as having sweet lips and a beautiful figure, and it is made clear that she takes much pleasure in love. When she descends to the netherworld, all sexual activity ceases everywhere on earth. Her fertility-oriented worship included annual rites during which the king and the Harine—Ishtar's high priestess and spiritual ruler of Babylon—united in a sacred marriage known as *hieros gamos. In this aspect her familiar and symbolic animal is the *dove. Ishtar was also thought to rule the *menstrual/ovarian cycle.

In the Old Testament her worship is regarded as an abomination, and it was Ishtar's worshippers and *ishtar-ishtu who were said to be found even at the doors of the Hebrew God's great temple, much to the consternation of his priests and prophets.

As well as being renowned for her powers of creation, divine rulership, prophecy, and desire, Ishtar was also regarded as a healer. We know that her effigy once was transported from Babylon to Egypt in order to heal the sick Amenhotep III. Many are her sacred titles: "Exalted Light of Heaven," "She Who Begets All," "Guardian of the Law," and "Shepherdess of the Lands." Many, too, are the places where shrines were erected to her and her names invoked. Most famous of these places are Niniveh, Aleppo, and Babylon, where a beautiful temple to her was erected in about 550 B.C.E.

SEE ALSO *BIT-SHAGATH, *BRIDAL PROSTITUTION, *KILILI

ISHTARISHTU

The "holy women of *Ishtar" who served the goddess in her temple, or in any other temple, as ritual prostitutes.

ITHYPHALLIC

Technical term to indicate that a certain figure, generally a deity, is depicted with an erect phallus. Numbered among such deities are the Egyptian *Min, the bisexual Greek Phanes (Scott, pp. 34, 218), and, probably most famous, the Greek and Roman god *Priapus, who has lent his name to the medical condition called priapism.

IZANAMI AND IZANAGI

"The female who invites" and "the male who invites." The two ancient Japanese deities who "discovered sexuality" and then set about creating the Japanese Islands, several other deities, and the world at large.

J

In the lap of the daughters of Jerusalem is the Gate of the Lord, and the righteous shall there go into the temple, even to the altar.

A. Unternährer, "Geheimes Reskript" (1821)

NOTE: An entry expected to have the initial *J* may sometimes be found under *Y*.

JADE FLUID OR JADE LIQUID

Taoist term for *saliva, regarded as a beneficial essence to be collected and swallowed during breathing exercises and/or to be exchanged between two partners while kissing. The Chinese term is *yu-chiang*.

SEE ALSO *JADE FOUNTAIN LIQUID

JADE FOUNTAIN

Chinese code for a woman's lips, also known as *red lotus peak.

SEE ALSO *SEXUAL BIOCHEMISTRY

JADE FOUNTAIN LIQUID

Chinese/Taoist term for the specifically female form of *jade fluid, a transparent and beneficial subtle essence secreted from the *red lotus peak during erotic *ecstasy.

JADE GATE

1. The Chinese expression (Chin., *yiu-men*) for one of the *three gates known in Taoist *subtle physiology, also called jade pillow. **2.** A code for the *yoni.

JADE PILLOW SEE *THREE GATES

JAGAD YONI

The great and cosmic "vulva of space/time," a symbol and a title of honor for the *Shakti as Mother of All—*jagad* meaning "universe" and "world."

SEE ALSO *YONI WORSHIP

JAGAN NATH TEMPLE

Whereas the Chinese concept of *secret dalliance and the Indian *yogini chakra* concentrate on sexual union between one man and several women, the Jagan Nath temple is one of the few that also shows, and thus encourages, such erotic play between one woman and two or more men. In one example, a naked woman exposes her *yoni while two men are fondling her breasts; in another, the loving couple is merely attended by a second male; yet another scene shows a woman with three men, all erotically active. The temple is dedicated to *Shiva and stands in the center of Nepal's capital, Kathmandu.

JAINA AND/OR JAINISM

An orthodox, yet non-Vedic, Indian religion founded by the Great Hero Mahavira (alive during the fifth and sixth centuries B.C.E.), a contemporary of Buddha. Two major facets of the Jaina teachings involve the strict practice of noninjury of any living being and the belief that the truly devine dwells within an individual's soul rather than in "outside" agents such as God or Goddess.

SEE ALSO *DIGAMBARA

JAKI

A Persian menstruation spirit and female *demon who is said to urge men to evil deeds, testifying to the forces seen as inherent in the *menstrual fluid.

JAMUL

One of several major sites in California's San Diego County where a great number of granite boulders feature an even greater variety of *yoni-shaped sculptures. Although most of them are completely natural rock formations, some—for example the main yoni found at Jamul—clearly show evidence of paint, if not chiseling. Apart from the five Jamul samples, further ones are located throughout the area, with another concentration of yoni rocks along Canebrake

JAGAN NATH TEMPLE. *A typical example of erotic art as found in Nepal. This image from the *Jagan Nath temple in Kathmandu shows three men and one woman during sexual play, including *masturbation. A local guide told the author that the images are meant to serve as examples of sexual possibilities for illiterate citizens. Photograph by Rufus C. Camphausen.*

Creek. From archaelogical evidence collected in the vicinity, it seems that local tribes, the indigenous Kumeyaay and their relatives the Northern Diegueno, recognized and utilized these shapes as symbols of the Earth Mother and that they chose specifically to build their villages in this area, probably as guardians of these sacred places. Apart from this evidence, which includes tools typically used by shamans, research has also shown that these sites were already occupied in prehistoric times.

A paper by achaelogist Charlotte McGowan even gives testimony that a Kumeyaay medicine man, about 1900, clearly stated that these places were visited by young women who had not become pregnant. McGowan then continues to recall other fertility-oriented rites known by the Kumeyaay and their neighbors, in which sacred stones played an equally important role in the rituals surrounding menarche. With all of these data at hand, the Jamul yonis become part of the general veneration of the Goddess and

her yoni that was once known and practiced around the world, be it *Hinta Hinyaai or *Kamakhya

JAPA   SEE *MANTRA

JASMINE

There are many plants of the genus *Jasminium,* but all references to the scent of jasmine and its erotic effects speak of the white jasmine only, a scent that is known in India as *champaka.* Few people will be in a position to judge whether it is true that the "scent of white jasmine can transform a woman into a *nymphomaniac" (Genders, p. 4), but the statement—even if exaggerated—does indicate that these flowers and derived perfumes function as strong *aphrodisiacs.

JATAKUSUMA

One of the many Tantric/Sanskrit terms for *menstrual fluid, which is regarded as sacred.

JAVALAMUKHI

A unique and famous temple in Himachal Pradesh, India, located in a city by the same name (Jawalamukhi, 56 kilometers from Dharamsala). The temple, named after the goddess Javalamukhi (Skt., Jvalamukhi, the "Fire-Faced One"), houses eternal blue flames of natural gas emerging from fissures in the dark rock and burning above a pool of water. These flames, regarded as the multitipped tongue of the goddess Sati and/or *Kali, have given Javalamukhi exalted status as one of the Shakta *Pithas, in this case the one whose tongue fell down after her corpse had been dismembered.

For tourists and noninitiated pilgrims, local priests are eager to light emissions of gas in smaller chambers. Elsewhere, the main flame is kept alight continuously. The sanctuary is contained in a simple, whitewashed building crowned with a squat golden spire once gilded on demand of the Mughal Emperor Akbar (1542–1605). For hundreds of years, the temple has attracted pilgrims of both Hindu and Tantric Buddhist affiliations. Also, as Miranda Shaw suggests (p. 82), the temple has been the site of Tantric feasts such as the *ganachakra, an assembly of yoginis to which men were only occasionally allowed.

It seems that Javalamukhi is an ancient and originally Dravidian sanctuary going back to pre-Vedic times where once worshippers performed Tantric rituals that included *cunnilingus (not necessarily heterosexual), *maithuna viparita ("dancing on the lover"), and even more "secret" techniques, such as stimulation of the *yonishtana. These rituals continue to the present day.

Inspired by this double association with the tongue, author and pagan priest Mark Roberts has developed what he calls *Blue Flame Tantra: a variety of woman-centered and mainly oral techniques based on the matriarchal, pre-Vedic veneration of woman as sacred vessel and goddess.

On the other hand, and not at all conducive to oral sexual play, devotees of the goddess *Chinnamasta are known to cut off their own tongues at this temple in order to demonstrate their ultimate faith in her, since they expect that the goddess will restore their tongues to them in her endless compassion.

JEWEL ENCLOSURE

Chinese code/term for uterus (see *Yoni Topography/18).

JIGME LINGPA
(TIB., *JIGS-MED GLING-PA; 1729–1798)

A *Dzogchen master well known for his consideration of the *Longchen Nyingthig and for his work The Excellent Path of Omniscience (Tib., rnammykhyen-lam-bzang).

JITENDRIYA

A term mostly used to mean "control of the senses," but in Tantric terminology more specifically indicating the control, that is, *retention, of *semen.

JIVASAKTI   SEE *KUNDALINI

JNANA

Sanskrit term meaning "knowledge" or "spiritual wisdom."

JNANASIDDHI

A Buddhist *Tantra attributed to *Indrabhuti, which therefore must have been composed in the early eighth century. The text describes the main doctrines of early *Vajrayana and states, true to Tantric tradition, that the Tantric adept may attain liberation by the very practices that in other religious systems are usually said to lead people to hell. Sexual union with anyone, of any caste, is advocated, as long as the person in question is a "holder of the *vajra"—that is, a Tantric initiate.

JONANGPA
(TIB., JO-NANG-PA)

A school of *Vajrayana, named after the monastery Jo-mo-nang, considered to be heretical by most other schools. The school was rooted in Kashmir Shaivism and also had connections with the *Kagyudpa. Jonangpa's best-known adepts were Sherab Gyaltsen (Tib., Shes-rab rGyalmtshan) of Dolpo (1292–1361) and the famous Taranatha (Tib., Kun-dga snyang-po, b. 1575). According to the school's radical teaching, all that is conceivable is an illusion, and nothing exists but essence itself. The major texts of Jonangpa are the *Kalachakra and the sBor yan-lag drug. After Tarantha's death, during the reign of the fifth *Dalai Lama (1618-1682), all Jonangpa monasteries were closed and transformed into *Gelugpa centers, and many of the Jonangpa books were burned!

JUS PRIMAE NOCTIS

Latin phrase meaning "the right to the first night," referring to a custom in which it was the privilege, and duty, of kings and priests to either practice *defloration of young girls or have sexual union with them before they married their future husbands. Though the custom became corrupted in later times by landowners, slavers, and other men in power, it originally grew out of a fear and dread of the *blood of defloration, which was seen as having evil and magical powers that could be withstood only by rulers or sanctified persons.

JYOTIRLINGA
(SKT., "LUMINOUS PHALLUS")

As a male counterpart of the 51-*pitha, goddess-oriented pilgrimage, Hindu and Tantric pilgrims also know of 12 sacred places where the god *Shiva is said to be present in so-called self-manifested (Skt., *swayambhu*) and very much venerated lingas, housed in the major Shiva temples located throughout the Indian subcontinent. Claims to their respective locations range from Tamil Nadu in the deep south to the Kathmandu valley in the Himalayas. However, once we count all the sites alleged to be so blessed, the list exceeds the number 12 so it comes as no surprise that not all existing sources agree with one another.

The textual and mythical background to the *jyotirlinga* is a very interesting and threefold one.

First, there is an ancient and oh so humanly inspired myth in which the three major gods of the all-male Vedic trinity feel the need to compare each other's relative size as a means of indicating their powers. During this competition, Shiva manifested a huge column of light at Varanasi (Benares) extending infinitely high into the heavens and deep down into the earth—so far that his two competitors, Brahma and Vishnu, were unable to reach the two respective ends even though they tried for a thousand years before they had to admit defeat. Shiva, his superiority thus established, then caused the column of light to divide into 12 parts, which subsequently descended in various locations.

In a different version of the *jyotirlinga* manifestations, Shiva's lingam had been cut off by jealous sages because he had united with their wives. When the dismembered lingam touched the earth, it grew into the above-mentioned column of light, which then divided into the 12 sacred objects.

Second, and most certainly based on such myths, the *Shiva Purana cites Shiva as saying "I am omnipresent, but I am especially present in 12 forms and places."

And last but not least, there exists a Jyotir Linga Stotram, a sacred text that not only lists the 12 locations but contains *mantras and prayers to be recited in their honor. As is to be expected, the recitation of this text is said to be of great benefit. In his *Lord Siva and His Worship*, Swami Sivananda writes that "he who remembers the tewlve Jyotirlingas morning and evening becomes absolved from sins committed in seven previous births."

Here, then, is a list of the *jyotirlingas* as given in the available literature. There is little doubt about the validity of the first 9 or 10 places; the others are increasingly uncertain, and the numbers beyond 12 are not even mentioned in the Jyotir Linga Stotram. On the other hand, contemporary descriptions of Indian pilgrimage sites make it sound as if numbers 3 and 4 are possibly one and the same place.

1. Somnath in Saurastra, Gujurat
2. Mallikarjuna in Sailam, Andhra Pradesh
3. Amareshvara in Ujjain, Madya Pradesh
4. Omkar Mandhata on Onkareshvar Island, Madya Pradesh
5. Kshetram Rameshvara, on the island Rameswaram, Tamil Nadu
6. Kasi Visvanath in Varanasi, Uttar Pradesh
7. Triyambaka near Nasik, Maharashtra
8. Kedarnath, 4,000 meters high in the Himalayas of Uttar Pradesh
9. Bhimashankar near Murbad Taluka, Thane District, Maharashtra
10. Nagesa in Darukavana near Dwarka, Gujurat
11. Parli-Vaijanth (Vaidayantha), Beed district of Maharashtra (or perhaps near Deoghar, Bihar)
12. Ghusrunesa in Sivalaya, Karnataka (or Grishneshwar near the Ellora Caves, Maharashtra)
13. Pashupatinath outside Kathmandu, Nepal
14. Gautamesa, no location given (India)

K

Oh recluse, if you aspire to paradise, go fast to the place where dwell the women of lust.

KUTTNI MAHATMYAM

NOTE: An entry expected to have the initial letter *K* may sometimes be found under *C*.

KA'A

An all-female Tantric sect operating in Tibet that specialized in *congressus subtilis, a kind of astral sexual union. Without having any physical contact, its practitioners apparently turned into temporary *succubi in order to have a subtle, sexual union "with a virile young male." The energy thus accumulated was then used by them for purposes of "healing and magical rites" (Garrison, p. 119).

KA'BAH

Arabic name for the most sacred symbol and shrine in the world of Islam, to which more than a million people travel each year on a holy pilgrimage. Not suprisingly, given this male-oriented and -dominated religious system, the sacred black stone that is the major feature and attraction of the Great Mosque at Mecca is regarded as the "hand" of Allah, the monotheistic and jealous male deity quite similar to the stern God of the Old and New Testaments.

What is surprising is the fact that the major object of veneration is a meteorite, a stone fallen from heaven, fitted in a silver band with the shape of a woman's genitals. The artist(s) who prepared the stone's metal encasement took care to make it resemble, quite precisely, the shape of a *mandorle, shaping it into a symbolic representation of the *Jagad Yoni. Evidence from ethnology, linguistics, astronomy, mythography, and comparative religion makes it clear that the *yoni stone and the place of the sacred shrine had once been in the hands of pre-Islamic, "pagan" priestesses who worshipped their goddess *Al'Lat, with her manifestations of *Al'Uzza, Al'Menat, and Q're, at this site. Many are the myths and legends that demonstrate the change from a matrifocal (see *Matriarchy) religion and society to the present-day patriarchal systems. Some of them are intended to obliterate memories of the Goddess and her priestesses; others offer less distortion. One such legend tells that *Abraham bought the sacred place from its priestesses; others claim that he built it by command of Allah. For a detailed essay on these matters, refer to the bibliography for my article (Camphausen, "The Holy Stone at Mecca") on the Ka'bah.

SEE ALSO *CANOPUS, *SACRED STONES, *YONI WORSHIP

KABBAZAH
(ARABIC, "HOLDER")
Though *kabbazah* sometimes seems, according to some authors, to be a sexual technique, the term actually refers to a woman who has mastered the art of the *pelvic floor

K'A'BAH. *The *Ka'bah at Mecca, the sacred (female) black stone visible in the eastern corner. Illustration by Christina Camphausen.*

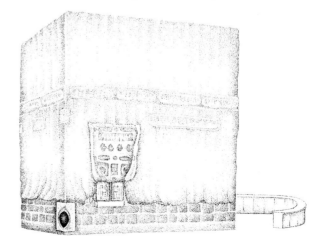

KAGURA. *A* *kagura *scene from the film* Nihon Tanjo *(Birth of Japan), 1955, by Inagaki Hiroshi.*

potential. The first mention of this term in Europe was made by Richard *Burton in his translation of the *Ananga Ranga, but the art has been known not only to the women of Arabia but also elsewhere as *pompoir and *bhaga asana.

Sexual union with a *kabbazah* is, for the man, an exercise in passivity, in letting her take absolute control once the *lingam is within the *yoni. The woman will guide herself and him toward erotic ecstasy, in her time and according to her rhythm. There is generally no body movement, especially not of the man—such as rotating the hips, thrusting in and out, or moving up and down—in this type of union. All that moves are the muscles of the pelvic floor and, with and through them, the walls of the vagina. The partners are, however, free to caress, kiss, and watch each other.

Such *maithuna of or with a *kabbazah* is a union of slow and tender patience, takes experience, and demands more time than most people usually spend with each other in sexual embrace. Nevertheless, the emotional and physical intensity of this sexual art, perhaps even prepared for by a week's abstinence or the use of an *aphrodisiac, seems worth all the "effort."

SEE ALSO *VIPARITA RATI, *YAB-YUM

KADAMPA
(TIB., *BKA'-GDAMS-PA*, "BOUND BY COMMAND")
Inspired by Atisa (982–1054), one of the heads of *Nalanda University, and founded by his pupil Bromston (1008–1064), the Kadampa was the first Tibetan Buddhist school to place high emphasis on monastic life and discipline. The Kadampas regarded the wandering, independent *Nyingmapa adepts as degenerate leftovers from the "first diffusion" (before 836 C.E.) of Tantric Buddhism into Tibet. The school eventually merged, after the reformation led by Tsongkapa (1357–1419), into the *Gelugpa.

KAGURA
(JAP., "THAT WHICH PLEASES THE GODS")
An old *Shinto ritual involving the performace of a striptease, in which the dancing priestess exposes her *yoni in full view of the participants. This celebration is held annually and commemorates an ancient myth about the goddesses *Amaterasu and *Ama-no-Uzume. In this myth, powerful *yoni magic is used to initiate a process of change, not so much on an individual level, as in the story of *Baubo, but on a social, even planetary, scale.

The myth tells us that Ama-no-Uzume, the "dread female of heaven," was instrumental in bringing the light back into a world that was plunged into total darkness. Amaterasu-o-mi-Kami, the Shinto goddess of the sun and as such of light, once in her anger hid in a cave, thus withholding light and warmth from Earth and from humanity. After all else had failed to persuade the sun to come back out of hiding, Ama-no-Uzume did what might be called a striptease act in front of the other assembled deities, who burst into laughter when she finally lifted her skirt and exposed her sacred genitals. Curious as to what the unaminous laughter was all about, the sun goddess came out of her cave, and once again there was light. This mythical "sacred striptease" gave rise to the *kagura*, wherein a priestess plays the part of Ama-no-Uzume and the audience consists of faithful temple visitors.

It seems interesting that this myth has become deeply embedded in the Japanese consciousness and that its basic pattern is operative even in a nonreligious context, such as the *tokudashi* of contemporary Japan's red-light districts.

KAGYUDPA
(TIB., *BKA-R GYUD-PA*, "ORAL TRANSMISSION")
Name indicating one of the four major traditions of *Vajrayana and/or a member of this lineage. The Kagyud (short for Kagyudpa) tradition as a whole consists of many subdivisions, each bearing a different name depending on the respective founders or the specific monastery where a particular "brand" of Kagyud teaching originated.

In the very beginning, there were only two schools, the *Shangpa Kagyud and the *Dagpo Kagyud, the latter of which multiplied into at least 12 subdivisions, each with slight changes of emphasis on one or another teaching and practice.

However, apart from these 12, Tibetan literature sometimes mentions a few additional schools bearing the name Kagyud or being closely related to this tradition. These are the Surmang Kagyud (see *Trungpa) and the Orgyanpa (or Ugyen Nyendrup). The Kagyudpa have, more than other Tibetan schools outside the old *Nyingmapa, incorporated and transmitted many of the teachings from original *Bön and *Tantra; their teachings comprise *Mahamudra, *Dzogchen, Naro-chos-drug, and many others. Ultimately, as one can judge from any list showing the Kagyud lineages, all these teachings are based on two streams of oral transmissions originating with *Tilopa and *Naropa: one via *Marpa to *Milarepa to Gampopa (see *Dagpo Kagyud), the other via *Niguma to Khungpo Naljor (see *Shangpa Kagyud).

Similar to Milarepa's *Mila Gnubum, most of the important Kagyud masters have composed "teaching songs": oral transmissions that have now been published as the *Vajra Songs.

KAKILA   SEE *MUKHARATA

KAKIRA
Sanskrit/Tantric term for *cunnilingus.

KALA
1. Sanskrit term meaning "time," as in *kala chakra*/3, which also expresses the idea of "black." Both the god Kala and the goddess *Kali take their names from the meaning of this term. **2.** An alternative name for Yama, the god of death. **3.** Tantric code for the subtle yet potent energy that exists in the form of pulsating vaginal vibrations produced by a woman who is sexually aroused or during her orgasm. The subdivisions of this energy are known as the "magical" *kalas*.

KALA CHAKRA
(SKT., "WHEEL OF TIME")
1. A focus for meditation and ritual in a *Dakshinacara gathering, consisting of a "circle of flowers and essences" that are meant to symbolize the *yoni of the goddess. **2.** A lesser-known *chakra* that is located below the *ajna chakra and above the *vishuddha chakra. **3.** A *Vajrayana *initiation ritual first held in the year 946 C.E., marking the start of the Tibetan calendar. **4.** A male deity (*Kala/2) often depicted with 24 arms and in sexual union with an eight-armed goddess.

KALACHAKRA TANTRA
A very extensive seventh-century *Tantra that attempts to describe all phenomena of the world in an all-inclusive vision. The "outer" section deals with cosmology and natural sciences such as astronomy, geography, and engineering. The more secret parts of the text, known as the "inner" and "outer" sections, describe the human body and mind, the functions of the *nadis, six types of meditation practice, and visualizations concerning the use and flow of sexual energy. According to Edwin Bernbaum and his *Way to Shambhala*, the text teaches, for example, that male *semen and female *menstrual flow "carry the impulse to enlightenment and can spread bliss throughout the body, transforming it into a vehicle to liberation" (Bernbaum, p.124).

This scripture, belonging to the highest group of Tantras, has been especially valued by the *Jonangpa school of *Vajrayana and is taught in other schools as well. The Kalachakra Tantra and its associated rituals also laid the basis for the Tibetan calendar, which started in 946 C.E. and is said to have originated in India at least three hundred years before it reached Tibet. The work also contains some of the teachings that later became known as the "Six Doctrines of Naropa," or Naro-chos-drug. See quotation on page 265.

KALAMUKHA

A *Shiva-oriented *Vamacara sect of southern India very similar to the *Kapalika.

KALAS
(SKT., "RAYS," "EMANATIONS")

Although the term's meaning of "rays" may mislead us into seeing the *kalas* as a "subtle energy" of the electromagnetic spectrum, there are several indications that we have here an ancient concept very much like the contemporary scientific idea of the *pheromones. Kenneth Grant writes that the *kalas* "equate with the psychologically modified somatic secretions of the erogenous zones that have not yet been investigated by physical science" (quoted by Redgrove, p.147). Grant, in 1972, was probably not acquainted with the idea of the pheromone, but the following information makes it clear that the *kalas* are connected with human *scent. Not only are the *kalas* thought to be present in *breath, *perspiration, and urine, they are also associated with the *suvarninis*, or "sweet-smelling ladies." Furthermore, Grant writes that an ancient science called *sri vidya* was concerned with the study of the "exudation and inhibition of magical *kalas* inherent in human fluids" (quoted by Redgrove, p. 147).

See also *Marmas, *Scent Aura, *Suvarninis

KALI and/or KALIKA

An Indian deity who is often regarded as a dark, black (Skt., *kala*), fierce goddess of death, and as the destructive "Power of Eternal Time." However, to her worshippers in both Hinduism and *Tantra she is much more, and represents a multifaceted Great Goddess responsible for all of life from conception to death. Her worship, therefore, consists of fertility festivals as well as sacrifices (animal and human), and her initiations expand one's consciousness by many means, including fear, ritual sexuality, and a variety of drugs.

A very apt and poetic description of the Great Mother Kali has been given by Gary Zukav in his *Dancing WuLi Masters*, where he wrote:

Kali, the Divine Mother, is the symbol for the infinite diversity of experience. Kali represents the entire physical plane. She is the drama, tragedy, humor, and sorrow of life. She is the brother, father, sister, mother, lover, and friend. She is the fiend, monster, beast, and brute. She is the sun and the ocean. She is the grass and the dew. She is our sense of accomplishment and our sense of doing worthwhile. Our thrill of discovery is a pendant on her bracelet. Our gratification is a spot of color on her cheek. Our sense of importance is the bell on her ankle. The full and seductive, terrible and wonderful earth mother always has something to offer (p. 329).

It has been said that Kali is "the divine Shakti representing both the creative and destructive aspects of nature," and as such she is a goddess who both gives life and brings death. Clothed only with the veil of space, her blue-black nakedness symbolizes the eternal night of nonexistence, a night that is free of any illusion and distinction. Kali as such is pure and primary reality (the enfolded order in modern physics): formless, void, yet full of potential. It is therefore not surprising that this goddess is also the foremost among the Mahavidya, the 10 most powerful and important goddesses of the Indian pantheon.

In time, Kali has become such a dominating figure in the Indian pantheon that many other goddesses have been assimilated into her and she herself has been ascribed an ever greater number of aspects and manfestations. Many of these, for example, the "One Hundred Names of Kali," are names that begin with the letter *K*. In their translations, these names define the goddess much more directly and intimately than any intellectual summary can do. The One Hundred Names occur in the Adyakali Svarupa Stotra, a hymn to Kali that is part of the *Mahanirvana Tantra. What

Kali. *In this Nepali image, the dark side of *Kali is featured in a variety of ways. The sagging breasts indicate time and aging, the fleshless ribs suggest death, the empty belly cavity shows her as not giving birth but rather inviting us back into her womb. The necklace and skirt made from human bones and skulls speak for themselves.*
Photograph by Kevin Bubriski.

emerges when one reads this hymn is an exposition of this goddess in a variety of strikingly different aspects:

- Kali as revealer, benefactress, and embodiment of the Kula school of Tantrics and their teachings, rituals, and lifestyle
- Kali as merciful helper and destructress of evil, fear, pride, and sin
- Kali as young, beautiful, swanlike, and sensual woman
- Kali as embodiment of desire and liberator from desire, as a free woman who enjoys and lets herself be enjoyed
- Kali who enjoys and partakes of drugs and aphrodisiacs (camphor, musk, wine)
- Kali who enjoys and encourages the worship of young women (with wine, drugs, and sexual play)
- Kali as queen of the holy city Varanasi (Benares) and as lover, beloved, and devourer of the god Shiva (the lord of that city)
- Kali as shape-shifter (assuming any form at will)
- Kali of terrific countenance, wearing a garland of bones, using a human skull as a cup
- Kali as dark night, as mother and destructress of time, as the fire of the world's dissolution

Although Kali is worshipped throughout India and Nepal, and even among the non-Islamic Indonesians of Bali, she is most popular in Bengal, where one also finds *Kalighat (Skt., kaligata), her most famous temple just outside Calcutta.

SEE ALSO *DURGA, *KALIKA PURANA, *KAMALA

KALIGHAT

The most famous *Kali temple of Calcutta and regarded as one of the 51 sacred *pithas. Here the goddess is worshipped in her aspect as *Kalika, the "devourer of him who devours." In the *Kalika Purana, a text obviously named after her, the goddess is also named as one of the 64 *yoginis. As the name Calcutta is simply an Anglicized form of kaligata, the city received its very name from this goddess. Ritual practices at Kalighat included human *sacrifice up to the time of the British occupation of India.

KALIKA PURANA

A so-called minor Purana originating within the folds of Shakta and Tantra as they developed in Assam and Bengal,

systems of belief in which the goddess is recognized as principal deity and source of universal energy. The text consists of 9000 stanzas in 98 chapters, and has been dated to the tenth century. The work is mainly concerned with describing the worship of the goddess *Kali or Kalika, and especially the veneration of Kamakhya, an erotic aspect of the Great Goddess Mahamaya.

The Kalika Purana is also known, and both feared and slandered, for its detailed description of human sacrifice—an ancient and very common ritual most humans don't like to be reminded of.

The text is also interesting in that it lists a great number of *yoginis, many of whom do not appear in other lists of those deities. See the quote on page 237.

KALIVILASA TANTRA

Besides the more or less usual topics dealt with in this work, which probably originates in eastern India, the Kalivilasa Tantra contains some interesting information not found elsewhere or in such explicit language. Though the work in general stresses the importance of sexuality as a means of Tantric *sadhana, chapter 10 quite clearly prohibits the use of *madya (wine) and also forbids sexual union with a partner married to someone else. It goes on in chapter 11, nevertheless, to make special allowance for this: Here the text states that such union is allowed provided both partners are initiates and that the man is able to retain the discharge of *semen. The scripture admonishes the devotee to give an upward motion to the semen energy in order to make it reach the brain and the higher *chakras.

SEE ALSO *EJACULATION, *OLI TECHNIQUES

KALI YUGA

(SKT., KALIYUGA; TIB., SNYIGS-MA'I-DUS, "DARK AGE")
According to Hindu tradition, the most degenerated of all cosmic ages. The Kali Yuga began in 3102 B.C.E. and has an expected duration of 432,000 years. Then, according to that tradition, the world will end in the coming dissolution by fire, known as mahapralaya. This Sanskrit term, from great (Skt., maha) and dissolution (Skt., pralaya), hints at the eventual total and final dissolution of the universe and all of its matter and inhabitants, even including all deities.

Interestingly enough, the starting point of this "dark age" coincides with the time in history when humanity invented writing.

KAMA

1. Sanskrit, "enjoyment," "sensual desire," and "longing." **2.** Name for the Indian god of love, lust, and desire; a cosmic force personified. The classic erotic textbook *Kama Sutra is named after this god.

See also *Gayatri Mantra, *Kamamarga, *Kama Salila, *Klim

KAMAKHYA

The physical aspect of the Great Goddess Mahamaya when prepared for sexual enjoyment. She is shown with a reddish-yellow body, standing on a *red *lotus, and with a garland in her hand. For steeds, she rides both a lion(ess) and a bull. The goddess is thought to dwell at the *Kamakhya Pitha.

KAMAKHYA PITHA

Famous and sacred site, near Gauhati in *Assam, comprising a cave and temple. The present-day foundations of the temple date from the sixteenth century, but the place has been sacred for many centuries longer. This temple is the most sacred of the 51 *pithas because it was here, according to Hindu mythology, that Sati's *yoni fell to Earth when she was *dismembered. The celebrated shrine's name refers to the goddess *Kamakhya, and it is the cave sanctuary that is revered as the menstruating yoni of the earth, the *Yonimandala. The temple of *Guheshvari in Nepal competes with this *pitha for the honor of harboring the divine essence of the goddess's yoni.

KAMAKHYA TANTRA

A text of 12 chapters that is mainly concerned with describing the glory of the *yoni and of the goddess *Kamakhya, as well as her famous *Kamakhya Pitha. A quote from the text can be found under the entry *Panchamakara.

KAMALA

This deity of the Hindu/Tantric pantheon is one of the many aspects of *Kali and appears in the list of Kali's 100 names. The term *kama embraces our concepts of desire, love, and eros, which makes Kamala the female personficiation of loving desire. Philip Rawson describes her most beautifully as "pure consciousness of self, bathed by the water and fulfilment . . . her whole body golden. She is enjoyer and enjoyed, the state of reconstituted unity" (*The Art of Tantra*, p. 133). The term also means *lotus, and Kamala, the

"beloved lover," is therefore sometimes identified with *Lakshmi, another lotus lady.

KAMALASILA

Indian-born adept Kamalasila (c. 710 c.e.) became famous during the council at the Samye Monastery (792–794 c.e.), where he was declared the winner, for the Indo-Tibetan Tantric teachings, in the debate against the Chinese Ch'an (Hwa shang) representatives.

Earlier, as has been shown in Miranda Shaw's *Passionate Enlightenment*, Kamalasila had received important initiations by an assembly of *yoginis and *dakinis under the patronage of *Mahasukhasiddi—a fact demonstrating that female teachers had a much stronger role in the development of Tibetan Tantra than is usually admitted.

See also *Chöd

KAMAMARGA

The "path of desire," one of several possible paths to illumination and liberation.

See also *Kama, *Kamala

KAMARUPA

1. As a goddess, Kamarupa (Skt., "She Whose Form Is Desire") is one of the 100 manifestations of *Chinnamasta. **2.** Reminiscent of this goddess, Kamarupa and Kamrup are the ancient names for *Assam.

KAMA SALILA

The "love juice" from a woman's *yoni, of which four different types are mentioned in the *Ananga Ranga and similar erotological texts. These types are based on, and ascribed to, the following four *female archetypes:

1. The *padmini woman's juice smells like a newly blossoming *lotus
2. The *chitrini's juice is hot and smells like *honey
3. The *shakhini's juice is very abundant and quite salty
4. The *hastini's juice tastes like elephant's tears in spring (see *Musk)

See also *Female Love Juices

KAMA SUTRA

(SKT., "APHORISMS OF LOVE")

A text of Indian sexual morals and techniques that can be compared to contemporary sex manuals. Written, or rather

KAMESHVARI. *Veneration of the goddess *Kameshvari; reconstruction of a partly destroyed image from a *sixty-four yogini temple at Bheraghat, Madhya Pradesh, India (c. twelfth century).*

compiled, by Vatsyayana (who lived during the third and fourth centuries C.E.) "in modesty and supreme reverence," the work combines concepts, knowledge, and wisdom of the Indian erotic arts from the time between 1000 B.C.E. and 400 C.E. First translated into English in 1883, 10 years after the *Ananga Ranga, it has become the most famous of all Indian erotic works.

SEE ALSO *ALGOLAGNIA, RICHARD *BURTON, *KOKA SHASTRA, *SHANKHINI NADI, AND THE QUOTATION ON PAGE 186

KAMESHVARI

As a manifestation of *Shakti in her specifically Tantric and lustful form, Kameshvari is one of the principal deities of *Tantra and is sometimes regarded as a manifestation of *Chinnamasta. A unique and beautiful statue of this goddess was erected in the twelfth-century *sixty-four *yogini* temple of Bheraghat (in Madhya Pradesh, India), where she is shown

with men and women performing active *yoni worship. Although the original statue was disfigured during the Muslim invasion of medieval India, the photograph here enables us to discern two worshippers below the large *yoni (representing *Adya Shakti) and musicians at left and right. Kameshvari is also a member of the eight *nayikas, personifications of "illicit love."

KAMI

The Japanese term for "deity" or "spirit," used in names such as *Amaterasu-o-mi-Kami (a goddess) or Kami-no-Michi, the original term for *Shinto.

KAMRUP   SEE *ASSAM, *KAMARUPA

K'AN

1. Chinese term for "water." **2.** One of the eight basic trigrams of the *I Ching, composed of two female *yin lines

29. K'an / The Abysmal (Water)

K'AN. *The trigram* *k'an, *symbolizing water.*

enclosing one *yang line. This is the mirror image of the trigram *li ("fire"). **3.** As one of the 64 hexagrams of the I Ching, k'an is composed of twice the trigram k'an.

The energy symbolized by k'an plays an important role in Taoist sexual techniques that aim at the *fusion of k'an and li and the resulting creation or concentration of life force. In this context k'an is often represented in the form of alchemical symbols such as the white tiger, the crescent moon, or the hare. Further symbolism of k'an includes the color black, the metal lead, and, among the physical organs, the kidneys.

SEE ALSO *CHI-CHI

KANDA
Sanskrit term for the subtle junction where the *nadis end.

KAN-LU
(CHIN., "GOLDEN NECTAR")
Chinese/Taoist term for the ambrosia that drips via the mouth into the body and helps achieve longevity or even immortality (Benjamin Walker, 1977, p. 242). The term refers to the "spillover" of *ching-ch'i from the *emerald pillow. The golden nectar can be recognized as a sweet and pleasurable taste on tongue and palate.

KANNON   SEE *KUAN-YIN

KANPATHA YOGIS
According to R. van Gulik, these yogis were the genuine snake charmers who roamed the countryside of India and sustained themselves by their snake and rope tricks, with juggling and palmistry. "Adepts of sexual mysticism" (p. 343), they found that people would pay for watching them exercise and study their rising and coiling cobras: an exercise that originally had been an aid in the raising of one's inner *kundalini, or *serpent energy.

KANZEON   SEE *KUAN-YIN

KAPALIKAS
(SKT., "SKULL MEN")
A Shaivite ascetic/yogic sect, the beliefs of which were strongly influenced by elements of *Shakta worship. The Kapalika's use of drugs, erotic stimulation, human *sacrifice, and graveyard meditation made them "heretic" outsiders to mainstream Indian religion. No literature is extant, but it is known that they lived among the ashes of the dead, wore jewelry of human bones, and drank their wine out of skull caps. J. N. Farquhar quotes Ramanuja (c. 1055–1137) as saying that the Kapalika meditates on himself as seated in the pudendum muliebre—that is, the *yoni. Generally speaking the Kapalikas, like the *Digambara, are part of the *Vamacara, or "way of the left hand." More specifically they constitute a subsect of the Tantric *Kula.

SEE ALSO *CANNABIS SATIVA

KARANA
Although normally a Sanskrit word meaning "cause" or "caused by," it is often used as a term designating the consecrated wine drunk during Tantric rituals. Such sacred wine, one of the five *makara, "is supposed to be the cause of knowledge" (Banerjee, p. 558).

KAREZZA
A sexual technique and spiritual observance propagated by the American physician Alice Bunker Stockham (d. 1912) and the occultist T. L. Harris (1823–1906). Dr. Stockham's 1896 book *Karezza* is subtitled *An Ethics of Marriage* and was meant to spiritually enhance the sex life of married couples. Both male and female practitioners charge each other with desire but refrain absolutely from *orgasm and/or *ejaculation, unless they want to conceive. This type of sexual union has also been named, by Dr. Stockham herself, *coitus sublimatus and is known among the Roman Catholic clergy as *amplexus reservatus. The actual techniques for this prolonged erotic play are similar to those used in *male continence and *imsak, but *karezza* also recommends intermissions of total quiescence with the *lingam erect in the *yoni. During this time the partners

exchange "spiritual fluids." Between two such *karezza* unions, one should allow several weeks to three or four months of sexual abstinence. Dr. Stockham was evidently acquainted with some of the Taoist texts, since she promised that her technique would result in youthfulness, prolongation of life, and increased vitality.

SEE ALSO *RETENTION OF SEMEN

KARGLING ZHIKHRO

A *terma of the sa-gTer (Tib., "earth-treasure") class that was discovered in the fourteenth century by *terton Karma Lingpa. It is a cycle of texts that represents an introduction to *Dzogchen, the culmination of *Vajrayana teachings.

Actually, Kar-gling zhi-khro is an abbreviation for the full title: *Zabchos zhi-khro dgongs-pa rang-grol* (Tib., "The Profound Teaching of Self-Liberation in the Primordial State of the Gentle and Fierce Deities"). It is the most complete of all the zhi-khro (synonym for *bardo) teachings and includes, among other texts, the justly famous yet often wrongly interpreted *Bardo Thödol and the lesser known but surely equally important text known as *Rig-pa ngo-sprod.

The Kargling Zhikhro, which has become widely disseminated, is particularly revered and transmitted among the *Nyingmapa and *Kagyudpa schools.

KARINI   SEE *HASTINI

KARMA KAGYUD

One of four major schools of the *Kagyudpa tradition, the Karma Kagyud itself comprises two branches known as Red Hat (Tib., *zhwa dmar*) and Black Hat (Tib., *zhwa nag*). The school's first monasteries, Karma gDan-sa in Kham (1147) and mTshur-phu (1189), were founded by Dusum Khyenpa, the first Gyalwa *Karmapa.

The lineage, which includes such great teachers as *Tilopa, *Marpa, and *Milarepa, has since then handed down the teachings of *mahamudra, and in the fourteenth century, Rangjung Dorje (third Gyalwa Karmapa) also introduced the *Dzogchen teachings to his students. Rangjung Dorje was also involved with the Orgyanpa school (*see* *Kagyudpa).

Apart from the Karmapa, the school knows more such reincarnations: the Shamarpa(s), Trungpa Tulku(s), Tai Situ(s), and Jamgon Kongtrul(s), several of which are still continued today. The school is now mainly active in Sikkim

(a monastery at Rumtek was founded in 1961 by the 16th Karmapa) and in the West. Another contemporary exponent of a Karma Kagyud subdivision (Surmang Kagyud) was the late Chogyam *Trungpa, one of the Trungpa Tulkus.

The school is also known by the alternative name of Karma Kamtsang (Tib., *ka-rma-kam-tshang*).

KARMA MUDRA

A Sanskrit/Tantric term indicating a gathering of men and women in "mutually rewarding activities"—that is, becoming intimate with each other.

KARMAPA

(TIB., *KARMA-PA*, "MAN OF KARMA")

Short version of the official title, Gyalwa Karmapa, for a lineage of continuous *reincarnations similar to those of the *Dalai Lama but within the *Karma Kagyud school. Again like the Dalai Lama, the Karmapa is regarded as an incarnation of Avalokiteshvara.

1.	Dusum Khyenpa	1110–1193
2.	Karma Pakshi	1203–1283
3.	Rangjung Dorje	1284–1339
4.	Rolpe Dorje	1340–1383
5.	Dezhin Shekpa	1384–1415
6.	Dongwa Donden	1416–1453
7.	Chodrak Gyatso	1454–1506
8.	Mikyo Dorje	1507–1554
9.	Wangchuk Dorje	1555–1603
10.	Choying Dorje	1604–1674
11.	Yeshe Dorje	1676–1702
12.	Changchub Dorje	1703–1732
13.	Dudul Dorje	1733–1797
14.	Thegchog Dorje	1798–1868
15.	Khakyab Dorje	1871–1922
16.	Rigpe Dorje	1923–1981
17.	Ogyen Trinley Dorje	(born 1985, enthroned 1992; also spelled Urgyen Thrinley Dorje)

KASHMIR

Like *Assam, *Bengal, and *Kerala, Kashmir was once one of the four major Tantric kingdoms. Today the country is divided between India and Pakistan and has quite a large Muslim population.

SEE *VIRA FOR A QUOTE FROM A KASHMIRI TEXT

KASSAPU

An interesting Sanskrit term that means both "saliva" and "sorcerer," indicating the ancient wisdom concerning the magical properties of *saliva and other bodily fluids.

SEE ALSO *JADE FLUID

KATHAVATTHU TANTRA

A Buddhist Tantra that originated in *Bengal but is preserved only in Chinese and Tibetan translations. Though Buddhist Tantra usually sees the female in a less exalted role than do the Hindu texts, this Tantra speaks mainly of the "female principle" and features all the usual sexual rituals associated with Indian *Tantra and/or *Shakta.

KAULA SEE *KULA

KAULAMARGA SEE *KULACARA

KAULAVALI NIRNAYA TANTRA

A text of 22 chapters that is attributed to the author/adept Jnanananda Paramahansa. This Tantra is very sexually oriented, is full of respect for women, and contains, among other things, of course, many rules and mores concerning social ethics. Furthermore, the text includes a strange condemnation of sexual union during the daytime and also speaks in detail of the *ekalinga and the *panchatattva.

Of the five *makara, it is written in chapter 4 that *maithuna alone will lead the devotee to her or his desired goal. This Tantra of the *Kula school allows, with a few exceptions, promiscuous sexual intercourse with married partners other than one's own, saying that "to the pure in heart everything is pure" (Banerjee, p. 217). Chapter 9 states that sexual union is a sin only for the foolish but that its joys will lead the wise to liberation.

The next chapter condemns several apparently often encountered features of social life ranging from rape and other violence to slander and waste of time. The text informs us about the status and treatment of women among the Kula: "Respect and consideration for women mark the precepts. All women are to be looked upon as manifestations of the Great Mother. An offending woman should not be beaten even with flowers. A woman of any age, even a girl, or even an uncouth woman should be bidden adieu after salutation" (Banerjee, p. 217).

The remaining chapters are mainly concerned with how to achieve and recognize the various magical/paranormal abilities called *siddhi.

KAULIKA SIDDHI SEE *KULA

KAULINI SEE *KULA

KAUMARI SEE *KUMARI

KERALA

An Indian province spread out along India's southwestern coastline. With *Bengal and *Kashmir, Kerala is a third region that was a stronghold of Tantric teachings and devotees.

KERALA SAMPRADAYA

A little-known Tantric sect originating in *Kerala. Although less influential than the *Kula or *Aghora, the sect spread in due time from Kerala across the whole of India.

KHADROMA SEE *DAKINI

KHADRO NYINGTHIG
(TIB., MKHA'-GRO SNYING-THIG)

Name for the transmission lineage of *Dzogchen teachings that goes back to *Padmasambhava. Generally, these teachings have been transmitted in the form of hidden *terma texts that have subsequently been discovered by certain *tertons. In the fourteenth century, this tradition was combined with the *Vima Nyingthig to form *Longchenpa's unified *Longchen Nyingthig.

KHAJURAHO

One of the famous and unique series of Indian temples that openly depict the erotic arts and practices of *Tantra in their many elegant and graceful stone sculptures. The village of Khajuraho in Madya Pradesh lies only about 80 kilometers away from Kalinjar, the town that was at the heart of central India's medieval Tantrism—a fact that helps to explain the prevalance of the erotic element in the art and architecture of the buildings.

The 85 original temples were built in a time span of 200 years, roughly during the period 950 to 1150, and of these original temples about 20 are still standing and are quite well preserved. In no way are all these temples affiliated with any particular one of India's many religious sects, and

KHAJURAHO. *Typical detail from a frieze on the wall of a *Khajuraho temple,
in which human sexual play is shown in its great variety.
Photograph courtesy of DMK Verlag, Nürnberg.*

one finds temples dedicated to Hindu deities such as *Shiva next to those that belong to the *Jaina. The temples built early during this period (950–1050) are those that most strongly feature the sensuous, erotic element and show, among others, scenes involving *orgylike group sex, sexual positions in which the help of attendants is needed, and even depiction of the preparation of *aphrodisiacs. The sculptures also illustrate sexual exercises and techniques such as *fellatio, *cunnilingus, and the *yogini chakra, and quite often the female partner plays the dominant role. With very few exceptions, such as the scenes with animals, all sculptural representations correspond closely to the *asanas and *bandhas that are described, shown, and taught in the erotic classics such as the *Ananga Ranga and the *Koka Shastra.

SEE ALSO *JAGAN NATH TEMPLE, *KONARAK

KHAPUSHPA SEE *MENSTRUAL FLUID

KHECHARI MUDRA

One of the *mudras/3, this is a yogic exercise/posture "which leads to spiritual attainment and enables a person to overcome disease and death" (Banerjee, p. 560). The khechari mudra is said to achieve this end by controlling the "celestial dew," known as *amrita and *ros, manufactured in the adept's brain.

SEE ALSO *VAJROLI MUDRA

KHLYSTI

A Slavic "heretical" Christian sect using sexual forces in its ritual, with man and woman representing or embodying, respectively, Jesus and the Holy Virgin, Mary, during their rites of collective intercourse. These rituals were a temporary departure from their usual abstinence and *chastity, in which the spiritually married partners would sleep in the same bed but never touch one another. During the rituals, the Khlysti used *dance, chanting, and flagellation to reach a state of ecstasy. The famous magician *Rasputin is said to have come from this background.

SEE ALSO *CARNIVAL, *STRI PUJA/1

KHUAI

Term for the energy released by the female partner during intercouse and especially during her orgasm. It is this vitalizing energy that certain male Taoists, Tantricas, and practitioners of *sexual magick try to absorb into their own system, sometimes purely for their own benefit.

SEE ALSO *FANG-CHUNG SHU, *GYNERGY, *YIN ESSENCE

KI

Japanese equivalent for the Chinese concept of *ch'i, one of the three Taoist vital energies.

KILILI

The goddess *Ishtar as symbol of the promiscuous and independent woman—the ancient idea of the *virgin—whose wanton behavior often inspires both excitement and a tremendous anxiety in those who desire her.

KIMALI

A term from the Melanesian Islands that indicates scratching, a form of *algolagnia, as an invitation to sexual union and as an expression of affection and passion during erotic play. As an invitation, it is done to a desired man by the interested woman. During a certain orgiastic rite, the *kamali kayasa,* the males would receive as many beatings and scratches as they could physically bear—this being done with fingernails, shells, or other sharp objects—but still be able to visit the huts of all their female "attackers." During sexual union, never performed in the *missionary position, each partner would mark the other's back with deep scratches, and the marks would proudly be displayed in the days to come. The anthropologist Bronislaw Malinowski further describes this custom in his important study *The Sexual Life of Savages.*

SEE ALSO *MITAKUKU, *RITUAL PROMISCUITY

KISS-MAERTH, OSCAR
(1914–1990)

Hungarian monk and activist Kiss-Maerth, a theorist who viewed humanity as cannibalistic primates, is mainly known as the auther of the controversial book *The Beginning Was the End.* Although his attempt to explain all the main features of human evolution by connecting evolution to the practice of *anthropophagy remains a doubtful one, his research had some interesting results. Kiss-Maerth established, through personal experimentation, that the eating of human and/or monkey *brain has a strong *aphrodisiac effect on those who do so. Ultimately, however, his research led to his becoming a vegetarian and to his belief that eating meat or brain also has disastrous side effects on human intelligence and behavior.

KLIM

A *Sanskrit seed syllable occurring in several *mantras and associated with the gods *Kama and Krishna.

KO HUNG
(284–364 C.E.)

Taoist scholar and physician who is known for his encyclopedic work, the *Nei P'ing. Ko Hung belongs to the religious/alchemical branch of Taoism called *Tao-chiao, and he attempted with his work to compile and describe all Taoist thought, practice, ritual procedures, and exercises known in his time.

Discussing health and sexual activity, Ko Hung makes this conclusion: "In sum, there is no benefit from taking all sorts of medicines and eating beef, mutton, and pork, if one does not know the arts of sexual intercourse." He also maintains, "Sexual intercourse may be compared with water and fire, either of which can slay man or bring him life, depending solely on his ability to deal with them" (quoted in Ware, p. 123).

Nonetheless, Ko Hung was also much influenced by Confucian thought and social rules. He therefore believed and taught that immortality could not be achieved solely by means of physical, sexual, and spiritual techniques but needed to be accompanied by the observance and practice of social virtues. He thus tried to combine Taoism with Confucian sociopolitical philosophy (*K'ung-tzu) and had a strong influence on the development of Taoist moral codes.

SEE ALSO *BEDROOM ARTS, *CH'I, *K'AN, *LI

KOKA SHASTRA

This is the popular name for an early medieval erotic textbook written by the twelfth-century Indian author Kokkoka, thus it's title, which translates as "the scripture (shastra) of Koka." The text's true and original name is Ratirahasya, a *Sanskrit word that translates as "secrets of Rati," *Rati being a name for the Indian goddess of love. The work composed by Kokkoka is the medieval equivalent of the third-century *Kama Sutra, and the author looks back with nostalgic reverence to that era. A comparison of these texts yields much information about the changes that took place in Indian society during those nine centuries.

SEE ALSO *POLYGAMY AND THE QUOTATION ON PAGE 92

KONARAK

Famous and beautiful Indian temple to the sun god Surya. Formerly known as the Black Pagoda, it was built between the eleventh and thirteenth centuries in the state of Orissa, on the bay of *Bengal. Similar to *Khajuraho, it features many erotic sculptures showing *apsarasas and other figures in sexo-yogic *asanas.

SEE ALSO *YOGINI CHAKRA

KONSEI MYOJIN

Japanese god similar to the European *Priapus.

KORRIGAN

A Celtic (Gaul/France) goddess associated with nature and especially water—for example, with springs in the vicinity of *dolmens and other *megaliths. It was said that in daytime she appeared as an old, wrinkled crone, but at night, at the height of her powers, she seemed a beautiful woman. Her worship involved *ritual prostitution.

KRIYA NISHPATTI

Term for "physical sexual congress" (Garrison, p. 235) as opposed to a merely abstract, symbolic, and visualized *maithuna. Literally, the *Sanskrit kriya means "deed."

KUAN-YIN

(CHIN., "CONTEMPLATING THE SOUND OF THE WORLD")
Originally the Chinese version of the male god Avalokiteshvara, Kuan-yin later evolved into the still-popular female goddess and *bodhisattva of mercy. Most often, she is seen as a very pious and proper female whose influence on the Chinese and Japanese collective psyche can be compared to that of the Christian Mary.

However, this same Kannon or Kwannon, as she is known in Japan, sometimes comes in a very different guise,

at least for certain schools and sects. A statue in the Kanshoji temple (at Tatebayashi, Japan) dating from the Edo period shows her with her skirt hitched up, displaying her *yoni very much in the manner of *Baubo or the *Sheela-na-gigs.

SEE ALSO *DAISEI SHOKUSHU

KUBJIKA TANTRA

This text of 17 chapters is of *Kula origin. However, the Kubjika *Tantra is also one of those scriptures that have given rise to the discussion about whether or not Tantra has been influenced by the import of certain techniques from Chinese *Taoism. Chapter 16 describes a certain mode of virgin worship that is stated to be derived from *Mahacina, the Indian name for ancient China.

Apart from this, the text describes *yoni mudra, as well as the worship of, and with, one's married partner; but generally this Tantra is especially focused on worship of, and meditation on, *virgin girls ranging in age from one to 16.

In chapter 7 great importance is attached to the Kula women, and the text states that such women of any age, including prostitutes, must be saluted. Girls who are 5 to 12 years old are regarded as *Kumari, and those between "ten and sixteen should be looked upon as a goddess" (Banerjee, p. 222).

Chapter 16 describes three specific and "effective means" of achieving rare success. In one, a girl of 16 should be worshipped by visual, focused meditation on every part of her body, while one repeats a *mantra without being influenced by passion.

Especially great is the merit of such ritual if the girl is menstruating and the goddess is visualized as residing in her *yoni (see also *Nyasa).

The second type of ritual has been described as follows: "Another very effective means is to worship one's own wife, who is initiated and drunk, looking upon her as a goddess. The husband should repeat mantras 108 times after touching her heart with his heart, her vagina with his penis and her face with his face" (Banerjee, p. 223). In the above-mentioned Mahacina mode of worship, a physical virgin, not yet menstruating and between the age of 1 and 16, is revered as a goddess. All girls have different names or titles indicating their age. A girl of 1, for example, is called Sandhya, and Annada is the name for a young woman of 16. The names for girls of various ages can be found under the entry *Kumari

KUAN-YIN. *Unique painting of *Kuan-yin by the twentieth-century *Shinto priest Kubo Morimaru.*

Puja; however, the reader should know that these names are not uniform throughout all texts. Comparing the names given here with those at *Kumari Puja and *Niruttara Tantra, the careful reader will detect a few variances.

SEE ALSO *MENSTRUAL FLUID, *MOON MAGIC

KULA OR KAULA

1. The most influential of the "left-hand," or *Vamacara, schools of *Tantra. **2.** Member of the Kula family, a particularly widespread Tantric group in which membership was/is gained either by birth or initiation. The Sanskrit *kula* translates as both "family" and "lineage."

The strong influence that the Kula have had on the general development of *Tantra can be judged from, among other things, the number of important Tantric scriptures that have grown out of this movement. The Kula had such a strong position and widespread following that they began to develop a terminology named after themselves from otherwise already well-known Indian/Tantric terms and con-

cepts: The *kundalini here becomes *kaulini*, liberation (Skt., *moksha*) is described as *kaulika siddhi*, *amrita becomes *kulamrita*, and *menstrual fluid is not simply *pushpa* or *rasa* anymore but is called *kulapushpa* or *kularasa*. The *panchatattva, which most Kula celebrate with wine and sexual union, is named *kuladravya*.

The infamous sects of the naked *Digambara and the skull-using *Kapalikas are, in fact, specialized subdivisions of *kulacara, "the way of the Kula."

SEE ALSO *KAULAVALI NIRNAYA TANTRA, *KUBJIKA TANTRA, *KULARNAVA TANTRA, *PARASURAMA-KALPA SUTRA, *YOGINI TANTRA

KULACARA

Like *kaulamarga*, this is a term for the system of spiritual, psychophysical Tantric exercises according to the *Kula teachings.

KULANGANAS   SEE *NAVAKANYA

KULA PUJA

1. General term for *puja, or ritual/worship, of the *Kula tradition. **2.** Sometimes the term is used to specifically indicate a *puja* of devotees belonging to the highest class of initiates, the *divya. In this sense *kula puja* is a synonym for the *divya chakra*.

KULARCANA

A type of *kula puja* mentioned in the *Niruttara Tantra that is quite unique in allowing women truly the same sexual freedom as that usually given to male devotees. The text states explicitly that "a woman has no fault in being united with a person other than her husband" (Banerjee, p. 258), a practice that was usually strictly prohibited in Indian society and even in some Tantric circles.

KULARNAVA TANTRA

An important and perhaps the foremost theoretical and philosophical *Tantra of the *Kula school. The text consists of two thousand verses in 17 chapters and was probably written before the year 1000. The text is set up as a series of questions by *Shakti that are answered by Shiva. The Tantra is much concerned with establishing proof that Kula teachings are the best, warns of false teachers, explains all its relevant terminology and concepts, and lays down its rules and regulations. It stipulates that Kula knowledge can be gained "by one who has pure mind, and whose senses are controlled." In chapter 2 we can read that the "Kula path is fraught with danger. In fact, it is more difficult than walking on a sword-edge, clinging to a tiger's neck and holding a serpent."

Though verses 107 through 112 explain the five *makaras in esoteric terms as symbolic and mental exercises, other chapters speak at least of drinking wine (*madya) in very real terms. In addition to describing the procedures for making wine and explaining the different types of it, the text prohibits *pashupana*, or "drinking like a beast," as it leads to an unsteady mind. Chapter 12 asks the devotee "to drink so long as the senses do not become unsteady nor the face deformed" (all quotes from Banerjee, pp. 226–27).

SEE OTHER QUOTATIONS ON PAGES 63 AND 70.

KULODAKA

The *Kula term for male secretions of love—that is, *semen.

KUMARI

(SKT., "VIRGIN")

1. Though scholars often introduce her as the virgin goddess of India, with that expression's overtones of chastity, it seems that Kumari is also very much concerned with the loss of physical *virginity. The *kumari puja, a religious festival dedicated to her, involves the ritual *defloration of selected virgins. Sometimes the term is written as *kaumari*. Kumari is also seen as the virgin aspect of *Durga and/or *Shakti. **2.** In Nepal, Kumari is the name and title of the *living goddess, a young girl who is selected at about the age of three and is kept in a kind of sacred imprisonment until the time of her first menstruation.

KUMARI PUJA

Chapter 15 of the *Kaulavali Tantra states that rituals performed without carrying out the kumari *puja ("virgin worship") are to be compared to a body without a soul. This ceremony or festival, which includes ritual *defloration of selected *virgins, was held, among other places, at Kanya Kumari, a temple whose name translates as "young virgin," at Cape Comorin in southern India.

Furthermore, the *Nila Tantra regards the *kumari puja* as indispensable to Tantric ritual. Chapter 15 of that text gives the different names indicating the age of the *Kumari girls:

Sandhya	1
* Sarasvati	2
Tridha-murti	3
* Kalika	4
Subhaga	5
Uma	6
Malini	7
Kubjika	8
Samvarsa	9
Aparajita	10
Rudrani	11
Bhairavi	12
Mahalaksmi	13
Pithanayika	14
Ksetraya	15
Tarini	16

Judging by the expression *veshya kumarika,* or "virgin whores"—a title given to women participating in *Kula rites—we may assume that such defloration, as happens so often, was accompanied in some way by more sexual rites

KUMARI PUJA. *During popular religious festivals in India, young *virgin girls are ritually worshipped by family members as representatives of the Goddess. Kangra, gouache on paper, c. eighteenth century.*

KUNDALINI. *Coiling upward from the base of the spine, the* kundalini *is represented here as twin serpents weaving themselves around an invisible *lingam. Ajit Mookerjee Collection, New Delhi.*

as well. There are also indications that sometimes girls were royally paid for the loss of their virginity: a practice that comes close to *ritual prostitution and makes them truly *veshya. The *kumari puja* is likewise known in Nepal, where *Kumari is also the title of the *living goddess.

KUMARI TANTRA

An anonymous but certainly *Kula-affiliated work (ninth to twelfth centuries) of nine chapters that is to be noted mainly because it is one of the few texts that openly speak of human *sacrifice, at the time still regarded as a sometimes required ritual.

The Kumari Tantra recommends, among other things, worship of the goddess in a cemetery, and describes the sacrifices to be made to the goddess *Kali. Such worship, to Kali and on a cremation ground, is said to be even better than rituals done in one of the famous and sacred *pithas. The scripture recommends the *blood of a human being—or of a sheep, buffalo, cat, or mouse—to be used in a Kali *puja, and it states quite explicitly that human sacrifice is the best. Another integral part of worship, according to this text, is the recital of *mantra while meditating before a naked Kula woman. The Tantra also states in the same chapters, 4 and 5, that sexual union is indispensable for any devotee, and in chapter 6 it specifies the nine types of women (*navakanya) who may or should take part in such rituals.

SEE ALSO *BHOGI, *KALIGHAT, *MAHAMAMSA

K'UN

1. One of the eight trigrams of the *I Ching, consisting of three *yin lines and signifying Earth, or pure yin. **2.** One of the I Ching's 64 hexagrams, consisting of twice the trigram *k'un.* **3.** In the context of *inner alchemy, *k'un* refers to the cauldron, as opposed to the furnace, or *ch'ien.*

KUNDALINI
(SKT., "THE COILED ONE")

Name for the famous "serpent power" of *Tantra, the spiritual energy that most often lies "coiled up" and unawakened in the *muladhara chakra* at the base of the spine. This force or energy (Skt., *Shakti) is seen as female in origin and is sometimes worshipped as a goddess: Kundalini Shakti.

Once awakened, the *kundalini* can be made to rise upward, along the major *nadi of the subtle body, toward union with the male, "heavenly" or cosmic forces present in the *sahasrara chakra.* It may be true, as Nik Douglas (*Tantra Yoga,* p. 53) believes, that the discovery of a "physical basis of the libido" by Wilhelm *Reich was merely his personal discovery of the *kundalini.*

In some instances, and in some people, the *kundalini* energy has been known to arise spontaneously, though this is for most people a question of diligent training and control. The arousal of the *kundalini* can, if one is not properly trained, experienced, or mentally stable, lead to undesirable side effects and may even lead, in the most extreme case, to an early *rebirth or *reincarnation of the practitioner.

SEE ALSO *SERPENT, *YONI MUDRA

KUNDODBHAVA

One of the many Sanskrit terms for *menstrual fluid, this one specifically for that of a married woman.

SEE ALSO *CHANDALI, *GOLODBHAVA, *JATAKUSUMA

K'UNG-TZU

(551–479 B.C.E.)

The man who has become known in the West as Confucius, the founder and main teacher of Confucianism. Confucianism is basically a traditional, social philosophy with a set of detailed rules concerning behavior, virtues, law, and order. This school of thought has strongly influenced Chinese society, politics, morals, and ethics and has often been in opposition to *Buddhism and *Taoism. Groups and individuals of these three "warring" schools have also made many attempts to combine these teachings into one system. One such example can be found in the efforts of author and alchemist *Ko Hung.

SEE ALSO *I CHING

K'UN-TAN

A nineteenth-century Taoist school, the members of which upheld ancient Chinese sexual practices of *ritual promiscuity. According to R. van Gulik, an Imperial Edict of 1839 described couples gathering "in the night, many people together in one room, and without the lamps burning. Then they have sexual intercourse in the dark" (van Gulik, p. 90).

KUNTHUS

A Greek goddess of fertility. Together with the *Sanskrit term *kunti, the name Kunthus is reflected in the presently used slang word *cunt*. The sacred origin of this term shows clearly that is was not intended to be a derogatory or vulgar word.

SEE ALSO *YONI TERMINOLOGY

KUNTI

An alternative Sanskrit term for *yoni; also the name of an Indian goddess.

SEE ALSO *KUNTHUS, *YONI TERMINOLOGY

KURMA   SEE *TORTOISE

KWANNON   SEE *KUAN-YIN

KWAN SAIHUNG

(B. 1920)

Contemporary Taoist master and the only member of the Zhengyi-Huashan sect outside of China. From the age of nine he was instructed in the ancient Taoist disciplines of *inner alchemy, the martial arts, herbalism, and medicine; years later, after having become a fully initiated adept, Kwan Saihung became involved in politics and served for a time as undersecretary to Premier Chou En-lai. In the mid-1960s Kwan Saihung left China to live in the United States. His life as disciple, initiate, and Taoist adept has been described in an interesting biography, *The Wandering Taoist,* by his student Deng Ming-Dao.

*He who spends his life without honoring the *lingam is verily unfortunate, sinful, and ill-fated.*

SHIVA PURANA

LABIAESTHETICS

The female labia minora—the small, inner lips of the vulva—are adorned and/or enlarged in some cultures.

Among the Hottentots, a woman was judged beautiful and powerful if she had large inner lips extending far beyond the outer ones. They were purposely elongated and were reported to have been very large indeed, so that early ethnologists called them the Hottentot apron. Often African

LABIAESTHETICS. *This contemporary woman is adorned with tattoos and multiple piercings, enhancing her natural beauty in the fashion of many tribal peoples. Photograph by Todd Friedman.*

tribes, such as the Urua of central Africa, also practiced such artificial enlargement of the inner genital lips.

An adornment similar to the male *ampallang* is known among the Turkhana peoples of Kenya. There the women enlarge their inner lips only slightly, but then make a number of holes in which they hang little metal rings and ornaments; the dangling ornaments then jingle as the women proudly walk through the village.

LABIA MAJORA SEE *YONI TOPOGRAPHY/3

LABIA MINORA SEE *YONI TOPOGRAPHY/4

LAKSHMI
(SKT., "FORTUNE")

The Indian goddess Lakshmi is a deity of happiness, luck, or fortune similar to the European goddess Fortuna. But Lakshmi also has a clearly discernible erotic element to her image and imagery. Not only is she the mother of *Kama, the god of love, but one of her major symbols is the *lotus, a well-known symbol of the *yoni. The myths of Lakshmi, like those of *Aphrodite/Venus, the Greek/Roman goddess of love, speak of her being born from ocean spray.

SEE ALSO *YONI TANTRA

LALANA SEE *NADI/IDA

LALITA SAHASRANAMA

The available translation of this work is based on a manuscript dating from 1785, one of the many works of the Indian initiate and scholar Bhaskararaya (eighteenth century). The manuscript is, in fact, a late edition with commentaries of a text that is part of the much earlier Brahmanda Purana of approximately the eleventh century.

The text is dedicated to the goddess Lalita and consists mainly of listing and explaining the goddess's one thousand names and epithets, a textual procedure often chosen in works of *Tantra and *Shakta. Such a "name," consisting of one or more Sanskrit words, can be very revealing as to the nature and quality of the goddess. They range from "All-pervading," "Multiform," and "Supreme Goddess" to such poetic and descriptive phrases as "the moonlight that gladdens the flowers" or "her breasts are the fruit growing on the creeperlike hair that springs from her deep navel."

LAMDRE
(TIB., LAM-'BRAS, "THE PATH AS GOAL," "THE PATH INCLUDING ITS RESULT")

The Lamdre teachings, mainly transmitted by the *Sakyapa, are based on the original Tantric teachings of the *Mahasiddha *Virupa. From him, via Brogmi (992–1077) and the continuing lineage of Sakya masters, the teachings developed during the fourteenth and fifteenth centuries into two traditions, exoteric and esoteric—a division that may be compared to the *Outer and *Inner Tantras of the *Nyingmapa. The exoteric tradition, known as Lamdre Tshogshed (Tib., Lam-'bras 'tshogbshad), is based on the "Three Visions" part of Virupa's *Vajragatha. This part of the Lamdre transmission is available in an English translation of a sixteenth-century text by Ngorchen Konchog Lhundrub: The Beautiful Ornament of the Three Visions.

The esoteric teachings, known as Lambre Lobshed (Tib., Lam-'bras sLob-bshad) and traditionally taught to only a few, are based on the "Three Tantras" of the Vajragatha. It is this series of teachings that contain the Saskya equivalent to *Dzogchen and *Mahamudra practice. These Lobshed teachings have been taught and committed to writing by the well-known Jamyang Khyentse Wangchug (sixteenth century), Mangtho Ludrub Gyatso (sixteenth century), and Jamyang Loter Wangpo (1847–1914). The three Tantras of this division are known, within the Sakya/Lamdre tradition, as:

Tantra of the Cause	the All-Base Mind
Tantra of the Path	the Body Method
Tantra of the Result	the Great Seal (Skt., mahamudra)

Contemporary Sakya publications such as the Beautiful Ornament of the Three Visions (1991) refrain from committing these teachings to print.

LAMIA

Basque name for female spirits or deities who appear as beautiful human women, yet have the feet of a bird—sometimes a duck. Living in caves, or at rivers and small lakes, the lamia are somewhat comparable to the Greek *nymphs. In another sense they seem more like witches, demanding offerings and gifts from the local people. In exchange, they will occasionally help in the building of bridges or provide someone with riches. They are also known to enter love relationships with young men who remain ignorant of the lamia's nonhuman nature. If someone does discover a lamia's identity, he is doomed to die. Sometimes the lamia have been known to kidnap men of their choice and keep them imprisoned for the purpose of sexual union and for creating offspring. Stories surrounding the lamia tell of them living to the age of more than 1,000.

Similar figures, with the same name, are known from northern Africa, where they are seen as *succubi.

LAO-TZU
(C. 480–390 B.C.E.) (CHIN., "OLD MASTER")

Popular name and title for the Chinese sage and former keeper of the archives at the court of Chou. His real name was Li Erh, and in later life he was known as Lao-tan. Lao-tzu is often regarded as the founder of *Tao-chiao (religious *Taoism), although he himself would never have considered this to be one of his functions. After he left the court, mainly because of quarrels with the Confucian followers of *K'ung-tzu, he wrote his short yet poignant Tao-te Ching, one of the basic texts of Taoism.

LASYA

A Tibetan deity who is numbered among the eight *boddhisattva dakinis (see there for details).

LATA ASANA

The "creeper exercise." A specific exercise in which the female adept embraces her partner in a manner similar to a creeper plant in the act of enfolding a tree.

See also *Asana

LEELA
(SKT., "PLAY," "JOY")

A term indicating "play" in the sense of an activity free from planning and from goal orientation. It also refers to the play and joy inherent in erotic activity and pleasure.

LH

Common abbreviation for the luteinizing hormone involved in the *menstrual/ovarian cycle. This hormone stimulates the formation of the *corpus luteum. LH is produced in the *pituitary gland.

LI

1. Chinese term meaning "fire." **2.** One of the eight basic trigrams of the *I Ching, composed of two male *yang lines enclosing one *yin line. This is the mirror image of the trigram *k'an ("water"). **3.** One of the 64 hexagrams of the I Ching and composed of twice the trigram li.

The energy symbolized by li plays an important role in Taoist sexual techniques that aim at the *fusion of k'an and li and the resulting creation and concentration of life force. In this context li is often represented in the form of alchemical symbols such as the green dragon, the sun, and the

30. *Li / The Clinging, Fire*

Lɪ. *The trigram *li, symbolizing fire.*

crow. Further symbolism of k'an includes the color *red, the metal mercury, and, among the physical organs, the heart.

See also *Chi-chi

LIBER   See *Libera

LIBERA

A goddess of wine and lover/partner to the male god Liber, a Roman approximation of *Dionysus.

LIBERALIA

Roman *fertility festivals in honor of the god Liber (a name for *Bacchus) and the goddess *Libera that were held annually in March. Huge phallic images were carried through the cities and displayed in the countryside, where people enjoyed all the possibilities of *ritual promiscuity.

LICORICE

Since it was discovered that licorice root contains large amounts of the female hormone *estrogen, we can better understand why Egyptian pharaohs drank *mai sus*, a drink made from the sap of fresh licorice roots; why people in India drank licorice tea with *honey; and why the Chinese chewed licorice root for strength and vigor.

See also *Sarsaparilla

LIGHT

Little is known precisely about erotic, sexual responses to light and color, but there are snippets of information that can serve as pieces of this unsolved puzzle and may "throw some light" on these matters. Tantric texts claim that *violet or

LATA ASANA. *Practitioners enfolding each other in the* *lata asana; *eleventh-century stone sculpture from* *Khajuraho, Madhya Pradesh, India. Photograph courtesy of Nik Douglas.*

ultraviolet is the color of female sexual energy. For this reason the wavelength of violet light is thought to be beneficial and stimulating for the female genitals, and therefore such light should be included in the arrangements for a ritual union.

Though the *pineal gland in humans is no longer a real "eye," it does have connections with both sexuality and light reception. It may be this gland that responds subtly to the shades of light and color, translating them biochemically into sexual response.

SEE ALSO *GINSENG

LILAC

According to the sixteenth-century herbalist Gerard, the lilac's scent is oppressively sweet, "troubling the head in a strange manner and exciting the sexual instincts" (quoted in Wedeck). To make this *aphrodisiac lilac oil, the sweet-scented white or purple flowers of the shrub *Syringa vulgaris* are used. Lilac oil contains *indole.

LILITH

The figure of Lilith is a complex one; her image differs from culture to culture, becoming more demoniac as time goes on and patriarchal values begin to become dominant.

In ancient Sumer, she was regarded as the "left hand" of the Great Goddess *Inanna and as her helper in bringing the men to the goddess's temples, where they were to worship her by participating in "Tantric" rites with the temple women. As a result of this role, Lilith became known as a seducer of men and a harlot.

Among the Semitic-speaking peoples of Mesopotamia, she was at first a figure similar to Lil, a Sumerian goddess of destructive winds and storms. When Hebrew/Semitic morals became dominant in the Near East, she was equated and merged with Lamashtu, a female *demon known in Syria as a killer of children, and so acquired her characterization as a winged demon of the night (in the Talmud), as a dangerous vampire and *succubus (in the *Zohar), as mother of the *incubi, and as a screeching night owl (in the *Bible).

Other legends show her to be the magically beautiful first woman to share the original Paradise with Adam, in which she is seen as a woman "made by God" in a manner similar to the Genesis story of how God created the first man. Here, then, she is humanity's first woman, an independent and free *virgin who would not submit to Adam's attempts at sexual domination. In the later biblical version of the story of the first man and the first woman, she was replaced by a less independent and less equal Eve, a woman not "made" from the earth but from a rib of the man Adam. It is said that Lilith is but one of 20 names by which that first woman was known, and each name is supposed to contain a "secret of sexual mysticism" (Barbara Walker, 1983, p. 142).

These "secrets" most likely represent the erotic teachings and sexual techniques that were taught to initiates and worshippers in the temples of *Inanna, *Ishtar, and *Astarte—teachings and practices that threatened the new patriarchal leaders and their attempts to make woman into a dependent, monogamous servant of their households.

"There is no doubt," says Ean Begg, that the "Queen of Sheba in the cabbala, the Zohar and Arabic legends" is iden-tical with the Near Eastern goddess Lilith, who "is also associated with the concubine of *Abraham, *Hagar 'the Egyptian,' whose son Ishmael, having been begotten on the Black Stone of the *Ka'bah, became the ancestor of the Arab peoples" (p. 38). In the Hebrew mysticism of the cabalah, Lilith is associated with the lunar position on the Qliphotic Tree, the "world of shells" that contains the "negative" and dark energies.

SEE ALSO *MISSIONARY POSITION

LILY

Next to the *lotus, this is the flower most often associated with the *yoni, and it was especially popular in Middle Eastern and Mediterranean cultures. Its symbolism, however, is quite ambivalent, and aside from yoni, love, and passion it may signify—in other instances—the yoni, or woman, in the aspect of the virgin. Specific deities connected with the lily are *Aphrodite, *Lilith, Eostre, and Juno.

SEE ALSO *PADMINI

LING AND/OR LING-CHIH

Often translated as "mushroom of immortality," this is not always a reference to the Chinese psychoactive mushroom *ling-chih* but has also become a Chinese/Taoist term for "the transcendental" in general. As is so often the case, the idea of immortality is associated with sexual symbolism: *ling* is used as a secret code for the *lingam, and in Taoist art *ling-chih* is often a symbol of the female *yin energy.

LINGAM

Lingam, which is a *Sanskrit term of reverence for the statues and images of the god *Shiva's genital organ, is also used as a technical term for the male phallus. The thousands of lingams one finds throughout India and Nepal, on almost every street corner and in every village square, are worshipped even today as sacred symbols of Shiva, most especially the 12 *jyotirlinga. People kiss and touch the statues, which are generally sculpted from stone; they offer rice, flowers, or fruit to them and will often color them with red ocher. Sometimes a lingam is represented together with its female equivalent, the *yoni, and such an image then is called *yonilinga. Throughout this encyclopedia we have, with a few exceptions, as in the discussion of *phallic worship, referred to the male organ of pleasure and generation by this Indian term. See *Lingam Terminology for other

words that can be used instead of *penis* or *phallus*.

SEE ALSO *AMARNATHA CAVE, *EKALINGA, *LINGAM TOPOGRAPHY, *MEGALITHS, *OBELISK, *SHIVALINGA

LINGAM TERMINOLOGY

For an introduction to the following list of terms, *see* *Genital Terminology.

Ambassador (Chinese)
Arrow of Love (Tantric)
Athanor (Latin, alchemy)
Bull (Tantric, sometimes used for testicles)
Crimson Bird (Chinese)
Dart (Arabic)
Diamond Scepter (Sanskrit, *vajra*)
Discoverer (Arabic, *el mokcheuf*)
Flute (Chinese [*see* *Fellatio])
* *Guhya* (Nepali)
* *Il Santo Membro* (Italian [*see* *Carnival])
Jade Flute (Chinese)
Jade Peak (Chinese)
Jade Scepter (Chinese)
Jade Stem (Chinese, *yu-heng*)
Key of Desire (Persian)
* *Ling* (Chinese)
Magic Wand (Western esoteric schools)

* *Mehana* (Sanskrit)
Membrum virile (Latin)
Mushroom of Immortality (Chinese, *ling*)
Phallus (Phoenician, Greek)
Plough (Tantric)
Rod (Wand) (Sanskrit, *danda*)
Searcher (Arabic, *el fattache*)
Spear (Sanskrit, *shula*)
Tortoise (Chinese)
Wand (Western esoteric schools)
Yang Peak (Chinese)

SEE ALSO *BANALINGA, *EKALINGA, JYOTIRLINGA, *SHIVALINGA

LINGAM TOPOGRAPHY

From an extended biological/medical and sexological point of view, we can arrive at the following picture of the male genital/reproductive system. In order to make visible the many similarities and homologues between female and male genitals, the numbers used here are based on those used in the entry *Yoni Topography (p. 259). They also correspond to the numbers used in the illustrations on p. 261.

1. PUBIS Latin name for the patch of hair that covers the mons marsianus and often parts of the scrotum; the area also contains *scent glands.

1. **Pubis**

2. **Mons marsianus**

3. **Scrotum (scrotal sac)**

4. **Penile skin**

5. **Foreskin**

6. **Lowndes crown**

7. **Glans penis**

8. **—**

9. **Penile shaft**

10. **—**

11. **Clitoris (corpus cavernosum)**

12. **Cowper's glands**

13. **Urethra**

14. **P-spot**

15. **Prostatic glands (prostate)**

16. **—**

17. **—**

18. **—**

19. **Spermatic duct (vas deferens, ductus deferens)**

20. **Testes**

21. **Seminal vesicles**

22. **Epididymis**

23. **—**

24. **Perineum**

25. **Perineal muscles**

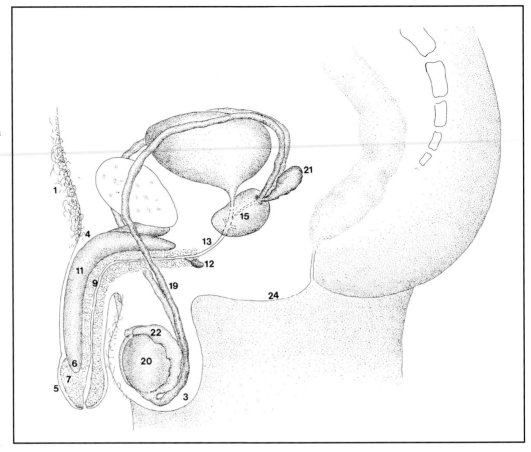

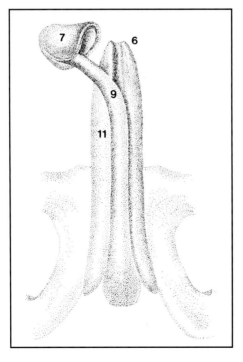

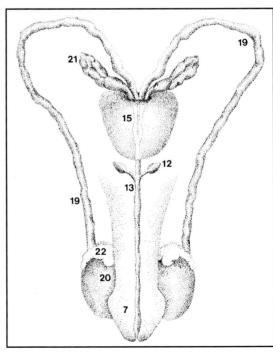

LINGAM TOPOGRAPHY. *Illustrations by Christina Camphausen.*

2. Mons marsianus The male, too, has a cushion of fatty tissue for the protection of his pelvic bone, although this is rarely mentioned or recognized. Consequently, as we have done here, it should be named after the god Mars, as the female equivalent (mons veneris) has been named after the goddess *Venus.

3. Scrotum (scrotal sac) An external saclike fold of tissue and skin that contains the two testes, the epididymes, and the beginnings of the spermatic ducts.

4. Penile skin The skin covering the lingam develops, at its end, into the foreskin, just as the female labia minora end in the clitoral hood.

5. Foreskin Comparable with the female's clitoral hood, this part of the penile skin surrounding the lingam covers and protects the glans penis, if *circumcision has not taken place. This is also one of the places where scent glands are located.

6. Lowndes crown Tucked away tightly beneath the glans penis—and therefore invisible—is the hitherto unrecognized "crown" of the male clitoris (11), named after Josephine *Lowndes-Sevely in 1987. This, rather than the glans penis, is the true homologue for the female crown, which up to now has been known as the glans clitoris.

7. Glans penis The highly sensitive tip of the penile shaft, which contains a large number of nerve endings and is instrumental in male orgasmic excitation. Similar to the woman's glans, it includes the meatus, the only external opening in the male genital system, serving to discharge *semen as well as urine.

8. No recognized male equivalent to the female vestibule.

9. Penile shaft Most of the lingam consists of a spongy and erectile tissue—the *corpus cavernosum, or male clitoris—loosely covered with skin. This shaft, which together with the glans penis makes up the outer, visible phallus, is the equivalent of the female vagina. It also contains the urethra, together with several nerves, veins, and arteries.

10. No recognized male equivalent to the female hymen.

11. Clitoris (previously called "corpus cavernosum") Whereas most anatomists and psychoanalysts of the past have regarded the female clitoris as a small, "atrophied" penis, the latest research and theory propose that the males of our species also possess a cli-

toris, very similar to the female one. In her book *Eve's Secrets*, Josephine Lowndes-Sevely convincingly argues that the male, erectile corpus cavernosum constitutes an obvious equivalent to the clitoris. Both "organs" are composed of erectile tissue that becomes engorged with blood in a sexually aroused state, and both contain the meatus of the urethra.

12. Cowper's glands Two tiny glands at the root of the penile shaft. Before the *ejaculation of semen, they produce an alkaline secretion—a clear and colorless liquid—in order to neutralize any acidic remains of urine in the urethra.

13. Urethra In both sexes this tube carries urine from the bladder toward its external opening, the meatus. In the male, it is joined in the *prostatic glands by the two spermatic ducts, and from there it serves also to transport semen on its way out of the body.

14. P-spot There is no "officially" recognized equivalent to the female *G-spot. Some men, however, report a similar internal pressure point—probably the prostatic glands—that can activate a specific type of *orgasm or orgasmic sensations when stimulated via the rectum, or by strong pressure on the *perineum.

15. Prostatic glands (prostate) A collection of glands surrounding the junction of the spermatic ducts with the urethra. The prostatic glands are important in male ejaculation and also constitute what we have tentatively called the P-spot. For more detail *see* the main entry *Prostatic Glands.

16. No recognized male equivalent to the female os.

17. No recognized male equivalent to the female cervix.

18. No recognized male equivalent to the female uterus.

19. Spermatic duct (vas deferens, ductus deferens) From each of the testes' epididymes a duct approximately 40 centimeters long runs toward the seminal vesicles and the prostatic glands. The two ducts then open into and join the urethra.

20. Testes Tiny tubules in the two egg-shaped testes produce the male's sperm cells—each containing 23 chromosomes along with enzymes, trace minerals, *prostaglandins, and ions—which are then moved into the epididymes. Aside from sperm, the testes also produce *androgens, male *sex hormones.

21. Seminal vesicles Two little sacs that collect sperm after its passage through the spermatic duct. Here the sperm cells are nourished with fructose sugar in a sticky yellowish substance that thickens the seminal fluid and constitutes almost 60 percent of the semen, compared with less than 2 percent of actual sperm cells.

22. EPIDIDYMES   Attached to the testicles, these are storage places for the newly made sperm cells, and it is here that they continue to grow and mature before being called upon when ejaculation is imminent.

23. No recognized equivalent to the female perineal sponge.

24. PERINEUM   Strictly speaking the perineum, a point midway between lingam and rectum, may not be considered to be a part of the genital system in either male or female. Nevertheless, for all practical purposes—that is, acknowledging the sense of touch and the possible technique involving the perineal muscles—it is closely involved, and its importance should not be overlooked. *See* the main entry *Perineum.

25. PERINEAL MUSCLES   Though many men may not be aware of it, there is a system of muscles equivalent to the female ones (*see* *Yoni Topography/25) discussed under *Pelvic Floor Potential. For the man, these muscles are mainly used as an aid in the *retention of semen, in techniques such as *intrajaculation, and in the *vajroli mudra*. Mantak Chia and Michael Winn's *Taoist Secrets of Love: Cultivating Male Sexual Energy* (1984) is one of the few books that deal with the use and exercise of these muscles.

LIPS

Similar to the nipples of the *breasts and to the *yoni/*lingam, the lips not only are one of the major erotogenic zones (*marmas*) but constitute an important point of contact for an alchemical exchange of liquids and subtle essences. The mouth and lips, in Taoist sexual practice, are regarded as one of the three locations from which the *medicine of the three peaks originates.

FOR SPECIFIC INFORMATION, SEE ALSO *JADE FOUNTAIN, *RED LOTUS PEAK, *SALIVA, *SCENT GLANDS, *SHANKHINI NADI

LIQUID RUBY   SEE *MENSTRUAL FLUID

LIQUOR VITAE

Latin/alchemical term meaning "fluid of life." It is used for the wet, physical, biochemical dimension of *semen as opposed to the subtle, rather electromagnetic constituent known as *aura seminalis.

LI SHAO-CHÜN

(D. 133)

Most famous of the *fang-shih, Li Shao-chün was a Taoist adept and proficient alchemist. He declared the attainment of immortality to be the major objective of *inner alchemy and advocated the use of all possible means to reach this goal.

LIVING GODDESS

Up to the present time Nepal has known the tradition of the "living goddess," and a young girl dedicated in this way can be seen, but not spoken to, by anyone who travels to Kathmandu and visits her residence, a beautiful three-story building at Basantpur in the center of the city. This tradition of the *Kumari, or "virgin goddess," as the living goddess is called, dates from the thirteenth century but was intensified when the first of these sacred *virgins was installed by King Jaya Prakash Malla as royal Kumari in Kathmandu. Kumari worship was continued when the Malla kings were conquered by the now-ruling Gurkha dynasty, and it is practiced by both Hindu and Buddhist followers whose religions have generally blended into the unique pantheon of Nepali beliefs.

The royal Kumari is thought to be the living embodiment of the goddess *Taleju. This is signified, apart from the general tradition and belief, by the fact that the Kumari is seated on a throne bearing the *sri yantra, the sacred diagram that is seen in Nepal as a symbol of Taleju.

LONGCHEN NYINGTHIG

A work by *Longchenpa in which the author combined two separate lineages of *Dzogchen teachings, *Khadro Nyingthig and *Vima Nyingthig, into one unified system, adding his own valuable comments. A condensation of the preliminary practices contained in this text, the Longchen Nyingthig Ngön-dro (Tib., *Klong-chen sNying-Thig sngon-'gro*) by *Jigme Lingpa, is an important liturgical text that forms the basis for the introductory meditations of Dzogchen. The preliminary practices, entitled *The Excellent Path of Omniscience* (Tib., *rnam-mykhyen-lam-bzang*) are available in English as *The Dzogchen Innermost Essence Preliminary Practice*.

LONGCHENPA

(TIB., *KLONG-CHEN RAB-'BYAMS-PA*, 1308–1363/64); (OTHER SPELLINGS: *LONGCHEN RABJAMPA, LONGCHEN RAB-JAM, KLONG CHEN-PA*)

A fourteenth-century *Nyingmapa master of special importance in the transmission and development of *Dzogchen. It was he who combined the teachings of the *Vima Nyingthig lineage with those of the *Khadro Nyingthig, thus creating a unified system of teachings that is known as the *Longchen Nyingthig.

Longchenpa is credited with more than 250 works, as author and compiler, among them the famous *Seven Treasures and the Kun-byed rGyal-po (Tib., "The King Who Creates Everything"), the latter belonging to the Mind Class (Tib., *sems-de*) of the Atiyoga (Dzogchen) *Inner Tantras. During his stay in Bhutan (Tib., *Mon*), Longchenpa fathered a daughter and a son; the latter, Trungpa Odzer (1356–1409?), also became a holder of the Nyingthig lineage.

LOTOPHAGI

(GREEK, "LOTUS EATERS")

Considering the symbolic association of the *lotus with the *yoni, the people described as lotophagi in Homer's famous *Odyssey* look more like members of a Tantric sect than strange dietarians. When the Greek myth of Odysseus tells of lotophagi who find "sweet forgetfulness" by eating the "sweet lotus fruit," we must wonder whether or not these connoisseurs of northwest Africa really digested the plant itself or merely "ate" the sweet fruit it symbolizes.

LOTUS

In India the lotus, a plant of the water lily family, is a symbol representing transformation and unfoldment as well as purity and fertility. The *Sanskrit term *padma* ("lotus") not only is a symbolic name for the *chakras but also serves as an alternative name for the goddess *Lakshmi and is quite often used as a secret code for the *yoni. Deities specifically connected with lotus symbolism are Amrita, Brahmani, *Kamakhya, and *Kamala.

The lotus flower was held equally sacred in Egypt, Persia, and Japan, although often with varying symbolic meaning. Oil of lotus—available in pure form among the essential oils used in aromatherapy—has also earned a reputation as an irresistible *aphrodisiac.

SEE ALSO *LOTOPHAGI

LOTUS NECTAR

Tantric phrase for the sweet-tasting *female love juices of the *yoni when the woman is sexually aroused.

LOWNDES-SEVELY, JOSEPHINE

An American medical researcher and psychologist who in 1987 published her interesting findings about the "Lowndes crowns," the male clitoris, and female *ejaculation in the book *Eve's Secrets*. Her modern theory of male and female homologues in urogenital anatomy is not yet a generally accepted fact, but it has been incorporated in this encyclopedia's description of male and female sexual anatomy. In the entries here on *yoni topography and *lingam topography, the idea of homologues has been carried even further to include nearly all parts of the two systems.

SEE ALSO *FEMALE LOVE JUICES, *PROSTATIC GLANDS

LSD

A psychoactive agent (lysergic acid diethylamide-25) discovered about 1940 by Albert Hoffman (b. 1906). In nature, the active substance occurs in ergot, a dark violet parasitic fungus that can often be found on rye, some of whose *alkaloids have proved useful in inducing childbirth.

Although proved to be nonaddictive, the drug is illegal in most countries of the world. Robert Anton Wilson writes that LSD is the "most potent psychoactive drug synthesized to date" (1988, p. 173). In the hands of an experienced user, and in the right setting, LSD is probaby the most powerful and rewarding *aphrodisiac and a tool for deconditioning and reprogramming of earlier, undesired *sexual imprinting. The novice, however, will have difficulties in adjusting to the increased sensitivity of her or his nervous system and the resulting overload of sensory input and brain activity. LSD has been extensively researched and publicized by Timothy Leary, whose *Politics of Ecstasy* still remains the classic work on this drug's effects on the individual and society.

A similar drug, but one less demanding on body and mind and less unpredictable, is the more recently developed *MDMA, or *ecstasy.

LUIPA

(C. 800 C.E.)

Also named "The Fish-gut Eater," the poor Luipa (sometimes spelled Luyipa) was one of the 84 *Mahasiddhas and probably a native of *Uddiyana. As a student of the Mahasiddha Savaripa (ninth century), he received initiation into the Chakrasamvara Tantra and became known as "Master of Secrets" (Skt., *guhyapati*).

LUNG-HU
(CHIN., "DRAGON AND TIGER")

A Taoist symbol for the merging of *yin and *yang energies and the *fusion of *k'an* and *li*.

LUTEUM   SEE *PROGESTERONE

Wine is the Goddess
Herself in liquid form, the Mother of
enjoyment and liberation.

MAHANIRVANA TANTRA

MACHIG LAPDRON
(1055–1145)

Machig Lapdron left her hometown La-phyi in Tsang, Tibet, after her scandalous cohabitation with Lama Thod-pa Bhadra (with whom she had one daughter and two sons) at Grwa-thang monastery. Her most important teacher was to be Phadampa Sangye (d. 1117), founder of the *Chöd tradition, who taught her his specific manner of attaining *mahamudra. At some point he told her to "go to the charnel grounds and to the mountains," reports *The Encyclopedia of Eastern Philosophy and Religion*, to "leave studying behind," and to "become a wandering *yogini" (p. 75). She

followed his advice, left her family, and went to live in caves and among the outcasts of society.

Machig Lapdron later formed a specific female branch of Chöd, and her teachings are still alive today. Together with *Niguma and *Yeshe Tsogyal, she is one of the few women who influenced the development of Tibetan *Vajrayana deeply and through whom several of the more ancient shamanic practices have passed into some of the Tibetan schools. She is generally believed to be an incarnation of Yeshe Tsogyal, and legend has it that she received direct attention and initiation from the goddess *Tara and others.

One of her more recent lineage holders was A-Yu Khadro (whose amazing life spanned the years 1837 to 1952!), who lived and taught in both Tibet and Nepal, and whose biography can be found in Tsultrim Allione's *Women of Wisdom*. Today this tradition is represented in the West by Namkhai Norbu (*see* *Bön).

Her name, Machig Lapdron, may also be seen spelled as Machig Lapdronme, Maji Lab Dran, and Machik Labdron.

MADANAHATRA

An Indian term for the clitoris.

MACHIG LAPDRON. *Contemporary rendering of a*
*traditional image of *Machig Lapdron.*
Illustration by Nigel Wellings.

MADHYAMA VAMACARA   SEE *VAMACARA

MADYA

The Sanskrit term for wine, or similar alcoholic drinks, as one of the five *makara*. People in the contemporary Western world are so used to wine made from grapes that we often assume this to be the "normal" state of affairs. In ancient India, however, other types of wine were common. According to the Nihs'vasa Tattva Samhita, for example, wine made of molasses and honey was regarded as superior to that made from fruit. In another sacred scripture, the *Parasurama-kalpa Sutra, possible types of wine are described as "that which causes joy, pleasant to look at, fragrant, light, i.e., that which does not cause illness, obtained from trees like palm, coconut, produced from molasses, distilled from rice, obtained from the bark of trees" and/or "produced from flowers" (quoted in Banerjee, p. 283).

According to general Tantric tradition, whatever wine is used in a ritual context must first be consecrated and dedicated to the deity. Even then the practitioner must say an appropriate *mantra before actually drinking the beverage. Such a mantra, prescribed for the *Vamacara devotees, is given in the *Parananda Sutra: "I take this holy nectar which is an antidote for the never-ending wheel of time; it is a means of cutting away the snares by which humans are bound to their animal nature." The making and drinking of wine as part of Tantric worship is discussed in the *Kularnava Tantra, which warns against overindulgence yet simultaneously prescribes the use of this alcoholic beverage in quite strong doses.

What *wine was to the Tantrics and ancient Greeks, beer was to cultures of Sumer, Babylon, and Syria. On a great many friezes and cylinder seals from this region, one finds depictions of ritual sexuality accompanied by the drinking of beer by one or both of the partners, often right during coitus.

SEE ALSO *KARANA, *KUBJIKA TANTRA, *MAHACINACARA-SARA TANTRA

MAEBH   SEE *MAEVE

MAENADS

Name for the members of an ecstatic cult centering on the god *Dionysus. The maenads represent the darkest facet of the female energy, in which woman is not a creatix but an

Madya. *Varunani or Varuni,*
the goddess of wine (Skt., madhya).
Photograph by Peter Keilhauer.

agent of death and destruction. In memory of their god, who himself was dismembered by the Titans, the maenads' mystery celebrations included the *sacrifice of a bull, or sometimes perhaps a human child or a man, who was shredded to pieces by the frenzied maenads' bare hands.

During their celebrations the maenads would also roam the country, drug-crazed and sexually excited, and were sometimes known to assault and kill men they encountered. The myths surrounding the singer Orpheus, after whom the *Orphic mysteries have been named, tell of his death at the hands of the female maenads, who literally tore him to pieces. The maenads' Roman equivalents were the *Bacchantes, female followers of the god *Bacchus.

SEE ALSO *DISMEMBERMENT, *KALI, *STYGIAN SEXUALITY

MAEVE AND/OR MAEBH
(IRISH, "INTOXICATION," "DRUNKEN WOMAN")

An Irish goddess connected to Tara, the island's legendary, mythical, and magical center. Part of her service was concerned with the use of drugs, with "wanton" sexuality, and with *ritual prostitution. The legends concerning her speak of Queen Maeve as a mighty warrior, who nevertheless was also known "to buy victory with her willing thighs" and to stop "the battle whenever she was menstruating" (Monaghan, p. 188).

MAGIC MUSHROOMS

A collective name for a variety of mushrooms with psychoactive, mind-expanding, and/or *aphrodisiac effects. The most famous of them are *Amanita muscaria and *Psilocybe mexicana, but most climates and countries know their own psychoactive mushrooms. One can find similar mushrooms in countries such as Nepal and Indonesia, and even Europe. They are usually dried and added to food such as omelets (Indonesia) or fruit yogurt; consumption has effects similar to those of *mescaline, *LSD, or *MDMA.

MAHACINA

The Indian name for ancient China. Some Tantric practices are thought to have originated in the sexually oriented *inner alchemy of Chinese *Taoism. Although the scientific discussion concerning the question "Who influenced whom, when, and where?" is far from being resolved, there is, in fact, a Tantric text called *Mahacinacara-sara Tantra, a "Tantra according to the Chinese way." In a similar connection, the *Kubjika Tantra speaks of a specific type of worship, involving very young girls, that is believed to have been imported from China.

MAHACINACARA-SARA TANTRA

A rather short Tantra, of only six chapters, which speaks of the many travels and spritual experiences of a man called Vasistha. After having worshipped *Tara and visited the *pitha of *Kamakhya in *Assam, the main character finally goes to *Mahacina, where he encounters the Buddha. In chapter 2 he finds the famous sage "contrary to the nature of a person like him" seated in a rather erotic environment, "surrounded by a thousand damsels and drunk" (Banerjee, p. 237). He is soon told that this mahacinacara is nevertheless proper for one who worships the Goddess. The Buddha also explains that mental worship, the worship of women, and worship in a naked state are the best types one can practice.

Chapter 3 of the text states that sexual union (*maithuna) is superior to the drinking of wine (*madya) and that both should be done only in a sacramental setting, not outside of worship. The text also mentions the *navakanya, with slight changes in the specific types of women, but actually says that an accomplished woman of any caste may be worshipped.

The text further praises the yoni pitha as the best and most auspicious place to do worship. Considering that this yoni pitha is actually the *Kamakhya Pitha of Assam—bordering on China, Tibet, and Bhutan—we can deduce that Chinese worshippers of the Goddess knew this place and went there to pay their respects to the stone that is seen as the menstruating *yoni of the Earth.

MAHAMAMSA

A Sanskrit term used in the *Nila Tantra for the flesh (mamsa) of a human sacrificial victim.

SEE ALSO *MAKARA, *SACRIFICE

MAHAMUDRA
(SKT., MAHAMUDRA; TIB., PHYAG-GYA CHEN-PO, "GREAT SEAL, GREAT SYMBOL")

> Mahamudra and Dzogchen differ in words but not in meaning (TANGPO TERTON SHERAB OSER, THE LAMP OF MAHAMUDRA, P. XIV).

1. As mahamudra asana, or "great seal posture," this refers most often to a psychophysical technique in which all nine orifices of the body are sealed for the control of one's breath and energy (see also *Mudra/3). However, there seem to be "eighty-eight great mudras in all, each one having a specific occult purpose" (Benjamin Walker, 1982, p. 44). As the locking of the genital opening is achieved by control of the pelvic muscles in both men and women, and as the technique requires a man to have an erect *lingam, the exercise is often done with a couple sitting in a *yab-yum position.

SEE ALSO *PELVIC FLOOR POTENTIAL

2. In Tibetan *Vajrayana, and especially the schools of *Kagyudpa orientation, one finds a more abstract concept of mahamudra. Here it is regarded as one of the highest teachings, the purpose of which is to attain what is called the "realization of emptiness," a spiritual liberation from all

MAHACINACARA-SARA TANTRA. *The Buddha in* *yab-yum, *a scene fitting the account in the* *Mahacinacara-sara Tantra.*

convention. The tradition is based on the experiences and teachings of several of the *Mahasiddhas. Someone who attains *mahamudra* is sometimes transformed into a "sacred fool," a famous example of which is *Drukpa Kunleg, a master of *crazy wisdom. The *Saskya-pa equivalent to this type of *mahamudra* is Lam-'bras, and a similar teaching with

roots in *Bön and *Nyingma traditions is known as *Dzogchen, sometimes abusively called Tibetan Zen.

3. Sometimes the term is also used to indicate a female practitioner of *maithuna, similar to *mudra/4, and sometimes to refer to this woman's *yoni.

MAHANAGNI

One of the goddesses mentioned in the then-controversial Atharva *Veda. The name translates as "the great naked woman," and the goddess, not surprisingly, is associated with *yoni worship, fertility ceremonies, and marriage. During such rituals her *yoni, as well as wine and dice (used for fortune-telling), was sprinkled with sanctified water. Mahanagni symbolizes the Earth, grants progeny, and is seen as responsible for good crops and an abundant harvest.

SEE ALSO *STRI PUJA/1, *YONI PUJA

MAHANIRVANA TANTRA

In the West this is one of the better-known Tantric scriptures, mainly by virtue of its early translation (1927) by Sir John G. Woodroffe (1865–1936), who wrote under the pseudonym of Arthur Avalon. The text describes, among other things, *bhairavi chakra and *divya chakra. The work categorically condemns the practice of having "public women" attend Tantric rites, thus apparently intimating that this was common. The Tantra also contains several hymns to various deities, among them the Adyakali Svarupa Stotra dedicated to *Kali.

SEE ALSO *DEVADASIS, *NAVKANYA, *RAJA CHAKRA, *VESHYA, AND THE QUOTATION ON PAGE 132

MAHARAGA

The term for a specific state of consciousness that the Tantric adept attempts to reach and for which there is no equivalent in modern Western languages. To describe it, one is forced to say such things as "the highest form of concentrated passionate energy" or label it as a state of mind in which "ultimate truth is experienced as a whole" (Mookerjee and Khanna).

MAHASIDDHAS

Contrasting with the scholastic and academically oriented Buddhist tradition between the sixth and twelfth centuries in India, the Mahasiddhas represent the path of self-realization through experience.

Rather than being monks, these "greatly [maha] accomplished [*siddha, 'accomplishment'] ones" were adepts of spontaneity and individuality. Coming from a wide spectrum of social backgrounds, these men and a few women followed the path of the Tantric yogi/magician in order to attain liberation and enlightenment within one lifetime.

Their experiences, attainments, and teachings are the root of *Vajrayana and especially of the *mahamudra teachings. Though the famous *Padmasambhava is not among these 84 adepts, his own life, his practice, spirit, and teachings are very much connected to them. The tradition of the Mahasiddhas has been carried through time mainly by the *Nyingmapa and the *Kagyudpa schools of Tibetan *Buddhism. Not all 84 Mahasiddhas are consequential for our inquiry in the context of this encyclopedia, but a few names are important to our puzzle:

- The Mahasiddha Saraha, the arrowmaker, was the principal teacher to Nagarjuna (c. 900 C.E.), one of Buddhism's most important philosophers. Saraha is said to have reincarnated in *Drukpa Kunleg. A quote from one of his songs can be found under the entry *Cannabis Sativa.
- Another Mahasiddha thought to have incarnated in *Drukpa Kunleg is Savaripa, the hunter.
- Tilopa (988–1069), the oil presser whose teachings have given rise to the *Kagyudpa lineage, was also one of the later teachers of *Naropa, one of the 84 Siddhas himself.
- Virupa is seen as the ancient master on whose teachings the *Saskya-pa school of Vajrayana is founded.
- Anangavajra, an early Mahasiddha held in high esteem in Tibet, is credited with authorship of the Buddhist *Tantra known as *Prajnopaya-viniscaya Siddhi, written early in the eighth century.
- Lakshmincara, a sister of *Indrabhuti and nicknamed "crazy princess," was one of the few women now regarded as a Mahasiddha, though many more female adepts would probably qualify if there had been no bias against women among the historians of Indo-Tibetan Buddhism, as is now known through the works of scholars such as Jane Campbell and Miranda Shaw.

SEE ALSO *SIDDHI

MAHASIDDHAS. *A contemporary rendering in traditional Tibetan *thangka style of the Mahasiddha Ghantapa. Ironically known as "the Celibate Monk," Ghantapa is in fact a once-celibate monk turned Tantric adept. Here he practices ritual sexuality with Darima, a seductress who accompanied him in five previous lives. Painting by Robert Beer.*

MAHASUKHA

The Sanskrit *sukha* signifies a "state of rapturous emotions" that is connected both to the perfection of wisdom and to sexual union. The *Prajnopaya-viniscaya Siddhi explains that this *sukha*, when it is "of the nature of endliss bliss, is called Mahasukha, which is beneficial in all respects, most eminent, and leads to complete enlightenment" (quoted in Banerjee, p. 363).

SEE ALSO *PRAJNA

MAHAVRATA

An ancient rite of fertility that is mentioned in the Atharva *Veda. In its older form, banned by later generations of puritanical priests, sexual union is used in order to stimulate the Earth's fertility.

SEE ALSO *FERTILITY FESTIVALS, *HIEROS GAMOS, *VRATYAS

MAHAYANA

The so-called greater vehicle and the major, northern branch of *Buddhism, which originally was prevalent in India, along with the *Hindu and *Jaina religions. From the first century onward, it's teachings spread in several waves to Burma, China, Indonesia, Japan, Korea, Mongolia, Nepal, Taiwan, Thailand, Tibet, and Vietnam: countries in which Mahayana actually came to flourish and where it gave rise to a great variety of schools. The term is used to differentiate these teachings from those of the earlier *Hinayana, from which it developed during the first century by way of the Mahasanghika and Sarvastivada schools. The concept of Mahayana Buddhism as the "great vehicle" refers to its many-sided approach to liberation, offering different ways and means for different types of people ("types" referring here to psychological makeup rather than to gender, caste, nationality, or race).

MAHAYANA. *Seventeenth-century phallic sanctuary
of the Buddha Ohana-san
on the island of Shikoku, Japan.*

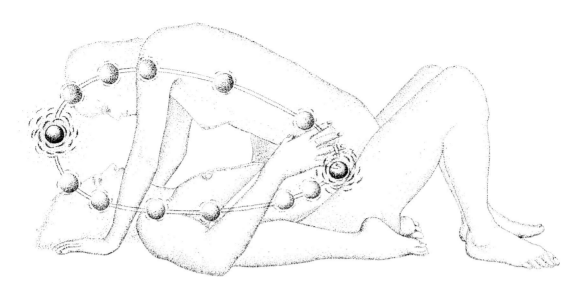

Mᴀɪᴛʜᴜɴᴀ. *Uniting fields of subtle energy during *maithuna.*
Illustration by Christina Camphausen.

The Mahayana teachings have developed into many off-shoots and include such different schools as *Vajrayana of northern India, Tibet, and neighboring regions; the schools of Ch'an and Pure Land Buddhism in China; the Zen lineages and *Tantra-influenced schools in Japan; and the Buddhist folk religions of Korea and Twaian.

Sᴇᴇ ᴀʟsᴏ *Mɪ-ᴛsᴜɴɢ, *Sʜɪɴɢᴏɴ

MAHAYONI
(SKT., "GREAT YONI")

A term used for the *yoni of the Goddess and for the moment during a *yoni *puja* when the woman's yoni, charged and ready to receive the *lingam, is energized and thus transformed into a manifestation of the Goddess's yoni.

MAHAYONI MUDRA   SEE *YONI MUDRA

MAITHUNA

Tantric/Sanskrit term for sexual union in a ritual context. It is the most important of the five *makara and constitutes the main part of the *panchamakara and/or *panchatattva rituals. Though some writers consider this to be a purely mental and symbolic act, *maithuna* clearly refers to the sacred art of male-female union in the physical, sexual sense and is synonymous with *kriya nishpatti*. An enlightening quote concerning the real practice or visualized form of *maithuna*

can be found in the *Chanadamaharosana Tantra. Here the goddess *Vajrayogini has the following lines of advice for the aspiring initiate:

> Kissing and embracing, he should always worship Vajrayogini. Physically if he can, or mentally and verbally if he cannot. The aspirant who satisifies me wins the supreme attainment. I am identical to the bodies of all women and there is no way that I can be worshipped except by the worship of women. Visualizing that she is fully my embodiment, he should make love to his woman. Because of uniting the *vajra and padma [Skt., *lotus], I will grant enlightenment (Shaw, p. 154).

Maithuna, like the other *makara*, is often surrounded with ritual requirements such as *nyasa and *mantra. One such mantric text, a male version, can be found in the *Parananda Sutra, according to which the man must chant the following prayer: "I take this divine woman who has drunk wine, who always makes my heart full of bliss, and helps in my *sadhana."

MAITHUNA VIPARITA

A specific form of *maithuna. The term is similar to the Tamil expression "dancing on the lover," which is a sexual *asana often found in the iconography of *Kali and other goddesses. It indicates that the woman takes the upper, active role.

MAJOON

A Moroccan *aphrodisiac delicacy prepared by mixing *honey, *Cannabis sativa, fruits, and various spices into a potent sweetmeat. It usually stimulates conviviality and appetite—so one easily takes some more—and offers the potential for a stimulating sexual experience. Whether or not one can make something of it depends, however—as with all drugs—on the individual and his or her partner.

MAKARA

Term for any one of the five major elements constituting the Tantric great rite, the *panchamakara or *panchatattva. All makara are described by words beginning with the letter M and are often simply referred to as the five Ms:

* madya	wine (and/or other alcholic drinks)
mamsa	meat (mostly beef), *mahamamsa
matsya	fish
* mudra	cereal wafer (an *aphrodisiac grain preparation)
* maithuna	ritual sexual union

Some sects, especially in the *Vamacara and *Kula schools, practice only three of these five. According to such teachings, only *madya, *mudra/2, and *maithuna are important, with the latter being supreme.

MALA   SEE *BODHISATTVA DAKINIS

MALE ARCHETYPES

The Indian classical books on erotology, such as the *Koka Shastra and others, were all written by men, and the detailed studies of women (see *Female Archetypes) in these texts reflect the authors' personal inclinations and interest. Their corresponding classification of men into three basic types, furthermore, is very much lacking in detail and knowledge; they seem to have avoided looking at themselves and their friends too closely.

1. The Hare (Skt., sasa): The man of the "hare" type is affectionate, attractive to women, and has slender, well-shaped hands. He produces *semen that is sweet to the taste and of pleasant odor.
2. The Bull (Skt., vrsa): The "bull" type is passionate in sexual union and a man of strong bones and deep

armpits. He is capable of repeated *orgasm.
3. The Stallion (Skt., asva): The "stallion" type is over-endowed with seminal matter and is constantly tormented by lust. His semen tastes salty, smells like a *goat, and has the yellow color of butter.

The above short list clearly indicates the need for contemporary women to reexamine these standard categories with an effort toward developing a more accurate classification of male (arche)types in a general, particularly in an erotic/psychological, sense.

MALE CONTINENCE

A term coined by John Humphrey *Noyes for his favorite technique concerning sexual union, which combines *coitus prolongatus and *coitus reservatus. In this technique, the male partner is expected not to *ejaculate, whereas the woman may certainly experience one or more *orgasms.

SEE ALSO *IMSAK, *KAREZZA, *RETENTION OF SEMEN

MAMA KILYA

An Inca goddess associated with nature, the moon, and sexuality. She was especially worshipped as ruler of women's *menstrual/ovarian cycles.

SEE ALSO *MOON MAGIC

MANDALA

1. A concentric diagram/painting/drawing used in Tantric rituals to focus consciousness toward both cosmic and individual, psychic energies. Such symbolic representations of cosmic forces are sometimes expressed in three-dimensional form, for example in the architecture of temples.

SEE ALSO *THANGKA, *YANTRA

2. Similar to *chakra, the term is also used to indicate a ritual circle in which male and female devotees sit around a leader/priest in order to partake in the five *makara.

MADORLE AND/OR MANDORLA

This *almond-shaped design is also known as the vesica piscis and is used to represent such ideas as divinity, virginity, sacredness, and last but not least the *yoni as gateway of life. It is a symbol that appears quite often in Christian iconography, where it is used to symbolize the "flame of the spirit," as, for example, in the aureole, or halo, that often surrounds the whole body of a sanctified personality such as

MALE ARCHETYPES. *As this Indian painting shows, the male fantasy of being endowed with a member*
as large as that of a stallion is not prevalent only in the West;
it seems a fallacy as universal as it is unnecessary.
Late eighteenth-century painting on paper, Punjab, India. Photograph courtesy of Nik Douglas.

Mary, the *virgin Queen of Heaven. Geometrically, it consists of two intersecting circles and is related to the golden mean.

MANDRAKE

Like *yohimbine, mandrake (*Mandragora officinarum*) is thought to aid in a more copius lubrication of the *yoni. This "plant of *Circe" was known to the Hebrews as dudaim, based on the root *dud,* which means "love." The plant's value, whether as an *aphrodisiac or as a hallucinogenic drug, must have been high indeed if we consider the biblical story in which Rachel offers one night of her husband's amorous attentions to Leah in exchange for some mandrakes (Genesis 30:14–16). King *Solomon, too, praises the mandrake (Song of Songs 7:14) and, as we know from Emperor Julian the Apostate, it was frequently used in Roman love potions. Often the mandrake was thought to aid in conception and even to make barren women fertile—a belief that, according to Sir James G. Frazer (1854–1941) in *The Golden Bough,* was still alive among Orthodox Jews of nineteenth-century America.

La Mandragore, a tale by Jean de la Fontaine (1621–1695), speaks of the erotic impact of this famous root.

MANI
(SKT., "JEWEL")

A term used as a synonym for the *vajra, the diamond scepter that is so important to Tibetan *Vajrayana.

See also *Om Mani Padme Hum

MANIPURA CHAKRA

The "navel" chakra, one of the four *chakras of the early Tantric tradition and now number 3. In *Taoism it is one of the *tan-t'ien, and among the *Sufi it is known as "center of the self."

LOCATION: Solar plexus, slightly above the navel, eighth thoracic vertebrae

ENDOCRINE GLAND: *Adrenals

RULING *SHAKTI: Lakini

COLOR: *Red

LOTUS: 10-petaled, blue

ASSOCATIONS: Sight, life force, life-preserving energy

See also *Sixty-four Yogini Pitha

MANTRA

To define mantra in the most general sense, one can best describe it as a sound or melody consisting of one or more syllables. Some mantras actually consist of no more than one single sound and/or letter; others are more or less short texts that are chanted according to a prescribed melodic and rhythmic structure.

A mantra is most powerful when chanted, either audibly or purely mentally and silently, but mantras are believed to be effective in written form as well. Mantras become especially powerful when repeated a great number of times, a technique that is known in Sanskrit as japa. Mantra practice is recommended to aid the devotee in focusing the mind and in concentrating cosmic/psychic energies.

Mantras are an integral and required part of Tantric ritual and are prescribed at certain stages in most rituals, especially during the stages that lead up to *maithuna. A typical description of such a practice is given in the *Guptasadhana Tantra. The text gives an example in which a man worships a woman by reciting his personal mantra 100 times each on her head, forehead, face, throat, heart, and navel and 200 times on her *breasts. This is to be followed by 100 recitations on her *yoni. *Tantra also knows special mantras that are to be recited when partaking in one of the *makara. Samples of such mantric texts, taken from the *Parananda

Sutra, can be found under the entries *Madya, *Maithuna, and *Mudra/2.

See also *Gayatrimantra, *Om Mani Padme Hum

MARMAS

A Sanskrit term that refers to what is known in the West as erogenous or erogenic zones. In the Tantric frame of reference, these marmas are divided into three classes and are valid for both women and men:

1. Primary marmas: *lips and tongue, *breasts and nipples, *yoni and/or *lingam
2. Secondary marmas: ear lobes, nape of the neck, base of the spine, junction of the thighs, inside surface of the thighs
3. Tertiary marmas: outside surface of the little finger, palms of the hands, navel, anus, frontal insides of the nostrils, aperture of the ears, soles of the feet, big toe

The prescribed course of stimulation, embracing all these locations on the human body, is to move from the secondary to the primary to the tertiary marmas, thus turning the body into one huge sensitive organ that is able to transmit as well as receive sexual energies.

See also *Kalas

MARRIAGE

Marriage, as defined in the monogamous sense that most contemporaries connect with the term, is by no means a universal institution. For information on different types and customs concerning marriage, see *Bridal Prostitution, *Defloration, *Group Marriage, *Monogamy, *Nasamonian Marriage Custom, *Nuptial Continence, *Polyandry, *Polygamy, *Serial Polygamy, *Sororal Polygyny, and *Virginity.

MARS

Whether or not one personally agrees with the characterizations of the god Mars and the goddess *Venus as representations of the human male and female, these are ancient archetypes—both are Roman, based on Greek models—expressing masculinity and femininity, and they can be viewed in a way similar to the concepts of *yang and *yin. Besides representing such things as aggression and war, Mars also stands for assertiveness, commencement of action, and male libido in general, often seen as the main male qualities. It is in the framework of such associations

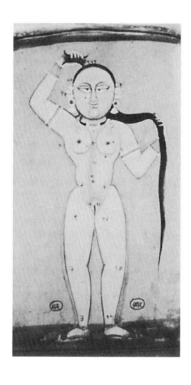

Marms. *Depiction of* *marmas *and/or* *kalas. *Circa eighteenth century, Rajasthan, India. Dr. H. Hunger Collection.*

that we propose a mons marsianus as the male counterpart of the female mons veneris, or "mound of Venus." The Greek/Thracian prototype for Mars is the god Ares.

SEE ALSO *LINGAM TOPOGRAPHY/2

MASLUB

The Arabian saints known by this name were, like the Indian *Digambara, a group of holy men who wandered the countryside entirely naked and who enjoyed the sexual status and privileges described in this encyclopedia under the entry *Carte Blanche. Reports of such Maslub saints come from Morocco, Damascus, and Egypt (Briffault, vol. 3), indicating that they were known in all or most of the early Arabian and/or Islamic lands.

When one of these unclad holy nomads came into a village, town, or city, women who desired to become pregnant would go and kneel before him. Touching his sacred *lingam or engaging in sexual union with him was believed to help the woman achieve pregnancy; naturally, it sometimes did. The Maslub, on the other hand, was free to choose any woman he encountered and would often make love to her right there and then, publicly and among much clapping and singing of the onlooking local men and women. Similar to certain Tantrics, the Maslub thought themselves to be above all normal rules and moral standards

and were known to have sexual union even in the courtyards of holy mosques—an unthinkable sin for all other men.

SEE ALSO *ADAMITES, *NAGNA

MASS OF THE HOLY GHOST

A secret ritual of Western *sexual magick that has been described by Israel Regardie (1907–1988) in his book *The Tree of Life: A Study of Magic* (1972) and, in more detail, by Louis T. Culling (*see* *Great Brotherhood of God). Similar in intent to the Tantric ritual described in the *Yoni Tantra, the main goal of this ritual is to produce, mingle, and (re)absorb the female and male sexual essences of *ejaculation. A conversation between two active practitioners of sexual magick, with very interesting and detailed information concerning this and similar rituals, is included in Peter Redgrove's *The Black Goddess.*

SEE ALSO *YONITATTVA

MASTURBATION

Although practiced by most people, masturbation has until recently been a much maligned and tabbooed form of sexuality. However, in both mythology and religious practice, and among adepts of *sexual magick, masturbation has often played a large role, although it is usually described with more elegant-sounding names such as autoeroticism or autosexual magical practice.

Whereas sexual magicians East and West mainly used this practice to empower their prayers, spells, or talismans, an ancient Egyptian creation myth speaks of the god Amun who gave rise to all of the universe and its various deities and beings by the act of masturbation. Although this information has not found its way into many books on Egyptology or religion in general, a widely televised BBC production with the title "The Secrets of Karnak" has left no doubt that this act of creation has been re-created daily, for centuries, by the priests of that famous temple now turned tourist attraction. Although the priest did not masturbate with the "hand of god," as the scriptures proclaim, but was helped by the hand of an assisting priestess, this example clearly shows that not every culture regarded this practice as a "vice."

Even today, in the United States a group exists by the name of Summum whose members base their practice on this ancient Egyptian ritual. They have tried for many years to be recognized as a religious institution.

MATANGI

(SKT., "INTOXICATED DESIRE")

This goddess represents, on the one hand, sovereignty and royal dominion: attributes based on her being the ancient "mother of elephants"—animals highly regarded and sacred in India. On the other hand, Matangi is the "incarnation of emotional frenzy," who stumbles around like a wild and drunken *elephant, her eyes rolling in their sockets and her dark body reeling with longing and desire for union. In Tamil Nadu, India, a *matangi* is a woman possessed by the goddess Mathamma. Once chosen, she holds this position for life.

MATRIARCHY

The dispute over whether or not human societies have ever been matriarchal is still unresolved, although general consensus tends to give "no" as the probable answer. It is quite likely that this negative answer stems from the fact that the question in itself is the wrong one. Matriarchy, perceived as a mirror image of patriarchy, implies that women ruled over men in the same prejudiced and power-hungry way that men in fact have ruled, and still rule, over women. This is, almost by definition, not the way of women.

Nevertheless, establishing that a true matriarchy may not have existed during known history must not lead us to the conclusion that things have always been the same. One of the few clear testimonies to the fact that both the Goddess and her women played a superior role—in this case in pre-Islamic Arabia—can be found in a statement by Omar, a faithful disciple of the prophet Muhammad: "When we came among the 'Helpers' [the Ansar of Medina], they proved to be a people whose women dominated them, and our wives have come to copy the habits of the women of the Ansar" (Allegro, 1973, p. 221). Furthermore, many cultures have known *matriliny and *matrilocality, two almost global customs that clearly indicate women as the focus of a given society and/or as powerful, respected, and often ruling or dominant members of their respective societies.

SEE ALSO *AL'LAT

MATRILINY

The custom of reckoning by matrilineal descent has often been interpreted as evidence for the existence of *matriarchy—for example, by writers such as Johann Jakob Bachofen (1815–1877) and Robert Briffault. To determine whether or not this is accurate cannot be an objective for our present pursuit, and the answer to this question must come from elsewhere.

A culture in which matrilineal descent is seen as the most important factor in establishing a person's bloodline and heritage does not usually call any children illegitimate; this concept appears only when the question of fatherhood is considered important. In matriliny, all matters concerned with such things as ownership, inheritance, royal bloodlines, and so forth are dependent on the identity of one's mother. As there can hardly ever be any doubt as to the identity of someone's mother, as opposed to the uncertainty of fatherhood in the absence of genetic tests, such "social problems" in matters of descent do not exist.

MATRILOCALITY

This term indicates the custom practiced by many peoples in which the newly married husband is taken into the family of the woman, and he often has to move into her home, village, or tribal community. This arrangement precludes the socioeconomic dependence that has often been the fate of married women in patrilocal cultures over the past two thousand to three thousand years and that has resulted in the patriarchal master/slave, owner/property relation that exists even today between the two sexes.

An example of the struggle to change from matrilocal to patrilocal customs can be found in a careful reading of the biblical stories concerning Sarah, *Abraham and *Hagar, Rebecca, Esau, Jacob, and Laban.

MATRIYONI

Sanskrit term indicating the *yoni of one's mother. Certain schools teach that penetration of the *matriyoni*—which is, in other words, *incest between mother and son—is a very powerful and beneficial experience. In this practice, so goes the reasoning, a circle that was broken at birth is once more completed. Tantric masters such as *Drukpa Kunleg undertook this practice, and their stories show that such teachings were (and are) really carried out despite strong, almost universal incest taboos. This nonetheless seems to be a rather specialized view. Most Tantric schools and their scriptures, such as the *Yoni Tantra, do not encourage the practice, and some go to the extreme of saying that no woman who has conceived a child should be a *Shakti during a *yoni *puja*, so that one's mother is—by definition—off limits.

A less drastic but still—to some—shocking worship of the *matriyoni* was reported by author Ian Buruma. Katsu Shintaro, an internationally known Japanese actor, publicly kissed his dead mother's genitals on the day of her funeral. The most interesting aspect of this event is the fact that Japanese news agencies, which widely distributed the story, reported the gesture with respect rather than surprise or sensationalism.

MATSURI

Common term for a variety of *Shinto festivals still held today throughout Japan. The *matsuri* constitute a type of *fertility festival during which worshippers carry huge phalli through the town and eat—or offer to the deities, or both—smaller *lingam symbols in the form of sweets. Women, of course, use such merry and *carnival-like celebrations as an opportunity to pray once more for a(nother) child.

SEE ALSO *PHALLIC WORSHIP

MAYPOLE DANCES

Part of the tradition of *fertility festivals and also connected with *phallic worship, the Maypole games and dances that are still held in the twentieth century in rural parts of Europe testify to the strong current of the ancient religions. Like other "pagan" modes of worship, they have been changed but could not be abolished by Christianity. The Maypole is, of course, a phallic symbol and an expression of phallic worship. The round dance and the wheel hung from the top of the Maypole, however, add the female element to the proceedings.

In pre-Christian or early Christian times, the dances originally ended with a general *orgy or with a pursuit of the young women by the male youths, with fertilizing sexual unions in the fields.

SEE ALSO *GIANT OF CERNE ABBAS

MBOZE

An African goddess of the Woyo peoples concerned with nature, fertility, and especially rainfall. Her myths show that she is also very involved with sexuality, including *incest.

MDA

(3.4-METHYLENE-DIOXYAMPHETAMINE)
A synthetic compound derived from isosafrole, an oil found in plants such as *sassafras and *nutmeg. It was first discovered in Germany in 1910 but became available only in the late 1960s, when it became known as "speed for lovers." Like the later but related *MDMA (*ecstasy), it is basically a therapeutic drug, but it lacks the buildup to a peak found with MDMA, and its effects last about twice as long. MDA has been called a "drug of truth" and is known to enhance tactile sensitivity, feelings of closeness, and the ability to truly communicate with one's partner. MDA is not readily available, but MDMA incorporates all of these effects as well.

MDMA AND/OR MMDA
(3-METHOXYL-4.5-METHYLENE-DIOXYAMPHETAMINE)
The official name for a modern and purposely designed psychoactive drug generally known as *ecstasy (XTC). MDMA is a synthetic compound based on one of *nutmeg's essential oils, myristicine. It became popular during the late 1970s and achieved fame as a kind of *aphrodisiac because it was especially designed to help lovers open up to each other psychologically and at the same time to provide intense physical pleasure. As was to be expected, and although many therapists have found this drug to be very useful, most countries have meanwhile banned the sale of MDMA and declared its use illegal.

Although it is often described as a "soft" version of *LSD, its effects are actually much closer to those of *mescaline and *magic mushrooms. Claudio Naranjo, who conducted a number of clinical studies in the early1970s, has characterized MDMA as an enhancer of the feeling he calls the "eternal now," an image that describes well the drug's ability to enhance warm, friendly, gentle erotic activity. In contrast to its precursor, known as *MDA, the effect of the drug includes a slow buildup to a peak, occurring more or less in the middle of a session that lasts three to five hours.

MEATUS   SEE *LINGAM TOPOGRAPHY/7, *YONI TOPOGRAPHY/7

MEDICINA CATHOLICA

Alchemical/magical term for the "quested essence," the feminine principle, used as a code for female sexual secretions.

SEE ALSO *FEMALE LOVE JUICES

MEDICINE OF THE THREE PEAKS

Chinese alchemical term for the sexual secretions originating in a woman's "three peaks": the lips, breasts, and yoni. The term *medicine* is not used simply as a code or *secret language but is meant quite seriously. Taoist sources often refer specifically to the healing powers of sexual union and erotic activity that can, by the resulting harmonization of *yin and *yang, help and heal may ailments—at least the common and minor ones. A description of "the great medicine of the three peaks" is included in R. van Gulik's *Sexual Life in Ancient China*, although he felt it necessary to obscure this information from nonacademic readers by presenting most of it in Latin only.

Detailed information about the individual peaks and their various medicines, and not only from the Chinese point of view, is available under the entries listed here.

1. Red lotus peak (the mouth and lips): *Jade Fluid, *Jade Fountain, *Kassapu, *Lips, *Saliva

MEDICINE OF THE THREE PEAKS. *Partaking of the*
**medicine of the three peaks.*
Nineteenth-century painting, China.
Roger Peyrefitte Collection.

2. Twin peaks (the breasts): *Breasts, *Peach Juice of Immortality, *White Snow, *Witches' Milk

3. Purple mushroom peak (the *yoni): *Ejaculation (female), *Female Love Juices, *Palace of Yin, *Purnacandra, *Purple Mushroom Peak, *White Metal, *Wine of the Navel

MEGALITHS
(GREEK, "GREAT STONES")

To most people, the term *megalith* immediately conjures up images of Stonehenge (England), Carnac (France), or the temples of the Great Goddess on the Maltese Islands. The uncounted megaliths of England, Scotland, Wales, France, and Germany as well as those found throughout southern Europe, remainders of the Celtic culture and religion, have so dominated contemporary consciousness that those of other early societies are rather neglected. However, megalithic "buildings," or monuments, are also to be found in China, India, Egypt, Indonesia (Nias), and South America. Yet, we are not concerned here with pyramids or figures from Easter Island but with those *sacred stones that have been set up as representations of the male and female forces of life and the universe, symbolized—as always—as *lingam and *yoni.

Such stones or stone arrangements are known under the names of *cromlech, *dolmen, *holed stones, or *menhir. Although their use and function may not have been entirely "sexual," this aspect certainly played a great part in the motivation for erecting or building them. Their locations often coincide with water and energy currents in the earth, and the stones themselves may have been set up to "heal" distrubances, to amplify the subtle energies available at these places, or both.

MEHANA

Alternative Sanskrit term for *lingam, sometimes used to indicate *semen.

MENHIR

Just as the *dolmen is a female symbol expressed in the form of *megalithic stones, the menhir (French for "standing stone") is a representation of the phallic creative force. Although such menhirs can be found all over Europe, the largest collection of these stones is that of Carnac in France. It once was popular usage, even in Christian times, to have

MEGALITHS.
Japanese *megaliths provide clear evidence of ferility-oriented genital worship (see *Phallic Worship, *Yoni Worship).

sexual union within a circle of menhir stones, as an "unfailing remedy" for barrenness. Another local custom prescribed that a young couple visit a menhir and there they should each touch the stone with their genitals, a ritual thought to assure the man of the birth of a male child and the woman of her husband's fidelity.

SEE ALSO *HOLED STONES

MENSTRUAL FLUID
(FROM LATIN *MENSIS*, "MONTH")

Menstrual blood—the monthly recurring "red tide"—is one of the major biochemical fluids and energies that must be discussed in the context of a book such as this. What is usually called menstrual blood is, of course, much more than blood alone. The monthly discharge that is typical of all female primates consists—in medical terms—of the disintegrated ovum, blood, mucus, bits and pieces of the endometrium (lining of the uterus), cells from the lining of the vagina, and hormonelike substances such as *prostaglandins (*see also* *Menstrual/Ovarian Cycle).

It is interesting to note the detail in which Tantric science deals with menstrual fluid. Eastern texts recognize at least 16 varieties, and all these terms end with *pushpa* (Skt., "flower"), a common designation for the red menstrual flux and flow. Several of these are given in texts such as the Matrikabheda Tantra and the Samayacara Tantra, where we find the following:

svayambhupushpa
kundapushpa
golapushpa
sonitapushpa
vajrapushpa
sarvakalodbhavapushpa
svapushpa (first bleeding after *defloration)

Whereas menstruating women are seen as impure in mainstream Indian religion, Tantra does not see it that way. The *Nila Tantra very clearly states that a woman undergoing her menstrual period "should be regarded as pure." Nevertheless, there are people who see no erotic element in this precious liquid, and it is true that many ancient peoples—not to mention contemporary consensus—did or do not approve of any sexual interaction during menstruation. To explain the very different Tantra view of this issue we must take a closer look at menstruation and at the history and variety of ideas and rituals surrounding it.

The fact that each woman, if not too young or too old, once every moon (or month) bleeds from that very place of mystery which—for male and female alike—is the gateway both to life and to erotic pleasures has always and in all cultures been regarded as a sign of magical power. Whether or not the particular local tradition surrounded this (menstrual) blood with taboos born from fear or saw it as a sacred gift from the goddess, the monthly red tide was one of the obvious signs of the uniquely female *moon magic and *gynergy.

MENHIR. *A phallic* *menhir at Filitosa,
Corsica, France.*

Since it has become possible to discuss, research, and describe menstruation and women's varied experience of this monthly event, it has been established very clearly that many women experience an increase of libido and a heightened sense of sexual desire before and during their menstrual flow. Patriarchal and Christian-dominated education, medical science, and psychology have always tried to tell us the opposite, putting an emphasis on ovulation and fertility and thereby helping to devalue the power and potential of menstrual energy.

Many are the words and phrases used to signify and describe this specific and rhythmically recurring bleeding. Often they are based simply on its redness, as in the Chinese *red tide, red flow,* and *red snow* as well as the red wine mentioned in the biblical *Song of Songs. Although the term *red wine* is born from a need for concealment and represents code language, it is still a quite poetic expression and can be compared to the Taoist term *peach blossom flow.*

Other terms show a more philosophical approach and often imply a certain respect, or a feeling of sanctity, in the face of this "inexplicable" and mysterious phenomenon, using a terminology that hints at the alchemical/magical properties that—according to many wise old wo/men—are inherent in menstrual blood. Terms such as *coral essence, liquid ruby,* *elixir rubeus,* and *khapushpa* ("womb flower") speak a clear language.

Our own culture, with its negative and antisexual Judeo-Christian programming, is certainly less imaginative, and our medical science does little more than warn that the womb flower is a poisonous plant! Patriarchal gynecologists invented the term *menotoxins* for the "poisonous" substances that are said to be discharged along with, or contained in, the menstrual fluid. However, one man's poison is often another man's healing elixir, depending not only on the way the substance is used but very much on the consciousness of the user or researcher. Most likely the "poisons"—among which are iron, lecithin, and traces of arsenic—are the same substances that, as elixir rubeus, are known as the magically potent ingredient in the female *blood, regarded to be especially strong during a full moon menstruation.

An interesting passage in the Tibetan "Secret Life and Songs of the Lady Yeshe Tsogyal" unmistakably reveals the high regard the ancient Tantric adepts had for the powers of the red tide. In that autobiography, *Yeshe Tsogyal reports one of her visions as follows: "Then I had a vision of a red woman, naked, lacking even the covering of bone ornaments, who thrust her *bhaga against my mouth, and I drank deeply from her copious flow of blood" (Dowman, 1984, p. 71).

This, of course, reminds us not only of *cunnilingus but of those Tantric rituals in which menstrual blood—whether or not mixed with male *semen—is drunk by the patricipating male and female adepts because of its inherent subtle and magical powers, or, in modern scientific terms, its biochemical and electromagnetic properties.

SEE ALSO *ADAMU, *CHANDALI, *GOLODBHAVA, *KUNDODBHAVA, *NIDDAH, *SCENT AURA, *YONIMANDALA, *YONIPUSHPA, *YONI TANTRA

MENSTRUAL/OVARIAN CYCLE

In order to understand the uniqueness as well as the powers of the *menstrual fluid, one must first have a good idea, or an image closely approximating the observed reality, of the menstrual/ovarian cycle as such.

When trying to describe this lunar/hormonal cycle of a

human female in a generalized model, one arrives at something like the "scientific" analysis of measurable causes and effects as given below. Not only, however, does this model describe a rather hypothetical, statistical, and often fictional creature—as is the case with most models—but also it discounts all or most of the evidence that does not fit the currently accepted paradigm. We must realize and not forget that the psychophysical, electromagnetic, and biochemical reality of a human being is infinitely more complex than the following model—already seemingly complicated—can ever convey.

One must also bear in mind that generally there are two possible types of menstrual attunement to the lunar phases: that occurring during the full moon and that occurring during the new moon. Although some authors favor one over the other and claim it to be the "right type," we must recognize that menstruation will occur during both phases and that neither occurrence means that the woman in question is out of tune with the lunar cycle. The type of menstruation and the accompanying psychosomatic state, however, may well be distinctly different at these two points in time.

For unfamiliar medical terminology you may encounter in the following description, consult the various entries under *Yoni Topography.

Phase 1 (days 1–4 of the cycle): Simultaneously with the red flow a new cycle begins. Triggered by the hypothalamus, the anterior *pituitary gland sends *FSH (follicle-stimulating hormone) down to the ovaries. This activates the follicles in the ovaries, which actually produce, ripen, and release the egg cells that will later grow into the ovum. During this growth the follicles also produce *estrogen.

Phase 2 (in general, day 5 of the cycle): The estrogen manufactured by the follicles enters the bloodstream and is carried up to the pituitary. Once a certain level of estrogen has been reached, the pituitary interprets this as a message to secrete less FSH and to start concentrating on the production of *LH (luteinizing hormone).

Phase 3 (ovulation; about day 14 of the cycle): When the estrogen level has reached its peak and enough LH has traveled to the ovary, where it serves to stimulate the follicle's growth, there comes a point when the ripened follicle bursts and an ovum is released and received into the fallopian tube. The walls of the empty follicle then collapse and turn into the *corpus luteum, where the manufacture of the hormones *progesterone (formerly called luteum) and estrogen now

takes place. The cervix begins to produce an alkaline, fertile mucus, stretchy like egg white, designed to aid sperm cells in reaching the uterus and the fallopian tubes.

SEE ALSO *SCENT AURA

Phase 4 (mature ovum travels down the tube): It takes the ovum a total of approximately seven days to travel through the fallopian tube—carried along by the tube's muscular contractions and by the ciliary current created by millions of fine hairs called cilia—before it reaches the uterus. Just before reaching the uterus the egg comes to rest for a few days in the tube, where it may be met by sperm and may be fertilized. During this time the progesterone has reached a level that causes the pituitary to stop producing LH. Without this hormone the corpus luteum withers and disintegrates.

Phase 5 (in the uterus): Whether the ovum has been fertilized or not, it is eventually propelled into the uterus. If fertilized, the ovum will implant itself in the lining of the uterus, and the development toward pregnancy and birth will start.

Phase 6 (menstruation; about day 28 or 29): If the egg has remained unfertilized, the lining of the uterus breaks down and both lining and egg will leave the body through the vagina with the *menstrual fluid. This occurs when the level of progesterone has reached its monthly low. After a few days of bleeding the pituitary begins once more to secrete FSH, and a new cycle begins.

MENSTRUUM OF THE GLUTEN
Unspecified, general alchemical term for vaginal fluids.

SEE ALSO *FEMALE LOVE JUICES

MESCALINE
The psychoactive *alkaloid of the *peyote cactus. Most often, the mescaline for sale—illegally—is a synthetic, but its effects are very close to those of the (rare) real thing. It often changes sensory and spatial perception, enhances the sense of touch, and lends a sense of supernatural beauty to things or beings. It may thus not be an *aphrodisiac in the strict sense, but it is certainly able to enhance the whole feeling and atmosphere before, during, and after erotic play or sexual union. Inner visions can be multicolored, sensuous spectacles that run before the inner eye like first-class erotic films—depending, of course, on the psychological makeup of the experimenting individuals.

METEORS   SEE *SACRED STONES

METU

Similar to the *nadis known in Tantric yoga, the metu are the 36 subtle "arteries" known to the priests, adepts, and physicians of ancient Egypt. These channels were thought to transport life energy to the various organs of the human body.

MILA GNUBUM AND MILA KHABUM

The Hundred Thousand Songs of Milarepa (Mila Gnubum) and the Biography of Milarepa (Mila Khabum) are prime examples of a specific type of sacred literature that originates with the 84 *Mahasiddhas and similar figures important in the development of Tantra and *Vajrayana.

The Mila Gnubum represents the complete poetic writings of the famous Tibetan yogi and philosopher Milarepa (c. 1039–1123).

The Mila Khabum was written down several decades after Milarepa's death by the "Mad Yogi from gTsan." It tells of Milarepa's adventures, hardships, and joys during his personal "odyssey" toward enlightenment and affords us insight into the style of life, teaching, and initiation during this formative century of Tibetan Buddhism.

SEE ALSO *VAJRA SONGS

MIN

Egyptian *ithyphallic fertility god shown on murals and in statues with an oversized, erect *lingam.

MISRACARA

A term used in the *Nila Tantra describing a concept of conduct and a way of living recommended as "pleasing to the goddess." On one hand, the concept requires the devotee to lead a socially "normal" life, which is sketchily defined as entering into married and monogamous life and wearing clothes. On the other hand, the person in question is to live part of that life in the manner of an independent Tantric: going naked, being at home in the creation grounds, and having promiscuous sexual union with whomever is available.

SEE ALSO *DIGAMBARA, *MONOGAMY, *RITUAL PROMISCUITY

MISSIONARY POSITION

The "male superior position" during sexual union, also known as *Venus observa. Cultural anthropologist Bronislaw Malinowski (1884–1942) wrote that Melanesian girls ridicule the missionary position, which demands that they should lie passive and recumbent. In their book Hebrew Myths, Graves and Patai point out that this position comes as a sort of package deal with patriarchy: "It is characteristic of civilizations where women are treated as chattels that they must adopt the recumbent posture during intercourse, which Lilith refused" (p. 65). This is the only sexual position traditionally allowed to "good" Christians and "good" Muslims, and it is this that *Lilith refused to Adam, a refusal that ultimately led to her becoming slandered and viewed in the mythology as a *female sexual demon.

SEE ALSO *VIPARITA RATI

MITAKUKU

Several tribes of the Melanesian Islands love and praise mitakuku, the practice of biting off their lover's eyelashes—a form of *algolagnia that to them seems as normal and essential as the kiss does to European and American lovers. One of their common terms of endearment for one another is agu mitakuku: "my bitten-off eyelashes" (Malinowski, p. 250). Extreme nakedness of the body is seen as beautiful, and other hair, except on the head, is usually shaved off, including the eyebrows and the pubic hair.

MI-TSUNG

Chinese "school of secrets," a school of *Tantra-oriented *Buddhism that originated in the eighth century, when Indian Tantrics came to China. Here the school soon lost its influence, but it lived on in Japan as *Shingon. From the seventh through the tenth centuries, the school was also very active in Korea.

SEE ALSO *MAHACINACARA-SARA TANTRA

MONOGAMY

The custom in some cultures whereby a person can be married to only one person of the other sex. This may seem quite natural to some readers, because it is how most of us were taught to view marriage. Marriage, however, does not have to be defined in this Judeo-Christian and Roman way, and other cultures recognize multiple and simultaneous marriage with more than one partner. Monogamy as a custom, and institutionalized as the only lawful possibility of sexual partnership, has become widespread and is considered the norm in most contemporary cultures; however, the high divorce rates encountered in modern Western societies seem to indicate that in this style of *marriage it is mainly the *idea* of monogamy that prevails. The actual situation would better be recognized for what it really is: successive monogamy or *serial polygamy/polyandry. Historical and contemporary examples of other "marital" lifestyles are described under *Group Marriage, *Polyandry, and *Polygamy.

SEE ALSO *MISRACARA

MONS MARSIANUS   SEE *LINGAM TOPOGRAPHY/2

MONS VENERIS   SEE *YONI TOPOGRAPHY/2

MOON FLOWER MEDICINE AND/OR MOON FLOW

Chinese term for the female secretions from the *palace of yin in the *purple mushroom peak during erotic stimulation. The ancient Taoists apparently had no doubt that women also can, at times, have profuse *ejaculations, at least if the *palace of yin is stimulated.

SEE ALSO *FEMALE LOVE JUICES, *SEXUAL BIOCHEMISTRY

MOON MAGIC

A specialized type of *yoni magic can be recognized in the strange powers that people of various cultures have attributed to the monthly *menstrual fluid, especially the blood of a first menstruation, when the girl is transformed into a woman. Much material has already been published on the many taboos surrounding this moment, and we have been amply informed by several authors about separations from tribe and family, fears of contagion, and many negative effects that menstrual fluid is supposed to have on humans, animals, and nature as such.

The following collection of data will establish that there is also a more positive and sympathetic side to the magic—or call it biochemistry and electromagnetism—of the "red snow." In many old cultures, the *blood that flows during *defloration is seen as an equivalent, in magical/energetic terms, to menstrual fluid.

EUROPE   In the Calabrian part of Italy, for example, women used to save a few drops of their own menstrual fluid in a small bottle, which they carried wherever they

went. It was believed that when such drops were secretly administered to a man of their choice, the man would be bound to them forever.

SEE ALSO *ELIXIR RUBEUS, *ORDO TEMPLI ORIENTIS

FAR EAST   *See* *Kamakhya Pitha, *Kubjika Tantra, *Teachings of Sister Niguma, *Yonipushpa

NEAR EAST   *See* *Adamu, *Gnosticism, *Jaki

THE AMERICAS   *See* *Mama Kilya, *Ordo Templi Orientis

MORS JUSTI
(LATIN, "DEATH JUSTIFIED")

A term used by Aleister *Crowley for a more or less symbolic type of death (mors) that occurs during sexual union—specifically, at the moment of *orgasm. The Latin *mors*, in its alternative meaning as "loss of memory," can also be meant to simply speak of the "little death," a negative image for the loss of ego that can occur at the peak moments of sexual union.

MORS OSCULI
(LATIN, "DEATH BY KISS")

A term used in connection with erotic techniques designed to alter someone's state of consciousness by means of sexual exhaustion, as in *erotocomatose lucidity.

SEE ALSO *MORS JUSTI

MUDRA

Based on the Sanskrit roots *mud* ("joy") and *ra* ("to give"), the term *mudra* has a variety of meanings:

1. General name for a number of ritual gestures of the hands that are employed in yogic practice. The *mudra* is a focus of energy and simultaneously transmits meaning to those who have learned to "read" the gestures. In many statues showing the Buddha or Hindu/Buddhist deities, the positions of their hands show such *mudras*. In our context, the *yoni *mudra*, *yonilinga *mudra*, and linga *mudra* are of special interest.

SEE ALSO *LASYA

2. As one of the five *makara, the term *mudra* refers to a cereal wafer or a similar preparation made from grain. Sometimes it is made with the addition of ganja (*cannabis) or other *aphrodisiac substances, including—in some schools—the addition of menstrual fluid. The following *mantra, taken from the *Parananda Sutra, is recited before

consumption: "I take it as an offering to the Lord; it destroys the torments of heart, and causes joy, and is enriched with other food stuff."

3. As "seal" mudra is the technical term for a variety of yogic techniques to control certain organs and physical processes in order to manipulate both the flow of subtle energy and the resulting psychic responses. Examples of such exercises can be found under the entries *Khechari Mudra, *Mahamundra, *Vajroli Mudra, and *Yoni Mudra/2.

SEE ALSO *BANDHA

4. In Buddhist Tantra, the term is also used for the female partner in Tantric ritual, similar to *prajna or *dakini.

5. A radically different interpretation of mudra, as the stage preceding *maithuna in a *panchamakara ritual, is given by the Indian author Chandra Chakraberti, who describes it as an "excitation of the clitoris by the raised forefinger" (Chakraberti, p. 302).

MUIRA PUAMA

An *aphrodisiac and strong stimulant derived from the Brazilian "tree of virility." The bark is chewed or brewed as a tea by tribal people along the Amazon and Orinoco Rivers, but it can also be smoked.

MUKHARATA

Sanskrit term for the type of mutual genital kissing in the sexual posture commonly known as "69." It enables the partners to practice *cunnilingus and *fellatio simultaneously. A synonym for this term is kakila.

MUKTATRIVENI

The triple knot made by the three principal *nadis near the *ajna chakra.

M OON FLOWER. *The Chinese term "Moon Flower" is equivalent to the Indian terms "Dark Flower" and "Womb Flower" (Skt., pushpa), both indicating that menstruation is seen in many parts of the East not as a curse but as a creative act in itself; something as precious, fragile, and beautiful as a flower. Christina Camphausen, "Moon Flower," 1993. Color pencil on paper.*

MULADHARA BANDHA

One of the more important *bandhas.

MULADHARA CHAKRA

The "root" chakra, one of the later additions to the ancient system of four. It is now counted as the lowest (number 1) of all *chakras.

LOCATION: Base of spine, the *perineum between genitals and anus, fourth sacral vertebra
ENDOCRINE GLAND: *Gonads; that is, the ovaries and/or testes
RULING *SHAKTI: *Dakini
COLOR: Yellow
LOTUS: Four-petaled, vermilion and crimson red
ASSOCIATIONS: Smell, sexuality, life promotion, vital energy

MUSCARINE

The active chemical in the mushroom *Amanita muscaria. It is a strong toxic substance, and only the smallest amounts are not fatal but rather work as a psychoactive drug.

MUSCULUS SPHINCTER URETHRA   SEE
*PELVIC FLOOR POTENTIAL

MUSK, MUSKONE

As used by many writers, and in common parlance, the term musk has become a general term and is often used to indicate any sexual odor. One then speaks, for example, of *elephant's musk, although these animals do not actually produce musk in the specific sense as outlined below. The actual substance that deserves the name musk is won from the abdominal glands of the musk deer (Moschus moschiferus), a small variety of deer native to Asia. The deer's sex attractant, muskone, is very similar to *civetone.

In Arabia, Persia, and Tibet, musk is taken internally and is believed to be a high-quality *aphrodisiac. Before making an attempt at following this ancient practice, one should know that there are many qualities of musk and that they are all mixed with other substances. Therefore, one should consume musk only if one is quite certain and satisfied about both its origin and its quality. Since pure and genuine musk sells today for more than $200 an ounce, most available musk oils are synthetic reproductions or are won not from the animal but from plants such as Mimulus moschatus,

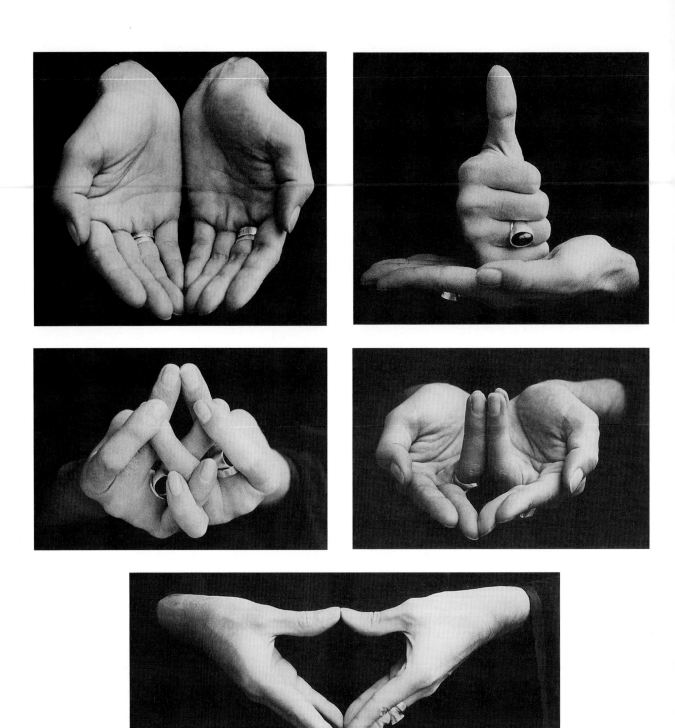

MUDRAS. *The author practicing various Tantric* *mudras*/1; from top to bottom:* linga *mudra,* mahayoni *mudra,* *yonilinga *mudra,* *yoni *mudra. Photographs by Christina Camphausen.*

although this particular plant has lost its smell since the beginning of the twentieth century.

The perfume industry often makes use of galaxolide, a synthetic substitute with the scent of musk.

SEE ALSO *SCENT GLANDS

MUSURI-KAMI

A Japanese *Shinto deity whose devotees practice *phallic worship. This *kami is also connected with the *matsuri festivals.

MYLITTA

Near Eastern goddess of fertility and sexuality to whom women had to sacrifice their physical virginity by serving as *ritual prostitutes in her temples.

MYRRH

The sacred myrrh, one of the Magi's gifts to the newborn Christian savior, is a gum obtained from Arabian trees known to botanists as *Commiphora abyssinica*. How famous this plant and its *aphrodisiac scent is, and has been, is made clear in the description of *olfactory delights. A familiar substance in all Oriental countries, and imported from there to Europe, myrrh is praised especially in the *Song of Songs and in the tales from the *Arabian Nights:* texts that abound with allusions to it.

MYRTLE

Both labia of a woman's *yoni were once compared to this sacred plant of *Aphrodite. The first-century Greek physician Rufus of Ephesus used the names "lips of the myrtle" for the outer labia majora and "fruit of the myrtle" for the inner labia minora.

SEE ALSO *YONI TOPOGRAPHY/3, 4

MYSTERIES OF ELEUSIS

Though these famous rites are most often regarded as Greek, they are actually of Thracian (approximately modern Bulgaria) origin. The initiates to the mysteries were originally all female, as evidenced by paintings from Pompeii that show women only, but the rituals seem to have changed in time to be open to both sexes.

Not surprising in a rite intended to promote fertility, the major and most secret feature of the Eleusinian ritual was the sexual union performed by priest and priestess. Robert

Briffault quotes diverse sources who speak of "the underground chamber and the solemn meeting of the hierophant and the priestess, each with the other alone, when the torches are extinguished, and the vast crowd believes that its salvation depends on what goes on there" (vol. 3, p. 211). Other sources (in Wasson, Hofmann, and Ruck) speak of the use of psychoactive drugs and *aphrodisiac substances during these rituals.

Sexual intercourse will procure absolution of all sins.

TAO AN (292–363)

NADIS
(SKT., "VEIN, TUBE")

According to Tantric subtle physiology, the human body knows 14 major *nadis*—among a great number (72,000) of general ones—of which again three have been given the status of principal *nadis*. The *nadis* are "channels" conducting subtle, electromagnetic energies throughout the human body, especially from one *chakra to the next. In traditional depiction, the number of lotus petals each *chakra* is thought to have indicates the number of *nadis* that emanate from it, distributing the subtle energies to all the organs throughout the body. In ancient Egypt, a similar system of subtle channels was known as the *metu,* and a Chinese equivalent to the *nadis* can be found in the invisible meridians on which the practice of acupuncture is based.

The following are considered the three principal *nadis* of

Yoga and Tantra and are the most commonly known and described:

1. *Sushumna,* the central *nadi,* symbolically associated with the legendary river *Sarasvati/1.
2. *Ida,* the "left" and feminine *nadi* (the river Ganges), of pale color, which expresses lunar energy and ends in the left nostril. In *Vajrayana the *ida* is known as *lalana.*
3. *Pingala,* the "right," red, solar, and masculine *nadi* (the river Yamima), which ends in the right nostril. In *Vajrayana the *pingala* is known as *rasana.*

The remaining 11 channels—sometimes referred to as the *secondary nadis*—are as follows: *alambusha, chitrini nadi* (in the interior of the cerebrospinal axis), *gandhari, hastijiva, kuhu, payasvini, pusha* and *shankhini nadi, sarasvati, vajra* (also in the interior of the cerebrospinal axis), *varuna,* and *vishodara* and *yashasvani nadi.* Other terms of interest in connection with the *nadis* are *brahma nadi, *kanda, *muktatriveni,* and *yuktatriveni.*

NAGIS
(SKT., "DARK, FORMLESS")
Like their male counterparts, the Nagas, these female deities are seen as immortal spirit beings. Half serpent and half human, they are often associated with water and are seen as guardians of mystic knowledge. The Nagis symbolize the "primordial sacrality concentrated in the ocean" and the "earliest aboriginal cultural forms" (Eliade, p. 351). Although not many Nagis are known individually, one is called Thusandi and is said to be mother to the emperor of China and the king of Pagan (Burma).

NAGNA
(SKT., "BARE, NAKED")
One of the Indian sects in which the members possess and wear no clothes. The celibate *nagna* go naked as a sign to the world that they have overcome all sexual desire.
SEE ALSO *ADAMITES, *MASLUB

NAIRATMIKA   SEE *TANTRIC VISUALIZATION

NAIVEDYA   SEE *BODHISATTVA DAKINIS

NALANDA UNIVERSITY
One of the most important places of learning in the history of *Buddhism, Nalanda University in *Bengal, founded in the second century, has brought forth many great teachers, such as *Padmasambhava and *Naropa. Originally, according to Chinese travelers of the period, it was known for its piousness and lofty intellectualism, but when the Tantric teachings began to win ground in India the university became the foremost center in the development of Tantric Buddhism. From here eager students went out toward Nepal, Tibet, China, and southeast Asia to spread the new teachings. It was from here, too, that Padmasambhava made his "missionary" trip to Tibet, which was the starting point for bringing that nation into the fold of *Vajrayana.

Nalanda was destroyed by Islamic invaders during the twelfth and thirteenth centuries. In Tibet, another Nalanda University was founded in Phan-yul in 1435 by the monk and scholar Rongston Sengge (1347–1449), a famous teacher of his time who came from a *Bön background but studied with many Tantric and Buddhist masters.

NAO
Chinese term for the *brain, which is considered to be the seat of female *yin energy. The communication, or connection, between this female energy and the "force of fire" situated in the base of the spine is thought to produce the spinal marrow whence the vital energies are distributed throughout the human body. The *nao* is thought to receive cosmic, subtle energies through the topmost of the Chinese *tan-t'ien.*

NAROPA
(1016–1100)
This Indian *Mahasiddha is renowned for his Six Doctrines (or Yogas) of Naropa (the Naro-chos-drug): teachings that were also expounded by Sister *Niguma and that now belong to the spiritual heritage of the *Shangpa and *Kagyudpa schools of *Vajrayana.

At one time Naropa, "the dauntless disciple," became the head of *Nalanda University, but later he chose to become a student once again. His new teacher was yet another Mahasiddha, the oil presser Tilopa. Naropa was of considerable influence on the development of *Vajrayana not only through the lineage of Niguma but also by being the teacher of Marpa (1012–1096) for more than 16 years. Marpa in turn was the principle teacher of the famous yogin Milarepa (1025–1135), and together they inspired and transmitted the teachings of the various schools of the Kagyudpa. More on this tradition can be found under the entries *Teachings of Sister Niguma and *Tantric Visualizations.

NASAMONIAN MARRIAGE CUSTOM
A term for a peculiar custom among some peoples whereby the bride is required to have intercourse with many men on her marriage night. The name is derived from the oldest account of this practice, given by the Greek historian Herodotus (484–424 B.C.E.), that concerned the Nasamonians of Cyrene, Libya (Briffault, vol. 3, pp. 224ff.).

The custom has been widespread, and examples are given under the entry *Bridal Prostitution, because often a certain gift or payment to the bride was involved. The observance probably has its roots in a fear of the female *blood that has also led to certain rituals surrounding *defloration.

SEE ALSO *OTIV BOMBARI

NAVACHAKRA
The nine chakras constituting the nine major triangles that make up the *sri yantra. The five downward-pointing ones are female and belong to the *Shakti, whereas the four male, upward-pointing ones represent *Shiva.

NAVAKANYA
Though the Sanskrit term kanya usually designates an unmarried woman, the concept of navakanya (nine types of women) is used by several Tantric scriptures to indicate those "types" of women suited, allowed, and prescribed to be partners in worship. On reading Tantric scripture it becomes clear that the term kanya, in this context, does not indicate that women are required to be unmarried. Several Tantras state explicitly that worship and *maithuna can be done with one's own wife or husband or with the partner of someone else. Though most texts merely lay out rules for men regarding with whom they may or may not partake in maithuna, by implication married women were also free to engage in extramarital sexual activity, as long as this occurred in the sacramental setting. This is revolutionary in the socioreligious structure of *Hinduism, where orthodox Brahmanic law would punish a woman heavily for such behavior.

Different Tantric texts name the following women as belonging to the navakanya: "actress, Kapalika woman, pros-

titute, washerwoman, barber woman, Brahmana woman, Sudra woman, cowherd woman, woman of the garland-maker class" (*Yoni Tantra, patala 2; *Kumari Tantra, patala 6). In order to appreciate these choices, one must consider that Hindu society usually prohibited women and members of the low castes from taking part in important religious rituals. This list then, with the high-caste Brahman women included among the "low" Sudra, the actress, and the prostitute, shows the radical social position that was taken by Tantra and that made many people come into its fold.

Another often-used term for these women is kulanganas.

NAYIKAS
These eight Indian deities are said to be personifications of "illicit love" (if such a thing can be said to exist) and are probably remnants of an earlier Indian society in which sexuality had not yet been classified into what "may" and "may not" be done. Because there are two groups of Indian deities called Nayikas, here are the individual names of the deities in the group that is relevant to our topic, to make identification easier: Aruna, Balini, Jayini, *Kameshvari, Kaulesi, Medini, Sarvesvari, and Vimal.

NAYIKA SIDDHI
Sanskrit term used in *Tantra for the female energy that is called *yin in Chinese *Taoism. The fact that the term *siddhi is used here instead of *Shakti indicates the magical, extrasensory, and special powers inherent in the female. The woman can impart these powers to her male partner during *maithuna and sexual *initiation, this in turn being beneficial to both adepts.

NECROPHILIA
Although most societies regard necrophilia as a pathological expression of sexuality, some extreme Tantric sects and/or individuals have made use of it as part of certain rituals or in the framework of a special *initiation ceremony, usually in connection with a graveyard meditation. In contrast to *spectrophilia, the "partner" in necrophilia is the body of a deceased person.

NEI P'ING
An extraordinary text written by the Chinese scholar and initiate *Ko Hung (284–364 C.E.), the first author of the "religious" branch of Taoism to break with the taboo against

writing down the oral traditions. The Nei P'ing is thus a text full of comments and discussions of Taoist "secret," alchemical, magical, and psychophysical "recipes" and represents a selection of then old and contemporary Taoist beliefs and practices. Considering that the religious/magical tradition (Chin., *tao-chiao*) blossomed in the second century B.C.E., beginning in 220, the Nei P'ing probably contains much from those times.

The work itself, written in 320 C.E., still shows these Taoists' general contempt for the written word, especially for the so-called Chinese Classics, which here are called "straw dogs" and "effigies of the past" (Ware, p. 328). However, the work also includes a very interesting and lengthy Taoist library, more than 100 works on silken scrolls Ko Hung collected during his studies. On those texts, his teacher once commented: "A large number of volumes of the various Taoist writings are bound to contain something valuable, but . . . don't waste your time and overwork your mind by learning all of them completely" (Ware, p. 312).

NEI-TAN
(CHIN., "INNER CINNABAR")
Chinese term for *inner alchemy, as opposed to *wai-tan,* or outer alchemy. In some instances, the term is also used for the "inner elixir," comparable to *ros and *dew of ecstasy.

NIDDAH
This specific part of the *Talmud deals in detail with rules and rituals centering on the "white" and "red" female fluids. Here, as is to be expected, all those fluids are seen as unclean. The text makes clear that no man may ever see, and no woman may ever show, "the fountain of her blood"—that is, the menstruating *yoni. If they do "both of them shall be cut off from among their people" (Leviticus 20:18). Such attitudes have, via the Jewish and Christian faiths, dominated many people's lives and are only now slowly beginning to change.

SEE ALSO *FEMALE LOVE JUICES, *MENSTRUAL FLUID

NIGUMA
Vajradhara Niguma is the Tibetan name of the eleventh-century Indian *yogini Vimalashri, a one-time disciple and lover of *Naropa. Naropa taught different things to each of his students, and Niguma received a special teaching that came to be known later as the Six Tantric Yogas of Niguma.

NIGUMA. *Sister *Niguma with shamanic drum and skull cup. Illustration by Saki Takezawa.*

At some point Niguma herself reached enlightenment and began to pass on her knowledge to others. Her most famous disciple was the Tibetan yogi and *Bön student Khyungpo Naljor (978–1079), the only student to whom she imparted her specific and most secret teachings.

When Khyungpo Naljor arrived at Niguma's dwelling place, the charnel ground of Sosaling, she appeared to him as a dark brown *dakini* "dancing above him in the sky" and "adorned with ornaments of human bones" (Mullin, p. 96).

SEE ALSO *TEACHINGS OF SISTER NIGUMA, *TANTRIC VISUALIZATIONS

NI-HUAN AND/OR NI-WAN
In Chinese subtle physiology, an "invisible cavity" situated in the crown of the head. It is regarded as the most important area of the upper *tan-t'ien and is believed to channel cosmic energies into the human body. This process is thought to happen by means of a connecting opening from the *ni-huan* to the *nao* (Chin., "brain")—a connection that can perhaps be equated with the *pineal gland and the *sahasrara chakra.

Sometimes the term is used less specifically and refers to the brain in general or to deities associated with the brain. Literally, the term means, suprisingly enough, "ball of clay."

NILA TANTRA

A work of 22 chapters that is set in the form of questions posed to *Shiva by *Parvati. It is a *Shakta-oriented text that was written early in the eleventh century. Along with a detailed exposition of gurus (male and female teachers) and rules concerning purification and *mantra, the Nila Tantra extensively treats the *kumari puja and also introduces the concept of *misracara. When discussing *sacrifice, the text—like the *Kumari Tantra—also makes provisions for human victims.

SEE ALSO *MAHAMAMSA, *RITUAL PROSTITUTION (FAR EAST)

NINE VEHICLES
(TIB., THEG-PA RIM DGU)

The *Nyingmapa tradition classifies all systems of spiritual teachings into nine categories, paths, or vehicles (Tib., theg-pa; Skt., yana): that of the Sutras (vehicles 1 to 3), *Outer Tantras (vehicles 4 to 6), and *Inner Tantras (vehicles 7 to 9). The first three levels, embracing both the *Hinayana and the *Mahayana teachings of *Buddhism, constitute what is also known as the *Sutra system (Tib., mdo-lugs, "exoteric teachings").

1. The first level is most often indicated as "the vehicle of the listeners" (Tib., nyan-thos-pa'i theg-pa; Skt., sravakayana), referring to the practitioners of Hinayana as "listeners" (Skt., sravakas) to the teachings of the Buddha. Sometimes, however, this first category is called the "Worldly Vehicle" (Tib., 'jig-rten-lha mi'itheg-pa), in which case it refers—quite chauvinistically—to all non-Buddhist religious systems.

2. The second level often refers to a Hinayana practitioner different from "the listeners" in that he or she finds the path alone, without the need to hear the Buddha's instructions. In this case, level 2 refers to "the Vehicle of the Solitary Buddhas" (Tib., rang gyal-ba'i theg-pa; Skt., pratyekabuddhayana): those who renounce social contact and live a life of solitary practice.

   However, if level 1 is defined as "Worldly Vehicle," this second level or vehicle refers to the "lesser" or "small vehicle" (Tib., theg-pa dman-pa; Skt., hinayana) in general, to those who want enlightenment mainly for themselves, as contrasted with the *bodhisattva ideal of stage 3 Mahayana.

3. The third level refers to the "greater vehicle" (Tib., theg-pa chen-po; Skt., mahayana) of those who aspire to the ideal of the bodhisattva, one who wants enlightenment for all and everyone. It is therefore known alternatively as "the Vehicle of Enlightened Beings" (Tib., byang-chub sems; Skt., bodhisattvayana).

   These three levels are distinguished from the teachings of the *Outer Tantras (vehicles 4–6) and the *Inner Tantras (vehicles 7–9), at the apex of which we find *Dzogchen.

NIRUTTARA TANTRA

This *Tantra is a relatively short work of 15 chapters and belongs to the *Kula tradition. It is very much a women's Tantra, with a rather liberal outlook concerning a woman's lifestyle and sexual freedom—a life far less regulated than Indian society would normally permit. The *veshya woman who follows *kulacara is sketched in the text as one who roams about freely—in the sense of the independent, not the physical, *virgin—and enjoys herself as the goddess *Kali does. It also describes extensively the different "types" of *veshya who often figure in rituals of Tantra and Shakta as a sort of ritual prostitute. The text also explains various modes of worship directed to several goddesses but is especially focused on Kali, the great "black mother of time, life, sexuality, and death." The work speaks furthermore about rituals such as the *kularcana, *vira chakra, and *raja chakra.

A study of the Niruttara Tantra makes it clear that also very young girls (a relative definition, depending on a given social context) took part in ritual sexuality. The text states that a woman who practices kularcana should choose *Shiva as her "husband." We know, of course, that Shiva can be the designation of any man in a Tantric ritual, just as any woman becomes the *Shakti. Depending on their age, the young women are then said to become like several powerful goddesses. At age 16, a very young woman is considered as *Kali; at age 15, as *Tara; at 14, *Sodasi; at 13, Unmukhi; and at 12, *Bhairavi.

NOTE: It is important to realize that many other cultures knew marriage, which usually includes sexual union, at a very young age, and some still do. Even in 1989, statistics showed the average age for marriage in Bangladesh as 11.6 years and in Pakistan as 15.3 years—numbers that should be viewed in the context of the fact that life expectancy in these countries generally ranges from 46 to 52 years of age.

NI-WAN   SEE *NI-HUAN

NIZARI ISMA'ILIS
An Islamic secret society whose spiritual concepts and teachings have much in common with those of *Sufism, another "heretical" offspring of Islamic religion. The group is perhaps best known under the name of the Order of Hashishins, an appellation that gave rise to our word *assassin*. The group, especially under the reign of its political and spiritual leader Hasan-I Sabbah (eleventh century) was famous for its political assassinations and for the use of *cannabis and sexual initiations designed as a means for *sexual imprinting. In their mountain stronghold at Alamut, Afghanistan, the Hashishins would undergo certain rituals in order to ensure loyalty and unquestioning execution of orders among its members. The initiation consisted, according to a report by Marco Polo (1254–1324), of multiple sexual union with several "lovely girls" under the influence of cannabis and "delicious drinks" in a luxurious and paradisiacal setting. Robert Anton Wilson rightly pointed out that the drugs used would not have been hashish alone but were probably a well-designed mixture of both stimulants and sedatives (1988, pp. 63 ff.). One can imagine that an experience like that, in the young men so treated, would have left a strong craving for repetition: a promise that was made to them if they were successful at their jobs and survived to return.

NOSE
It is a medically established fact that swelling of the nasal spongy tissues and congestion of the nose occurs during sexual excitement in human beings. The nasal passages of women swell, and occasionally bleed, during menstruation (Benjamin Walker, 1977, p. 92)—a condition that sometimes occurs even in men close to such women.

SEE ALSO *CIVET, *OLFACTORY DELIGHTS, *PHEROMONES, *VNO

NOYES, JOHN HUMPHREY
(D. 1886)
American religious leader and member of a group known as the Perfectionists, who in 1841 founded the Oneida Community in New York State. He believed and taught that the Second Coming of Christ had already taken place in the year 70 and that since then sexuality was no longer sinful. He preached that love should be shared freely without the restraints of marriage and that sexual union, when practiced in a manner that uses *male continence, could lead to spiritual heights and insights of mystical intensity. Noyes preached that sexual union without any intent at procreation was to be regarded as *masturbation, and he wanted to make his male continence a general social accomplishment, or even a fine art. With this as a new and general standard for sexuality, he wanted to establish that each person would be "married" to all others: the ultimate *polygamy and *polyandry. Though most of this may sound rather strange to most people, Noyes did have his basic facts right when he wrote: "A man and woman in intimate physical union have one of the noblest and sweetest encounters possible, amounting to a spiritual experience" (Noyes, 1876).

SEE ALSO *BOGOMILES, *KAREZZA

NU-GUG
The "pure and immaculate ones." A Sumerian term designating the women who held the office of sacred harlot at the temple of Erech in Mesopotamia.

SEE ALSO *SHEELA-NA-GIG

NUIT
Ancient Egyptian star and sky goddess who is seen as mother to all the major Egyptian deities, such as Isis, *Osiris, Nephtys, and Set. In Aleister *Crowley's *Book of the Law* she is quoted as having said, "Take your fill and will of love as ye will, when, where and with whom ye will! But always [dedicate it] unto me" (Liber Al, verse 51) and "I am divided for love's sake, for the chance of union" (Liber Al, verse 29).

SEE ALSO *GEB, *INCEST, *VIPARITA RATI

NUMEROLOGY
This form of divination (others may prefer to call it a method of psychological analysis) has little special erotic or sexual information to provide. Nevertheless, even something as abstract as numbers has been divided according to male and female polarities. In both China and Greece, even numbers are regarded as female, whereas odd numbers are male. Says Plutarch (46–126 C.E.): "Sacrifice to the celestial gods with an odd number and to the terrestrial with an even."

For those who do numerological research, a short index (index 16, p. 283) provides access to all entries of potentially numerological interest.

NUPTIAL CONTINENCE

A custom that demands at least one or two nights, and sometimes from several days to one month, of continence directly after marriage. The many examples of this practice as cited by Robert Briffault demonstrate clearly that such sexual abstinence "is unrelated in its origin to any notion concerning the meritorious character of chastity" (vol. 3, p. 236).

In fact, the prohibition is often directed at the man only, whereas his newly wedded wife is free, or even required, to have sexual union with other men. Whether they are the husband's brothers, friends, or strangers depends on local usage. In this aspect the custom sometimes merges, or even is identical, with that of *bridal prositution. The major cultural regions or peoples who have been known to observe this custom include Eskimos; the tribes of *Assam; European Estonians; the oceanic peoples of Fiji, Borneo, Flores, and the Solomon Islands; and several African tribes.

Yet another form, and rationale, of nuptial continence is known among the African Swahili. Here husband and wife do have sexual contact during the wedding night, but actual sexual union occurs between the husband and the young woman's "chaperon," who, on her part, teaches the art of love to both young people and thus serves as an initiatrix.

SEE ALSO *ASAG, *MALE CONTINENCE, *NASAMONIAN MARRIAGE CUSTOM

NURE

A Japanese term that translates as "to grow wet." Considering some of the words derived from this root—*nuregoto* ("intercourse") and *nuregoke* ("moist widow") as examples—it is clear that the word refers to *ejaculation and *female love juices.

NUTMEG

One of the few *aphrodisiacs especially chosen and promoted by women for their own enjoyment. Nutmeg—in the West mainly known as just another kitchen spice—was highly praised in all Oriental cultures and was especially beloved by women in China. According to Robert Anton Wilson, it "is considerably stronger than marijuana and a dose of ten grams can produce quite *LSD-like states" (1988, p. 183). The drug, however, has unpleasant side effects such as nausea and an increased, rapid heartbeat that can lead to feelings of panic. A recommended amount for a softer and more pleasant effect could not be found.

Two of nutmeg's essential oils, isosafrole and myristicine, have served as blueprints for the drugs known as *MDA and *MDMA, the latter also known as *ecstasy.

SEE ALSO *SASSAFRAS

NYASA
(SKT., "APPLYING," "RITUAL PROTECTION")

A technique, using touch and visualization, that is one of the preliminary parts of many Tantric rituals, especially *maithuna. Different parts of a partner's body are touched and, through identification with the corresponding parts of the deity, are vitalized and charged with divine potential. This is thought to make those parts of the body divine, or to protect them from any "magical" harm, or both. Starting on the right side of the body, the succession in a typical *nyasa* is as follows: big toe, foot, calf, knee, thigh, buttock, *yoni or *lingam, nipple, *breast (if a woman), hand, elbow, arm, *lips, *nose, top of the head. From here on the same parts are touched/consecrated, in reverse order, on the left side of the body.

SEE ALSO *SPARSA DIKSHA

NYINGMAPA

This oldest school of Tibetan Buddhism—the "ancient ones" or "old order"—bases its teachings on the early influx (eighth and ninth centuries) of the then-new *Vajrayana teachings, a process known as the "first diffusion." Their principal teachers are *Padmasambhava, *Yeshe Tsogyal, Santarakshita (d. 802 C.E.), and Vimalamitra (eighth century), but it was only in 978 that the Nyingma lineage was officially established.

The Nyingmapa represent the earliest and nonmonastic school of Tantric Buddhism, the adherents of which were mainly wandering yogis, magicians, and exorcists, often with close ties to the shamanic *Bön-po. Only early in the fourteenth century did the Nyingmas organize themselves into a monastic order, forced to do so by a need to compete with the other powerful schools then active in Tibet.

The lineage continues today with high lamas living in India, Nepal, Darjeeling, and the West.

NYMPHAE

It is interesting to note that the term *nymphae* (the English *nymphs) was the original Greek name for their water goddesses before it was ever used as a term for the small lips, or labia minora, of the *yoni. This term for the inner lips was first used by Rufus of Ephesus, in the first century, for "the little piece of flesh in its [the cleft's] middle" (Lowndes-Sevely, p. 15). By choosing this term, the Greek physician Rufus seems to recognize that women also have, or can have, an *ejaculation.

SEE ALSO *YONI TOPOGRAPHY/4

NYMPHEUMENE
(GREEK, "SEEKING A MATE")

A Greek goddess of promiscuous sexuality, representing the mature and adult phase (second stage) of woman as exemplified in the triple goddess Hera. The first stage (maiden, or *virgin) was called Hebe, and the third stage (crone) was known as Theria.

NYMPHOMANIA

A term usually indicating "sexual obsession" in a woman, based on the Greek nymphe and the Latin nympha, where those terms simply meant "bride" or "nubile young woman."

The term's present-day usage probably derives from the fact that priestesses of the Goddess, when assisting in sexual rituals, were designated as *nymphs and thought to be "brides of God" and representatives of the powers of fertility.

An almost archetypal example of the nymphomaniac woman can be found in Valeria Messalina (executed in the year 48 C.E.), who was friend, wife, and victim of the Roman emperor Claudius (10 B.C.E.–54 C.E.). Aside from making love whenever, wherever, and with whomever she wanted (her husband's power helped considerably) she also loved to masquerade as a prostitute and to have herself satisfied by all kinds of men in the cheapest of Roman whorehouses. According to Pliny the Elder (23–79 C.E.) her personal record was 25 men in one night.

NYMPHS

One could say that the nymphs (Greek, *nymphae) symbolize female sexual enjoyment, and—regardless of how paradoxial it may first seem—as an archetype they have something in

NYMPHS. *Three *nymphs listening to the enchanting flute of *Pan, the divine archetype of male virility. Painting by Andreas Groll, "Pan and the Nymphs," 1897. Oil on canvas. Private collection.*

common with the ancient concept of the *virgin. In later phases of Greek, Roman, and general European decline, the nymphs were seen merely as cute nature spirits inhabiting trees, water, mountains, and so on: the original sacred places of the goddess who was Mother Nature and Mother Earth.

In a cross-cultural context, these deities can be compared to the Indian *apsarasas and *yakshinis as well as to the *dakinis and *yoginis of *Mahayana Buddhism.

SEE ALSO *NYMPHOMANIA, *SATYR

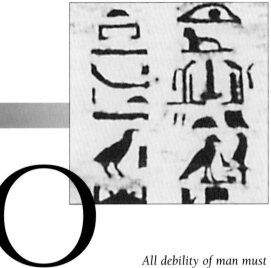

All debility of man must be attributed to faulty exercise of the sexual act. Woman is superior to man in the same way as water is superior to fire. Those who are experts in sexual intercourse are like good cooks who know how to blend the five flavours into a tasty broth.

*SU NÜ, IN THE SU NÜ CHING

OBEAH
1. A term used in Jamaica and other Caribbean islands for magical, supernatural powers, comparable to the Indian *siddhis. 2. The so-called obeah women and obeah men are regarded as shamanlike magicians and diviners, making the term also into a name for a subsect of *Voodoo. The major deity of this cult is the (originally African) goddess *Oduda.

OBELISK
Like the *menhir, the obelisk is a phallic symbol with associations of male fertility, regeneration, and the power of stability. To the Egyptians it was a representation of the sacred *lingam of the god Ra, the generative power of the sun.

SEE ALSO *PHALLIC WORSHIP

OCCULT
(FROM LATIN OCCULERE, "TO HIDE")
Often used almost as a synonym for esoteric, this word has given rise to such concepts as occultism, occult knowledge, and occult schools.

ODUDA
A major goddess worshipped among the northwest African tribes of the Benin, Dahomey, and Yoruba. Her name translates as "the Black One," and her image is that of a *serpent. She is the African equivalent of concepts as diverse as the Near Eastern *Lilith and the Indian *kundalini. In the city of Ado, where Mother Earth menstruates, according to the African tradition, Oduda is responsible for the practice of *ritual prostitution. The cult of which she is the chief deity is known as *Obeah and is practiced mainly in the Caribbean Islands.

OESTROGEN   SEE *ESTROGEN

OESTRONE   SEE *ESTRONE

OESTRUS   SEE *ESTRUS

OIL OF HALCALI   SEE *VAUGHAN, THOMAS

OJAS
(SKT., "LIFE FORCE," "POWER")
Term for the vital, subtle, and highest form of energy associated with human life. The transformation and sublimation of, for example, sexual energy into ojas—by means of rituals, special techniques, and visualization—was and is one of the major aims of those groups and individuals who consciously refrain from all erotic activity, or at least from *orgasm and/or *ejaculation. Ojas is believed to accumulate in a given individual, and a person's spiritual, intellectual, and social accomplishments are believed to be fed and made possible by this energy, which is called ojas-shakti.

SEE ALSO *CHASTITY, *CH'I, *CHING, *RETENTION OF SEMEN, *SEMEN

OLFACTORY DELIGHTS

The sense of smell is, from an evolutionary standpoint, our most ancient, and simultaneously our most sophisticated, physical sense. The capacity for discrimination of the olfactory sense far outranks that of eye or ear, and it is therefore not suprising that people at all times and everywhere have concerned themselves with scents—aromatic herbs, oils, and perfumes—and often with their erotic effects.

Even the stern prophet Muhammad spoke of his love for perfumes and for the women who wear them, and the *Bible also contains reports of women applying these arts: Judith anoints herself with precious ointments and Ruth with fragrant oils, and Esther "purifies" herself with oil of *myrrh and other sweet odors. That biblical authors were well acquainted with the erotic delights of scent we can judge by the following quote: "I have perfumed my bed with myrrh, aloes, and cinnamon. Come, let us take our fill of love until the morning; let us solace ourselves with loves" (Proverbs 7:17–18). Elsewhere, wealthy and sophisticated Romans were enchanted by *ambergris and *civet, *myrrh and *cinnamon, and ointments made from *spikenard. From ancient Egyptian women comes an interesting and unique custom that was also known in eighteenth-century France and is still in practice today: According to this tradition, a woman carries a little bag filled with a delightful scent in her *yoni.

Aside from the fact that some individual plants, their oils, or other derivatives enhance erotic emotions and sexual arousal, some people and (sub)cultures have tested and invented mixtures of *aphrodisiac scents that act on body and soul like a well-orchestrated symphony of olfactory stimulation. One example of this is the recommended use of the *Tantric perfumes, different scents being applied to different parts of the body. One of the *Tantras, the Pithamala-Mahatantra, even has a whole chapter devoted to deha ranjana: a Sanskrit term that translates as "perfumes for ensuring pleasure in sexual union." Among Turkish perfumers an exciting recipe was and still is familiar, consisting of *olibanum, *musk, and myrrh: a mixture said to directly affect the genitals. More recently, the connection between scent and sexuality has been revealed by studies concerning animal and human *pheromones, and the role of tabooed types of odors (from sweat, armpits, genitals) has become more clear. The sexual impact of odor has also been much expounded in the literary works Germinal and La Terre by Emile Zola (1840–1902) and La-Bas and A Rebours by J. K. Huysmans (1848–1907). The most incredible and interesting novel concerning odors, however, is Perfume, by Patrick Suskind (b. 1949), in which the main character succeeds in making the "perfect scent" by distilling it from the bodies of 24 *virgins.

SEE ALSO *PERSPIRATION, *SCENT GLANDS, *SHUNAMISM, *VNO

OLI

Sanskrit term meaning "womb fire," a designation for female sexual heat energy. The *oli techniques are designed to (re)absorb this energy.

OLIBANUM

This is the biblical frankincense, which has been praised for its scent and for its *aphrodisiac qualities, as in incense and as a perfume.

OLIPHANT, LAURENCE
(1821–1888)

An English statesman and journalist who worked for The Times of London, Oliphant in 1865 became a disciple of the American mystic Thomas Lake Harris (1823–1906), to whom he gave (or lost) all his money. Back in England, he married a well-endowed woman, apparently for money. He also made several journeys to India, where he became acquainted with *pranayama. He and his wife are known for their development of a breathing technique they called *sympneumata; Oliphant published a book by this title in 1885. In later years the couple went to live in Palestine, where they saw themselves as being rather like sexual missionaries, and they attempted to teach their insights to the local people.

Oliphant as a character is described in William Harrison's novel Burton and Speke, which is now in print under the title Mountains of the Moon.

SEE ALSO *BREATH, *CONSPIRATION, *KAREZZA

OLI TECHNIQUES

A group of three related exercises—mainly for the male adept—aimed at manipulating and directing the flow of sexual energy in *maithuna, or simply at absorbing *oli.

Using the seal called *vajroli mudra, the male draws the "female seed" up or in, a process called sahajoli. In the case of male emission, the now mingled male and female energy/essence/juices can also be (re)absorbed by a technique called amaroli.

A similar Taoist technique is known as *huan-ch'ing pu-nao.

OM

In one sense, Om is simply one letter in the *Sanskrit alphabet. At the same time, however, it is one of the best-known and most widely used *mantras. Repetitive vocalizing (Skt., japa) of the sound Aaouummmm serves to unite the practitioner with the general vibrational background of the universe and is thought to have a beneficial effect on the brain and on the complete *endocrine system.

OM MANI PADME HUM

The Sanskrit version of the oldest and most famous *mantra of *Vajrayana Buddhism, the Tibetan version being om mani peme hung. To the majority of Tibetans, and according to most of the schools (see *Gelugpa and *Saskya-pa, for example), this sacred formula, literally "jewel (*mani) in the lotus (Skt., padma)," expresses an abstract, philosophical, and spiritual concept. Enlightenment, symbolized by the mani, or jewel, is seen here as arising from, or in, human consciousness, represented by the *lotus. Whenever one comes into contact with Tibetan culture, travels among Tibetan or Nepali people, or takes part in a *puja, one will hear this mantra chanted thousands or millions of times. In written form, the mantra can be found on prayer flags and prayer wheels, from which the message "jewel in the lotus" is thought to penetrate all regions and all worlds.

To other schools and individuals, the message has a second and not less exalted meaning, signifying the eternal yearning of the universe to make the best possible use of *dualism and its promise of union. With the help of entries for the individual syllables of the mantra in this encyclopedia, the reader will not find it difficult to decipher the actual text.

ONEIDA COMMUNITY   SEE *NOYES, JOHN HUMPHREY

ONION

From the Indian *Vedas to the Chinese, Islamic, and European traditions of erotically active substances, the onion is held in high regard. Aside from being generally stimulating and blood cleansing, it is probably the cheapest *aphrodisiac, and accordingly onions were banned in most of the monasteries in East and West.

OPHIDIAN CURRENT

Derived from the Greek ophis ("snake"), this term is a Western approximation of, or an equivalent to, the *kundalini and symbolizes the sexual currents of energy used and amplified in several ceremonies in the context of *sexual magick.

SEE ALSO *EROTOCOMATOSE LUCIDITY, *OPHION, *SHAKTI ASANA

OPHION
(FROM GREEK OPHIS, "SNAKE")
The *serpent of creation in the *Orphic Mysteries.

OPIUM

This illegal, *alkaloid psychoactive drug is derived from the opium poppy (Papaver somniferum), a plant that was sacred to *Aphrodite, the Greek goddess of love and sexuality. Along with its general effect of relaxation, it can have beneficial side effects on the user's erotic energies by stimulating erotic dreams, visions, fantasies, and also "performance." Charles Baudelaire, comparing it to *Cannabis sativa, wrote: "Opium is a peaceful seducer; hashish is a disorderly demon."

In China, the *aphrodisiac effects of opium were also well known: The ancient erotic novel Dschau-yang dschii-schii (The Golden Lord Mounts the White Tiger) claims, with true Chinese perfectionism, that it will give life to a tired lance (*lingam) and assures its functioning for at least 3000 thrusts.

ORDO TEMPLI ORIENTIS

An occult group founded at the turn of the century by the wealthy Austrian Karl Kellner (d. 1905), a widely traveled Freemason who had also studied *sexual magick in both India and Arabia. The group's most famous member, and the successor to Theodor Reuss (d. 1924) as head of the order, was Aleister *Crowley, but several other famous people were also originally affiliated with it. Among them were the founder of anthroposophy, Rudolf Steiner (1861–1925), the cabalistic writer Papus (1865–1916), and Gerald B. Gardner (1884–1964), the "founder" and grand master of modern witchcraft.

Apart from its general hermetic and cabalistic teachings, the O.T.O., as the Order of the Temple of the Orient is known, also made use of sexual techniques gleaned from *Tantra and *Taoism. The "secret teachings" of this order, stripped of alchemical codes, *secret language, and ritual preparations, are easily explained. Sexual magick was practiced in almost every conceivable way, in the form of autoerotic, homosexual, and heterosexual activities. The latter included sexual union with virgins and menstruating women, *ritual promiscuity, and the technique known as *erotocomatose lucidity. Tantric symbols and codes were transliterated into Occidental imagery, and the *vajra and *ghanta, for example, came to be called the magic rod and the mystic rose.

The O.T.O. is still active today, and several groups in England, Germany, Switzerland, and the United States claim the title of representing the "official" and true lineage from the original mother temple. The knowledgeable writer and teacher Kenneth Grant (b. 1924) as of 1989 was the head of the order's English branch. Technically, all international rights to name, succession, copyrights, and so forth have been granted to the American caliphate by a recent decision of an American court. A good introduction to the history, theory, and practice of this order is Francis King's *The Secret Rituals of the O.T.O.* One of the order's manuals, reproduced in King's book, lists the following texts as required for an adept's study: the *Ananga Ranga, the ancient Hathayoga Pradipika and *Shiva Samhita, the *Kama Sutra, and *The Perfumed Garden.* To judge by the publications and teachings of Kenneth Grant, it also becomes clear that the members know of the Tantric *kalas and *marmas and that they (or some of them) practice rites related to the *yoni *puja* and, for example, the *Mass of the Holy Ghost. Some of the "advanced" degrees in the order's initiatory hierarchy are—or at least were in 1923, under Crowley—related to different sexual techniques:

- Eighth degree: theory and practice of autosexual magical techniques (*masturbation) that are used, for example, for the consecration of talismans
- Ninth degree: teachings/exercises concerning heterosexual techniques of male-female sacred union (nine is the number of evolution) to achieve magical creativity
- Eleventh degree: techniques concerning anal intercourse (homosexual and/or heterosexual), thought to revitalize the body

The fact that this last degree is numbered "higher" than the heterosexual initiation and practice reflects the personal tastes of certain leading practitioners. Given the society of 1923 and its morals and taboos, it is easy to comprehend that a higher number may indicate merely a more "secret" teaching.

SEE ALSO *GREAT BROTHERHOOD OF GOD

ORGASM
(GREEK, "TO SWELL WITH WETNESS")

In everyday language and imagery, the idea of orgasm is all too often associated, even equated, with *ejaculation. However, ancient and contemporary research shows quite clearly that these two sexual, erotic states are separate. Although they often occur almost simultaneously, especially for men, it is better if we disassociate them in our minds and remind ourselves that the succession of arousal states occurs in the following manner in both women and men:

1. swelling (engorgement of genital parts by blood)
2. contractions (muscle event)
3. orgasm (psychosomatic energy event)
4. ejaculation (fluidic and energy event)
5. deflation (drainage of blood, relaxation)

According to *Lowndes-Sevely, the time lag between events three and four is longer in women and is the main reason for the well-known—or so one hopes—fact that orgasm is achieved and reached in different ways in men and women, with different approach times and peaks.

The Chinese have long known about these differences in male and female pre- and postorgasmic states of affairs. The man's *yang energy is thought of as *li, or fire, whereas the woman's *yin energy corresponds to *k'an or water. Fire, according to Chinese physicians and alchemists, easily flares up in a great heat but is also easily and quickly extinguised by water. Water, however, takes quite a long time to become heated up over fire, but it also will cool down only very slowly. In the ancient *I Ching these two elements, when combined in their proper order with water above fire, form into the hexagram *chi-chi and signify "completion."

The question whether or not there are vaginal and/or clitoral and/or *G-spot orgasms is still not resolved and becomes superfluous when we consider the *yoni as a synergetic and holistic system.

SEE ALSO *EJACULATION, *FUSION OF K'AN AND LI, *MORS JUSTI

ORGY

This often misused and misunderstood term is derived from the Latin *orgia*, indicating the "state of inspired exaltation" preceding a ceremony of initiation. Considering this, any gathering of women and men that deserves the name *orgy* should be regarded—and conducted—as a sacred gathering intent on a transformation and change of consciousness in both the individual's and the group's mind. In this, the orgy is closely related to such Tantric rites as *karma mudra* and *chakra puja*. However, considering the historical material as well as reports from participants, a typical Middle Eastern and European orgy is less disciplined and controlled and—may the reader appreciate the image—much more orgiastic than its Indian counterparts.

Sexual orgies were also known to the tribes of New Guinea—for example the Marind-anim—and were clearly seen by them as a sacred activity, designed to please their ancestral deities. In the 1930s an old member of the tribe once said to a Dutch missionary, "This then is our prayer" (Cornelissen, p. 40). First the participants, especially the women and girls, were sexually excited or, according to one missionary, "made very horny" (Cornelissen, p. 125), and then the public orgy would commence with most members of the tribe joining in. Such ritual orgies were deemed necessary to the well-being of the tribe and were thought to rebalance any problem or disease. After venereal diseases had been introduced to New Guinea by white men, probably Australians, the tribes tried to heal themselves by even more orgies, with disastrous consequences.

SEE ALSO *KIMALI

ORIGEN OR ORIGENUS
(185–254 C.E.)

A Greek Christian church father and philosopher who, according to the report of Eusebius of Caesarea, castrated himself in order to be able to teach and preach before girls and women—that is, to avoid the potential sins of his natural, carnal tendencies in dealing with women. If Eusebius's story is true, Origen would have based his action on the biblical words "there are eunuchs who have made themselves eunuchs for the sake of the kingdom of heaven" (Matthew 19:12). Origen's allegorical interpretation of the *Song of Songs has influenced Christian mysticism and has helped to establish the mystical tradition of *spiritual marriage.

SEE ALSO *CASTRATION, *PURITANICAL FANATICISM

ORPHIC MYSTERIES

What are known as the Orphic Mysteries are the ritual celebrations of a mystery religion based on Greek as well as Egyptian beliefs, deities, and symbols. Developed during the fifth century B.C.E., Orphism attempted to combine the mysteries of Apollo with those of *Dionysus; it centered on legends of the singer Orpheus, with an androgynous, hermaphrodite *Eros often becoming the central focus. An Orphic bowl, dating from the first century and found in the 1860s, shows 16 nude worshippers, nine female and seven male, apparently making ritual gestures, some of which are directed, as in the Tantric *nyasa, toward breasts, navel, and genitals.

The Orphic Mysteries were directed toward personal initiation and the attainment of a blameless life, without which *rebirth or *reincarnation would cause an eternal return to the world. During his or her initiation into the Orphic Mysteries the candidate had to enter the earth (symbolic death) and come out once more (rebirth), and would then partake of the milk from the Earth Mother's breasts.

SEE ALSO *MAENADS

OS   SEE *YONI TOPOGRAPHY/16

OSIRIS

Egyptian god famous for his myth of *dismemberment, in which phallic symbolism plays a major role. The myths concerning Osiris include numerous accounts of *incest, *ritual promiscuity, and what is usually called adultery.

SEE ALSO *NUIT

OTIV BOMBARI

Name of the marriage ceremony—"the ceremony of many men"—among the Marind-anim, a tribe of the Papua family in New Guinea. As in the custom known as *Nasamonian marriage, the bride has sexual union with all men of her husband's totem clan, with a maximum of five or six per night (Cornelissen, p. 35).

O.T.O.

Abbreviation for the occult group *Ordo Templi Orientis.

OUTER TANTRAS
(TIB., *PHYI RGYUD*)

The Lower or Outer Tantras, also known as "Outer Tantras of Secret Mantra" (Tib., *gsang sngags phyi'i rgyud sde*) or

"Outer Secret Mantra" (Tib., *gsang sngags phyi pa*), correspond to the fourth to sixth levels of the *Nine Vehicles.

LEVEL 4: KRIYA-TANTRA (TIB., *BYA-BA'I RGYUD*) OR *KRIYA YOGA* (TIB., *BYA-BA*, "ACTION")   On this level, the practice consists mainly of formal, ritual action.

LEVEL 5: CARYA-TANTRA (TIB., *SPYOD-PA'I RGYUD*)   The teachings of this category are partly external and partly internal in terms of actual practice and include much attention to personal behavior and conduct (Tib., *spyod-pa*). Another name for this level of teachings is *upa* yoga, or Ubhaya (Skt., *ubhaya*; Tib., *gnyis ka*, "twin, both"), a combination of conduct according to *kriya* yoga and an outlook/view that belongs to yoga Tantra.

LEVEL 6: YOGA-TANTRA (TIB., *RNAL-'BYOR-PA'I RGUYD*)   At this stage, most of the practice is interiorized and the adept experiences actual union (Tib., *rnal-'byor*) with the deity who is the object of his or her meditation.

The teachings and practices of these Outer Tantras are often concerned with purification of the self, thus preparing the adept to receive the wisdom of the *Inner Tantras. To reach this level of the teachings, the practitioner must usually undergo the first level of initiation (Tib., *dbang-bskur*; Skt., *abhiseka*, "initiation, empowerment, sprinkling"): the Vase or Flask Initiation (Tib., *bum-dbang*; Skt., *kalasabhiseka*). This is actually a whole series of initiations that includes the five "Initiations of the Five Families."

OVARIES   SEE *YONI TOPOGRAPHY/20

OYSTERS

If you wonder what Napoleon, Casanova, and Madame Du Barry have in common, their love for oysters—and extolling their *aphrodisiac properties—is the answer. Oysters show a very high content of protein, phosphorous, and *zinc, and this is the most likely reason for their legendary strengthening effects on both sexes. Apart from this it is certainly their *yoni-like appearance that made them erotically interesting in the first place, but some of the remarks on *caviar may be valid here, too. For a much cheaper aphrodisiac of an even better quality, in terms of mineral content, one should turn to anchovies. Robert Anton Wilson observed in 1973 that "the reputation of the oyster is probably due to sympathetic magic: they look (and even taste) like the female genitals" (Wilson, 1988, p. 183).

OSIRIS. *The Egyptian god *Osiris in an *ithyphallic stance.*
Egyptian Museum, Cairo.

P

*All thoughts vanish with the
onslaught of pure passion.*

Kuttni Mahatmyam

PAAN

An Indian term used for a chaw often composed of an edible leaf, betel nut, slaked lime, catechu paste, and other spices. *Paan* can be bought on almost every street corner in India, Pakistan, and Nepal, but the contents are not always the same. Some *paan* can be obtained, for prices up to $50 a chew, that are composed of costly substances all of which have *aphrodisiac qualities.

PADMA   SEE LOTUS

PADMASAMBHAVA

(C. 730–C. 805 C.E.)

The Sanskrit name of this famous Great Guru translates as the "Lotus-born," and he is said to be the son of *Indrabhuti, another famous sage involved with the spreading of *Tantra and the establishment of *Vajrayana in Tibet. When traveling through Tibet in order to subdue the fierce, local demons (that is, non-Buddhist deities) and *dakinis of the then-prevalent shamanic *Bön religion, the Guru Rinpoche, as Padmasambhava is often called, sometimes resorted to female "manifestations" of himself as, for example, *Sinhamukha.

At other times the hero himself felt that he needed certain initiations and knowledge that was possessed by Tibet's female adepts, and he did not shrink from begging for it, as the interesting story of *Suryu-candrasiddhi shows quite

clearly. As a true Tantric, the master initiated, made love to, and in turn was initiated by several beautiful *dakinis*, and he took care that all the countries that he wanted to enlighten, and to subjugate to Buddhist rule, were represented in his choice of partners. His five major partners were the Lady *Yeshe Tsogyal (Tibet), Mangala (probably of the Himalayas), Kalasiddhi (India), Mandarava (Zahor), and Sakyadevi (Nepal). Though Padmasambhava is generally regarded as the historically identifiable founder of Tibetan *Buddhism, or Vajrayana, and is held in high esteem by all Tibetan schools, he is especially venerated by the *Nyingmapa, where he is regarded as a second Buddha. The year of his birth is not on record but must have been quite some time before 757 C.E., the year of his arrival in Tibet (after his departure from the famous *Nalanda University). He left Tibet in 804 after having founded the first Tibetan Buddhist monastery at Samye.

PADMINI

The "lotus woman," one of the *female archetypes of Indian erotic literature. The *padmini* woman is said to enjoy sexual union much more by day, when her *lotus opens up under the rays of the sun, than by night. She also prefers the lushness of flowery surroundings to the cool satin sheets of the bedchamber and especially enjoys strong pressure on her yoni and much stroking of her breasts. The *padmini's* love juice is said to smell like a newly blossoming lotus.

See also *Light

PALACE OF YIN

Although sometimes used to mean simply "womb," this term specifically refers to the location in the body where the ogasmic secretion called *moon flower medicine lies waiting to be released. The concept may well be the most early "discovery" of a *G-spot and represents the ancients' insights into female *ejaculation and the female *prostatic glands.

See also *Female Love Juices, *Purnacandra

PAN

This Greek/Arcadian god—in some ways a European equivalent to the Indian god *Shiva—represents the male aspect of nature, the male forces of fertility and sexuality. Often he is symbolized as an *ithyphallic figure, half man, half *goat—the goat being an animal well known for its fertility,

Padmasambhava.
*Subject of many *thangkas,
the ultimate culture-hero of
Tibet is variously shown as a
shamanic yogi, a compas-
sionate teacher, or, as here,
a fully ordained monk.
Traditional thangka by a
contemporary Nepalese
artist. Photograph by Rufus C.
Camphausen, with kind
permission of the Everest
Thangka Gallery,
Patan, Nepal.*

virility, and untiring sexual appetite. Similar figures are *Bacchus, *Dionysus, and *Priapus.

PANCHAMAKARA or PANCHATATTVA

This is the infamous ritual of the five Ms (from *makara), which has shocked and shamed many a European as well as Indian writer on Tantric religion. The five objects, or obser- vances, of this ritual gathering are *madya (wine), mamsa (meat), matsya (fish), *mudra/2, and *maithuna.

The panchamakara is celebrated by at least eight men and women. The term panchatattva ("five elements") is often used as merely another name for the panchamakara ("five observances"), but some writers make the distinction that the panchatattva is celebrated using not only wine but other drugs—such as *cannabis in the waters of grain—as well. Concerning this ritual the *Kamakhya Tantra says the following: "The true devotee should worship the Mother of the Universe with liquor, fish, meat, cereal, and copulation." Other Tantric schools, especialy those of *Dakshinacara (right-hand) affiliation, have assigned alternative meanings to the five Ms. The wine, meat, fish, and so on are then replaced with "coconut juice, cheese, ginger, rice, and honey" or, more abstractly, with "composing the mind, inbreathing, outbreathing, holding in the breath, and meditation" (Benjamin Walker, 1982, p. 66).

PAPISH

A custom among the Asmat of New Guinea according to which two married men could exchange their wives, if the wives consented and after each had borne a first child to her husband. Such an agreement was not seen as a second marriage in the sense of *polygamy but was nevertheless a lifelong affair. An actual exchange took place for only one night at a time, and sexual union was allowed only if all partners in the *papish* relation were present in the village.

PARAKIYA

The term indicates a married woman who takes part in Tantric worship and sexual union with someone other than her own husband. Another type of woman called *parakiya* is an unmarried girl who is still in the care, and under the protection, of her guardians.

SEE ALSO *GOPIS, *SAHAJIYA

PARANANDA SUTRA

A *Vamacara work dating from sometime between the tenth and twelfth centuries. The text considers only three of the five *makara as important and gives a *mantra for each of these three: *madya, *mudra/2, and *maithuna. Similar to other Tantric texts, it states specifically that women represent the divine, are "the life-breath of the world," and "should not be made angry," as quoted in Banerjee (p. 275). Banerjee also says that the Tantra contains "vulgar details" of the devotee's sexual activities, but no English translation is given to substantiate this personal moral judgment.

PARASURAMA-KALPA SUTRA

A Tantric work of the thirteenth century that comes from the *Kula tradition. Not only is the text unique for being written in an aphoristic style, but it is regarded as a systematic compendium of *Tantra philosophy and worship, ded-

icated especially to the goddess Tripurasundari. The text regards the five *makara as mandatory and describes, among other things, the sexual ritual known as *dutiyaga.

Interesting for its discussion of the *veshya, and the phenomenon of *ritual prostitution in general, is the following admonition contained in this text: "A woman, who is indifferent, should not be enticed by money and the like" (Banerjee, p. 282). The scripture also contains a detailed description of *madya, the wine drunk in many Tantric rituals.

SEE ALSO *CROWLEY, ALEISTER

PARAURETHRAL GLANDS AND DUCTS

Often-used term for the two glands and their many ducts at the fringe of the female urethra, part of the *urethral sponge. Although their specific function is yet unknown, they are involved with the production of *female love juices and with *ejaculation. The term *paraurethral glands* is replaced more and more with the term female *prostatic glands*, and that is the term we have used in this encyclopedia.

PARTHENOPE
(GREEK, "VIRGIN")

The fact that this Greek term is also the name for one of the seductive and tempting sirens indicates once again that *virginity is not necessarily a nonsexual, nonerotic state of being.

SEE ALSO *PEISINOE

PARVATI
(SKT., "OF THE MOUNTAINS")

The goddess Parvati is seen as the daughter of the Himalayas and represents the *Shakti in one of her many manifestations as partner and lover of *Shiva. The *Nila Tantra and a number of other Indian sacred texts are written in the form of dialogues between Shiva and Parvati.

PASIPHAE

A Cretan goddess, "she who shines for all," who is known mainly for her passion, which led her to mate even with a bull, thus conceiving and giving birth to the famous Minotaur of Cretan mythology. Pasiphae is regarded as the sister of the seductress *Circe.

PASHU

A person still possessed by his or her "animal nature," as opposed to those called *vira and *divya. The *pashu* is either

PARVATI. *Merging three goddesses into one, this beautiful seventeenth-century bronze shows a smooth-limbed, full-breasted goddess *Parvati in her aspect as Uma, who in turn is one of the many manifestations of *Durga. Private collection.*

an uninitiated person or an initiate of the third and lowest degree. Most scriptures do not allow a *pashu* to take part in Tantric rituals that involve the drinking of wine and sexual union.

PATCHOULI

An *aphrodisiac scent and one of the traditional *Tantric perfumes. The oil is won from an Oriental soft-wooded shrub known as *Pogostemon heyneanus.*

PC MUSCLE   SEE *PELVIC FLOOR POTENTIAL

PEACH

A fruit connected in China with youthfulness and immortality, as can be seen in the myths of *Kuan-yin and, for example, the expression *peach juice of immortality. However, as the Chinese type of peach is a very deeply clefted fruit, it also serves as a symbol for the *yoni.

SEE ALSO *YONI SYMBOLOGY

PEACH BLOSSOM FLOW   SEE *MENSTRUAL FLOW

PEACH JUICE OF IMMORTALITY

A Chinese expression for the secretions from the nipples of a woman's *breasts.

SEE ALSO *WHITE SNOW, *WITCHES' MILK

PEISINOE

(GREEK, "SEDUCTRESS")

Like *Parthenope, this deity is a member of the sirens, the group of Greek goddesses famous for their attempt at seducing Odysseus and his men with their erotic wailing and their ecstasy-promising songs.

PELVIC FLOOR POTENTIAL

> If the pelvic floor muscles are slack and you do not
> know how to use them, you are missing out on one
> whole aspect of sexual experience
> SHEILA KITZINGER, WOMAN'S EXPERIENCE OF SEX

Known in Sanskrit as *bhaga asana,* and in Tamil as *pompoir, this Western term refers to the system of pelvic floor muscles in the genital area of women that consists of two groups, each of which can be activated, or controlled, independently. The first group consists of the ischiocavernosus (1) and bulbocavernosus (2) muscles as well as those responsible for control of the urethra, the musculus sphincter urethra (4). In the second group we find the pubococcygeus (3) or PC muscle, the pubovaginalis (5), and the puborectalis (6) (see illustration). Exercising and training these muscles not only can enhance erotic sensations and possibilities for both partners in general but can be used specifically for the following goals:

1. Aiding the *ejaculation of *female love juices and in

PELVIC FLOOR POTENTIAL. *Cross sections showing two layers of muscles involved with the *pelvic floor potential. Illustrations by Christina Camphausen.*

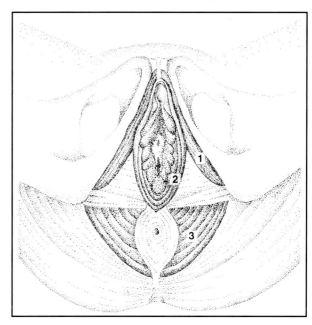

Outer layer of pelvic floor muscles.

1. **Ischiocavernosus**
2. **Bulbocavernosus**
3. **Pubococcygeus (PC muscle)**

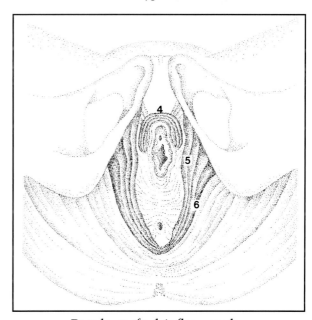

Deep layer of pelvic floor muscles.

4. **Sphincter urethra**
5. **Pubovaginalis**
6. **Puborectalis**

the woman's control over the stimulation of her *yoni and her orgasmic timing (Ladas, Whipple, and Perry, in *The G-Spot*, observe that "female ejaculation occurs mostly in women with strong pubococcygeus muscles").

2. Controlling the prolongation of penile erection and/or the excitation of male *ejaculation (*see* *Imsak).

3. Absorbing orgasmic fluid(s) (*see* *Ka'a).

Especially famous for their accomplishments in this art were the *kabbazah* and the women of Ethiopa and southern India, and today the technique is recommended by authors as diverse as Alan Ramsdale, Mantak Chia, Nik Douglas, and Sheila Kitzinger (see bibliography). These authors describe a number of detailed exercises—for example the Taoist deer exercise, the vaginal kiss, and even "vaginal weight lifting"—all designed to gain full control over these muscles. Incidentally, such training will also aid the woman during childbirth.

Men have similar muscles, of course, which are mainly used as an aid in the *retention of semen.

SEE ALSO *LINGAM TOPOGRAPHY/25, *VAGINAL BALLS

P'ENG TSU

A legendary Chinese sage and adept of sexual *Taoism reported "to have lived more than nine hundred years" (Levi and Ishihara, p. 15). Much of his advice to men on matters of sexual union and the *retention of semen and many of his proverbial commentaries have been translated in Levi and Ishihara's 1989 volume *The Tao of Sex*.

PENILE PERISTALSIS

A technique similar to the *oli techniques. The practitioner of penile peristalsis aims at directing sexual fluids upward through the *lingam. This is achieved by means of a series of rhythmic movements of the lingam's tube walls. Some texts use the term *upward peristalsis* to indicate this technique or process.

PENIS   SEE *LINGAM, *LINGAM TOPOGRAPHY/4–9

PERFUME   SEE *OLFACTORY DELIGHTS, *TANTRIC PERFUMES

PERFUMED GARDEN

An Arabic erotic manual, comparable to the Indian *Kama Sutra, written by the Tunesian Sheikh al-Nefzaoui in the six-teenth century and translated into English by Sir Richard *Burton in 1866.

The text begins by praising God as well as the human genitals: "Praise be given to Allah who has placed man's greatest pleasure in the natural parts of woman and has destined the natural parts of man to afford the greatest enjoyment to woman." The book, apart from telling several erotic fairy tales of differing qualities, goes on to name, explain, and describe 25 coital positions and techniques. At the end of this section the author adds, "If there be anybody who thinks that those which I have described are not exhaustive, he has only to look for new ones."

The book also contains a large collection of *yoni and *lingam terminology. In addition to providing the Arabic names and their translations, it describes these 35 types of lingams and 38 types of yonis in terms that often afford insights into the psyche of male and female personalities and behavior. Although the work is clearly written by a man and is intended mainly for men, its author certainly realizes that different women have different tastes, and he often admonishes his readers to find out which kind of union the woman prefers most and to help her reach satisfaction and fulfillment.

PERINEAL SPONGE   SEE *YONI TOPOGRAPHY/23

PERINEUM

This point/location midway between genitals and anus, though not usually seen as part of the genital system in either male or female, should not be overlooked, nor its importance misjudged. The Chinese and Sanskrit terms for the perineum, *ching-tao, *hui-jin, and *yonishtana, appear often in Taoist and Tantric texts, sometimes as a female place of pleasure and intelligence, sometimes as instrumental in male retainment techniques such as *intrajaculation.

SEE ALSO *INFIBULATION, *LINGAM TOPOGRAPHY/24, *SUBINCISION, *YONI TOPOGRAPHY/24

PERIPLANONE B

A *pheromone secreted into the air by female cockroaches. A study carried out by the Centraal Laboratorium in Delft, Netherlands, can serve to illustrate the incredibly small amounts involved in the study of pheromones and the power these substances can exert on the receiver's behavior.

In order to obtain a mere 200 micrograms of periplanone B, entomologist C. J. Persoons needed 75,000 virgin female cockroaches. Male roaches in the study reacted to only 100 femtograms (that is, 0.000000000000001 gram) of periplanone B with an excited mating dance, and scientists speculate that just 0.001 gram of the substance would be sufficient to attract 100 billion interested and highly motivated male roaches to the source of transmission.

PERSPIRATION SEE *CONISALUS, *SCENT AURA

PERTUNDA
A little-known Roman "sexual deity" (Wedeck, p. 219) described as a "pagan goddess of sexual intercourse" by George R. Scott in his *Phallic Worship*.

PERVERSIONS
Today we are, fortunately, in a position to recognize that the definition of what is normal and what is perverse depends almost entirely on a given culture's frame of reference, whether in the name of religion, superstition, "good" and "healthy" upbringing, or even common sense. In an age when information is readily available on the different moral codes and sexual preferences of our ancestors as well as our global neighbors, it makes no sense to define such things as *cunnilingus, homosexuality, exhibitionism, *spectrophilia, or group sex as "perverted" or "abnormal" behaviors. Even our own societies, as we can observe in the course of our lives, change their outlooks from generation to generation, with little or no stability of sexual mores that can be detected. Some people will find this disturbing, and others will see it as a liberating concept that allows them to finally feel free to make their own choices and to follow enthusiastically their heart's own path.

Attention, however, should be given to certain immutable rights that every human—if not every living being—has or should have and that should serve as a general social constant for judging what is perverse and pathological and what is not. The application of such human-rights thinking then leads to the conclusion that "perverse" is that which is done by one person without consent of the other. It is sad, but we must also know by now that such consent on the part of another person cannot ever be asked, or accepted, from a so-called representative, not even either or both of a child's parents. Like anyone else, parents are also too human and do not always automatically decide matters in the true interest of their child.

When using this type of definition we must of course classify war, terrorism, murder, and all those dark sides of the human experience as the real perversions. In the context of the erotic/sexual framework of the present book, however, we can label rape, torture, and the witch-hunt of the *Inquisition as perverse, together with *castration, *circumcision, *clitoridectomy, *infibulation, and those forms of sadism and *incest that are forced on an unconsenting person or animal.

PEYOTE
A cactus (*Lophophora williamsii*) with psychoactive properties that has been used for at least three thousand years in certain rituals of Mexican Indians. It is also used in rituals of the contemporary Native American Church, a religious society numbering 250,000 members (according to 1997 statistics) in Canada and the United States, for whom such use is legal. One problem with peyote as an *aphrodisiac is the almost certain nausea produced by some of the chemicals in the plant, although this does not occur with *mescaline, its active chemical substance and/or synthetic derivative, when that substance is taken alone.

PHALLIC WORSHIP
Although the expression *phallic worship* has often been used to describe all types of sacred sexuality, erotic ritual, and worship of genital symbols in general, we shall use it throughout this encyclopedia in its true, phallic, and male sense only (*see also* *Yoni Worship). Worship of the phallus as a symbol of male creative and fertile energy has been quite common in most parts of the world, and it should rightfully be studied and discussed in as much detail as others of the so-called great religions of the world. Its physical/sexual nature, however, which is today generally considered quite impossible with sacredness and spirituality, makes such open and serious consideration incompatible, and the available data have been studied by only a handful of self-motivated and independent researchers and authors.

The term itself is misleading and somehow derogatory and discriminating, seeming to convey that we are dealing here with something "pagan," "heathen," and "primitive." Phallic worship as a classification taken in its most literal sense can actually be accepted only if we also accept a

PHALLIC WORSHIP. *This large marble sculpture in the sanctuary of the goddess *Tap-tun is not itself an expression of *phallic worship, but it has the same appearance and dimensions of the huge phalli carried by many bearers during the *matsuri festivals of Japan.*
Photograph by Rufus C. Camphausen.

classification of Christianity as "cross worship," Islam as "stone worship," and Judaism as "worship of a six-pointed star": confusing symbol with content, map with territory, the menu with the meal itself.

With this in the back of our minds, we now take a closer look at how the concept of maleness, or *yang, has been expressed and where it has been manifested.

FAR EAST   *Thailand: See* *Hinta Hinyaai, *Tap-tun.

Japan: See *Matsuri, *Sarutakhiko.

India: Not only statues of gods and lingams received worhip in this country. It has been reported that the priests of Kanara "used to go naked down the streets ringing a bell" (Benjamin Walker, 1982, p. 62) so that barren women could come to kiss their sacred member in order to become fertile.

SEE ALSO *AMARNATHA CAVE, *CARTE BLANCHE, *EKALINGA, *GANESH, *SHIVALINGA

NEAR EAST   *Egypt:* Phallic worship was practiced in the temples of Karnak, Thebes, and Heliopolis until the fourth century.

SEE ALSO *GEB, *MIN, *OSIRIS

Israel: Probably reminiscent of the earlier sanctity of the genitals, the early Hebrews swore their oaths by placing one hand on the other's *lingam, a practice that biblical writers have disguised as "Put, I pray thee, thy hand under my thigh" (Genesis 24:2–3, 47:29). The small Gnostic sculptures of winged phallis speak their own language.

EUROPE   *England:* The *Giant of Cerne Abbas and a similar figure of equal dimensions cut into a mountain at Wilmington (in the former kingdom of Sussex) testify to phallic worship, as do the traditions of *Maypole games and dances.

France: As an aid to help them achieve pregnancy,

women in the Brittany region of France used to eat a little of the dust surrounding their town's phallic statue.

Greece: Megalithic "standing stones" at Filitosa on the island of Corsica were deliberately shaped as phalli, complete with glans penis.

SEE ALSO *DIONYSUS, *HERMES, *MENHIR, *PHALLOPHORIA, *PRIAPUS

Italy: Worship of the "holy member" during *carnival is notable in this context.

PHALLIMANCY

A Hindu system of divination based on shape, length, thickness, and other features of someone's phallus, or *lingam, mentioned in the *Ananga Ranga.

PHALLOPHORIA

A festival of *phallic worship held on the Greek island of Rhodos in honor of the god *Dionysus.

PHALLUS   SEE *LINGAM, *LINGAM TOPOGRAPHY/4–9

PHEROMONES

(FROM THE GREEK *PHERO*, "TO CARRY," AND *HORMON*, "TO EXCITE")

A class of chemical substances released into the environment, mostly in minute amounts, by one organism (transmitter) and received by the olfactory organs of another (receiver). Pheromones are a means of communication and are also used by the transmitter to influence behavior of the receiver, although such communication is restricted to members of the same species.

Many animals make use of such pheromones in order to announce territorial claims, status in the chain of command, and/or sexual needs or interest. Many of the (known) pheromones are involved in the processes surrounding fertility and are thus instrumental in the regulation of sexual attraction. An indication of how powerful such pheromones can be, and of how sensitive the sense of smell can be, can be found in the text describing *periplanone B.

There are indications, furthermore, that not only do mosquitos, queen bees, cockroaches, and pigs transmit and receive invisible messages through such pheromones, but also that these substances play an active and important role in human sexuality, especially in the cycles of fertility and menstruation. Perspiration from the armpits of female sub-jects, as well as male perspiration during sexual intercourse, has been shown to be influential in the synchronization and regulation of the *menstrual/ovarian cycle.

Studies in recent years have confirmed the existence of human pheromones, secreted through our skins and perceived by the *VNO in our *noses, although researchers often shy away from using this proper name with its animalic associations. Instead, names have been invented such as *echtohormones* and others.

SEE ALSO *OLFACTORY DELIGHTS, *SCENT AURA, *SCENT GLANDS

PHILATELES   SEE *VAUGHAN, THOMAS

PILLOW BOOKS

The famous erotic pillow books of the Orient are not, as is often thought, a purely Japanese invention but were also known in India, Nepal, and China. The books generally contain paintings of erotic scenes and unusual sexual postures, interspersed and annotated with love poems, quotations from classic erotic texts, and sometimes passage from famous erotic novels. Some books also featured texts from the esoteric traditions concerned with *dual cultivation, *maithuna, and the use of sexual energies in general. Exquisite materials were used in the production of such books, which came, and were stored, in beautiful boxes made, for example, of *sandalwood, silk, brocade, jade, and precious metals. Such finely and artistically produced erotic albums basically served two aims. First, they were a means to acquaint young and inexperienced men and women with the incredible variety of human sexuality, and as such they were an aid in teaching the art and science of physical love. Second, but by no means of less importance, they were meant and used to stimulate loving couples, to enhance their lovemaking, and to remind them of the possibilities connected with sex and eroticism beyond "habitual manners" of sexual union.

The partners looking together at the erotic scenes depicted on such pages—unlike the common approach to contemporary pornography, which is generally consumed alone—surely must have experienced a feeling of comradeship and enjoyed the mutual understanding created in learning about which scenes and activities each partner liked the most. Whether or not that effect was intended will remain unknown to us; we do know that it works, and it would seem well worth reintroducing this custom in modern-day cultures and bedrooms.

In their cross-cultural *Erotic Sentiment in the Paintings of China and Japan* (1994) and *Erotic Sentiment in the Paintings of India and Nepal* (1989), authors Nik Douglas and Penny Slinger have tried to re-create such a work, using material from all the countries mentioned above. That the countries involved have abandoned the tradition and under Western influence have gradualy developed much more negative and restricted attitudes toward sexuality is generally acknowledged, but it is interesting to know that an Indian couple is still presented with an elaborately ornamented and wrapped pillow book upon their marriage. In this case, however, as recorded by Douglas in 1968, the pages are all white and empty (Douglas and Slinger, 1981, p. 7).

PINEAL GLAND

This gland, also known as the pineal body, conarium, or epiphysis, is one of the seven glands constituting the *endocrine system. It must not be confused with the better-known *pituitary gland, or hypophysis, which lies only a few centimeters farther forward and down.

In humans, the tiny pineal gland is about the size of a grain of puffed rice and is shaped like a pine cone. It is attached to the midbrain, as its base, and lies exactly between the right and left hemispheres of the *brain, about halfway between the cerebellum and the thalamus (see illustration p. 28).

Biologically the pineal gland is regarded as an evolutionary relic of the light-sensitive *third eye that is still present and functioning in some lizardlike reptiles, where it is called the pineal eye. Even today its precise function in humans is unknown to medical and biological scientists, but it is known that the pineal gland produces and secretes melatonin. This is a hormone concerned with pigmentation and changes in skin color, as well as with the circadian rhythm of night and day that governs our habits of sleep. The tiny gland, attached to the lower midbrain, has been called the third eye and the doorway to the divine spirit. When René Descartes (1596–1650) tried to overcome the apparent paradox of Christian dogma with the then-new scientific insights into the functioning of body and brain, he proposed the pineal gland as the place where the soul resided, driving and controlling the body through the brain and the nervous system, yet separate from both.

Scientific research has shown that in many animals—chickens, squirrels, rats, and hamsters, for example—the pineal gland secretes an enzyme, N-acetyltransferase, that "provides a natural timing mechanism: a biological clock that may regulate both physiological and behavourial processes" (Binkley), and it is this and similar information that indicates the pineal gland is an important factor in the "biological clock" operative in all animals, including the species *Homo sapiens*.

One of the alarms built into the biological clock of humans is the time for puberty and sexual maturation. It has been shown that young boys with a pineal tumor come to puberty much too early, and tests with animals have shown that melatonin can slow the onset of puberty. Other signs of the pineal gland's connection to sexual development in humans are to be found in the fact that the gland is largest in children and begins to involute in puberty, but that it remains generally larger in women than in men. In terms of subtle physiology, the pineal gland is associated with the *sahasrara among the Tantric *chakras and, in Taoist terms, with the *ni-huan.

SEE ALSO *ECSTASY (PSYCHOSOMATIC)

PINGALA   SEE *NADIS

PITHAS OR PITTHS

A Sanskrit term meaning "seat" or "shrine." It indicates many places sacred to Tantrics and other Indian pilgrims. The Shakti *pithas*, or *pitashtanas*, are thus called because they are connected with the Great Goddess, *Shakti, under whatever name she may be worshipped locally. Several traditions are connected with the *pithas*, and the number of holy places with this statue is variously given as 4, 51, 64, or 108.

The four "seats" mentioned in the *Puranas are places at which the Great Goddess was thought to be actually present in one or another of her manifestations. The places in question are, according to research done by traveler and author Nik Douglas, the Uddiyana Pitth (at Odiyana, Orissa), the Sirihatta Pitth (Sylhet, *Assam), the Purnagiri Pitth (Purnasaila, East *Bengal), and the Kamakhya Pitth (Gauhati, Assam).

The series of 51 sacred places of pilgrimage is based on the archaic myth of the goddess's *dismemberment (the myth of Sati) into 51 pieces, which then fell to Earth at these places, creating a series of aniconic altars that became sacred sites, each associated with a certain part of her body. Her left and right *breasts, for example, fell at Ramgiri and Jalandhara (both in the Punjab), her *yoni at Gauhati (Assam), her tongue at *Javalamukhi, and other limbs and organs at *Kalighat (Bengal) and other places. In each of these locations the goddess—in one of her aspects—is worshipped in a shrine or temple that holds a relic (a stone or object) representing one of her limbs or some other part of the body. One can thus wander through India (especially Bengal), Nepal, Assam, and Bangladesh in order to pay homage to her, recombining and unifying with such a pilgrimage her image and energies inside oneself.

The most famous of these shrines, and one to appear in every listing of the *pithas*, is located in a cave near Gauhati (Assam), where the goddess *Kamakhya is worshipped and where the unique *Yonimandala can be found. Two more such sites are described in the entry *Sixty-four Yogini Pitha.

For extensive information, *see* D. C. Sircar's *The Sakta Pithas.*

PITUITARY GLAND

Formerly regarded as the master gland of the endocrine system, which, under the influence of the hypothalamus (*see* *Brain), governs all other glands of the *endocrine system and thus all hormone activity in the brain and body. It is composed of an anterior and a posterior lobe, both of which have specific functions and produce a wide variety of hormones. It is now known, however, that the hypothalamus plays a much larger role, and the concept of a master gland has had to be changed.

Hormones of the anterior lobe control the activity of other glands such as the *adrenals, the thyroid, and the ovaries and/or testes as well as specific actions of the pancreas. Two of the hormones manufactured in the anterior pituitary are *FSH and *LH.

The posterior lobe controls the heart (and blood circulation), the kidneys, and the uterus.

PLAYING THE FLUTE

"Flute" is a Chinese example of *lingam terminology, and this is a poetic Chinese expression for *fellatio.

P'O

(CHIN., "BODY SOUL")

In Taoism, this is the subtle and luminous element of the female, or *yin, principle, located in the "space of the force" in the lower body.

SEE ALSO *HUN

POLYANDRY

(FEMALE–MALE–MALE)

A term indicating the custom of some cultures in which a woman can have two or more husbands. This is structurally different from general promiscuity and must not be confused with it. With a group marriage as defined by the term *polyandry,* the woman formally marries her men with all the cultural responsibilities connected to marriage. Examples of this custom—its opposite is known as *polygyny and *polygamy (male–female–female)—can be found almost everywhere, worldwide and throughout the ages:

FAR EAST   In Tibet, and in regions of India such as Ladakh, a woman can have more than one husband. Sometimes, as an exact complement to the custom known as *sororal polygamy, a woman would marry two or more brothers; for that Briffault uses the term *fraternal polyandry.* However, Tibetan marriage customs are much more complicated and could best be classified as *group marriage.

Polyandry was common among tribal peoples of Malaysia.

SEE ALSO *SERIAL POLYGAMY

OCEANIA AND AUSTRALIA   Polyandry is found among many tribal people of the Pacfic islands.

AFRICA   Polygamy is more common, but polyandry was known on Madagascar.

POLYGAMY (GENERAL)

1. A custom according to which marriage includes more than one partner or spouse from the opposite sex. Polygamy therefore contrasts with *monogamy, which is a one-to-one social contract. In the original meaning of the word, polygamy does not indicate whether one man is married to several women (*polygyny) or one woman to several men (*polandry).

2. In a study of data about 853 human societies worldwide, both past and present, 84 percent practiced polygamy and/or found it acceptable. In only 16 percent of these societies was monogamy considered the norm (Stump).

The definitions of *polygamy*, *polyandry*, and *polygyny* have become less precise, and the word *polygamy* is now often used for what should be called *polygyny*: one man and several women. Because it is the more familiar word, we use *polygamy* throughout this work to mean one man with two or more wives.

POLYGAMY (MALE–FEMALE–FEMALE)

Term indicating the custom of some cultures in which a man can have two or more women as wives. This is structurally different from general promiscuity and should not be confused with it. With a group marriage as defined by the term *polygamy*, the man formally marries his women with all the cultural responsibilities connected to marriage. Polygamy therefore is quite different from customs like the *Nasamonian marriage, *otiv bombari, or *ritual promiscuity. Special regard must be given to two unusual types of polygamy, both of which are too specific to be treated here: *sororal polygyny, in which one man marries a number of sisters, and the largely unrecognized, modern form of *serial polygamy.

Here then are some examples of polygamy from throughout the world:

FAR EAST   The twelfth-century *Koka Shastra admonishes the polygamous husband with the following words: "He must give pleasure to all his beloveds, so long as they live, with walks in pleasure-gardens, love, care and gifts" (Comfort, p. 154). Polygamy seems to have been

POLYGAMY. *This Japanese scene shows one male practicing what is often called a "Herd of Cows" in India,*
*the term inspired by the god Krishna's famous erotic dalliances with *Radha and the other *gopis.*
*The aim here is to receive as much female *yin essence as possible.*
Drawing by Penny Slinger, based on an eighteenth-century Japanese print by Kitao Shigesama.

an ancient practice in the Himalayan region. In the mythical songs of the northern Magar, a people in the Nepalese Himalayas, the very first shaman of the world, for example, is reported as having had two wives (Oppitz, p. 16).

The nobility among the Mongols, especially the Great Khans (a khan being the equivalent of a ruler or emperor), practiced polygamy. It is known, for example, that Kublai Khan (1215–1294) had several primary wives, along with hundreds of lesser wives from his many subject nations.

NEAR EAST   In Egypt, as in Europe and Africa, the male nobility often married several wives.

Among the ancient Hebrews, tribal chiefs and war-lords (see *Abraham) often had more than one wife, and the possible number was virtually unlimited.

In Islamic cultures, religious law limits a man's legal wives to four, yet there is no injunction against a harem or against "lesser" wives or concubines.

EUROPE   Polygamy was practiced especially among the Teutonic, Irish, and Slavic nobility.

SEE ALSO *SERIAL POLYGAMY

THE AMERICAS   High in the north among the Inuit Eskimos as well as among many of the Indian tribes of South America, polygamy was (and sometimes still is) the norm.

OCEANIA AND AUSTRALIA   Among the Mandobo and Muju tribes of New Guinea, it was a sanctioned practice for the husband in a barren, older couple to find a sec-ond, younger wife—often a woman with children—in order to have someone to provide and care for him and his first wife in old age.

AFRICA   Polygamy is a widespread custom, especially among tribal nobility, kings, and chiefs.

POLYGYNY

The older and more precise term for what is now most often called *polygamy. It is sometimes still used, as for example in the expression *sororal polygyny.

POMEGRANATE

Because this word means "apple of many seeds" and proba-bly because of its *red sap, reminding one of menstruation and birth, this fruit has become in many cultures a symbol of fecundity and fertility. The pomegranate is an attribute of deities such as *Aphrodite and Hera, and the fruits were also carved on the pillars of *Solomon's great temple. Its biblical name is rimmon, which derives from the root word rim, meaning "to bear offspring." Sometimes the pomegran-ate, like the *peach or the *apricot, is used as a symbol for the *yoni, and according to Pliny the Elder its pits were considered to have *aphrodisiac effects when eaten.

SEE ALSO *BLOOD, *MENSTRUAL FLUID

POMPOIR

A Tamil term for the technique(s) of using the female pelvic floor muscles for the enhancement of pleasure and/or the control of timing during sexual union.

Richard *Burton's translation of the *Ananga Ranga includes the following quote concerning the art of *pelvic floor potential: "She must ever strive to close and constrict the *yoni until it hold the *lingam, as with a finger, opening and shutting at her pleasure, and finally acting as the hand of the Gopala-girl, who milks the cow. This can be learned only by long practice, and especially by throwing the will into the part affected." Mastery of the technique is helpful in *imsak and is required for a woman to be a *kabbazah.

SEE ALSO *BHAGA ASANA

PRAJNA
(SKT., "CONSCIOUSNESS," "WISDOM")

1. Similar to *mudra/4, this term is sometimes, especially in Buddhist texts, used to indicate the female partner in ritual *maithuna. In this the term is similar to *vidya and *yogini.
2. In *Mahayana Buddhism, the term prajna is defined as a wisdom that is inherent in immediate experience: a wisdom that we call intuition when it is proved right.

PRAJNOPAYA-VINISCAYA SIDDHI

A Buddhist Tantra of the late seventh or early eighth cen-tury. Attributed to Anangavajra, one of the 84 *Mahasiddhas, the work contains several features that high-light the earliest *Vajrayana teachings. It describes several *siddhis, prescribes indiscriminate sexual relations, and even allows sexual union between mother and son, brother and sister, or father and daughter. The work also clearly defines *prajna, the "perfection of wisdom," as a female pre-rogative, to be obtained by men only through women.

SEE ALSO *INCEST, *MAHASUKHA, *MATRIYONI, *SHEKINAH

PRAKRITI
(SKT., "NATURE," "MATTER")

In the teachings of *Shakta, *prakriti* is the term for the female principle of creation and also a name for the Great Goddess *Shakti. *Prakriti* is thought to unfold in the world in accordance with the principles known as *gunas*: universal, generalized principles.

PRANAYAMA

Sanskrit term indicating a whole range of respiratory exercises and techniques that are an integral part of any yoga. Tantric adepts, like their *Taoist counterparts, also use their understanding of the forces inherent in *breath in their sexual *asanas.

SEE ALSO *CONSPIRATION, *T'AI-HSI

PRAYOGA

A special type of yoga that serves to attract female elementals (*succubi) and to make use of their energies (*nayika siddhi*) by practicing *congressus subtilis.

PREMA

To the Tantric adept, the term signifies that type of love and love play in which all distinction between lover and beloved is transcended.

PREPUTIAL EXCISION   SEE *CIRCUMCISION

PRIAPUS

Greek phallic god, son of *Aphrodite and *Dionysus, who presides over the fertility of both fields and livestock and is regarded as the personification of the male sexual impulse. He is probably the most celebrated among the phallic deities and is usually depicted in *ithyphallic stance and with unusually large genitals. He—or rather his priest—also had the duty and priviledge of being instrumental in the *defloration of his young female worshippers.

The sacred animal of Priapus is the goose, reputed to possess highly developed sexual and generative powers. Much of what is known as *phallic worship in southern Europe is centered around this god. His many statues in the countryside and in small public chapels were constantly presented by his female devotees with garlands of flowers. In cases of venereal diseases, impotence, or other afflictions of the genitals, people would offer reproductions of their "private parts" to Priapus together with prayers for help. These offerings were often paintings or small figurines made from wax, wood, or even marble.

SEE ALSO *EMA

PRIMA MATERIA

This alchemical term for "first matter" is often used to indicate the elixir produced by mixing male and female sexual liquids.

PROSTAGLANDINS

Natural, body-generated substances found in *semen as well as in *menstrual fluid. Prostaglandins are involved in such basic and important body functions as the immune response and the activities of the lungs, heart, uterus, and digestive system.

PROGESTERONE

A substance produced in the *corpus luteum and formerly known as luteum. Progesterone is a hormone instrumental in the *menstrual/ovarian cycle and is dominant during pregnancy and in the latter stages of the menstrual cycle. The substance has a typical odor: German shepherd dogs who were given this scent as a cue were able to identify women in either of the two conditions.

SEE ALSO *PROGESTOGENS, *SCENT AURA

PROGESTOGENS

A group of steroid hormones, produced in the *adrenal glands and in the woman's ovaries, with actions/effects similar to those of *progesterone.

SEE ALSO *YONI TOPOGRAPHY/20

PROMISCUITY   SEE *RITUAL PROMISCUITY, *SERIAL POLYGAMY

P REMA. *To the advanced Tantric adept, ritual sexuality does not focus, as in romantic love, on a specific individual to whom one is bonded. Rather, it represents a joyful meditation free from planning and from goal orientation, a kind of play in which all distinction between lover and beloved is transcended. Nineteenth-century painting on paper, Ragasthan, India. Photograph courtesy of Nik Douglas.*

PROSTATIC GLANDS (MALE)

What is often simply called the prostate is actually a group of glands collected into an organ about 2.5 centimeters long. This collection of glands surrounds the junction of the spermatic ducts with the urethra. At the time of *ejaculation, "the prostate" supplies—via only two ducts—a powerful jet of thin, white seminal fluid that helps propel the sperm cells through the urethra. This glandular fluid makes up about 38 percent of the male's semen—the other constituents being sperm cells (2 percent) and fluid from the seminal vesicles (60 percent); see *Lingam Topography 21—and is also responsible for its characteristic odor. The glands contain—and need—a large amount of *zinc. The prostatic glands may also be what we have tentatively called the P-spot.

See also *Lingam Topography/13, 15, 19

PROSTATIC GLANDS (FEMALE)

Women also have a number of prostatic glands, similar in makeup and function to those of the male and embedded in the urethral sponge. These *paraurethral glands, as they are sometimes called, have only recently been "rediscovered" or reestablished. The glands are connected to the urethra by a large number of ducts, which transport the glandular liquids that are the major constituent of female ejaculation. They probably constitute the actual "erotogenic" pressure point that has become known as the *G-spot.

See also *Female Love Juices, *Yoni Topography/13–15

PROSTITUTION   See *Bridal Prostitution, *Ritual Promiscuity, *Secular Prostitution

PSILOCYBE MEXICANA

A mushroom that has been regarded as sacred for more than three thousand years by Mexican Indians and some others. Use of this mushroom is said to bring one face to face with the Divine and/or one's true, inner self. Its active substance, *psilocybin, has been synthesized and is sometimes available in the form of small pills. After the first few hours of rather breathtaking mental activity and dramatic visions, it can provide one with a heightened sensitivity that is very conducive to erotic experience and activity, and it may thus be regarded as an *aphrodisiac. Among the ancient Mexicans it was known as teonanacatl, the "flesh of the gods."

See also *Amanita Muscaria, *Magic Mushrooms

PSILOCYBIN

The active *alkaloid of the mushroom *Psilocybe mexicana. It is sometimes available, although illegally, in pill form.

PUBERTY RITES   See *Circumcision, *Defloration, *Infibulation, *Menstrual Fluid, *Subincision

PUBIS   See *Lingam Topography/1, *Yoni Topography/1

PUBUCOCCYGEUS   See *Pelvic Floor Potential

PUBORECTALIS   See *Pelvic Floor Potential

PUBOVAGINALIS   See *Pelvic Floor Potential

PUDENDA

Latin term for the external, visible parts of the female genitals.

See also *Yoni, *Yoni Topography/1–7

PUJA

The sanskrit word puja is usually translated as "worship" and/or "ritual." There's nothing wrong with that translation, linguistically, except that for a native speaker, the experience does not feel like "worship" but rather like "Holy Mass." Seen from within the culture, puja carries all the emotional connotations that for most Christian-educated people are inherent in the terms mass or religious service; whereas worship and ritual, to most, belong to the terminology of anthropologists rather than to someone actively practicing her or his faith.

A typical puja of *Vajrayana and *Tantra consists of chanting *mantras, doing *mudras/1 and visualization exercises, reading and reciting sacred texts, and presenting offerings and libations.

See also *Kumari Puja, *Rahasya Puja, *Stri Puja, *Yoni Puja

PUMPKIN

The raw seeds of pumpkin contain phosphorus as well as the *vitamins B and F, a fact that makes them excellent food for health in general, and also a largely unrecognized *aphrodisiac that aids in the production of *sex hormones.

PUMSCALI

Name for those women among the early (pre-)Vedic *vratyas* who engaged in *ritual prostitution. In this capacity, they initiated men to the sacred dimensions of sexuality and transmitted sexual practices and rituals that have become part of *Shakta and *Tantra.

PURANAS

A collective name for a category of Indian sacred scriptures that were available not only to the priestly caste of the Brahman, as were the *Vedas, but to the common people as well. There are 18 principal Puranas, written down only from the fourth century onward, containing ancient legends and traditions that reveal the beliefs and practices of early, popular Hinduism.

The texts were generally subdivided into three classes, depending upon which particular deity of the Hindu trinity they exalt most. The Bhavishya Purana, for example, emphasizes Brahma, while the Vishnu Purana and the Bhagavata Purana exalt Vishnu, and the Shiva Purana and Agni Purana are concerned mainly with *Shiva. Apart from these texts that exalt three male gods, there are also Puranas associated with *Shakta and *Tantra dedicated to some of the major goddesses of India—for example the sixth-century *Devi Purana and the tenth-century *Kalika Purana. Also of special interest are the Markandeya Purana, a fifth- or sixth-century text that includes the *Devi Mahatmya, and the eleventh-century Brahmanda Purana, which includes the *Lalita Sahasranama.

PURITANICAL FANATICISM

Though the terms *sadism* and *masochism* are quite recent coinages, the psycho(patho)logical drives behind these "modern" phenomena are as ancient as the repression—in whatever manner—of sexuality. The early Christian demand for celibacy and chastity and its negative obsession with the "evil" of woman and of sexuality not only spawned the sadistic *perversion that became known as the *Inquisition but also gave rise to a number of truly mad saints whose only chance for expressing their sexuality lay in negative, self-destructive, and masochistic practices. In order to dispel her sexual desires, the sixteenth-century Carmelite nun Maria Magdalena of Pazzi, for example, rolled herself over thorny bushes until she bled from multiple cuts, and she also enjoyed being whipped—bound and naked—by the abbess and in the presence of her sisters (de Ropp, pp. 180 ff.). Another woman, Angela de Fulgino, went so far as to burn her own genitals with hot coals.

As things go—and as is natural with such a basic, instinctive, and survival-oriented drive as sexuality—even the most rigid measures often could not dispel the desires of body and mind. St. Jerome, a pious hermit who withdrew into the desert in order to stay away from the temptations of women and eros, gave an honest report of the problems he developed. He wrote: "Parched by the burning sun, how often did I fancy myself amidst the pleasures of Rome. . . . I, who from dread of hell, had consigned myself to a prison in which my only companions were scorpions and wild beasts, fancied myself amongst bevies of young women. . . . My mind was aflame with desire and lust seared my flesh. . . . Helplessly, I lay at the feet of Christ . . . struggling to subdue my rebellious body" (Jerome, Epistola XXII). Some men, like the philosopher *Origen and members of the sect called *Valerians, went so far as to castrate themselves in an attempt to be saved from the fires of hell.

SEE ALSO *ALGOLAGNIA, *CASTRATION

PURNACANDRA

(SKT., "FULL MOON")

Term used in the *Koka Shastra for a duct or channel, part of the *yoni, that is said to be filled with a juice of love.

SEE ALSO *FEMALE LOVE JUICES, *PALACE OF YIN

PURPLE MUSHROOM PEAK

One of the many Taoist expressions, in *secret language, for the *yoni. From here, and more specifically from the *palace of yin, comes the female *ejaculate known as *moon flower medicine.

SEE ALSO *YONI TERMINOLOGY

PUSHPA   SEE *BODHISATTVA DAKINIS, *MENSTRUAL FLUID

PUSHPAVATI

Sanskrit term indicating a menstruating woman, from *pushpa*, or "flowering." Another and similar term for such a woman is *rtula*.

Q

*Once the Wheel of Love
has been set in motion,
there is no absolute rule.*

*KAMA SUTRA

QADESH AND/OR QADESHET

A goddess of love and sexuality known in Egypt and in the Akkadian and Babylonian empires whose worship included *ritual prostitution. Qadesh has attributes such as the *lily and the *serpent and is shown as a "lady of the beasts," a type of goddess known in many cultures as protectress and ruler of the animal world and its fertility.

QADESHTU

Women dedicated to, or in service of, the goddess *Qadesh, trained adepts in the arts of love. The term *qadeshtu* or *kadishtu* (Hebrew *kadesha*), translates as "the pure" or "the holy ones."

SEE ALSO *ISHTARISHTU, *RITUAL PROSTITUTION

QODOSH

Also spelled *kodosh* or *quodosch,* this is the third degree of initiation that follows on *alphaism and *dianism. In qodosh, in contrast to dianism, reaching sexual climax (*ejaculation and/or *orgasm) is allowed and desired, and the man's "loss" of semen is seen not as harmful but rather as a gift.

SEE ALSO *IMSAK, *RETENTION OF SEMEN

QOPH

The 19th Hebrew glyph, or letter, which has some interesting cabalistic associations:

1. The eye of the needle
2. Luna, Earth's only natural satellite; tarot card 18, the Moon
3. The *yoni and its "secret female energies"
4. The cerebellum (*brain)

QUEBRACHO AND QUEBRACHINE

A plant quite similar to *yohimbine that was used in South America as an *aphrodisiac. Quebrachine is the name of the *alkaloid derived from the quebracho, a tree native to Argentina, Bolivia, and Chile.

QUININE

This substance, one of the medicines used to fight malaria, was considered an *aphrodisiac by the Persians. Minute amounts of the *alkaloid quinine are included in various sparkling drinks like tonic and ginger ale.

R

*One must rise by
that by which one falls.*

*HEVAJRA TANTRA

RADHA
(SKT., "SHE-ELEPHANT")

As the main character in the forbidden and adventurous love dalliance of the god Krishna—himself an incarnation of the god Vishnu—with the *gopis, Radha has become the chief female deity in the Tantric *Sahahiya cult and is thus to be compared to the Tantric *Shakti.

SEE ALSO *ELEPHANT

RAHASYA PUJA

The most secret form of the *yoni *puja*, constituting the meditation aspect of the secret and outer type. In this ritual, the practitioner is alone with the woman who has agreed to serve as his focus on energies, to serve as a representative of the *devi. This woman may be his married wife, another lover, an initiate, or perhaps a *veshya: a paid and professional woman specializing in such services.

The practitioner sits in front of and between the woman's opened legs. With complete concentration and with unwavering awareness, the worshipper goes through a cycle of ritual actions, each of which represents one of the five elements. With the element ether in mind, he moves his hands across most of her body in large circles, ranging from her legs to her breasts, repeating these movements over and over. During the next stage, with the element air in mind, he restricts the movements of his hands to her belly and thighs, once more repeating his strokes several times. During stage three, his attention becoming focused now on the *yoni and the element fire, he strokes the genital area again and again in a repetitive upward movement. Next, the direction of stroking is changed and he strokes the yoni downward, symbolizing the element water. Finally, after a process that may have taken the better part of an hour, the element earth is given expression as he presses one hand, softly but firmly, against the woman's yoni, resting there until the ritual finds its natural end.

RAJA CHAKRA

A Tantric ritual during which five different women are worshipped by a male devotee.

According to one source, the women in question are a given man's mother, sister, daughter, and daughter-in-law, as well as his teacher's wife (Banerjee, p. 573). A very different constellation is described in the following quote, translated from the *Mahanirvana Tantra: "Five beautiful and most charming maidens of five castes . . . should be engaged. The worshipper should next offer honey, wine, and meat. This is Raja Chakra. By its influence one acquires piety, worldly gain, desire, and emancipation and lives in the celestial region for sixty thousand years" (Bose and Haldar, p. 144). The authors follow this description, and that of the similar *deva chakra, with the statement that these "mystic practices . . . do not form any indispensable part of daily or common Tantric worship" and that "their efficacy is known only to the initiated and can hardly be understood by the laity" (p. 145).

SEE ALSO *INCEST, *VIRA CHAKRA

RAJAS

1. General *Sanskrit term for "female seed," secretions connected with *menstrual fluid, of which 16 varieties are recognized in Eastern texts. **2.** One of the three Hindu *gunas, with *rajas* representing the principle of motion, activity, daring, and striving.

RASANA   SEE *NADIS (PINGALA)

RASAYANA   SEE *SESAME

RASPUTIN, GRIGORY YEFIMOVICH
(1872–1916)

Siberian mystic visionary, psychic, healer, and enterprising lover who was, if not a member, very attracted to the teachings of the *Khlysti. Rasputin was popularly believed to be the "Tsar's evil genius and probably the Tsarina's lover" (Colin Wilson, 1977, p. 20) but was held by the czar himself to be a man of God. In the course of his political career, Rasputin attracted many disciples, mostly female and with many of whom he seemed erotically involved.

Rasputin was feared and despised by many as much for his political influence as for his "heretical" and libertine views and lifestyle. He was killed by Russia's then-richest man and notorious dandy, Prince Felix Yusupov, who was punished for his deed with only a few months of exile.

RATI

An Indian goddess of love, passion, desire, and pleasure, she is a *Hindu version of *Aphrodite and the female counterpart to *Kama, the god of love. It is this goddess whose "sexual secrets" have been described in the Ratirahyasa, a medieval text that became known as the *Koka Shastra. Here the name *Rati* also appears in terms used for sexual techniques and positions. One example of this is *ratipasa*, or the "noose of Rati": a position in which the woman locks her legs behind her partner's back.

On the Indonesian island of Bali, Rati is often depicted as a demoniac figure with huge, pointed breasts, a fact that is interpreted by some writers as a sign of aggressiveness.

REBIRTH

Although often thought to be synonymous with *reincarnation, there is a clear and important difference and distinction between these two concepts. In *Hinduism and *Buddhism, rebirth signifies a somewhat "automatic" return to a seemingly endless number of lives. Thus, the term applies only to the death and rebirth of an untrained, nonenlightened individual who has no control of his or her fate and future.

RED

Red has long been regarded in the West as the color of sexuality. This is borne out not only by the red lights of individual bordellos and entire city districts around the world but by the red light in many bars and discos. The color is known to add a more sensual tone to the skin and to hide small imperfections, making people appear more beautiful and attractive to others and themselves.

However, it seems that red, traditionally the color of the planet Mars (male aggressiveness), is actually merely the color that is especially stimulating to the male, whereas the human female is more stimulated by *violet. People seem to have known this already in ancient India, where the color red symbolizes, with very few exceptions, a female energy and force. Many goddesses—for example, *Sodasi and *Kamakhya—are visualized or painted with red bodies, and many symbols of the feminine are represented in red.

SEE ALSO *TANTRIC VISUALIZATION, *TEACHINGS OF SISTER NIGUMA, *SPARK OF LIFE

Most often, red also signifies life and the life force in general. More specifically this color symbolism, of course, has to do with *blood, especially that of the *menstrual fluid. The *Nila Tantra, a *Shakta-oriented text, enjoins the devotees of the goddess to worship her "with red flowers besmeared with red sandal-paste, red leaves and champaka flowers, red ornaments, the blood of buffaloes and sheep, and meat of goats" (Banerjee, p. 255).

SEE ALSO *POMEGRANATE, *SANDALWOOD

RED CINNABAR   SEE *CINNABAR

RED LOTUS PEAK

Chinese/Taoist term for a woman's *lips and mouth from which, probably as constituents of *saliva, the *jade fountain liquid is emitted.

RED SNOW   SEE *MENSTRUAL FLUID

RED TIDE   SEE *MENSTRUAL FLUID

RED WINE   SEE *MENSTRUAL FLUID

REICH, WILHELM
(1897–1957)

As a young student of Sigmund Freud's school of psychoanalysis, Reich was regarded, in the early 1920s, as the most gifted and brilliant among the new generation of psychoanalysts. By the time of his death, however, he had stirred up so much political, analytic, and sociosexual controversy that he was regarded with suspicion in several nations and seen as a dangerous individual. With his discovery of a so-called bioenergy, or orgone, Reich bridged the gap between science and "magic" and had discovered for himself the Tantric current of energy known as *kundalini.

Reichian therapy, now mainly known as bioenergetics, includes techniques of *breath control and bodywork in order to remove physical and pschological blocks and to free one's body of its accumulated "body armor." In a manner similar to the Tantric *chakras, Reich also conceptually subdivided the body into seven sections, from the cranium down to the genitals.

In Reich's works *Function of the Orgasm* and *Character Analysis*, he demonstrates clearly and convincingly the importance of healthy sexuality in the development of a free, self-actualized human being.

> Suppression of the natural sexuality in the child, particularly of its own genital sexuality, makes the child apprehensive, shy, obedient, afraid of authority, good, and adjusted in the authoritarian sense; it paralyzes the rebellious forces because any rebellion is laden with anxiety; it produces, by inhibiting sexual curiosity and sexual thinking in the child, a general inhibition of thinking and of critical faculties. In brief, the goal of sexual suppression is that of producing an individual who is adjusted to the authoritarian order and will submit to it in spite of all misery and degradation.

A fictional, but interesting, treatment of Reichian theory and practice has been provided by Colin Wilson in his novel *The Sex Diary of Gerard Sorme*.

SEE ALSO *HEDONIC ENGINEERING, *SEXUAL IMPRINTING

REINCARNATION

Although often thought to be synonymous with *rebirth, this term is used—in *Hinduism and *Buddhism—to indicate a "controlled" return to another life by human beings sufficiently advanced to master the *bardo and to control time, place, and the parents connected with their approaching new birth. Most schools of Tibetan *Vajrayana have such people among their principal teachers who are thought to return over and over again in an unbroken line of incarnations. Probably the most famous of such beings are the *Dalai Lama of the *Gelugpa and the *Karmapa, the Tai Situ, and the Trungpa Tulku(s) of the *Kagyudpa, but there are several other lines that are also still continued.

The most famous Western magician of the twentieth century, Aleister *Crowley, claimed to be the reincarnation of the esoteric scholar and author Eliphas Levi (c. 1810–1875).

SEE ALSO *BARDO THÖDOL, CHOGYAM *TRUNGPA

RETENTION OF SEMEN

In general, Taoist adepts advise against much or any ejaculation, which they consider a loss or even a "waste" of precious energies. Thus, according to the seventeenth-century Chinese physician Li Tung Hsuan, "a man should discover and master his own ideal frequency of ejaculation," but the seemingly wise master also contradicts himself by saying that this "should not be more than two or three times in ten coitions."

Other Chinese sources are much more radical and teach that only once in a hundred sexual unions should a man ejaculate, and that older men especially have to be careful in retaining their essence of *yang. Similar theories, although often based on other motivations as well, have been expressed by individuals and groups among Tantrics, both Hindu and Buddhist, and by some Christian "heretics." A quote from the Guyhya-Siddhi runs as follows: "Let the aspirant insert the *lingam into the *bhaga, but not discharge the *bodhichitta* [Skt., 'wisdom, mind']."

SEE ALSO *ACCLIVITY, *BENI UDHRI, *ENCRATISM, *KAREZZA, *MALE CONTINENCE, *OLI TECHNIQUES, *STRI PUJA. A COMPLETE LIST OF ALL RELATED ENTRIES IS GIVEN IN INDEX 9.1 ON PAGE 278.

RHINO HORN

The popular label for the *aphrodisiac substance won from the horn of an unfortunate rhinoceros. The use of such horn may even have given rise to the expression "being horny." Ground into a powder, this "horny" substance results in an irritation of the urethra similar to that caused by *Spanish fly.

Nevertheless, even those who would like to take that personal risk would do better to refrain from doing so. The fact that the powerful and unique rhinoceros is almost extinct is a direct result of the high prices some people are ready to pay for a sexual stimulant and/or placebo.

RIG VEDA   SEE *VEDAS

RIGPA NGOSPROD

At the root of the *Kargling Zhi-khro texts is the Rig-pa ngo-sprod gcermthong rang-grol (Tib., "Self-Liberation through Seeing with Naked Awareness, Being a Direct Introduction to the State of Intrinsic Awareness"). The text constitutes an introduction to *Dzogchen that has been translated into English by John M. Reynolds. An earlier translation was also made by Kazi Dawa Samdup (1868–1922) and his editor W. Y. Evans-Wentz (1878–1957), but it has never received the attention that was given to the *Bardo Thödol published by the same team.

The Tibetan *ngo sprod* constitutes what would in English be a "pointing-out instruction": a direct introduction to the nature of mind given by an initiated master to a disciple.

RITUAL OF THE FIVE Ms   SEE *PANCHAMAKARA

RITUAL PROMISCUITY

Most of the customs, rituals, and festivals brought together under this heading are undoubtedly connected to the idea of ritual and sacramental promiscuity, and they are often concerned with the promotion of fertility. Some, however, are borderline cases that could as well be mentioned under *ritual prostitutiton, and it is advisable to read all related entries in order to get as complete a picture as possible. Index 7 (p. 276) has been prepared to aid such study.

FAR EAST   Indian/Tantric theory and practice can be found in the entries *Choli Marg, *Gopis, *Misracara, *Radha, *Soma Sacrifice, *Vira.

NEAR EAST   In ancient Egypt, quite often the religious celebrations at the temple of *Hathor ended in a public *orgy. The famous golden calf of the Old Testament (Exodus 23:4–20) was probably an idol, or rather a sacred image, of Hathor or another Near Eastern goddess symbolized as a life-giving "cow," and the "abominations" so despised by Moses were public rituals involving the drinking of wine and more or less public sexual union.

SEE ALSO *BIT-SHAGATHA

EUROPE   During harvest festivals in Phoenicia, a woman could choose whether to lie with a stranger or shave her head as a sign of mourning for the sacrificed vegetation god; either choice would be honored and praised by all others. At Cyprian Paphos, *Aphrodite's birthday was celebrated by first bathing her image in the very sea from which she was born. This would be followed by a ritual bath for all participants before they joined in a general *orgy (Wedeck, p. 140). Cretan festivals of the god Hermes were known for their hedonic nature and sexual indulgence.

SEE ALSO *ATTIS, *FLORALIA, *LIBERALIA, *NASAMONIAN MARRIAGE CUSTOM, *SATURNALIA

THE AMERICAS   Orgiastic fertility festivals were held, for example, in Peru; ritual copulation took place during the seeding of fields in Central America.

OCEANIA AND AUSTRALIA   In the Melanesian Islands, married women would have sexual union with men and boys after the burial of a deceased family member. Their regular spouses were neither asked permission nor allowed to interfere.

SEE ALSO *KAMALI, *OTIV BOMBARI, *SEXUAL HOSPITALITY, *SPERM MAGIC

AFRICA   When the Turkhana warriors, who live north of Mount Kenya, are circumcised and thus officially reach manhood, they may make love with any woman of the village, the women dancing before them in order to attract their attention.

RITUAL PROSTITUTION

To have intercourse with a prostitute is a virtue that takes away sin.

INDIAN TEMPLE HYMN

It is no exaggeration to say that ritual prostitution—also called religious, sacred, or temple prostitution—was known to cultures on every continent of planet Earth. Most famous and most often published are the known facts from and about the cultures bordering the Mediterranean Sea, be they European, African, or Near Eastern. But India, Oceania, and the Americas also know their "sacred harlots," whatever local name or titles they may have responded to. Although

in the course of time many of them may have become less sacred and more commercial, the beginnings of this custom were quite certainly religious. Often the lines between sacred, *secular, and *bridal prostitution are difficult to draw, and customs that involve *ritual promiscuity also often overlap with this present subject of inquiry. Index 7 on page 276 will aid the reader in finding all related entries.

FAR EAST   In India, temple prostitution was a requirement for all Santal girls at Telkupi Ghat, who were under the obligation to be a public prostitute at least once in their lives, similar to the duties prescribed for all women of *Babylon. Among the caste of weavers in Tamil Nadu, it is regarded as proper and normal that at least one daughter of the family be dedicated to the service of the god as one of his *hierodules, and the girls are vowed to such service from birth. Southern India also knows the *bayaderes*, or *nautch* girls, who are temple dancers similar to the *devadasis and are seen as wives of the god or the king.

A special case that comes close to paid prostitution can be found in the *kumari puja. This is actually a ritual of *defloration involving young *virgins; the *Nila Tantra requires that such a *Kumari (virgin) be given a "fee in gold, silver or pearls" (Banerjee, p. 251). The devotee is held responsible for all expenses of the girl's future marriage.

SEE ALSO *INARI

NEAR EAST AND EUROPE   Historians such as Strabo (63 B.C.E.–21 C.E.) and Herodotus (484–410 B.C.E.) have supplied us with a long list of peoples and places where ritual prostitution has been practiced. They claim, however, that such practices did not happen in Greece and Egypt. This is simply a nationalist/chauvinist notion and an apologetic attempt at concealment, which can easily be proved to be false. They tell us that such practices had been known in Armenia, throughout Assyria, and among the Canaanites and the Jews; in Cyprus and Lydia (Turkey); and at Carthage (North Africa), Eryx (Sicily), and Pontus (on the eastern shore of the Black Sea). Other sources inform us of its occurrence at Mecca and in Egypt (Briffault, vol. 3, p. 214).

SEE ALSO *BABYLON, *GHAZYE

Most famous are the priestesses of Aphrodite's temple in Corinth (Greece), one of the infamous cities known for its legions of sacred and secular prostitutes. On the island of Cyprus, too, the temples of *Aphrodite Urania were served by such women; the only visual information on

RITUAL PROMISCUITY. *Ritual promiscuity as depicted in the Elephanta caves (sixth century) near Bombay, India.
From Payne Knight, Worship of Priapus (1786), now at the Cambridge University Library.

this phenomenon comes from there. Farther west we find sacred *hierodules on the Italian mainland and in Sicily.

THE AMERICAS   Among the Tahu tribe of western Mexico, the girls designated for the sacred office of priestess were held in high esteem and were consecrated with much ceremony at great annual festivals, when all tribal chiefs of the area were present. After the public celebration, with songs and dances, the girl retired to a special hut "and the chiefs went one by one to lie with her and all the others who wished to do so followed them" (Castaneda de Nacera, quoted in Briffault, vol. 3, p. 214). Having thus become priestesses and ritual prostitutes, for the rest of their lifetimes these women never refused anyone who paid a certain amount. Even after they may have married—which was permitted after a

number of years—this obligation undertaken at their consecration did not end.

OCEANIA AND AUSTRALIA   The Bilin are priestesses among the Dayak of Sarawak (Borneo) who—according to a nineteenth-century researcher—"also constitute a class of public women" (H. Ling Roth, quoted in Briffault, vol. 3, p. 213).

AFRICA   Not only in India do certain clans or castes regularly and traditionally bring forth ritual prostitutes. The women of the Algerian clan of the Walad 'Abdi practice this profession—although here it much resembles *secular prostitution—and are regarded as holy; the social standing and prosperity of the clan depend upon their services.

SEE ALSO *MBOZE, *ODUDA

RITUALS

Index 6 (p. 275) gives access to all entries related to festivals, rituals, and customs.

ROMANO, GIULIO

(C. 1499–1546)

A Renaissance painter and architect, the favorite student of Raphael (1483–1520), whose work is executed in an exaggerated Raphael-esque style and laid the groundwork for what is called mannerism by art critics. In his famous sketches he examined the various postures of lovemaking. Clement VII, who held the papacy from 1523 to 1534, ordered the destruction of Romano's work, and the artist was forced into exile.

ROS

(LATIN, "DEW")

This "ineffable celestial dew" seems to be a type of endocrine "nectar" believed to drip down from the *pineal gland or *pituitary gland, or both, into the body—under certain conditions—and to aid in achieving both immortality and enlightenment. It is the "fiery dew" of the *Fratres Roris Coctis, who connected it with both male semen and the holy cross (Benamin Walker, 1977, p. 242). Emanuel Swedenborg (1688–1772) defined it in his work *The Brain Considered Anatomically, Physiologically, and Philosophically* as a "highly refined alcohol of animal nature that is utterly beyond the ken of our senses."

SEE ALSO *ECSTASY

ROSE

This flower is to the Occidental world what the *lotus is to the cultures of Asia: a foremost feminine, mystic, and sacred symbol, yet with a great variety of interpretation (*see* *Lily). Sacred to the Greek Aurora and the Roman *Venus, it is a symbol of love, joy, and desire as well as beauty. In the rites of the Egyptian Isis and the Christian Mary it stands for chastity, virginity, and a love that is free from all carnal associations. The Virgin Mary is sometimes called "mystic rose," an expression that also occurs in the writings of Rosicrucians, cabalists, and alchemists. In some texts of the latter groups, the term is also used as code for the *yoni.

SEE ALSO *RED

ROYAL ROAD SEE *BRAHMA NADI

S

*United with *Shakti, be full of power.*

KULACUDAMANI TANTRA

NOTE: Sanskrit terms like *Siva* or *Sakti* are here transliterated as *Shiva* or *Shakti*.

SA

Egyptian name for the "invisible semen" of the god Ra, a subtle energy and/or fluid that the deity is believed to bestow on the new pharaoh at the moment of his coronation. The recipient was then filled with a magical fire that gave him—as in the concept of *ojas—the energy, dignity, and divine guidance he needed to be a good and just ruler.

SABBATIANS

A Hebrew sect of cabalist/Christian background whose members recognized that sexual union is a potentially sacred and initiatory experience. For them the "advent of the Messiah" is "considered not as a historical or collective fact . . . but as a symbol of inner individual awakening" (Evola, p. 226). They saw the mystical force that is symbolically represented by the Messiah as inherent in women, and men's awakening and salvation as possible only by partaking of this energy through sexual union. Similar to the Tantric vision of the *Shakti as divine energy present in the female, the Sabbatians—and other cabalists as well—saw in all women the manifestation and divine energy of the *Shekinah.

That such teachings were not all too extravagant or even heretical, compared with mainstream Hebrew cabalah, can be seen from the following quotes collected by Julius Evola:

> "The Holy One, may He be blessed, does not choose to dwell where the male and female are not united" (Zohar I, 55b).

> "He who has not taken a woman is as if he were only a half" (Zohar III, 81a).

> "Three things have in themselves something of the beyond: the sun, the Sabbath, and sexual union" (*Talmud; Berakoth, 57b).

SACRED LOCATIONS AND PLACES OF POWER

For the inspired travelers among the readers, a listing of all sacred places, temples, and caves mentioned in this encyclopedia has been provided in index 14 on page 282.

SACRED MARRIAGE   SEE *HIEROS GAMOS

SACRED PROSTITUTION   SEE *RITUAL PROSTITUTION

SACRED STONES

Many peoples have been fascinated with the beauty and power of stones and have either worshipped stones as deities or conceived of deities as living or inherent in stones. This is probably true for the *megaliths—although we simply cannot know in the absence of texts—but is certainly appropriate for those sacred stones that were meteorites: fallen from Heaven! Most famous of those is the sacred black stone of *Al'Lat at the *Ka'bah, but Europe also knew such deities and shrines. To name but a few: *Aphrodite at Paphos, *Cybele at Pessinus and in Rome, *Astarte at Byblos, and the famous *Ephesian Artemis, the latter's most ancient sculpture having been cut from a black meteorite.

SACRIFICE

In the new and revised edition of *The Wise Wound* (Shuttle and Redgrove), the authors speak of unpublished material that shows convincing evidence that menstrual rites—celebrations of the *moon magic inherent in *menstrual fluid—were probably the source of most or all sacrificial rites. As, for example, in the motivation behind *subincision, male members of the community had to make do with other types of *blood in their attempts to prove that they too had magical powers.

In the light of such information on the origin of blood sacrifice, we can perhaps begin to sense some of the probable motivations behind so controversial a practice as that recommended, for example, in the *Kumari Tantra. Sexuality, the act that often leads to life and ultimately to death, is also inseparably linked with blood, creation, and destruction.

A simpler form of blood sacrifice, not involving the death of human or animal, is required and hailed in the Tara Tantra. Chapter 5 states that offering one single drop of the devotee's own blood is better than a whole cup of any other sacrificial blood.

SEE ALSO *ATTIS, *BHOGI, *BREASTS, *CASTRATION, *CIRCUMCISION, *JAVALAMUKHI, *KALIGHAT, *SOMA SACRIFICE, *TLAZOLTEOTL

SADHAKA

General Sanskrit term for any "worshipper" or "practitioner" who takes part in ritual activities, whether they are Tantric or not.

SADHANA

A Sanskrit word that can best be approximated by the English term *spiritual exercise*. The term itself expresses concepts like "arriving at one's goal" or "a means to attain perfection."

SEE ALSO *EJACULATION, *GUPTA-SADHANA TANTRA, *KALIVILASA TANTRA, *MAITHUNA

SADOMASOCHISM (SM)

The two novelists Marquis de Sade (1740–1814) and Leopold von Sacher-Masoch (1835–1895) have achieved much fame indeed by lending their names to, respectively, inflicting and receiving pain in association with sexual activity.

Today the hitherto hidden and more or less private practices in which sexuality and pain are intimately connected receive much attention in literature and other media, and the harsh judgment that reckons them into the category of *perversions has become somewhat softened. An ever larger number of people openly speak about their sexual preferences in general, and about sadomasochistic ones in particular, and this public dialogue has in a way pressured society into a sort of acceptance of these practices, however tentative and full of suspicion and misunderstanding that

acceptance may be. This same attention, however, has led a great number of people into thinking that they themselves, or their spouses or lovers, are "sadists" or "masochists" whenever they seek or practice some more adventurous and controversial form of erotic stimulation. The recent infatuation of the media with high-drama sexuality has in fact led many people to believe that wearing black leather or playing bondage or domination games constitutes SM.

Because of a general absence of a realistic or even enlightened view of human sexuality in most contemporary cultures, all of our classifications in this regard are black and white, with no shades that exist in between: Either you are "normal" or you are not. In ancient and medieval India, to name but one example, the manuals of love taught techniques such as bondage, biting, scratching, and slapping (within limits) as part of the normal erotic and sexual spectrum. Anyone who happened to enjoy this—actively, passively, or both—did not feel the need to internally label herself or himself as sadist or masochist.

It would be advisable to use the term *algolagnia for all these expressions of flesh and emotions, and as long as two or more consenting adults are involved in such play there seems to be no need for any stigmatization. The latter only aids the business interest of SM clubs and shops, which are all too pleased with the free advertisements that help to sell their leather and metal trappings.

SAFFRON

This not only is one of the major *Tantric perfumes but was consumed as an *aphrodisiac by the Greek and Arab peoples. If someone was given saffron for an entire week, he or she was, according to legend, unable to resist erotic advances. The saffron plant (*Crocus sativus*) is of Asian origin but is also cultivated in Europe. It is also used as a flavoring and coloring agent in certain dishes.

SAHAJA or SAHAJIYA

Developed from the Sanskrit terms for "natural" and "togetherness," this is the name for an erotically oriented sect that developed in *Bengal (India, Bangladesh) about the tenth century, a time when Buddhist Tantra in general underwent an intensification of its erotic/sexual elements. During this time, also, religious sculptures as well as sacred scriptures began showing *dakinis and *Buddhas in sexual union. Texts, beliefs, and rituals of this movement are a mixture of influences derived from *Vajrayana, Hindu *Tantra, and the Vaishnavas (Vishnu sects) of Bengal. In Sahajiya, the figures of *Shiva and *Shakti have been replaced by the god Krishna and Radha, the *gopi. The *chakras have become ponds, and the female *mudra/4 has turned into *parakiya, but the basic message that true spiritual initiation and liberation cannot be attained without love, both mental and physical, is the same here as in other

Tantric sects and schools. Sahajiya teachings are strongly based on the ideal of extramarital partners for ritual *maithuna (see *Parakiya), however much denounced such practice may be by society in general. Remarkably enough, Sahaja has also been called "the easiest and most natural way of spiritual exercise" (Banerjee, p. 573).

A similar idea was once espoused by the *Bogomiles, a European group of "heretics."

SAHAJOLI   SEE *OLI TECHNIQUES

SAHASRARA CHAKRA
(SKT, "THOUSAND")

The "crown" chakra. One of the four *chakras of the earlier Tantric tradition but now regarded as number 7. The center may be compared to the Taoist's *ni-huan of the upper *tan-t'ien and the *Sufi's center known as "the teacher."

LOCATION: At (or above) the top of the skull
ENDOCRINE GLAND: Pineal gland (third eye)
SEED-SYLLABLE: Om
COLOR: Pale purple
LOTUS: Thousand-petaled, rainbow
ASSOCIATIONS: Integration, liberation, cosmic consciousness
SEE ALSO *ECSTASY (PSYCHOSOMATIC)

SAKYA-PA   SEE *SASKYA-PA

SALIVA

Taoist *inner alchemy, of both the sexually and nonsexually oriented schools, regards saliva as a carrier of important and beneficial fluids and/or energies. During breathing techniques such as *t'ai-hsi, the adept swallows his or her own saliva, and partners involved in erotic play or exercises will exchange their saliva in order to facilitate mutual absorption of their respective *yin and *yang energies and essences. Some Taoist teachings even proclaim that spitting, constituting a loss of saliva, can result in a loss of vitality.

In other occult systems, saliva is believed to contain and carry subtle energies originating in the *brain and heart, and it has been called the "water of life . . . and an antidote to poisons and other evils" (Benjamin Walker, 1977, p. 243). As with *scent, saliva changes according to one's emotional state, and an experienced "drinker" may be able to detect changes in taste depending on whether the saliva is produced by someone in fear or in panic, in love or in *ecstasy.

SEE ALSO *JADE FOUNTAIN LIQUID, *MEDICINE OF THE THREE PEAKS

SAMARASA

The state of "bi-unity" or "two-being-one" that is one of the goals of Tantric *sadhana and especially of the sexual exercises. The term is akin to samadhi, or enlightenment.

SAMA VEDA   SEE *VEDAS

SAMBARA

Nepalese term for what in Sanskrit is known as *yamala.

SAMGHATAKA

A form of plural intercourse and a Tantric ritual in which a single woman or man makes love with two or four partners of the opposite sex.
SEE ALSO *SECRET DALLIANCE

SAMHITA(S)
(SKT, "COLLECTION")

1. A class of Vaishnava texts (oriented to the god Vishnu) in which we can recognize the influence of *Tantra and *Shakta. Some of the more interesting texts are the Gheranda Samhita, *Shiva Samhita, Ashktavakra Samhita, and Nisvasatattva Samhita. 2. In a more general sense, samhita is the word for various collections of songs, taken from the *Vedas, for certain occasions and *sacrifices. 3. The term samhita is also used to indicate mystical union as distinct from physical union.

SANDALWOOD

This fragrant and stimulating wood is much loved in the Orient, and its essential oil is one of the traditional *Tantric perfumes. The *apsarasas, female heavenly dancers often depicted in the erotic sculptures of temples like *Khajuraho (India) and Angkor Wat (Kampuchea [Cambodia]), are said to have breasts that smell, like the human *pheromone *alpha androsterol, of sandalwood.

SANDHYABHASA
(SKT, "TWILIGHT")

A name for the secret "twilight language," of esoteric terminology, in which Tantric knowledge and sacred texts are often transmitted. Such "intentional language," as it is sometimes called, can at times lead to as many as four different interpretations of the text, as, for example, in the *Guhyasamaja Tantra. Most often this language is said to be that in which *yoginis and *dakinis convey their messages and revelations. S. C. Banerjee, on the other hand, writes that sandhyabhasa is an "amalgam of Sanskrit . . . and Bengali language" (p. 361).

Similar "hidden" interpretations have also been found in the *Bible by making use of the various numerological systems known to adepts of the cabalah.

SEE ALSO *SECRET LANGUAGE

SANSKRIT

The sacred language of *Hinduism, in which most of its religious texts are written. The term itself means "perfect" and "complete," and the Sanskrit alphabet is called devanagari, or "language of the gods." Since the language was developed along with the philosophical, scientific, and religious thought of India and its Aryan invaders, it features a highly differentiated and sophisticated terminology for extraordinary states of consciousness, subtle physiology, and mental or spiritual processes of which no immediate equivalents are known in Western languages. Although this creates a problem in translation, it also offers a possibility for learning.

As a written language, devanagari consists of 48 glyphs, or letters, that are often difficult to translate into Latin-based Western languages like English, which has only 26 letters. Several systems are in use.

SEE ALSO *ARYAN INVASION THEORY

SARASVATI

1. The Indian goddess of creative energy, associated with music, *dance, and many other art forms. Sarasvati is often considered the patroness of the *sixty-four arts, among which the art of love is considered first and foremost in importance. She is also the deity ruling scholarship and, simultaneously, intuitive wisdom.

SEE ALSO *KUMARI PUJA

2. A river mentioned in the *Vedas that was, until recently, thought to be purely mythical. However, satellite-aided research has meanwhile established that it actually existed until about 2000 B.C.E., when it dried out—an occurrence that contributed to the cessation of the proto-Indian Harappa civilization.

SEE ALSO *ARYAN INVASION THEORY

3. The Sarasvati River is also a symbol for the *sushumna nadi.

SEE ALSO *YUKTATRIVENI

SARSAPARILLA

A tropical vine (Smilax officinalis) from which the male sex hormone *testosterone is manufactured for medical treatment. For centuries this plant was used by Mexican Indians in order to combat sexual weakness and impotence in men; it is therefore one of the few *aphrodisiacs science must recognize. This tradition was generally ridiculed by scientists, as is still done in the cases of *ginseng, *yohimbine, and *fo-ti-tieng, until the Hungarian scientist Dr. E. Solmo discovered the testosterone content of the plant in 1939. For a plant that contains *estrogen, see *Licorice.

SARUTAHIKO

Japanese phallic god quite similar in concept to *Priapus and other such deities associated with *phallic worship. This "walking penis"—as Ian Buruma aptly describes this figure—is commonly known in Japan as a deity before whom all evil creatures and *demons shrink with fear and flee. However, when Sarutahiko is confronted with the naked *yoni of *Ama-no-Uzume, he himself loses all strength and wilts away like a dead flower, showing us that her *yoni magic is the more potent force of the two.

SASKYA-PA

One of the major schools of Tibetan *Vajrayana, tracing its lineage back to the *Mahasiddha Virupa. The school was named after the monastery Gray Earth (Saskya) in southern Tibet and also recalls one of its foremost masters, Sakya Pandita (1182–1251). The Saskya-pa regard the *Hevajra Tantra as their most precious text, and much of their teaching is based on this text.

Before the rise of the *Gelugpa, the Saskya-pa (and the connected clan) had long been the actual rulers of Tibet, and they often clashed with and fought opponents such as the *Kagyudpa. About 1350, the school lost much of its power. The Saskya monks were especially involved with preparing a systematic collection of Buddhist and Tantric texts. Their scientific objectivity, however, was less than perfect, and their famous encyclopedist Bu-ston (1290–1364) excluded most *Nyingma and Dzogchen (see *Mahamudra/2) texts from the official canon.

SASSAFRAS

Although the well-known herbal tea made from *Sassafras officinalis* is a generally stimulating tonic, an *aphrodisiac effect cannot be achieved with it. For such an effect, one has to turn to small doses of its oil.

R. Stark writes in *The Book of Aphrodisiacs* that "100 mg of oil can undoubtedly bring about an aphrodisiac/psychedelic effect" (1981), but larger doses can also affect, and perhaps harm, the inner organs. Isosafrole, the active and potent ingredient of the plant, is also found in *nutmeg and has been used in the drug *MDA, a forerunner of *MDMA, better known as *ecstasy.

SATTVA   SEE *GUNAS

SATURNALIA

This Roman *fertility festival, held during the month of December and dedicated to the deities of the harvest, was a welcome occasion marked by much sexual revelry. During the seven consecutive days of the festival all social norms, differences of class, and sexual restrictions were abandoned, and all participants surrendered to the joy of freedom and of life.

SATYR AND SATYRIASIS
(FROM THE GREEK *SATUROI*)

Usually depicted as half man, half *goat, the mythic creatures known as satyrs are regarded as symbols of elemental, unrestrained male libido and passion. Associated with the god *Pan, "the divine and horny goat," they have contributed to the Christian idea of the devil. Their unquenchable thirst for erotic adventures—sometimes called sexual obsession or *erotomania—makes them the male equivalent of a *nymphomaniac. Such a condition in human men is termed *satyriasis*.

SAYONI

Name for the two revolving yonis of Ushasa-naktam, the best known of twin goddesses mentioned in the Rig *Veda. Separately, these deities are known as Ushas and Nakra, but they are seen as so deeply intertwined that even their yonis revolve around each other. In her book *Sakhiyani*, author Giti Thadani gives this ancient myth a sexual interpretation, regarding it as evidence of early, and then accepted, sexual activity between women—an interesting theory to which

SATYR. *Etruscan statue of a cloven-hoofed satyr in the typical *ithyphallic state also known as* satyriasis.

one should remain open, but certainly not the only interpretation possible. The myth may as well be an expression of early ignorance concerning the male role in the creation of life and an expression of prepatriarchal veneration of the female as goddess and her dynamic *yoni energy as ultimate cosmic creatrix.

SCALLOP

This shell, or marine mollusk, is an ancient European symbol for the *yoni, used from the far northern shores inhabited by the Norsemen to the borders of Greek civilization.

S~AYONI~. *Reminiscent of the Chinese t'ai chi symbol showing *yin and *yang revolving in an endless dance,*
this drawing is a representation of the divine twins Ushas and Nakra. Unique in mythology,
each sister's *yoni revolves around the other's, possibly indicating all-female sexual relationship.
Christina Camphausen, "Sayoni" or "Yin Yin," 1997. Color pencil on paper.

The English word *scallop,* with its roots in the Norse *skalpr* ("sheath," "vagina"), thus has similar connotations with the Greek name for the shell, which is *kteis. Kteis* not only refers to this specific shell (and to the *cowrie as well) but also was a widely accepted term for the outer and visible female genitals, a term equivalent to the Latin *vulva. When Alessandro Botticelli (1445–1510) painted his famous conception of the birth of Aphrodite/*Venus, he used the *kteis*/scallop consciously as representing the yoni of the sea, out of which the goddess of love was born.

SCARLET WOMAN

The image of the tarot card 11, Strength, or Lust, painted by Lady Frieda Harris and imagined/designed by Aleister *Crowley, is clearly based on the following biblical text: "I saw a woman sit upon a scarlet-colored beast, full of names of blasphemy, having seven heads and ten horns. And the woman was arrayed in purple and scarlet color, and decked with gold and precious stones and pearls, having a golden cup in her hand full of abominations" (Revelation 17:3–4) What seemed abominations to St. John, however, may very likely be the essence of life, and the cup so detested by John is the very *grail of people with other insights and inclinations.

This, then, an image from the Book of Revelation, is the origin of the concept known as the "scarlet woman." To the mind of Crowley, the scarlet woman needed to be alive just as he, the apocalyptic "great beast," was alive. He consecutively appointed several of his lovers, often prostitutes, to this "office," and together they communed with *demons and deities, traveled astrally, and practiced their/his own brand of *Tantra or *sexual magick.

SEE ALSO *BABYLON

SCENT

The sense of smell is of much importance to the erotic arts and to sexuality in general. Information concerned with perfumes and sexually attracting chemicals can be found throughout this encyclopedia (see *Olfactory Delights, *Scent Aura, *Scent Glands, *Tantric Perfumes, *Perspiration, *Pheromones). Index 5.2 (p. 274) deals with smell-related aphrodisiacs.

SCENT AURA

Apart from general *perspiration and in addition to the sexually oriented action of the *scent glands, there are even more intimate fountains of fragrance to be considered— sources that have an important place in our overall olfactory aura and almost certainly play a role in the still largely unknown processes by which mutual attraction or incompatibility is determined. These are the various male and female love juices and the woman's monthly red tide.

In the male, the main sources of fragrance are the *prostatic glands, the fluids of which are responsible for the characteristic odor of *semen. Other sources of male sexual scent are the two *Cowper's glands and the male hormone *testosterone, which adds its musky odor to all of this.

Concerning the *female love juices and/or ejaculate, the following parts and fluids are involved as constituents of a woman's odor: the two vulvovaginal glands, the female *prostatic glands, the *aliphatic acids, and *progesterone.

The monthly *menstrual fluid is a special case. What we usually call menstrual "blood" consists, when analyzed, only partly of blood and contains several other substances, each of which contributes to its specific scent. The changing hormone levels during the *menstrual/ovarian cycle also have their influence on a woman's scent. It has been shown (Nathan, 1989) that menstruating women are especially attractive to mosquitoes, but *goats, stags, monkeys, and bears also pick up this special scent and often approach or follow the woman in question. An extra dimension of the menstrual/ovarian cycle is a woman's varying sensitivity to male, musky scents. Women can smell the male hormone testosterone most easily when their own level of *estrogen is high.

SCENT GLANDS

These apocrine glands produce tiny amounts of fluid secretions that form the characteristic and unique odor of a human being. The glands are located in the armpits, nipples, ears, lips, and anus as well as under the male foreskin and the female genital lips.

THE ARMPITS   A prescientific, medieval German belief reflects people's practical knowledge of the sexual impact of perspiration from the armpits. In order to attract the erotic attentions of a certain man, the interested woman would make him eat an *apple she had carried in her armpit for a while, which thus had collected a large amount of her perspiration. Modern scientific evidence has demonstrated that perspiration from the armpits of male and female subjects is influential in the synchronization and regulation of women's menstrual/ovarian cycles.

SEE ALSO *ANDROSTENONE

BREASTS/NIPPLES   The scent from the nipples actually guides the young baby to her/his source of food. If a *breast is held under a sleeping baby's nose, he/she will make automatic sucking movements. After about six weeks, a baby is able to distinguish the mother's breasts from those of other women.

THE GENITAL/ANAL REGION   In both women and men, these are beyond doubt prominent areas concerned

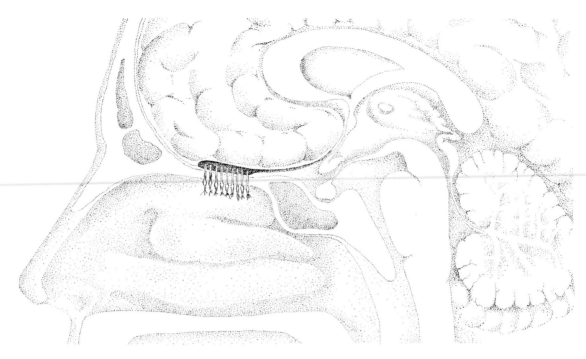

SCENT. *Olfactory receptors in the human *nose feed signals directly into the *brain.*
Illustration by Christina Camphausen.

with the production of odors and scents. Aside from the odorous ingredients that make up male and female ejaculate or love juices, the sebaceous (oil-secreting) scent glands located in the anus, the male foreskin, and the soft, inner skins of the female labia minora and majora all produce odors. In addition, these parts also contain many eccrine sweat glands, which add their odorous molecules to the *scent aura of a human being in general, and to that of the individual in question.

Among other substances, the fluids contain, and evaporate, the volatile *pheromones and are known to be influenced by psychological states such as fear, stress, pain, or excitement. Secretions from the scent glands contain *indole, *muskone, steroids, and "at least a hundred other identifiable components" (Redgrove, p. 65). In *shunamism, the scent of a *virgin is considered able to heal and/or rejuvenate a person's life force.

SCROTUM   SEE *LINGAM TOPOGRAPHY/3

SEAFOOD (AS APHRODISIAC)   SEE *FRUIT DE MER

SEAT OF PLEASURE
Chinese expression indicating the clitoris (see *Yoni Topography/5–7, 11).

SECRET DALLIANCE
Although this Chinese term for sexual union with more than one partner implies "secrecy," the practice was quite common among the Chinese aristocracy and the Taoist masters. In *pillow books and other erotic literature we find many visual and verbal examples of this sexual "technique" or "exercise," although there it most often involves one man with two or more women, and seldom the other way around.

SEE ALSO *YOGINI CHAKRA

SECRET LANGUAGE
Often alchemists, Tantrics, heretics, and other "outsiders" have had to resort to writing down their teachings in veiled terms that could be understood only by those who were given the right symbolic hints and explanations; this is a major reason for many of the secretive rites of initiation. *Menstrual fluid, in the Near East, becomes spoken of as "red wine," whereas *lingam and *yoni can be expressed

and symbolized in Tibet as "thunderbolt" (*vajra) and "bell" (*ghanta). Other secrets are revealed by using the numerological traditions of the cabalah on biblical texts and, in the *Tantras, by being aware of the "twilight language" (*sandhyabhasa) of the *dakinis. In Taoist scriptures such as the famous Tao-te Ching we also find this kind of mystical twilight language, where the uterus becomes a "deep vale" and the vagina is spoken of as a "mysterious gate."

SEE ALSO *UNION OF SKILLFUL MEANS AND PROFOUND COGNITION

SECTS AND SCHOOLS

A listing of all sects, schools, spiritual subcultures, and religious systems of belief can be found in index 2 on page 271. Most entries of that listing are concerned with groups, movements, branches, or schools—often part of a larger religious system—in whose teachings the erotic, sexual element plays an important role. This encyclopedia also contains many short, general descriptions of major religious systems: entries meant to provide quick-reference background information.

SECULAR PROSTITUTION

Whether or not secular prostitution has developed from, or independently of, its spiritual counterpart, *ritual prostitution, is a question that cannot be answered with any "scientific" certainty. Nevertheless, an association between prostitution and religion existed until deep into the time of Christianity; popes and bishops were known to have run brothels, and more than one monastery or church had a brothel attached to it. Such facts perhaps point to Christianity's origins in worship of the Goddess and perhaps in ancient fertility celebrations.

The secular prostitute—in contrast to the sacred *hierodules, or harlots, of *Ishtar or the "holy ones" of *Qadesh—distinguishes herself by engaging in sex for survival, money, power, pleasure, or a combination of these. These prostitutes, *hetaerae, and *courtesans represent a phenomenon so well known and so much discussed that it requires little attention here.

The borderline between secular and sanctified is thin and not always easy to establish, as is demonstrated in the fact that in Mesopotamia even the commercial prostitute was considered to be a "worshipper" of the fertility deities, worshipping them in the same way as the temple women, yet living off the money thus made. Other borderline cases are the Egyptian *ghazye or the *Kumari (the *living goddess) of Nepal—some of whom take up prostitution once they are mature women and are released from their seclusion. Greece also knew male prostitution, although it was a profession rarely meant to be at the service of women but rather was for the legion of homosexual men of the intellectual and aristocratic elite, the military, and the Olympic athletes.

SEE ALSO *CARTE BLANCHE, *SEXUAL HOSPITALITY

SEMEN

Before we turn to the actual, physical, and wet semen that has the potential to unite with an ovum and cocreate new life, we must realize that many of the ancient cultures, who knew themselves to be dependent on the fertility of the soil (and worshipped the Earth as a goddess) regarded every rain shower as the semen of their respective high god, whether he was called U (Sumerian), Jehovah or Jaweh (Hebrew), or *Zeus (Greek), and were thankful for such a libation. As such, semen was viewed as divine, helpful, necessary, and altogether positive.

In this connection, the Greek dramatist Aeschylus (525–456 B.C.E.) wrote: "The pure Sky yearns passionately to pierce the Earth" and "Rain falls from the bridegroom Sky, impregnating the Earth, and she brings forth her brood for mortal man." With this in mind, we can better understand why in South Africa and Australia "women lie in a shower of rain when they desire to conceive" (Briffault, vol. 3, p. 58).

Concerning the healing powers ascribed to semen, John *Allegro supplies the following information: "The name Jesus/Joshua (the Greek and Hebrew forms) means 'the semen that heals' or 'fructifies,' the god-juice that gives life. To be smeared with this powerful liquid, above all to absorb it into his body, was to bring the worshipper of the 'Jesus' into living communion with God, indeed, to make him divine" (1972, p. 21).

Semen, in a clinical sense, is a mixture of sperm cells and a number of other secretions from the epididymes and the *prostatic glands, but the word is often wrongly used as a synonym for *sperm*. For information on the different liquids that make up what we call semen, *see* *Lingam Topography/12, 15, 20–22.

In recent years the "quality" of male semen—in terms of the amount of sperm it contains—seems to be deteriorating, a fact that is probably due to the increasing pollution and poisoning of nature and therefore, directly and indirectly, of our bodies. The German magazine *Natur* reported in June 1989 that the average sperm count per milliliter of semen was about 250 million only 50 years ago but that it has now dropped to about 40 million.

"In esoteric theory," writes Benjamin Walker, "semen consists of (1) the *liquor vitae, 'fluid of life,' containing the physical seed that it nourishes within the body of the male, and (2) the *aura seminalis, or super-physical essence, which has a fiery nature" (1977, p. 250).

SEE ALSO *ARGENINE, *GUPTA-SADHANA TANTRA, *SPERM MAGIC

SEMINAL VISCOSITY

Like Tantrics and Taoists, the inner alchemists of the West recognized a subtle current of energy as part of *semen, and *seminal viscosity*, like *aura seminalis, is one of their terms for this subtle energy.

SEE ALSO *OJAS

SEPHER HA ZOHAR   SEE *ZOHAR

SERIAL POLYGAMY/POLYANDRY

Since the "sexual revolution" in the Europe and America of the 1960s, many men and women have evolved a new pattern in their sexual lives. We are not talking here about the general and widely practiced promiscuity of the subsequent two decades (until the appearance of the AIDS threat) but of the type of *polygamy that is hidden under a cloak of *monogamy. This "serial," or consecutive, polygamy becomes apparent only when we look at the divorce rates of modern Western societies. Not only do several countries have divorce rates between 50 percent and 75 percent, but the rates of remarriage among the divorced also reach similar heights (80 percent in the United States in the 1970s). These facts show that "the US . . . de facto has evolved from a culture of traditional monogamy to one of consecutive marriage or serial polygamy" (Leary, *Neuropolitics*, 1977, p. 98).

SERPENT

The imagery and mythological status of the serpent is an ambivalent and difficult concept. On one hand, the serpent seems to be quite clearly a male phallic symbol, and quite often it is used that way. However, he can also be she, representing femininity, or is occasionally even neutral.

Some manifestations of serpent imagery are of special interest to our study and are spoken of in the entries *Kanpatha Yogis, *Kundalini, and *Ophion.

SESAME

Sesame seeds and the oils and products derived from them contain a large amount of *vitamin E, and this is the main reason that sesame is held in high regard as a virility food—a fact attested by its Indian name: *rasayana*, or "life extender."

One of the famous *aphrodisiac treats of Near Eastern peoples is halvah, a tasty, sweet, crumbly confection made from honey and ground sesame seeds. Author Scott Kilham, likewise, recommends eating tahini—a healthy butterlike paste made from the ground seeds—with honey in order to increase one's sexual endurance.

SEVEN TREASURES
(TIB., *DZODCHEN DUN, MDZOD-CHEN BDUN*, "SEVEN GREAT TREASURES")
A collection of seven texts of various lengths that belong to the most important writings by *Longchenpa. Excerpts from these texts have been translated and published in the work *Buddha Mind*.

SEX GLANDS   SEE *GONADS

SEX HORMONES
Several of the hormones produced in the human body have specialized functions responsible for the sexual development of both male and female. They regulate the activation and growth of gender-specific physical features and are instrumental in the *menstrual/ovarian cycle in women and in the general functioning of the reproductive system.

SEE ALSO *ANDROGENS, *ENDOCRINE SYSTEM, *ESTROGENS, *HONEY, *SCENT AURA, *VITAMINS

SEXUAL ABSTINENCE   SEE *CHASTITY

SEXUAL BIOCHEMISTRY AND ELECTROMAGNETISM
One of the goals of Tantric and Taoist sexual practice is to harmonize, balance, exchange, and utilize the life energies activated and set free during erotic play and sexual union.

Tantrics—both Eastern and Western—not only have recognized the importance of the biochemical properties of

SERPENT ENERGY. *Serpent energy
manifesting from the *yoni
of a *yogini.
Wood, south India, c. 1800.
Ajit Mookerjee Collection, New Delhi.

male *semen and *female love juices or secretions but also have carried out extensive studies and research concerning the flow of subtle energies that accompany all psychophysical events in the human body, *brain, and mind. If, in the material presented in this book, the distinction between the physical and the nonphysical/energetic seems not always as clear as one would wish, we must remind ourselves that the Tantric/Taoist or alchemical/magickal adept regards these concepts—especially those of the subtle energies—as well-known realities and does not necessarily require or desire such differentiation. We should remember that even "hard-nosed" physicists were finally forced by the universe to accept that light is neither a wave nor a particle but rather can be fully understood only after we go beyond such dualist distinctions and accept it in both its aspects.

Index 11 (p. 279) lists—as far as it is possible to distinguish—all entries concerned with fluid secretions from glands, lips, breasts, and genitals (*Dew of Ecstasy, *Ejaculation, *Jade Fountain Liquid, *Moon Flower Medicine, and so forth).

On the other hand, index 12 (p. 280) is concerned with the electromagnetic aspects of our topic, with the currents and fields of energies that make up the human subtle body and that are involved or activated during erotic/sexual interplay (covering such entries, for example, as *Aura Seminalis, *Blue-Green Halo, *Kundalini, and *Shankhini Nadi).

SEXUAL HOSPITALITY

Difficult as it may be to imagine from within our present set of almost worldwide "morals" (mainly based on teachings and prohibitions of the major world religions), other and earlier peoples knew a hospitality that went beyond that of offering roof and bed, salt and water, or whatever the local standard may have been. Often, however, the "generosity" thus displayed, known as sexual hospitality, was mainly toward men. Women, so we must assume from most reports, had little say in this cultural requirement and often simply had to comply with it. One of the problems in establishing a conclusion about it, however, is the mindset of most of the early explorers and amateur anthropologists, whose own backgrounds did not even let this question arise in their minds and thus not in their papers. But where a woman's options were limited to a rigid role within marriage and family life, especially in a small, isolated village, the women may also have enjoyed the possibility of variation and change.

One must realize, however, that the major motivation for such practice is not really one of offering, or getting, sexual pleasure, but to establish a familylike bond. Many cases are known where the guest also had to drink some of his host's blood, serving as a first symbol of integration to the tribe or family.

Some interesting examples of sexual hospitality are offered below, and many more have been collected by authors such as Joseph Campbell and Robert Briffault. In his book *The Mothers,* Briffault's bibliography only—on this topic—is almost three pages long. Among the Marind-anum of southwest New Guinea, friends and members of the husband's totem are allowed sexual union with the married wife. Sometimes this is done as "mere" hospitality; most often it is a way of thanking for help and services rendered (Cornelissen, p. 36). Another aspect of this custom was its use in collecting the large amounts of sperm necessary for use in *sperm magic.

Similar customs were known among the Papuas of the Frederik Hendrik Islands. Here the younger warriors assured their protection in war by "lending" their women to older and experienced fighters, who would then aid them during the fight. During festive dances, and in order to please the older men of the tribe, young and unmarried men often sent their future brides to the older men of the tribe for sexual union. Among the tribes of the Trobriand Islands, it was the normal state of affairs for a girl of the house to spend the night with a visiting guest. Sometimes this custom actually amounts to a type of *secular prostitution—for example, when such sexual union of a man's wife is in exchange for tobacco, clothes, or seed plants.

In the Near East, beginning in ancient times and lasting at least into the nineteenth century, Arab custom included the practice of offering one's wife or another woman of the household for one night to guests, whether friend or stranger. The peoples of Tahiti and Madagascar, as well as some Eskimo and Indian tribes of North America, were also famous for their sexual hospitality.

SEE ALSO *BRIDAL PROSTITUTION, *RITUAL PROMISCUITY

SEXUAL IMPRINTING

The Islamic, Ishmailian "heretics" known as *Nizari Isma'ilis were apparently masters of sexual imprinting, binding their "initiates" to them by creating an unforgettable erotic experience, using drugs and multiple sexual partners to create a kind of *erotocomatose lucidity. Apart from such consciously designed imprints, most members of our species are subject to incidents of sexual imprinting of a less obvious and more unconscious type: our education and first sexual experiences. The techniques for, and the abuse of, sexual imprinting are described in detail in the works of Timothy Leary and Robert Anton Wilson (see bibliography).

SEE ALSO *HEDONIC ENGINEERING

SEXUAL MAGICK

1. Sometimes this term is used to indicate all systems concerned with the magical, spiritual, and/or religious use of the sexual instinct and energies. In such cases the term embraces *Tantra, especially the *Vamacara teachings, as well as the sexually oriented schools of *Taoism, Islamic groups such as the *Nizari Isma'ilis, and the sexual *alchemy of the Western hermetic tradition. **2.** More specifically, the term is applied only for the later European and American forms, exponents of which have been Aleister *Crowley and the members of the *Ordo Templi Orientis and of such groups as the *Great Brotherhood of God. Some groups connected with witchcraft and satanism also have their place here. Among the rituals and techniques of SM, or sex magic (two other often-used designations for sexual magick), are *erotocomatose lucidity, *alphaism, *dianism, *qodosh, the *Mass of the Holy Ghost, and the famous *black mass.

SEE ALSO *MASTURBATION

SHAIVA

A comprehensive name given to the teachings of a great number of schools throughout India, and especially in Kashmir, whose common denominator is the worship and veneration of the god *Shiva. As a coherent movement, Shaiva (or Shaivism) goes back to approximately the second century B.C.E., although it is generally believed that its essential core is much older, deriving from the *phallic worship prevalent on the Indian subcontinent. Even now, the major symbol associated with Shiva is the *lingam, icons and statues of which are found throughout the country. The school has often rivaled the other main schools of *Hinduism, *Shakta and Vaishnava (centered on the god Vishnu), but there are also groups who attempted to merge the views of these systems and also those that have close ties with *Tantra. Little of the vast literature of the Shaivas is extant and/or has been fully researched, translated, and published.

SHAKTA

One of the four mainstream religious systems of *Hinduism, Shakta (or Shaktism) designates the worship of *Shakti as the principal deity and energy of the universe and creation. The creative force, recognized as being sexual in nature, is therefore often represented in images of sexual union, similar to Tantric practice. Different subschools may use teachings that mirror this concept on the physical plane by using sexuality in their rituals; others see it as mere symbology and reject all actual union. One of the features that clearly delineate the difference between *Tantra and Shakta is the fact that Shakta teachings always regard the feminine principle—Shakti or *Devi—as supreme, whereas in Tantra the devotee is free to choose whether *Shiva, Shakti, or neither is so regarded.

SHAKTI
(SKT., "ENERGY, FORCE, POWER")

Hundreds of pages could be and have been filled with descriptions, discussions, and definitions of this most complex goddess of the East—and probably of the entire known world—yet we will try here to give a concise sketch of the essential traits and functions of this deity and of the associated concept of the female/feminine energy in the universe as the primal cause of All and Everything.

In short, we can say that Shakti as goddess and symbol represents the ultimate female principle of energy and motion, without which there could be no manifested universe. Her name is in fact a feminine noun of India's sacred language, *Sanskrit, which in our terms means "(creative) energy" and/or "power."

According to most authorities on *Tantra and Indian religion, this universal principle consists of such important ingredients as *cit* (consciousness, intelligence), *ananda* (joy, bliss), *iccha* (will), *jnana* (knowledge), and *kriya* (action).

Reading or studying Indian religious and philosophical texts and their associated commentaries, one may also come across terms that combine the name of the goddess with other terms or concepts, and one finds expressions such as *adya Shakti (primal energy, primordial force), *cit* Shakti or *vacya* Shakti (the energy of consciousness), *vacaka* Shakti (manifested consciousness), and *para* Shakti (supreme energy, cause of all), each of these terms implying—by the appellation of Shakti—that the concept or energy in question is a feminine one.

In sacred scriptures and in contemporary works concerning Eastern religion and mythology, however, we find that the name Shakti is used not only as indicated above, for the Great Goddess, but also as a title of honor for those women who participate in Tantric rituals, similar to the usage of such terms as *yogini.

Further confusion is caused by the fact that *Shakti* is also used as a term in Tantric subtle physiology. Each *chakra*, for example, has a "ruling goddess" who represents and expresses the specific energy of that subtle plexus, and these, too, are called Shakti.

SHAKTI ASANA
(SKT., "ENERGY EXERCISE")

Tantric sexual *asanas*, one cannot state it often enough, are rarely designed as an outlet for one or more persons' libidinous desire or need, although this may often be a resulting side effect. What such exercises aim at, instead, is to awaken, harness, and fine-tune the sexual energy of the body/mind in order to achieve heightened awareness and one-pointed concentration: necessary prerequisites for the transcendence of all duality and the realization of the one-ness of all. On the way to such insight, usually aided by well-tested *Tantric visualizations and *mantras, the practi-

tioners pass through many states of consciousness. If both are lovers in the classical sense and are not merely together for the ritual as such, this kind of sexual play will also lead to true communion between the participants at the deepest and highest levels of being.

In her text "Tantric Sharing of Consciousness," female practitioner J. Devi describes a contemporary version of such an exercise, one that is free of traditional requirements as to timing and chanting and *nyasa or *sparsa diksha. It does, however, clearly show how to "plug in" to the subtle body and how to combine sexual energy with the subtle electromagnetism of the human body—a typically Tantric technique that can result in visionary experiences as well as in full-body orgasm.

Her description sometimes makes it sound like something out of vampire lore, but on reading it one should realize that the active party is not "going for the red stuff in the jugular," as she says, but for the sexual energy, the *kundalini, *ophidian current, or *fivefold light—whatever people have called it. At the same time, there is no question here of "feeding" on this energy to the partner's detriment. On the contrary, the whole exercise will be fruitful only if and when both parties cooperate fully and consciously, thus creating a circle of spiraling energy flowing from one body into the other.

The author describes her practice as follows:

> The neck is the primary erotic zone. It is best approached from behind, not too directly. The tongue and lips are used to pick up a pulse where the juice seems to flow strongest. In the mind's eye, it often appears as a bluish white energy with an almost ultraviolet quality to it [a description that is reminiscent of the *blue-green halo known in *sexual magick].
>
> The active partner in the vamp role focuses all their attention on the parts of the tongue in contact with the other's nape. For the moment, those taste buds become eyes, searching for a filament of light, or a response that requires the energy of thought. Nothing happens until the napee responds by sending all of their attention, their consciousness to directly experience the tongue. With both parties responding with the energy of their attention, an energy circuit is established. However, this circuit is not complete until there is another junction to return the energy to and to keep it circulating. Connecting (without penetrating) at the pelvic region seems to be the best way to "plug in."
>
> Once you get the hang of it, you can work with greater amounts of voltage and get quite creative with the energy patterns. The energy can light up the brain and be visible to the mind's eye. . . . It is possible to keep this energy running for hours at each time. Just by using the same technique of moving the energy to other areas, it is possible to "orgasm" anywhere on the body, whichever body it may be. Similarly, you can spread your consciousness to all points of contact and put all the energy into connecting with the other completely and become like a wave of ecstatic energy. Experience has shown that this rite of sharing the blue-white energy is more effective when starting with the nape of the neck as the receiving zone. Later, the *yoni and the nipples are excellent receiving zones.

The entire text of "Tantric Sharing of Consciousness" can be found on J. Devi's website; see Index 28, "Internet Resources," (Miscellaneous).

SHAKTISM   SEE *SHAKTA

SHAMANISM

All indications considered, the cross-cultural phenomenon that can be identified under the collective name *shamanism* lies at the very root of all those mystery religions and schools that are oriented toward the individual's direct experience in the here and now, often using ecstatic, orgiastic rituals designed to expand the mind. Although the words *shaman* and *shamaness* are of Siberian origin, the title of these adepts is now generally used for the actual practitioners in many cultures. Studies of the medicine men and women, witches, sorcerers, diviners, and magician-priests of tribal people in Africa, America, Asia, Europe, and Oceania have all led, in principle, to a general acceptance of a pattern of ideas and behavior that today is called shamanism.

This pattern often includes a spirit flight, or journey of the soul, from which the shaman(ess) returns further enlightened and sometimes with messages for the tribe. Such experiences are often induced with the help of drum rhythms, *dance, and the use of drugs, and sometimes by means of a sexual relation with an "astral" partner of the other sex in the spirit realm.

SEE ALSO *AMANITA MUSCARIA, *BARDO, *BŌN, *SPECTROPHILIA, *VOODOO

SHANGPA KAGYUD
(TIB., *SHANGS-PA*)

One of the original two schools that form the *Kagyudpa tradition. Shangpa was officially founded by Khyungpo Naljor (Khyung-po Nyal-jor, 978–1079). However, although coming from a *Bōn and *Dzogchen background, Khyungpo Naljor received the school's major teachings through initiations by two female adepts: the *yogini *Mahasukhasiddhi, and Vajradhara *Niguma, the latter imparting her most secret knowledge to him alone. One of the school's major texts concerns Niguma's *mahamudra teachings, some of which were put into writing in her essay entitled "Mahamudra as Spontaneous Liberation."

Apart from *mahamudra,* the school's teaching and practice is centered on the Nigu-chos-drug, the "Five Tantras"

(Mahakala, Chakrasambhava, Hevajra, Mahamaya, and Guhyasamaja Tantras), and on the oral transmission (Tib., *sNyan rgyud*) of other "secret" teachings originating with Tantric adepts of the past, both male and female. This tradition still exists today, the late Kalu Rinpoche (1905–1989) having been its foremost representative in this century. Not long after his death, this compassionate lama returned in the form of a new incarnation, who will most certainly continue the Shangpa tradition.

SHANKHINI

The "conch woman," one of the *female archetypes of Indian erotic literature. The *shankhini* seems to be hot tempered, but she does not become a passionate lover until the third quarter of the night, when she enjoys much foreplay, especially *mukharata and the more elaborate types of sexual union. The *shankhini's* *yoni is said to be always moist and covered with much hair. Her love juice is very abundant and is said to taste quite salty, or acid.

    SEE ALSO *CONCH SHELL, *SHANKHINI NADI

SHANKHINI NADI

One of the subtle channels called *nadis. It runs downward from a woman's palatal region directly behind the philtrum (the small groove between the upper lip and the nose) and creates a direct link for the transmission of energy to her *yoni and vice versa (see illustration). In their book *Sexual Secrets,* Nik Douglas and Penny Slinger quote an ancient text, the Goraksa Vijaya, as stating, "There is a duct from the moon-center of the head to the hollow in the palatal region and upper lip" that is the "curved channel through which the Great Elixir passes" and that it "descends to the *lotus" (p. 196). According to this text, the *shankhini nadi* is also known as the 10th, secret opening of the body.

    To activate this subtle nerve, one can best combine exercises constricting the *yoni with a visualization of the *nadi* as a vibrant, oscillating beam of energy running back and forth from the clitoris to the upper lip of the mouth. It is interesting, in this context, to note that ancient erotic texts such as the *Kama Sutra and *Ananga Ranga especially recommend the kissing, nibbling, and biting of the upper lip.

    SEE ALSO *PELVIC FLOOR POTENTIAL, *TANTRIC VISUALIZATION

SHANKHINI NADI. *A visualization of the *shankhini nadi. Illustration by Christina Camphausen.*

SHEELA-NA-GIG

This is a collective name for the many female figurines found as artifacts mainly in the region that today forms Ireland and in some cases also in England, Scotland, and Germany, the general area that has long been under Celtic influence. These *sheelas* are mostly cut from stone and show a squatting or standing female figure, legs spread, exhibiting her yoni. In most cases these women or deities are, by most standards, quite unpleasant to look at, resembling as they do underfed, half-dead skeletal creatures or half-smiling *demons from someone's nightmare. What makes these figures especially interesting is the fact that most of them were found embedded—as some still are—in the walls of early monasteries and village churches, and we can imagine that they have given more than one abbot or priest his share of devilish headaches. Nevertheless, most of these *sheelas* have meanwhile been dismantled—many first disfigured and damaged by soldiers and other good Christians—and are hidden away in a cellar of the Dublin Museum.

    Little is known of the background and ritual purpose of these sculptures, and we therefore have to approach this question with mythographical imagination and with the intuitive mind of a criminologist. As a possible object for

SHEELA-NA-GIG. *A typical image of the* *sheela-na-gig, *this one from the Church of St. Mary and St. David, Kilpeck, Herefordshire, England. Photograph by Rick Murphy.*

SHEELA-NA-GIG. *Less famous than the Sheela of Kilpeck, this image from Kilsar shows a sheela* above the gate. *All visitors must pass below her spread legs, and many of them touch the sheela's* *yoni. *Photograph by Tara McLoughlin.*

meditation on the endless cycle of birth and death, they show an interesting relation to the woman in a Tanric *stri puja*. If we consider them mainly as exhibitionist, they may have a connection to figures such as the Greek *Baubo or the Japanese *Ama-no-Uzume. Their name, *sheela-na-gig*, has always been a considerable puzzle to etymologists, since it fits into none of the languages ever spoken in the British Isles. In Mesopotamia, however, at the temple at Erech, the term *nu-gug* ("the pure and immaculate ones") was used to designate the women who held the office of sacred harlot (*see* *Ritual Prostitution). It is therefore my suggestion that they are a pre-Celtic version of the Oriental ritual prostitutes and that they may have been "imported" from the Mesopotamian region. This, of course, does not exclude the possibility and probability that they were objects for meditation as well as figures demonstrating simple *yoni magic—that is, keeping negative energies at bay.

SHEKINAH

The cabalistic term for the "creative force" and/or "supreme energy," conceived of as a female principle similar to the Tantric *Shakti. In the words of one author, this Hebrew goddess is "the Great Mother in whose fertile womb the universe was conceived" (Gonzalesz-Wippler, p. 50). The concept of the Shekinah is, however, not that simple and is too detailed to be covered in the context of this book, but it contains some interesting facets that bear on our present study.

To the cabalists, whose main concern is the balance and eventual union of all polarities (such as male/female, fire/water, and *yang/*yin), the purpose of formulating a concept such as the Shekinah does not end by merely establishing that there is a divine, universal, female energy that is present in all humanity and in the world at large. Like *Tantra, *Taoism, and *Gnosticism, the cabalah conceives of man and woman as being "incomplete" and "half" as long as he or she has not been united with the complementary, other half. However antisexual and antifemale certain aspects of Jewish life and religion may have become, we find that sexual union, by preference on the holy Sabbath, has a sacred and spiritual dimension. It is then, when woman and man are united in the presence of the Shekinah, that they become "one body" and partake of divinity. Author Benjamin Walker states that "the Shekinah . . . envelopes all women, and abides for a short time in man only while he is in union with woman" (1977, p. 153). In a comment on Numbers 20:25–28, Walker also explains that when Aaron, on God's command, was stripped of his garments on Mount Hor, "it was in order that he receive the kiss of the Shekinah. From this kiss Aaron, the first high priest of Israel, died, for no person can endure union with the Spirit and survive in mortal form" (p. 181). Thus the goddess shows herself to be one of the Near Eastern Great Mothers, like *Ishtar and *Astarte, who rule all aspects of life: creation, sexuality, and death.

SEE ALSO *SABBATIANS

SHEN
(CHIN., "SPIRIT, DEITY")

1. Besides *ch'i and *ching, this is the third type of energy associated with the three *tan-t'ien, and it belongs to the topmost of these Chinese *chakras, the invisible cavity at the top of the skull. Shen is something like the "luminous personal spirit, compounded of all an individual's thoughts, feelings and sense of identity" (Rawson and Legeza, p. 28). Shen, one's individual spirit (or mind), is thought to arise from the union of ching and ch'i. It is believed to enter the body with a child's first breath and to leave it at the moment of death. **2.** The term is also used as a general designation for all deities who inhabit the universe and the bodies or minds of human beings.

SHINGON
(JAP., "TRUE WORD")

A Japanese *Mahayana Buddhist school, the teachings of which derive from the Chinese *Mi-tsung. The school shows many influences from *Tantra and *Vajrayana and was founded by Kobo Daishi (774–835 C.E.), a master known in Japan as Kukai. Shingon is divided into ken-kyo (exoteric teachings) and mitsou-kyo (esoteric teachings). Today Shingon is one of the largest Buddhist schools in Japan. The school makes use of *mandalas and *mudras/1,

and also holds the *vajra as a sacred object. A left-hand branch of Shingon is known as *Tachikawa.

SHINTO

Chinese term for the indigenous, nature-oriented Japanese religion, Kami-no-Michi, that translates as "way of the divine." The main deity of Shinto is the goddess *Amaterasu, representing the sun, and her main shrine is at Ise, near Kyoto. Although there are at least 130 different sects, Japan also knew a state Shinto; it was repressed by the American army in the wake of World War II.

SEE ALSO *AMA-NO-UZUME, *KAGURA, *KAMI, *MATSURI, *UKE-MOCHI-NO-KAMI

SHIVA

The Indian male creative principle, the opposite pole and partner/lover of *Shakti. Worshipped most often in the form of a *lingam, he is India's foremost deity connected with *phallic worship. Shiva is known under many names—for example, Mahadeva, Nandi, and Nataraj—and has many functions and attributes, differing from school to school and sect to sect. He is worshipped all over India and in neighboring countries, especially among the non-Islamic population of *Kashmir. Shiva and *Parvati, a form of Shakti, are often featured in sacred texts as a conversing couple, one answering the other's questions and thus instructing their devotees.

SEE ALSO *JYOTIRLINGA, *PAN, *SHAIVA, *SHIVALINGA, *YONILINGA

SHIVALINGA

Everywhere in India's cities, towns, and villages one sees small and large statues of *Shiva's *lingam. Fresh flowers and newly applied ocher powder testify to the living religious practice of *phallic worship that still surrounds this god and his sacred member. The occurrence is so frequent that we can mention here only some of the most outstanding examples.

Along with the famous place of pilgrimage at *Amarnatha, mention must be made of the Matan-geshvara Temple, one of the most holy of *Khajuraho's 85 temples. The site contains an erect lingam 2.5 meters tall and with a diameter of more than 1 meter. The *Gupta-sadhana Tantra states that "infinite result is obtained by worship of a Sivalinga that should be made of crystal etc. but never of clay" (Banerjee, p. 187).

SEE ALSO *BANALINGA, *EKALINGA, *YONILINGA

SHIVA SAMHITA

A Sanskrit text of five chapters that is of interest mainly to students of hatha yoga and/or *Tantra. In its theoretical part, this "Collection of Shiva's Wisdom" presents a philosophy that is strongly influenced by Advaita Vedanta; in its practical part it explains in detail the precept and rules for the study of yoga and gives clear instructions on how the various steps of yogic development can be achieved. The seventeenth-century text deals with anatomy, breath control, and a large number of exercises and techniques.

The text also describes the yoni *mudra*, a secret Tantric technique that according to this work "should not be revealed or given to others." However, the text has meanwhile been translated and published and is available to all who can read. In connection with the above exercise, the scripture tells of the splendor of the divine *yoni, which is "brilliant as tens of millions of suns and cool as tens of millions of moons" and explains furthermore that "above the yoni is a very small and subtle flame, whose form is intelligence."

SHUNAMISM

The *Bible speaks of the practice called shunamism in the story of the old and ailing King David (c. 1000 B.C.E.). For him rejuvenation was sought, and found, by his absorbing a young *virgin's body heat. The text points out that there was no actual sexual union by saying that she "ministered to him: but the king knew her not" (I Kings 1:4). The virgin in question was Abishag from the Shunammite tribe, known for the healing properties of their *breath and *scent; hence the term. The emperor Rudolf of Habsburg (1218–1291), surely inspired by the Old Testament, also used this method. When in fever, he would order all wives and daughters of his noblemen to come and kiss him.

SEE ALSO *OLFACTORY DELIGHTS

SIDDHI

(SKT., "ABILITIES OF PERFECTION")

The Sanksrit term for a type of spiritual/mental accomplishment that we can best approximate with modern expressions such as, for instance, ESP (extrasensory perception) or Colin Wilson's (b. 1931) Faculty X. Concepts such as "mystical power," "paranormal potential," and "magical skill" are also often used to cover these phenomena. The term *siddhi* is also the root of the title for the "greatly accomplished ones," or *Mahasiddhas, each of whom had achieved one or more of these "perfections." *Vajrayana texts speak of eight types of *siddhi* only, but one can find a much more detailed classification in the Hindu *Tantras, where 84 are recognized. Among them, many phenomena can be found that correspond to those charted by contemporary parapsychology—for

SHIVA. *Seated on a tiger skin, accompanied by serpents, and with hair that appears like the gnarled roots of an old tree, this vision of Shiva shows him as the perfect ascetic and yogi that many of his followers aspire to. Painting on silk by Harish Johari.*

example, psychokinesis, telekinesis, and the astral "double." Here is a list of the more interesting parallels:

1. akrsti	attracting others
2. anima	decreasing one's size at will
3. antardhana	making oneself invisible
4. isitva	greatness, mastery
5. kamarupitva	assuming forms at will
6. kamavasaita	the power to control one's passion
7. khecara	the power to fly
8. kramana	the power to enter another person's body—that is, possession
9. laghiman	the power to cancel out gravity—that is, levitation
10. mahima	increasing one's size at will
11. mohana	rendering a person unconscious
12. manojavitva	achieving high speed
13. padalepa	the ability to move about anywhere, unnoticed
14. prapti	the power of obtaining everything
15. prakamya	irresistible willpower
16. stambhana	causing temporary paralysis in someone
17. vasitva	control over others
18. vikaranad-harmitva	infinite mental powers

See also *Divya Siddhis, *Hevajra Tantra, *Obeah

SILENT PRAYER

Because God is thought to be present during sexual union between a married couple, Zoroastrians and followers of Islam are supposed to offer a silent, inwardly recited prayer before making love. This is especially surprising because these belief systems do not generally encourage sexuality or the respectful treatment of women.

See also *Shekinah

SINHAMUKHA

One of the manifestations of *Padmasambhava, but in the form of a wrathful female *dakini, as they are encountered in the *bardo.

SIXTY-FOUR ARTS

"A person should study the sixty-four arts and sciences, as also the sixty-four aspects of sexual union." We can see from this quote from the *Kama Sutra that both men and women are admonished to train themselves in these sixty-four arts, whose patroness is the goddess *Sarasvati. Although the "art of love" is the foremost, and many other art forms like singing, dancing, music, writing, reading, drawing, and sculpture are naturally included, the list of skills and inclinations described as the sixty-four arts is also full of everyday activities such as sewing, gardening, carpentry, and cooking. Along with such skills, there is mention of religious ritual, magic, sports, and games as well as of languages, mental exercises, logic, and management; this is a list for veritable lifelong study.

Important here is the fact that love—erotic activity, sexuality, however we prefer to name it—is presented as a skill that can and should be learned with a creative attitude and with as much dedication (or more) as one would study logic, language, or the martial arts—a concept quite unknown in the West, or one left to playboys and prostitutes, who are then both despised and envied for their proficiency.

See also *Chitrini

SIXTY-FOUR YOGINI PITHA

Two circular open-air *yogini *pithas, or sanctuaries, can be found in Orissa: a smaller one in Hirapur dating from the tenth century and the famous, larger one in Rhanipur-Jharial, which dates from the eighth century.

The number 64, traditionally also the number of the yoginis, may be connected to the 64 petals or *nadis of the *manipura chakra, and these temples could be initiatory *mandalas built to represent this important center, from which 64 channels of energy rise upward.

We can be certain that the number of 64 yoginis is no coincidence and that the sacred engineers had something special in mind when they built these temple mandalas, whose inner walls are partitioned into 64 niches, each holding the statue of a different yogini. It is known that these sanctuaries were used by left-hand Tantrics for celebrating their *chakra puja, *kula puja, and *stri puja/1: group rituals using psychophysical techniques to transmute life energy or libido toward the attainment of spiritual liberation and enlightenment.

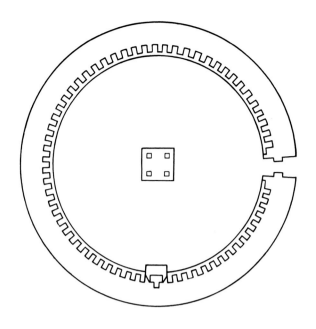

SIXTY-FOUR YOGINI PITHA. *A ground plan.*

SIXTY-FOUR YOGINI PITHA. *A view of the *sixty-four yogini temple
at Ranipur-Jharial (eighth–eleventh centuries), Orissa, India.
Photograph by Bala Chowdhury, London.*

The keynote here—as so often in Tantric and Taoist *inner alchemy—is the transformation and transmutation of energy. Men and women unite and separate, intermingle and dissolve their fluids and energies in a manner very similar to the *yin and *yang lines in the 64 hexagrams of the *I Ching, or as happens in the spiraling ladder of life, the double helix of DNA molecules, which separate and reunite in order to create something new. Order and balance, traditionally represented by the number eight, are taken here to a new and higher level, 64, eight to the power of two.

SEE ALSO *KAMESHVARI

SKOPTSI AND/OR SKOPZI
(RUSSIAN, "THE CASTRATED ONES")

An eighteenth-century sect in Russia and Rumania in which ritual *castration and *circumcision were promoted and practiced. The Skoptsi called themselves the "people of God" and believed that the removal of their genitals brought them profound spiritual powers. Not only the men's genitals were mutilated for such "religious" reasons: in *A Private Anthropological Cabinet*, Robert Meadows shows a Skoptsi woman with amputated nipples, and he reports that the women's genitals were also mutilated.

SM

1. Mostly, a popular abbreviation used for the various practices people usually connect with *sadomasochism. **2.** In the circles of the Western occult traditions, the abbreviation for *sexual magick, a Western type of *Tantra; sometimes merely called sex magic.

SMARNANAM

According to the sacred texts of the *Vedas, this is one of the aspects of sexual union. It translates literally as "allowing the thoughts to dwell upon it."

SNAKE   SEE *SERPENT

SODASI
(SKT., "PERFECT ONE")

The goddess Sodasi is seen as a 16-year-old woman and as an embodiment of the 16 types of desire. The number 16, in Indian thought, is the number representing perfection and totality and is also associated with other goddesses. In the Sodasi Tantra, the goddess is identified with Tripurasundari, the "radiant light in the three eyes of Shiva"—that is, she is the source of his wisdom, soul, and consciousness. Sodasi's body is of a deep *red color, and she is often depicted in ecstatic intercourse, sitting astride the god Mahakala ("great time"), her throne being carried by several other important male deities such as Brahma, Indra, and Rudra.

In the *Niruttara Tantra, it is a girl of 14, not 16, who is described as "the perfect one."

SODOM AND GOMORRAH

The famous twin cities on the southeastern shore of the Dead Sea, which were destroyed not by the Hebrew deity (Genesis 18:20–19:28) but by *Abraham's troops, who were told to eradicate these places along with their heathen worshippers of the Goddess. "And lo, the smoke of the country went up as the smoke of a furnace" (Genesis 19:28). The "unspeakable" sins committed there were mostly of a sexual nature and concerned *ritual promiscuity, *ritual prostitution, *incest, and as the name makes obvious, sodomy.

SOLOMON
(990–922 B.C.E.)

Ancient Middle Eastern king proverbial for his wisdom and famous for his *Song of Songs, which forms part of the *Bible. Like some of the old Chinese emperors, Solomon kept a large *harem that at one time included 60 queens plus an additional 80 "lesser wives" and concubines. All in all he is said to have been the lover of at least a thousand women during his lifetime.

Various bits of information on Solomon can be found throughout this book under the headings *Cinnamon, *Ecstasy, *Mandrake, *Menstrual Fluid, *Myrrh, *Wine of the Navel, *Yoniyugma, and *Zohar.

SOMA

1. Name for a sacred drug used by early shamans, yogis, and Brahmans that is—according to R. Gordon Wasson and colleagues (p. 13)—probably derived from fly agaric, also known as *Amanita muscaria. The same drug was known to the ancient Persians as *haoma*. **2.** Similar to *ros and *golden nectar, this Sanskrit "nectar of ecstasy" is a subtle biochemical fluid/energy released by the *pineal and/or *pituitary gland during erotic *ecstasy.

SEE ALSO *AMRITA

SOMA SACRIFICE

Like many of the religious observances and rituals of India's early Vedic period (roughly 1200–800 B.C.E.), during which most of *Hinduism was shaped, the great soma *sacrifice was sexually oriented. Intoxicated with *soma, the participants would sing songs of *ecstasy, and "a noblewoman would ritually make love with a priest" (Douglas and Slinger, 1981, p. 13) who represented a divine being.

In a different Vedic ceremony, the ancient "horse sacrifice" (Skt., *ashvamedha*), the queen was required to make sexual contact with the member of a freshly sacrificed horse, which represented the absent king.

SONG OF SONGS

One of the books in the Old Testament, usually attributed to Solomon (990–922 B.C.E.), son of David (c. 1010–c. 962 B.C.E.) and king of Israel, famous for his wisdom and his intuitive judgments concerning human affairs. Although attributed to this sage-king, the work has been dated, in a written form, not earlier than about 350 B.C.E., a time when it had been transmitted orally for at least six hundred years.

In terms of our present topic the Song of Songs (sometimes called Song of Solomon and/or Canticles) is one of the more important and beautiful texts contained in the Old Testament. However, church fathers and rabbis throughout history have protested against any literal interpretation of the text, and as with certain *Tantras, it has been explained as a mere allegorical expression of the worshipper's love of God—for example, by *Origen. Considering their cultural origins and the historical reality of Solomon's time, that is, the existence of *fertility festivals and *ritual prostitution among the Near Eastern peoples, one can easily imagine the texts to literally and actually speak of human love, which they do on an exoteric level. On the other hand, they also represent an encoded cabalistic wisdom similar to that used in Genesis and the Sepher Yetsirah.

Whereas many orthodox Jewish and Christian scholars and believers are thus confused or unhappy with the Song's inclusion in the canonical *Bible, it is regarded as a very important text among cabalists and is one of the 18 parts of the *Sepher ha Zohar. Other works attributed to Solomon, his odes and psalms, are part of the apocryphal Old Testament literature.

Quotes from this love poem can be found in this book under the headings *Ecstasy, *Mandrake, and *Myrrh.

SEE ALSO *CINNAMON, *MENSTRUAL FLUID, *WINE OF THE NAVEL

SORORAL POLYGYNY

A term used to indicate a special type of *polygamy in which, when a man marries a woman from another tribe or family, he not only marries her but thereby becomes simultaneously married to one, more, or all of her sisters, although marriage sometimes means little more than being socially sanctioned to make love to any of these other women. The information presented below, when not otherwise stated, is based on Robert Briffault's study *The Mothers*.

FAR EAST   It is known that the Mongol leader Genghis Khan married two sisters, and he did so according to the ancient traditions of both Eastern and Western Mongols. But this custom has likewise been observed in early China, Japan, Kampuchea (Cambodia), Malaysia, Burma, *Assam, and Thailand, and it was found among the Siberian Chukchi and the Ostyaks as well.

Among several tribes of India, from north to south, including the Indo-Aryan invaders, sororal polygyny was once in vogue, and marriages with as many as 10 sisters have been reported.

NEAR EAST   A famous example of this custom among the early Hebrews is found in the marriage of Jacob to Leah and her sister Rachel.

THE AMERICAS   The custom was widespread among the North American Indians—the Pawnee, Dakota, Natchez, Ojibwa, and Algonquian tribes, to name but a few. When a warrior married a young woman he often received all her sisters as wives, too, having merely to wait until the girls reached puberty.

Similar customs prevailed in Central and South America, with the Jivaros, Canebo, Guaranis, and Chriguanos as named examples. Briffault quotes a study by the University of Chile in which it is stated that "when an Indian is able to obtain several sisters together as wives, they prefer it to marrying women who are not related to one another" (Briffault, vol. 1, p. 617).

OCEANIA AND AUSTRALIA   On several Melanesian islands it was common that a man who took one woman as his individual partner became the husband of all her sisters, too. In Western Australia, all girls of a family traditionally became married to the husband of the eldest sister. Aboriginal tribes in Queensland married the sisters to different men, but all these husbands were allowed to be sexually involved with all their wives' sisters. Aside from these examples, the custom was also common in New Guinea, Ceram, Celebes, Samoa, the Gilbert Islands, and the Philippines as well as among the Maori of New Zealand.

AFRICA   Sororal polygyny was known among the Guanches of the Canary Islands and among many tribes of the African mainland, although the custom varied in its details. Among the Basoga of east Africa, only one sister accompanied the bride to her husband's home, and among the Herero in southwest Africa, it was specified that a man must take the older sister along when marrying the younger. Different varieties are reported from among the Bushmen, Ba-Congo, Kaffirs, and Zulu, and also from Mozambique.

SPANISH FLY

A famous powder, readily available in Morocco and also in most contemporary sex shops, that is stirred into (some)one's drink in order to arouse passion. The powder, which consists of ground, dead green blister beetles (*Lytta vesicatoria* and other types), can actually be quite detrimental to one's health—even fatally so—if it is used too often or in high doses. Its active chemical ingredient, *cantharidin, not only can cause vomiting, abdominal pain, and shock but often leads to an inflammation of the urethra that in men causes a pathogenic arousal. These false erections are largely responsible for the substance's fame as an *aphrodisiac, yet, who would want a false erection? Since *cantharides is often illegal, for example in the United States, the ingredient used in most commercial "Spanish fly" products is simply cayenne pepper.

SEE ALSO *RHINO HORN

SPARK OF LIFE

A symbol of the Japanese Tantric *Tachikawa sect, with representations of male and female energies smelting in a circle of fire. It represents the spiritual dimension of Tantric sexuality through yellow images of sun and moon and the physical dimension by two mirroring images of the *Sanskrit letter *A* (the beginning and end of things), one in white for the male semen and one in red for the female ovum.

SPARK OF LIFE. *The *spark of life, a symbol of the Japanese *Tachikawa school.*

SPARSHA DIKSHA
(SKT, "CONTACT, TOUCH")

"Initiation by touch," a Sanskrit concept indicating that the sense of touch, from the laying on of hands to more advanced forms, can be used as a medium or vehicle for initiation.

SEE ALSO *NYASA

SPECTROPHILIA

Not to be confused with *necrophilia, this is a rather specialized form of *congressus subtilis. In the case of spectrophilia, however, the "nonphysical entity" and sexual partner is not an *incubus or *succubus but the spirit of a deceased. In *Beyond the Body,* Benjamin Walker reports that the famous medieval magician Dr. Johann Faust (1480–1589) claimed to have thus evoked several Greek heroes and heroines, one of whom was the famous Helen of Troy (c. 1200 B.C.E.).

Another alleged practitioner of spectrophilia was the Belgian Catholic priest and abbé Joseph-Antoine Boullan (1824–1893), who was excommunicated because of his turning to satanism and magic. Boullan, the model for the main character in the novel *La-Bas* by French occultist

J. K. Huysmans (1848–1907), taught the members of his cult to connect sexually with such astral entities as *nymphs and *satyrs, succubi, incubi, and spirits of the deceased. Successful "contacts" were reported with the astral bodies of historical personalities such as Cleopatra (69–30 B.C.E.) and Alexander the Great (356–323 B.C.E.).

SEE ALSO *KA'A

SPERM SEE *LINGAM TOPOGRAPHY/19–22, *SEMEN

SPERM MAGIC
Among many tribes of New Guinea, *semen was regarded as a sacred substance and was used in several rituals and in healing. J. F. Cornelissen, who has studied the notes of Dutch missionaries in New Guinea written between 1905 and 1963, reports that the various tribes used sperm in a variety of ways (pp. 40 ff., 60 ff.):

- to protect oneself against the spirits of the dead by rubbing it on one's forehead
- rubbing it into ritual scarifications
- to enhance the fertility of coconut and sago palms
- eating it baked with sago, as an *aphrodisiac and a general strengthening tonic
- to heal wounds, both by applying it to the wound and by eating it; sometimes a drink was prepared of sperm and coconut milk
- in fighting epidemics, when every member of the village would eat a little sperm mixed with grated coconut meat and the substance would be applied to his or her body by the local shaman
- rubbing it onto the body during initiation rituals
- as a binding and strengthening agent when coloring the teeth black
- mixing sperm from a father's *masturbation with coconut milk and giving it to a baby as a strengthening drink

The large supplies of sperm regularly needed for all these usages were often provided by asking one's wife to have sexual union with other men. The sperm was collected afterward and often mixed with grated coconut.

SEE ALSO *AURA SEMINALIS, *GNOSTICISM, *MOON MAGIC, *OJAS

SPIKENARD
One of the major *Tantric perfumes, which is won from the underground stems of the Himalayan plant *Nardostachys jatamansi.*

SEE ALSO *OLFACTORY DELIGHTS

SPIRITUAL MARRIAGE
A Christian concept introduced by *Origen's allegorical interpretation of the *Song of Songs, which gave way to a love mysticism that speaks of a "marriage" between God or Christ, on one hand, and the "soul bride" on the other. The love mystics even speak of secret embraces and of kisses that are exchanged between the soul bride and the divine bridegroom. It has been shown by James Leuba, in his *Psychology of Religious Mysticism,* that such concepts, visions, and visualizations can lead to actual erotic sensations, even to *orgasm. In reports of several mystics, both male and female, one can ascertain that they became "sexually excited by their 'spiritual' love for Jesus or the Virgin Mary" (Leuba, p. 143).

Nevertheless, spiritual marriage was not confined to Christian mystics. Shamans, female and male, throughout the world speak of spirit partners with whom they have sexual union, often with full knowledge and sometimes jealousy of their real-life partners. *Voodoo devotees are also known to "marry" with certain *loa,* or spirits. Similar customs were also known among the Saora people of Orissa (India) and in Ethiopia.

SEE ALSO *SPECTROPHILIA, *SUFISM

SRI CHAKRA SEE *SRI YANTRA

SRI VIDYA
Sanskrit name for an ancient Tantric science that has as its object of study the human erotic secretions—such as *semen, *menstrual fluid, and *female love juices—and their subtle components.

SEE ALSO *KALAS, *MARMAS, *PHEROMONES

SRI YANTRA
The most important of all Tantric *yantras, the *sri* yantra is a diagram symbolizing the playful and creative sexual activity of the universe and the resulting continuous creation. The small dot in the middle is the cosmic seed, or *bindu,* the undifferentiated potential energy that gives rise to the nine *navachakras,* five female and four male triangles. (As is typical and fitting for a symbol of the *Tantra and *Shakta

traditions, its designers honored the goddess by including just one more female *triangle in a symbol that at first sight seems symmetrical.) All in all, these nine intersecting triangles, weaving in and out of one another, add up to 28 downward-pointing (female) triangles and 24 upward-pointing (male) triangles, the interplay of which represents the root of all creation and unfoldment.

The *sri yantra* is also known under the names *sri chakra* and *tripura chakra*.

SEE ALSO *LIVING GODDESS, *TALEJU

STRIPTEASE   SEE *CORDAX, *KAGURA, *TOKUDASHI

STRI PUJA

1. Very similar to the *yoni *puja*, this ritual of woman worship (Skt., *stripuja*) is in fact a holy mass dedicated to *Shakti, during which the devotees direct their concentrated attention toward a specially selected nude woman, focusing their meditative awareness especially on her *yoni. The preparations for this ritual include several days of sexual abstinence and other means (drugs, aphrodisiacs, and a special diet) of heightening their mental and physical responsiveness to erotic stimulation.

Although there are various possible paths along which such a ritual can proceed, they are known only to a select group of practitioners. One account of a *stri puja* was given in the early twentieth century by an anonymous observer (and perhaps a participant), who described it as follows:

> The woman is seated on an altar with legs spread wide apart to display the sacred symbol, the yoni, which the priest kisses and to which he offers food and libations in sacred vessels called *argha, which are shaped like a yoni. After these offerings have been consecrated by touching them to the living yoni, they are distributed among the worshippers and eaten.
>
> Often such a ritual is held in order to examine an adept's achievement of control over himself, and there may be neither intercourse nor ejaculation if he is to pass this test. Contrary to what one might expect, the woman thus honored is not selected for beauty, youth, or virginity, because it is not the individual who is the focus of everyone's perceptive attention but the goddess in the form of the sacred "lotus of wisdom" between her legs.

SRI YANTRA. *Most important of all Tantric diagrams (Skt., yantra), the sri yantra is a complex interplay of upward- and downward pointing triangles (for example, male and female) symbolizing the playful and creative sexual activity of the universe and the resulting continuous creation. Painting by Harish Johari.*

2. Another type of *stri puja*, or a preparatory phase for it, is mentioned by Benjamin Walker. Here the Tantric plays the part of a domestic servant in a woman's household, slowly progressing toward an intimate relationship with her. "At first he sleeps in the same room with her, but on the floor, while she sleeps on the bed. After two weeks he joins her in bed, but at her feet; then beside her, but clothed. Then he lies beside her nude, fondling and caressing her. Then he has intercourse with her, but without emission" (1982, p. 51). This ritual technique for building up erotic tension has been used as the plot for a beautifully written story, *Jewel of the Moon*, by novelist William Kotzwinkle.

SEE ALSO *ASAG

STYGIAN SEXUALITY

The erotic/sexual impulse is—at least in humans—so strong as to pervade almost every area of life, thought, dream, and fantasy. Whether the forces are affirmed or negated does not matter much.

Even beyond and after death the sexual drive, its energies,

and its manifestations seem to continue, and there are marvels of information concerning the phenomenon of Stygian sexuality, which draws its name from Styx, the netherworld's River of Death. There are, of course, certain connections we are not concerned with here, such as sexual magicians who unite with *succubi and *incubi or, in the case of *spectrophilia, with the spirits of persons long dead. We also do not refer to graveyard meditations involving *necrophilia or of imaginary voyages to astral realms where sexual encounters with *demons or deities can be experienced.

Much closer to home, in regard to death and dying, are the revelations made by author Robert Monroe. Monroe has written about the out-of-body experiences he and others have had—of being close to death or actually pronounced dead, yet "coming back" during or after medical attention and surgery. Monroe reports that sex still does play a prominent role even after one has left one's physical body and that the sex drive can be surprisingly strong. The union itself is described as an exchange of electric currents accompanied by feelings of mild shock, when contact results in "a quick momentary flash of the sex charge" (p. 197).

Such imagery—or is it indeed fact?—fits the idea of Emanuel Swedenborg (1688–1772), who surmised that loving souls who meet beyond death will fuse their astral bodies and merge into a single bright light. It also recalls William Butler Yeats's statement "the intercourse of angels is a light."

SUBINCISION

A practice mainly known from the initiation ceremonies and puberty rites of Australian Aborigines. By slitting open the underside of their *lingam along the whole length of the urethra, the men simulate having a woman's *yoni. Their motivation seems to be a need to acquire some of the female magic of periodic bleeding, to which end they will again and again reopen the wound during strictly guarded ceremonies that no woman may attend. The men thus initiated and subincised are called "possessor of a vulva," and they are known to have homosexual relations with youths not yet incised. This "penis which is also a vagina"—so Norman O. Brown reminds us (1966, p. 60)—is probably one of the earliest solutions to the problem of squaring the circle.

SUBTLE PHYSIOLOGY

Many of the more advanced and sophisticated cultures subscribe to a concept in which a human being has, apart from the material or physical body, also a subtle body. Peoples of India, Tibet, China, and Egypt, as well as the alchemists of the Middle Ages and some of the advanced thinkers of the twentieth century, have studied that subtle body and take its existence and functions for granted. For a quick overview see the following:

Centers of energy: *see* *Chakras (Physiological), *Tanden, *Tan-t'ien

Subtle arteries: *see* *Metu, *Nadis

Fields/energies: *see* *Ch'i, *Ching, *Kundalini, *Shen

Index 12 on page 280 shows all related entries.

SUCCUBUS

Latin term (plural, succubi) for an ethereal, nonmaterial female intent on sexual intercourse with human beings. Succubi are said to suck a man dry of all his potent juices. *Semen collected in this way may then, according to medieval beliefs, be stored by the devil for later use by incubi (their male counterparts) in order to impregnate human females. Succubi were seen as the instigators of men's "wet dreams."

Apparently, similar female spirits can be evoked through a special manner of worship, according to the Prapancasara Tantra—worship that produces such erotic feeling in the immaterial females that they are drawn to the devotee.

See also *Female Sexual Demons, *Incubus, *Lamia, *Lilith, *Spectrophilia

SUFISM

The name of this mystical movement, developed out of Islamic religion, is based on the term *suf,* meaning "wool," since the early Sufis wore a cloth made from wool only. In the framework of Islam, Sufism has always been regarded as a kind of heresy, and its members have often been actively persecuted. Different schools of Sufism operated and extended their influence into Egypt and India, Persia, Afghanistan, and Syria, often picking up local customs and beliefs.

Though Sufism generally tends toward asceticism in its general and sexual dimension, Sufis do, like Christian mystics and Indian followers of *bhakti, employ the energies of love by directing it solely toward the Divine. The inspired mystical love poetry of Sufi adepts such as Jalal'al-Din Rumi (1207–1273) speak of this divine love. Nonetheless, among the many groups, schools, and sects of Sufi orientation we

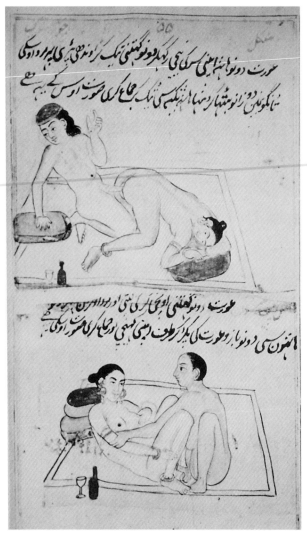

SUFISM. *Page from an eighteenth-century Islamic erotic manual, Kashmir.*

also find those who are known to have used certain types of sexual initiations, drugs, and techniques that we could classify as Tantric. Western adepts of *sexual magick often claim that their secret teachings derive, by way of the crusading Templars, from Sufi sources.

Like *Tantra and *Taosim, Sufism also incorporates teachings concerning the human subtle body and counts four subtle centers that can be compared to the Indian *chakras:

The Teacher	* Sahasrara Chakra
The Mysterious Center	* Vishuddha Chakra
The Secret Center	* Anahata Chakra
Center of the Self	* Manipura Chakra

Since all four of these parallels correspond with the early Tantric tradition of four instead of seven *chakras*, the tradition of the Islamic mystics may have been imported from India.

SEE ALSO *AMBER, *GURDJIEFF, *NIZARI ISMA'ILIS, *SPIRITUAL MARRIAGE

SUKRA

Like *mehana,* this is another Sanskrit term for *semen.

SUMERIAN WRITING

The earliest written symbols for *male* and *female*—quite an important step in cultural development that occurred about 3500 B.C.E.—were merely a few lines that represented an "erect penis ejaculating sperm" and "the pubic triangle with the slit of the vulva" (Allegro, 1973, pp. 35ff.).

SU NÜ

The "plain girl" or "simple maid," one of the *Three Lady Immortals. A quote from her Su Nü Ching can be found on page 163.

SEE ALSO *WONDROUS DISCOURSE OF SU NÜ

SURYACANDRASIDDHI

The great adept *Padmasambhava is often said to have subdued those *demons and *dakinis that were fierce and demoniac (that is, anti-Buddhist), yet at other times it is clear that he himself was first initiated by such goddesses/female adepts and received special, magical knowledge from the Great Mothers. Of special interest in this regard is canto 34 of *The Life and Liberation of Padmasambhava*, where the hero "prostrated himself to the enthroned *dakini*" (Suryacandrasiddhi) and "begged her for teachings; outer, inner and secret."

Suryacandrasiddhi (or "highest" *dakini*)—also known as Laygya Wangmo or "great sovereign *dakini* of deeds"—then changes her new disciple in true magical/shamanic fashion into the sacred syllable *hum*, swallows him whole, and lets him pass through her body. In the process Padmasambhava is purified; he is initiated into certain teachings and obtains magical powers before being reborn and "ejected through her secret lotus"—that is, her *yoni. How powerful and advanced an adept this Magical Mother of Padmasambhava represents is emphasized in the text by the fact that even her maidservant *Kumari was a woman of wonder: "With a

Sumerian Writing. *Symbols for* man *and* woman *in early *Sumerian writing.*
Illustration by Christina Camphausen.

crystal dagger she cut open her breast, within which appeared the many-colored splendor of the gods of the calm Diamond Plane."

SUSHUMNA
(SKT., "ROYAL ROAD")

The central and most important *nadi, which runs along/within the spinal column that connects the lowest to the highest *chakra. It is the major pathway for the potential ascent of the *kundalini energy and a symbol for the river *Sarasvati. It runs from the *muladhara chakra upward to the *sahasrara chakra.

SUTRA
(SKT., "THREAD")

A basic spiritual, religious, and/or sacred text regarded as divine revelation. However, often the sutras are in fact compact summaries of other, earlier, and more lengthy scriptures.

SUTRA OF SECRET BLISS

A sacred text of the Japanese *Tachikawa school, the full title of which is *Sutra Proclaiming the Secret Method Enabling a Man and a Woman to Experience the Bliss of Buddhahood in This Very Body.* It contains, apart from the school's general teachings on sexuality and enlightenment, a detailed description of male and female genitals, classified in five types each.

This and other texts of the school, for example the *Yoshinshu, Sangai Isshin-ki,* and *Hokyoshu Sangen Menju,* date back to the twelfth and thirteenth centuries, after which the school was outlawed and had to go underground.

SUVARNINIS

A Sanskrit term that translates as the "sweet-smelling ladies," for a certain type of female Tantric initiate and partner in *maithuna. Such a *suvarnini* (sometimes spelled *suvasini*) "is the source of wisdom in the heterosexual practices . . . who emits the *kalas" (Kenneth Grant, quoted by Redgrove, 1989, p. 147).

SVADHISHTANA CHAKRA

The "spleen" *chakra, one of the later additions to the ancient system of four *chakras and now number 2.

> LOCATION: Midway between pubis and navel, first lumbar vertebra, plexus hypogastricus
> ENDOCRINE GLAND: Spleen, pancreas
> RULING *SHAKTI: Rakini
> COLOR: White
> LOTUS: Six-petaled, vermilion and carmine red
> ASSOCIATIONS: Taste, health, reserve

SVAYAMBHU KUSUMA

Term used in the *Nila Tantra for the menstrual "blood" (*menstrual fluid) of a young girl. The Sanskrit term *svayambhu* means literally "existing out of itself."

SWEAT   SEE *SCENT AURA

SYMPNEUMATA

A technique of breathing practiced and taught by Mr. and Mrs. Laurence *Oliphant during the 1880s. It is quite similar to *conspiration and *insufflation; the Oliphants believed that the mingling of their breaths created something like a spiritual body of energy, which they called sympneuma.

SYZYGY

The literal translation of this *Gnostic term is "yoked together," but it is generally used to indicate a male/female pair of cosmological opposites such as the Indian *Shiva/*Shakti, the Chinese *yin/*yang, or the biblical pair of King *Solomon and the Queen of Sheba.

SEE ALSO *DUALISM, *LILITH

T

One should fix the mind on whatever delights it; there proceeds supreme joy.

VIJNANA BHAIRAVA

TACHIKAWA

(JAP., *TACHIKAWA-RYU*)

A Japanese Tantric school founded by Nin-kan (1057–1123) as a branch of *Shingon and as an attempt to create a Japanese school corresponding to the Indian *Vamacara, or left-handed Tantra.

Although the Tachikawa and their activities were soon outlawed by the authorities, the school continued covertly at least until 1689. According to R. H. van Gulik, Nin-kan taught that sexual union and "one's living body" were means for "directly obtaining Buddhahood," and the Tachikawa held mass meetings where Tantric rites were practiced. The sect still has a rather bad name in Japan because of its involvement with sexuality, and most of its texts are hidden away in various monasteries, "securely sealed and marked with the century-old notice *ake-bekarazu*" (van Gulik, p. 359)—a note that reads in direct English as "Do Not Open!"

SEE ALSO *SPARK OF LIFE, *SUTRA OF SACRED BLISS

TAHINI SEE *SESAME

T'AI-HSI

(CHIN., "EMBRYONIC BREATHING")

A Taoist breathing technique that is used, among other things, for achieving longevity or immortality. The breath is directed to reach the lower *tan-t'ien instead of only, as is usual, the lungs, heart, liver, and kidneys. At the same time the practitioner will try to produce and accumulate as much saliva as possible. Both these agents, *breath and *saliva, are thought to help achieve general health.

TALEJU AND/OR TALEJU BHAVANI

A goddess specific to Nepal, where *Hinduism, *Buddhism, and *Tantra have mingled in a unique way. Taleju is something of a hybrid deity worshipped by believers of all these religions. Though seen as a "sexually mature Mothergoddess" (Majupuria, 1982, p. 24), she is also the goddess who is thought to be embodied and manifested in the Nepalese *living goddess, or *Kumari. Taleju is the chief protective deity of Nepal and its royal family and is sometimes equated with *Durga, though the latter goddess is much more fierce. It is thought that the king's power derives from her, and a king who fails to receive her *mantra is most likely to lose his kingdom.

The goddess is also worshipped in the form of the *sri yantra.

TALMUD

The major work of postbiblical Jewish literature, compiled about 500 C.E. It is mainly a compilation of ancient Hebrew/Jewish laws and customs based on the Mishna, a work that codified, during the first and second centuries, the ancient oral traditions.

SEE ALSO *LILITH, *NIDDAH, *SABBATIANS

TAMAS SEE *GUNAS

TANDEN

Japanese spelling and equivalent of the Chinese "fields of cinnabar" (*tan-t'ien) in the human subtle body. Several Japanese schools, however, have concentrated on only one: the lower, *tanden,* which has become known as *hara,* in the lower abdomen.

In a volume by Thomas Cleary that collects, in English translation, rare Taoist texts written by female adepts, one can find information indicating that this lowest *tanden* is appropriate to work with, in meditation for example, but by male practitioners only. According to a text that Cleary has translated as "Spiritual Alchemy for Women," female practitioners of Taoist or Zen meditation should concentrate instead on the sternum, a location slightly below and between the *breasts (1989, pp. 91–99).

TAN-T'IEN

The Chinese collective name for what has been called the "fields of cinnabar," "fallow fields," "elixir fields," or "crucibles": centers in the human subtle body that can be compared to some of the Tantric *chakras. Different from the Indian system of four, or sometimes seven, centers, three *tan-t'ien*, each of which is located along an imaginary central column within the body, are counted by the adepts of *Taoism:

UPPER TAN-T'IEN Located in the head, behind and between the eyes: a location at—or close to—the *pineal gland. Part of this is the important brain chamber known as *ni-huan*. The center is associated with the *shen* energy.

MIDDLE TAN-T'IEN Located at the lower end of the sternum, behind the solar plexus. The center is often symbolized as a cauldron of water, to be heated by the fire from the lowest *tan-t'ien*. It is the center of the *ch'i* energy.

LOWER TAN-T'IEN Located in the stomach region, just below the navel. This center is often visualized and symbolized as a cauldron of inner fire and is also seen as the furnace that is instrumental in the *fusion of *k'an* and *li*. It is the seat of the *ching* energy. In Zen and the martial arts, this is known by the Japanese names *kikai-tanden* or *hara*.

SEE ALSO *T'AI-HSI

Looking at the Taoist subtle body (see facing illustration), it is interesting to note that the three *tan-t'ien*, together with the *heavenly fire of the heart and the *three gates, form a series of seven centers, reminiscent of the Indian system of seven *chakras and the scientific concept of the seven glands of the *endocrine system.

SEE ALSO *TANDEN

TANTRA

1. A mystical/spiritual system of psychology, philosophy, and cosmology that aims at the union of opposites on all levels of being and becoming, from cosmic to quantum levels, on astral, mental, and physical planes. This central theme is expressed in many sacred texts and in art, alchemy, science, and ritual observance. Women and men are seen as microcosmic expressions and/or mirrors of macrocosmic energies represented by the goddess *Shakti and the god *Shiva, in whatever guise they may appear.

See *Tantra (1: System)

T AN-T'IEN. *Chinese concept of the subtle body, showing the *tan-t'ien, the *Three Gates, and the *Heavenly Fire of the Heart. Illustration by Christina Camphausen.*

2. A sacred treatise containing spiritual and psychophysical teachings concerned with the transmutation of energy, liberation of the mind, attainment of one's full potential, and other Tantric practices.

See *Tantra (2: Scriptures)

3. Literally, this *Sanskrit term has a meaning that can best be approximated by such concepts as "continuum," "web," and "context." This ambiguity has led to the many different translations and definitions of Tantra that can be found in literature.

TANTRA (1: SYSTEM)

Balanced union of and between the "opposite poles" (*see* *Tantra/1, above) is taught as a sure way to achieve

Tʌɴᴛʀᴀ. *The symbolic approaching the real:*
male part of *yab-yum *statue. Seventeenth-century bronze, Tibet.*

liberation of mind and body, a liberation from the supposedly endless cycle of unconscious *rebirth. In order to facilitate such union on all levels of being, Tantra makes use of a variety of physiological, psychological, and devotional or spiritual techniques, many of which have been described or outlined in this encyclopedia.

In a historical context, Tantra as a system developed from about the fifth century and reached its peak of social diffusion by about 1200, but even today it continues to influence Indian ritual and life. Originally, Tantra seems to have been a kind of religious and social revolt against the foreign, Aryan peoples, priests, and deities. With its roots in pre-Aryan spirituality, Tantra reestablished the tradition of the Great Goddess (*Shakti, *Kali) and reinfused ancient aboriginal, tribal practices and beliefs into what is generally

called *Hinduism. Certain areas, provinces, and states of India, which is in a sense the mother country of Tantra, have made outstanding contributions to the development of Tantra. Among them, *Bengal and *Assam are most noteworthy, but also *Kerala and *Kashmir certainly belong to these Tantric regions. Unknown to many people is the fact that many of the features we associate today with yoga, Hinduism, and *Vajrayana were discovered, invented, and/or developed and sophisticated by Tantric adepts. They include, for instance, the use of *mantra and *mudra/1, the sacred art forms of *mandala and *yantra, and the sophisticated system of subtle physiology with its *chakras and *nadis.

SEE ALSO *Aʀʏᴀɴ Iɴᴠᴀsɪᴏɴ Tʜᴇᴏʀʏ, *Dᴀᴋsʜɪɴᴀᴄᴀʀᴀ, *Sʜᴀᴋᴛᴀ, *Vᴀᴍᴀᴄᴀʀᴀ

TANTRA (2: SCRIPTURES)

Nik Douglas (1971) quotes Gampopa (1079–1153), a major teacher of the *Kagyudpa lineage, as saying that the "Tantras represent a philosophy comprehensive enough to embrace the whole of knowledge, a system of meditation which will produce the power of concentrating the mind upon anything whatsoever, and an art of living which will enable one to utilize each activity of Body, Speech and Mind, as an aid to the path of liberation."

The Tantric scriptures are generally classified as either Hindu or Buddhist Tantras, depending on the religiocultural sphere from which they originated: *Hinduism and/or *Vajrayana *Buddhism. Although many original *Sanskrit texts have been lost throughout the ages, they often exist in translation, often in Tibetan or Chinese and sometimes in Bengali, the language of *Bengal. The number of Tantras historically was once considered to be 64, but today the actual number of known texts is much, much larger.

The Hindu Tantras quoted or described in this encyclopedia can be found under the headings *Yogini Tantra, *Yoni Tantra, *Parananda Sutra, *Niruttara Tantra, *Nila Tantra, *Mahanirvana Tantra, *Mahacinacara-sara Tantra, *Kularnava Tantra, *Kumari Tantra, *Kubjika Tantra, *Kaulavali Nirnaya Tantra, *Kamakhya Tantra, *Kalivilasa Tantra, and *Guptasadhana Tantra.

Buddhist Tantras relevant to our inquiry can be found under the names of *Kathavatthu Tantra, *Prajnopaya-viniscaya Siddhi, *Jhanasiddhi, *Hevajra Tantra, and *Guhyasamaja Tantra.

In addition to the major texts mentioned here, this encyclopedia contains many quotes from other Tantras. For a complete listing of works cited, turn to index 13 on page 281.

TANTRIC PERFUMES

Whereas musk and patchouli are used in almost all Tantric rituals, the *Kula tradition features a special formula according to which the ritual partners should be anointed, resulting in an erotic symphony of delicious odors with each and every movement. According to this tradition, the hair is treated with oil of *spikenard, the cheeks and breasts with *patchouli, and the hands with *jasmine (champaka). Moreover, the feet are scented with *saffron, the thighs with *sandalwood, and the pubic hair with *musk.

It is interesting to compare some of the contemporary "erotically oriented" perfumes with this ancient living blend: the ingredients in such exclusive and famous perfumes as Eau Sauvage Extreme (Christian Dior), Magie Noire (Lancome), and Poison (Dior) are the very *aphrodisiacs known to humanity since ancient times. Several of them contain the chemical substance known as *indole.

Ingredient	Eau Sauvage	Magie Noire	Poison
* amber	yes	—	—
* ambergris	—	—	yes
* civetone	—	yes	yes
* jasmine	yes	yes	—
lily of the valley	—	yes	—
* muskone	yes	yes	—
orange blossom	—	—	yes
* patchouli	yes	yes	—
* sandalwood	yes	—	—
* tuberose	—	yes	—

TANTRIC VISUALIZATION

As we know from the writings of the second *Dalai Lama (Gendun Gyatso, 1475–1542), the early adepts of the *Kagyudpa school used much sexual imagery in their visualizations, and they also knew the value of the actual physical enactment of their spiritual visions.

The following quotations from a text by Gendun Gyatso, translated into English by Glenn H. Mullin as "Transmission of the Wisdom Dakini," in *Selected Works of the Dalai Lama II,* will show this clearly, even if most lamas of our day—and this is even more true of their contemporary disciples—prefer to avoid the topic.

The text, written by a man and for men, first recommends that one visualize oneself as the male deity Heruka and goes on to say that a *triangle of white light then "appears at the level of one's eyebrow." This downward-pointing triangle—a universal symbol of the Goddess and/or her *yoni—is to be visualized inside one's head as connecting the adept's two ears, with the third angle pointing to the "root of one's tongue."

The triangle is then described as follows (Mullin, pp. 107 ff.):

- It "appears in the nature of blissful wisdom and gives rise to ecstasy."
- It "symbolizes the wisdom of innate great bliss, or higher tantric consciousness."
- It "has the shape of the consort's vagina, thus

symbolizing innate wisdom, and its three sides represent the three doors of liberation."

In another part of the same text we learn of a technique to receive the four "powerful initiations." Visualizing the goddess Vajraishvaridhatu locked in sexual embrace with the Buddha Vajradhara upon one's head, "from the point of their sexual union flows forth the precious nectar," which then enters one's own body.

Similar to the above is the method known as Purification by Means of the Goddess Nairatmika, the Egoless One. Here the text (p. 137) recommends the following:

> In the space before you visualize the Dakini Nairatmika. She is blue in color and holds a curved knife and skull cup. One recites the mantra Om ah svaha, causing blue lights to radiate forth from her body. They enter one's own body via one's sexual organ, and then the Egoless One herself enters one's body via the same passage. She melts into light, and one's body becomes filled with a bluish radiance. . . . All becomes pristine emptiness.

An example of a secret visualization technique best suited for female practitioners has come down to us from the Black Hat sect, a branch of the Karma Kagyud:

> Imagine that your body is in the form of the Wisdom-Goddess, a complete virgin-girl, naked, with hair flowing. Imagine yourself as Her, in the center of an effulgence of light, holding an elixir bowl close to the heart and garlanded with red flowers. Think in yourself that the Guru enters you through your open yoni and resides in your heart. Then imagine the Wisdom-Goddess above the crown of your head having just consummated the act of love; she is naked, with disheveled hair, and her yoni is moist and overflowing with sexual secretions. Her three eyes are filled with erotic emotion and look toward the vast expanse of the sky, which, as she begins to dance, becomes filled with similar forms of herself. (Douglas, p. 114)

In these examples of visualization scenarios, the flow of energy is mostly from the deity to the practitioner, but Tantra is certainly not meant to be a one-way road. In one of the techniques belonging to the Yoga of Consciousness Transference taught by *Naropa and *Niguma—used most effectively at the moment of one's death—we hear that at the right moment one's mind "in the form of a white letter 'ah' shoots up the central channel" and, via the *Brahma aperture, out from the top of one's skull. It then enters the holy mother *Vajra Yogini, "via the passage of her sexual organ, that is red in colour" and dissolves when reaching her heart. One's mind has then become "one with the wisdom of bliss and void of the Vajra Yogini" (Mullin, p. 146).

For another example, see *Yogini Tantra.

TAO

This Chinese term for "the way" or "teaching" indicates the main concept of *Taoism. Although there are attempts at defining and explaining the Tao, one of its basic characteristics is the fact that it cannot be described and is nameless and unnameable: "The Tao that can be told is not the eternal Tao. The name that can be named is not the eternal name" (from Tao-te Ching, Feng and English, trans., verse 1).

In his Tao-te Ching, the most famous of Taoist texts, the sage *Lao-tzu used the term for the first time in a metaphysical sense, as that of an all-embracing first principle and primordial source of all things. In the terms of contemporary science this comes close to what David Bohm calls the "enfolded reality" from which all unfoldment has yet to proceed. The Taoist adepts of sexually oriented *fang-chung shu also took inspiration from the text, especially from the sixth chapter, with its famous statement concerning the "gateway" of the mysterious female. The following English version of the passage is based on the German translation by Victor von Strauss (p. 63):

> The valley-spirit is immortal, it is called the
>   mysterious female.
> The mysterious female's gate is the origin of heaven
>   and earth.
> Ever enduring, it is never exhausted.

Aleister *Crowley, in his rendering, ends this passage with the following words: "Its operation is of pure Joy and Love, and faileth never" (Crowley, 1976, p. 36).

SEE ALSO *SECRET LANGUAGE, *YIN ESSENCE

TAO-CHIA

Specific term for what is now known as philosophical *Taoism, a branch of Chinese philosophy that has at its root the works and teachings of *Lao-tzu and *Chuang-tzu (±369–286 B.C.E.). The term has been introduced in order to distinguish this branch from *Tao chiao, so-called religious Taoism. Although such a distinction may be somehow artificial and/or irrelevant, scholars and authors have found it useful to point out the similarities and differences among the various schools of *Taoism.

The philosopher-Taoists, often connected with a temple or monastery, strive to achieve union with the *Tao mainly through meditation and by the practice of *wu-wei*, the art of spontaneous and unmotivated (non)action. The concepts of this meditative, philosophical, but sometimes also socially engaged Taoism was sufficiently compatible with the teachings of *Mahayana Buddhism, arriving from India after the first century C.E., to merge with it and play an important part in the formation and development of Chinese Ch'an Buddhism (Jap., Zen).

TAO-CHIAO

One of the two major branches of *Taoism, Tao-chiao developed most strongly during the second and third centuries. The term embraces several different schools, movements, or sects that are known as the Inner Deity Hygiene School, the School of the Magic Jewel, the Way of the Realization of Truth, the Way of Right Unity, the *Way of Supreme Peace, and the *Five Pecks of Rice Taoism (*Encyclopedia of Eastern Philosophy and Religion*, pp. 358 ff.). Adepts of these and other schools and sects, similar to the Indian *Mahasiddhas, usually were not attached to a specific temple or monastery and have often been called wandering Taoists. They are known by the Chinese expression *fang-shih*. One of the better-known and important individual adepts and scholars of "religious" Taoism is the physician, alchemist, and author *Ko Hung.

Tao-chiao, although influenced by Lao-tzu and Chuang-tzu just as *Tao-chia is, combined the Taoist teachings with already existing schools of Chinese *alchemy, and it is mainly this branch of Taoism that is concerned with immortality, *breath exercises, yogic exercises, and the sexual practices of *fang-chung shu. Although many ancient and modern writers on Taoism deny it, the Taoist *inner alchemy most certainly includes practical sexual exercises and uses sexual union as an integral part of meditation and ritual. "No man," writes Philip Rawson, "can reach the goal without receiving generous gifts of *yin essence, no woman without *yang" (Rawson and Legeza, p. 28). Compare this with *Tantra (1: System) and *see also* *Fang-shih.

TAOISM

Based on the idea of the *Tao, this influential and original system of Chinese religion, philosophy, and *inner alchemy has strongly shaped the whole of Chinese culture.

What we call Taoism—usually rather indiscriminately—consists, to the Chinese scholar, of two major streams of thought, lifestyle, and practice. One school, called *Tao-chia, represents the philosophical, mystical branch, and the other, *Tao-chiao, is the more religious, magical, and alchemical branch of Taoism.

TAP-TUN

A Far Eastern goddess about whose origin little is known, even in Thailand, where a temple to her is virtually stacked with gifts and offerings, mainly *lingams for use in *phallic worship.

Thai people, fond of magical charms and amulets anyway, also use phallic amulets. They are called *palad khik,* or "representative phallus," the smaller of which are worn on the body and the larger ones displayed in temples or shrines. In Tap-tun's small, quiet sanctuary in Bangkok (now located in the backyard of the Hilton Hotel), almost a hundred lingams can be found, varying in size from about 20 centimeters to about 2.5 meters. They all represent offerings to the goddess that have been brought here by her devotees, in some cases with considerable effort, as some large ones are made not of wood but of stone. It is a unique sight, as they surround the small center shrine where one also finds gifts of incense, *lotus buds, and *jasmine flowers.

It is speculated that Thai phallic worship is based on influences from India, although Tap-tun's alternative name, Chao Mae Tuptim, rather hints at a Chinese origin.

TARA
(SKT., "STAR," "SAVIOR")

Although Tara is today best known as the goddess and bodhisattva (*see* *Lasya) of compassion of nearly all Buddhist schools, where she is known as White Tara and/or Green Tara, she represents in reality a much older and larger concept of female deity. As Eliade and others have shown, she is better described as the ancient and almost archetypal pre-Aryan Great Mother of aboriginal India, corresponding to the Great Goddesses of the Middle East who ruled over all aspects of life from conception until death. As such a goddess, her domain is not only compassion and wisdom but

all of nature and the universe, fertility, sexuality, and death. The fact that Tara is venerated by almost all Indian schools—*Hinduism, *Jaina, *Buddhism, *Shakta, and *Tantra—and that her name has become a title of honor for other goddesses as well, testifies to this.

In Hinduism and Tantra, she is regarded as one of the ten major goddesses and aspects of *Shakti, the Mahavidyas, among whom we also find *Kali, *Chinnamasta, and *Sodasi. In this role, Tara appears with a shining blue body standing in the midst of a funeral fire, and her belly is pregnant with the potential of endless creation and recreation.

In the *Kalika Purana she is characterized as a member of the *yoginis.

TATHAGATA-GUHYAKA   SEE *GUHYASAMAJA TANTRA

TEACHINGS OF SISTER NIGUMA

Besides such techniques as described under the heading *Tantric Visualization, early initiates of *Vajrayana followed many of the traditional Tantric teachings derived from the *Mahasiddhas. Sister *Niguma was initiated into the Six Yogas of Naropa, and she practiced and taught the Path of Relying upon the Body of Another Person with and to her students. Her teachings reached Tibet in the eleventh century, through Khyungpo Naljor, who made them the base of his *Shangpa school. These explicit and extraordinary oral teachings became disseminated widely in Tibet and were finally written down by Gendun Gyatso, the second *Dalai Lama; they were published in English for the first time, in a translation by Glenn H. Mullin, in 1985.

In the chapter from this book entitled "Transmission of the Wisdom Dakini," sexual union is not only visualized but practiced, and "the yogi on the high levels of the completion-stage practices is led to great bliss." If both male and female adepts are properly trained and ripe for this path, the practice is said to induce "the clear light of mind" that arises "with great strength" (Mullin, p. 123).

Along with the many teachings she imparted to the Dalai Lama in his "dreams" (dream yoga being one of Naropa's doctrines), she also taught him the traditions concerning the *Vajra Yogini and the "techniques for controlling the mystic drops of genetic force" (p. 98).

The term *genetic force* seems to be an attempt by Mullin to avoid the all-too-obvious sexual connotations of words like *female love juice* or *semen. He takes similar liberties in the following text when, instead of male semen and female *menstrual fluid, he makes believe that the Dalai Lama speaks of hormones: "When the white *bodhimind* substance (male hormones) moves it also causes the sun-like red *bodhimind* substance (i.e., female hormones) to follow" (p. 122).

TEACHINGS OF THE GOLDEN FLOWER OF THE SUPREME ONE

The teachings concerning the Secret of the Golden Flower seem to have originated with the Taoist Dragon Gate School (Chin., *Lung-men),* an offshoot from the better-known Way of the Realization of Truth (Chin., *Ch'üan-chen tao),* a school that combined the teachings of religious Taoism with certain concepts of Buddhist and even Confucian origin.

The oral roots of the teachings presented here go back to at least the eighth century, and in printed form the work can be traced back to the seventeenth century; probably during an intermediate period hand-written texts were circulated among a small number of initiates only.

The golden flower, which refers to the Taoist concept of an immortal spirit-body, can be awakened, according to the text, by various psychophysical exercises and techniques that aim at a controlled use of the life energies and are designed to lead the practitioner toward complete integration of his or her personality. The text speaks of "a field one

TEACHINGS OF THE GOLDEN FLOWER. *Detail from a Chinese crown depicting the *Golden Flower. Silver gilt, Liao dynasty (907–1125). Shanghai Museum.*

inch square, which is the heavenly heart, the dwelling of light, the golden flower" and locates it "between the eyes," indicating the *ni-huan of the upper *tan-t'ien inside the brain. It is here where all one's thoughts are collected and where, after the energy has circulated throughout one's body, it crystalizes into the "golden flower." As with the Indian *Brahma aperture, it is here that light and cosmic rays are received into the body. This "body of light" is sometimes symbolized as a flaming sun of fiery pearl, its radiance expressing the union of the two male and female currents of energy, represented as two dragons.

Unfortunately, the available manuscripts of this work, in Chinese known as *T'ai-i chin-hua tsung-chih,* are incomplete. Later editions of the available German and English translations somehow make this up by including portions of another, similar text with the title *Hui-ming Ching,* "The Book of Consciousness and Life."

TEONANACATL   SEE *PSILOCYE MEXICANA

TERMA
(TIB., *GTER-MA,* "MOTHER TREASURE")

A secret treasure in the form of hidden teachings, texts, or objects intended to be rediscovered at a future time by an inspired *terton (Tib., "revealer"). According to the *Vajrayana tradition, such texts were most often prepared, sealed, and hidden by *Padmasambhava and *Yeshe Tsogyal during the time when Buddhism, after a relatively short flowering, was threatened and outlawed in Tibet. Several now existing and translated *Tantras have been transmitted in this way.

TERTON
(*TERTÖN;* TIB., *GTER-STON,* "REVEALER OF TREASURE")

Term for an individual who discoveres, recovers, and reveals one or more previously hidden texts known as *terma (Tib., "mother treasure"). Generally these are texts that had been hidden for the sake of future generations and/or because certain teachings were judged too advanced for people then living. Members of the early *Nyingmapa and *Bön, especially, used this "hide and recover" method for the transmission of teachings—a very sensible one in view of the various phases of persecution these groups and their teachings endured.

TESTICLES (ANIMAL)

The testes of certain animals, usually those that are physically strong and/or known to be sexually very active, were eaten in several cultures as an *aphrodisiac. In Morocco and Algeria, men ate the testes of lions and praised them highly. Louis XV offered the testicles of a ram to Madame de Pompadour as an aid in overcoming her frigidity, and ram's testes were also recommended, and tastefully prepared, by the French writer Alexandre Dumas (1824–1895).

SEE ALSO *ASS, *GOAT

TESTICLES (HUMAN)   SEE *LINGAM
TOPOGRAPHY/20

TESTOSTERONE

A major male sex hormone (see *Androgen), although it is present in both men and women. The higher testosterone level in men is instrumental in and responsible for the embryonic development and healthy functioning of the male genitals.

An interesting study has shown that testosterone levels in the bloodstream can be increased by visual stimulation. In 1974 researchers Kirke, Kockott, and Dittman of the Max Planck Institute for Psychiatry showed a 30-minute film with erotic/sexual images to several male subjects and afterward found their testosterone levels notably increased (J. Chang, p. 116). This may also happen in such techniques as *Tantric visualization (there has been no research yet), and it certainly happens during *maithuna and related erotic rituals. Testosterone for medical treatment is mainly manufactured from the tropical vine *sarsaparilla.

THANGKA

A class, or type, of Tibetan sacred art. The paintings are prepared—and empowered by the constant recital of appropriate *mantras—by highly trained adepts as a "dwelling place" for deities and/or (corresponding) psychic energies.

THC

Abbreviation for delta-9-tetrahydrocannabinol, the main active ingredient in *Cannabis sativa and its products such as *bhang, *charas, and *majoon.

THERAVADA   SEE *HINAYANA

THIRD EYE
(SKT., *URNA*)

In both Western and Eastern traditions we find the belief that a third eye exists that can be trained and can help achieve abilities such as deep, intuitive understanding as well as clairvoyance and similar paranormal phenomena.

The physical equivalent of this third eye seems to be the tiny *pineal gland of the *endocrine system, a gland that has been assoicated with one of the *chakras and that has been called the Doorway to the Divine Spirit by René Descartes (1596–1650). Trying to overcome the apparent paradox of Christian dogma with the then budding new scientific insights into the functioning of body and brain, Descartes proposed the pineal gland as the place where the soul resides, driving and controlling the body through the *nervous sytem/*brain, yet separate from it.

THREE GATES

In the teachings concerning *subtle physiology, *Taoism knows not only the three "cinnabar fields" (see *Tan-t'ien) but also three "gates" located in the spinal column. They are known as the jade gate (at the base of the skull), the middle gate (at heart height), and the lowest gate (at the base of the spinal column).

SEE ALSO *HEAVENLY FIRE OF THE HEART AND THE ILLUS-TRATION ON PAGE 225

THREE LADY IMMORTALS

The three legendary instructors of the *Yellow Emperor, who transmitted to him the various Taoist teachings and techniques of sexual alchemy such as *dual cultivation and *ho-ch'i. Individually these ladies are *Su Nü, the "simple girl"; *Hsuan Nü, the "mysterious maiden"; and *Ts'ai Nü, the "fancy girl."

According to John Blofeld, some written texts by the Three Lady Immortals are still extant, but R. van Gulik believes that these "immortal" ladies were very likely mythical figures of divine origin based on older Chinese goddesses, and the texts ascribed to them were probably written by a much later generation of Taoist scholars and adepts. We do, however, have a full English translation of one of these works available today, namely the *Wondrous Discourse of Su Nü.

THREE PEAKS   SEE *MEDICINE OF THE THREE PEAKS

TIDE OF YIN

Chinese/Taoist expression for the female *orgasm.

SEE ALSO *YIN ESSENCE

TILOPA
(988–1069)

Known as the Oilpresser, based on his profession, and as the Great Renunciate, Tilopa is the *Mahasiddha whose teachings gave rise to the *Kagyudpa lineage. He was also one of the later teachers of the Mahasiddha *Naropa. Tilopa once apparently resided in *Uddiyana.

TLAZOLTEOTL

Ancient Aztec/Mexican goddess of love and sexuality whose worship included *ritual prostitution. In her dark aspect she is associated with death and human *sacrifice.

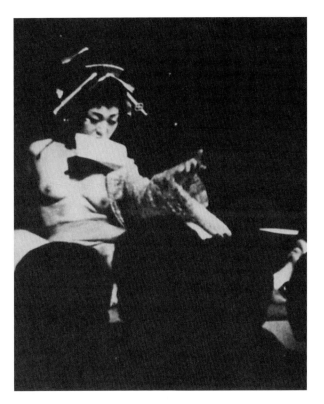

TOKUDASHI. *Scene from a* *tokudashi *in the red-light district of Osaka, Japan.*

TOKUDASHI

This is the infamous special event staged in some of the more luxurious erotic shows of contemporary Japanese striptease parlors in Kyoto, Tokyo, and elsewhere. The show—also nicknamed The Open—clearly reflects the mythological pattern laid down in the Japanese collective unconscious, even down to the details. Where the *kagura is a myth in which light is made to shine once more in the general darkness, the tokudashi uses flashlights illuminating the mysterious gate of life. In his book *Behind the Mask* Ian Buruma describes a tokudashi in detail:

> The girls shuffle over to the edge of the stage, crouch
> and, leaning back as far as they can, slowly open their
> legs just a few inches from the flushed faces in the
> front row. The audience . . . leans forward to get a bet-
> ter view of this mesmerizing sight, this magical organ,
> revealed in all its mysterious glory. The women . . .
> slowly move around, crablike, from person to person,
> softly encouraging the spectators to take a closer look.

To aid the men in their explorations, they hand out magnifying glasses and small hand-torches, which pass from hand to hand. All the attention is focused on that one spot of the female anatomy; instead of being the humiliated objects of masculine desire, these women seem in complete control, like matriarchal goddesses (pp. 12 ff.).

TORAH   SEE *BIBLE

TORTOISE

The word *tortoise* technically refers to the land-based reptile only, and the term *turtle* is reserved for the amphibian, marine, or freshwater forms. In our context, however, information concerning both these varieties has been collected under this entry, because ancient myths are not always as discriminating as modern science is.

ASIA   *India:* The tortoise (Skt., *kurma*) indicates an aspect of Vishnu, one of the major gods of *Hinduism. Here, the amphibian animal (turtle) also plays an important role in creation myths and symbolizes the vital, physical, libidinous part of a human being and/or of being human.

China: The tortoise (*gui*) usually accompanies every major cultural hero and is regarded as a symbol not only of immortality but of order, steadfastness, and immutability. The tortoise's shell has been used in divination, and its 24 rim plates are correlated with the 24 agricultural divisions of the year. The term also has several sexual associations: as a secret code for the *lingam, in a word for "pimp" (*wu gui,* or "black tortoise"), and as a swear word that roughly equates to "father of a whore" (*gui-gong,* or "tortoise-master").

Japan: The tortoise (*kame*) is regarded as sacred in *Shinto.

EUROPE   The tortoise is a sacred animal of Roman *Venus, representing the principle of procreation and fertility, and of the greek god Hermes, who created his first musical instrument from a tortoise shell. Elsewhere, it has been thought that the Earth is carried by a tortoise on her back.

TRIANGLE

This is the most abstract symbol used to represent the *yoni, and quite often its meaning remains unrecognized except by those who have a certain degree of esoteric knowledge. The downward-pointing triangle is used (in *alchemy and astrology, for example) to represent water and earth, the feminine principle, the natural world, and so forth—all those concepts that are essentially female. Pythagoras not only considered the triangle as sacred because of its perfect shape but also saw it as a symbol of universal fertility, and the well-known "seal of Solomon" uses two intersecting triangles to represent the merging of male/solar and female/lunar energies, making this symbol a Western version of the Chinese *yin and *yang. In the East, the triangle is also used with the allusion to yoni and female energy, as for example the Kali *yantra or in the many triangles composing the *sri yantra. In Tantric *Buddhism, it is seen as the "source of the dharma," as the "gate of all that is born," or—in the words of Chogyam *Trungpa—as the "cosmic cervix." The *Hevajra Tantra says: "Concentrate on the triangle of origination in the midst of space."

SEE ALSO *DOLMEN, *TANTRIC VISUALIZATION

TRILINGA

A symbol or statue that consists of three *shivalingas, often each sculptured with the face of the deity. The sculptures must not be confused with the face lingas, which feature three aspects or faces of *Shiva on one lingam stone.

TRIPURA CHAKRA   SEE *SRI YANTRA

TRUFFLES

The truffle, a rare edible fungus beloved by pigs and human gourmets, may easily be the most expensive of all *aphrodisiacs. Already famous for its erotic properties in Roman times, it was also recommended by Napoleon (1769–1821), and a Turkish recipe for a stimulating potion includes Algerian truffles. Truffles are usually detected wtih the help of specially trained pigs. The reason for this lies in the fact that truffles emit a chemical odor that is almost identical to the pig's own sexual attractants. Peter Redgrove offers an exploration of the aphrodisiac qualities of truffles in his book *The Black Goddess and the Sixth Sense.*

TRUNGPA, CHOGYAM
(1940–1987)

One of the Tibetan lamas to flee from the Chinese persecution in 1959, Chokyi Gyatso Trungpa was the first English-

TRILINGA. *A linga stone, this one showing a "face linga" with different aspects of the god *Shiva. Nepali reproduction.*

speaking Tibetan to establish himself as a teacher and prolific author in the West. He taught the traditions of both *Nyingma and *Kagyud schools and was regarded as the 11th incarnation of the Trungpa Tulku, an active lineage of *reincarnations that continues the Surmang Kagyud tradition.

He also turned out to be somewhat of a "holy madman" who, like the famous "Three Madmen" of his own tradition or like the Bhutanese master *Drukpa Kunleg, practiced and taught Tantric *crazy wisdom—a fact that many "spiritual" American and European Buddhists, at first his devoted disciples, were shocked to realize. Chogyam Trungpa was the author of many books on *Tantra and *Vajrayana and also helped translate several ancient works into English, among them the important *Bardo Thödol.

Four years after his early death, his reincarnation was discovered, verified, and enthroned (1991) in the person of Chokyi Sengay (born 1989 in Tibet), now the 12th Trungpa Tulku.

TS'AI NÜ
The "elected girl" or "chosen maid"; one of the *Three Lady Immortals.

TUBEROSE
The botanical name of this rose is *Polianthes tuberosa,* but the Malayan people call it "mistress of the night" because of its seductive effect on both men and women. Some people, especially women, seem to find the scent of this flower quite irresistible, and it has therefore often been used in both East and West as an *aphrodisiac. The flower also grows in Mexico, and its oil contains *indole.

TURIN PAPYRUS
An erotic paper from about 1200 B.C.E. that shows a variety of sexual positions and situations; the depictions are mainly of an Egyptian woman with a foreign man (Hollander, pp. 270ff.).

TURTLE   SEE *TORTOISE

TUTINUS AND/OR TUTUNUS
Ancient Roman *ithyphallic god, perhaps another aspect of *Priapus. It was common until the fourth century for a bride to deflower herself on the erect *lingam of a sculpture of Tutinus, anointed with sacred oil, rather than have her *yoni opened by her husband. Such women were somtimes called virgin brides.
   SEE ALSO *DEFLORATION, *VIRGINITY

TWILIGHT LANGUAGE   SEE *SANDHYABHASA

TWIN PEAKS
Chinese/Taoist term for a woman's *breasts, the source of *white snow and the *peach juice of immortality.

*What does it mean to
re-vamp a society? It means that we
must become vamps again, sexual-spiritual
beings, that we must act out of eros.*

DEENA METZGER, "RE-VAMPING THE WORLD"

UDDIYANA

(SKT., *UDDIYANA*, "FLYING VEHICLE, GOING HIGH AND
FAR"; TIB., *OR.GYAN, UR.GYAN*)(OTHER SPELLINGS:
ODDIYANA, OR.GYAN, OR.GYEN)

According to some researchers and writers, Uddiyana was an
ancient kingdom in the region of the Swat Valley, west of
*Kashmir, now part of northern Pakistan. In contemporary
maps and non-Buddhist publications, the name is often written as Udyana. Some writers on the history of Buddhism,
however, are not convinced by the scarce historical evidence
provided by Tibetan records and prefer to regard Uddiyana as
a purely legendary and mythical place, a symbolic realm of
the *dakinis*: divine/demonic "sky dancing women" of the
Hindu and Tibetan pantheon. A third opinion holds that
Uddiyana does not refer to the small Swat Valley only but to
a larger region that may have reached from western Tibet to
Afghanistan. Whatever the exact region, the Tibetan tradition
and its records make quite clear that Uddiyana was a place
where people of flesh and blood were born. Several of the
important teachers (*Garab Dorje, *Luipa, *Padmasambhava, *Tilopa) and influential teachings that are now part of
the *Vajrayana tradition, and especially of *Dzogchen, have
their origins in this mountainous region bordering on northwest India, Kashmir, and Turkestan.

Before the Muslim invasion in the twelfth century,

Uddiyana seems to have been a center of Tantric theory and
practice that attracted adepts and masters from different
backgrounds, and from here they also went forth to teach
their newly found insights elsewhere. Uddiyana's close
proximity to the famous Silk Road, then the most important
trade route between China, Afghanistan, the Near East, and
Europe, aided this constant traffic in ideas, and it also helps
explain the traces of Chinese influence present in
Dzogchen.

Many of the texts originating in Uddiyana and written in
its language have later been translated into Tibetan, passing
into the tradition of the early *Nyingmapa school during the
"first dispersion" (c. 600–836 C.E.). This was a period during
which many Buddhist scriptures were translated into the then
newly improved Tibetan alphabet and grammar, a language
strongly influenced by *Sanskrit and more or less designed c.
645 C.E. by Thonmi Sambhota (Tib., *Thon-mi sam-bho-ta*).

NOTE: One of the lesser-known schools of Vajrayana was
known as Orgyanpa.

UKE-MOCHI-NO-KAMI AND/OR UKEMOSHI

A Shinto goddess worshipped in Korea and Japan as a creatrix of flora and fauna. She is seen as a general symbol of
fertility and is especially associated with all vegetation that
serves as food for human beings. In her myth she merely
turned her head toward the land and boiled rice came forth
from her mouth; when she faced the ocean it was fish that
her mouth brought forth. Even after having been slain she
continued to provide plants and animals useful to humanity:
From her head arose oxen and horses, from her forehead
grew millet, and from her eyebrows arose the silkworm.
Rice grew from her belly, and from her *yoni, wheat and
beans came into existence.

SEE ALSO *KAMI

UNION OF SKILLFUL MEANS AND
PROFOUND COGNITION

A very good example of the sort of words and phrases used
to transmit secret techniques and images that are based on
sexual energy. This is a way of referring to sexual union
between male (means) and female (cognition) adepts, but
this content of the phrase would usually be known only to
initiates of a certain degree.

SEE ALSO *SECRET LANGUAGE

UPANISHADS

Sanskrit term that best translates as "secret doctrine." The texts so called are seen as more or less authoritative summaries of the philosophy and moral codes of the *Vedas and of *Hinduism in general. They were prepared mainly by India's ancient sages and came to be regarded as major sacred scriptures in their own right. Originally these texts were to be transmitted to members of the upper three castes only.

UPWARD PERISTALSIS   SEE *PENILE PERISTALSIS

URDHVARETAS

A term that refers to the "upward flow" of sexual energy, used in connection with the *oli techniques.

URETHRA   SEE *LINGAM TOPOGRAPHY/13, *YONI TOPOGRAPHY/13

USHAS
(SKT., "DAWN")

A Hindu goddess of dawn who is also called the "awakener of beings." Ushas is often depicted as an eternally young woman, the daughter of Heaven, exposing her *breasts for men to admire. In the *Vedas it is written that "she enters every house, disdaining neither old nor young as she grants prosperity to the inhabitants."

In the oldest of these texts, the Rig Veda, Ushas is a part of a twin goddess who shares a "rotating yoni" with her sister (see *Sayoni).

Her Greek counterpart is the infamous *Eos, also a goddess of dawn, who was known to sexually assualt men of her liking.

UTERUS   SEE *YONI TOPOGRAPHY/18

UTTAMA VAMACARA   SEE *VAMACARA

V

*For just as a man is a parasol bearer on account of taking a parasol, and a bather at the time he takes a bath, in the same way *Mahamaya's body when prepared for sexual enjoyment, colored reddish yellow by the red saffrons applied for the sake of sexual excitement, is called *Kamakhya.*

KALIKA PURANA

VAGINA   SEE *YONI TOPOGRAPHY/9

VAGINAL BALLS

In stores that sell sexual toys and tools, various types of vaginal balls are available, all of which originate in the Far East: China, Buma, Thailand, and Japan. All of them are used for two purposes: as a tool that allows exercising the muscles of the *pelvic floor, and as a toy for the rather effortless creation of erotic titillation, or even *orgasm, for the woman who uses/wears them. The differences between these balls are simple to describe: they are solid, hollow, or battery-driven.

Ben-wa is the Japanese name for a set of two solid metal balls that are inserted into the *yoni and are used as a stimulating tool. The woman, lying down or sitting in a rocking chair, gently rolls her hips and makes the balls within her touch, separate, and meet again. The resulting vibrations transmit themselves outward to the entire vagina, clitoris, and labia and inward toward the uterus. Such continued languid movement can lead to one or more orgasms.

These solid *ben-wa* are quite different from the hollow

mien-ling, or duo-balls. The Chinese *mien-ling* (do not confuse with *mien-lung,* a name for dildo), or the Japanese *rin-no-tama,* are small vibrating balls inside the larger ones (today made from plastic) used for centuries by Far Eastern women for self-stimulation.

Vaginal balls are sometimes advertised and sold as "automated *masturbation equipment"—an unfortunate name. However, in the wake of battery-driven dildos, or vibrators, truly automated balls have appeared on the market. Under the name "duotone balls" one can get plastic-encased solid metal balls that actively vibrate as long as the woman, and the batteries, are able to endure.

VAIROCHANA
(EIGHTH/NINTH CENTURY) (VAIROTSANA, TIB., *BAI-RO TSA-NA*)
One of the original students of *Padmasambhava, and an important translator instrumental in spreading the teachings of *Dzogchen.

VAJRA
1. In *Hinduism, an emblem and/or magical weapon, the "lightning flash" controlled by the god Indra. It is said to be of indestructible power and is comparable to the thunderbolts of some male European/Aryan deities. **2.** In *Vajrayana teachings, the *vajra* expresses and symbolizes the hardness

and clarity of a diamond, which gives to the word connotations of indestructibility, shining clarity, beauty, and truth. The Tibetan word for the *Sanskrit *vajra* is transcribed as *dorje.*

A synonym for *vajra* is *mani* ("jewel"), and both terms are also used as a code synonymous with *lingam, still carrying the associations of power, hardness, and great worth. Its female counterpart is the **ghanta.*

SEE ALSO *OM MANI PADME HUM, *VAJRA YOGINI

VAJRAGATHA
(TIB., *RDO-RJE'I TSHIG-RKANG,* "ROOT TREATISE OF THE VAJRA VERSES")
A short text of 12 Tibetan folios, representing the oral teachings transmitted by the *Mahasiddha *Virupa. The treatise, based on the *Hevajra Tantra, forms the basis of the *Lamdre tradition of the *Saskya-pa. The transmission reached Tibet, via four successive Indian masters, in the form of a translation by *Brogmi and was expanded with extensive commentaries in the centuries to follow.

The first folio of the text, or part one, is known as the Three Visions. It deals with general Buddhist teachings that are shared between *Hinayana and *Mahayana, preparing the student for the *Vajrayana teachings of part two. This second part, the Three Tantras, comprising the rest of the text, present in a nutshell the entire Vajrayana teachings and

V<small>AJRA</small>. *For those who climb the long, steep stairway to the famous temple of Swayambhunath (near Kathmandu, Nepal), awaits this large *vajra (Tib., dorje) of about 2 meters in length. Located high above the Kathmandu Valley, this is an apt symbol for the age-old presence of the *Vajrayana teachings in this Himalayan kingdom. Photograph by Rufus C. Camphausen.*

their many aspects, up to and including the level of *mahamudra* (see *Inner Tantras). The text has been published by Ngorchen Konchog Lhundrub as *The Beautiful Ornament of the Three Visions.*

VAJRA SONGS

A general name for songs and/or poems written by a number of Tantric adepts and teachers in order to provide "teaching stories" that could easily be learned by heart and transmitted orally—a tradition that started with the *Mahasiddhas of old and continued with adepts of the *Kagyudpa lineage through the ages and up to the present day.

The Legends of the Eighty-four Mahasiddhas, for example, are Tibetan manuscripts that describe, in song and prose, the lives and spiritual adventures of the renowned and important Indian Tantrics who lived and taught during the seventh through the twelfth centuries. These Mahasiddhas were instrumental in the development of Tibetan Buddhism. Among this group of revered masters, some of whom were fishermen, kings, thieves, and princesses, we find such illuminated figures as *Naropa (1016–1100), Saraha (c. 780), and *Tilopa (988–1069), whose lifestyle and teachings influenced even more famous masters, as, for example, Milarepa (c. 1039–1123), well known for his 100,000 songs (see *Mila Gnubum).

Similar to the songs of these masters, which for centuries have kept that tradition alive, first orally and then in written form, are the Vajra Songs of lamas belonging to the *Kagyudpa school of *Vajrayana: a collection of texts known as the Kagyu Gurtso. According to Chogyam *Trungpa (1940–1987), an incarnated master of that tradition, these songs represent "the best of the butter which has been churned from the ocean of milk of the Buddha's teachings" (Trungpa, p. xiii).

The Kagyu Gurtso, published as recently as 1980 under the title *Rain of Wisdom,* includes texts composed by masters of Tibetan Tantra spanning one thousand years from the early tenth through to the late twentieth centuries.

VAJRAYANA

The Diamond Vehicle: a name for the esoteric, *Tantra-influenced *Buddhism of Tibet, Bhutan, Nepal, Ladakh, and Mongolia. The term distinguishes this school from *Hinayana and *Mahayana, although Vajrayana itself is also a subdivision of the latter. In early studies on Tibetan

Buddhism by Europeans and Americans, it has sometimes wrongly been called Lamaism. A similar notion applied to Christianity would result in a religion's being named Priestism or Bishopism.

The Diamond Vehicle is most often said to consist of four major schools, the *Nyingmapa, *Saskya-pa, *Kagyudpa, and *Gelugpa, but there are also more than 20 other subgroups and minor schools with equally valid, important, or interesting teachings and traditions.

For several centuries the Gelugpa have been the largest and most dominant school of Tibetan Buddhism in Tibet itself, and the best known in the West, mainly because the *Dalai Lama, the traditional spiritual and political leader of Tibet, comes from this background. In the context of this encyclopedia, we are mostly concerned with the Nyingma, the Kagyudpa, and some of their many greater and lesser subgroups—for example, the Drugpa Kagyud and the Karma Kagyud.

SEE ALSO *DRUKPA KUNLEG, *MAHASIDDHAS, *REINCARNATION, *TRUNGPA

VAJRA YOGINI

A so-called wisdom goddess who cuts through the initiate's ignorance and severs him or her from all hindering attachments. The exalted status of this deity can be deduced from the following prayer to her, an invocation that is used in connection with *Tantric visualization:

> O Mother Yogini, please guide me to the Pure Land of the Dakinis, the Land of Bliss and Void. Meditational deity Vajra Yogini, please guide me to the Dakini's Pure Land of Bliss and Void. Holy Guru Vajra Yogini, please guide me to the Dakini's Pure Land of Bliss and Void. Buddha Vajra Yogini, please guide me to the Dakini's Pure Land of Bliss and Void (Mullin, p. 145).

VAJROLI MUDRA

A Tantric *mudra/3 in which the partner's sexual fluids are sucked by muscular force into one's *lingam or *yoni for both spiritual and physical benefits.

SEE ALSO *OLI TECHNIQUES

VALERIANS

One of the many sects associated with *Gnosticism. Inspired by the Arab Valerius (c. 250 C.E.), founder of the

VAJRA YOGINI. *The female Buddha* *Vajra Yogini holding a flaying knife in her right hand and a skull cup in her left. Contemporary black* *thangka according to traditional design. Photograph by Rufus C. Camphausen, with kind permission of the Everest Thangka Gallery, Patan, Nepal.*

school and a disciple of *Origen, the group's members practiced *castration of themselves and others to avoid their eternal damnation through lust. The group is sometimes known as Valesii.

VAMACARA OR VAMAMARGA

The left-hand path of Tantric worship, which includes actual sexual union and the *panchamakara ritual. The name for the followers of this path is Vamacharis or Vamacharias. This school must be considered as representing the original *Tantra and *Shakta; there is no mention of a "right-hand" path, or *Dakshinacara, before the thirteenth century, although the centuries during which Tantrism developed and flourished were the fourth through the twelfth. The designation "left" derives from the fact that the women participating in the rites were seated to the left of their male partners.

Vamacara as a whole is subdivided once more into Madhyama Vamacara, whose ritual includes all five of the *makara, and Uttama Vamacara, according to which only *madya (wine), *maithuna (sexual union), and *mudra/2 (cereal) are required and/or recommended.

SEE ALSO *CHAKRA PUJA, *RAJA CHAKRA

VAUGHAN, THOMAS
(1623–1665)

Alchemist who published his works under the pseudonym Eugenius Philaletes and who described the "great alchemical secret" in clearly sexual terminology. He calls the vessel used for alchemical operations a "menstruous substance" and advises one to "place the universal sperm" into this "matrix of Nature." Vaughan seemed convinced that the main secret of *alchemy "is the secret of Nature," which "the philosophers call The First Copulation." Being a good Christian as well as an alchemist, Vaughan describes himself in his diary as a great sinner, another indication that his alchemy had much to do with sexual energies and that the substances of his beloved alchemical "oil of Halcali" were sexual secretions.

Author and researcher Colin Wilson, furthermore—with his uncanny and experienced eye for the sexually abnormal—hints at the possibility that Vaughan may have practiced *necrophilia with his wife on the very day of her death (Wilson, 1978, p. 435).

SEE ALSO *INNER ALCHEMY

VEDA(S)
(SKT., "SACRED KNOWLEDGE")

Written in an archaic form of Sanskrit, the Vedas are India's most ancient collection of sacred scriptures. These texts consist of hymns, legends, and treatises on ritual, magic, cosmology, and medicine. Although dating the texts has proved difficult, they are generally believed to have been transmitted orally since approximately 1500 to 1200 B.C.E., and in written form, since only about 600 B.C.E. The general and collective name applies to four (sometimes only three) major divisions of these ancient documents, individually known as Rig, Sama, Yajur, and Atharva Veda.

Rig Veda A collection of 1017 hymns orally transmitted since about 1500 B.C.E. A written form in *Sanskrit appeared only after 600 B.C.E. This most ancient part of the Vedas contains rules and regulations concerning *sacrifices, public and domestic ceremonies, and the religious, cosmological speculations by the Indo-Aryan peoples of this early age. The Rig Veda is also very much concerned with the preparation and use of *soma. The texts feature a number of racist opinons and doctrines that are at the root of India's rigid caste system. Although the Rig Veda is mainly patriarchal, it does mention *Shakti, who later became a major goddess in the traditions of *Tantra and *Shakta.

SEE ALSO *ARYAN INVASION THEORY

Sama Veda A collection of songs to be recited during the preparation and commencement of the soma sacrifice. The text differs only slightly from the Rig Veda.

Yajur Veda Subdivided into Black Yajus and White Yajus, this Veda constitutes a manual mainly intended as a guide for the priests performing sacrifices. A *Upanishad belonging to the White Yajus is known as Brihadaranyaka Upanishad and is famous for its profound teachings concerning the Self.

Atharva Veda This fourth Veda is the youngest of the texts (c. 200 B.C.E.), and for a long time it was not recognized as a true part of Vedic literature. Its contents were not clearly fixed and delineated, and some of its parts were seen as belonging to the Yajur Veda, a division that resulted in the Trayi or Threefold Veda. The Atharva contains 731 hymns copied from the Rig Veda, as well as some other texts that once had been judged too controversial or uninspired and were therefore excluded from the official Vedic canon; this history is similar to that of the various Apocrypha that were excluded from the *Bible. The Atharva deals mainly with medicinal concerns: the power of healing and associated rites and magical spells.

VENUS

The Italian/Roman goddess of love whose imagery and mythology is strongly based on the Cyprian/Greek *Aphrodite. We will examine here only some of her specialized and more unknown aspects.

The *hierodules of Mount Eryx in Sicily named her Venus Ericyna, and it was in her name that they practiced *ritual prostitution. In ancient Pompeii she was worshipped as Venus Fisica (a term for genitals) and was believed to be the force that arouses love, passion, and sexuality. Those Romans who, throughout time, tried to tame and restrain their fellow citizens' erotic activities resorted to inventing a goddess who was to turn the tide toward chastity, and they called this deity Venus Verticordia: "she who turns the heart." As Venus Volgivaga she is a Roman approximation of Aphrodite Porne and is seen as patroness of prostitutes; the name can best be translated as "Venus who walks the street." According to Ovid (43 B.C.E.–18 C.E.) her day of honor was April 23.

SEE ALSO *MARS, *YONI TOPOGRAPHY/2

VENUS AVERSA

Latin technical term for anal coitus, the male positioned behind the female. Not to be confused with *coitus a tergo.

VENUS OBSERVA

Technical term for the infamous *missionary position, with the male lying in the superior position on top of the woman.

SEE ALSO *VIPARITA RATI

VESHYA

Tantric/Sanskrit term similar in content to the Near Eastern/European concept of the ritual prostitute. A passage in the *Niruttara Tantra takes pains to state that the veshya are not "common prostitutes," who bear the same name, but are so called only because of the independence they have in common.

An elaborate exposition and classification of such women is given in chapter 14 of the Niruttara. The text also defines the veshya for us, in general, as a woman "who, at the sight of articles for worship, desires sexual intercourse" (Banerjee, p. 267). The names of the seven different types and some of their characteristics are as follows:

1. Gupta veshya: A woman born as daughter of Tantric devotees, passionate and devoid of shame, who prefers a *pashu husband
2. Mahukula veshya: A woman who likes to undress and to be naked
3. Kula veshya: A woman born into a householder's family
4. Mahodaya-Kula veshya: A devoted Tantric woman who chooses to follow the path of detachment and to become the wife of a *vira

VENUS. *Unlike her Greek counterpart, *Aphrodite, the less independent and less powerful Roman Venus is often envisioned as having been born from a seashell rather than from the last seed of a god being castrated. Nineteenth-century classicistic kitsch by William Bouguereau. Oil on canvas, 1879.*

5. Raja veshya: A woman free and independent like a queen

6. Deva veshya: A woman who first "unites with the deity"—who may be a *shivalinga or the officiating priest—before she receives the *semen of a worshipper, who also repeatedly kisses her *yoni and forehead

7. Brahma veshya: A woman who observes all practices of the *kulacara (probably the highest female initiate)

Another specific type of veshya, not mentioned in the Niruttara, is the veshya kumarika or "virgin harlot," who takes part in the *kumari puja. A different interpretation of

some of the veshya types is given under the entry *Deva Chakra.

SEE ALSO *RITUAL PROSTITUTION

VESICA PISCES   SEE *MANDORLE

VESTA

Ancient Italian agrarian goddess connected with sexuality; her male partner is the phallic god *Priapus. Vesta was reformed/deformed quite deliberately by the later Romans into a guardian of virtue and *virginity. However, the famous "vestal virgins" have not always been physical virgins. Their older and real nature was much more expressed in *fertility festivals such as the Vestalia or *Saturnalia, which made use of phallic emblems and "ritual obscenities."

VESTIBULE   SEE *YONI TOPOGRAPHY/8

VESYA   SEE *VESHYA

VIDYA
1. Sanskrit for "knowledge," a concept generally seen as feminine and personified as a goddess. *Vidya* is divided into lower (intellectually acquired) and higher or true (experiential and intuitive) knowledge. **2.** The term *vidya devi,* or "wisdom goddess," is used for a type of goddess who represents the *Shakti and who can be found often in sexual union with gods or men. The deities are worshipped in order to help the applicant to attain true knowledge and enlightenment. **3.** The term is used also for a female partner in *maithuna, similar to *prajna, *Shakti, and *yogini.

VIMALAMITRA
An eighth-century Indian adept also known as the Sage of Kashmir, although he traveled and lived just as much in China, *Uddiyana, and Tibet. He is an important teacher within the lineages of the *Nyingmapa and *Dzogchen traditions and the compiler/author of the *Vima Nyingthig.

Vimalamitra also translated, together with Ma Rinchen Chok, important Nyingmapa texts such as the *Guhyasamaja Tantra and the Guhyagarbha (Tib., gSang-ba snying-po, "The Secret Heart," or "Essence of Secrets").

VIMALANADA
Name (a pseudonym) of a teacher of the *Aghora tradition whose life and teachings are described in a book by Robert E. Svoboda.

VIMA NYINGTHIG
(TIB., *VIMALA SNYING-THIG,* "THE HEART ESSENCE OF VIMALAMITRA") (OTHER SPELLINGS: *BIMA NYINGTHIG, VIMA NYINGTIG*)
Name for the transmission lineage of *Dzogchen teachings that goes back to *Vimalamitra, a lineage that has been transmitted orally (bKa'-ma) throughout the ages. The Vima Nyingthig teachings belong to the Mannagde class (*see*

*Inner Tantras). In the fourteenth century they were combined with the *Khadro Nyingthig and are now part of *Longchenpa's unified *Longchen Nyingthig.

VIOLET
1. As a flower oil, violet was loved by women in Greece, who used to oil their entire bodies before entering into sexual union. Albertus Magnus (c. 1200–1280), Dominican monk, philosopher, occultist, and alchemist, tells us that violet, if gathered during the last quarter of the moon, is a 'love-producing"—that is, *aphrodisiac—herb. **2.** As a wavelength of light, violet is the color of female sexual energy.
SEE ALSO *GINSENG, *LIGHT

VIPARITA RATI
A *Sanskrit term that indicates sexual union "in reverse order," though even that definition has led to several interpretations: **1.** Most often, this is interpreted as sexual union with the woman on top of the man, which is "reversed" only if one regards the *missionary position as a standard. **2.** At other times, the above is extended to include the love play known as *pompoir. **3.** Sometimes it is seen as indicating orgasmic restraint on the part of the woman, as is required in *karezza.

Although in Tantra and other schools of sacred sexuality the *female superior position (i.e., explanation 1 above) is recognized as very beneficial, Indian mainstream education consistently tries to keep people from making love this way. As Giti Thadani has reported extensively, all kinds of "problems" will afflict a child created this way. It will, so goes this patriarchal myth, become either sterile, homosexual, or a *hermaphrodite, all due to this "faulty sexual act"—one that gives the woman both pleasure and heightened control over what is happening.
SEE ALSO *CHI-CHI, *KABBAZAH, *MISSIONARY POSITION

VIRA
Sanskrit term indicating a man of the "hero" type as opposed to those called *pashu (animal) and *divya (supreme). The vira is an initiate of the second degree, with advanced mental/spiritual faculties, and constitutes a good male partner for the *vidya or *mudra/4 in Tantric ritual.

In the *Niruttara Tantra we find the statement that men of the vira and divya types become, in the ritual called *kularcana, the husband of all women. One of the Tantric texts from *Kashmir, the Rudrayamala, admonishes the *vira* to worship his wife—or any woman—"burning with the fire of passion and gay with wine" (Banerjee, p. 398).

SEE ALSO *VIRA SHAKTI

VIRA CHAKRA

Similar to *raja chakra* and *deva chakra,* this is a ritual in which one man worships five women or *Shaktis. According to the *Niruttara Tantra, the women in question are the mother, daughter, sister, daughter-in-law, and married wife of the man.

SEE ALSO *INCEST

VIRA SHAKTI

A designation for the *veshya* woman participating in Tantric ritual and *maithuna.* The woman is seen as representing and transmitting "heroic energy" to her male partner.

SEE ALSO *DIVYA SHAKTI, *VIRA

VIRGIN, VIRGINITY

Although everyone seems to know the meaning of these words when they are encountered in everyday use, the terms *virgin* and *virginity* actually do have two very distinctive meanings in older texts.

1. In ancient usage, these terms refer not to the physical state of an unbroken hymen—that is, to a girl/woman who has not yet been deflowered by sexual union or otherwise—but to the social/psychological state of being unbound to, and independent from, all and any male(s). It is mainly in this context that we must understand certain virgin goddesses such as the Greek *Artemis and Kore, the Arabic Q're, and one of the manifestations of *Al'Lat.

2. Only when marriage, *monogamy, and patriarchal possessiveness became the rule concerning the relations between women and men did it seem important—mainly to priests and future husbands—whether or not a woman was "untouched," "pure," and "innocent." Proof of a young

VIPARITA RATI. *Just as Christian priests tried to ordain the way in which sexual union could be practiced—hence the so-called *missionary position, with the man on top— so did Orthodox Hinduism try to steer people this way. *Viparita rati, sexual union with the woman "riding" on the man, was considered a faulty act. Many myths were invented to instill fear and encourage people to abstain from this empowering practice. Eighteenth-century ivory, Orissa, India. Dr. Manfred Wurr Collection, Hamburg.*

woman's virginity was often demanded, and numerous customs developed around the *blood connected with *defloration. In fact, however, only 42 percent of women are born with a hymen that is likely to bleed; in another 47 percent it is highly flexible, and in the remaining 11 percent the hymen is so thin that it will easily break at an early age through normal body movement (based on el Saadawi, p. 26).

SEE ALSO *KILILI, *KUMARI PUJA, *LIVING GODDESS, *PARTHENOPE

VIRUPA
(LATE EIGHTH/EARLY NINTH CENTURY) (SKT., "THE UGLY ONE"; TIB., BIR WANA)

Also known as the dakini master, Virupa was an East Indian *Mahasiddha who was first student, then abbot and teacher at *Nalanda University, where he was known as Sri Dharmapala. However, he dropped out later and turned to higher Tantric practices. He formulated the quintessence of his attainment, experiences, and visions in a short treatise known as *Vajragatha, a teaching that forms the basis of the *Lamdre tradition transmitted by the *Saskya-pa.

VIRYA
The seed, or "spiritual manhood," that according to some male-oriented teachings may not be "spilled" or "wasted."

SEE ALSO *RETENTION OF SEMEN

VISHUDDHA CHAKRA
(SKT., "PURE")

The "throat" chakra, one of the four *chakras of the earlier Tantric tradition and now number 5. In Taoism this is one of the three *tan-t'ien, and it is known among the *Sufi as the "mysterious center."

LOCATION: Throat, third cervical vertebra, plexus laringeus
ENDOCRINE GLAND: Thyroid
RULING *SHAKTI: Shakini
COLOR: Sky blue
LOTUS: 16-petaled, smoky purple
ASSOCIATIONS: Hearing, creativity, and self-expression

VISHVA YONI
The "universal *yoni" of the *Shakti, of whom the woman in a Tantric rite is a manifestation, taking into herself the cosmic *lingam.

VISRISTI
In Sanskrit, this is the term for female *ejaculation, the physical discharge of *female love juices.

SEE ALSO *KAMA SALILA

VITAMINS
Only in the twentieth century has medical and nutritional science discovered many of the micronutrients necessary for the healthy functioning of the human body, and our knowledge of this area is not yet complete. Vitamins regulate the function of a variety of organs, and deficiency as well as oversaturation is known to cause imbalances, loss of energy, and ultimately diseases. Concerning sexuality, the following substances are probably the most important to be aware of:

VITAMIN B All vitamins of the B complex are involved with the production of *sex hormones in both women and men, and some of this group are known for their specific effects on sexual ability and general vigor and health. The most important ones in this context are B_1, B_2, B_{12}, choline, and pantothenic acid, all of which are essential to the functions of the *pituitary gland. Vitamins B_2 and B_{15} (pangamic acid, illegal in the United States) are known as "youth vitamins," and animal testing has shown a significant extension of life span with the use of these vitamins. In natural sources, B_{15} is contained most abundantly in apricot kernels, which form part of the Hunza diet. These peoples of Pakistani *Kashmir are famous for their long lives.

VITAMIN E Necessary for proper functioning of the *pituitary, vitamin E has been called the fertility vitamin and seems to be something of an *aphrodisiac, too. It is also involved with the *menstrual/ovarian cycle, and deficiencies have been known to cause sterility and impotence. The best source for vitamin E on the planet is *wheat germ. In order for this vitamin to be assimilated the body also needs to be supplied with vitamins A and F.

VITAMIN F A name for what was previously known as unsaturated fatty acids, needed for the proper assimilation of vitamins A and E.

More detailed information on these and other vitamins and their complex functions cannot be given within the context of this book. Consult your physician and/or works on vitamin therapy.

VNO

The much-used abbreviation for the recently rediscovered vomeronasal organ located inside the human *nose but apparently unrelated to the hitherto known sense of smell and its connections to the *brain. Located near the nasal septum, this tiny organ (two small sacs about 2 millimeters deep that open into shallow pits on either side of the septum) was described by medical researchers about 300 years ago but was neglected by more "modern" science as a nonfunctional evolutionary remnant: the so-called Jacobson's organ, thought to appear only at an early stage of embryological development and then to disappear.

Not so. During the 1980s, and more intensely during the 1990s, scientists from Japan to Austria to the United States became convinced they had found what has been termed—euphorically—a sixth sense, though this notion is not really convincing. The fact that we simply don't know enough, even close to the twenty-first century, about the human sense of smell does not make it necessary to postulate an added organ of perception that may just as well be a hitherto unrecognized property of our normal and very refined olfactory sense. To the structures of that sense in its present definition, pheromones seem odorless, although they most certainly register with the VNO.

The fact remains that the foremost "discoverer"—if that term is applicable—of the human VNO and its pheromone-receiving capabilities has already laid claim to several patents concerning substances that either are *aphrodisiac or may influence the *menstrual/ovarian cycle. As of late 1997, major pharmaceutical companies have already shown their interest in these findings, and much more research is underway.

VOODOO

(FROM AFRICAN *VODUN*, "DEITY," "SPIRIT")

Also written as Vodoun or Vaudoux, this is a magically oriented religious system of belief with strong roots in African culture. In the course of its evolution, after being "exported" from Africa along with black slaves, Voodoo has absorbed some American tribal customs as well as Christian imagery. Today it is mainly practiced in countries of Central and South America, especially Brazil, Haiti, and other Caribbean islands. Nonetheless, certain forms of original Voodoo can still be found in Africa, although some governments have begun to outlaw its practices. Voodoo makes much use of extraordinary states of mind such as trance and spirit possession, often with a strongly erotic element. Practices such as the magical use of corpses, *sacrifices, and *anthropophagy indicate Voodoo's basis in early African *shamanism.

Two very different but almost complementary works on Voodoo are those of Maya Deren and Gert Chesi (see bibliography).

SEE ALSO *ERZULI, *SPIRITUAL MARRIAGE

VRATYAS

(SKT., *VRATYA*)

Little information can be found on these outcasts of early Vedic society, but what we know makes them look like prototype Tantrics who, as was done elsewhere on the planet, worshipped the Goddess and celebrated life with *wine and *orgies. Women among the *vratyas* sometimes became *pumscali*—ritual prostitutes—and they may well be the precursors of the later *devadasi* tradition.

Philip Rawson, referring to *vratyas* but probably speaking of the *pumscali,* makes them sound like an all-female "sect" and connects them to the *dakinis and *yoginis of later myth and ritual. According to Rawson, they may represent "a female line of power holders" who initiated male Tantrics by "ritual intercourse with them" (*The Art of Tantra,* p. 80).

Mircea Eliade, with his reference to *Shiva, contributes information that must refer to the *vratya* men. According to him, an obscure chapter of the Atharva Veda (*see* *Vedas) refers to this "mystical fellowship" but does not tell us much more than that they dressed in black, wore turbans, practiced yogic techniques such as *breath exercises, and "homologized their bodies with the macrocosm." Thus, he sees them as a precursor of the later ascetics and yogis of Shiva (pp. 103 ff., 256 ff.).

Indra Sinha, on the other hand, clearly defines them as non-Dravidian, Aryan outcasts who were known to have celebrated "bacchantic, orgiastic rites" and hints they may have continued traditions from the early Indus Valley civilization (p. 72), for example, the *Mahavrata festival.

V<small>OODOO</small>. *Within the variety of Voodoo-inspired religions, the goddess Oshun is one of many powerful orishas. Queen of rivers, hence this painting's scenery, Oshun also epitomizes female sensuality.*
Private collection.

VULVA

Properly used, this Latin/medical term for the *yoni refers to the outer and visible parts of the female genital system, also called *pudenda,* that surround the opening to the vagina.

    S<small>EE ALSO</small> *Y<small>ONI</small> T<small>ERMINOLOGY</small>, *Y<small>ONI</small> T<small>OPOGRAPHY</small>

VULVOVAGINAL GLANDS   <small>SEE</small> *Y<small>ONI</small>

T<small>OPOGRAPHY</small>/12

W

The woman you love,

you must not possess.

THE GODDESS BASHOLI

WAY OF SUPREME PEACE
(CHIN., T'AI-P'ING TAO)

One of the schools of "religious" *Taoism, the followers of which practiced the *ho-ch'i ritual.

WEB OF HEAVEN AND EARTH

In order to understand this Chinese ritual, which was used only as a last resort when fatal catastrophes were imminent and needed to be warded off, we need some background information on the prevalent beliefs concerning the figure of the Chinese emperor and his socially oriented sexual duties. In his excellent work *Sexual Life in Ancient China,* R. H. van Gulik makes clear that it was the emperor who was responsible for balancing the forces of Heaven (*yang) and Earth (*yin).

That balance, which to the farmers expressed itself in plentiful livestock, abundant harvests, and general conditions such as good weather and the absence of war and other disasters, had to be achieved through the emperor's rituals of sexual union with the empress and with many other women available for this purpose; van Gulik mentions a number of 120. If something nonetheless went wrong and the emperor seemed unable to keep the forces of Heaven and Earth in harmony, the farming families of villages and countryside came to help. An auspicious night would be chosen, and hundreds of men and women would meet in the fields in a general *orgy under the open sky.

SEE ALSO "CLOUDS AND RAIN, *YELLOW TURBAN SOCIETY

WHEAT GERM

Wheat germ and wheat germ oil may not evoke the most erotic images in one's mind, but they may well constitute one of the best *aphrodisiacs available. Wheat germ not only is the best of all possible sources for *vitamin E but also contains a significant amount of *zinc. Although wheat germ is contained in any good product made with wheat, one must turn to its oil to provide the body with a real boost. The oil may be relatively expensive, but it can be used as a salad oil as well as in cooking.

WHITE LEAD

Taoist code for the male *yang fluid used in sexual alchemy.

WHITE METAL

Chinese/Taoist general term for liquids in the *yoni during ecstasy, such as the individually named *moon flower medicine.

WHITE SNOW

In *Taoism, the sweet, white, and beneficent essence from a woman's *breasts—that is, her nipples. The best "quality" is said to be obtained from a childless woman.

WHITE WINE   SEE *WINE OF THE NAVEL

WINE (IN EUROPEAN RITES)   SEE
*DIONYSUS, *FLORALIA

WINE (IN TANTRIC RITES)   SEE *MADYA,
*KARANA

WINE OF THE NAVEL

Term—sometimes also called white wine—used in the biblical *Song of Songs that refers to female sexual fluids. *Navel* is used here to indicate the *yoni.

WINE OF SACRAMENT

In alchemical *secret language, a term used for the *female love juices.

SEE ALSO *GRAIL

WITCHES' MILK

An expression for colostrum, the yellowish fluid, said to be a strong *aphrodisiac, that collects in the *breasts of a pregnant woman shortly before she gives birth. Colostrum is the first fluid secreted by the breasts for nourishment of a suckling infant; after a few days the fluid thins and clears and becomes the secretion we call milk. Colostrum is said to have a rejuvenating effect, and adult men have been known to drink it (Benjamin Walker, 1977, p. 174).

SEE ALSO *PEACH JUICE OF IMMORTALITY, *WHITE SNOW

WITCHES' OINTMENT

It took years of murder and brainwashing by the *Inquisition to make people who called themselves witches stop such invigorating exercises as flying off into other realms and taking part in *ritual promiscuity. Most of the actions for which those witches were known—and either despised or appreciated—have their basis in the use of an ointment made from various strong hallucinogens that have, among other effects, *aphrodisiac properties. This magical ointment is applied not only to sensitive and absorbing areas of the skin, such as the wrist, temples, nostrils, groin, and anus, but also explicitly on the glans of the *lingam or the lips of the *yoni.

WONDROUS DISCOURSE OF SU NÜ

An originally Chinese work destroyed and lost in its homeland but preserved in Japan, where the texts had been copied on several occasions. The work (Chin., *Su Nü miao lun*) consists of instructions given by *Su Nü, a legendary female teacher and deified initiate, to the *Yellow Emperor. The work seems to date, in writing, from the fourteenth or fifteenth century, but its contents partly reflect the perhaps one thousand years' earlier Su Nü Ching (Chin., "Classic of Su Nü") and the Su Nü Fang (Chin., "Prescriptions of Su Nü").

The complete text, translated into English, can be found in *Art of the Bedchamber,* a work by Douglas Wile highly recommended for its translations and the author's extensive introduction and commentaries to the classical works on sacred sexuality in its Chinese variety.

WORMWOOD   SEE *ABSINTHE

WU-TOU-MI TAO   SEE *FIVE PECKS OF RICE TAOISM

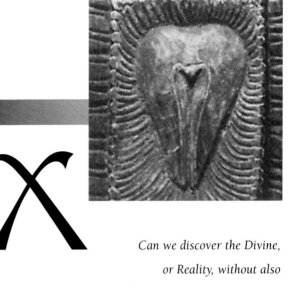

Can we discover the Divine, or Reality, without also discovering the mystery of our own body? Conversely, can we find fulfilment in sex without finding the Divine, or Reality?

GEORG FEUERSTEIN, *ENLIGHTENED SEXUALITY*

XTC   SEE *MDMA

X CHROMOSOME

This is one of the largest and most active and important of the 46 chromosomes in human beings. The X-linked genes determine a variety of traits, one of which is important in sexual differentiation. Most humans are, on this genetic level, either female (*XX) or male (*XY), but there are also other possibilities. Some women have only one chromosome, X (in a condition known as Turner's syndrome), whereas to have only a single *Y chromosome is invariably lethal. Girls with Turner's syndrome need treatment with ovarian hormones during adolescence in order to parallel the normal development into womanhood, although they most often remain sterile.

XX

Biological code for a genetically female human being, signifying the presence of two female (X) chromosomes.

SEE ALSO *X CHROMOSOME, *XY, *Y CHROMOSOME

XY

Biological code for a genetically male human being, signifying the presence of one female (X) and one male (Y) chromosome.

SEE ALSO *X CHROMOSOME, *XX

Y

Buddhatvam yosit-yoni-samasritam
(Buddhahood resides in the female organ.)

SUBHASITA-SAMGRAHA

NOTE: An entry expected to have the initial letter Y may sometimes be found under J.

YAB-YUM

A Tibetan term that literally translated means "father-mother." It is a phrase used for sexual union, similar to the sanskrit *maithuna,* but can also be compared to the Chinese concept of the *yin and *yang energies permeating all of the universe. In the typical *yab-yum* pose, the couple are face to face, with the woman sitting in or on the man's lap. Deities in the *yab-yum* position, often found in sculptures and on *thangkas,* can be found in almost every temple and monastery of *Vajrayana affiliation.

SEE ALSO *FEMALE SUPERIOR POSITION, *YAMALA

YAJUR VEDA   SEE *VEDAS

YAKSHINIS

A certain category of deities similar to paradisiacal goddesses such as the *apsarasas* or *houris.* Many of the female figurines known from Indian erotic temple art are thought of as *yakshinis.*

YAMALA
(SKT., "COUPLE," "PAIR")

1. A term referring to statues and paintings showing a male and female deity in sexual union. The pose, often depicted in Tantric iconography, is known as *yab-yum* in Tibet and as *sambara* in Nepal. **2.** Name for a specific class of *Shakta scriptures, also called Yamala *Tantras, most of which were composed during the tenth and/or eleventh century. In general, the texts are neither purely *Vamacara- nor *Dakshinacara-oriented; they seem to represent a developmental phase during which "left-hand" Tantra was beginning to be replaced by the "right-hand" version. As with the Upanishads and Puranas, there is a traditional classification of these texts into principal and minor works. Both categories together number 91, with each of the works bearing the name of a certain god or goddess: Brahma Yamala, Ganesha Yamala, Lakshmi Yamala, Rudra Yamala, Skanda Yamala, Uma Yamala, and Vishnu Yamala.

YANG

One of the two Chinese concepts that express the omnipresent dual forces at work in the universe and all of creation. Yang represents the energy that manifests as male, light, Heaven, and positive electrical charge, among numerous other associations.

SEE ALSO *DUALISM, *INNER ALCHEMY, *TAOISM, *YIN

YANTRA
(SKT., "INSTRUMENT," "AID")

A symbolic diagram depicting, focusing, and containing a certain field of energy. Traditionally a yantra should be painted at the time of worship, and the worshipped deity—or the energy it represents—is then imagined to reside within the yantra. The diagrams are also used as aids for inner visualizations, providing a model or map for the images to be evoked on one's inner, mental "screen."

The Tantraraja Tantra mentions that a yantra should be painted, drawn, or engraved on pieces of *gold, silver, copper, cloth, or birch leaves. As painting material the text

YAB-YUM. *Male and female *Bodhisattvas in *yab-yum position of ritual union.*

recommends paste from *sandalwood, camphor, *musk, *saffron, and a variety of other substances.

SEE ALSO *SRI YANTRA, *THANGKA

Y CHROMOSOME

Among the thousands of genetic traits inherited by a newborn human, only maleness itself, the Y chromosome, is exclusively transmitted from father to son. The Y is one of the smallest, and otherwise insignificant, of all 46 human chromosomes (gorillas and chimpanzees have 48) and must be paired with at least one *X chromosome in order for life to become possible.

SEE ALSO *X CHROMOSOME, *XX, *XY

YELLAMMA AND/OR ELLAMMA

An ambiguous Indian goddess, mainly known among the Tamil people, connected with healing, wisdom, childbirth, and the *ritual prostitution of the *devadasis. She also has her rather dark side and is thought to cause dangerous diseases such as leprosy.

YELLOW BOOK
(CHIN., HUANG-SHU)

The secret manual of the *Yellow Turban Society contained, according to several Buddhist sources largely detesting it, many coded references to sexual techniques and activities, for example making the "Dragon and Tiger sport together according to the rules of the 3-5-7-9 strokes," opening "the Red Gate and inserting the Jade Stalk," and opening "the Gate of Life, embracing the adept's infant."

YELLOW EMPEROR

Last of the three legendary Chinese emperors, sages, and culture heroes, who has been identified as the Emperor Huang Ti (2697–2598 B.C.E.). He is celebrated as the patron and ancient teacher of many arts and sciences such as *alchemy, medicine, technology, nutrition, and Taoist "sexual yoga." In his Classic of Internal Medicine he codified, for the first time, the Chinese knowledge concerning medicine, surgery, and acupuncture.

Huang Ti is said to have practiced *dual cultivation as taught to him by the *Three Lady Immortals and to have absorbed the *yin essence of 1,200 women, resulting in his manufacture of the elusive "golden pill." This in turn led to his achievement of "immortality," an expression used by the

Chinese to indicate a human being who achieves a divine status.

The Yellow Emperor's words "Not to struggle against one's natural desires and so to attain longevity, what joy!" sound essentially like the quote from the *Hevajra Tantra on page 85.

SEE ALSO *GOLDEN ELIXIR

YELLOW TURBAN SOCIETY
(CHIN., HUANG-CHIN, "YELLOW SCARVES")

A rebellious Taoist movement toward the end of the second century. Under the leadership of High Priest Chang Chüeh (d. 184 C.E.) and two of his brothers, the Yellow Turbans tried to overthrow the Han dynasty, attempting to establish a Taoist empire. Although this dream did not come true, many of Chang Chüeh's male and female disciples formed a school and continued to live according to his teachings, which gave rise to great public gatherings that included mass confessions of sins, *ritual promiscuity, and uninhibited *orgies. We depend on later and critical Buddhist commentators for information on the group's practices and its sacred *Yellow Book. They practiced the *Web of Heaven and Earth, whereby "men and women indulge in promiscuous sexual intercourse" (van Gulik, pp. 88–89) and during which couples quite publicly exchanged partners, all in an effort to generate and exchange the "vital essence."

Although the movement fell apart after about two hundred years, it was one of the key factors that seriously destabilized the Han dynasty and finally led to its downfall.

SEE ALSO *I-KUAN-TAO, *K'UN-TAN

YESHE TSOGYAL
(757–817 C.E.)

An important female Tibetan initiate and one of the five *dakinis who were partners and lovers of *Padmasambhava, the yogic hero who is credited with bringing Buddhist *Tantra to Tibet. Yeshe Tsogyal is especially known for her autobiography, translated by Dowman (1984) as Sky Dancer: The Secret Life and Songs of Yeshe Tsogyal, and it is she who wrote the biography of the Great Guru, The Life and Liberation of Padmasambhava. The two works provide us with much information on the crucial times when *Vajrayana, the Tibetan/Tantric form of *Buddhism, fought to establish itself among the shamanic religion and society of the *Bön-po.

In 772 C.E., at the age of 16, Yeshe Tsogyal met Padmasambhava. She received her *initiation through him in 773, starting her on a remarkable spiritual "career" during which she became famous throughout Tibet and Nepal, gaining the powers and status of a *dakini*. She is thought to have reincarnated since then as several important female adepts, including *Machig Lapdron (1055–1145) and Yomo Memo (1248–1283). For one of the extraordinary visions of Yeshe Tsogyal, quoted from her biography, see the entry *Menstrual Fluid.

SEE ALSO *REINCARNATION, *ZAP-LAM

YIN

One of the two Chinese concepts that express the omnipresent dual forces at work in the universe and all of creation. Yin represents the energy that manifests as female, dark, Earth, and negative electrical charge, among numerous other associations.

SEE ALSO *DUALISM, *YANG

YIN ESSENCE AND/OR YIN FLUID

Taoist general term for the inexhaustible female sexual fluid/energy that, when combined with the male *yang essence, results in the *golden elixir, the quested essence of the *dual cultivation exercises.

YIN NANG

(CHIN., "SECRET POUCH")

Chinese/Taoist technical term for testicles or scrotum, regarded as being in the care of heavenly deities.

YOGANIDRA ASANA

Although this posture (Douglas and Slinger, 1979, p. 61) may perhaps seem—or be—a rather difficult one, it has many advantages and should be exercised regularly by both partners. Not only is the exercise very relaxing, releasing tension and warming the body, but also it stimulates most of the internal organs and the complete set of glands known as the *endocrine system. All these effects add up to complete sexual invigoration. In its similarity to the posture taken by the *adya Shakti, it also provides one's partner with the opportunity to meditate and focus, free of thoughts and desire, on the sacred *yoni or *lingam.

The Sanskrit *nidra* means "sleep" and "deep relaxation."

SEE ALSO *STRI PUJA/1

YOGINI

1. Most often the term is used for several goddesses (or a certain "class" of female spiritual beings) that appear, for example, during the 12th day one spends in the *bardo,* the intermediate state between death and rebirth. Although the traditional number of these *yoginis* is said to be 64, various extant lists give different names from school to school and from century to century.

That these *yoginis* are not minor deities—as is often written—becomes clear when we recognize among them many powerful and important Indian and Tibetan deities. Major text sources describing these goddesses are the *Bardo Thödol and the *Kalika Purana; individual goddesses described in this encyclopedia are *Guheshvari, *Lasya, and *Vajra Yogini.

2. In both Hindu and Buddhist *Tantra this term is used also as a title, such as *Shakti or Vidya, for the female partner in *maithuna* practice.

3. Probably as a result of the two definitions given above, the term has also been used to indicate or honor certain other women. It sometimes refers to a certain class of accomplished female ascetics who spread Tantric knowledge among the masses: It is used for a shamaness or medicine woman, and it can sometimes indicate a woman possessed by the Goddess. For example, *see* *Machig Lapdron and *Niguma.

SEE ALSO *SIXTY-FOUR YOGINI PITHA, *YOGINI TANTRA

YOGINI CHAKRA

A secret Tantric ritual in which a single man practices *maithuna* with more than one woman, a constellation known in China as *secret dalliance. Such triple unions, or trinities, are often depicted in the temples of *Konarak and *Khajuraho and can also be found in many of the Nepalese temples in Kathmandu and Patan.

SEE ALSO *EROTOCOMATOSE LUCIDITY, *JAGAN NATH TEMPLE

YOGINI TANTRA

A text of 28 chapters, the authorship and age of which are unknown. To a great extent the text deals with the worship of the goddesses *Kali and *Kamakhya. It also describes the *Yonimandala and a great number of other *pithas and sacred places where worship is supposed to have excellent results. The text has many recommendations concerning the five *makara and about who may perform *maithuna with whom. It especially forbids *incest betwen mother and son.

The Yogini Tantra includes, in chapter 6, another example of *Tantric visualization. In this case, a male devotee is asked to imagine a 16-year-old woman with luster like that of a great many suns that "is to be fancied from her head to *breasts. Thus reflecting, one should concentrate on her figure from her *yoni to the lowest portion of her feet. That figure is to be contemplated as adorned with ornaments." Chapter 8 describes the origin of the *yoginis, which are stated to have come into being out of the "wavicles" (particle/wave paradox, as in light) of *Kali's energy.

Like many other *Kula-inspired texts, the Yogini Tantra allows the moral codes of mainstream *Hinduism to be broken and suspends many of the usual rules concerning marriage between castes. It allows women to talk and have sexual relations with whom they please.

YOHIMBE AND YOHIMBINE

The African yohimbe tree (Corynanthe yohimbe) is the souce of this well-known and legal *aphrodisiac. The active ingredients are yohimbiline and yohimbine, crystalline *alkaloid substances present in the tree's bark. It is widely used in Africa for the strong sexual stimulation it offers. Yohimbine is said to work for both male and female partners by strengthening the man's erection and by stimulating the woman's vaginal fluids. It does so by stimulating the spinal nerves and by flooding the pelvic area with blood. It can best be used as a tea, and it has been recommended to combine its intake with 1,000 milligrams of *vitamin C, which makes its effects both softer and more pronounced.

Similar to the effects of *MDMA, yohimbine also brings about the release of profound emotions and aids in overcoming mental barriers. Orgasms under the influence of the African "magic" are often accompanied by the feeling that one's body is dissolving, simultaneously merging with that of the lover. As is the case with so many delightful things, yohimbine has toxic effects when used in large quantities.

YONI

The mons veneris of the Mother is the triangle of Aphrodite, the "mound of Venus," the mountain connecting man and woman, earth and sky.

NOR HALL, THE MOON AND THE VIRGIN

Yoni is the term used throughout this book when we refer to the female genitals. It is a term borrowed from Sanskrit, where it means "womb," "origin," and "source" and/or refers more specifically to the female pubic region, the vulva and/or vagina. The conscious choice to use this term rather than a term from a Western language seems a natural one, since the word yoni neither carries any of the linguistic undercurrents of clinical detachment of words such as vulva or vagina nor has any of the pornographic, immature, and often derogatory connotations of words like cunt and similar expressions. On the contrary, the term yoni stems from a cultural and religious background where women have long been regarded and honored as an embodiment of divine female energy (*Shakti) and where the female genitals are seen as a sacred symbol of the Goddess.

Because Eastern Tantrics and other ancient cultures worship(ped) the divine in the form of a goddess, the term yoni has also acquired another, more cosmic level of meaning and has become a symbol of the universal womb, the matrix of generation and source of all. Yet here we must also, linguistically, be on our guard. Some modern writers—both Eastern and Western—go very far in their attempts to overly abstract and mystify the very real flesh-and-blood aspect of the yoni as a biological organ of creation and the gateway of life. We can find, for example, definitions of the yoni as the "primal root of the source of objectivation" or as a "symbol of cosmic mysteries" (Mookerjee and Khanna, p. 200). This may sometimes be done in an honest attempt to convey a true sense of sacredness to a part of the body so often shamefully hidden away. In other instances, however, this is merely another patriarchal trap and a shameful denial of the fact that sexuality and fertility were and are part of humanity's general religious and sacred practice.

More detailed information can be found under the headings *Adya Shakti, *Jagad Yoni, and most of the following entries beginning with yoni.

Y<small>ONI</small>. *The divine *yoni.*
Nineteenth-century wood carving from south India.
Ajit Mookerjee Collection, New Delhi.

YONI ASANA

A secret yoga posture or *asana* usually taught orally from guru to disciple.

YONILINGA

A statue or sculpture, usually from stone, that shows the *lingam of *Shiva in the *yoni of *Shakti. Beneath the visible part of such a statue—that is, beneath the actual yoni and lingam—is buried a complete, traditionally determined architectural structure of materials and symbols.

SEE ALSO *GENITAL WORSHIP, *YONILINGA MUDRA

YONILINGA MUDRA

One of the ritual gestures called *mudra/1, it is a truly "hand-made" *yonilinga, a symbol for the union of *yoni and *lingam, *yin and *yang. See illustration on page 154.

YONI MAGIC

Concerning the magical effects of nudity in general and of exposing the sexual organs in particular, there are many examples from a variety of peoples whose customs make obvious that the genitals—especially those of the female—exude an inherent magical power. Such myths and stories show clearly that our ancestors in various cultures regarded the *yoni as a kind of magical "weapon" imbued with protective and healing energies and that the exhibition of the

Y<small>ONILINGA</small>. *A symbol of unity expressed by depicting both *yoni (woman, goddess) and *lingam (man, god) as one, *yonilinga can be found throughout villages, cities, and temples of India and Nepal. Photograph by Rufus C. Camphausen.*

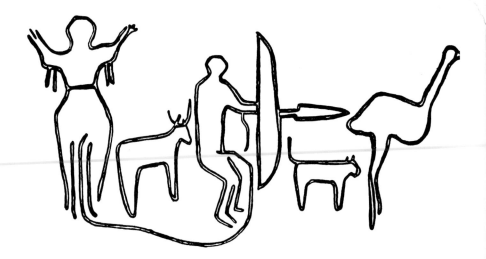

YONI MAGIC. *An African rock painting depicting the transmission of energy from a woman, or goddess, to the hunter. Tassili, Sahara, c. 7000 B.C.E.*

yoni has effects akin to those of certain magical spells.

Not only was "flashing" the yoni at the devil known as a fail-safe method to hinder his approach, but more generally it was seen as a means to avert evil forces such as the evil eye. The high esteem in which the ancients—on quite a universal scale—held this "yoni power" is well documented.

FAR EAST *Tibet: see* *Suryacandrasiddhi

Japan: see *Ama-no-Uzume, *Kuan-yin, *Sarutahiko

India: Many of the erotic sculptures at *Khajuraho show men and women exposing or exhibiting their genitals. Here, too, this was thought to dispel evil influences. In the province of Madras in southern India, women expose themselves in order to quiet down storms.

SEE ALSO *MATRIYONI, *YONIMANDALA

NEAR EAST Egyptian women used the same method to drive away evil spirits from their fields, and a similar intent is suggested by Theban wall paintings of funerals.

EUROPE Both Pliny (23–79) and Plutarch (46–126) note that heroes, gods, and ghosts have had to flee from the sight of the naked yoni. Different in content, yet certainly related to such "magic," is the myth of *Baubo and Demeter.

The many figures on early European church and cloister walls, called *Sheela-na-gigs, also may have been made with the intent that their yoni magic would protect the buildings from the "dark powers."

AFRICA Robert Briffault tells of a sixteenth-century traveler to Africa who relates that even a wild lion was thought to shy away from the sight of a naked yoni. An entirely different story is told by the accompanying illustration, which shows a hunter stalking his prey. This rock painting from Tassili (in the Sahara, dating from about 8000–5000 B.C.E.) has sometimes been classified as an expression of "hunting magic," a fact that overlooks the main point of this piece of religious art: the power line that runs from the woman's or goddess's genitals. Here we see that the magical force flowing from the yoni is an aid—and a permission from the Great Mother—in the men's hunting endeavors, telling the world that the taking of life can be granted only by the one able to create life as well.

OCEANIA A unique story of yoni magic is recorded in Hawaiian mythology. Not fertility oriented but clearly sexual, the story tells of the "traveling yoni" possessed by the goddess Kapo. When young Pele, beautiful goddess of the Pacific volcanoes, was once sexually assaulted by the macho god Kamapua'a, Kapo detached her yoni (Hawaiian *kohe*) from her body and sent her off to distract the rapist, in which ploy she succeeded. This myth gave rise to the goddess's epithet *Kapo-kohe-lele*, "Kapo of the Traveling Vulva." The major magical mystery in this story, however, lies in the fact that a surreal flying yoni would actually distract a randy male from mating with a complete and blossoming young woman in his powers. The solution to this riddle surely lies in the fact that Kapo, also known as Red Kapo and Red Eel Woman, is the goddess of menstruation and that her traveling yoni carried all the special powers inherent in the *menstrual fluid. Kapo, as has been indicated by the foremost researcher of Hawaiian religion, Martha Beckwith, represents the "passive" form of the reproductive energy, whereas her sister Laka represents the "active form," i.e., ovulation (Beckwith, p. 187). What is also most interesting in this connection, and what shows the power of myths over the human mind, is the fact that Hawaiian males are known to dream sometimes of a woman without a yoni, just as elsewhere males dream about a vagina dentata, the fearful (i.e., possibly castrating) yoni with teeth that occurs in Indian myth.

YONIMANDALA

A sacred stone in the Manobhavaguha cave at Mount Nila (*Assam), which is part of the *Kamakhya Pitha. The Yonimandala is seen as the dwelling place of the goddess *Kamakhya and is regarded as "axis mundi"—the center of the universe. It is here that one can witness the menstruation of the goddess and/or of Earth, an event that is celebrated yearly during the Indian month of Assar.

The goddess is said to reside in this *pitha, where the sacred stone has the shape of her *yoni and where a *red and intoxicating water wells out of the stone's cleft. The *Yogini Tantra relates that the well within the cave "reaches down into the netherworld" and that the actual opening "measures twelve fingers all around" (Banerjee, p. 339). This water is sacred to the practitioners and believers of *Shakta and *Tantra, who say that "one who drinks from it will not be reborn." A scientific analysis shows the water to contain traces of red arsenic. The water welling out from a cleft is seen as the *menstrual fluid of the Great Mother.

YONI MUDRA

1. One of the hand gestures called *mudra/1. This specific one, like the mahayoni mudra, resembles the shape of a *yoni.
2. A secret Tantric technique—for adepts only!—that according to the ancient Shiva Samhita "should not be revealed or given to others." Fortunately, the text has come down to us in written form, has been translated and published, and is available to anyone interested enough to search for it. The scripture tells of the splendor of the divine yoni, which is "brilliant as tens of millions of suns and cool as tens of millions of moons," and it explains furthermore that "above the yoni is a very small and subtle flame, whose form is intelligence." The technique includes contracting, or "sealing," the *yonishtana. What is actually prescribed is this: The devotee seals her or his anus with the left heel, presses the tongue against the palate, and fixes the eyes on the tip of the nose.

According to chapter 6 of the *Kubjika Tantra, the aim of yoni mudra is the arousal of *kundalini energy, which is made to rise from the *muladhara chakra (low end of spine) upward and toward union with the thousand-petaled *sahasrara chakra (top of skull): a technique designed to activate and stimulate the *pineal gland.

SEE ALSO *KHECHARI MUDRA, *VAJROLI MUDRA

YONI PITHA   SEE *KAMAKHYA PITHA

YONI PUJA

Ritual worship of the *yoni in symbolic (sculpture, altar, picture, and so forth) or living form (a woman's genitals) using concentration, meditation, and visualization on the venerated object. In some Tantric texts we also find mention of such ritual worship under its alternative name of bhagayaja. Aside from the obvious—that a unique and special singleness of mind can be achieved by such contemplative concentration—it becomes clear from texts such as the *Yoni Tantra that a major aim of the yoni puja is the ritual creation of a liquid (or subtle fluid) called *yonitattva or, in special cases, *yonipushpa. Such is the merit of this ritual that the *sadhaka who makes the yoni puja her or his sole mode of worship is excused from any other obligation. Before the actual union—*maithuna—there is much preliminary ritual, or "foreplay," during which wine and *cannabis are used and both yoni and *lingam are anointed with a *red paste of *sandalwood. After the puja (worship, mass), two-thirds of the resulting love juices is mixed with wine and drunk; the other third is used, in an *argha, as an offering to the Goddess. Sometimes the *yoni puja is celebrated with a menstruating woman, a practice forbidden by many texts and sects but specifically advocated in the Yoni Tantra, as it is by certain sects of *Gnosticism.

YONIPUSHPA
(SKT., "VULVA FLOWER")

> The flower blossoms after twelve years, month after
> month that flower falls. To whom shall I speak
> about that flower? Except for the enlightened, it
> is forbidden to say.
>
> BENGALI SONG

1. A Sanskrit term with a significance very similar to *yonitattva, the mixture of female and male sexual fluids. In this case, however, the sacred and quested essence is enriched by the fact that *maithuna is performed during the woman's menstrual flowering. Drinking these fluids is said to lead to liberation (Skt., *moksa*). **2.** "A black flower that symbolizes sexual intercourse" (Banerjee, p. 584).

SEE ALSO *GNOSTICISM, *MENSTRUAL FLUID

YONISHTANA
(SKT., "YONI PLACE")

A center of subtle energy where the "union of *Shiva and *Shakti" takes place and not far from where the *kundalini* resides. Literally translated, it indicates the place of the female genitals; yet, for all practical purposes, it is equated with the *perineum, midway between genitals and anus, female or male.

SEE ALSO *HUI-JIN, *JAWALAMUKHI, *YONI MUDRA

YONI SYMBOLOGY

Peoples everywhere throughout all ages have found natural shapes that resemble the yoni, and inevitably such objects were declared sacred; locations of larger objects became places of pilgrimage. Caves, shrines, and stones like the *Yonimandala and the *Ka'bah; shells like the *cowrie and the *scallop; flowers like the *lotus, the *lily, and the *rose; fruit like *apricot, *coco-de-mer, or *cardamom—all these and many more are symbolic representations of the *Shakti, of woman and her *yin essence. Also any small stone with a hole in it, and all ring stones, are seen as symbols of the yoni. A male follower of the Goddess would test whether or not such an *objet trouve* would fit his *lingam, and if so, he would consecrate the stone and carry it as an amulet.

But not only in nature can one find the yoni symbolized. Recurring images of the yoni in the context of sacred art, East and West, are the *triangle and the *mandorle.

SEE ALSO *SRI YANTRA, *YONI MUDRA

YONI TANTRA

> The sadhaka who utters the words "Yoni Yoni" at the time of his prayers, for him the Yoni shall be favourable, granting him enjoyment and liberation.
>
> YONI TANTRA, PATALA III

The Yoni Tantra is a religious text from *Bengal that is mainly concerned with describing the *yoni *puja*, a ritual dedicated to creating—and consuming—the sacred fluid

YONI SYMBOLOGY. *The Buddha in meditation before the Golden Gate, an obvious example of *yoni symbology. Japanese terracotta.*

called *yonitattva. According to this text, *maithuna is an indispensable part of Tantric ritual and may be performed by and with all women between the ages of 12 and 60, married or not, with the exception of *virgins. The text explicitly forbids the incestuous mother-son constellation.

In general, however, this Tantra does not impose many restrictions on the *sadhaka* who is dedicated to the yoni *puja*; it advocates use of the five *makara and leaves the choice of partner, place, and time very much up to the practitioner. Nevertheless, the male *sadhaka* is explicitly admonished "never to ridicule a yoni" and to treat all women well and never be offensive toward them. (*See also* *Incest, *Matriyoni, *Navakanya.)

The text also gives a specific *yoni topography with 10 subdivisions: hairpit, field, edge, arch, girdle, nodule, cleft, wheel, throne, and root. These parts are regarded as associated with one or another of the more important goddesses. For example:

Yonicakra-kali	*Kali
Yonicakra-tara	*Tara
Yonikuntala-chinnamastaka	*Chinnamasta
Yonisamipato-matangi	*Matangi
Yonigarta-mahalakshmi	*Lakshmi
Yonigarta-sodasi	*Sodasi

YONITATTVA

According to texts such as the *Yoni Tantra, this term refers to the mixture of female and male fluids created during sexual union or *maithuna. Such fluid is then drunk—after it has been washed off the *yoni and *lingam with water and then, sometimes, mixed with wine—by both partners, and sometimes by other *sadhakas as well. The creation of this *yonitattva* is one of the major goals of the ritual called *yoni *puja*.

SEE ALSO *GNOSTICISM, *MASS OF THE HOLY GHOST, *YONIPUSHPA

YONI TERMINOLOGY

For an introduction to this list of words, *see* *Genital Terminology.

* Alembic	Latin, alchemy
Chalice	Western esoteric schools
Cinnabar Cleft	Chinese/Taoist
Concha	Latin (*see* *Conch)
Counte	Middle English
Cucurbite	Latin, alchemy
Cunnus	Latin (from Greek *konnos*)
Cunt	modern English (slang)
Cunte	Middle English
Cwithe	Old English (also means "womb")
Dark Gate	Chinese
Doorway of Life	Chinese
* Ghanta	Sanskrit
Golden Gate	Chinese
* Guhe	Nepali
Hor	Hebrew
Inner Heart	Chinese
* Jade Gate	Chinese
Ka-t	Egyptian (also means "mother")
Kohe	Hawaiian
Konnos	Greek
Kteis	Greek (also means *"scallop")
* Kunthus	Greek
* Kunti	Sanskrit
Kut	Dutch (slang)
Kvithe	Teutonic
Lotus of Her Wisdom	Tantric/Sanskrit (*see* *Lotus)
Mysterious Gateway	Chinese/Taoist
Mysterious Valley	Chinese/Taoist
Mystic Rose	Western esoteric schools
Navel	*see* *Song of Songs
Padma	Sanskrit, *lotus
Phoenix	Chinese
Pillow of Musk	Chinese
Precious Crucible	Chinese/Taoist
Pudendum muliebria	*see* *Pudenda
Pure Lily	Chinese
* Purple Mushroom Peak	Chinese
Qitbus	Gothic
Queynthe	Code for *cwithe*
Quiff or Quim	from Celtic *cwn*, "cleft, valley"
Red Ball	Chinese
Red Pearl	Chinese
Retort	Latin, alchemy
Secret Cavern	Chinese/Taoist
Sensitive Cave	Chinese
Sulcus	Latin, "furrow"
Vesica	Latin, "bladder"
* Vulva	Latin

YONITIRTHA

A sacred bathing place, thought of as the Goddess's *yoni, in the shrine of the goddess Bhimadevi.

YONI TOPOGRAPHY

When one takes an extended biological, medical, and sexological point of view, a picture of the female genital or reproductive system appears that consists of a great number of different elements. It has been common to compare female features with those of the male, resulting in statements like "the clitoris is a rudimentary penis." But considering what we now know about human reproduction—about X and Y chromosomes and the development of the embryo—it seems time to view things in their more appropriate proportions and interconnected causalities. The female system is not only the primary one—the egg always being *X/*yin programmed—but is also the more sophisticated of the two. Only if a *Y/*yang chromosome is introduced into the ovum will the potentially female system be changed, or reprogrammed, into a male one.

In order to make visible the many similarities and homologues between female and male genitals, the numbers used in the entry *Lingam Topography correspond to those used here for the various parts of the *yoni system. The succession here chosen corresponds to a movement from the most outward and visible parts of the system toward the most inward, with the numbers corresponding to the illustrations of the facing page.

1. PUBIS   The triangle of hair that covers the mons veneris (2) and much of the labia majora (3). The area also contains scent glands. In China, female pubic hair is generally known as *yinmao*; there are also phrases for it such as "black rose," "fragrant grass," "sacred hair," or "moss"; whereas women without any pubic hair are known as "white tigers." To the Chinese, an equilateral triangle with an upward-directed growth is a sign of beauty, and abundant hair is seen as a sign of sensuality and passion.

2. MONS VENERIS   The "mound of Venus," or mons pubis, refers to the cushion of fatty tissue that protects the pubic bones and separates, lower down, into the labia majora (3). A Chinese name for the female mons translates as "hill of sedge."

3. LABIA MAJORA (LABIUM MAJUS)   The large or outer lips—running from the mons veneris to the perineum—that contain sebaceous (oil-secreting) *scent glands and a small number of sweat glands. After puberty the pigmented outer skin of these fatty, protective folds will grow pubic hair, while the inside remains smooth and hairless. Like the labia minora, these lips often swell during sexual arousal. Between the labia majora and the forks of the clitoris are the two "clitoral bulbs" of

spongy, erectile tissue that are responsible for the lips' swelling.

SEE ALSO *MYRTLE

4. LABIA MINORA   The small or inner lips—mostly hidden by the labia majora (3)—of smooth, hairless skin, mostly colored in various shades of pink. These inner lips contain sweat glands and sebaceous scent glands that are also instrumental in moistening these sensitive tissues. During sexual arousal they can become engorged with blood and swell to two or three times their usual size, often undergoing changes in color. At their upper end, the labia minora, or labium minus (Latin), join to form the clitoral hood (5). The small fold connecting the labia minora to the vaginal opening is known as the fourchette.

These sensitive lips are sometimes called *nymphae, and it is quite interesting to note that this word (the English *nymphs*) was the original Greek name for their water goddesses before it was ever used for the woman's small, inner lips. In China, the labia minora are known as "red pearls" (Chin., *ch'ih-chu*) or "wheat buds," their lower meeting point as "jade veins" (Chin., *yü-li*), and the upper (almost) meeting point near the clitoral crown (6) as "lute strings."

SEE ALSO *LABIAESTHETICS

5. CLITORAL HOOD   A small, freely movable fold of skin formed by the joining of the two labia minora (4). It completely covers the shaft of the clitoris (11) and forms a protective "hood," which wholly or partially covers the clitoral crown (6). In China, the hood was known as "dark garden," "god field," and "grain seed."

6. CLITORAL CROWN (LOWNDES CROWN; GLANS CLITORIDIS)   This is what most people actually call the clitoris (11), though it is merely the relatively small, visible part of the clitoris. This crown, so named by Josephine *Lowndes-Sevely, consists of tissue known as the *corpus spongiosum and contains a large number of nerve endings, the latter making it into one of the most highly sensitive parts of the female anatomy. During sexual arousal it can change color and increase in size, often projecting itself far out of the clitoral hood (5). It is this outer part that is cut away on those unfortunate girls who undergo *clitoridectomy, not the whole clitoris, as is sometimes reported.

Just below the crown, where the labia minora (4) seem

1. Pubis

2. Mons veneris
   (mons pubis)

3. Labia majora
   (labium majus)

4. Labia minora
   (labium minus;
   *nymphae)

5. Clitoral hood

6. Clitoral crown
   (Lowndes crown;
   glans clitoridis)

7. Vaginal glans

8. Vestibule

9. Vagina

10. Hymen

11. Clitoris

12. Vulvovaginal
    glands (Batholin's
    or vestibular
    glands)

13. Urethra

14. Urethral sponge
    and G-spot

15. Female
    prostatic glands
    (prostate)

16. Os

17. Cervix

18. Uterus

19. Fallopian tubes
    (egg tubes)

20. Ovaries

21. —

22. —

23. Perineal sponge

24. Perineum

25. Pelvic floor
    muscles (not in
    illustration; see
    *Pelvic Floor
    Potential)

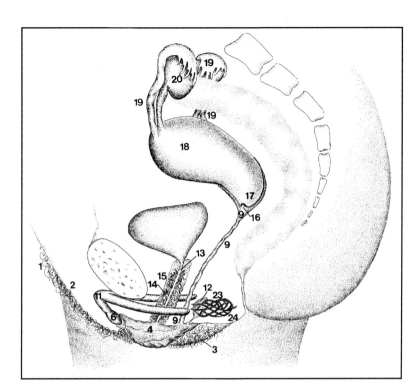

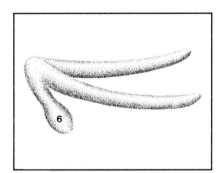

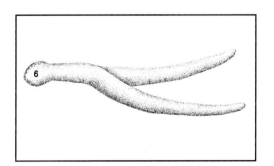

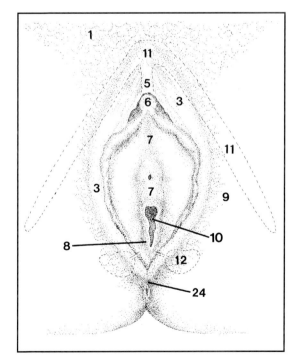

Yoni Topography.

Illustrations by Christina Camphausen.

to meet, is another highly sensitive area, usually known as the frenulum of the clitoris or, in China, as Lute Strings. To the *Tachikawa adepts of Japan, the most appropriate name for the clitoris was *hoju*—a term that in Buddhism also signifies the "magical jewel of the dharma."

7. VAGINAL GLANS   What Lowndes-Sevely has named the woman's glans is the small area of skin below the clitoral crown and above the opening to the vagina, including the meatus of the urethra. Like the crown, this recently "discovered" female glans is a highly sensitive zone with a great number of nerve endings. The glans is very flexible and moves during sexual union "in and out of the vagina—creating a pleasurable sensation for the woman" (Lowndes-Sevely, 1989, p. 25).

8. VESTIBULE   This "outer room" or "entrance chamber" to the vagina (9) indicates the hollow surrounded and enclosed by the (parted/open) labia minora (4). It contains the openings of, and receives secretions from, the urethra (13), the vagina, and the two ducts coming from the vulvuvaginal glands (12). The vestibule encloses/contains the vaginal glans (7), two elongated bodies of erectile tissue and many mucus-secreting glands. Chinese terms for this vaginal entrance are "heavenly court" (Chin., *t'ien-t'ing*), "secluded valley" (Chin., *yu-ku*), and "examination hall."

9. VAGINA   A deeply folded, elastic, muscular tube (10–12.5 centimeters) connecting the vestibule (8) to the cervix (17). The healthy vagina is capable of great distention and is highly lubricated by its mucous membranes. It plays, in concert with the vaginal muscles, a most important role in sexual union—a role often neglected in medical textbooks. It also constitutes, of course, the pathway to be traveled by *menstrual fluid, by the sperm cells on their way to the ovum, and at birth by the newborn human. The vagina of most women also contains the odorous substances known as *aliphatic acids. A Japanese expression for the vagina is "gate of jewels," making it obvious once more that in matters of sexual anatomy, Oriental cultures are usually much more respectful, and reminding us of the fact that sexuality was regarded and studied as both an art and a science.

Unfortunately, because of the widespread lack of knowledge concerning these matters, the term *vagina* is often used—even by women—when one actually means to refer to the vulva.

10. HYMEN   The opening to the vagina is covered in many young women, until broken by accident or *defloration, by a membranous fold of skin called the hymen. After defloration, fragments of it will often remain along the vaginal opening. The widely held idea that all women are born with a hymen that breaks and bleeds when put under pressure is refuted by medical statistics, as described under the entry *Virginity. The use of the term, in English, dates back to the seventeenth century and is most likely derived from the name of Hymen, a Greco-Roman god of marriage.

11. CLITORIS   A relatively large structure of erectile tissue, most of which is hidden from view. The clitoris consists—apart from the crown (6)—of a shaft and two forked crura (medical term meaning "legs"). The shaft, or corpus, of the clitoris becomes erect and enlarged, like its visible crown, by the increased blood pressure that occurs during sexual stimulation. The highly sensitive shaft usually moves involuntarily when touched. The deeper and invisible parts—unfortunately unknown to most people—constitute a fork, each of the crura running downward and inward below the clitoral bulbs at their respective sides of the outer lips.

In both woman and man, shaft and crura consist of a tissue called the *corpus cavernosum.

Other terms for the female clitoris are the "Chinese golden tongue," "seat of pleasure," "golden terrace" or "jade terrace" (Chin., *hsüan-t'ai*), the Latin *naviculus* (little boat), the Sanskrit *madanahatra*, and, for example, the contemporary lesbian slang expression "boy in the boat." If the Chinese seem eloquent already, one should realize that the Maori people of the Pacific Ocean have more words in their language for the clitoris than any other peoples anywhere!

12. VULVOVAGINAL GLANDS (BARTHOLIN GLANDS, VESTIBULAR GLANDS)   Two tiny glands (1–2 millimeters) located left and right of the vagina (9) between the vaginal wall and the lower labia minora (4). The glands secrete a thick protein compound via two ducts (Bartholin ducts) into the vestibule (8). The major purpose of these glands, apart from lubrication of the vaginal opening, seems to be the generaion of a stimulating sexual odor. As such they may be related to the *estrus cycle, to the *scent glands, and to the human *pheromones.

There are several Chinese terms for these glands, for example, "infant girl," "mixed rock," and "sun terrace." The Sanskrit *purnachandra* (Skt., *purnacandra,* "full moon"), defined in the *Koka Shastra as a duct or channel within the yoni and said to be filled with the "juice of love," probably refers to the ducts of these glands.

13. URETHRA The urethra is the tube that transports the urine from the bladder toward its external opening, the meatus of the vaginal glans (7). In women, this tube is only about 4 centimeters long and is surrounded by the urethral sponge (14).

14. URETHRAL SPONGE AND G-SPOT The urethral sponge is a sheath of tissue (*corpus spongiosum) surrounding the female urethra. It consists of several glands, ducts, and blood vessels as well as fleshy tissue, including the *paraurethral glands and ducts instrumental in female *ejaculation.

The G-spot is an internal sensitive area in the vagina, about halfway between the mons veneris and the cervix. This location—part of the urethral sponge—is a vital element of the female genital system and can, for many women, be instrumental in achieving *orgasm and/or the discharge of orgasmic fluids. For a more detailed discussion, *see* the main entry *G-spot.

15. FEMALE PROSTATIC GLANDS (PROSTATE) Embedded in the urethral sponge (14), women also have several prostatic glands, similar in makeup and function to those of the male. Only recently "discovered" as such (see the work of Josephine *Lowndes-Sevely), they were hitherto known as paraurethral glands. The glands are connected to the fringe of the female urethra (13) by a large number of ducts that transport the glandular liquids. Although the glands' specific function is as yet unknown, they probably constitute the actual pressure point that has become famous as the *G-spot, and their liquids form part of the *female love juices that make female ejaculation a reality to be denied only by the most die-hard male chauvinists. For more detail, *see* *Prostatic Glands.

16. OS A tiny opening at the tip of the cervix, sometimes called the mouth of the uterus. It provides a passageway from the vagina (outer os) into the uterus (inner os) and vice versa, but cannot be penetrated by either finger or lingam. After enlargement, in the case of giving birth, it will close again very tightly.

17. CERVIX Lower part, or "neck," of the uterus. The cervix projects forward into the vagina and can often be felt there by a probing finger, depending on position and situation.

18. UTERUS Including cervix and os, the uterus is a more or less pear-shaped, hollow, muscular organ. Its usual size is that of a small avocado pear; its size and location within the body change with position and/or sexual excitation. Part of the uterus is the endometrium, the inner lining that undergoes several changes throughout the menstrual/ovarian cycle. The uterus is the actual "womb" wherein all humans have initially grown before leaving this dark, warm, aquatic environment via the cervix (17), os (16), and vagina (9) for the world outside. The *alembic (Latin) of the European alchemists has been fashioned to resemble the uterus, and the term is therefore often used as a code when referring to the yoni.

Chinese/Taoist alchemists have called the uterus by such (secret) names as "children's palace" (Chin., *tzu-kung*), "cinnabar cave," "jewel enclosure," or "red chamber" (Chin., *chu-shih*).

19. FALLOPIAN TUBES (EGG TUBES) Named after the Italian anatomist Gabriel Fallopio (1523–1562), these are two tubes each about 10 centimeters (4 inches) in length. They are attached to the right and left upper ends of the uterus (18), and their far ends lie close to the ovaries. The tubes serve to transport and guide the eggs from one of the ovaries toward the uterus. The eventual meeting between egg and sperm happens most often in the lower end of these fallopian tubes.

20. OVARIES Part of the female *endocrine system, the two ovaries not only produce the eggs (Latin, ova) but also manufacture *estrogens, *androgens, and *progesterone and thus help determine female embryonic development in general and that of specific genital/sexual features. Ovary activity is controlled, in a complex and synergetic fashion, by the pituitary hormones *FSH, *LH, and prolactin (PRL). Once a month, during a woman's fertile years, a randomly selected ovum will float out of the ovaries and into one of the fallopian tubes (19), resulting either in an embryo or in the monthly discharge of *menstrual fluid. In China, the ovaries (Chin., *hsueh*) are seen as containing the female yin energy. Color photographs of the very beautiful ovaries can be found in Lennart Nilsson's book *Behold Man,* a beautiful book despite its male-chauvinistic title.

21. No recognized equivalent to male seminal vesicles.

22. No recognized equivalent to male epididymes.

23. Perineal sponge An area of sensitive tissue (*corpus spongiosum) beneath the perineum that fills with blood during sexual excitation.

24. Perineum The female perineum, the flesh and skin between yoni and anus, is not usually seen as part of the genital system. Nonetheless, for all practical purposes—for the sense of touch and for any technique involving the muscles of the pelvic floor—it is closely involved, and its importance should not be overlooked. The Chinese and Sanskrit terms for the perineum, *ching-tao, *hui-jin, and *yonishtana, appear often in Taoist and Tantric texts, underlining the importance of this location and the attention paid to it. In our times, especially in the United States, the perineum is cut, often unnecessarily, as a preparation for childbirth.

25. Pelvic floor muscles This system of muscles in the genital area of women, sometimes referred to as love muscles, consists of muscles such as the pubococcygeus or constrictor cunnis (responsible for contractions of the vagina), the pubovaginalis, and the puborectalis. The use and training of these muscles is discussed under the entries *Imsak, *Kabbazah, *Pelvic Floor Potential, *Pompoir, and *Vaginal Balls.

YONI WORSHIP

Although the worship of both female and male genitals is probably the original starting point of many cults and sacred customs, it is mainly *phallic worship that has been exten-

Yoni Worship. *Similar figures to the Celtic* *sheela-na-gig *can be found in India and Nepal, where numerous temple sculptures feature women displaying the* *yoni. *Carving from the Maju Deval temple, Kathmandu. Photograph by Rufus C. Camphausen.*

sively studied, and that is the better known of the two. Nonetheless, archaeological evidence points to the conclusion that the *yoni preceded the *lingam as a sacred symbol and object. That the yoni and her power was the first to be recognized as having magical importance can easily be understood once we remind ourselves that early humanity did not know about the male's involvement in conception and procreation.

EUROPE Symbols of the yoni are probably the oldest (35,000–25,000 B.C.E.) of all depictions of the primal goddess and of woman's fertile powers. Rock-incised triangles and circles representing the vulva have been found in many caves in France (La Ferrassie, Abri Blanchard, Castanet, Cellier, Laussel, Poisson, Les Rois). They are of very early Aurignacian origin but may even stem from their predecessors, *Homo sapiens neanderthalensis*. Both peoples seem to have used the same caves as natural shelters and temples. From roughly the same time period are the "vulva rocks" of Kostienki, a site 500 kilometers south of Moscow at the river Don, which in 1932 yielded several rock medallions similar to the incised vulvas of the French cave artists.

SEE ALSO *DOLMEN, *HOLED STONES, *SHEELA-NA-GIG

FAR EAST Of India, and especially of southern India, Mircea Eliade writes that "everywhere" the Great Goddess's icons are "simple stone images of the female organs of generation" (p. 349). For more information on yoni worship in the East, *see* *Adya Shakti, *Guhesvari, *Hinta Hinyaai, *Kameshvari, *Matriyoni, *Yonilinga, *Yonimandala, *Yoni Puja.

Japan: see *Ema, *Kuan-yin

NEAR EAST *Arabia: see* *Ka'bah

AFRICA The rock paintings at Tassili (see illustration, p. 256) described under *Yoni Magic are, naturally, an expression of yoni worship.

SEE ALSO *YONI SYMBOLOGY

AMERICA At several sites in California, for example at *Jamul, a great number of vulva-shaped rocks, stones, and engravings have been found that clearly indicate that some indiginous tribes have used them for menstrual and fertility-related initiation and/or as symbols of the Great Earth Mother.

YONIYUGMA

Sanskrit term for a diagram that shows a downard-pointing female *triangle intersecting a male triangle with its apex pointing upward. This is the symbol known in the West as the hexagram, or King *Solomon's seal.

SEE ALSO *SRI YANTRA

YUKTATRIVENI

The meeting point of India's three sacred rivers (Ganges, *Sarasvati, Yamima), a symbol for the triple *nadi knot called *muktatriveni*.

YU-CHIANG   SEE *JADE FLUID

YUN-YU   SEE *CLOUDS AND RAIN

*When he has embraced his
female partner, inserted his sceptre
(*vajra) into her *lotus (padma),
he should heavily drink from her lips;
they seem as if sprinkled with milk.*

*KALACHAKRA TANTRA

ZAP-LAM
(TIB., "PROFOUND PATH," "PATH OF SKILLFUL MEANS")
Although the Tibetan terms *zab lam* and *thabs lam*, from which the word Zap-Lam is derived, are by no means synonymous, the teachings and practices associated with both have an essential point in common. Both refer to practices carefully guarded with great secrecy by most Tibetan teachers and authors, mainly because the techniques involved

use the innate and natural energies we have come to call libido, erotic desire, lust, and sexuality. Yet the terms *zab lam* and *thabs lam* do have different meanings; not all are meant to shroud matters in secrecy. In order to appreciate just how carefully Tibetan literature should be read, we'll look at several meanings connected with these words.

In its most general usage, the expression Profound Path (*zab lam*) simply refers to what is more commonly known as the *Mahamudra teachings and their lineage, dating back via Milarepa and Marpa to Indian *Mahasiddhas such as *Naropa, *Tilopa, and Saraha. In several instances, only recognizable by way of the context, *zap lam* is used as an abbreviation for a variety of terms or titles that are too lengthy to speak or write. These "long forms" include *zab lam na ro'i chos drug,* "Profound Path of the Six Teachings of Naropa"; *zab lam na ro chos drug gi khrid rim yid ches gsum ldan,* "Six Yogas of Naropa with the Three Confidences" (a text by the *Gelugpa reformer Tsongkhapa); and *zab lam na ro chos drug gi khrid rim yid ches gsum ldan,* "Axe to Cut Through Taking Self and Phenomena as Real" (a liturgical text used in the practice of *Chod, written by Shabkar).

The term *zab lam* can easily be qualified by adding other words, thus leading to related concepts. Such "compounds" include *zab lam pa* ("followers of the profound path"); *zab lam pho ba* ("profound path of the transference of consciousness"); and *zab lam bde stong phyag rgya chen po* ("profound path of the great seal of bliss and emptiness"). Employing the phrase "bliss and emptiness" (*bde stong),* in this last phrase is contained a hint regarding the sexual nature of the practices associated with the so-called Anuyoga fulfillment stage of the *Inner Tantras. The Union of Bliss and Emptiness, symbolizing male and female, is synonymous with the more oft-encountered phrase *Union of Skillful Means and Profound Cognition.

In this context, the name Zap-lam refers to ritual techniques practiced, for example, by two of *Padmasambhava's female students and consorts. Judging from the available literature, *Yeshe Tsogyal practiced with two partners in Bhutan, and Sakya Devi apparently did so in Nepal (which suggests that these teachings, originally from India, came to be known throughout the Himalayas as well).

In this sense, Zap-lam has been described as "the yoga of coincident emptiness and pleasure on the profound path" (Dowman, *Sky Dancer,* p. 249). Here, sexual energy is used as motivation for, and desire as the object of, meditation,

thus becoming transformed into awareness and pure pleasure. The technique, however, should only be carried out by adepts trained in the control of all levels of energy, and especially—as Yeshe Tsogyal herself points out—in the conscious redirection of the male and female seed essences through the channels of the subtle body.

Further evidence for the sexual nature of the Zap-lam teachings is found upon examination of the Tibetan term *thabs lam,* from which the name Path of Skillful Means comes. In order to carefully decipher *thabs, thabs lam,* and its various derivatives, it is good to recall that *lam* translates as "path" or "way," whereas *thabs* translates as "means," "skills,"or "skillful means." Considering the existence of the term *thabs dang shes rab* ("union of skillful means and profound cognition"), it is most interesting that *thabs shes* is given as a synonym for *thabs lam* in some dictionaries. This hints at the fact that the path of skillful means (*thabs lam*) is actually, without saying it in so many words, a path of combining skillful means (*thabs*) with wisdom or knowledge (*shes*).

Most interesting in this pursuit to reveal the "deep secret" of Zap-lam is the fact that both Mahayoga and Anuyoga teachings (see *Inner Tantras) refer to two different paths of means; the difference between the two paths lies in whether one is using the so-called "upper door" or "lower door" of the body. The name for these Anuyoga teachings clearly shows this: *thabs steng sgo'i man ngag dang 'og sgo'i man ngag gnyis* translates as "two secret instructions concerning the skillful means of employing the upper/higher and lower/secret doors/gates of the body."

And what are these *steng dang 'og sgo gnyis,* the two upper and lower doors of the body? Although the uses of *steng sgo* ("upper door") sometimes hint at "mouth," the term actually refers to the so-called Brahma aperture, the fontanelle, at the crown of the skull. In terms of the lower door, in the Tibetan dictionary *'og sgo* simply translates as "groin" or "genitals." But the careful reader is also supplied with several synonyms and coded expressions for these parts: *gsang gnas* ("secret center") and *mkha' gsang* ("secret space" or "sky"). Once we pursue all the linguistic constructs of these synonyms it becomes obvious that the most potent of the two secret spaces (*mkha' gsang gnyis*) is the "inner space" or "inner vacuity" (*mkha' nang*) or the "gate of samsara"(*'khor ba'i sgo),* terms that are reserved for the *yoni.

Finally, looking at a few more phrases associated with the

lower doors, such as *gsang ba bde skyong gi 'khor lo,* "the wheel/chakra of sustaining bliss at the secret organ, and *'og sgo bde chen,* "great bliss of the lower gate," we're suddenly back to the union of bliss and emptiness discussed in connection with the spelling *zab lam.* Here, united in the **yab-yum* position, both the male consort *(yab)* and the female consort *(yum)* merge their two secret spaces (Tib., *mkha'gsang gnyis*) on the path of interdependence (Tib., *'khor ba'i lam*) in order to achieve liberation from the dualistic fixation (Tib., *gnyis 'dzin*) in which perceiver and perceived seem different entities.

ZEUS

The high god and father figure among all other Greek Olympic deities. Zeus is the archetype of the macho, alpha male and is shown in his myths as engaging in deception, sexual coercion, brutality, and *incest. He is married to the similarly powerful goddess Hera. This pattern of behavior has sometimes been apologetically explained as "reflecting the divine union with all life" (Matthews and Matthews, p. 189), but it is actually the typical behavior sponsored by all overly male-oriented religions and cultures: Zeus forcefully dominates everyone around him, especially the women.

SEE ALSO *ABRAHAM, *DIONYSUS

ZHANG ZHUNG
(OTHER SPELLINGS: SHANGSHUNG, SHANG SHUNG, XANXUN)

Ancient kingdom in the area now known as western Tibet, specifically Guge, and including Ladakh, Mt. Kailas (Tib., *ti se*), and Lake Manasarovar (Tib., *ma-pham-tsho*). The kingdom is about five hundred years older than the Tibetan Bod Kingdom. Sometimes, however, the name was also used for a much larger region, including the north and northeast of what we are now accustomed to think of as Tibet.

ZINC

A valuable and important mineral needed by the human organism. It is present in only a few of our general food products. The fact that *oysters and other *fruits de mer are used and useful as *aphrodisiacs is most likely due to the unusually high content of minerals, especially zinc, in these animals. Zinc is also the "sexually active" ingredient responsible for the aphrodisiac properties of *mushrooms, *onions, and *wheat germ. Zinc is greatly involved in the growth and development of the reproductive organs and is known to play a part in regulating the *menstrual/ovarian cycle and in the proper functioning of the male prostatic glands. Male *semen, the prostate, and most of all the sperm cells show very high concentrations of zinc—many times more than anywhere else in the male body.

SEE ALSO *ARGININE

ZOGQEN   SEE *DZOGCHEN

ZOHAR

The full title of this book is Sepher ha Zohar, which translates as "Book of Splendor." It was written or compiled between 1270 and 1300 C.E. by Moses ben Shem Tov de Leon (c. 1240–1305), translates as "Book of Splendor." The Zohar is regarded by many as the leading mystical text of the Hebrew cabalah, although the biblical Genesis is regarded as equally important. According to its author, the book represents the teachings of a circle of Palestinian adepts during the second and third centuries, and the text has thus been written in an artificial form of Aramaic. Despite justified doubts, the cabalistic tradition has come to accept the Zohar as a genuine text. The concepts and ideas of the work are strongly linked to the Torah, but the book also includes other texts—for example, a cabalistic commentary on the *Song of Songs.

One of its 18 parts, the Book of Concealment, has some unique information concerning the mystical *dew of ecstasy, which is produced in the *pineal and /or *pituitary gland.

SEE ALSO *LILITH, *SABBATIANS

Appendix:
Index Lists by Topic

INDEX I: INDIVIDUALS

Abraham

Aeschylus
  see Semen

A-Yu Khadro
  see Machig Lapdron

Albertus Magnus
  see Brain (as Aphrodisiac)

Allegro, John M.

Al-Nefzaoui
  see Perfumed Garden

Anangavaja
  see Mahasiddhas

Anger, Kenneth
  see Crowley

Apuleius, Lucius
  see Ass

Asanga
  see Guhyasamaja Tantra

Augustus
  see Ars Amatoria

Baudelaire C.
  see Cannabis Sativa, Opium

Bennett, J. G.
  see Gurdjieff

Blake, William
  see Goat

Bleibtreu, John N.
  see Ecstasy (Psychosomatic)

Bohm, David
  see Tao

Boullan, Joseph-Antoine
  see Black Mass, Spectrophilia
Buddha, Gautama
  see Buddhism, Dzogchen,
  Mahacinacara-sara Tantra
Burton, Sir Richard
Buruma, Ian
  see Matriyoni, Tokudashi
Chakraberti, Chandra
  see Mudra/5
Chang Tao-ling
Chia, Mantak
  see Lingam Topography/25, Pelvic
  Floor Potential
Chuang-tzu
  see Taoism
Cleary, Thomas
  see Breasts, Tanden
Clement VII (Pope)
  see Romano
Cleopatra
  see Fellatio
Cohn, Norman
  see Amaurians
Collin, Rodney
  see Canopus/2, Gurdjieff
Crowley, Aleister
Culling, Louis T.
  see Great Brotherhood of God
Dalai Lama(s)
King David
  see Shunamism
Deng Ming-Dao
  see Kwan Saihung
Descartes, Rene
  see Pineal Gland
Douglas, Nik
  see Asana, Chakra (Physiological),
  Kundalini, Pelvic Floor Potential,
  Pillow Books, Pithas, Shankhini
  Nadi
Dowman, Keith
  see quotation on page 50,
  Dzogchen, Indrabhuti
Drukpa Kunleg

Dumas, Alexandre
  see Testicles (Animal)
Eliade, Mircea
  see Aghora
Epiphanus of Salamis
  see Gnosticism
Esther (Biblical)
  see Olfactory Delights
Eve (Biblical)
  see Lilith
Fallopio, Gabriel
  see Yoni Topography/19
Feldenkrais, Moshe
  see Gurdjieff
Feuerstein, Georg
  see quotation on page 249
Frazer, James G.
  see Mandrake
Fulgino, Angela de
  see Puritanical Fanaticism
Gampopa
  see Kagyudpa, Tantra
Garab Dorje
Gardner, Gerald
  see Ordo Templi Orientis
Gendun Gyatso
  see Dalai Lama, Tantric
  Visualization
de Graaf
  see Ejaculation (Female)
Grafenberg, Ernest
Gulik, R. van
  see I Ching, Medicine of the
  Three Peaks
Gurdjieff, George Ivanovich
Hagar
Harris, Frieda
  see Grail, Scarlet Woman
Harris, Thomas Lake
  see Karezza, Oliphant
Hasan-I Sabbah
  see Nizari Isma'ilis
Helen of Troy
  see Apple, Spectrophilia
Herodotus
  see Sacred Prostitution

Hoffmann, Albert
  see LSD
Homer
  see Ecstasy (Psychosomatic)
Hsuan-nü
Huang Ti
  see Yellow Emporer
Huysmans, J. K.
  see Black Mass, Olfactory Delights,
  Spectrophilia
Indrabhuti
Jamyang Khyentse Wangchumg
  see Lamdre
Jamyang Later Wangpo
  see Lamdre
Jerome, St.
  see Puritanical Fanaticism
Jesus
  see Amanita Muscaria, Spiritual
  Marriage
Jigme Lingpa
Jodorowsky, A.
  see Gurdjieff
Johnson, Virginia
  see Ejaculation (Female)
Judith (Biblical)
  see Olfactory Delights
Kalyanamalla
  see Ananga Ranga
Kanipa
  see Aghora
Khyungpo Naljor
  see Niguma
King, Francis
  see Grail, Ordo Templi Orientis
Kinsey, Alfred
  see Ejaculation (Female)
Kipling, Rudyard
  see Gurdjieff
Kiss-Maerth, Oscar
Kitzinger, Sheila
  see Pelvic Floor Potential
Kobo Daishi
  see Shingon
Ko Hung

Kotzwinkle, William
   see Stri Puja/2
Kublai Khan
   see Polygamy (Male-Female)
Kukai
   see Shingon
K'ung-tzu
Kwan Saihung
La Fontaine, Jean de
   see Mandrake
Lakshmincara
   see Mahasiddhas
Lao-tzu
Leary, Timothy
   see Aphrodisiacs, Hedonic
     Engineering, LSD
Lepine, Jules
   see Fo-ti-tieng
Leuba, James
   see Spiritual Marriage
Levi, Eliphas
   see Reincarnation
Li Chung Yun
   see Fo-ti-tieng
Lilly, John
   see Inner Tantras
Li Tung Hsuan
   see Retention of Semen
Lloyd Wright, Frank
   see Gurdjieff
Longchenpa
Lowndes-Sevely, Josephine
Luipa
Machig Lapdron
Mangtho Ludrub Gyatsho
   see Lamdre
Maria Magdalena of Pazzi
   see Puritanical Fanaticism
Marpa
   see Naropa
Masters, William
   see Ejaculation (Female)
Meadows, Robert
   see Skoptsi

Messalina, Valeria
   see Nymphomania
Metzger, Deena
   see quotation on page 236
Milarepa,
   see Kagyudpa, Naropa
Monroe, Robert A.
   see Stygian Sexuality
Morimaru Kobu
   see Daisei Shokushu
Muhammad
   see Al'Lat, Ka'bah
Nagarjuna
   see Mahasiddhas
Narian, Nanddo
   see Fo-ti-tieng
Naropa
NeLidoff, Ida
   see Ecotocomatose Lucidity
Ngorchen Konchog Lhundrub
   see Lamdre
Nicoll, Maurice
   see Gurdjieff
Niguma
Nilsson, Lennart
   see Yoni Topography/20
Nin-kan
   see Tachikawa
Norbu, Namkhai
   see Bön, Dzogchen, Machig Lapdron
Noyes, John Humphrey
O'Keeffe, Georgia
   see Gurdjieff
Oliphant, Laurence
Omar
   see Matriarchy
Onan
   see Coitus Interruptus
Orage, A. R.
   see Gurdjieff
Origen(us)
Ouspensky, P. D.
   see Gurdjieff
Ovid
   see Ars Amatoria

Padmasambhava
Papus
   see Ordo Templi Orientis
P'eng Tsu
Perry, John
   see Grafenberg
Phadampa Sangye
   see Machig Lapdron
Pirsig, Robert
   see Kali
Pliny the Elder
   see Nymphomania
Plutarch
   see Numerology
Polo, Marco
   see Nizari Isma'ilis
Prahevajra
   see Garab Dorje
Pythagoras
   see Triangle
Ramsdale, Alan
   see Pelvic Floor Potential
Raphael
   see Romano
Rasputin, Gregory Yefimovich
Redgrove, Peter
   see Mass of the Holy Ghost
Reich, Wilhelm
Reuss, Theodor
   see Ordo Templi Orientis
Romano, Giulio
de Ropp, Robert S.
   see Chakras (Physiological), Gurdjieff
Rudolf of Habsburg
   see Shunamism
Rufus of Ephesus
   see Myrtle
Rumi, Jalal'al-Din
   see Sufism
Ruth (biblical)
   see Olfactory Delights
Saadawi, Nawal el
   see Clitoridectomy
Solomon
Santarakshita
   see Nyingmapa

Saraha
  see Mahasiddhas, Cannabis Sativa
Savaripa
  see Luipa, Mahasiddhas
Siddhartha Gautama
  see Buddhism
Shamzaran Badmaev
  see Gurdjieff
Shaw, Miranda
  see Ganachakra
Shenrab
  see Bön
Shintaro, Katsu
  see Matriyoni
Slinger, Penny
  see Asana, Pillow Books, Shankhini
  Nadi
Solmo, E.
  see Sarsaparilla
Steiner, Rudolf
  see Ordo Templi Orientis
Stockham, Alice Bunker
  see Karezza
Su-nü
Suskind, Patrick
  see Olfactory Delights
Swedenborg, Emanuel
  see Stygian Sexuality
Tao An
  see epigraph on page 155
Tenzin Gyatso
  see Dalai Lama
Tilopa
Trungpa, Chogyam
Ts'ai-nü
Tsongkapa
  see Gelupga
Unternährer, A.
  see quotation on page 99
Vairochana
Valerius
  see Valerians
Vatsyayana
  see Kama Sutra
Vaughan, Thomas

van der Velde, Theodoor
  see Ejaculation (female)
Vimalamitra
  see Nyingmapa
Vimalananda
Vimalashri
  see Niguma
Virupa
Whipple, Beverly
  see Grafenberg
Wilson, Colin
  see Fang-chung Shu, Reich
Wilson, Robert Anton
  see Breasts, Hedonic Engineering,
  LSD, Nizari Isma'ilis, Oysters,
  Sexual Imprinting
Woodroffe, Sir John George
  see Mahanirvana Tantra
Yellow Emperor
Yeshe Tsogyal
Yundon Dorje Bal
  see Dzogchen
Zoroaster/Zarathustra
  see Gnosticism
Zola, Emile
  see Olfactory Delights

INDEX 2: RELIGIOUS GROUPS, SECTS, AND SCHOOLS

Most entries in this index are concerned with groups, movements, branches, or schools—often part of a large religious system—in whose teachings the erotic, sexual element plays an important role. However, the encyclopedia also contains a number of short, general descriptions of major religious systems—entries meant to provide quick-reference background information.

Adamites
Aghora, Aghoris
Ali Ullaheeahs
  see Choli Marg

Amaurians
Bacchantes
Beni Udhri
Bogomiles
Bön
Buddhism
Chen-jen
Chöd
  see Machig Lapdron
Chu-lin Ch'i-hsien
Crazy Wisdom
Daisei Shokushu
Dakshinacara
Digambara
Dzogchen
Eleutherians
Familists
  see Free Spirit Movement
Fang-shih
Five Pecks of Rice Taoism
Fratres Roris Coctis
Free Spirit Movement
Gauda Sampradaya
Gelupga
Gnosticism
Great Brotherhood of God
Hashishins
  see Nizari Isma'ilis
Hinayana
Hinduism
Jaina
Ka'a
Kagyudpa
Kalamukha
Kanpatha Yogis
Kapalikas
Kerala Sampradaya
Khlysti
Kula
Lamdra
Lotophagi
Mahasiddhas
Mahayana
Maslub
Misracara

Mi-tsung

Nagna

Native American Church
  see Peyote

Nessereah
  see Choli Marg

Nine Vehicles

Nizari Isma'ilis

Nyingmapa

Obeah

Ordo Templi Orientis

Perfectionists
  see Free Spirit Movement, Noyes

Sabaras
  see Cannabis Sativa

Sabbatians

Sahaja, Sahajiya

Shaiva

Shakta

Shamanism

Shingon

Shinto

Skoptsi

Sufism

Tachikawa

Tantra

Tao-chiao

Taoism

Vajrayana

Valerians

Vamacara

Voodoo

Vratyas

Yellow Turban Society

Yezidi
  see Carte Blanche

Zen
  see Buddhism, Mahamudra, Tanden

Zhengyi-Huashan
  see Kwan Saihung

INDEX 3: WOMAN AS GODDESS, DEMONESS, AND CULTURAL HEROINE

Most entries in this index are concerned with lesser-known female deities in whose worship and ritual the erotic, sexual element and/or power of fertility plays an important role. In some instances, however, other deities are listed here if the related information can contribute, in the context of our pursuit, to our understanding. No discrimination is made between Great Goddesses, minor female deities such as *nymphs, and ancient deities made into demons by succeeding religious and political systems. All too often such discrimination is arbitrary and does not reflect the status of such a goddess in the originating culture. For some background information, see *Female Sexual Demons and *Yoni Worship.

Abtagigi

Acca Larentia

Adamu

Adya Shakti

Agrat Bat Mahalat

Al'Lat

Al'Menat
  see Al'Lat

Al'Uzza

Ama-no-Uzume

Amaterasu-o-mi-Kami

Anat

Anna Furrina

Aphrodite

Apsarasas

Ariadne

Artemis
  see Absinthe, Cordax, Ephesian
    Artemis, Virgin

Asherah

Ashtoreth

Astarte

Atargatis

Babylon

Basa Andere

Basholi
  see quotation on page 248

Baubo

Bebhionn

Benten
  see Benzai Tennyo

Benzai Tennyo

Chandali

Chao Mae Tuptim
  see Tap-tun

Charis

Charites

Chinnamasta

Circe

Cotytto

Cybele

Dakini

Demeter
  see Al'Lat, Baubo

Diana of Ephesus
  see Ephesian Artemis

Durga

Empusae

Eos

Erzuli

Female Sexual Demons

Flora

Fortuna Virilis

Freya

Gopis

Graces

Guheshvari

Hagar

Hathor

Hecate
  see Al'Lat

Inanna

Inari

Isis
  see Dismemberment, Incest, Nuit,
    Rose

Ishtar

Izanami

Jagad Yoni

Jaki

Kabbazah

Kali

Kamakhya

Kamala

Kameshvari

Kilili

Kore

   see Virgin, Al'Lat

Korrigan

Kuan-yin

Kumari

Kunthus

Kunti

Kwannon

   see Kuan-yin

Lakshmi

Lamia

Lasya

Libera

Lilith

Living Goddess

Maenads

Mahanagni

Matangi

Mathamma

   see Matangi

Mboze

Mylitta

Nairatmika

   see Tantric Visualization

Nuit

Nympheumene

Nymphs

Oduda

Oestre

   see Estrus

Parthenope

Parvati

Pasiphae

Peisinoe

Pertunda

Qadesh

Q're

   see Al'Lat

Radha

Rati

Sarasvati

Sati

   see Dismemberment, Guhesh-
     vari/2, Kamakhya Pitha, Pithas

Scarlet Woman

Shakti

Sheela-na-gig

Shekinah

Sodasi

Suryacandrasiddhi

Taleju

Tap-tun

Tara

Three Lady Immortals

Tlazolteotl

Tutinus

Uke-mochi-no-kami

Ushas

Vajraishvaridhatu

   see Tantric Visualization

Venus

Vesta

Vidya Devis

Virgin Mary

   see Circumcision (Female)/2

Yakshinis

Yellamma

Yogini

INDEX 4: MAN AS GOD, DEMON, AND CULTURAL HERO

Most entries in this index are concerned with deities in whose worship and connected ritual the erotic, sexual element and/or power of fertility plays an important role. In some instances, however, other deities are listed here if the related information can contribute, in the context of our pursuit, to our general knowledge and understanding.

Adam

   see Lilith

Aghora

Attis

Baal

   see Anat

Bacchus

Bhairava

   see Bhairavi

Buddha

   see Mahacinacara-sara Tantra

Conisalus

Cupid

Dionysus

Eros

Frey

Ganesh

Geb

Hermes

   see Ritual Promiscuity

Hercules

   see Giant of Cerne Abbas

Izanagi

Kama

Konsei Myojin

Liber

   see Libera

Mars

Min

Musuri-Kami

Ophion

Osiris

Pan

Phanes

   see Ithyphallic

Priapus

Ra

   see Obelisk

Sarutahiko

Satyr

Shiva

Tutinus

U

   see Semen

Zeus

INDEX 5: APHRODISIACS

For a general introduction to these substances that do, and/or are thought to, enhance the erotic/sexual experience, see the entries *Aphrodisiacs and *Anaphrodisiacs. For a more detailed view check several or all of the following entries.

INDEX 5.I: HERBS, FRUIT, FLOWERS, CACTI, AND MUSHROOMS

Amanita Muscaria
Basil
Beans and Bean Flowers
Cannabis Sativa
Cardamom Seeds
Cinnamon
Cocoa
    see Alkaloids
Coconut
Fennel
Garlic
Ginger
Ginseng
Lilac
Licorice
Lotus
Magic Mushrooms
Muira Puama
Myrrh
Nutmeg
Onion
Peyote
Pomegranate
Psilocybe Mexicana
Pumpkin
Quebracho
Sarsaparilla
Sassafras
Sesame
Truffles
Violet

Wheat Germ
Wormwood
    see Absinthe
Yohimbe

INDEX 5.2: SCENTS
SEE ALSO *OLFACTORY DELIGHTS, *SCENT, *SCENT AURA

Amber
Ambergris
Civet
Frankincense
    see Olibanum
Indole
Jasmine
Lilac
Musk
Myrrh
Olibanum
Patchouli
Pheromones
Saffron
Sandalwood
Spikenard
Tantric Perfumes
Tuberose
Violet
Virgin
    see Shunamism

INDEX 5.3: ANIMAL/HUMAN SUBSTANCES

Ambergris
Anchovies
    see Oysters
Bee Pollen
    see Honey
Bird Nest Soup
Brain
    see Brain (as Aphrodisiac)
Camel
Cantharidin
Caviar
Civet

Eggs
Escargots
Fat
    see Camel
Fruit de Mer
Fugu
Honey
Menstrual Fluid
Milk
    see Camel, Goat
Musk
Opium
Oysters
Perspiration
Prawn
    see Fruit de Mer
Rhino Horn
Saliva
Semen
Spanish Fly
Testicles (Animal)
Witches' Milk

INDEX 5.4: OTHER PREPARATIONS AND SUBSTANCES

Absinthe
Alcohol
Alkaloids
Angel Water
Arginine
Bhang
Charas
Choline
    see Vitamins/B
Cocaine
Ecstasy (Drug)
Halvah
    see Sesame
Indole
LSD
Madya
Majoon
MDA
MDMA

Mescaline
Muscarine
Paan
Pantothenic Acid
  see Vitamins/B
Psilocybin
Quinine
Theobromine
  see Cocoa
Vitamins
Wheat Germ
Wine
  see Madya
Witches' Ointment
Zinc

INDEX 6: FESTIVALS, RITUALS, AND CUSTOMS

A few entries provide a general introduction to such social customs, festivals, and rituals related to and/or
including erotic/sexual activity;
see for example *Fertility Festivals,
*Carte Blanche, *Orgy, *Puritanical
Fanaticism, and *Circumcision. Entries
in this list sometimes overlap with those
in index 7.

Alphaism
Anthropophagy
Asag
Bedroom Arts
Bhairavi Chakra
  see Ganachakra
Black Mass
Buddha-face
Carnival
Carte Blanche
Castration
Chakra/2
Chakra Puja
Chastity
Children of God
Choli Marg

Circumcision
Clitoridectomy
Cordax
Dance
Defloration
Deva Chakra
Dianism
Diksha
Dismemberment
Divya Chakra
Drugs and Sexual Initiation
Dual Cultivation
Dutiyaga
Encratism
Fertility Festivals and Rites
Floralia
Fraternal Polyandry
Ganachakra
Group Marriage
Harem
Hieros Gamos
Ho-ch'i
Holi
  see Gopis
Incest
Infibulation
Initiation
Jitendriya
Jus Primae Noctis
Kagura
Kala Chakra
Karma Mudra
Kimali
Kuladravya
  see Kula
Kula Puja
Kularcana
Kumari Puja
Liberalia
Mahamudra
Mahavrata
Matriarchy
Matriliny
Matrilocality
Matsuri

Mitakuku
Monogamy
Moon Magic
Mudra
Mukharata
Mysteries of Eluesis
Nasamonian Marriage Custom
Nuptial Continence
Orgy
Orphic Mysteries
Otiv Bombari
Panchamakara
Papish
Parakiya
Phallic Worship
Polyandry
Polygamy
Polygyny
Prayoga
Puberty Rites
Puja
Qodosh
Raja Chakra
Ritual Promiscuity
Sacred Prostitution
Sadomasochism
Saturnalia
Serial Polygamy/Polyandry
Sexual Magick
Sexual Hospitality
Sexual Imprinting
Soma Sacrifice
Sororal Polygyny
Sperm Magic
Spiritual Marriage
Stri Puja
Stygian Sexuality
Subincision
Tantric Visualization
Tattva Chakra
  see Ganachakra
Teachings of Sister Niguma
Thesmophoria
  see Chastity
Vira Chakra

Virginity
Web of Heaven and Earth
Yab-Yum
Yoni Puja
Yonitattva
Yoni Worship

INDEX 7: RITUAL PROMISCUITY AND SACRED PROSTITUTION

Both *Ritual Promiscuity and *Sacred Prostitution are entries in the encyclopedia that provide a general introduction to the rites, cults, and deities listed here. See also *Fertility Festivals and *Secular Prostitution. Entries in this list sometimes overlap with those in index 6.

INDEX 8: EROTIC SYMBOLOGY IN NATURE, ART, AND LANGUAGE

Plants, fruits, and natural features such as caves and mountains have been seen—often determined by their shape—as being associated with one or another deity and have thus been declared sacred by our ancestors. In the case of animals, it was their observed behavior or extraordinary fertility that usually led to such status.

Aside from such natural symbols, most cultures have developed a "sacred art" and appropriate wo/man-made symbols to express one or more of their beliefs and/or to symbolize, more or less abstractly, the male and female energies, powers, and physical attributes.

Another aspect of "symbolism" can be found in language, where expressions and code words are often "double-talk," hiding an erotic, sexual meaning below the surface of the apparently obvious. This topic can best be approached from the entries *Lingam Terminology, *Secret Language, *Yoni Symbology, and *Yoni Terminology.

Coco-de-mer
Cock
Color Symbolism
    see Gold, Light, Red, Violet
Conch Shell
Cowrie Shell
Cross
    see Ankh
Crux Ansata
    see Ankh
Dolmen
Dorje
Dove
Ekalinga
Elephant
Ema
Fig
    see Apricot
Flowers
Gauripatta
Ghanta
Goat
Goose
    see Priapus
Hermaphrodite
Ithyphallic
Jagad Yoni
Jagan Nath Temple
Kala Chakra
Khajuraho
Konarak
K'un
Lily
Ling/Ling-chih
Lingam
Lotophagi
Lotus
Lung-hu
Mandorle
Megaliths
Menhir
Myrtle
Obelisk
Om Mani Padme Hum
Oysters

Padma
Peach
Pomegranate
Purple Mushroom Peak
Qoph
Rose
Sacred Stones
Scallop
Serpent
Spark of Life
Sri Yantra
Sumerian Writing
Syzygy
Tortoise
Triangle
Trilinga
Union of Skillful Means and
    Profound Cognition
Vajra
Yoni
Yonilinga
Yonilinga Mudra
Yonimandra
Yoni Mudra
Yoni Terminology
Yonitirtha
Yoniyugma

INDEX 9: TECHNIQUES, EXERCISES, AND POSITIONS

Along with discussions of literature, rituals, festivals, and general customs concerning eros and sexuality, throughout this encyclopedia there are a number of entries that constitute actual exercises and/or techniques for individuals and/or heterosexual couples/groups. Such entries are listed here.

Under index 9.1 the reader will find a listing of all entries concerned specifically with the male's *retention of semen. Those entries are not included in the general list that follows.

Algolagnia
Ampallang
Amplexus Reservatus
Ars Amandi
Asana
Auparishtaka
Bandha
Bhaga Asana
Breath
Chakra Asana
Chamber of Six Combinations
Clouds and Rain
Coitus a Tergo
Coitus Interruptus
Coitus Prolangatus
Coitus Sublimatus
Congressus Subtilis
Conspiration
Cunnilingus
Diksha
Divya Siddhis
Dual Cultivation
Ecstasy (Psychosomatic)
Erotocomatose Lucidity
Fang-chung Shu
Fellatio
Female Superior Position
Fusion of K'an and Li
Hedonic Engineering
Ho-ch'i
Hsing-ch'i
Huan-ch'ing Pu-nao
Imsak
Insufflation
Intrajaculation
Japa
    see Mantra
Jitendriya
Karezza
Karma Mudra
Khechari Mudra
Kimali
Kriya Nishpatti
Kumari Puja
Lata Asana

Mahamudra

Maithuna

Maithuna Viparita

Mantra

Marmas

Missionary Position

Mitakuku

Mors Osculi

Mudra

Mukharata

Necrophilia

Nyasa

Pelvic Floor Potential

Penile Peristalsis

Pillow Books

Pompoir

Pranayama

Prayoga

Ratipasa
  see Rati

Sadhana

Samghataka

Secret Dalliance

Sexual Imprinting

Sexual Magick

Shunamism

Siddhi

Smarnanam

Sparsha Diksha

Spectrophilia

Sperm Magic

Sympneumata

T'ai-hsi

Tantric Visualization

Teachings of Sister Niguma

Urdhvaretas

Venus Aversa

Venus Observa

Viparita Rati

Yab-Yum

Yogini Chakra

Yoni Asana

Yonitattva

Zap-lam

INDEX 9.I: SEMEN RETENTION— CONCEPTS, TECHNIQUES, AND EXERCISES

Acclivity

Amplexus Reservatus

Beni Udhri

Breath Retention

Ching

Ching-tao

Coitus Prolongatus

Coitus Reservatus

Coitus Sublimatus

Encratism

Free Spirit Movement

Imsak

Male Continence

Ojas

Oli Techniques

Retention of Semen

Vajroli Mudra

INDEX 10: BODY, BRAIN, AND GENITALS

Abdomen
  see Tanden

Adrenal Glands

Alembic

Bartholin Glands
  see Yoni Topography/12

Blood

Brain

Breasts

Breath

Cerebellum
  see Brain

Cerebrum
  see Brain

Ching-tao

Chromosome
  see X Chromosome, XX, XY, Y
  Chromosome

Cinnabar Cave
  see Cinnabar/2

Clitoral Crown
  see Yoni Topography/6

Clitoral Hood
  see Yoni Topography/5

Clitoris
  see Lingam Topography/11, Yoni
  Topography/11

Constrictor Cunnus
  see Yoni Topography/25

Corpus Cavernosum

Corpus Luteum

Corpus Spongiosum

Cortex
  see Brain

Cowper's Glands
  see Lingam Topography/12

Defloration

Eight Valleys

Ejaculation

Emerald Pillow

Endocrine System

Epididymis
  see Lingam Topography/22

Foreskin
  see Lingam Topography/5

Gate of Jewels

Glans Clitoridis
  see Yoni Topography/6

Glans Penis
  see Lingam Topography/7

Golden Flower

Golden Tongue

Gonads

G-Spot

Hsueh

Hui-jin

Hymen
  see Yoni Topography/10

Hypothalamus
  see Brain

Ischiocavernosus Muscle

Ithyphallic

Jade Fountain

Jewel Enclosure

Kakira

Kalas

Kassapu

Labiaesthetics

Labia Majora
    see Yoni Topography/3

Labia Minora
    see Yoni Topography/4

Limbic System
    see Brain

Ling

Lingam

Lingam Terminology

Lingam Topography

Lips

Lowndes Crown
    see Lowndes-Sevely

Madanahatra

Marmas

Matriyoni

Mehana

Mons Marsianus
    see Lingam Topography/2

Mons Veneris
    see Yoni Topography/2

Nao

Nose

Palace of Yin

Paraurethral Glands and Ducts

PC Muscles
    see Pelvic Floor Potential

Pelvic Floor Potential

Penile Glans
    see Lingam Topography/7

Penis
    see Lingam Topography/9

Perineal Muscles
    see Lingam Topography/25

Perineal Sponge
    see Yoni Topography/23

Perineum

Phallus
    see Lingam

Pineal Gland

Pituitary Gland

Prostatic Glands
    see Lingam Topography/15, Yoni
    Topography/15

Pubis
    see Lingam Topography/1, Yoni
    Topography/1

Pudenda

Purnacandra

Red Lotus Peak

Scent Glands

Scrotum
    see Lingam Topography/3

Seat of Pleasure

Seminal Vesicles
    see Lingam Topography/21

Spermatic Duct
    see Lingam Topography/19

Sternum
    see Tanden

Testes
    see Lingam Topography/20

Thalamus
    see Brain

Thyroid
    see Endocrine System, Garlic

Twin Peaks

Urethra
    see Lingam Topography/13, Yoni
    Topography/13

Urethral Sponge
    see Yoni Topography/14

Uterus
    see Yoni Topography/18

Vagina
    see Yoni Topography/9

Vaginal Glans
    see Yoni Topography/7

Vestibule
    see Yoni Topography/8

Vulva

Vulvovaginal Glands
    see Yoni Topography/12

X Chromosome

XX

XY

Y Chromosome

Yin Nang

Yoni

Yonishtana

Yoni Terminology

Yoni Topography

INDEX II: FOUNTAINS OF LOVE—HUMAN BIOCHEMICAL/SEXUAL FLUIDS AND SECRETIONS

This index lists—insofar as it is possible to distinguish—all entries concerned with fluid secretions from glands, lips, breasts, and genitals.

On the other hand, index 12 is concerned with the electromagnetic aspect of our topic: the currents and fields of energies that make up the human subtle body and that are involved or activated during erotic and sexual interplay.

Adamu

Aliphatic Acids

Alpha Androsterol

Amplexus Reservatus

Amrita

Androgens

Androstenone

Aqua Vitae

Arginine

Bindu

Blood

Blood of the Red Lion

Chamber of Six Combinations

Chandali

Ching

Cholesterol

Cinnabar/2

Clouds and Rain

Conisalus

Corpus Luteum

Coral Essence
    see Menstrual Fluid

Dew of Ecstasy
Dual Cultivation
Ecstasy (Psychosomatic)
Ejaculation
Elixir
Elixir Rubeus
Estradiol
Estrogen(s)
Estrone
Female Love Juices
FSH
Garlic
Golden Elixir
Golodbhava
Grail
Inner Alchemy
Inner Yang
Jade Fluid
Jade Fountain Liquid
Kalas
Kama Salila
Kan-lu
Khapushpa
Kundodbhava
LH
Licorice
Lingam Topography
Liquor Vitae
Lotus Nectar
Medicina Catholica
Medicine of the Three Peaks
Mehana
Menstrual Fluid
Menstrual/Ovarian Cycle
Menstruum of the Gluten
Moon Flower Medicine
Moon Magic
Nei-tan
Niddah
Nure
Oestrogen
   see Estrogen
Oil of Halcali
   see Vaughan, Thomas
Oli

Orgasm
Palace of Yin
Peach Juice of Immortality
Penile Peristalsis
Perspiration
Pheromones
Prima Materia
Progesterone
Progestogens
Prostatic Glands
Purnacandra
Rajas
Red Cinnabar
   see Cinnabar/2
Retention of Semen
Ros
Sa
Saliva
Scent Glands
Semen
Sexual Biochemistry and
   Electromagnetism
Soma
Sperm Magic
Sri Vidya
Sukra
Tantric Visualization
Testosterone
Tide of Yin
Vajroli Mudra
Virya
Visristi
White Lead
White Metal
White Snow
White Wine
Wine of the Navel
Wine of the Sacrament
Witches' Milk
Yin Essence
Yoni Puja
Yonipushpa
Yonitattva
Yoni Topography

INDEX 12: EROTIC FIELDS OF ENERGY—HUMAN ELECTROMAGNETIC/SUBTLE ENERGY FIELDS, CENTERS, AND CHANNELS

This index lists entries concerned with the electromagnetic currents and fields of energies of the human subtle body that are involved in erotic and sexual activity.

By contrast, index 11 is concerned with human biochemical fluid secretions.

Ajna Chakra
Anahata Chakra
Aura Seminalis
Bindu
Blue-Green Halo
Brahma Nadi
Brahma Aperture
Chakra/1
Ch'i
Ching
Chin-tan
Chitrini/2
Dragon Veins
Fivefold Light
Golden Elixir
Golden Flower
Gynergy
Halo
   see Blue-Green Halo
Heavenly Fire of the Heart
Hsueh
Hun
Kala
Kanda
Khuai
Kundalini
Light
Liquor Vitae
Mahasukha
Metu
Moon Magic
Muktatriveni

Nadis
Najika Siddhi
Ni-huan
Ojas
Oli
Ophidian Current
P'o
Ros
Sa
Seminal Viscosity
Sexual Biochemistry and
 Electromagnetism
Shakti
Shankhini Nadi
Shen
Shunamism
Sushumna
Tanden
Tan-t'ien
Tantric Visualization
Three Gates
Urdhvaretas
Yang
Yin

INDEX 13: PRIMARY LITERATURE—SACRED AND/OR EROTIC

Ananga Ranga
Arabian Nights
 see Burton
Ars Amatoria
Bardo Thödol
Bible
Carmina Priapea
Chinnamasta Stotra
 see quotation on page 32
Devi Bhagavata
 see quotation on page 17
Golden Ass
 see Ass
Goraksa Vijaya
 see Shankhini Nadi
Guhyasamaja Tantra

Guptasadhana Tantra
Guyhya-Siddhi
 see Retention of Semen
Hathayoga Pradipika
 see Ordo Templi Orientis
Hevajra Tantra
Huang-t'ing Ching
I Ching
Inner Tantras
Jnanasiddhi
Kalachakra Tantra
Kalika Purana
Kalivilasi Tantra
Kamakala Vilasa
 see Bindu
Kamakhya Tantra
Kama Sutra
Kargling Zhikro
Kathavatthu Tantra
Kaulavali Nirnaya Tantra
Khadro Nyingthig
Koka Shastra
Kubjika Tantra
Kulacudamani Tantra
 see quotation on page 192
Kularnava Tantra
Kumari Tantra
Kuttni Mahatmyam
 see quotations on pages 103 and 169
Longchen Nyingthig
Mahabharata
 see Durga
Mahacinacara-sara Tantra
Mahanirvana Tantra
Matrikabheda Tantra
 see Menstrual Fluid
Nei P'ien
 see Ko Hung
Niddah
Nila Tantra
Niruttara Tantra
Parananda Sutra
Parasurama-kalpa Sutra
Perfumed Garden

Pillow Books
Prajnaparamhita Sutra
 see Dzogchen
Prajnopaya-viniscaya Siddhi
Prapancasara Tantra
 see Succubus
Puranas
Ratirahasya
 see Koka Shastra
Rigpa Nngosprod
Rudrayamala
 see Vira
Samayacara Tantra
 see Menstrual Fluid
Samhita(s)
Secret of the Golden Flower
 see Golden Flower
Sepher ha Zohar
 see Zohar
Seven Treasures
Shiva Purana
 see quotation on page 121
Shiva Samhita
 see Ordo Templi Orientis, Yoni Mudra
Sodasi Tantra
 see Sodasi
Song of Songs
Subhasita-samgraha
 see quotation on page 250
Sutra
Talmud
Tantraraja Tantra
 see Yantra
Tantra/2
Tao-te Ching
 see Tao
Terma
Turin Papyrus
Upanishads
Vajragatha
Veda(s)
Vijnana Bhairava
 see quotation on page 224
Vima Nyingthig

Yellow Book
Yogini Tantra
Yoni Tantra
Zohar

INDEX 16: NUMBERS AND NUMEROLOGY

Numerology as a form of divination and/or a method of psychological analysis has no especially erotic information to provide. Nevertheless, for those involved in numerological research we have prepared this small special index that provides access to all entries of numerological interest.

INDEX 17: THE AMERICAS— NORTH, MESO, AND SOUTH

INDEX 18: ARAB AFRICA, EGYPT, PERSIA, AND THE NEAR EAST
SEE INDEX 20 FOR BLACK AFRICA

Carte Blanche
Castration
Choli Marg
Cinnamon
Circumcision
Clitoridectomy
Cybele
Defloration
Diana
    see Ephesian Artemis
Dismemberment
Dove
Eggs
Fellatio
Female Superior Position
Geb
Ghazye
Gnosticism
Hagar
Hashishins
    see Nizari Isma'ilis
Harem
Hathor
Horae
Houris
Inanna
Incest
Infibulation
Ishtar
Ishtarishtu
Isis
    see Dismemberment, Incest,
    Nuit, Rose
Jaki
Ka'bah
Kabbazah
Kilili
Lilith
Lingam Terminology
Lotus
Majoon
Maslub
Matriarchy
Matrilocality
Menstrual Fluid

Metu
Min
Mylitta
Nasamonian Marriage Custom
Niddah
Nizari Isma'ilis
Nu-gug
Nuit
Obelisk
Olfactory Delights
Osiris
Perfumed Garden
Phallic Worship
Polygamy
Pomegranate
Qadesh
Qadeshtu
Qoph
Ritual Promiscuity
Sa
Sabbatians
Sacred Prostitution
Sacred Stones
Shekinah
Shunamism
Silent Prayer
Sodom and Gomorrah
Soma
Sororal Polygyny
Spanish Fly
Sufism
Sumerian Writing
Yoni Magic
Yoni Terminology
Yoni Worship

INDEX 19: AUSTRALIA AND OCEANIA (INCLUDING TRIBAL INDONESIAN AND FILIPINO PEOPLES)

Algolagnia
Ampallang
Androstenone
Anthropophagy

Borneo
    see Ampallang
Bridal Prostitution
Circumcision
Coconut
Cowrie Shell
Dayak
    see Ampallang
Defloration
Ejaculation (Female)
Kimali
Missionary Position
Mitakuku
Moon Magic
Nuptial Continence
Orgy
Otiv Bombari
Papish
Polyandry
Polygamy
Ritual Promiscuity
Serpent
Sexual Hospitality
Sororal Polygyny
Sperm Magic
Subincision

INDEX 20: BLACK AFRICA
SEE INDEX 18 FOR ISLAMIC AFRICA

Androstenone
Anthropophagy
Bridal Prostitution
Circumcision
Civet
Clitoridectomy
Cowrie Shell
Defloration
Dismemberment
Drugs and Sexual Initiation
Erzuli
Incest
Labiaesthetics
Mboze
Nuptial Continence

Obeah
Oduda
Polyandry
Polygamy
Ritual Promiscuity
Sacred Prostitution
Semen
Sororal Polygyny
Spiritual Marriage
Voodoo
Yohimbe
Yoni Magic

INDEX 21: EUROPE

Acca Larentia
Acclivity
Adamites
Alchemy
Amanita Muscaria
Amaureans
Ambergris
Amplexus Reservatus
Androstenone
Angel Water
Anna Furrina
Anthropophagy
Aphrodisiacs
Aphrodite
Apple
Ariadne
Ars Amandi
Ars Amatori
Artemis
    see Ephesian Artemis
Asag
Ass
Atargatis
Aura Seminalis
Bacchantes
Bacchus
Basa Andere
Basil
Baubo
Beans and Bean Flowers

Bebhionn
Bible
Black Mass
Blood
Blue-Green Halo
Bogomiles
Bridal Prostitution
Cannabis Sativa
Carmina Priapea
Carnival
Castration
Charis
Charites
Circe
Circumcision
Cocaine
Conisalus
Conspiration
Cordax
Cotytto
Courtesans
Cowrie Shell
Cromlech
Crowley, Aleister
Cupid
Cybele
Defloration
Diana
    see Ephesian Artemis
Dionysus
Dolmen
Dove
Drugs and Sexual Initiation
Ecstasy (Psychosomatic)
Eleutherians
Elixir Rubeus
Eggs
Empusae
Eos
Ephesian Artemis
Eros
Erotocomatose Lucidity
Escargots
Female Archetypes
Female Superior Position

Flora
Floralia
Fortuna Virilis
Fratres Roris Coctis
Free Spirit Movement
Frey
Freya
Fruit de Mer
Giant of Cerne Abbas
Gnosticism
Group Marriage
Hermaphrodite
Hetaerae
Incest
Inner Alchemy
Inquisition
Jus Primae Noctis
Khlysti
Korrigan
Lamia
Liber
Libera
Liberalia
Lingam Terminology
Liquor Vitae
Lotophagi
Maenads
Medicina Catholica
Megaliths
Menhir
Moon Magic
Mors Justi
Mors Osculi
Mysteries of Eleusis
Numerology
Nuptial Continence
Nymphs
Nympheumene
Nymphomania
Ophidian Current
Ophion
Orgy
Orphic Mysteries
Pan
Parthenope

Yin
Yin Essence
Yin Nang
Yoni Terminology
Yü Yen
    see Dual Cultivation

INDEX 23: INDIA AND PAKISTAN

Adya Shaki
Aghora
Alchemy
Algolagnia
Amanita Muscaria
Amarnatha Cave
Amrita
Ananda
Androstenone
Apsarasas
Argha
Asana
Assam
Auparishtaka
Banalinga
Bandha
Bengal
Bhaga
Bhaga Asana
Bhairavi
Bhairavi Chakra
Bhakti Yoga
Bhang
Bhoga
Bhogi
Bhukti
Bija
Bindu
Brahma Aperture
Brahma Nadi
Buddhism
Cannabis Sativa
Cardamom Seeds
Carte Blanche
Chakra
Chakra Asana

Chakra Puja
Chakresvara
Chandali
Charas
Chinnamasta
Chitrini
Choli Marg
Circumcision (Female)
Coco-de-mer
Coconut
Cowrie Shell
Dakini
Dakshinacara
Defloration
Deva Chakra
Devadasis
Digambara
Diksha
Dismemberment
Divya
Divya Chakra
Divya Shakti
Divya Siddhis
Dove
Drugs and Sexual Initiation
Durga
Duti
Dutiyaga
Ekalinga
Elephant
Fellatio
Female Archetypes
Fivefold Light
Ganachakra
Ganesh
Gauda Sampradaya
Gauripatta
Gayatri Mantra
Golodbhava
Gopis
Guheshvari
Hardhakala
Hastini
Hinayana
Hinduism

Incest
Indrabhuti
Jagad Yoni
Jaina
Jatakusuma
Jitendriya
Jivashakti
Kakira
Kala
Kala Chakra
Kalamukha
Kalas
Kali
Kalika purana
Kama
Kamakhya
Kamala
Kamamarga
Kama Salila
Kama Sutra
Kameshvari
Kanda
Kanphata Yogis
Kapalikas
Karana
Kashmir
Kassapu
Kerala
Kerala Sampradaya
Khajuraho
Khechari Mudra
Konorak
Kriya Nishpatti
Kula
Kulacara
Kuladravya
    see Kula
Kula Puja
Kularcana
Kumari
Kumari Puja
Kundalini
Kundodbhava
Lata Asana
Leela

INDEX 24: JAPAN

Fugu
Gate of Jewels
Inari
Izanami and Izanagi
Kagura
Kami
Ki
  see Ch'i
Konsei Mojin
Kuan-yin
Lotus
Matriyoni
Matsuri
Musuri-Kami
Nure
Phallic Worship
Pillow Books
Sarutahiko
Shingon
Shinto
Spark of Life
Tachikawa
Tanden
Tara
Tokudashi
Tortoise
Uke-mochi-no-kami
Yoni Magic
Yoni Worship

INDEX 25: HIMALAYAN COUNTRIES (TIBET, BHUTAN, MONGOLIA, NEPAL, LADAKH, UDDIYANA)

Anthropophagy
Bardo
Bardo Thödol
Brahma Aperture
Bön
Buddhism
Circumcision
Cock

Conch Shell
Crazy Wisdom
Dakini
Dalai Lama
Dismemberment
Dorje
Drukpa Kunleg
Duti
Dzogchen
Fraternal Polyandry
Garab Dorje
Gelugpa
Ghanta
Group Marriage
Guheshvari
Guhyasamaja Tantra
Gurdjieff
Hevajra Tantra
Incest
Indrabhuti
Inner Tantras
Jagan Nath Temple
Jigme Lingpa
Jnanasiddhi
Ka'a
Kagyudpa
Kala Chakra
Kalachakra Tantra
Kargling Zhikhro
Khadro Nyingthig
Lasya
Living Goddess
Longchen Nyingthig
Longchenpa
Luipa
Machig Lapdron
Mahamudra
Mahasiddhas
Mahasukha
Mahayana
Mandala
Mantra
Matriyoni
Menstrual Fluid

Mudra
Musk
Nalanda University
Naropa
Niguma
Nine Vehicles
Nyingmapa
Oddiyana
  see Uddiyana
Om Mani Padme Hum
Outer Tantras
Padmasambhava
Pillow Books
Pithas
Polyandry
Polygamy
Puja
Rigpa Nngosprod
Sambara
Seven Treasures
Shamanism
Sororal Polygyny
Suryacandrasiddhi
Taleju
Tantra
Tantric Visualization
Tara
Teachings of Sister Niguma
Terma
Terton
Thangka
Tilopa
Uddiyana
Union of Skillful Means and
  Profound Cognition
Vairochana
Vajra
Vajragatha
Vajrayana
Vajra Yogini
Vima Nyingthig
Yab-Yum
Yantra
Yeshe Tsogyal

Yogini

Yoni Magic

Yoni Worship

Zap-lam

Zhang Zhung

INDEX 26: OTHER FAR EASTERN COUNTRIES (INCLUDING BURMA, KAMPUCHEA [CAMBODIA], INDONESIA, MALAYSIA, AND THAILAND)

Ampallang

Androstenone

Anthropophagy

Assam

Bird Nest Soup

Buddhism

Carte Blanche

Circumcision

Civet

Clitoridectomy

Defloration

Infibulation

Hinayana

Palad Khik
    see Tap-tun

Phallic Worship

Rati

Ritual Promiscuity

Sororal Polygyny

Tap-tun

Tuberose

INDEX 27: CHINESE DYNASTIES

The chronology below is based on James Ware, *Alchemy, Medicine, and Religion in the China of* A.D. *320* (1966, pp. 387 ff.).

Hsia (the prehistoric north)

Shang (or Yin)	c. 1100 B.C.E.
Chou	722–481 B.C.E.
Warring States	403–250 B.C.E.
Ch'in	221–207 B.C.E.
1st Han	202 B.C.E.–8 C.E.
Wang Mang	9–23 C.E.
2nd Han	23–220 C.E.

Three Kingdoms:

We	220–265 (north China)
Shu	221–263 (west China)
Wu	222–280 (south China)
Chin	265–316 (all China)
Northern Wei (Turkish occupied)	399–581
Sui	581–618 (reunited China)
T'ang	618–907
Five Dynasties and Ten Kingdoms	907–979
Sung	960–1126
Yuan (Mongol rule)	1279–1368
Ming (Chinese)	1368–1644
Ch'ing (Manchu)	1644–1912
Chinese Republic	1912–1949
Hong Kong (GB)	1898–1997
People's Republic	1949–
Taiwan/Formosa	1949–

INDEX 28: INTERNET RESOURCES

The Internet, often decried as a dangerous repository of both fascism and pornography, is in fact a huge and continuously growing database for all aspects of personal interest and research. Apart from containing well-known resources such as the *Encyclopedia Brittanica* and others, the World Wide Web is also overflowing with the graphics, texts, and thoughts of thousands of commercial, educational, and private institutions—as well as with the doubts, dreams, questions, visions, and specialized knowledge of individuals.

The topics of religion, sacred sexuality, spiritual sex, Tantra, and related pursuits are well represented with a great variety of websites, some of which are listed here. Although the World Wide Web contains many more sites related to sexuality and Tantra, sacred or not, the following addresses (URLs) have been selected by the author for either quality, depth, and variety of information or—sometimes—simply for being unique. Most of the sites given here have their own pages with links for additional sources.

The URLs presented here have been checked for accuracy as this book goes to press, yet URLs sometimes do change;

just as people move house. If you encounter such an instance, use one of the many available search engines (my personal favorite is MetaCrawler (see p. 293) to (re-)locate what you are searching for.

I. Sacred Sexuality and Tantra Sites
Sacred Sexuality

The classical, yet still growing, collection of pages by Catherine Yronwode; covers many aspects of sacred sexuality and Tantra, with a special focus on what is known as *Karezza. Includes many links and concise discussions of available publications.

URL: http://www.luckymojo.com/sacredsex.html

Hindu Tantrik Home Page

A most extensive collection of translations (from Sanskrit originals) and information on Hindu Tantra created by Michael Magee and associates. Contains a large, concise glossary of key terms.

URL: http://www.hubcom.com/tantric/

Tantra Works

A vast site by author and art collector Nik Douglas, contains texts and images of major deities and concepts; includes a beautifully designed puzzle/game centered on the "secret of the mind;" that is, the deity Yamantaka. In addition, the site is used to sell original Tantric statues and, naturally, to promote the author's many publications. Contains an extensive list of links and a large bibliography.

URL: http://www.tantraworks.com
URL for the puzzle: http://www.tantraworks.com/yama.html

Church of Tantra

Site with a number of articles concerning aspects of Tantra (a movement that has never been a "church") and sacred sexuality, as well as a commercial venture announcing workshops and selling books and video films.

URL: http://www.tantra.org/

Sacred Sex Tantra Ring

A navigation center giving access to several Tantric sites with varying content and of differing quality.

URL: http://nav.webring.com/cgibin/
navcgi?ring=sacredsex;index

Popular Tantra

Various articles by well-known, contemporary teachers of so-called New Tantra: Robert Frey, Charles and Caroline Muir, David Ramsdale.

URL: http://www.dorje.com:8080/netstuff/dharma/
buddha10/

International Journal of Tantric Studies

Coming from Harvard University, this is a journal of scholarly publications. Although often all too intellectually oriented, it is also refreshingly free of all New Age inspired Fairy Tale Tantra espoused in some of the above sites.

URL: http://www.asiatica.org/publications/ijts/

2. Tibetan Buddhism, Lineages, and Schools
Diamond Way Dharma Glossary

A small glossary with mostly Sanskrit terms and very short explanations. Brought online by a New York based Karma Kagyu Center, with links to *Kagyu and other *Karmapa related lineage information and a calendar of events.

URL: http://www.fusebox.com/diamondway/glossary/
glossary.html

Buddhism according to the Contemporary Gelugpa

Part of the official site of the Government of Tibet in Exile, this is a detailed and interesting source on how the present *Gelugpa Order views the development of Buddhism in Tibet (and in exile). Most interestingly, they now include *Bön in the so-called Five Principal Traditions.

URL: http://www.tibet.com/Buddhism/index.html

Nyingma in the West

Although not representative of all *Nyingma organizations in the West, Nyingma.org is an influential and large organization under the guidance of Tarthang Tulku. The organization has a huge monastery in the U.S., is involved in a number of large translation and publication projects (under the name Dharma Publishing), and is represented in several other countries as well. The site, which has several photographs of the monastery, shows what Vajrayana looks like in the USA rather than actually "in the West."

URL: http://www.nyingma.org/

Nyingma Palyul Lineage

A specific tradition within the *Nyingma originates with the Palyul Monastery in Tibet and its associated teachers.

URL: http://www.palyul.org/lineage.html

Aro gTer Lineage

Very small and relatively unknown, this is an especially interesting *Nyingma-rooted lineage because it is mainly oriented toward female masters and adepts (though it seems to be headed—at least temporarily—by a male.) Nevertheless, this website has information and images concerning women such as *Yeshe Tsogyal, Jomo Memo, *Machig Lapdron, and others. Well worth a visit.

URL: http://www.aroter.org/

Karma Kagyu Lineage

Both in content and design, this is probably the best of several online efforts to introduce the development of this lineage and its major teachers.

URL: http://www.karmapa.com/lineage/

Union of Bliss and Emptiness

Although the title is used poetically rather than covering the site's actual content, the main interface and many of the pages are beautifully designed—with love for the subject. The overall contents are of varied importance and value, and the best part is the so-called Chöd Club, dedicated to the teachings, texts, rituals, and symbology of *Chöd as practiced within the Gelugpa tradition. Great graphics!

URL: http://www.personal.umich.edu/~miyash/

Dzogchen Foundation

A site introducing *Dzogchen, "Buddhism for the West" according to author Lama Surya Das, including biographies and photographs of important Tibetan teachers/lamas. Naturally, the site also promotes the various publications and lectures by Surya Das.

URL: http://www.dzogchen.org/

Tibetan Buddhism WWW Links

A very complete and regularly updated collection of links.

URL: http://www.buddhanet.net/l_tibet.htm

3. ART, IMAGES
The Art of Tibet

One of the most beautiful sites featuring a great number of thangkas and mandalas brought together from a variety of collections. Although there is a well-designed search function for finding specific deities or persons featured in the images, a truly excellent way to visit the site is to follow the 24 page essay by Chris Wilkinson. Although time consuming, his "Transmission of Enlightenment," illustrated with most of the images in the collection, is perhaps the best online introduction to the topic at hand.

URL: http://www.tibetart.com/

Asian Art

A large and varied website containing galleries and exhibitions centering on Tibet, Bhutan, Nepal and other Himalayan countries and their arts; offers a collection of fine art books for sale.

URL: http://www.asianart.com/

Statues of the Divine

A commercial catalogue of divine and mythical images from East and West. The illustrations are beautiful.

URL: http://jblstatue.com/sacredsex.html

Padmasambhava Buddhist Center

Although commercially oriented toward selling their prints, this is a well-done and interesting resource with more than one hundred thangkas of *Padmasambhava, *Vajrayogini, and many other heroes and deities of Tibetan Tantra; thumbnails as well as large versions.

URL: http://pbc.interliant.com/pbc/pbc.nsf/gallery?OpenView

4. MISCELLANEOUS
Alchemy

A vast virtual library and collection of texts and images concerning Arabic, Chinese, European, and Indian alchemy; including an extensive glossary of alchemical processes, many essays and images.

URL: http://www.levity.com/alchemy/

Tantric Vampire Yoga

Containing more detailed information than given in this encyclopedia, this is the site where you find the complete theory and practice of what I have called *Shakti Asana. Here you can read what the "Sacred Slut" (her own choice of words) has to say about it.

URL: http://members.aol.com/ideajdevi/

Marriage Systems

Only a small part of a larger anthropology site, this is an interesting, though not complete, discussion of various forms of *marriage in a variety of cultures.

URL: http://www.umanitoba.ca/faculties/arts/anthropology/tutor/marriage/index.html

Museum of Menstruation

Not a "museum" in the modern sense of the term (i.e., image oriented), but more in the ancient Greek sense of temple and library.

URL: http://www.mum.org/index.html

Sheer Phallacy

Whereas most people would deny that phallic worship is still practiced today, this site—filled with phallic images—shows just how deeply the symbol of masculinity has penetrated our culture. Freud would have loved it but never saw it; you can!

URL: http://members.tripod.com/~sheerphallacy/

Do What Thou Wilt

For every human activity there is a divine precedence to be found in one or another myth of some ancient culture. At this website, the people behind "Summum.org" make the point that *masturbation has an ancient Egyptian (male) deity and thus, a ritual dimension.

URL: http://www.summum.org/mastur.htm

Omphalos of the Goddess

An article by Bob Trubshaw and part of his great "At the Edge Archive," deals with the *Ka'bah and also with the author of this encyclopedia.

URL: http://www.gmtnet.co.uk/indigo/edge/blstone.htm

The Church of the Most High Goddess

A variety of essays and musings by Sabrina Aset (high priestess) concerning religion and sexuality; includes titles such as "The Theology of Sex" and "A Brief History of Religious Sex."

URL: http://www.goddess.org/home.html

Liber Conjunctus

"Being an Essay on Sex and Sex Magick, by Frater Nigris" An essay comparing "normal" human sexuality with magically oriented sexuality. Interesting yet also typical for the thinking in *Crowley inspired circles.

URL: http://www.hollyfeld.org/heaven/Avidyana/Huntun/conjunctus.fn

5. BIBLIOGRAPHIES

If you cannot find a certain publication in the pages mentioned above, nor at the large online bookstores, the following addresses will help you locate the work you're looking for:

The complete Library of Congress catalogue
URL: http://lcweb.loc.gov/catalog/

The Asian Studies Bookstores
URL: http://www.ciolek.com/wwwVLPages/AsiaPages/VLBookshops.html

A large Buddhist bibliography sorted by title rather than author
URL: http://members.aol.com/Wangchuk/fullbib.html

6. SEARCH THE NET

MetaCrawler is a search engine "smarter" than most others in the sense that it makes use of several other such "robots," then presents you with the combined results.

URL: http://www.metacrawler.com/

Bibliography

Adler, Margot. *Drawing Down the Moon*. New York: Viking Press, 1979. Reprint. Boston: Beacon Press, 1986.

Allegro, John M. *The Dead Sea Scrolls*. Harmondsworth, England: Penguin Books, 1956. Rev. ed. 1958, 1959.

———. *The Sacred Mushroom and the Cross*. New York: Doubleday, 1970. Rev. ed. London: Sphere Books, 1973.

———. *The End of a Road*. New York: Dial Press, 1972.

———. *Lost Gods*. London: Michael Joseph, 1977. Reprint. London: Sphere Books, 1978.

Allione, Tsultrim. *Women of Wisdom*. London and Boston: Routledge & Kegan Paul, 1984. Reprint. London and Boston: Arkana, 1986.

Andersen, Jørgen. *The Witch on the Wall: Medieval Erotic Sculpture in the British Isles*. Copenhagen: Rosenkilde & Bagger, 1977.

Andritzky, Walter. "Die heilsame Macht der Riesensteine." Freiburg, Germany: *Esotera* No. 6, 1989.

Atkinson, Clarissa W., Constance H. Buchanon, and Margaret R. Miles, eds. *Immaculate and Powerful: The Female in Sacred Image and Social Reality*. Boston: Beacon Press, 1985.

Avalon, Arthur. *See* Woodroffe, Sir John.

Banerjee, S. C. *A Brief History of Tantra Literature*. Calcutta: Naya Prokash, 1988.

Barks, C., trans. *Stallion on a Frozen Lake: Love Songs of the Sixth Dalai Lama*. Athens, Ga.: Maypop, 1994.

Beane, W. C. *Myth, Cult, and Symbols in Sakta Hinduism*. Leiden: Brill, 1977.

Beckwith, Martha. *Hawaiian Mythology*. Honolulu: University of Hawaii Press, 1940. Reprint 1976.

Begg, Ean. *The Cult of the Black Virgin*. London and Boston: Arkana, 1985.

Bernbaum, Edwin. *Der Weg nach Shambhala* (The Way to Shambhala). Freiburg, Germany: Hermann Bauer, 1995.

Beurdeley, Michel, ed., and Kristofer Schipper. *The Clouds and the Rain: The Art of Love in China*. London: Hammond, Hammond & Co., 1969.

Bhattacharya, Brajamadhava. *The World of Tantra*. New Delhi: Manoharlal, 1988.

Bhattacharyya, Bhaskar, Nik Douglas, and Penny Slinger. *The Path of the Mystic Lover: Baul Songs of Passion and Ecstasy*. Rochester, Vt.: Inner Traditions International, 1993.

Bhattacharyya, Narendra Nath. *The Indian Mother Goddess*. 2nd rev. ed. New Delhi: Manohar, 1977.

Binkley, Sue. "A Timekeeping Enzyme in the Pineal Gland." *Scientific American,* April 1979.

Bleibtreu, John. *The Parable of the Beast*. New York: Collier MacMillan, 1968.

Blofeld, John. *Taoist Mysteries and Magic*. Boulder, Colo.: Shambhala, 1982.

Bornoff, Nicholas. *Pink Samurai: An Erotic Exploration of Japanese Society*. London: Grafton, 1992.

Bose, D. N., and Hiralal Haldar. *Tantras: Their Philosophy and Occult Secrets*. Calcutta: Firma KLM Private Ltd., 1981.

Bose, Manindra Mohan. *The Post-Caitanya Sahajia Cult of Bengal*. Delhi: Gian, 1986.

Brauen, Martin. *Feste in Ladakh*. Graz, Austria: Akademische Verlagsanstalt, 1980.

Briffault, Robert. *The Mothers: A Study of the Origins of Sentiments and Institutions*. 3 vols. London: Allen & Unwin, 1927.

Brown, Norman O. *Love's Body*. New York: Vintage Books, 1966.

———. The Resurrection of the Body. In *The Highest State of Consciousness,* edited by John Warren White. New York: Anchor Books, 1972.

Burman, Edward. *The Assassins: Holy Killers of Islam*. Wellingborough, England: Aquarian Press, 1987.

Burton, Sir Richard, and F. F. Arbuthnot, trans. *The Illustrated Kama Sutra, Ananga Ranga, Perfumed Garden*. Rochester, Vt.: Park Street Press, 1991.

Buruma, Ian. *Behind the Mask*. New York: New American Library, 1985.

Califia, Pat. *Public Sex: The Culture of Radical Sex*. Pittsburgh, Pa.: Cleis Press, 1994.

———. *Sensuous Magic: A Guide for Adventurous Couples*. New York: Masquerade Books, 1996.

———. *Sex Changes: The Politics of Transgenderism*. Pittsburgh, Pa.: Cleis Press, 1997.

Cameron, Averill, and Amelie Kuhrt. *Images of Women in Antiquity*. London: Croom Helm, 1983.

Campbell, Joseph. *The Hero with a Thousand Faces*. Rev. ed. New York: Bollingen Foundation, 1968.

———. *The Masks of God: Oriental Mythology*. New York: Penguin, 1970.

———. *The Masks of God: Primitive Mythology*. New York: Penguin, 1970.

———. *The Masks of God: Occidental Mythology*. New York: Penguin, 1976.

Campbell, June. *Traveller in Space: In Search of Female Identity in Tibetan Buddhism*. New York: Braziller, 1996.

Camphausen, Rufus C. "De heilige steen in Mekka." ("The Holy Stone of Mecca.") Amsterdam: *Bres* No. 139, 1989.

———. *The Divine Library*. Rochester, Vt.: Inner Traditions International, 1992.

———. *The Yoni: Sacred Symbol of Female Creative Power*. Rochester, Vt.: Inner Traditions International, 1996.

———. *Return of the Tribal: A Celebration of Body Adornment*. Rochester, Vt.: Park Street Press, 1997.

Chakraberti, Chandra. *A Cultural History of the Hindus*. Calcutta: V. Krishna Brothers, 1945.

Chang, Garma C. C. *The Six Yogas of Naropa and Teachings on Mahamudra*. Ithaca, N.Y.: Snow Lion, 1977.

Chang, Jolan. *The Tao of Love and Sex: The Ancient Chinese Way to Ecstasy*. London: Wildwood House, 1977.

Chesi, Gert. *Voodoo: Africa's Secret Power*. Worgl, Austria: Perlinger, 1980.

———. *Susanne Wenger: Ein Leben mit den Gottern*. Worgl, Austria: Perlinger, 1980. Reprint 1984.

Chia, Mantak, and Maneewan Chia. *Healing Love through the Tao: Cultivating Female Sexual Energy*. Huntington, N.Y.: Healing Tao Books, 1986.

Chia, Mantak, and Michael Winn. *Taoist Secrets of Love: Cultivating Male Sexual Energy*. New York: Aurora Press, 1984.

Cleary, Thomas, ed. and trans. *Immortal Sisters: Secrets of Taoist Women*. Boston and London: Shambhala, 1989.

———, trans. *The Inner Teachings of Taoism* by Chang Po-Tuan, commentary by Liu I-ming. Boston and London: Shambhala, 1986.

———, trans. *The Taoist I Ching*. Boston and London: Shambhala, 1986.

Coburn, Thomas B. *Devi Mahatmya*. Delhi: Motilal, 1984.

Cohn, Norman Rufus Colin. *The Pursuit of the Millennium*. London: Secker & Warburg, 1957.

Collin, Rodney. *The Theory of Celestial Influence: Man, the Universe, and Cosmic Mystery*. London: Watkins, 1954. Reprint. 1980.

Comfort, Alex, trans. *The Koka Shastra*. London: Allen & Unwin, 1964. Reprint. 1982.

Cooper, J. C. *Chinese Alchemy*. Wellingborough, England: Aquarian Press, 1984.

Cornelissen, J. F. L. M. *Pater en Papoea*. Kampden, The Netherlands: Kok, 1988.

Cozort, Daniel. *Highest Yoga Tantra: Esoteric Buddhism of Tibet*. Ithaca, N.Y.: Snow Lion, 1986.

Crowley, Aleister. The Psychology of Hashish. In *Hasheesh: The Herb Dangerous*, ed. by David Hoye. San Francisco: Level Press, 1974. *See also* Regardie, 1974/1982.

———. *The Book of the Law*. London: O.T.O., 1938. Reprint. York Beach, Maine: Weiser, 1976.

———. Liber E and Liber O. London: *The Equinox*, Vol. 1, No. 1, 1909. Reprint. York Beach, Maine: Weiser, 1976.

———. *Tao Teh King*. London: O.T.O., 1947. Reprint. York Beach, Maine: Weiser, 1976.

———. *777 and Other Qabalistic Writings of Aleister Crowley*. York Beach, Maine: Weiser, 1973. Reprint. 1977.

———. *The Book of Lies*. London: 1913. Rev. ed. 1952. Reprint. York Beach, Maine: Weiser, 1978.

———. *De Arte Magica*. N.p.: Sure Fire, 1988.

Crul, Helen, ed. *Uit naam van de godin*. Bloemendaal, The Netherlands: Gottmer, 1985.

Csaky, Mick, ed. *How Does It Feel?* London: Thames & Hudson, 1979.

Culling, Louis T. *Sex Magick*. St. Paul, Minn.: Llewellyn, 1971. Reprint. 1988. Dalai Lama. *See* Mullin, Glenn.

Danielou, Alain, trans. *The Complete Kama Sutra*. Rochester, Vt.: Inner Traditions International, 1994.

———. *The Phallus: Sacred Symbol of Male Creative Power*. Rochester, Vt.: Inner Traditions International, 1995.

Dawood, N. J., trans. *The Koran*. Harmondsworth, England: Penguin Books, 1974. Reprint. 1988.

de Barandiaran, Jose M. *Mitologia Vasca*. Madrid, 1960.

Delaney, Janice, Mary Jane Lupton, and Emily Toth. *The Curse: A Cultural History of Menstruation*. New York: Dutton, 1976. Rev. ed. Urbana, Ill.: University of Illinois Press, 1988.

Deng, Ming-Dao. *The Wandering Taoist*. San Francisco: Harper & Row, 1986.

Deren, Maya. *The Voodoo Gods*. London: Thames & Hudson, 1953. Reprint. Frogmore, England: Granada, 1975.

de Ropp, Robert S. *Sex Energy: The Sexual Force in Man and Animals*. New York: Delacorte Press, 1969.

de Rosa, Peter. *Vicars of Christ: The Dark Side of the Papacy*. New York: Bantam Books, 1988. London: Corgi Books, 1989.

Devereux, Georges. *Baubo: Die mythische Vulva*. Frankfurt am Main: Syndikat, 1981.

Devi, Kamala. *The Eastern Way of Love: Tantric Sex and Erotic Mysticism*. New York: Simon & Schuster, 1985.

de Vries, Theun. *Ketters*. Amsterdam: Querido, 1982.

Dierichs, Angelika. Erotik in der Kunst Griechenlands. Jona, Switzerland: *Antike Welt*, Vol. 19, No. 608, 1988.

Dorje, Rinjing, Addison G. Smith, and Hans G. Behr, trans. *Tantra Yoga*. New Delhi: Manoharlal, 1971.

———. *Tales of Uncle Tompa*. Basel: Sphinx Verlag, 1983.

Douglas, Nik. *Spiritual Sex: Secrets of Tantra from the Ice Age to the New Millennium*. New York: Pocket Books, 1997.

———. *Tantra Yoga*. New Delhi: Munshiram Manoharlal, 1971.

Douglas, Nik, and Penny Slinger. *Mountain Ecstasy*. Paris: Dragon's Dream, 1978.

———. *Sexual Secrets: The Alchemy of Ecstasy*. Rochester, Vt.: Destiny Books, 1979.

———. *The Pillow Book*. Rochester, Vt.: Destiny Books, 1981. Reprint. 1984.

———. *The Erotic Sentiment: In the Paintings of India and Nepal*. Rochester, Vt.: Park Street Press, 1989.

———. *The Erotic Sentiment: In the Paintings of China and Japan*. Rochester, Vt.: Park Street Press, 1990.

Dowman, Keith. *Sky Dancer: The Secret Life and Songs of Lady Yeshe Tsogyal*. London: Routledge & Kegan Paul, 1984.

———. *Masters of Mahamudra: Songs and Histories of the Eighty-four Buddhist Siddhas*. Albany, N.Y.: State University of New York Press, 1985.

———, trans. *The Divine Madman: The Sublime Life and Songs of Drukpa Kunleg*. Clearlake, Calif.: Dawn Horse Press, 1983.

———, trans. *Masters of Enchantment: The Lives and Legends of the Mahasiddhas*. Rochester, Vt.: Inner Traditions International, 1988.

Dowson, John. *A Classical Dictionary of Hindu Mythology and Religion: Geography, History and Literature*. New Delhi: Heritage Publishers, 1992.

Drury, Nevill. *The Shaman and the Magician: Journey between the Worlds*. London: Routledge & Kegan Paul, 1982.

———. *Vision Quest: A Personal Journey through Magic and Shamanism*. Calmington, England: Prism Press, 1984.

Duca, Lo. *A History of Eroticism*. Paris: Pauvert, 1961.

———. *Das Tabu in der Erotik*. Basel: Desch Verlag, 1967.

———. *Die Erotik im Fernen Osten*. Wiesbaden, Germany: VMA Verlag, 1967. Dvorak, Josef. *Satanismus: Geschichte und Gegenwart*. Frankfurt am Main: Eichborn, 1989.

Dworkin, Andrea. *Intercourse*. New York: Free Press, 1987. Ebin, Victoria. *The Body Decorated*. London: Thames & Hudson, 1979.

Edwardes, Allen. *Das Juwel im Lotus* (The Jewel in the Lotus). Munich: Heyne, 1980.

Eisler, Riane. *The Chalice and the Blade: Our History, Our Future*. New York: HarperCollins, 1988.

———. *Sacred Pleasure: Sex, Myth and the Politics of the Body—New Paths to Power and Love*. San Francisco: HarperCollins, 1995.

Eliade, Mircea. *Yoga: Immortality and Freedom*. New York: Princeton University Press, 1958. 2nd corr. ed. 1969. Reprint. 1973.

Emde Boas, Coen van. *Geschiedenis van de seksuele normen*. Antwerp: Nederlandse Boekhandel, 1985. *The Encyclopedia of Eastern Philosophy and Religion: Buddhism, Taoism, Zen, Hinduism*. Boston: Shambhala, 1989.

Evans-Wentz, W. Y. *The Tibetan Book of the Dead*. New York: Oxford University Press, 1927. Reprint. 1960.

Evola, Julius. *The Metaphysics of Sex*. London and The Hague: East-West Publications, 1983.

Fabricius, Johannes. *Alchemy: Medieval Alchemists and Their Royal Art*. Wellingborough, England: Aquarian Press, 1989.

Farquharar, J. N. *An Outline of the Religious Literature of India*. Delhi: Motilal, 1920.

Fend, Werner. *Die Nestrauber von Borneo*. Mainz, Germany: TV feature ZDF, September 29, 1989.

Feng, Gia-fu, and Jane English, trans. *Tao-te Ching*. New York: Knopf, 1974.

Feuerstein, Georg, ed. *Enlightened Sexuality: Essays on Body-Positive Spirituality*. Freedom, Calif.: Crossing Press, 1989.

———. *Sacred Sexuality: Living the Vision of the Erotic Spirit*. Los Angeles: Tarcher, 1992.

Fisher, Helen. *Anatomy of Love: A Natural History of Mating, Marriage, and Why We Stray*. New York: Fawcett Columbine, 1994.

Foucault, Michel. *The History of Sexuality*. New York: Random House, 1978. Reprint. Harmondsworth, England: Penguin Books, 1987.

Frank, Karlhans. *Der Phallus: Von der Magie der Mannlichkeit im Wandel der Epochen*. Frankfurt am Main: Eichborn Verlag, 1989.

Frazer, James G. *The Golden Bough: A Study in Magic and Religion*. London: Macmillan, 1922, Abr. ed. 1987.

Fremantle, Francesca, and Chogyam Trungpa. *The Tibetan Book of the Dead: The Great Liberation through Hearing in the Bardo*. Boulder and London: Shambhala, 1975.

French, Marilyn. *Beyond Power: On Women, Men and Morals*. New York: Ballantine Books, 1985.

Frischauer, Paul. *Knaur's Sittengeschichte der Welt*. Munich: Droemer Knaur, 1968.

Furst, Peter T. *Flesh of the Gods*. New York: Praeger, 1972. Reprint. 1974.

Gadon, Elinor W. *The Once and Future Goddess: A Symbol for Our Time*. Wellingborough, England: Aquarian Press, 1990.

Gang, Peter, trans. and ed. *Das Tantra der Verborgenen Vereinigung (Guhyasamaja Tantra)*. Munich: Diederichs Verlag, 1988.

Garrison, Omar. *Tantra, The Yoga of Sex*. New York: Julian Press, 1964.

Gelb, Norman. *The Irresistible Impulse*. New York: Paddington Press, 1979.

Genders, Roy. *A History of Scent*. London: Hamish Hamilton, 1972.

George, Christopher S., trans. *The Candamaharosana Tantra, Chapters 1–8: A Critical Edition and English Translation*. American Oriental Series, No. 56. New Haven: American Oriental Society, 1974.

Georgieva, Ivanichka. *Bulgarian Mythology*. Sofia: Svyat Publishers, 1985.

Gilbert, N., and C. J. Wysocki. "The Smell Survey Results." *National Geographic*, October 1987.

Gimbutas, Marija. *Goddesses and Gods of Old Europe 6500–3500 B.C.* London: Thames & Hudson, 1982. Reprint. 1984.

———. *The Language of the Goddess*. San Francisco: Harper & Row, 1989.

Giroux, Leo. *The Rishi*. London: Collins, 1985.

Gleason, Judith. *Oya: In Praise of the Goddess*. Boston and London: Shambhala, 1987.

Goblet d'Alviella, Compte Eugene. *The Mysteries of Eleusis*. Wellingborough, England: Aquarian Press, 1981.

Gold, Cybele, and E. J. Gold. *Beyond Sex*. Crestline, Calif.: Institute for the Development of the Harmonious Human Being, 1980.

Gonzalez-Wippler, Migene. *A Kabbalah for the Modern World: How God Created the Universe*. New York: Julian Press, 1974. Reprint. Bantam Books. 1977.

Grant, Kenneth. *The Magical Revival*. London: F. Muller, 1972.

———. *Aleister Crowley and the Hidden God*. London: F. Muller, 1973.

Graves, Robert, and Raphael Patai. *Hebrew Myths*. New York: Doubleday, 1964.

Guellouz, Ezzedine. *Pilgrimage to Mecca*. New York: McGraw-Hill, 1966. Reprint. Boston: Salem House, 1982.

Guenther, Herbert V. *From Reductionism to Creativity: rDzogs-chen and the New Sciences of Mind*. Boston: Shambhala, 1989.

———. *The Tantric View of Life*. Boston and London: Shambhala, 1972.

Hall, Manly Palmer. *The Secret Teachings of All Ages*. San Francisco: private printing, 1928. Los Angeles: Philosophical Research Society, 1962. Reprint. 1975.

Hall, Nor. *The Moon and the Virgin*. New York: Harper & Row, 1980. Reprint. 1984.

Hancarville (alias Pierre-François Hugues). *Denkmaler des Geheimkults der romischen Damen*. France: 1784. Germany: 1906. Reprint. Dortmund, Germany: Harenberg, 1979.

Harding, Esther. *Woman's Mysteries: Ancient and Modern*. New York: Jung Foundation, 1955. Reprint. London: Rider, 1982.

Harrison, William. *Burton and Speke*. New York: St. Martin's Press, 1982. Republished as *Mountains of the Moon*. New York: Ballantine Books, 1989.

Hawley, John Stratton, and Donna Marie Wulff. *The Divine Consort: Radha and the Goddesses of India*. Delhi: Motilal, 1982. Reprint. Boston: Beacon Press, 1986.

Heissig, Walther. *The Religions of Mongolia*. London: Routledge & Kegan Paul, 1970.

Henricks, Robert G. *Lao-Tzu: Te-Tao Ching. A New Translation Based on the Recently Discovered Ma-wang-tui Texts*. New York: Ballantine, 1989. *Het complete parfumhandboek*. Alphen, The Netherlands: Samson, 1987. *High Times Encyclopedia of Recreational Drugs*. New York: Stonehill Publishing Company, 1978.

Hillman, James, ed. *Facing the Gods*. Dallas, Tex.: Spring Publications, 1984.

Hite, Shere. *The Hite Report on Male Sexuality*. New York: Knopf, 1981. Reprint. New York: Ballantine Books, 1983.

———. *Women and Love: The New Hite Report: A Cultural Revolution in Progress*. New York: Knopf, 1981. Reprint. New York: St. Martin's Press, 1983.

Hollander, Eugen. *Askulap und Venus: Eine Kultur und Sittengschichte im Spiegel des Arztes*. Berlin: Propylaen Verlag, 1928. *Holy Bible: Old and New Testaments in the Authorized King James Version*. London: Harwin Press, 1976.

Hope, Murry. *Psychology of Ritual*. Shaftesbury, England: Element Books, 1988.

Housden, Roger. *Travels through Sacred India*. Wellingborough, England: Thorsons, 1996.

Howley, John. *Holy Places and Temples of India*. New Delhi: Rekha Printing, 1996.

Hoye, David, ed. *Hasheesh: The Herb Dangerous*. San Francisco: Level Press, 1974.

Hunt, Lynn. *The Invention of Pornography: Obscenity and the Origins of Modernity, 1500–1800*. New York: Zone Books, 1996.

Hutchins, Loraine, and Lani Kaahumanu, eds. *Bi Any Other Name: Bisexual People Speak Out*. Boston: Alyson Publications, 1991.

Huxley, Francis. *The Way of the Sacred*. New York: Doubleday, 1974. Reprint. New York: Dell, 1976.

Huysmans, Joris Karl. *La-Bas* (Down There), trans. by Keene Wallace. New York: Dover Publications, 1978.

———. *A Rebours* (Against Nature), trans. by Margaret Mauldon. New York: Oxford University Press, 1998.

Hyatt, Christopher S., L. M. DuQuette, and G. Ford. *Taboo: The Psychopathology of Sex and Religion*. Scottsdale, Ariz.: New Falcon, 1991.

Jigme Lingpa. *Nying Tig or The Innermost Essence* (Tib., *Klong-chen sNying-Thig*). Amsterdam: DeKosmos, 1984.

———. *The Dzogchen Innermost Essence Preliminary Practice* (Tib., *Klong-chen sNying-Thig sngon-'gro*). 2nd rev. ed. Dharamsala: Library of Tibetan Works and Archives, 1989.

Johari, Harish. *Tools for Tantra*. Rochester, Vt.: Destiny Books, 1986.

Kale, Arvind, and Shanta Kale. *Tantra: The Secret Power of Sex*. Bombay: Jaico, 1976. Reprint. 1987.

Kalweit, Holger. *Dreamtime and Inner Space*. Boston and London: Shambhala, 1988.

Keilhauer, Anneliese, and Peter Keilhauer. *Die Bildsprache des Hinduismus: Die indische Gotterwelt und ihre Symbolik*. Cologne: DuMont Buchverlag, 1983. Reprint. 1986.

Kersenboom-Story, Saskia C. *Nityasumangali: Devadasi Tradition in South India*: Delhi: Motilal, 1987.

Keuls, Eva C. *The Reign of the Phallus: Sexual Politics in Athens*. New York: Harper & Row, 1985.

King, Francis. *Ritual Magic in England*. London: New English Library, 1970.

———. *Magic: The Western Tradition*. London: Thames & Hudson, 1975.

———. *Tantra for Westerners: A Practical Guide to the Way of Action*. Wellingborough, England: Aquarian Press, 1986.

———, ed. *The Secret Rituals of the O.T.O.* London: C. W. Daniel, 1974.

Kinsley, David. *Hindu Goddesses: Visions of the Divine Feminine*. Delhi: Motilal, 1985. Reprint. 1987.

———. *The Goddesses' Mirror: Visions of the Divine from East and West*. Albany, N.Y.: State University of New York Press, 1989.

———. *Tantric Visions of the Divine Feminine: The Ten Mahavidyas*. Berkeley: University of California Press, 1997.

Kiss-Maerth, Oscar. *The Beginning Was the End*. London: Michael Joseph, 1973.

Kitzinger, Sheila.. *Woman's Experience of Sex*. New York: Putnam, 1983.

Knight, Chris. *Blood Relations: Menstruation and the Origins of Culture*. New Haven, Conn.: Yale University Press, 1991.

Knight, Richard Payne. *A Discourse on the Worship of Priapus* (1786). *See* Knight and Wright: *Sexual Symbolism*.

Knight, Richard Payne, and Thomas Wright. *Sexual Symbolism: A History of Phallic Worship*. New York: Julian Press, 1962.

Koltuv, Barbara Black. *The Book of Lilith*. York Beach, Maine: Nicolas Hays, 1986.

Kooij, K. R. van. *Worship of the Goddess according to the Kalikapurana*. Leiden, The Netherlands: E. J. Brill, 1972.

Kotzwinkle, William. *Jewel of the Moon*. New York: Putnam, 1985.

Kramer, Samuel Noah. *Mythologies of the Ancient World*. New York: Doubleday, 1961. *See also* Wolkstein and Kramer.

Kripal, Jeffrey. *Kali's Child: The Mystical and the Erotic in the Life and Teachings of Ramakrishna*. Chicago: University of Chicago Press, 1995.

Ladas, Alice Kahn, Beverly Whipple, and John D. Perry. *The G-Spot and Other Recent Discoveries about Human Sexuality*. New York: Holt, Rinehart, and Winston, 1982.

Laing, Ronald D. *The Facts of Life: An Essay in Feelings, Fact and Fantasy*. New York: Pantheon Books, 1976. Reprint. New York: Ballantine Books, 1978.

Lander, Louise. *Images of Bleeding*. New York: Orlando, 1988.

Leary, Timothy. *Psychedelic Prayers*. New York: Lyle Stuart, 1972.

———. *What Does Woman Want?* Beverly Hills, Calif.: 88-Books, 1976.

———. *Exopsychology*. Culver City, Calif.: Peace Press, 1977.

———. *Neuropolitics*. Culver City, Calif.: Peace Press, 1977.

———. *The Game of Life*. Culver City, Calif.: Peace Press, 1979.

———. *The Politics of Ecstasy*. Berkeley: Ronin Publishing, 1990.

Leese, Kurt. *Die Mutter als religioses Symbol* (The Mother as Religious Symbol). Stuttgart, Germany: JCB Mohr, 1934.

Leeuwen, Apolonia van. "Lilith: Symbool van de verstoten vrouw." In *Uit naam van de godin*, ed. by Helen Crul. Bloemendaal, The Netherlands: Gottmer, 1985.

———. *Vrouwen over vrouw-zijn*. Amsterdam: Bres Boek, 1989.

Lesser, Michael. *Nutrition and Vitamin Therapy*. New York: Grove Press, 1980.

Lessing, F. D., and L. A. Wayman. *Buddhist Tantras: Light on Indo-Tibetan Esotericism*. Delhi: Motilal, 1990.

Leuba, James H. *The Psychology of Religious Mysticism*. London and Boston: Routledge & Kegan Paul, 1929. Reprint. 1972.

Levi, Howard S., and Akira Ishihara. *The Tao of Sex*. Tokyo: Shibundo, 1968. 3rd rev. ed. Lower Lake, Calif.: Integral Publishing, 1989.

Lhalungpa, L. P., trans. *Mahamudra: Quintessence of Mind and Meditation*. Boston: Shambhala, 1986.

Lilly, John Cunningham. *Programming and Metaprogramming in the Human Biocomputer: Theory and Experiments*. New York: Julian Press, 1968. 2nd rev. ed. 1972.

———. *Simulations of God*. New York: Simon & Schuster, 1975. Reprint. New York: Bantam Books, 1976.

Lilly, John Cunningham, and Antonietta Lilly. *The Dyadic Cyclone*. New York. Simon & Schuster, 1976.

Longchenpa. *You Are the Eyes of the World,* trans. by K. Lippman and M. Peterson. Novato, Calif.: Lotsawa, 1987.

Loth, Heinrich. *Die Frau im alten Afrika*. Leipzig, Germany: Edition Leipzig, 1986.

Lowndes-Sevely, Josephine. *Eve's Secrets: A Revolutionary Perspective on Human Sexuality*. London: Collins, 1987. Reprint. 1989.

Lubell, Winifred Milius. *The Metamorphosis of Baubo: Myths of Woman's Sexual Energy*. Nashville: Vanderbilt University Press, 1994.

Maccoby, Hyam. *The Sacred Executioner*. London: Thames & Hudson, 1982.

McGowan, Charlotte. *Ceremonial Fertility Sites in Southern California*. San Diego: San Diego Museum Papers, No. 14, 1982. Reprinted 1991.

Maddock, Kenneth. *Australian Aborigines: A Portrait of their Society*. Harmondsworth, England: Penguin Books, 1982.

Maffesoli, Michel. *The Shadow of Dionysos: A Contribution to the Sociology of the Orgy*. New York: SUNY, 1993.

Majupuria, Indra. *Nepalese Women*. Kathmandu: M. Devi, 1982.

Majupuria, Trilok Chandra, and Indra Majupuria. *Erotic Themes of Nepal*. Madhoganj, India: S. Devi, 1986.

Malinowski, Bronislaw. *The Sexual Life of Savages*. London: Routledge & Kegan Paul, 1929. Reprint. Boston: Beacon Press, 1987.

Marglin, Frederique Apffel. "Female Sexuality in the Hindu World." In *Immaculate and Powerful: The Female in Sacred Image and Social Reality*, ed. by Clarissa W. Atkinson, et al. Boston: Beacon Press, 1985.

———. *Wives of the God-King: The Rituals of the Devadasis of Puri*. Delhi and New York: Oxford University Press, 1985.

———. "Types of Sexual Union and Their Implicit Meanings." In *The Divine Consort: Radha and the Goddesses of India*, by John Stratton Hawley and Donna Marie Wulff. Delhi: Motilal, 1982. Reprint. Boston: Beacon Press, 1986.

Markale, Jean. *Women of the Celts*. Rochester, Vt.: Inner Traditions International, 1986. Marschall, Wolfgang. *Der Berg des Herrn der Erde*.

Munich: Deutscher Taschenbuch Verlag, 1976. Masters, Robert. *The Goddess Sekhmet*. New York: Amity House, 1988.

Matthews, Caitlin, and Colin Matthews. *The Western Way: A Practical Guide to the Western Mystery Tradition*. Vol. 2, *The Hermetic Tradition*. London and Boston: Arkana, 1986.

Maury, L. F. A. *Croyances et Légendes du moyen-age*. Paris, 1896. Quoted in *The Mothers: A Study of the Origins of Sentiments and Institutions,* by Robert Briffault. Vol. 3. London: Allen & Unwin, 1927.

Mbiti, John S. *African Religions and Philosophy*. Oxford: Heinemann, 1974.

Metzger, Deena. "Re-Vamping the World." In *Enlightened Sexuality: Essays on Body-Positive Spirituality,* ed. by Georg Feurstein. Freedom, Calif.: Crossing Press, 1989.

Meuleman, G. Een alternatieve Paasviering. Amsterdam: *Bres* No.147, 1991.

Monaghan, Patricia. *Women in Myth and Legend*. London: Junction Books, 1981.

Monick, Eugene Arthur. *Phallos: Sacred Image of the Masculine*. Toronto: Inner City Books, 1987.

Monroe, Robert A. *Journeys Out of the Body*. Souvenir Press, 1972.

Mookerjee, Ajit. *Tantra Art*. Basel: Ravi Kumar, 1967.

———. *Tantra Asana: A Way to Self-Realization*. Basel: Ravi Kumar, 1971.

———. *Kundalini*. London: Thames & Hudson, 1982.

———. *Ritual Art of India*. London: Thames & Hudson, 1985.

———. *Kali: The Feminine Force*. Rochester, Vt.: Destiny Books, 1988.

Mookerjee, Ajit, and Madhu Khanna. *The Tantric Way: Art, Science, Ritual*. London: Thames & Hudson, 1977.

Mordell, Phineas. *Sefer Yetzirah*. Philadelphia, Pa.: *Jewish Quarterly Review*, 1914. Reprint. York Beach, Maine: Weiser, 1975.

Mullin, Glenn, trans. and ed. *Selected Works of the Dalai Lama II: The Tantric Yogas of Sister Niguma*. Ithaca, N.Y.: Snow Lion, 1985.

Mumford, John. *Ecstasy through Tantra*. St. Paul, Minn.: Llewellyn, 1988.

Muses, C. A. *Esoteric Teachings of the Tibetan Tantra*. York Beach, Maine: Weiser, 1982.

Nagaswamy, R. *Tantric Cult of South India*. Delhi: Agam Kala Prakashan, 1982.

Nagle, C. A. *Magical Charms, Potions and Secrets for Love*. Minneapolis, Minn.: Marlar Publishing, 1972.

Narain, L. A., and Aditya Arya. *Khajuraho: Temples of Ecstasy*. New Delhi: Lustre, 1986.

Nathan, Peter. *The Nervous System*. Oxford and New York: Oxford University Press, 1989.

Nebesky-Wojkowitz, Rene de. *Oracles and Demons of Tibet*. Kathmandu, Nepal: Tiwari, 1993.

Nelli, Rene. "Op zoek naar een nieuwe sexuele moraal." Amsterdam: *Bres* No. 7, 1967.

Neumann, Erich. *The Great Mother: An Analysis of the Archetype*. New York: Bollingen Foundation, 1955. Reprint. London and Boston: Routledge & Kegal Paul, 1963.

Ngorchen Konchog Lhundrub. *The Beautiful Ornament of the Three Visions*. Ithaca, N.Y.: Snow Lion, 1991.

Nilsson, Lennart. *Behold Man: A Photographic Journey of Discovery inside the Body*. Boston: Little, Brown, 1974.

Nissim, Rina. *Natural Healing in Gynecology: A Manual for Women*. New York and London: Pandora Press, 1986.

Norbu, Namkhai *The Necklace of Gzi: A Cultural History of Tibet*. Dharamsala: IOHHDL, 1984.

———. *The Crystal and the Way of Light: Sutra, Tantra, and Dzogchen: The Teachings of Namkhai Norbu*. New York: Routledge & Kegal Paul, 1986.

———. *Dzog Chen and Zen*. Nevada City, Calif.: Blue Dolphin, 1986.

———. *Dzogchen: The Self-Perfected State*. London: Arkana, 1989.

———. *Dream Yoga and the Practice of Natural Light*. Ithaca, N.Y.: Snow Lion, 1992.

———. *Drung, Deu and Bön*. Dharamsala: Library of Tibetan Works and Archives, 1995.

Norbu, Namkhai, K. Lipman, and B. Simmons, trans. *Primordial Experience: An Introduction to rDzogs Chen Meditation (rDo la gser zhun) by Manjusrimita.* Boston: Shambhala, 1987.

Noyes, John Humphrey. *Male Continence.* Originally published 1876. Reprint. New York: AMS Press, 1976.

Nydahl, Ole. *Entering the Diamond Way.* Nevada City, Calif.: Blue Dolphin, 1985.

Olschak, Blanche C. *Mystic Art of Ancient Tibet.* Boulder and London: Shambhala, 1973.

Oppitz, Michael. *Schamanen im Blinden Land.* Frankfurt am Main: Syndikat, 1981.

Otto, Walter Friedrich. *Dionysus: Myth and Cult.* Bloomington, Ind.: Indiana University Press, 1965. Dallas, Tex.: Spring Publications, 1981.

Owen, Lara. *Her Blood Is Gold: Celebrating the Power of Menstruation.* San Francisco: HarperCollins, 1993.

Pandit, M. P. *Gems from the Tantras* (1st series). Madras: Ganesh & Co., 1970. Reprint. 1975.

———. *Gems from the Tantras* (2nd series). Madras: Ganesh & Co., 1970. Reprint. 1976.

Paris, Ginette. *Pagan Meditations: The Worlds of Aphrodite, Artemis, and Hestia.* Dallas, Tex.: Spring Publications, 1986.

———. *Pagan Grace: Dionysos, Hermes and Goddess Memory in Daily Life.* Woodstock, Conn.: Spring Publications, 1990.

Patai, Raphael. *Gates to the Old City: A Book of Jewish Legends.* New York: Avon Books, 1980. *See also* Graves and Patai.

Payne, Richard Karl. *The Tantric Ritual of Japan: Feeding the Gods—The Shingon Fire Ritual.* Delhi: Aditya, 1991.

Petersen, E., and F. von Luschan, *Reisen in Lykein.* Vienna: 1889, p. 199. Quoted in *The Mothers: A Study of the Origins of Sentiments and Institutions,* by Robert Briffault. Vol. 3. London: Allen & Unwin, 1927.

Pollack, Rachel. *The Body of the Goddess: Sacred Wisdom in Myth, Landscape and Culture.* Shaftesbury, England: Element Books, 1997.

Pomeroy, Sarah B. *Goddesses, Whores, Wives and Slaves: Women in Classical Antiquity.* New York: Schocken Books, 1975. Reprint. 1984.

Qualls-Corbett, Nancy. *The Sacred Prostitute: Eternal Aspect of the Feminine.* Toronto: Inner City Books, 1988.

Rai, Ram Kumar. *Encyclopedia of Indian Erotics.* Varanasi: Prachya Prakashan, 1983.

Ramsdale, Alan, and Ellen Jo Dorfman. *Sexual Energy Ecstasy.* Playa Del Rey, Calif.: Peak Skill Publishing, 1985.

Rawson, Philip. *Erotic Art of the East.* New York: Putnam, 1968.

———. *The Art of Tantra.* London: Thames & Hudson, 1973.

———. *Tantra: The Indian Cult of Ecstasy.* London: Thames & Hudson, 1973.

———. *Sacred Tibet.* London: Thames & Hudson, 1991.

Rawson, Philip, and Lazlo Legeza. *Tao: The Chinese Philosophy of Change.* London: Thames & Hudson, 1973.

Redgrove, Peter. *The Black Goddess and the Sixth Sense.* London: Bloomsbury, 1987. Reprint. London: Collins, 1989. *See also* Shuttle and Redgrove.

Regardie, Israel. *The Tree of Life: A Study in Magic.* York Beach, Maine: Weiser, 1972.

———. *The Golden Dawn.* Rev. ed. St. Paul. Minn.: Llewellyn, 1971. Reprint. 1982.

———, ed. *Gems from the Equinox.* Phoenix, Ariz.: Falcon Press, 1974 and 1982.

Reich, Wilhelm. *Character Analysis,* trans. by Vincent R. Carfagno. New York: Noonday Press, 1980.

———. *The Function of the Orgasm: Discovery of the Orgone,* Vol. 1. New York: Noonday Press, 1986.

Reynolds, John Myrdhin. *Self-Liberation through Seeing with Naked Awareness.* Barrytown, N.Y.: Station Hill, 1989.

———, ed. and trans. *Golden Letters: The Three Statements of Garab Dorje, the First Teacher of Dzogchen.* Ithaca, N. Y.: Snow Lion, 1996.

Richter, Alan. *Sexual Slang.* New York: HarperCollins, 1995. Roberts, Alison. *Hathor Rising: The Power of the Goddess in Ancient Egypt.* Rochester, Vt.: Inner Traditions International, 1997.

Saadawi, Nawal el. *The Hidden Face of Eve: Women in the Arab World.* London: Zed Press, 1980.

Sastri, R. A. *Lalitasahasranama.* Nilgiri Hills, India: private printing, 1925. Rev. ed. Delhi: Gian, 1986.

Schipper, Kristofer. *Tao: De levende religie van China.* Amsterdam: Meulenhoff, 1988. *See also* Beurdeley and Schipper. Schoterman, J. A. *Yonitantra.* New Delhi: Manohar, 1980.

Scott, George R. *Phallic Worship: A History of Sex and Sex Rites.* London: Luxor Press, 1966.

Sharkey, John. *Celtic Mysteries: The Ancient Religion.* New York: Crossroad, 1975. Reprint. 1981.

Shaw, Miranda. *Passionate Enlightenment: Women in Tantric Buddhism.* Princeton, N.J.: Princeton University Press, 1994.

Shea, Robert. *All Things Are Lights.* New York: Ballantine Books, 1986.

Shostak, Marjorie. *Nisa, The Life and Words of a !Kung Woman.* Cambridge, Mass.: Harvard University Press, 1981.

Shuttle, Penelope, and Peter Redgrove. *The Wise Wound: Menstruation and Everywoman.* Rev. ed. London: Collins, 1986.

Sinha, Indra. *The Great Book of Tantra: Translations and Images from the Classical Indian Texts.* Rochester, Vt.: Destiny Books, 1993. Sircar, D. C. *The Sakta Pithas.* Calcutta: 1948. Reprint. Delhi: Motilal, 1973.

Sivananda, Swami. *Lord Siva and His Worship.* Shivanandanagar, Uttar Pradesh: The Divine Life Society, 1992.

Snellgrove, David L., and Hugh Edward Richardson. *The Nine Ways of Bön.* Boulder, Colo.: Prajna Press, 1980.

———. *A Cultural History of Tibet.* Boston and London: Shambhala, 1986.

———. *Indo-Tibetan Buddhism: Indian Buddhists and Their Tibetan Successors.* London: Serindia, 1987.

Stark, Raymond. *The Book of Aphrodisiacs.* Briarcliff Manor, N.Y.: Stein & Day, 1980.

Stevens, John. *Lust for Enlightenment: Buddhism and Sex.* Boston: Shambhala, 1990.

Stone, Merlin. *The Paradise Papers.* London: Virago, 1976.

———. *Ancient Mirrors of Womanhood: A Treasury of Goddess and Heroine Lore from Around the World.* Boston: Beacon Press, 1979. Reprint. 1984.

Strauss, Victor von. *Tao Te King* (German). Zurich: Manesse, 1959.

Stroud, Joanne, and Gail Thomas, eds. *Images of the Untouched.* Dallas, Tex.: Spring Publications, 1982.

Stubbs, K. R., and C. D. Chasen. *Clitoral Kiss: A Fun Guide to Oral Sex for Men and Women.* Larkspur, Calif.: Secret Garden, 1993.

Stump, Jane Barr. *What's the Difference?* New York: William Morrow, 1985.

Stutley, Margaret, and James Stutley. *Harper's Dictionary of Hinduism: Its Mythology, Folklore, Philosophy, Literature, and History*. New York: Harper & Row, 1977. Reprint. 1984.

Suarez, Carlos. *The Cipher of Genesis*. Boulder and London: Shambhala, 1975.

———. *The Resurrection of the Word*. Boulder and London: Shambhala, 1975.

Superweed, M. J. *Herbal Aphrodisiacs*. Stone Kingdom, 1971.

Svoboda, Robert E. *Aghora: At the Left Hand of God*. Albuquerque, N.Mex.: Brotherhood of Life, 1986.

Symonds, John, and Kenneth Grant. *The Confessions of Aleister Crowley: An Autohagiography*. New York: Bantam Books, 1971.

Ta-Kao, Ch'u, trans. *Tao Te Ching*. London: Allen & Unwin, 1937. Reprint. 1976.

Talalaj, J. and S. Talalaj. *Human Sex, Ceremonies and Customs*. Melbourne, Australia: Hill of Content Publishing, 1994.

Tannahill, Reay. *Sex in History*. London: Hamish Hamilton, 1980.

Taylor, Dena. *Red Flower: Rethinking Menstruation*. Freedom, Calif.: Crossing Press, 1988.

Taylor, Timothy. *The Prehistory of Sex: Four Million Years of Human Sexual Culture*. New York: Bantam Books, 1996.

Teish, Luisah. *Jambalaya*. New York: Harper & Row, 1985.

Thadani, Giti. *Sakhiyani: Lesbian Desire in Ancient and Modern India*. London: Cassell, 1996.

Thirleby, Ashley. *Tantra: The Key to Sexual Power and Pleasure*. Berlin: Ullstein, 1978.

Thompson, William Irwin. *The Time Falling Bodies Take to Light: Mythology, Sexuality and the Origins of Culture*. New York: St. Martin's Press, 1981.

Thondup, Tulku. *Buddha Mind: Anthology of Longchenpa's Writings on Dzogpa Chenpo*, ed. by Harold Talbot.. Ithaca, N.Y.: Snow Lion, 1989.

Thurman, Robert A. F., trans. *The Tibetan Book of the Dead*. New York: Bantam, 1994.

Tiwari, Jagdish Narain. *Goddess Cults in Ancient India (0–700 A.D.* Delhi: Sundeep Prakashan, 1985.

Torrens, R. G. *The Secret Rituals of the Golden Dawn*. Wellingborough, England: Thorsons, 1973.

Trungpa, Chogyam, and the Nalanda Translation Committee. *The Rain of Wisdom: The Vajra Songs of the Kagyu Gurus*. Boston and London: Shambhala, 1980.

Tucci, Giuseppe. *The Religions of Tibet*. London: Routledge & Kegan Paul, 1970. Reprint. 1980.

Tulku, Tarthang, trans. *Mother of Knowledge: The Enlightenment of Ye-shes mTsho-rgyal*. Berkeley: Dharma, 1983.

U. D., Frater. *Secrets of the German Sex Magicians*. St. Paul, Minn.: Llewellyn, 1991.

Udry, J. R., and N. M. Morris. "Distribution of Coitus in the Menstrual Cycle." *Nature*, Vol. 220, 1968.

van Gulik, Robert Hans. *Sexual Life in Ancient China*. Leiden, The Netherlands: E. J. Brill, 1961. Reprint. 1974.

Vermaseren, Maarten J. *Cybele and Attis*. London: Thames & Hudson, 1977.

Vorberg, Gaston. *Luxu et Voluptate*. Schmiden, Germany: Freyja Verlag, 1962.

Voss, Jutta. *Das Schwarzmond Tabu: Die Kulturelle Bedeutung des weiblichen Zyklus*. Stuttgart, Germany: Kreuz Verlag, 1988.

Waddell, L. A. *Lamaism*. Cambridge, Mass.: Heffer & Sons, 1939.

Wagner, Peter. *Eros Revived: Erotica of the Enlightenment*. London: Secker & Warburg, 1988.

Walker, Barbara G. *The Woman's Encyclopedia of Myths and Secrets*. San Francisco: Harper & Row, 1983.

———. *The Crone: Woman of Age, Wisdom and Power*. San Francisco: Harper & Row, 1985.

———. *Woman's Dictionary of Symbols and Sacred Objects*. San Francisco: Harper & Row, 1988.

Walker, Benjamin. *Beyond the Body: The Human Double and the Astral Planes*. London: Routledge & Kegan Paul, 1974.

———. *Encyclopedia of Esoteric Man*. London: Routledge & Kegan Paul, 1977.

———. *Encyclopedia of Metaphysical Medicine*. London: Routledge & Kegan Paul, 1978.

———. *Tantrism: Its Secret Principles and Practices*. Wellingborough, England: Aquarian Press, 1982.

Ware, James R. *Alchemy, Medicine and Religion in the China of A.D. 320: The Nei P'ien of Ko Hung*. Cambridge, Mass.: MIT Press, 1966. Reprint. New York: Dover Publications, 1981.

Warner, Marina. *Alone of All Her Sex: The Myth and the Cult of the Virgin Mary*. London: Weidenfeld and Nicolson, 1976. Reprint. London: Pan Books, 1985.

Wasson, R. Gordon, Albert Hoffmann, and A. P. Ruck. *The Road to Eleusis: Unveiling the Secrets of the Mysteries*. New York: Harcourt Brace Jovanovich, 1978.

Watson, Lyall. *Gifts of Unknown Things*. London: Hodder & Stoughton, 1976. Reprint. 1977.

———. *Lightning Bird: The Story of One Man's Journey into Africa's Past*. London: Hodder & Stoughton, 1982. Reprint. 1983.

———. *Dreams of Dragons: Ideas on the Edge of Natural History*. London: Hodder & Stoughton, 1986. Reprint. 1987.

———. *Neophilia: The Tradition of the New*. London: Hodder & Stoughton, 1989.

Wedeck, Harry Ezekiel. *Dictionary of Aphrodisiacs*. London: Peter Owen, 1962.

Weir, Anthony, and James Jerman. *Images of Lust: Sexual Carvings on Medieval Churches*. London: Batsford, 1986.

Wex, Marianne. *Let's Take Back Our Space: "Female" and "Male" Body Language as a Result of Patriarchal Structures*. Berlin: Frauenliteratur Verlag, 1979.

White, David Gordon. *The Alchemical Body: Siddha Traditions in Medieval India*. Chicago: University of Chicago Press, 1997.

White, John Warren. *The Highest State of Consciousness*. New York: Anchor Books, 1972.

Wile, Douglas. *Art of the Bedchamber: Chinese Sexual Yoga Classics, Including Women's Solo Meditation Texts*. New York: SUNY, 1992.

Wilhelm, Richard, trans. *The Secret of the Golden Flower: A Chinese Book of Life*. Rev. ed. New York: Harcourt, Brace & World, 1962.

Wilhelm, Richard, and C. F. Baynes, trans. *The I Ching; or, Book of Changes*. 3rd ed. Princeton, N.J.; Princeton University Press, 1967.

Williams, Charles. *Witchcraft*. London: Faber and Faber, 1941. Reprint. Wellingborough, England: Aquarian Press, 1980. Williams, Heathcote, and Werner Pieper. *Aus den Vorhautakten*. Lohrbach, Germany: Der Grune Zweig, 1989.

Willson, Martin. *In Praise of Tara: Songs to the Saviouress*. London: Wisdom Publications, 1986.

Wilson, Colin, ed. *Men of Mystery: A Celebration of the Occult.* London: W. H. Allen & Co., 1977.

———. *The Sex Diary of Gerard Sorme: An Inquiry into the Powers of Imagination and Lust.* London: Granada, 1980.

———. *The Occult.* London: Hodder & Stoughton, 1971. Reprint. London: Granada, 1984.

———. *Lifeforce.* New York: Warner Books, 1985.

———. *Mysteries: An Investigation into the Occult, the Paranormal and the Supernatural.* London: Hodder & Stoughton, 1978. Reprint. London: Granada, 1985.

———. *The Misfits: A Study of Sexual Outsiders.* London: Collins, 1989.

Wilson, Edward Osborne. *On Human Nature.* Cambridge, Mass.: Harvard University Press, 1978. Reprint. New York: Bantam Books, 1979.

Wilson, Robert Anton. *Sex and Drugs: A Journey Beyond Limits.* New York: Playboy Press, 1973. Reprint. Phoenix, Ariz.: Falcon Press, 1988.

———. *Ishtar Rising.* Phoenix, Ariz.: Falcon Press, 1989.

Wind, Edgar. *Pagan Mysteries in the Renaissance.* London: Faber and Faber, 1958. Rev. ed. Oxford and New York: Oxford University Press, 1980.

Winter, Urs. *Frau und Göttin* (Woman and Goddess). Göttingen: Vandenhoeck & Ruprecht, 1983.

Wolkstein, Diane, and Samuel Noah Kramer. *Inanna, Queen of Heaven and Earth: Her Stories and Hymns from Sumer.* New York: Harper & Row, 1983.

Woodroffe, Sir John. *Shakti and Shakta.* Madras: Ganesh & Co., 1918. Reprint. New York: Dover Publications. 1978.

———. *Introduction to Tantra Shastra.* Madras: Ganesh & Co., 1980.

Wright, Thomas. *The Worship of the Generative Powers During the Middle Ages of Western Europe* (1866). *See* Knight and Wright: *Sexual Symbolism.*

———. *Hymns to the Goddess and Hymns to Kali.* Madras: Ganesh & Co., 1913. Reprint. Wilmot, Wis.: Lotus Light Publications, 1981.

———. *Mahanirvana Tantra.* Madras: Ganesh & Co., 1927. Reprint. 1985.

———. *Principles of Tantra.* 2 vols. Madras: Ganesh & Co., 1913. Reprint. 1986.

Yeshe Tsogyal. *The Life and Liberation of Padmasambhava,* trans. by Kenneth Douglas and Gwendolyn Bays. Berkeley, Calif.: Dharma Publications, 1978.

———. *Lotus-Born: The Life Story of Padmasambhava* trans. by Erik pema Kunsang. Boston: Shambhala, 1993.

Young, Serenity, ed. *An Anthology of Sacred Texts by and about Women.* London: Pandora, 1993. Younge, W. C., ed. *Sex and Internal Secretions.* 2 vols. Baltimore: Williams & Wilkins, 1961.

Zacks, Richard. *History Laid Bare: Love, Sex and Perversity from the Ancient Etruscans to Warren G. Harding.* New York: HarperCollins, 1994.

Zangpo, Tsering Lama Jampal. *A Garland of Immortal Wish-Fulfilling Trees: The Palyul Tradition of Nyingmapa.* Ithaca, N.Y.: Snow Lion, 1988.

Zola, Emile. *La Terre* (The Earth), trans. by Douglas Parmee. New York: Penguin USA, 1980.

———. *Germinal.* New York: Viking Press, 1987.

Zukav, Gary. *The Dancing Wu Li Masters: An Overview of the New Physics.* New York: William Morrow, 1979.